Encyclopedia of
AMERICAN FOREIGN POLICY

Studies of the Principal
Movements and Ideas

Alexander DeConde, *EDITOR*

Volume II

CHARLES SCRIBNER'S SONS · NEW YORK

Copyright © 1978 Charles Scribner's Sons

Library of Congress Cataloging in Publication Data

Main entry under title:

Encyclopedia of American foreign policy.

    Includes index.
    1. United States—Foreign relations
—Dictionaries.   I. De Conde, Alexander.
JX1407.E53   327.73   78-5453
ISBN 0-684-155036-6

Acknowledgment is gratefully made to the American Council of Learned Societies for permission to
use biographical material from the *Concise Dictionary
of American Biography* (copyright © 1977, 1964
Charles Scribner's Sons) and *Dictionary of American
Biography, Supplement 5* (copyright © 1977 American Council of Learned Societies).

1 3 5 7 9 11 13 15 17 19 V|C 20 18 16 14 12 10 8 6 4 2

Printed in the United States of America

Encyclopedia of
AMERICAN
FOREIGN
POLICY

FOREIGN AID

Ian J. Bickerton

SINCE World War II, foreign aid has been an important instrument of United States foreign policy. During much of this time it has been a controversial and complex policy issue. Foreign aid is an ambiguous term, and the lack of a consistent definition has led to considerable confusion concerning what is meant by American aid. Different organizations and different countries include or exclude a variety of items in their definitions: the Organization for Economic Cooperation and Development, for example, includes both government flows of capital and private investment, private lending, and export credits. The problem of measuring aid and determining its goals is further complicated by the polemic nature of much of the literature on the subject. In this essay, foreign aid will be regarded as economic and military assistance on a government-to-government level, or through government-supported agencies or programs. United States economic assistance has taken the form of direct grants, loans, and technical cooperation in the person of engineers and other experts. Loans have been either banking-type loans, described as hard loans, or nonbanking-type loans, described as soft loans and characterized by lower interest rates, longer periods of repayment, and repayments in local currencies rather than American dollars. Loans have been made on a government-to-government basis or to private enterprise through semigovernment agencies. Loans have been made through both bilateral and multilateral agencies. Military assistance has taken the form of providing military advisory groups and the furnishing of military equipment of all kinds. In addition, the United States has provided aid for defense support to build up the economies of those countries re-

ceiving direct military assistance through the construction of power plants, railroads, dock facilities, fertilizer, chemical, and other industrial plants; as well as expenditures for schools, public health facilities, and improvements in sanitation.

Foreign aid emerged as a goal of United States foreign policy during the early 1940's. Prior to World War II, government-to-government assistance and loans were almost unknown, except in emergencies. American economic assistance had taken place mainly through private ventures and missionary organizations, and had involved such varied projects as disaster relief, general postwar rehabilitation and refugee aid, cultural, educational, and religious activities, and capital investment and market expansion. Like lend-lease, some of the United States government loans to European nations after World War I were for reconstruction purposes and not for arms, and hence were a form of foreign aid. During and immediately following World War II, the mechanisms utilized to undertake the economic relief and reconstruction of Europe included the World Bank, the Export-Import Bank, the International Monetary Fund, and the United Nations Relief and Rehabilitation Administration. Since 1945 American foreign aid programs have included three different kinds of activities, according to official pronouncements: (1) reconstructing the economies of war-devastated allies, (2) strengthening the military defenses of noncommunist countries, and (3) encouraging the economic development of so-called underdeveloped countries.

The explanation as to why the United States embarked upon foreign aid in the postwar period involves many considerations. In the broadest sense, American foreign aid programs were the assumption by the United States of the economic and political role previously played by Great Britain. Britain's loss of world leadership marked the end of European economic and political domination of the other nations of the globe. The last thirty years have seen a struggle between the United States—the major partner in the Anglo-American economic community—and the recently industrialized Soviet Union for the controlling influence over the newly formed nation-states of Asia, Africa, and Latin America which comprise the majority of the countries of the Third World. The United States and Soviet Russia have both attempted to integrate foreign aid programs into their foreign policy goals, and have used aid as a weapon in their quest for allies, friends, markets, United Nations votes, and various other ends. An expanding world economy and the breakdown of restraints to international trade were regarded as central to the continued strength of the American economic system. Aid, in the form of grants, loans, and the use of development corporations, was to be one means of keeping the system functioning.

In general terms, it can be said that the foreign aid relationship has existed for the best part of two centuries in the form of the colonial relationship. The terminology has changed; the "white man's burden" is now the "debt burden," and the nineteenth-century exploitation of raw materials is now called the "transfer of resources." Foreign aid has enabled former colonial powers, such as the United Kingdom and France, to maintain their historic political, economic, and cultural ties with former colonies. And it is precisely this network of Atlantic-European domination and imperialism that forms the basis of the current aid programs (called by the donor countries international cooperation for development) from which it is the prime political aim of developing nations to escape.

America's foreign aid programs were shaped by the Cold War mentality that gripped the country in the postwar years, and by the desire of the United States for increased overseas markets. By 1947, United States policymakers had concluded that the Soviet Union had embarked upon a policy of world domination.

Washington resolved to oppose Soviet expansion—especially into areas regarded as strategically important because of their raw materials. Foreign military and economic aid, by building a country's military strength, establishing internal political stability, and promoting general economic development, was seen as the best means to counteract Soviet plans without engaging in direct combat with the enemy. Aid recipients fell into two categories—forward defense countries bordering the communist bloc and the less strategically placed countries. In the forward defense countries, aid was designed to support existing governments—directly through arms and personnel and indirectly through economic aid to mitigate internal discontent. It was hoped that aid would preserve the status quo and prevent these countries from falling into the Soviet orbit. Greece, Turkey, Iran, India, and Southeast Asia belonged to the forward defense group.

In 1947 the administration of Harry S. Truman believed that the Soviet Union was moving to control Europe and the Middle East at a time when Great Britain was no longer able to continue large-scale financial aid to Greece and Turkey. The result was the first landmark of American foreign aid—the Greek-Turkish aid program and the Truman Doctrine. In calling for aid to these two countries, President Harry S. Truman told a joint session of Congress that the preservation of their integrity was essential to maintain order in the Middle East, and that only the United States could provide the aid necessary to prevent communist success. He declared that American security was at stake and that "it must be the foreign policy of the United States to support free people who are resisting attempted subjugation by armed minorities or outside pressures." The importance of the Greek-Turkish aid program was that it inaugurated the use of American money and matériel as a means to counter the spread of Soviet influence.

The second landmark of American aid, the European Recovery Program, the Marshall Plan, was developed in response to what was seen as a further Soviet-related crisis in Europe. It appeared to policymakers in 1947 that failure of European economic recovery could lead to political collapse and open the door to Soviet domination of Europe through internal subversion. Secretary of State George C. Marshall, outlining the aid plan in an address at Harvard University on 5 June 1947, stated that the goal of the United States "should be the revival of a working economy in the world so as to permit the emergence of political and social conditions in which free institutions can exist." American aid was needed to help in the reconstruction of Europe. Without it, the Truman administration believed, no parliamentary regime in Western Europe would survive.

Economic assistance programs were soon expanded to include the economic stabilization of non-European areas. The China Aid Act of April 1948 (Title IV of the Foreign Assistance Act) authorized technical and other (military) aid to China, and in January 1949 Truman extended economic aid to Korea. The emphasis of aid began to shift from relief and reconstruction to economic development. Economic aid was initiated for Indonesia, Burma, French Indochina, Thailand, and the Philippines, and announcing the Point Four program in his inaugural address on 20 January 1949, Truman extended technical assistance to Asia, Africa, and Latin America. The Point Four program, according to a State Department official, sought "to strengthen and generalize peace throughout the world by counteracting the economic conditions that predispose to social and political instability and to war." Truman called Point Four a "bold new program for making the benefits of our scientific advances and industrial progress available for the improvement and growth of underdeveloped areas . . . in cooperation with other nations." He stated that the United States should "foster capital investment in areas needing development." Experience showed, he believed, that American commerce with other countries grew as they progressed industrially and economically. "Greater production," he concluded, "is the key to prosperity and peace."

By 1949 Washington regarded the Soviet threat to Europe as military as well as economic; it now seemed that military security was needed in addition to economic recovery, and the United States pledged military support to Western Europe. Prompted in part by the development of the atomic bomb by the Soviet

Union, the United States set out to rearm Europe through the Mutual Defense Assistance program initiated in 1949 and, with the Mutual Security Act of 1951, also committed itself to providing aid—predominantly defense support—to the Third World nations. The bulk of foreign aid granted by the United States between 1947 and 1950, approximately $26.5 billion—not including American investments in the World Bank and the International Monetary Fund—was economic assistance, mostly in the form of direct grants to Europe. Throughout the 1950's, however, most foreign aid was for military defenses and went primarily to Korea, South Vietnam, Formosa, and the European allies.

In 1954 the Food for Peace program was launched with the passage of Public Law 480 (the Agricultural Trade Development and Assistance Act of 1954), which enabled the funds from the sale of surplus agricultural products to be used for development purposes; the local currency proceeds from the sales being used thereafter for development loans and other purposes approved by the recipient government. Designed to "increase the consumption of United States agricultural commodities in foreign countries, to improve the foreign relations of the United States and for other purposes," Public Law 480 became an important element in the foreign aid program. In July 1955 the International Cooperation Administration (ICA) was established as a semiautonomous agency within the Department of State and in 1957 the Development Loan Fund (the lending arm of the ICA) was set up in large part to assist India, which faced a serious foreign exchange crisis. This was the first real emphasis on development (or soft) loans, which by the end of the decade were to become the single most important tool employed in the United States foreign aid programs. By the mid-1960's, 67 percent of the economic aid funds included in the Mutual Defense and Development program were in the form of soft loans.

In January 1957 Congress approved an economic and military aid program for the defense of the Middle East which was promptly designated the Eisenhower Doctrine. In 1961, under the authority of the Foreign Assistance Act of that year, the Agency for International

Development (AID) was established, coordinating all United States aid programs under the administration of the State Department. Under the new administrative machinery the emphasis of foreign aid programs moved to program-oriented rather than project-oriented development (a change in terminology more than substance) and the conditions of soft loans were made more stringent. Also in 1961, the Alliance for Progress was launched. This program, directed towards Latin America, followed the Act of Bogotá passed by the Council of American States in 1960, and had as its stated goal the modernization of Latin America through reform of political and economic structures, and the injection of capital and technical assistance to be administered by AID.

President John F. Kennedy found the existing aid programs unsatisfactory in meeting what he saw to be the needs of the 1960's. The task of the United States, "the fundamental task of our foreign aid program in the 1960's," he said, "is not negatively to fight Communism . . . it is to make a historical demonstration that in the twentieth century, as in the nineteenth, . . . economic growth and political democracy can develop hand in hand." Underdeveloped countries would be assisted in reaching the state of "self-sustained economic growth." The 1960's were to be the "decade of development," and whereas in the 1950's military assistance had been roughly double the level of development aid, in the first half of the 1960's the ratio was reversed. The formation of the Peace Corps in March 1961 was probably the most effective attempt to create the image of newly found American altruism. The notion of volunteers assisting other countries "under conditions of hardship" was particularly successful as a public relations weapon to engender support for American foreign aid. However, neither the Peace Corps nor the Alliance for Progress lived up to the promise of their idealistic rhetoric when confronted with the economic and political realities of Latin America and the Third World.

Throughout the 1960's, foreign aid programs were conceived in the increasingly narrow and paramilitary interests of the United States. Aid became increasingly bilateral, controls over AID programs were tightened and all aid (other than military assistance) was tied to the purchase of United States goods and services. Development aid strategy was broadened to include support to strengthen resistance to internal communist subversion and revolutionary radicalism as well as to meet the external "avowed communist threat." Concerning the Foreign Assistance Act of 1964, Secretary of Defense Robert McNamara, in an effort to gain the support of right wing opponents of foreign aid, told a congressional committee that "the foreign aid program generally and the military assistance program has now become the most critical element of our overall national security effort." This highly exaggerated administration rhetoric was simply reinforced when President Lyndon B. Johnson stated that the foreign aid program was "the best weapon we have to ensure that our own men in uniform need not go into combat."

By 1970 foreign aid had begun to feel the effects of the Vietnam War as the nation's mood shifted toward withdrawal and a concern for rising domestic requirements. Despite considerable public and congressional debate over the objectives and techniques of foreign aid programs—particularly from economy-minded, conservative Democrats and right-wing Republicans who objected to what Congressman Otto Passman of Louisiana called "the greatest give-away in history"—for much of the postwar period foreign aid had been regarded as sacrosanct in American politics and diplomacy, at least by the policymaking establishment, who tended to oversell its virtues to an increasingly skeptical public and Congress. Democratic and Republican administrations had outbid each other in extending aid programs; liberal and conservative congressmen had joined in bipartisan voting on aid appropriations; and labor, management, churches, and universities had all voiced approval of foreign aid. By the end of the 1960's, however, the domestic and international environment had changed so dramatically that virtually all the familiar liberal, geopolitical underpinnings of United States foreign policy were collapsing. The interventionist policy articulated in the Truman Doctrine and Point Four, and widely supported for two decades, had found its final expression in Vietnam. At the deepest point in United States involvement in the Third World, many Americans began to question most seriously the rationale for any involvement. Arguments that for twenty years had given the greatest urgency and immediacy to the case for foreign aid—the threat of communism, the need for continued access to vital raw materials, the economic benefits to be gained through increased trade, and the political dividends to be reaped in terms of peace and democracy—lost much of their force. The United States then began a reappraisal of its whole foreign aid rationale. To the numerous critics on the Right who did not share the liberal vision and who regarded foreign aid as a squandering of American resources and strength, this reappraisal was long overdue.

Despite the investigations undertaken in an effort to revitalize support for foreign aid programs—the Rockefeller Report (1969); the Pearson Report, *Partners in Development* (1969); and the Peterson Report, *U.S. Foreign Assistance in the 1970's: A New Approach* (1970)—there was little likelihood of a basic change in aid strategies or programs. The Peterson Report, for example, although recognizing that "a predominately bilateral United States program is no longer politically tenable in our relations with many developing countries," recommended that the United States establish a Development Bank, a Development Institute, and a Development Council under American influence, and further utilize the United States–dominated World Bank and International Monetary Fund. All three reports urged the United States to widen its use of private investment, skills, and initiatives—despite clear statements from many Third World countries that they did not welcome private investment when it came disguised as aid.

An analysis of American aid throughout the entire postwar period reveals that the United States government has always maintained that public funds must be kept to a minimum and, as far as possible, remain under American control. Foreign aid programs have been predicated on the propositions that economic development should be achieved through capital growth within the countries themselves and that funds should be used to encourage private industry which would generate capital for investment. These propositions have, in turn, reflected rather vague concepts concerning the economic causes of war and the relationship between communism and poverty, underdeveloped areas and sources of strategic raw materials, and the prosperity and national security of the United States.

Official explanations of aid have continually stressed the importance of aid to national security. Secretary of State Dean Acheson observed in 1950 that, "as a security measure, it [aid] is an essential arm of our foreign policy. For our military and economic security is vitally dependent on the economic security of other peoples." Secretary of State Dean Rusk reflected these concepts when he told the House Foreign Affairs Committee, on 2 May 1968, that leaders who believed in peaceful progress "cannot be expected to endure unless they produce results . . . unless their people receive tangible economic and social benefits. . . . They can have no chance of success, no matter how great their efforts, without adequate assistance from the wealthy nations of the world."

America's need for strategic raw materials was brought home forcefully by the Korean War, and in 1952 the President's Materials Policy Commission (Paley Commission) recommended that the United States look to the countries of Latin America, Africa, the Near East, South Asia, and Southeast Asia for imports of minerals, and aid programs were initiated to this end in the 1950's. In his first State of the Union message, President Dwight D. Eisenhower declared that the explicit purpose of American foreign policy was the encouragement of a hospitable climate for private American investment capital abroad, and spokesmen for aid policies repeatedly have emphasized its correlation to United States domestic capital growth. Aid has been designed primarily to stimulate private investment through trade liberalization and to improve the investment climate in Third World countries. When the United States began its foreign aid program, many congressmen were reluctant to vote public funds for development purposes because they believed that such funds should not replace, or do the work of, private investment. Although Third World countries needed development funds, they were unwilling to accept private capital. Their stand, supported by the United Nations, exerted pressure on the American government to modify its position on governmental assistance, which it did gradually.

Yet the level of public funds expended on foreign aid has remained at less than 1 percent of the gross national product.

Three major assumptions about economic growth and development and its relationship to the United States have permeated official pronouncements concerning foreign aid. The first is that economic and technical assistance contribute to economic development and this, in turn, leads to political development. Political development has always been defined in terms of freedom, stability, democracy, anticommunism, and pro-Americanism. The second is that aid can be used to promote political stability, cement alliances with the United States, and contain communism and radical or revolutionary regimes. The third assumption that aid programs have rested upon is that aid contributes to the growth of liberal, democratic political systems in the Third World. All three assumptions spring from what has been described as the liberal tradition in American thought: that ethnocentric view Americans have of themselves which enables them to see the "peculiar historical and social experience" of the United States as setting it apart from the experiences of the rest of the world. The tenets of the liberal tradition relevant to foreign aid are that change and development occur gradually and can be achieved without revolution, and that the results of such gradual change are beneficial.

Many critics of American aid policies and programs do not share the liberal vision of the United States as "the watchman on the walls of world freedom," or as the "guardians at the gate" and indeed have rejected it as a distortion of reality. Nor do they accept the view that American interventions in the Third World stem from "the politics of inadvertence" or that they are "the burden and the glory of the Republic." Rather, these critics see the United States engaged in a policy of worldwide economic imperialism in which foreign aid is used as a means to contain and channel world economic growth into desirable paths. They see the United States, with only a fraction of the world's population, area, and natural resources, adroitly utilizing foreign aid to manipulate the global money market, to control much of the world's trade, and to reserve most of the world's raw materials for its own use. They

note that the United States supports with aid right-wing and military dictatorships in Latin America, Southeast Asia, and the Middle East, because they welcome American corporations. Critics note too the widening gap between the wealth and standards of living of Third World countries and highly industrialized nations. They see the Third World's trade declining from one-third of the world's exports in 1950 to one-fifth in 1962—a trend that continued throughout the 1960's—and the income from that trade declining because of the drop in world prices of primary products. Thus, a radical minority report of the Columbia Conference on International Economic Development held in Williamsburg, Virginia, and New York in 1970 to discuss the Pearson Report asserted its belief that continued foreign aid would increase the economic and political vulnerability of the less-developed countries by keeping them politically weak; would make their economies increasingly dependent and reliant upon assistance and markets in which their individual positions as buyers and sellers is weak; and, by expanding the importance of private investment from multinational corporations, would retard development rather than promote it.

Although a majority at the Columbia Conference accepted the Pearson Report recommendations on aid concerning the desirability of achieving a 6 percent rate of growth, a minority felt that what the Third World needed was not "self-sustaining" growth but "self-reliant" growth. Third World critics of American policy find that the recent economic exploitation by the United States, supported by the local privileged elite, is as suffocating as the old-fashioned colonial administrations. They regard foreign aid as one of the means utilized by the United States to oppose internal violence, revolution, and radical change throughout the Third World, seeing America's preeminent position dependent upon allowing only gradual, controlled, and orderly change and modernization.

There is considerable evidence to support the critics. The Middle East and its raw materials have been especially significant to the United States since the end of World War II. The Eisenhower administration built up an elaborate worldwide alliance system, including the Middle Eastern countries, as part of its

Cold War strategy to contain communism. Foreign aid was an important weapon of intervention in the affairs of the Middle Eastern countries. This can be seen especially in the case of Iran in 1953, when the United States was instrumental, through the Central Intelligence Agency, in bringing down the nationalist, anti-American prime minister, Mohammed Mossadegh. In return, the United States gained control of 40 percent of Iran's oil operations and the following year gave Iran $85 million in foreign aid. The shah's army was soon among the best equipped in the Middle East. Following the November 1956 Suez Crisis, in January 1957 Congress approved a joint resolution authorizing President Eisenhower to use $200 million in economic and military assistance to preserve "the independence and integrity of the nations of the Middle East." The purpose of this aid was to prevent communist subversion and infiltration which might threaten Western access to the oil of the region.

Eisenhower and Secretary of State John Foster Dulles also used foreign aid to gain friendship and allies in Latin America. There seemed little danger of communist influence in Latin America in the immediate postwar years, but by 1948 military coups began to abort democratic experiments and the United States became alarmed. By the mid-1950's the Cold War stress on stability led Washington to adopt a policy of supporting incumbents. Between 1948 and 1958 there had been a dramatic rise in the number of military governments in Latin America and, under the influence of the Pentagon, United States policymakers abandoned their apparent efforts to foster democratic institutions and undertook military assistance programs. Of the twelve Latin American countries receiving foreign aid in 1958, eight were under military governments, six of which had come to power after the inauguration of military assistance projects. Guatemala provides an interesting example of the way aid was used in this respect. In June 1954 President Jacobo Arbenz Guzmán was overthrown by a military coup led by Colonel Carlos Castillo Armas. Between 1944 and 1954 American aid to Guatemala had totaled $600,000; in 1954 United States economic and military assistance to Guatemala was $45 million.

Perhaps the most dramatic example of the effect of foreign aid in Latin America is the case of Chile. In September 1970 Salvador Allende Gossens, a Marxist, was elected president of Chile, and the following July the Chilean Congress approved the nationalization of Chile's copper industry and the payment of compensation to the major foreign copper firms, the Kennecott and Anaconda companies. Allende told the United Nations that the Kennecott Copper Company, which held 49 percent of the huge El Teniente mine, had made profits on its investments in Chile of 106 percent in 1967, 113 percent in 1968, and a staggering 209 percent in 1969. In addition, Chile had assumed a debt burden of the copper companies of $727 million, which they had financed through foreign loans (in one instance with the company's own parent company in the United States). At the time Allende took office, Chile had received approximately $80 million per year from the World Bank and the Inter-American Development Bank, and in the previous ten years had received $50 million from AID. Following the nationalization of the copper companies, all of Chile's aid and credits were cut off by these agencies. United States military aid to Chile, however, was increased. On 11 September 1973 Allende was overthrown by a military coup led by General Augusto Pinochet Ugarte. Foreign economic sanctions against Allende's government and a decline in the world price of copper were the primary factors that had led to inflation and economic collapse in Chile, and the strongly anti-Marxist military took control. In the same year the Joint Chiefs of Staff told a congressional committee that it should be the task of the United States in Latin America to foster the already strong rapport between the United States armed forces and the Latin American military by extending military assistance to that region.

Whether foreign aid condemns the Third World to perpetual backwardness and poverty by assisting the penetration of multinational corporations into these areas, or whether it will serve as the vehicle of technology and growth, cannot easily be answered. There is no simple solution to this problem because the impact of foreign aid remains obscure and perplexing. We know very little about either private capital investment or military aid. Information is fragmentary and incomplete. For the multinational corporations, for example, little is known of capital outlay, foreign-based employment, trade relationships between parent corporations and their affiliates, and even stockholdings in local companies. What is known, however, is that foreign aid is seen as a function of the urge for expansion, the struggle for market shares, which is central to the dynamic of capitalism itself. We know, too, that foreign aid often supports technologies and social structures that are inimical to rounded development by shoring up corrupt and privileged classes and encouraging some countries to concentrate their agricultural production on exports rather than on badly needed food for local consumption. It may be that foreign aid, as practiced, became an instrument of the American capitalist economy, but it has not assured the United States access to foreign markets. Its objectives were more political than economic, and it cost more than the United States recovered in trade and investment. The United States, in considering its priorities on foreign aid, must accept that there is a viable alternative open to countries of the Third World—namely, the examples offered by such countries as China, Cuba, and Tanzania. From the perspective of the mid-1970's it appears that foreign aid continues the traditions of late nineteenth- and early twentieth-century imperialism.

BIBLIOGRAPHY

Perhaps the most persuasive case for foreign aid is Max F. Millikan and Walt W. Rostow, *A Proposal: Key to an Effective Foreign Policy* (New York, 1957). Herbert Feis, *Foreign Aid and Foreign Policy* (New York, 1964), is also a defense of foreign aid. *U.S. Foreign Aid: Its Purposes, Scope, Administration and Related Information* (Washington, D.C., 1959), published by the Library of Congress, is a summary of the programs of the 1940's and 1950's and contains much of the official rhetoric surrounding foreign aid. Official statistics can be found in United States Agency for International Development, *United States Overseas Loans and Grants, 1945–1974* (Washington, D.C., 1975). Thomas G. Paterson, *Soviet American Conflict: Postwar Reconstruction and the Origins of the Cold War* (Baltimore, 1973), and "Foreign Aid Under Wraps: The Point Four Program," in *Wisconsin Magazine of History*, 56 (1972–1973), provides a detailed, critical analysis of the role of foreign aid. Charles C. Alexander, *Holding the Line: The Eisenhower Era, 1952–61* (Bloomington, Ind., 1975), is a good general treatment of the Eisenhower years including foreign aid. Gustav Ranis, ed., *The United States and the Developing Economies* (New York, 1973), contains several interesting articles; and David Baldwin, *Economic Development and American Foreign Policy, 1943–1962* (Chicago, 1966), is a valuable discussion of the political aspects of American policies of economic development. Robert A. Packenham, *Liberal America and the Third World* (Princeton, 1973), is a critique of the liberal assumptions underlying United States foreign aid policies. For an articulate and well-documented analysis, which questions the traditional explanations of foreign aid, see Richard J. Barnet, *Intervention and Revolution: The United States in the Third World* (New York, 1968); and Richard J. Barnet and Ronald E. Müller, *Global Reach: The Power of Multi-national Corporations* (New York, 1974). Sharply drawn papers analyzing the effect of foreign aid in the Third World countries can be found in Barbara Ward *et al.*, eds., *The Widening Gap: Development in the 1970's* (New York, 1971); and Gunnar Myrdal reveals many shortcomings of foreign aid in his attack *The Challenge of World Poverty* (New York, 1970). Dennis Goulet and Michael Hudson, *The Myth of Aid: The Hidden Agenda of the Development Reports* (Maryknoll, N.Y., 1971), is an attack on recent foreign aid programs. For articles showing the impact of aid on Latin American countries, see the *Latin American Research Review* and the journal *Inter-American Economic Affairs*.

[See also THE COLD WAR; ECONOMIC FOREIGN POLICY; THE EISENHOWER DOCTRINE; THE MARSHALL PLAN; PAN-AMERICANISM; THE TRUMAN DOCTRINE.]

THE FOURTEEN POINTS

Daniel M. Smith

ON 8 January 1918 President Woodrow Wilson delivered to a joint session of Congress his most famous wartime speech, proclaiming Fourteen Points to be the basis of the just and lasting peace that he and others ardently sought in order to end the Great War. After referring critically to the new Bolshevik regime in Russia opening peace talks at Brest-Litovsk with the as yet victorious Germans, the president listed the following fourteen points as the only reliable program for world peace:

1. "Open covenants of peace openly arrived at," whereby all diplomacy should henceforth proceed openly and candidly, with no more secret treaties or arrangements of the kind that liberal opinion blamed as causes of World War I.

2. Freedom of the seas in peace and in war, with the high seas to be open to regular commerce except as they might be closed via international agreements.

3. Removal of economic barriers, insofar as practical, to the equitable flow of trade and the access of all to markets.

4. Reduction of armaments to the lowest level consistent with the national security of all states.

5. Impartial adjustment of colonial claims and rivalries based upon the principle of the interests of both the colonial peoples involved and claimant powers.

6. Evacuation of Russia's national domain and cooperation to permit Russia to determine independently her own national policy and development, as "the acid test" of the good will of other powers toward Russia.

7. Evacuation and restoration of Belgium.

8. Evacuation of all French territory and restoration by Germany of invaded portions, together with the correction of the wrong done France in 1871 in regard to the German seizure of Alsace-Lorraine.

9. Readjustment of Italy's frontiers along "clearly recognizable lines of nationality."

10. Autonomy for the various nationalities of the Austro-Hungarian Empire.

11. Evacuation and restoration of Rumania, Montenegro, and Serbia, with the latter assured of access to the sea.

12. Autonomous development for the non-Turkish nationalities of the Ottoman Empire and the opening of the Dardanelles to ships of all nations.

13. An independent Poland inhabited by indisputably Polish peoples and with assured access to the sea.

14. Formation of "a general association of nations . . . under specific covenants for the purpose of affording mutual guarantees of political independence and territorial integrity to great and small states alike."

In Wilson's view, this fourteenth point was the key to the peace.

The immediate background to the Fourteen Points speech arose from events in World War I that revealed a growing desire for peace, particularly the November 1917 Bolshevik revolution in Russia and a meeting of the Socialist Congress in Stockholm, and opposition by European labor and radicals to an imperialistic war. The necessity of reassuring liberal opinion everywhere of the morality of the goals of the Allies and the Associated Powers was emphasized when the Bolshevik leaders in Russia began to publish copies of the secret Allied treaties, found in the archives of the czarist and provisional governments, for a postwar division of spoils to be achieved by the joint war. Nikolai Lenin and his cohorts denounced the war as a capitalistic imperialistic plot and took steps to withdraw Russia from the conflict on the Allied side as rapidly as possible, meanwhile calling for a "just and democratic peace" based on no annexations and no war indemnities. Consequently, when the president's close friend and adviser Colonel Edward M. House journeyed to Europe to confer with the Allied leaders about war measures, he bore instructions from Wilson to seek agreement upon a joint statement of war goals. He reported back to Wilson that the Allied leaders had revealed little enthusiasm; in fact David Lloyd George, the British prime minister, objected that such a statement would be unnecessary and inopportune in view of current German military successes in Italy and Russia. France's premier, Georges Clemenceau, concurred with Lloyd George. Apparently this cold reception to Wilson's suggestion reflected not only the Allied leaders' preoccupation with the war but even more their suspicions of Wilson and the likelihood that his proposal would entail a repudiation of the secret inter-Allied treaties. Hence, upon House's return to the United States, the president decided upon unilateral action, a decision he clung to despite doubts aroused by Lloyd George's Caxton Hall address on 5 January 1918, which anticipated many of Wilson's main points in referring to the need for some kind of international collective security organization to prevent future wars from ravaging mankind. House argued that a reiteration of liberal goals and a demonstration of harmonious Anglo-American war purposes was desirable.

The Fourteen Points address, in the opinion of Wilson's biographer Arthur S. Link, revealed Wilson's leadership role as spokesman for the liberal community in the United States and abroad. Members of this group had evolved a concept of an ideal peace settlement long before, at least as early as 1915, when the League to Enforce Peace (headed by former President William Howard Taft) had been founded in the United States, and when similar bodies, such as the League of Nations Society, came into existence in Great Britain. These organizations advocated an end to old-fashioned balances of power and alliances, to be supplanted by democratically open diplomacy and an international organization to protect all members by means of some kind of mutual guarantee. President Wilson's role was less that of an originator, consequently, than of a synthesizer or spokesman for liberalism, a cause that he made his own. After entry by the United States into the war, he set himself the task of translating the wartime policy of the United States into harmony with the goals of the international liberal community.

To help him formulate goals, Wilson had requested House in September 1917 to organize a group of scholars to begin studies in preparation for the peace settlement. House assembled a body of about 158 scholars, mostly historians and social scientists, who were housed in the American Geographical Society headquarters in New York City and fell under the immediate charge of House's brother-in-law, Sidney E. Mezes, the head of the City College of New York. Isaiah Bowman of the American Geographical Society became Mezes' executive assistant and assembled a staff that included such eminent personages as legal expert David Hunter Miller, James T. Shotwell, professor of the history of international relations at Columbia University, and Walter Lippmann, the noted reform journalist. Known as "the Inquiry," the group compiled nearly 2,000 reports on geographical, economic, and political problems that might arise at the peace negotiations; and hundreds of excellent maps were acquired or prepared. The papers differed in quality and usefulness, but the work of the Inquiry was of considerable value and made a definite impression on the resultant peace treaties. The functioning of the Inquiry also largely dispels the charge that one of the causes of Wilson's failures at the peace conference was lack of preparation for the peacemaking.

The Inquiry prepared a memorandum, largely the work of Mezes, Miller, and Lippmann, which House transmitted to Wilson. House then aided the president in reworking it into a more generalized document in keeping with the president's penchant for exhortation and sweeping pronouncements. The Inquiry recommendations also placed greater emphasis on strategic and economic factors, whereas Wilson chose to accentuate the concept of the self-determination of peoples based on nationality principles.

Most important, in Wilson's view, was the task of rallying the American and Allied publics behind his concept of a reasonable and fair peace settlement that would have a real prospect of enduring over the decades. Wilson sought to mobilize the consciences of men everywhere by expressing the nearly universal desire for a lasting and equitable peace settlement that hopefully would end the bloody war and usher in a new age of peace and justice. The American president saw his remarks also as a direct notice or warning to the Allied governments that American war goals differed sharply from their secret treaties and agreements for a postwar division of spoils and vengeful treatment of Germany after its defeat. As he wrote House on 21 July 1918, "England and France have not the same views with regard to peace that we have by any means. When the war is over we can force them to our way of thinking because by that time they will . . . be financially in our hands; but we cannot force them now and any attempt to speak for them . . . would bring on disagreements. . . ."

Since President Wilson had voiced widely held American and European liberal sentiments and beliefs, the Fourteen Points received great praise from the American press. Even such dedicated opponents as former President Theodore Roosevelt hailed the nobility of the president's remarks. Yet beneath this outward surface of harmony, a number of Republican and other critics at home reacted adversely to parts of the Fourteen Points, particularly those clauses or phrases that implied a weakening of tariff protection against foreign imports and the assumption of international responsibilities foreshadowed by the United States as a member of an association of nations.

Abroad the general reaction was also outwardly favorable. In Great Britain, liberals increasingly pinned their hopes for the future upon the American "messiah" who promised to rid mankind of the scourge of war. Liberal circles on the Continent reacted with similar hope and enthusiasm, but not so their governmental leaders, whose goals and schemes for territorial gains clearly clashed with the president's idealistic prescription. Clemenceau simply ignored the address, while British leaders privately voiced great skepticism, particularly in regard to Wilson's reference to freedom of the seas. The Italian government and the official press in Italy responded negatively to the Fourteen Points. Wilson's reference to boundaries based on clear lines of nationality conflicted with Italian ambitions to expand along the Adriatic Sea in areas inhabited by a majority of Slavic-speaking peoples. There was no immediate reaction from Japan; its interests were confined largely to territorial gains in the Pacific, and later at the Peace Conference it made an unsuccessful effort to have incorporated in the Covenant a clause relating to the racial equality of all peoples.

The Bolsheviks and the German leaders dreamed of a quite different peace—the former of a world workers' state and the latter of extensive German annexations—and reacted unfavorably to the speech, thereby limiting the immediate impact. Yet the long-range effects of this and similar speeches did encourage German liberals and socialists to distrust the policies of the imperial German government. The Committee on Public Information, the wartime American propaganda agency that operated under journalist George Creel, eventually flooded enemy countries, cobelligerents of the United States, and neutrals with 60 million pamphlets and leaflets that embodied Wilson's several pronouncements. Such oversell of the idealistic goals of peace undoubtedly prepared the way for later disillusionment, but as a war measure helping to arouse the American and Allied peoples and to some degree to weaken the morale and stamina of the Central Powers it was a bold psychological weapon.

Meanwhile, in subsequent speeches, the American chief executive added to or enlarged upon his original Fourteen Points as the basis for a just and enduring peace. A total of twenty-seven particulars, some repetitive, eventually were proclaimed. On 11 February 1918 Wilson in another address to Congress termed Germany's response to his Fourteen Points inadequate and advocated a peace based upon four general principles that called for each aspect of the peace settlement not only to reflect the dictates of justice but also to help promote a lasting peace. Peoples and lands were not to be transferred or bartered as pawns in a game of balance of power; each adjustment of territory must reflect the interests of the people directly involved; and the aspirations of peoples for separate nationality status ought to be met to the greatest degree possible without creation of new antagonism and discord that would endanger the future peace of Europe and the world community.

Again, liberals in Europe and the United States were immensely pleased while even the German and Austrian leaders, facing a worsening military situation, now admitted the acceptability of Wilsonian principles but expressed doubt that the Allied governments would negotiate on such an enlightened basis. Meanwhile enemy actions had seemed to highlight the differences between what was generally described as the "old diplomacy" of imperialism and the "new diplomacy" of morality and principle. When the Bolshevik leaders of Russia signed the harsh Treaty of Brest-Litovsk that was dictated by Germany and Austria in March 1918, they found themselves saddled with heavy territorial losses and great financial burdens. The imposition of such a drastic peace treaty on prostrate Russia revealed what the leaders of a triumphant imperial Germany would do elsewhere. Consequently, Wilson proclaimed that the only response by the United States and its cobelligerents lay in the full use of force to crush the evil imperialists: "Force, Force to the utmost, Force without stint or limit, the righteous and triumphant Force shall make Right the law of the world, and cast every selfish dominion down in the dust." Clearly Wilson had come to share the views of close advisers and others that a fair and just peace necessitated the final and complete defeat of the Central Powers.

At Mount Vernon, in a Fourth of July address, 1918, the president again emphasized the necessity for a peace founded upon a league of nations that would draw authority from the consent of the world's peoples. In short, Wilson advocated a league that would be based upon world moral opinion and that would comprise a definite part of the postwar treaties of peace. On 27 September 1918, after House had again urged the advisability of seeking an agreement on war aims with the Allies,

Wilson did make a major speech and requested the Allies to accede to his version of a liberal settlement. He called for a permanent peace to end this war, based upon impartial justice in every aspect and fulfilled by an association of nations. He then set forth five particulars for a lasting peace arrangement: no discrimination in a just settlement; no spheres of interest to override the common interest in peace; no alliances within the overarching league of nations; no selfish economic combinations or boycotts except as applied by the future league; and no secret international treaties and agreements.

While the major Allied leaders did not respond officially to Wilson's pronouncements, the reaction of British radicals and liberals to these later addresses was highly enthusiastic. Responding to such sentiment, Lloyd George spoke along similar lines, on 12 November 1918, after the signing of the Armistice with Germany. Wilson warmly congratulated the British leader and rejoiced at the broad similarity between American and British aims. Thus as the war ended, an informal Anglo-American agreement on essential war aims had come into existence. Unfortunately there was no attempt made at a more specific concert for the peacemaking.

Yet while credited by some writers with much success in driving a wedge between the enemy peoples and their rulers, recent reexaminations indicate that Wilson's idealistic pronouncements had little positive effect upon the German authorities until they were forced by military reverses to ask for an armistice. Only at that time, with Germany obviously defeated and facing the prospect of actual invasion and occupation, did the seeds of distrust and disillusionment with the war, sown by Wilson's speeches, bear fruit. Therefore, on 4 October the German government sued for peace based on the principles that Wilson had announced in his Fourteen Points speech and other addresses. Much delicate diplomacy ensued. The Allies were disturbed by the German overture and feared that the tricky enemy would take advantage of the idealist in the White House. Yet Wilson skillfully avoided the German traps and, by releasing the exchanges to the press, hastened the end of the war by undermining German morale both by indicating the approaching end of the war and by the fairly generous peace terms. At one stage in the negotiations, when the Allied governments showed great resistance, Colonel House was sent to Europe as the president's representative and threatened in effect that the United States might have to sign a separate peace. The British and French finally and reluctantly agreed to concur in the Fourteen Points, with two qualifications: the first embodied France's definition about the restoration of invaded areas and damaged property; the second contained a British reservation on the freedom of the seas. Lesser Allied objections were then brushed aside and the so-called Pre-armistice Agreement was completed. On 5 November Wilson informed Germany that the Allies and the Associated Powers would grant that country a peace based on the Fourteen Points with the two reservations. Germany was directed to send representatives to receive the military terms for an armistice. The Armistice was signed on 11 November 1918, ending four years of incredibly bloody warfare.

The Pre-armistice Agreement represented a triumph for Wilson's Fourteen Points. It was not a victory imposed on Great Britain, however, for Lloyd George's war addresses had also called for a liberal peace; and on Point 2, freedom of the seas, Britain had reserved full freedom for subsequent debate. As for France, it had also secured a reservation on the important question of war damages. Clemenceau is reported to have remarked cynically during the peace conference, "God gave us the Ten Commandments, and we broke them. Wilson gives us the Fourteen Points. We shall see." Other powers at the Supreme War Council had indicated that they too had questions about the details of Wilson's ideals applied in any peace negotiations.

Wilson, however, had at last won a formal, if grudging, Allied agreement to a peace based on his principles. No doubt he was justified in assuming that the secret treaties had either been nullified or relegated to a secondary place. On the eve of the greatest peace conference since the Congress of Vienna in 1815, Wilson understandably took great satisfaction in having contributed to military victory over Germany and more importantly in formulating the bases for the peace.

At the Peace Conference, where Wilson broke American tradition by personally leading the United States delegation, he is now generally conceded to have achieved the major portion of his Fourteen Points. Anglo-American harmony was particularly revealed in the drafting of the Covenant of the League of Nations. France, on the other hand, preferred a league that would serve as a cover for a military alliance. In Wilson's view, creation of a league of nations was the most important work of the conference. Although he has been accused of spending too much time upon the drafting of the Covenant of the League, in fact he labored on it in the evenings after the regular sessions were over and thus did not substantially delay the work of the conference. The American peace commission used as its working text a joint Anglo-American draft. France made an effort to incorporate clauses that would promote its security by establishing an international army and general staff under the league. The most that its delegates could obtain, however, was the deletion of a denunciation of military conscription and an acceptance of an advisory committee on possible military sanctions that might be adopted by the future league.

The principal article of the Covenant, Article X, embodied Wilson's concept of a mutual guarantee of the territorial integrity and independence of all member states. Other articles authorized the League Council, composed of five permanent members and four elected members, to invoke measures ranging from economic pressure to the use of armed force against violators of Article X. A general assembly represented all members for purposes of discussion. The Anglo-American idea of a more democratic organization, one that would be primarily dependent upon public opinion and conciliatory devices to preserve peace, had thus emerged victorious over France's desires for a military grand alliance within the League.

Opposition to the Covenant in the United States was to center on Article X and the mutual guarantee that critics saw as a dangerous commitment violating the Constitution. A lesser obligation would probably have eased the path to approval in the Senate, and it might well have improved the image of the league in the 1930's. After all, the positive guarantee of Article X in practice turned out to be unworkable, or at least it was not successfully used.

THE FOURTEEN POINTS

The major defect of Wilson's collective security concept proved to be that it in fact depended upon great power unanimity to enforce, and yet the meaningful challenges to world peace only could arise from among the great powers themselves. A league that promised less initially would have had the virtue of simplicity and to that extent would perhaps have avoided later disillusionment.

Wilson's record of achievement on the remainder of the Fourteen Points at the Paris Peace Conference was mixed. Germany was to be saddled with huge reparations and stripped not only of colonies but of territory, which was assigned to France, Poland, and the new state of Czechoslovakia, thus violating, in the view of many, the principle of self-determination and nationality underlining the Fourteen Points. Point 5, relating to adjustment of colonial claims with due regard to the interests of the peoples living therein, was embodied in the mandate system established under the league. Despite sharp exchanges in Paris between Wilson and those who sought to follow old-fashioned colonialism, a compromise, which represented a considerable victory for principle, was achieved. The Turkish territories and German colonies were classified as *A, B,* or *C* mandates to be administered under the League by the powers that had conquered them. Class *A* mandates were defined as requiring only a short period of tutelage before achieving complete independence. Class *B* mandates, defined as intermediate areas, included Central Africa, while the former German colonies in Southwest Africa and the Pacific became Class *C* mandates to be administered as unfortified but integral parts of the mandatory's territory. Although this solution has been denounced as hypocrisy, a fraud that concealed an imperialistic division of the spoils, Wilson wisely regarded it as the best solution obtainable. After all, the Allies and Japan actually occupied these territories and could not easily be pried loose. The mandate system at least restricted their rule of the colonial peoples involved and opened the way for eventual self-government for the more advanced colonies after World War II.

The mandate system has been seen as ultimately presaging the end of the age of colonialism. It may not always have worked out well in practice but morally the mandate system clearly signaled that the exploitation of one people by another was wrong, and it advocated the ideal of independence for all people. A very important if incomplete victory for Wilsonianism thus was achieved.

As for their impact upon most Americans, Wilson's pronouncements probably had little or no lasting effect. Evidence indicates that a majority of citizens felt more affected by emotional appeals to crush the enemy than by Wilson's talks about the abstract requirements for a just peace and a league of nations. Probably the president would have been wiser and more effective if he had placed greater emphasis upon the practical benefits to the United States in terms of security and trade from the new world order he proclaimed, but such an approach would have been alien to Wilson's idealistic nature. Moreover, a number of Wilson's peace prescriptions were overly vague, thus avoiding no doubt immediate difficulties with the Allies but creating popular misconceptions that bore bitter fruit in the subsequent general postwar mood of disillusionment. For example, his references to open or democratic diplomacy were popularly interpreted to mean that all diplomacy thereafter should take place in the full glare of publicity, when in fact the president, as he wrote Secretary of State Robert Lansing on 12 March 1918, meant by the phrase merely that the results of diplomacy henceforth should be made fully known.

Another of the moving slogans of the war, "self-determination of peoples," also has received criticism for allegedly helping to balkanize Europe via the arousal of nationality sentiments and the subsequent creation of a number of new small and jealous independent states. It would be incorrect to attribute the emergence of the new states of Poland, Czechoslovakia, Finland, Latvia, Lithuania, Estonia, and Yugoslavia to Wilsonian encouragement. Rather, the military collapse of the Central Powers and of Russia made inevitable the creation of these new states. Moreover, the peace treaty, if it were to grapple successfully with the basic cause of the recent conflict, had to recognize and satisfy such widespread desires for statehood and independence if it were to have any prospects at all of endurance and justice. In recognizing these facts, President Wilson was being realistic and idealistic. Unfortunately, however, his penchant for phrase-mongering ultimately called down upon his head the disappointments and sense of grievance that any settlement must inevitably produce. As assessed by historian-critic Thomas A. Bailey, the Fourteen Points and related points were sufficiently vague for wartime purposes, but they proved inadequate as a practical basis for peacemaking.

BIBLIOGRAPHY

Thomas A. Bailey, *Woodrow Wilson and the Lost Peace* (New York, 1944), is a sympathetic but sharply critical account from the viewpoint of a disillusioned Wilsonian. Ruhl J. Bartlett, *The League to Enforce Peace* (Chapel Hill, N.C., 1944), relates the history of the popular movement for collective security and traces its origins in Anglo-American thought. Sidney Bell, *Righteous Conquest: Woodrow Wilson and the Evolution of the New Diplomacy* (Port Washington, N.Y., 1972), a "New Left" presentation, depicts Wilsonian diplomacy as aimed at a new world order safe for American economic expansionism. Lawrence E. Gelfand, *The Inquiry: American Preparations for Peace, 1917–1919* (New Haven, 1963), examines closely the role of a group of scholars and experts assembled by Colonel House to study problems likely to arise at the Paris Peace Conference, concluding that the Inquiry had a considerable impact on the final shape of the peace treaty. N. Gordon Levin, Jr., *Woodrow Wilson and World Politics: America's Response to War and Revolution* (Toronto, 1968), is also critical of Wilson, from a viewpoint that depicts American policy as trying to promote an open-door economic system primarily for the benefit of the United States, while purporting to serve the interests of the rest of the world. Arthur S. Link, *Wilson the Diplomatist: A Look at His Major Foreign Policies* (Baltimore, Md., 1957), a series of essays on major aspects of Wilsonian diplomacy, finds the idealist often more realistic than assumed heretofore. Lawrence W. Martin, *Peace Without Victory: Woodrow Wilson and the British Liberals* (New Haven, 1958), studies the interrelationship between British and American thought on the Fourteen Points and the Paris Peace Conference. Arno J. Mayer, *Political Origins of the New Diplomacy, 1917–18* (New Haven, 1959), and *Politics and Diplomacy of Peacemaking: Containment and Counter-Revolution at Versailles, 1918–1919* (New York, 1967), traces the impact of the Fourteen Points on the European belligerents and the Bolsheviks in Russia, and heavily stresses the effects of revolution in the work of the Paris Peace Conference. Daniel M. Smith, *The Great Departure: The United States and World War I* (New York, 1965), a treatment of the entire war period, weighs the evidence and concludes that Wilson obtained many of his objectives at Paris.

[See also ANTI-IMPERIALISM; DISARMAMENT; FREEDOM OF THE SEAS; IDEOLOGY AND FOREIGN POLICY; IMPERIALISM; INTERNATIONALISM; INTERNATIONAL LAW; INTERNATIONAL ORGANIZATION; NATIONAL SELF-DETERMINATION; PEACEMAKING; PRESIDENTIAL POWER IN FOREIGN AFFAIRS; REALISM AND IDEALISM; REVOLUTION AND FOREIGN POLICY; SUMMIT CONFERENCES; TREATIES.]

FREEDOM OF THE SEAS

Armin Rappaport

THE TERM "freedom of the seas" refers to the concept that the seas, except for territorial waters, are free to all peoples and that no authority, sovereign, or nation may restrict that freedom. As Queen Elizabeth I of England said, "The use of the sea and air is common to all; neither can any title to the ocean belong to any people or private man. . . ." It was on the principle of freedom of the seas that King Francis I of France disputed the exclusive right in certain seas that the pope granted to Spain and Portugal in the fifteenth century. It was on that principle, too, that the mercantilist systems of the colonizing powers in the seventeenth and eighteenth centuries were questioned. By the time of the great dynastic wars in those centuries, the term "freedom of the seas" was being used in relation to commerce in time of war, and diplomats and publicists were arguing about the rights and duties of neutrals and belligerents.

From the beginning of the American nation, political leaders championed the view that the seas ought to be free in war as well as in peace. As John Adams said in 1783, "The United States of America have propagated far and wide in Europe the ideas of the liberty of navigation and commerce. The powers of Europe, however, cannot agree as yet, in adopting them to their full extent. . . . For my own part, I think nature wiser than all the courts and estates of the world, and, therefore, I wish all her seas and rivers upon the whole globe free." Benjamin Franklin was of the same mind. In 1782 he said, "In general, I would only observe that commerce, consisting in a mutual exchange of the necessaries of life, the more free and unrestrained it is the more it flourishes and the happier are all the nations concerned

in it." Applied in wartime, the principle translated into the right of citizens of neutral states to carry on their normal trading pursuits without molestation or interference by the belligerents, unless that trade was in war goods destined for a belligerent. Throughout its history, with but two exceptions—the Civil War and World War I—the United States has been the principal proponent and defender of that view.

The American position on freedom of the seas was first expressed on 18 July 1776, when John Adams presented to the Continental Congress the report of a committee of which he was chairman and whose other members were Benjamin Franklin, John Dickinson, Benjamin Harrison, and Robert Morris. The committee had been appointed some five weeks earlier and had been charged with preparing a "plan of treaties to be entered into with foreign states and kingdoms." The report proposed a model set of articles concerning neutral commerce in wartime to be included in treaties of amity and commerce with other powers. On 17 September of the same year, Congress adopted the proposals, which thereupon became the first official American statement on the freedom of the seas.

There were four articles in the proposal: (1) should one of the signatories be at war and the other neutral, the citizens of the neutral could trade with the enemies of the belligerent in all items except contraband of war, the latter being limited to arms, munitions of war, and horses (food and naval stores were specifically excluded); (2) citizens of the neutral could trade with the enemies of the belligerent in noncontraband not only from enemy ports to neutral ports but also between ports of an enemy; (3) enemy noncontraband found in neutral ships was not liable to confiscation by the belligerent ("free ships make free goods"); and (4) neutral goods, whether contraband or noncontraband, found in enemy vessels were liable to confiscation.

These principles, known collectively as the Treaty Plan of 1776, and clearly favorable to neutrals, were not invented by Adams and his colleagues. For more than a century they had been a part of the international maritime scene and had been practiced by neutrals and belligerents during the great dynastic wars of the seventeenth and eighteenth centuries, albeit with occasional modifications. They had also been incorporated in several treaties between European powers, most notably France and Great Britain in 1655, 1686, and 1713. Indeed, the American indebtedness to precedent was duly acknowledged by the printing in the journals of the Continental Congress, as an annex to the Treaty Plan, the maritime articles of the Peace of Utrecht of 1713, which ended the War of the Spanish Succession between France and England.

It is not surprising that Adams' committee proposed, and the Congress accepted, the maritime principles of 1776. For one thing, they were a natural and logical concomitant of the Declaration of Independence. It seemed only reasonable that the "unalienable right to life, liberty, and the pursuit of happiness" should extend to the high seas. More important, the principles were consistent with the visions the Founding Fathers had for the new republic's future. The country was to "be as little as possible entangled in the politics and controversies of European nations." It would take no part in Europe's wars. Rather, American merchants would be the great neutral carriers of the needs of the belligerents, and for that role they would need the protection of the maritime principles of 1776. Should the United States find itself a belligerent at some future time, a liberal interpretation of the rights of neutrals would still be useful and important. The Founding Fathers never expected that the American navy would be large and powerful enough to protect American shipping in wartime—neutral vessels would have to be depended upon to handle American commerce, and for that they would need the cover of the principles of 1776.

It was a source of satisfaction to American diplomats that they succeeded in incorporating the cherished maritime articles into the first bilateral treaty signed by the new republic. In 1778 the Franco-American Treaty of Amity and Commerce contained almost without change the language and the substance of the Treaty Plan. But that was only the beginning of the nearly universal acceptance of the American position. Three more agreements—with the Netherlands in 1782, with Sweden in 1783, and with Prussia in 1785—also included the maritime articles of 1776.

Meanwhile, in 1780, the Russian empress, Catherine the Great, had announced that her country's neutral commerce in the war then raging between England and her former colonies would be governed by four principles. Three of them—free ships make free goods, freedom of neutrals to trade between ports of a belligerent, and contraband limited to arms and munitions—came directly from the Treaty Plan of 1776. The fourth—that a port be considered legally blockaded only if there were a sufficient number of vessels at its mouth to make entry dangerous—had not been dealt with by Adams' committee in 1776. It was, however, included in a new treaty plan adopted by the United States in 1784. At Russia's invitation, seven other nations adhered to Catherine's principles. Thus, of the great powers only Great Britain refused to be bound by the liberal maritime principles. Hard though they tried, the American commissioners negotiating the peace that ended the war between mother country and colonies could not get the principles incorporated in the final treaty. English statesmen, envisioning their country more often belligerent than neutral—and big-navy belligerent, at that—rejected the American overtures. The treaty said nothing about the rights of neutrals.

The first challenge to the American position was not long in coming. In 1793 France and Great Britain went to war. The United States at once declared neutrality and soon became the chief neutral supplier of belligerent needs. France was legally bound by the terms of the Treaty of 1778 to treat American commerce according to the principles of 1776. Britain, having entered into no agreement with the United States on neutral and belligerent rights, was free to halt, by all means possible, trade between France and America. Unwilling to fight the war at so serious a disadvantage, French warships soon violated the provisions of the 1778 treaty and treated American commerce as the British did. When England and the United States signed a convention in 1794 (Jay's Treaty), which specifically included naval stores on the contraband list and stated that enemy goods were not protected by the neutral flag, France was furious that American diplomats had not forced Britain to accept the principles of 1776. The result was an intensification of French depredations upon American neutral commerce, which led, in 1798, to an undeclared Franco-American maritime war. Known as the Quasi-War, it lasted until 1800.

France and England made peace in 1802, but war broke out again in the following year. This second phase of the great struggle was marked by intense efforts by each belligerent to prevent neutrals from trading with its enemy. As the chief neutral suppliers and carriers, American citizens suffered severe restrictions on their trade. In 1812 the United States went to war, in part, to defend its citizens' neutral rights.

It was true, of course, that the war was fought only against England, but not because France's conduct was less reprehensible. Congress gave serious consideration to declaring war against both nations. In the end, however, a war against two enemies was unthinkable and England was chosen over France for the very good reason that her navy, not France's, dominated the seas and committed the largest number of violations of American neutrality.

President James Madison, when touching upon maritime reasons for requesting hostilities, referred specifically only to "mock blockades" and to "violations of our coasts" as evidence of Britain's perfidious conduct. More generally, he spoke of England "laying waste our neutral trade" and plundering "our commerce . . . in every sea." He surely had in mind three British practices, all contrary to the principles of 1776. One was the interdiction of American trade between ports of the enemy, which England justified on the basis of the Rule of the War of 1756. That rule, established during the French and Indian War of 1754–1763, declared that a trade closed in peacetime could

not be opened in wartime. In conformity with good mercantilist doctrine, France, as well as every other European nation, prohibited foreigners from engaging in the trade between ports. In wartime, however, when the superior British navy made it unsafe for French vessels to carry the traffic, it was thrown open to non-French bottoms. Thus, the rule deprived American merchants of a lucrative trade. When they sought to evade it by touching at a neutral port (most often in the United States) en route between the two enemy ports, the British were not fooled. Their cruisers picked up the American vessels and their prize courts condemned them on the grounds that the ultimate destination was, in fact, an enemy port and that the voyage between the two enemy ports was "a continuous voyage only ostensibly broken at a neutral port." The two other British practices were the inclusion of naval stores and foodstuffs on the contraband list and the confiscation of enemy goods found in neutral ships.

Now a belligerent, the United States made every effort "to pay the strictest regard to the rights of neutral powers." Naval commanders were instructed "to give them [neutrals] as little molestation or interruption as will consist with the right of ascertaining their neutral character," and the orders were carried out. Neutral rights were respected.

Insofar as the war was fought in defense of American neutral rights, it proved futile, for the treaty ending the war made no mention of the subject. In a letter to the commissioners sent to Europe to negotiate the peace, Secretary of State James Monroe expressed the hope that Great Britain, having violated almost every neutral right, "herself will see the advantage of adopting a more just and enlarged policy towards neutral powers." That expectation was not fulfilled. The British flatly refused to discuss the matter. Big-navy powers are never willing to constrict their belligerent rights.

Between the end of the war with Britain and the opening of the Civil War, the United States continued to push for the acceptance of the principles of 1776 and the provision on blockade in the Treaty Plan of 1784. To some observers it seemed anomalous that the United States, on the threshold of becoming a significant naval power, should continue to support liberal maritime principles. A clue to the riddle was provided by Secretary of State Henry Clay, who noted in 1828 that the United States did not expect to become involved in maritime wars because its "prosperity is so evidently connected with the preservation of peace." And, he implied, even if the country should become involved in a war—and as a big-navy belligerent—it would value "the general cause of humanity and civilization [which] will be promoted by the adoption of these maritime principles [above] pecuniary interest." Thus, between 1824 and 1850 the United States concluded treaties with ten Latin American republics and one with Prussia incorporating the liberal maritime principles. Efforts to commit Great Britain to the principles remained unsuccessful.

The war with Mexico (1846–1848) provided the United States with the occasion to practice what it preached. Its policy toward neutrals was governed by the instruction of the secretary of the navy to commanding officers of American naval forces in the Pacific, issued on 24 December 1846: "The President has desired to subject neutral commerce to the least possible inconvenience or obstruction compatible with the exercise of the belligerent right necessary to the success of our military operations." One year later, explaining the United States position to the newly appointed commander in the Pacific, the secretary wrote: "No present advantage . . . should induce us to depart from that liberal interpretation of the laws of nations which we have always contended for as protecting the interests of neutrals against the violent claims of belligerents." Indeed, in the matter of blockade, contraband, and enemy goods on neutral ships, the United States adhered strictly to the principles of 1776 and 1784.

Six years after the end of the Mexican conflict, the Crimean War broke out and the United States again found itself a neutral—but with two important differences from the period 1793–1812. This time, Great Britain and France were on the same side, fighting Russia; and they made clear their intention to pursue a liberal course toward neutral commerce insofar as neutral goods on enemy ships and enemy goods on neutral ships were concerned. In both instances the goods, except for contraband, were to be free from seizure. Russia adopted the same principles and incorporated

them in a convention signed with the United States in July 1854.

Encouraged by the action of the three belligerents, especially by that of Great Britain, and recognizing that for Britain and France the policies on neutral rights covered the duration of the war only, the United States government sought to incorporate the rules in a multilateral treaty and make them a "principle of international law." Secretary of State William L. Marcy, in instructions sent to the American ministers in Paris, London, and St. Petersburg in 1854, enclosed a draft treaty, noting: "The United States are desirous to unite with other powers in a declaration that . . . [the rules] be observed by each hereafter, as a rule of international law." In his annual message to Congress in December of the same year, President Franklin Pierce voiced the same hope.

The three belligerents did, in fact, "unite with other powers in a declaration" on maritime law at the peace conference that met in Paris in the winter and spring of 1856. Four principles constituted the Declaration of Paris, signed on 16 April 1856, by representatives of Austria, France, Great Britain, Prussia, Russia, Sardinia, and Turkey: (1) privateering is, and remains, abolished; (2) the neutral flag covers enemy goods, except for contraband; (3) neutral goods, except for contraband, are not liable to capture under the enemy flag; and (4) blockades, in order to be binding, must be effective.

It was not surprising that the United States was highly gratified. The liberal view on neutral rights that it had so vigorously championed for more than half a century had at last been written, if only in part, into international law. Particularly welcome was the end of British opposition. Still, the United States found itself in the curious situation of refusing to become a party to the declaration. The reason lay in the article on privateering. As Secretary of State Marcy pointed out in a lengthy note to the French minister in Washington, the strong-navy powers could afford to renounce privateering because they could effectively prey upon enemy commerce with their public armed vessels; small-navy states, like the United States, lacking an adequate number of warships, had to rely upon private armed vessels to destroy the enemy's goods. Only if the words "and that the private property of the subjects or citizens of a belligerent on the high seas shall be exempted from seizure by public armed vessels of the other belligerent, except it be contraband" were added to the first article would the United States sign the declaration.

That principle—the complete immunity of (noncontraband) private property—had been advanced by the United States for many years. It was a logical extension of the liberal position on neutral rights. First suggested by Benjamin Franklin in 1780 and again in 1782 for inclusion in the peace treaty ending the War of Independence, it was included in the Treaty Plan of 1784, incorporated into the Treaty of Amity and Commerce of 1785 with Prussia, and made the central feature of an instruction by Secretary of State John Quincy Adams in 1823 to the American minister in London to negotiate a treaty on neutral rights with Great Britain. "The great object of the whole convention," said Adams, ". . . is to take the first step toward the eventual abolition by the Law of Nations of private war upon the sea."

The signatories of the declaration did not summarily reject the American amendment. They deferred action pending a careful examination of the problem and the opportunity to consult among themselves. By March 1857, when President James Buchanan assumed office, no action had been taken and the new secretary of state, Lewis Cass, told the American ministers to suspend negotiations on the subject until the president had time to study "the questions involved." The president, preoccupied with problems closer to home, never did get around to the matter; and thus the United States lost the opportunity to incorporate into a multilateral treaty its historic and traditional position. Because the four principles of the declaration were considered indivisible by the signatories, the United States could not adhere to numbers 2, 3, and 4 while rejecting the first.

Viewed from a different perspective, the failure of the United States to become a party to the Declaration of Paris may be considered fortunate, for in the Civil War, which broke out in 1861, the United States remained free of any international legal commitments regarding neutral rights. For the first time in its history, the United States was the preponderant belligerent naval power, and that freedom would permit it to pursue any course at sea calculated to increase the chances of victory. As a matter of fact, the United States did expand its belligerent rights during the war and did constrict those rights of neutrals that it had championed since the earliest days of the Republic.

Early in the war, Secretary of State William H. Seward informed the principal neutral powers that American policy toward their commerce would be governed by articles 2, 3, and 4 of the Declaration of Paris. And the United States did, during the course of the war, respect the principles of "free ships make free goods" and the freedom from seizure of neutral goods (not contraband) in enemy ships. On blockade, however, the United States strayed far from its traditional position. It is true that Seward insisted that the blockade need not be respected if it were not maintained by an adequate force and that every effort was made to station a sufficient number of vessels at the blockaded ports to prevent entry and exit. It is true, too, that the British government accepted the existence of an effective (and, hence, a legal) blockade and respected it. But it is also true that in an effort to make the blockade more effective, the United States indulged in some highly questionable practices that the British had used when a belligerent in the French Revolutionary and Napoleonic wars (1792–1815) and against which the United States had protested vigorously. One, called the long-range blockade, was accomplished by "flying squadrons" of swift warships that patrolled the sea-lanes and intercepted neutral vessels far from a blockaded port, seizing them if there were grounds for believing their destination to be a blockaded port. Another was to place neutral ports (in England, the Bahamas, Mexico, and the West Indies) under surveillance and capture vessels as they left the protection of territorial waters, presumably for a port under blockade. In addition, Union warships took as prizes on the high seas neutral vessels coming from and going to neutral ports, on the ground that the ship and its cargo were ultimately destined for a blockaded port. American prize courts upheld the seizures, considering the voyage between the neutral port of origin and the blockaded port as one continuous, albeit broken, voyage. The doctrine was also applied to contraband. It was strange to find the United States applying the doctrine of continuous voyage, which had been so objectionable when practiced by the British in the wars against France.

In the matter of contraband, the United States did not publish an official list; but the secretary of the treasury, in a circular sent to collectors of customs at several Southern ports where the blockade had been lifted, enumerated articles considered contraband and therefore banned from the ports. Among them were arms, munitions, and war supplies, as was to be expected. But the list also included naval stores and a host of other items, such as ardent spirits, corn, bullion, printing presses, coal, iron, lead, copper, tin, brass, telegraphic instruments, wire, and marine engines—and those were not to be expected. They flew in the face of the historic American resistance to an expanded contraband list.

Why the United States turned its back on history and tradition, and exchanged the role of champion of the rights of neutrals for that of defender of the rights of belligerents, can be explained only in terms of a sacrifice of principle for expediency. Winning the war was the overriding factor in determining the nation's policy. Nothing else mattered.

From the end of the Civil War to the opening of World War I in 1914, the United States did not concern itself greatly with the freedom of the seas. It was a neutral in three wars during the period (Franco-Prussian, Boer, Russo-Japanese), but none of them presented any serious problems on the seas. The United States was a belligerent once during this period (against Spain), but that conflict was too brief to raise any serious maritime issues. There was, however, one significant development in American policy toward neutral commerce during the Spanish-American War—the division of the contraband list into absolute and conditional contraband. The former included articles primarily and ordinarily used for military purposes and destined for an enemy country; the latter included articles that might be used for purposes of war or peace, according to circumstances, and would be subject to seizure only if actually and specifically consigned to the military or naval forces of an enemy. In the latter category, foodstuffs and coal were the most important items. This division became a permanent feature of American policy when it was in-

corporated in the United States Naval War Code, adopted in June 1900.

If there was one preoccupation of American diplomacy concerning neutral and belligerent rights and duties, it was the effort to secure international acceptance of the principle of the immunity of private property at sea. The adoption of such a broad principle, long sought by American diplomats, would have applied to all private property, both neutral and belligerent, replacing the more specific provisions covering neutrals, such as "free ships make free goods." It was the subject of negotiation with the North German Confederation in 1870, and was incorporated into a treaty of amity and commerce with Italy in 1871. In December 1898 President William McKinley asked Congress for authority "to correspond with the governments of the principal maritime powers with a view of incorporating into the permanent law of civilized nations the principle of the exemption of all private property at sea, not contraband of war, from capture or destruction by belligerent powers." Five years later, his successor in the White House, Theodore Roosevelt, reiterated the plea. In the instructions prepared for the American delegation to the First Hague Conference in 1899, the chief item was on immunity of private property at sea; and the instructions for the delegates to the Second Hague Conference in 1907 included a congressional resolution of 1904 supporting the same principle. All these efforts proved in vain, however. The United States did not succeed in gaining international acceptance of the doctrine.

The United States did, nonetheless, have the satisfaction of seeing many of its other principles adopted at an international congress that met in London during the winter of 1908–1909, convened at the call of Great Britain. The ten maritime powers represented (Germany, England, Austria-Hungary, the United States, Spain, France, Italy, Japan, the Netherlands, Russia) agreed on a code of prize law that would be administered by an international prize court hearing appeals from national prize courts set up by belligerents. In seventy-one articles contained in ten chapters, precise and detailed rules were established governing blockade, contraband, nonneutral service, treatment of prizes, determination of a vessel's character, convoy, transfers to a neutral flag, and visit and search of vessels. Taken together, the rules that made up the Declaration of London were favorable to neutrals, which may account for the fact that the British House of Lords refused to ratify them (after the House of Commons had given its approval). Thus they were not binding on any of the other signatories. Still, the United States sought, at the outbreak of war in August 1914, to have the warring nations accept the declaration as the guide in their treatment of neutrals. Germany was willing, but England was not. As the preponderant navy belligerent, England was not willing to surrender the advantage to be derived from the lack of legal restrictions.

The plight of the neutrals, particularly the one most heavily involved in the carrying trade, was cruel indeed. As in the titanic struggle between France and England from 1792 to 1815, the only rule followed by the belligerents was expediency. No holds were barred, no measure was neglected that might contribute to the defeat of the enemy. Each contestant used to the utmost the weapon it knew best. The submarine stalked the seas, but mainly the waters surrounding the British Isles, sinking every vessel it could catch—enemy or neutral—carrying supplies to England. The British surface navy roamed the oceans enforcing measures designed to halt all traffic to Germany. Those measures were numerous and comprehensive, and reflected the cumulative experience of a nation for which the sea had been a lifeline for three centuries. The contraband list was extended to include the widest variety of articles; and the distinction between absolute and conditional categories, which England had adopted at the same time as the United States, was gradually blurred until it disappeared altogether.

The blockade of Germany was not effective, in that ships were not stationed at German ports to prevent entry and exit but were, rather, placed in the North Sea and the Downs, from which the traffic to the Continent was more easily controlled. It must be pointed out that the two belligerents were under no legal obligation to treat American commerce according to American wishes. There was no body of international maritime law binding the warring countries (the Declaration of London not being in force and not having been signed by the

United States), nor were they bound by any bilateral treaties with the United States concerning the treatment of neutrals. Visit and search were not conducted at the point of interception on the high seas; neutral vessels were taken into British or other Allied ports for a detailed and careful examination of cargo and papers. Neutral mails were opened and inspected for contraband and for clues as to destination of cargo. The principle of "free ships make free goods" gave way to the practice of detaining all goods on neutral vessels of enemy origin or ownership. Neutral firms that dealt with the enemy were put on a "blacklist" and forbidden to trade with the Allies, while neutral vessels that did not conform to certain conditions laid down by the British were subjected to "bunker control" and denied coal, oil, and other supplies. Finally, the doctrine of continuous voyage, hitherto applied to absolute contraband only, and where the second leg of the broken voyage was by sea, was applied to conditional contraband, and where the second leg was over a contiguous land frontier.

The United States, caught between the two belligerents, protested both the violations of its neutral rights and the destruction of the doctrine of the freedom of the seas. The protests to Germany were sharper, more insistent, and more demanding than those to England, although the policies of both were equally oppressive and damaging. The reason for such discrimination was stated by President Woodrow Wilson when he compared the British to thieves and the Germans to murderers. The former, he said, seized property, a matter that could be adjudicated at the end of the war, while the latter took lives, which were lost forever. There was, of course, another cause for the partiality to the British—Americans were entangled, emotionally and economically, with the British, which made a rupture of relations with them unthinkable. The United States finally went to war against Germany to uphold its rights as a neutral and to defend the principle of the freedom of the seas, not only for itself but for other nations as well (the "challenge is to all mankind," said the president). The move might be viewed as the fulfillment of the task set out by Secretary of State Robert Lansing in a note sent to the British government in October 1915: ". . . championing the integrity of neutrals . . . [which] the United States unhesitatingly assumes. . . ."

The deep concern the United States exhibited for its neutral rights, as well as for the rights of others, between 1914 and 1917 vanished the moment the country joined the Allied cause. Indeed, as a belligerent the United States outdid its allies in trampling upon neutral rights. The justification of a harsh policy toward neutrals lay in the necessity for winning the war and defeating the enemy of mankind's freedom—on the seas as elsewhere. The neutrals were not impressed by America's beneficence. They were shocked. As one Danish newspaper noted, "It was as a spokesman of the *freedom of the seas* and the *rights of neutral countries* that America came into conflict with Germany, and finally went to war. It would be a strange *début* for her to start by committing exactly the same kind of outrage which Mr. Wilson pretended to fight against in the interest of the neutrals." As a matter of fact, the belligerent policy of the United States need not have been so unexpected. It was heralded in a remark made by Secretary Lansing in 1915. He noted: "It was of the highest importance that we should not become a belligerent with our hands tied too tightly by what we had written. We would presumably wish to adopt some of the policies and practices which the British had adopted, though certainly not all of them, for our object would be the same as theirs . . . to break the power of Germany. . . ."

Almost every practice against which the United States protested as a neutral it pursued as a belligerent—the blacklist, "bunker control," sweeping contraband list, postal censorship, and broadest interpretation of the doctrine of continuous voyage—rather as it had done during the Civil War. In fairness, it must be noted, however, that certain British practices were not adopted by belligerent America. The United States did not join Britain in the blockade or in the routing of neutral vessels into ports to facilitate searching them. It must also be pointed out that President Wilson was not pleased by the necessity to treat the neutrals harshly. He undertook the measures reluctantly and sadly and, in many cases, held off using them as long as possible.

As World War I came to an end, the American view of the freedom of the seas underwent a considerable change. It came about as a consequence of Woodrow Wilson's dream of a new postwar international order. In that order, the concept of freedom of the seas would not be used to describe the problem of the rights of neutrals to trade in wartime. It would have a much broader meaning. As stated by the president in a message to the Senate on 22 January 1917, it would mean the right of every nation to have free access to "the open paths of the world's commerce. . . ." And, he went on to say, "The paths of the sea must alike in law and in fact be free. The freedom of the seas is the *sine qua non* of peace, equality, and co-operation." One year later, on 8 January 1918, Wilson further elaborated his concept of freedom of the seas in his Fourteen Points. The second of them called for "absolute freedom of navigation upon the seas, outside territorial waters, alike in peace and in war, except as the seas may be closed in whole or in part by international action for the enforcement of international covenants." It should be noted that by the last qualifying phrase, Wilson indicated that restrictions on freedom of the seas could be effected only by the League of Nations, the new international organization for maintaining the peace, when acting to chastise a peace-breaking nation.

Unfortunately, certain nations were not prepared to accept so broad and bold a definition of freedom of the seas. Britain, particularly, balked at its being incorporated in the peace treaty. The British could not afford to leave so vital an element of their national security in any hands other than their own. "This point we cannot accept under any conditions," said Prime Minister David Lloyd George. "It means that the power of blockade goes; Germany has been broken almost as much by the blockade as by military methods; if this power is to be handed over to the League of Nations and Great Britain were fighting for her life, no League of Nations could prevent her from defending herself." France and Italy took much the same view. Said French Premier Georges Clemenceau, "War would not be war if there was freedom of the seas."

For his part, Wilson would not "consent to take part in the negotiation of a peace which did not include freedom of the seas [and] . . . unless Lloyd George would make some reasonable concessions on his attitude upon the freedom of the seas, all hope of Anglo-Saxon unity would be at an end." To avoid such a breakdown among the Allies, which would give Germany so great an advantage, the British finally accepted the point as a basis for discussion at the conference—but on the understanding that they "reserve to themselves complete freedom on this subject when they enter the Peace Conference." The point was never seriously discussed at the conference, and the treaty ending the war made no mention of it. Thus Wilson's effort to redefine the principle came to naught.

Between the two world wars the freedom of the seas did not figure prominently in international affairs. After the breakdown of the Geneva Naval Conference in 1927, Senator William E. Borah of Idaho called for a conference of the great powers to codify the rights of neutrals and belligerents on the high seas in wartime, but nothing came of it. It was clear that the United States and Britain would not agree—the former supporting the liberal view of neutral rights and the latter championing a broad interpretation of the rights of belligerents. In 1929 Senator Arthur Capper of Kansas introduced a resolution in the Senate that would have revived in some measure the Wilsonian dream of the United States joining other nations in denying the freedom of the seas to an aggressor. Appreciating the fact that America could not participate in the League of Nations' enforcement machinery by virtue of nonmembership, he proposed that should the League of Nations declare a nation to be a violator of the peace, the United States would withhold from that country "arms, munitions, implements of war, or other articles for use in war." Thus, there would be no danger of the United States clashing with League of Nations' states in the protection of its neutral rights. Sentiment in America, however, was not ready for a policy of taking sides in an international struggle. A similar effort in 1933 by the American representative at the Geneva Disarmament Conference failed for the same reason.

The outbreak of World War II in 1939 found the United States, for the first time in its history, a neutral unconcerned with the defense of its rights at sea. It had, by drastic legislation enacted in 1935–1939, voluntarily withdrawn from the business of supplying the needs of the belligerents. It had also curtailed the travel of Americans on belligerent passenger vessels and had circumscribed trade with neutrals by keeping American ships out of certain areas, designated combat zones, adjacent to neutral ports. It had, in short, surrendered its traditional insistence that the rights of neutrals be respected.

Before long, however, the country abandoned the role of passive and withdrawn neutral and became virtually a cobelligerent, supplying the Allied Powers with the sinews of war. The restrictive legislation was repealed in November 1941, and a vast flow of American goods in American ships started across the Atlantic. Now the term "freedom of the seas" was once more on the lips of American statesmen as German submarines, operating in wolf packs, attacked the Anglo-American maritime lifeline. President Franklin D. Roosevelt said in May 1941, "All freedom—meaning freedom to live and not freedom to conquer and subjugate other peoples—depends on the freedom of the seas—for our own shipping, for the commerce of our sister Republics, for the right of all nations to use the highways of world trade, and for our own safety. . . . As President of a united, determined people, I say solemnly: we reassert the ancient American doctrine of the freedom of the seas. . . ." He had already, in September 1940, labeled submarine warfare as defiance of the "historic American policy" for which, "generation after generation, America has battled . . . that no nation has the right to make the broad oceans of the world . . . unsafe for the commerce of others." And in August 1941, when Roosevelt and Prime Minister Winston Churchill drew up the Atlantic Charter, a blueprint for the postwar world, the seventh of eight principles was the hope that "such a peace should enable all men to traverse the high seas and oceans without hindrance." Thus, the two leaders of the "free world" reiterated the broad concept of the freedom of the seas first proposed by Woodrow Wilson.

Like the Treaty of Versailles, which ended World War I, the several treaties negotiated after World War II made no mention of the freedom of the seas; and as the Covenant of the League of Nations had ignored the principle, so did the Charter of the United Nations. Thus the hope of Franklin Roosevelt suffered the same fate as did the dream of Woodrow Wilson. The unrestricted right of all men to enjoy the freedom of the seas is still not guaranteed by international agreement. Indeed, since the end of World War II, the United States has on three occasions taken actions that tended to limit the use of the seas by other nations. The first time was in June 1950, at the outbreak of the Korean War. President Harry S. Truman ordered the Seventh Fleet to patrol the Formosa Strait to prevent the Chinese communists from attacking Formosa and to keep the forces of Chiang Kai-shek from mounting an assault on the mainland. The Soviet Union promptly labeled the action a blockade, which the United States as promptly denied. As evidence to support its contention, America pointed to the fact that commercial traffic in the strait was unimpeded and untouched. The interdiction applied only to naval forces.

The second occasion came in October 1962, when President John F. Kennedy, upon learning that the Soviet Union had built missile sites in Cuba and had supplied Cuban Premier Fidel Castro with missiles, proclaimed his intention "to interdict . . . delivery of offensive weapons and associated material to Cuba." He called the policy a "strict quarantine," yet it had all the markings of a blockade. Vessels were to be stopped, and visited and searched, within certain prescribed zones and along certain routes. The Russians considered it a blockade and protested, on the ground that a blockade could be instituted only in wartime. To escape that anomaly, American lawyers called it a "pacific blockade," which international law permits as a means for one nation to seek redress, short of war, from another. The legal difficulty surrounding the use of that term was that in a "pacific blockade" only the blockaded nation's ships could be stopped and seized—not those of a third party. In this instance, Soviet ships were the object of search and seizure. Whatever the terminology, it was clear that the United States had used naval forces to interfere with shipping on the high seas, albeit for the lofty motive of self-defense.

The third example of postwar American practice centered on President Richard M. Nixon's mining of North Vietnamese ports in May 1972. Again there was confusion as to the legal status of the act. Nixon denied the Soviet allegation that it was a blockade. The *New York Times* called it a "semi-blockade." The difficulty was compounded by the fact that the action took place not on the high seas but within the "internal and claimed territorial waters of North Vietnam," to use the words of the Department of State's legal officer. And, indeed, there was no interference with freedom of navigation beyond North Vietnam's territorial waters. Judged by the classic nineteenth-century definition of blockade, the act could not be called a blockade. But, by the mid-twentieth century, many of the traditional and historic concepts that made up the doctrine of the freedom of the seas were being altered to suit new conditions of international relations.

One major change concerns the extent of territorial waters. From early times, the territorial waters of a state were calculated at three miles (a cannon's range). At a conference held in 1930 at The Hague for the codification of international law of the sea, the three-mile limit was adopted officially and the marginal sea was declared to belong to the state. At the same time several nations, wishing to exploit, without competition from other nations, extensive fishing beds and mineral resources in the subsoil, made claims to a more extended area—up to 200 miles. The United States made no such claims, but in 1945 President Truman announced the creation of "conservation zones in those areas of the high seas contiguous to the coasts of the United States" for the development of fishing. Similarly, the continental shelf in the same contiguous areas was to be exploited for its natural resources. No specific limits were put on the contiguous areas, but it was known that the government favored an extension of the territorial waters from three to twelve miles and the creation of an economic zone of 200 miles.

To settle the problem, conferences were held at Geneva in 1958 and 1960 and at Caracas in 1974, but no agreement was reached. At Caracas, the United States pushed the 12- and 200-mile limits, providing freedom of navigation and of scientific research in the economic zone was assured for all nations—"a balance between coastal states' rights and duties within the economic zone"—but some nations appeared uncertain about diluting their sovereignty in the zone. When the conference disbanded in August 1974, it was decided to reconvene in March 1975 for another attempt to write an oceans treaty.

The Geneva meeting of March 1976 produced no agreement, nor did another meeting held in New York during the spring and summer of the following year. Meanwhile, on 13 April 1976 President Gerald R. Ford signed into law a measure (to take effect on 1 March 1977) that would extend American fishing rights to 200 miles. The president regretted such unilateral action but believed it necessary because of the failure of the several conferences to reach an agreement. By 1976 the 12-mile territorial sea zone and the 200-mile economic zone had been adopted by such a large number of nations that despite the absence of an international convention, the zone was viewed as having the force of law.

An additional conference is planned for 1977, but the prospect of agreement on a comprehensive law of the sea does not appear promising. The differences among nations on such matters as the exploitation of the resources of the deep seabed and the extent of sovereignty in the 12- to 200-mile economic zone seem irreconcilable. The question of "national jurisdiction" in the zone is the most crucial one facing the negotiating states, and on that issue the United States' position is consistent with history and tradition. It favors "freedom of the seas" in the zone—that is, that the area be considered the "high seas," with all nations having equal rights of "innocent passage" (military and commercial) for scientific research and exploitation. For 200 years, from the very beginning of the Republic, the ten-

dency of American policy has been to enlarge rather than to restrict the rights of nations on the seas—that is, except in certain periods when the country was at war and the national interest dictated the extension of American rights at the expense of other nations.

BIBLIOGRAPHY

See R. C. Amacher and R. J. Sweeney, eds., *The Law of the Sea: U.S. Interests and Alternatives* (Washington, D.C., 1976); Elizabeth M. Borgese, *The Drama of the Oceans* (New York, 1976); Jonathan I. Charney, "Law of the Sea: Breaking the Deadlock," in *Foreign Affairs*, 55 (1977); *Digest of United States Practise in International Law* (Washington, D.C., 1973–   ), vol. 1 of a projected series to be published annually, which contains documents plus a narrative describing United States policy; Gilbert Gidel, *Le droit international public de la mer,* 3 vols. (Châteauroux, France, 1932), a monumental and exhaustive account of the law of the sea; Charles C. Hyde, *International Law Chiefly as Interpreted by the United States,* 2 vols. (Boston, 1922), a classic and standard account that deals with a wide range of matters pertaining to the freedom of the seas; Philip C. Jessup, *Neutrality, Its History, Economics, and Law,* 4 vols. (New York, 1935–1936), an excellent account dealing with the practices of all the major maritime nations from the eighteenth century to the end of World War I; John Bassett Moore, ed., *Digest of International Law,* 8 vols. (Washington, D.C., 1906), a comprehensive account that fully covers maritime matters and deals with all phases of international law as practiced by the United States (the *Digest* is not a narrative but, rather, a collection of documents and cases interspersed with comment; the work has been carried forward chronologically by Green Hackworth, 8 vols. [1940–1944], and Marjorie Whiteman, 15 vols. [1963–1973]); Carlton Savage, *Policy of the United States Towards Maritime Commerce in War,* 2 vols. (Washington, D.C., 1936), a narrative with documents that covers 1776 to 1918, giving a clear and concise account; and John T. Swing, "Who Will Own the Oceans," in *Foreign Affairs,* 54 (1976).

[*See also* BLOCKADES AND QUARANTINES; EMBARGOES; INTERNATIONAL LAW; NEUTRALITY; TREATIES.]

IDEOLOGY AND FOREIGN POLICY

Paul Seabury

As coined by Comte Antoine Destutt de Tracy, the eighteenth-century philosopher, "ideology" described the method of analyzing ideas which he and his philosophical friends were devising. Derived from the Greek "idea," and "logos"—science—it meant a "science of ideas." A philosophical discipline purporting to explore the elements that Destutt de Tracy believed composed all ideas, the expression partook of the Enlightenment's skepticism of man's mental abilities, and its optimism about improving them.

With the passage of time, the word has come to signify quite different things. Following the French Revolution, the ensuing reaction to unbounded rationalism led also to a reaction to the critical mode so essential to this philosophical school. The worship of reason came widely to be seen as subversive of social institutions. "Ideologues" became mistrusted as dangerous and impractical. Paradoxically, the original aspiration of some practitioners of this school, to ground the social order in reason, sharply contrasted with the practical consequences of their activities.

In the hands of subsequent writers, such as Karl Marx, an almost total reversal of the original meaning of the expression occurred. Ideology, far from being the science of ideas, in Marx's hands became a prevailing belief system used to justify or legitimate a given social order; thus, ideology connoted a "false consciousness." To change society, it was necessary to expose the falsity of the beliefs undergirding it. Ideology subsequently has come to signify a closed system of belief designed to supply ready explanations of the "real" world. It now is widely regarded as a programmatic portfolio of ways in which to act within that world.

Later views of ideology suggest a dual meaning of the word. In one sense, ideology is a system of beliefs required to sustain some existing order; in a second sense, it is a belief system required in order to overthrow the status quo. The former gives it a conservative cast, while the latter gives it a revolutionary one. In the abstract, each meaning is laden with pejorative connotations; in each sense, ideology is deemed to have an instrumental value. The question of the objective merits of a particular set of beliefs thus is bypassed.

In discussing the relationship between ideology and foreign policy in America's international policies, it is essential to note one difficulty entailed in any discussion of ideology in general. Some analysts, chiefly Marxists, have come to see ideology as a rhetorical cover for "real" motives underlying action—the falseness of declaratory policies arises from their deliberate employment to deceive in order to persuade. Others, basing their view on twentieth-century political experience, have come to accept the concept that ideology derives its power not from deliberate deception but from deep and even fanatical devotion to some common cause. Such movements as fascism and Marxism-Leninism, which are closed systems of belief, may thus represent modern, secular equivalents of traditional religious faiths. Seen in this context, such ideologies may be contrasted with the civic characteristics of most Western polities which permit many philosophical and political outlooks. The attempt by revolutionary movements of the twentieth century to mold a "new man" for "new societies" is thus incompatible with civic norms that seek to protect or encourage diversity. Ideology in this sense may be seen as a set of beliefs or convictions that, when acted upon,

398

may entail the zealous and even messianic attempt to impose rigid social formulas upon heterogeneous social reality, often with little account of the costs which the attempt may entail, or the damage which may be done to "real" interests of the nation or the persons it encompasses.

It is a most significant aspect of the role of ideology in American foreign policy that during the entire course of United States history the credos and values that have played themselves out in world politics have not been official contrivances imposed by monolithic political movements controlling an authoritarian state; rather, they have emerged out of diverse strands of the American political culture, itself originally the product of trends and modes of thought active in seventeenth- and eighteenth-century England. Thus it is important to note that controversies over policy and action, arising out of principled conviction, have been exactly that: ideological advocacy can arise in opposition to official policy as much as it can be officially employed to justify and sanction such policy. It is equally significant, although not surprising, that the ideological content of foreign policies has tended to grow in periods of danger and crisis, and to diminish in periods of relative tranquility.

What influence may ideology have upon a nation's international behavior? Some writers have sought to point out the dualistic sources of national foreign policy, one of these being interest and the other belief. Interest might be taken to comprise those matters pertaining to a nation's safety and well-being, while belief might be taken to signify views of a nation's mission in the world at large. Obviously, the relationship might vary greatly in the real world. Interest might suggest a course of action contradictory to belief, and the other way around. Often they can act in tandem. In World War II, for instance, many Americans fought against the Axis Powers convinced that the combination presented a real threat to America's well-being and safety. Others fought under the conviction that Nazism, fascism, and Japanese militarism were evil, and that a victory over them would present an opportunity to spread the values of Western-type liberalism and constitutional democracy. Much the same dualism governed America's participation in World War I as well.

The most fundamental long-term consequence of the American Revolution in world politics lay in the challenge it posed to established, traditional orders in Europe. The new nation was not simply another new factor to contend with in the society of nations; rather, it served in its very existence and successful survival as a civic contrast to the political orders of the Old World. Furthermore, in asserting the right of colonies to independence, its success inevitably inspired other colonial rebellions, especially in Spanish America. It is thus interesting in the case of French support of the American rebellion—which remained clandestine until 1777—that the realpolitik motives of Charles Gravier, comte de Vergennes, (the French foreign minister), clouded the court of Versailles to the ideological implications of the American rebellion for France itself. (Marie Antoinette—a later victim of republicanism—patronizingly referred to the rebels as "our dear republicans.") Other courts of Europe took a less sanguine view of the inherent implications of the Revolution; the Spanish government, while sharing French desires to diminish England's power, was all too aware that the success of American arms would inspire similar rebellions in its own New World empire. Spain's irresolute role in the ensuing war against Britain was as much inhibited by fears of spreading ideological brush fires as it was inspired by animus against British power. In France, and in Europe generally, the subversive influence of republican philosophy and doctrine was furthered, during the war years, by the physical presence of the American agent Benjamin Franklin—a benign, fur-capped philosophe—who seemed, in Paris, the very embodiment of advanced Enlightenment aspirations.

The contrast between New World political institutions—and virtues—and Old World politics from the beginning thus lay in the intertwining of anticolonialist doctrine with republican virtue. The doctrine of the social contract put into practice became inseparable in America from the very concept of self-government, which was employed in the Declaration of Independence to justify severing links with the empire.

Some ideologues like Thomas Paine asserted that the Revolution had as its purpose not just the independence of the American colonies, but also the export of revolution back to Europe. Paine, echoing similar views at the time popular among English pamphleteers and continental intellectuals, was under the impression that the wars afflicting European states owed their origins to the monarchical structure of the latter. The establishment of republican forms of government would naturally lead to peace. An ardent admirer of the French Revolution, which followed in the footsteps of the American, Paine—otherwise remembered for his insistence on a policy of American isolation towards Europe—became an active devotee of American intervention, to help its sister republic in Europe against counterrevolutionary forces.

The central theme of American ideology since the eighteenth century, in all its varied manifestations, has been the theme of liberty. Emblazoned as symbols on national monuments, put to music in national anthems, inscribed in documents and state messages, and stamped upon coinage, the ideas of liberty and freedom so dominated the civic language and thought of the United States as to make virtually impossible the development of authentic conservative thought that might explicitly seek to deny their tenets. Alexis de Tocqueville to the contrary, the idea of liberty has had far more enduring popularity than the idea of equality in American civic culture. The Declaration of Independence, in fact, subsumed the idea of equality under the idea of independence; only by breaking the shackles of imperial domination could the rights of inherently equal men to life, liberty, and the pursuit of happiness (or property) be successfully established. Columbia, the secular goddess of a predominantly Christian polity, is indistinguishable in appearance from liberty.

But liberty, also in the guise of freedom, has had many different manifestations. A principal historical manifestation lies in the notion of America as a haven from oppressive rulers and cultures. As a nation of immigrants, the United States became populated (excluding, of course, black slaves) by persons who had voluntarily entered the North American continent, choosing American nationality as colonists and settlers. American nationality thus came to be based not upon concepts of race or tribe but upon the concept of chosen citizenship. Such a

concept of citizenship entails the idea of equality before the law. The profound influence of the English philosopher John Locke upon the development of American civic virtues is to be seen in the notion of a compact, or social contract, among freely choosing men to establish, extend, and renew the fabric of the polity.

This aspect of the American civic myth, grounded in historical experience, significantly distinguished the American concept of independence from most subsequent movements similarly seeking civic freedom in other parts of the world. For while the nationalisms that proliferated in the nineteenth and twentieth centuries in Europe and elsewhere likewise asserted the notion of freedom as the justification of national self-rule, the American experience did not ground the concept of nationality upon a historical myth of a preexisting national entity, but upon the assertion of the rights of "free men." (Thomas Paine, the principal ideologue of the American Revolution, for example, had lived in the New World barely two years when he wrote his famous call to arms, *Common Sense*.) The vast migrations of the nineteenth and twentieth centuries from Europe, Asia, and Latin America further accentuated this aspect of American liberty.

Thus the national identity of the United States was formed not so much as an act of collective liberation from alien rule but as the formation of a new collectivity born of the very culture from which it chose to break away. The Old World, as the latter came to be known, was not alien to the new Americans; they had originated there. The act of dissociation from Europe could never be complete, and this gave to the new nation on the North American continent a novel, and ambivalent, role to play in the society of nations. No other modern nation could claim a universality grounded upon the multiple sources of its population.

Aside from the matter of American blacks and the aboriginal Indians, it is worth remarking that the colonization of America, and the subsequent waves of immigration, did not entail the conquest and subjugation of one race by another. The original settlers, principally from England and other parts of northwestern Europe, established a dominant culture that subsequently attracted peoples from other parts of the world. This experience greatly differs from acts of colonization elsewhere, except Australia and Canada.

This distinction of the American polity from most others becomes clearest when we contrast it with that of modern China. The peoples ruled by the Maoist regime are overwhelmingly derived from indigenous ancestors whose civilization goes back many millennia. A history of immigration into that nation in the past two centuries would be a slim volume indeed. After the Chinese Communist revolution, nearly all foreigners—save for tiny enclaves of transient technicians, diplomats, and traders—were expelled. Nor is the emigration of nationals permitted.

The success of the American civic experiment lay not simply in its proclaimed attainment of liberty but also in its subsequent maintenance of contractual unity. Momentous as was the Confederate rebellion (1861–1865) as a challenge to this Union, it did not terminate the basic principle, asserted in the Constitution, of the voluntary accession of states to a federal contract. The knowledge of this success kindled, among some American "world reformers," the notion that this experience of federation could be repeated elsewhere, notably in Europe, and even on a global scale through a "Parliament of Man."

When considered in its various aspects, the American ideology of liberty (or freedom) may be seen in its stress upon a variety, and admixture, of qualities that are not the same. The idea of national liberty, which, as we have seen, historically became confused in the American migratory experience with personal liberation from countries of origin, is nevertheless importantly different from the conception of civil and individual freedom. Yet the idea became transformed into a vast ideal by American patriotic thinkers of the nineteenth and twentieth centuries. George Washington, Thomas Jefferson, and Benjamin Franklin thus were offered up to a waiting world as exemplars of national liberty. Americans came to honor foreign national patriots elsewhere who, singing the praises of these liberators, borrowed and applied the American example in seeking freedom for their own countrymen. Early foreign devotees of the American revolution, such as Lafayette and Kościuszko, returned to their homelands to participate in political revolutions

in the name of liberty. Other national heroes, such as Bolívar, Garibaldi, Kossuth, and Sun Yat-sen, were widely celebrated in America for their success in vindicating the principle of national self-determination in their homelands.

In the nineteenth century the idea of national liberty and independence was associated in American minds with principles of republicanism. The subsequent new nations, it was confidently expected, would borrow heavily from the store of republican ideas housed in the New World. In proclaiming the Monroe Doctrine in 1823, the American statesmen James Monroe and John Quincy Adams took note of the fact that while the "Citizens of the United States cherish sentiments the most friendly, in favor of the liberty and happiness of their fellowmen on that [the European] side of the Atlantic," nevertheless in "the wars of the European powers, in matters relating to themselves we have never taken any part, nor does it comport with our policy to do so" (Samuel Flagg Bemis, *The Latin American Policy of the United States* [New York, 1943]). Monroe and Adams, however, were concerned to note that attempts by the European powers to extend their colonial possessions in the New World, or to reestablish them, would be resisted by the new republic. The reason for doing so was essentially ideological: the danger which such extension of European authority raised arose chiefly from the fact that the "political system of the allied powers [the Holy Alliance] is essentially different . . . from that of America. This difference proceeds from that which exists in their respective Governments." The basic and original justification of the Monroe Doctrine thus was grounded in ideological principles of republicanism, as well as in the conception that the contrasting systems of governance found expression geographically in the distinction between an Old and a New World.

This confident faith in the identity of republican virtue with the virtues of national liberation endured in American thinking about foreign relations through all of the nineteenth—and much of the twentieth—century, many facts and much experience to the contrary. The high-water mark of this faith, when viewed in hindsight, may be found in its Wilsonian formulations during and after World

War I. Woodrow Wilson's war aims, found in his famous Fourteen Points (1918), associated the principle of national self-determination with the principle of democratization. Autocracies—governments of an authoritarian character—were, in Wilson's view, not merely repugnant in themselves, but also were a chief cause of international wars. The war, he said, was "to make the world safe for democracy."

The Spanish-American War and World War I saw a significant breach in the official practices of the United States with respect to the internal organization of other societies. Until 1898, while official America and wide sectors of American opinion rejoiced in evidences of rebellion against imperial and autocratic authority, this was not reflected in governmental practice or policy. (Occasionally, as in the Irish Fenian raids of the mid-nineteenth century, insurgent groups used the United States as privileged sanctuary for organizing attacks on other countries—notably British Canada; but this is to be distinguished from overt governmental action.) The Spanish-American War was in part a response to waves of popular reaction, however stimulated, at repressive Spanish measures against Cuban insurgents; the defeat and ouster of the Spanish authorities from the island was hailed as its liberation. Yet ironically Cuba's liberation was followed by six decades of United States hegemony. In somewhat different fashion, once the United States entered the European war in 1917, ideological goals came to be included in its war aims.

It is important to note the enormous impact of Wilson's personality and doctrines on European opinion. Much is made, in American interpretations of Wilson's role in peacemaking, of his compromises and his ultimate failure to obtain Senate approval of the Treaty of Versailles. Yet Wilson's influence upon European political developments, particularly in Central Europe, was of profound importance. As the regimes of most European belligerents tottered, and some collapsed entirely, Wilson and his antithesis, Lenin, towered over the chaos of peace, each offering his alternative to Europe: Bolshevism or liberal democracy. The monuments erected to Wilson, particularly in Eastern Europe and the Balkans, testified to the enormous respect which his memory enjoyed. The American demand for the abdication of the

Hohenzollerns encouraged centrist German political forces not only to establish but also to defend successfully the new Weimar democracy against immediate threats from the Bolshevik totalitarian left. The succession states of Eastern Europe (Czechoslovakia, Poland, Yugoslavia and Rumania)—which obtained nationhood after the war—perceived Wilson as their liberator and principal advocate.

Optimistic devotees of liberty in America soon were to discover the world about them to be more complex in receiving the benefaction. As events in Europe and later in the Third World were to demonstrate, the establishment of national liberty was infrequently accompanied by civic freedoms. By the mid-1930's, for example, most of the Central and East European states "liberated" from foreign rule after the war had become dictatorships. In fact, of all the nations "freed" from foreign shackles by the peace treaties, only Finland and Czechoslovakia remained democracies in 1935. The vulnerability of all these tiny states, now detached from great empires, to powerful neighbors unsettled the politics of Europe. All became victims of German and Soviet imperialism, and many today are subject to Soviet hegemony. In the period following World War II, furthermore, the new states of Asia and Africa, gaining national liberty from European colonial powers, for the most part subsided into petty tyrannies or one-party states paying little respect to the civic virtues extolled by classic republics. Only India managed long to maintain the essential constitutional aspects of a free society.

Meanwhile, after the Bolshevik revolution, Marxist-Leninist doctrines were forcibly exported by the Soviet Union and furthered by indigenous communist parties, challenging the claims of liberal constitutionalism to be the "wave of the future." Communist totalitarianism, in its own ideological pretensions claiming to create the "new man," proved dramatically different from the classical authoritarian states which American conceptions of liberty had challenged in the nineteenth century. The new object was not so much that of simply preventing popular participation in government; rather, it was the object of totally transforming society and, in the process, of exterminating the autonomy of individuals and groups and harnessing them into state-controlled collectivities.

Among publicists and diplomatic historians who have criticized the central role of ideology (or ideals) in American foreign policy, there are two quite different interpretations placed on it. One, a "realist" view, would object to manifestations of ideology in international politics as being damaging to concrete national interests, which at all times should be derived from practical needs and aspirations such as national security, prosperity, and the protection of national rights abroad. Seen in such a light, Wilsonianism represented a diversion of American energies and resources to purposes far beyond the actual needs of the United States of America. An excessive zeal of ideology, furthermore, promised to embroil the nation in endless, costly, and dangerous controversies. The reformist passion, once set loose on foreign soil, risked America's transformation into an imperialist power.

Another, Marxist, interpretation of the American ideology of liberty was that it masked all too well an underlying material urge to dominate; even Wilsonianism—in the eyes of such Marxist historians as William Appleman Williams—was a guise under which American corporate interests were the better able to spread their nets of interest and control abroad. (In particular, liberal free-trade doctrines were depicted as modes by which less-developed nations might be subject to domination by powerful American business firms.) Thus one set of critics of American ideology has emphasized the all-too-real nature of sincere passion, romanticism, and true belief as dangerous excesses, while the other has sought to depict, in classic Marxist fashion, the function of ideology as a deliberately contrived mask for quite material interests and aspirations. Each falls far short of providing a satisfactory explanation of the complex relationship between values and interests.

The traditional American espousal of liberty had much more to it than the simple idea of independence. Indeed, the substantive content of the notion of liberty, translated into freedom, has entailed a range of concerns that have deeply affected America's foreign policies, even though at first glance they may seem to apply only to domestic conditions.

In their deliberations about the nature of politics, the early American constitution builders were perhaps as much affected by classical Greek and Roman writings as by more contemporary tracts such as the writings of John Locke. The Roman Republic, and its public institutions, served as a partial model for early American republican architecture and for its constitutional forms. The deliberative character of Roman legislative institutions, emulated in the houses of Congress, was seen to require an openness to public discussion of major questions of state, while the executive was seen to require central authority to act. From such considerations arose the conception that a "free civic society" required open deliberation and the consent of the governed. This view of things came to have a profound effect upon the conduct and control of American foreign relations. Contemporary European courts habitually conducted their foreign relations in secrecy; treaties were made by royal fiat; alliances were often concluded with no public knowledge; and wars were declared without legislative approval. The United States Constitution, breaking with Old World habits, presented a radical view of how foreign policy should be conducted. Wars could be declared only with congressional approval; in fact, Congress could even declare war without executive approval. Treaties could be ratified only after Senate deliberation and approval. An executive could appoint his ministers only with senatorial consent. These constitutional requirements, and subsequent elaborations in practice, profoundly affected the practices of other states. The appeal by Wilson for "open covenants, openly arrived at," taken to the Paris Peace Conference in 1919, proved to be a prescription that even Wilson as negotiator could not follow to the letter; yet it was a widely shared civic conviction of many Americans and, in part, a constitutional requirement of an American democracy.

The inherent tension between democracy and foreign policy, increasingly evident in the twentieth century, was already amply clear in the nineteenth. As Tocqueville wrote in his *Democracy in America*:

> Foreign politics demand scarcely any of those
> qualities which a democracy possesses; and they

require, on the contrary, the perfect use of almost all those faculties in which it is deficient. Democracy is favorable to the increase of the internal resources of the State; it tends to diffuse a moderate independence; it promotes the growth of public spirit, and fortifies the respect which is entertained for law in all classes of society; and these are advantages which only exercise an indirect influence over the relations which one people bears to another. But a democracy is unable to regulate the details of an important undertaking, to persevere in a design, and to work out its execution in the presence of serious obstacles. It cannot combine its measures with secrecy, and it will not await their consequences with patience.

The passions and enthusiasms, Tocqueville further noted, which nearly drove a weak and vulnerable America to war on the side of France in Washington's time, could work in quite opposite fashion in other circumstances. Ideological crusades, whether for war or for peace, for American withdrawal or for American further involvement in world politics, have on more than one occasion lent the United States a reputation for unpredictability and unreliability. In times of passion, as the American diplomat George F. Kennan noted, a democracy often seems akin to the dinosaur.

> . . . I sometimes wonder whether in this respect a democracy is not uncomfortably similar to one of those prehistoric monsters with a body as long as this room and a brain the size of a pin: he lies there in his comfortable primeval mud and pays little attention to his environment; he is slow to wrath—in fact, you practically have to whack his tail off to make him aware that his interests are being disturbed; but, once he grasps this, he lays about him with such blind determination that he not only destroys his adversary but largely wrecks his native habitat.

On close inspection it is difficult to draw sharp distinctions between interest and ideology, even though in the abstract it would seem clear that some ideologies, in their extremities, verge on the fanatic and lose their moorings to the real world. The abstract, traditional American fondness for freedom is an instance of this. Aside from the not unremarkable affection for national liberty, which manifests itself in many different kinds of polities, the conventional American views of freedom in the abstract,

when viewed more meticulously, can be seen to relate to quite precise values, difficult to distinguish from quite important interests. That the abstract American view of freedom may spill over, in many ways, into America's international activities is due in some measure to the fact that in many particulars it was closely wedded to quite valued—and therefore valuable—interests.

The most characteristic valued freedoms that American civic virtues have extolled, even in their abstract natures, have quite important and precise connotations. Freedom of information; freedom of movement, including the right to leave and enter the country; freedom of ideas, expression, and assembly; freedom of workers to change jobs; freedom of contract; and freedom of religion—all these have profound practical implications in concrete instances. Freedom of movement, for instance, is not without significance for the ease with which a worker may arrive at his place of work, or the ease with which a family may take a vacation. The restless mobility of American culture, as manifest in the ubiquitous automobile, is so inseparable a part of American culture that it would be difficult to imagine the nation otherwise.

In its relations with both traditionalist authoritarian and modern totalitarian nations, the United States long has confronted political systems in which most, if not all, such principles were flouted, disregarded, or systematically eliminated. The sympathy extended to nations and movements protesting on behalf of such principles has represented a constant theme in American foreign relations. The systematic repression of religions by contemporary totalitarian states may differ in degree but not in kind from religious persecutions in traditional societies and the American protest of them could perhaps be seen, not as mere ideological cant but as affirmation of qualities that the culture itself deeply venerated. The cherished right of freedom of information, while sometimes carried by Americans to wild extremes, nevertheless reflects both a healthy skepticism of secrecy and a practical "need to know." The scientific community, and other scholars as well, deem the principle essential to their profession—and not out of a mere abstract ideological "faith." When other nations or governments trampled upon such values, it might be seen that more was at stake than mere "principle."

Similarly, many American businessmen and entrepreneurs could not help but chafe at economic practices in other cultures which have impeded the full employment of market-economy principles. The war with the Barbary pirates, in Jefferson's administration, was no ideological crusade to carry capitalism to Arab outlaws, but the practical defense of harassed American commerce on the high seas. Accustomed to such freedoms at home, it was hardly surprising that Americans, cast abroad in different circumstances, might be less than relativistic when their conceptions of justice and fairness were flaunted.

Yet only in rare instances have Americans permitted abstract questions of justice, human rights, or freedoms to steer the nation into belligerency. In 1917 Wilson abandoned neutrality for war, not to conduct a crusade in Europe, but because in his view German unlimited sea warfare against American vessels in itself constituted an act of war; the principles came later. (It should be noted that the German government, in initiating unlimited U-boat warfare in early 1917, was fully aware of this fact.) The Roosevelt administration in the 1930's repeatedly protested Nazi and fascist aggression in Europe, while doing little about it; the Four Freedoms (freedom of speech, freedom of religion, freedom from want, and freedom from fear), proclaimed by the American president when war was imminent, became, with the Atlantic Charter, abstract war aims of America. But it is doubtful that most Americans thought the war a crusade. Eric Hoffer has noted how important, among American combat troops, was the idea of "getting the job done." The work instinct applied unideologically to an unambiguous goal. Rather the effective reasons for American belligerency arose out of quite other considerations than morality—a profound fear for the security of the United States in a world dominated by totalitarian states. Pearl Harbor, and not a preconceived ideological mission to liberate the persecuted victims of Axis tyranny, was the casus belli in the American instance. Nor did American disgust with the known villainies of Stalinist Russia stand as impediment to expediential Lend-Lease aid, after the German invasion in 1941. Similarly,

the quasi-fascist reputation of Franco Spain, after World War II, did not blind American strategic decision makers to the practical utility of the Iberian Peninsula as a naval and air facility for defense in Europe. These instances demonstrate that frequently in conflicts between or among cherished values and practical interests, interests may cross over the line to have profound "ideological" implications, while ideologies may serve important practical ones.

In several respects the Cold War has been an ideological conflict between the United States and the Soviet Union. Characterized by occasional periods of relaxation—détente—the rivalry between the two superpowers has been expressed in part as a contest about the manner in which societies should be organized. Here the principles of Marxism-Leninism and of liberal democracy have confronted each other in an asymmetrical contest. During the 1920's and 1930's this contest had slight bearing on the bilateral relations between the two states. If the United States government was among the last major powers to recognize the Soviet Union (1933), the absence of de jure diplomatic relations between them had minimal bearing on world politics. Yet from an ideological standpoint, official Soviet communist doctrine recognized the United States as the principal bourgeois adversary. Josef Stalin's Comintern—Maxim Litvinov's agreement with Cordell Hull to the contrary—continued to infiltrate the United States with subversive agents.

On the practical level of state-to-state relations, however, the United States and the Soviet Union followed parallel lines, particularly in the Far East. Japanese expansion in Manchuria, commencing in 1931, led to heightened tensions that posed a threat to Soviet interests in North Asia and to the Republic of China. American policy—embodied in the Stimson Doctrine (1932)—was one of opposition to Japanese expansion. Closer United States–Soviet relations during the early New Deal were prompted more by these developments than anything else.

The Soviet espousal in 1935 of popular frontism and collective security—symbolized in the foreign policy of Litvinov—marked a shift in Soviet tactics toward the Western democracies, including the United States. The hostility to democratic regimes and parties, which had prompted the German Communist party to collaborate with Nazis in the overthrow of the Weimar Republic, briefly gave way to policies of resistance to the threat to European security, which Hitler exemplified.

The bewildering shift of Soviet policy toward Nazi Germany in August 1939, and the subsequent German attack on Russia in June 1941, prompted oscillations in official Soviet ideology, with reverberations throughout the communist movement. After Pearl Harbor, with the United States now as cobelligerent or ally, the Soviet Union portrayed itself as a supporter of democracy, national self-determination, and other liberal values.

Yet quickly, after the defeat of the Axis Powers, Soviet doctrine reverted to dogmas that had characterized the pre-Litvinov period. In tandem with the Red Army, communist parties in Europe, by 1947, abandoned popular front tactics and joined to subvert Western-style political movements and regimes. In response, American policy—as in the Truman Doctrine of 1947—set out lines of resistance to further communist expansion.

In communist theory and practice, distinctions long have been made between state-to-state, people-to-people, and party-to-party relations. As the contest between the two superpowers over Europe intensified after 1947, the competition occurred on each of these levels. In analyzing American policy and behavior during the Cold War, difficulty arises as to the relationship of American ideology of liberty and freedom to the overall official strategies and actions. Yet there is confusion as to whether the principal adversary to United States interests has been communism or Soviet power. The fact that the two had been virtually indistinguishable during the Stalinist period, when the reins of Marxist ideology were firmly grasped in the hands of one man, made the issue simpler than when, after Stalin's death, the trends toward polycentrism manifested themselves in the communist world.

The American response to Soviet postwar expansion—hesitant at first, yet clear in the late 1940's—came to have powerful ideological components. Central to it was the quite controversial yet low-keyed doctrine of containment, originally conceptualized by George F. Kennan in 1947. This doctrine, purposing to

deny further inroads of Soviet power by concerting defensive force around the peripheries of the Soviet realm, clearly ruled out aggressive, messianic measures designed to "roll back" Soviet power. By setting such limits on American (and Western) purpose in this contest, the doctrine sharply contrasted with Soviet ideological strategies, which unswervingly continued to preach the doctrine that "socialism" (that is, Soviet-style communism) encompass the entire Western world. At home, containment found domestic critics, such as John Foster Dulles, who chided it for its "amoral" qualities, and who demanded a more intense ideological war against the Soviet system. In the line of thinking of many domestic critics of containment, America had as much of a moral obligation, under the principles of the Atlantic Charter, to "liberate" those countries that had fallen under the Soviet yoke as it had to defend those now threatened by it. The limited measures, such as the Marshall Plan and the North Atlantic Treaty Organization, to shore up the West were, in this view, insufficient.

Paradoxically, many American ideologues of the Right, most critical of the Truman (and, later, the Eisenhower) administration's limited and defensive responses to the problem, were themselves often opposed to even the minimal measures that these containment devices represented. In 1950, for instance, right-wing anticommunist political leaders, such as ex-president Herbert Hoover and Senator Robert A. Taft, opposed the sending of American ground troops to Europe to put teeth in the NATO alliance. Hoover, in particular, came to advocate doctrines of hemispheric defense ("Fortress America"), which would place minimal reliance on overseas allies and concentrate upon United States naval and air power for both defense and retaliation.

At first glance it would appear paradoxical that the American conservative Right, itself strongly anticommunist on ideological grounds, should behave in this fashion in this crisis. Yet there was an inner logic to such a position. Opposed to the steady encroachment of government in the American free enterprise system, many anticommunist conservatives concluded that massive budgetary outlays for widespread implementation of containment in both Asia and Europe would only lead to socialism at home. Lenin's dream of a communized

America could be fulfilled by tempting it to bankrupt itself. The crusade of Senator Joseph R. McCarthy—directed more to targets within the Truman administration than to communists—lent heightened credibility to a perverse if pervasive view that communist victories abroad were accomplished only through the connivance of the very American leaders who at the time were resisting the encroachments of Soviet power. (General George C. Marshall, Roosevelt's military chief of staff, subsequently secretary of state, and father of the Marshall Plan, was one of McCarthy's chief targets, as was Dean Acheson, Truman's secretary of state.) Anticommunism at home thus chose as its prime target those who were architects of anti-Soviet containment abroad.

With the Eisenhower administration the un-ideological doctrine of containment found stronger bipartisan support than it had had in previous, Democratic administrations. Dulles, himself critical of Kennan's tenets before coming into office, in practice not only came to accept them, but extended them in ways which Kennan himself objected to. To Kennan, and some other supporters of the containment theory, the doctrine did not purport indiscriminately to apply countervailing force in all areas peripheral to the Soviet Union, or now to its major ally, Communist China. But Dulles, as architect of new containment pacts such as the Southeast Asia Treaty Organization, extended the doctrine to areas remote from the central theater of Soviet-American contention. That Dulles, once a devotee of "liberationism" in Europe, came to accept the strategic limitations on American power best could be shown in his refusal, in 1956, to assist insurgent movements in Eastern Europe which rose up against Soviet power. Dulles' own strong religious convictions, which included the notion that the Cold War, among other things, was a struggle between Christianity and communism, found resonance among many Americans (and Europeans as well) who were aware of the profound hostility of Marxist parties, movements, and states to Christianity and to religion in general. But neither this conviction nor his secular anti-Marxist views prompted him to digress significantly from the policies and programs of his predecessor, Dean Acheson.

The complexity of the relationship between ideology and national interest in the Cold War may perhaps better be seen by comparing this global contest with previous occasions in world history when state interest and metaphysical movements became enmeshed. The great contest, for example, between Christianity and Islam, which raged for centuries until in the early modern period when the Islamic influence was finally driven from Europe, provides a useful parallel. Each of these great religions powerfully affected the behavior of individual states; yet state interest all too often diverged from the prescriptions of religious doctrine. In the eighteenth century, religious conviction did not restrain the Bourbon monarchs of France from tacit and profitable alliance with the Ottoman Empire against other Christian states. Yet schisms within Christianity, bearing some parallels to contemporary schisms within the communist world, did not inhibit the fury and messianic convictions of Protestants and Catholics in the holy war against Islamic civilization. In some respects, the upheaval that the Reformation and Counter-Reformation caused within Christian Europe intensified the hostility that each exhibited against a common and hated adversary. (Columbus' memorial to Queen Isabella of Spain, requesting her to fund his search for a new route to the Indies, was couched in terms of an extension of the combat against the infidels.)

That states themselves may not wholly control the vigor of ideology, but seek to channel or deflect it, may be seen in the ideological schisms of the communist world in the post-Stalin era. The demise of the concept of "monolithic communism" in world politics began in 1949, four years before Stalin's death. In that year of the Stalin-Tito split and the victory of communism on the Chinese mainland, it became apparent that Moscow was not long to remain the sole holy city of Marxism. The great break between Maoist China and the Soviet Union, commencing in 1958, grew to ominous proportions through the 1960's. These schisms, reflected in communist movements throughout the world, did not dampen the ideological vigor with which component movements of communism pursued their goals. The vigorous competition between communist China and the Soviet Union for support of communist movements outside their respective orbits contributed greatly to the spread of communist states and movements in Asia, Africa, and the West-

IDEOLOGY AND FOREIGN POLICY

ern Hemisphere. Both Moscow and Peking—courting favor of Hanoi and the Vietcong—outbid each other in supplying the military equipment to them during the Vietnam War. In the Western Hemisphere, doctrinal and ideological differences between Maoist and Soviet views of revolutionary strategy came to fruition in the 1960's—yet neither official doctrine repudiated the shared view that bourgeois democracy was the principal enemy of each.

The ideological thrust of American policy in the Cold War against communist doctrines had been to stress the centrality of "free men and free institutions." This was not a set of doctrinaire convictions concocted to meet the communist challenge; rather, it represented a set of views displayed since the birth of the Republic against all comers: Britain, the Holy Alliance, Spain, Czarist Russia, Imperial Germany, Japan, Nazi Germany, and the communist states. Ultimately, of course, the degree of such views had to depend upon the vitality of convictions that an American civic leadership maintained concerning their validity at home. The dominant civic culture of America rarely seriously challenged the validity of these views, even in periods like the Great Depression, when economic collapse occurred.

Whether an impediment to foreign policy or an asset, the American "democratic dream," with its optimistic conviction that the whole world might ultimately come to emulate American civic norms, has exerted a profound effect upon other cultures. In themselves, of course, such convictions contained no programmatic strategies for foreign policy. The great complexities of international politics were not susceptible to advice from abstract convictions, though men went to them when in need of inspiration. The ideology of freedom throughout the long span of American history likewise has proved Janus-faced, serving on occasion to turn American attention away from a recalcitrant world, to purify American institutions; serving on other occasions to involve Americans in "other people's business." A restless civic motor force, it has displayed no signs of diminishing.

BIBLIOGRAPHY

Raymond Aron, *The Opium of the Intellectuals* (New York, 1957), is an essay by the noted French political analyst on the relationship of contemporary Western intellectuals to ideological movements and causes. Charles A. Beard, *The Republic* (New York, 1945), probes colloquial analyses of the nature of the American political order; in chapter 20, "The Republic in a World of Nations," Beard seeks to revive, explain, and defend arguments of early Federalist writers about basic principles of a "realistic" foreign policy against critics urging a more messianic role for the United States in world politics. George F. Kennan, *American Diplomacy: 1900–1950* (New York, 1951), consists of lectures concerning the perennial tensions between oscillating popular moods and the need for steadiness in America's international policies. Irving Kristol, *On the Democratic Idea in America* (New York, 1972), contains essays concerning what the author calls "the problematic relationship of the modern intellectual to foreign affairs," and "the tortured connection between American liberal ideology and the American imperial republic." Hans J. Morgenthau, *In Defense of the National Interest* (New York, 1952), is a political scientist's "call" for a return to nonideological guidelines of "realism" in American diplomacy; the author seeks to establish the view that principles of realism, practiced in the early years of the American republic, were subsequently abandoned and replaced by moralism. Reinhold Niebuhr, *The Irony of American History* (New York, 1952), is an American theologian's view that the end of American isolationism coincides with the end of American "innocence" in the world of nations; the question of a future relationship between classic American ideals and American purposes in world politics is discussed. Robert Osgood, *Ideals and Self-Interest in America's Foreign Relations* (Chicago, 1953), a comprehensive intellectual history of American debate and thought about international politics and foreign policy, suggests an inescapable tension between realpolitik and ideology. Dexter Perkins, *The American Approach to Foreign Policy* (New York, 1962), seeks to delineate unique and praiseworthy qualities in "democratic" and populist styles of American diplomacy. David M. Potter, *People of Plenty* (Chicago, 1954), attempts to explain American character, and America's position in the world, as arising out of a successful quest for greater affluence and productivity. Paul Seabury, *Power, Freedom and Diplomacy* (New York, 1963), is a political scientist's attempt to reconcile the respective claims of ideology and national interest in United States diplomacy. William Appleman Williams, *The Tragedy of American Diplomacy* (New York, 1962), an American Marxist's thesis that United States international expansion (to which he objects) is explained by economic pressures; "Open Door" aspects of America's free-trade doctrines are said to prevail over all other considerations in setting basic foreign-policy guidelines; "Ideology" masks, and is used to justify, imperialistic motives.
[*See also* CONTAINMENT; REALISM AND IDEALISM; REVOLUTION AND FOREIGN POLICY.]

IMPERIALISM

David Healy

IMPERIALISM, in its most precise traditional usage, means the forcible extension of governmental control over foreign areas not designated for incorporation as integral parts of the nation. The term is commonly used to mean any significant degree of national influence, public or private, over other societies; but to some it refers principally to foreign economic exploitation with or without other actions. In all usages, however, the essential element is that one society must in some way impose itself upon another in a continuing unequal relationship. Thus American expansionism dated from the beginning of the national experience, while its evolution into true imperialism occurred only in the later nineteenth century.

The expansion of the United States from 1803 to 1853 into contiguous areas such as Louisiana, Florida, Texas, the Oregon territories, and the Mexican cession is not best described as imperialism, although it contained related elements. This expansion involved lightly populated areas in which an influx of settlement from the older portions of the nation soon constituted the great bulk of the inhabitants. The Northwest Ordinance of 1787, a profoundly anti-imperialist measure, had early defined the process by which such areas could be divided into prospective states and ultimately brought into the union as equal members. The resulting expansion represented the continuous extension of a single society over vast neighboring areas, rather than the takeover of one society by another.

The North American continent was not unoccupied; indigenous Indian tribes roamed every portion of it, while the areas taken from Mexico contained many scattered settlements, particularly in California and around Santa Fe. Neither the people nor the government of the United States showed much interest in such preexisting societies; the aim of the United States was to brush them aside and replace them with the society and culture of the incoming majority. This was particularly true in regard to the Indians; rather than take over Indian society, the whites virtually destroyed it. The process was tragic for its victims, and Americans' constant assertions that they were peopling an empty continent contained the seeds of hypocrisy. There were nevertheless important differences between the movement of such a settlement frontier and the establishment of a true empire. For example, while the United States acquired half of Mexico's national territory between 1845 and 1848, the transfer entailed less than 2 percent of the Mexican population. Broadly speaking, the Mexican War was fought to gain territory, not a captive people, and the land thus gained would be populated largely from the existing United States. For purposes of comparison, the activities of the British in India, where they ruled a teeming alien society, and the British in Australia, where they settled a continent and built a self-governing nation, were so dissimilar that the use of a single term to describe both cases does more to obscure than enlighten. Prior to the Civil War, American expansion came closer to the Australian example, though dispossessing a more numerous indigenous people the end result cannot be accurately classified as imperialism.

There were, of course, common features in the earlier expansion and later imperialism of the United States. Chief among these were a strong sense of national mission and special destiny, a general confidence in the unique superiority of American institutions, a belief in the inequality of races and peoples, and the very habit of expansion itself. The expansionism of "manifest destiny" could lead toward true imperialism, as in the abortive movement to annex all of Mexico during the Mexican War. If westward expansion was not the same as imperialism, it furnished some of the materials out of which the latter could grow.

The purchase of Alaska in 1867 ended the period when new territory was assumed to be on the path to eventual statehood. By that time the nation's policymakers were already debating a new and more truly imperialist form of expansion. Schemes to acquire Cuba, by purchase or otherwise, had been current from 1848 onward, while in 1870 the Ulysses S. Grant administration negotiated the annexation of the Dominican Republic, only to see the Senate reject the instrumental treaty. Critics of this latter scheme were quick to point out the break with tradition implicit in the quest for territory already compactly settled by an alien society. Such a society could be assimilated into that of the nation proper only with great difficulty and over a long period of time, or more probably it could not be assimilated at all. Thus the United States had to choose between incorporating an unassimilated people into its federal system, thereby endangering its integrity, or ruling them as colonial subjects in violation of the right to self-government supposedly inherent in the American political system. Foreshadowed by the earlier opposition to the all-Mexico movement of the late 1840's, the Senate debate over the annexation of the Dominican Republic developed the main lines of the controversy over imperialist expansion, and marked the maturing of an active anti-imperialism in the United States.

For a generation after 1870, projects for further expansion attracted little support in the United States, and most people assumed that imperialism had become a dead issue. A number of developments, however, prepared the nation for imperial ventures at the end of the century. Chief developments were the rapid industrialization and soaring productivity of the national economy, which made the United States the leading industrial power by 1900. Increasingly conscious of their numbers, wealth, and strength, and proud of their unique institutions and sprawling territory, Americans began to aspire to a place for their country among the world's great powers. The severe economic depression of the 1890's added material aims to the drive for prestige, as the nation's business leaders and political spokesmen hoped for economic salvation in increased exports of American manufactures. By the mid-1890's, a new mood had brought a reappraisal of America's world position.

While largely internal forces first prompted the nation's leaders to look outward, the global sweep of European imperialism was reaching its high point, providing both the model and the final impetus for the new activism. Initially, Americans reacted to European imperialism as a threat to be repelled, fearing its penetration into the Western Hemisphere. Still mindful of France's incursion into Mexico in the 1860's, Americans were startled by a French project in 1879 to build a ship canal across the Isthmus of Panama. Later they also came to see Great Britain as a potential interloper, inspiring Secretary of State Richard Olney to a famous warning against such penetration during the Venezuelan crisis of 1895. Fears of European encroachment undoubtedly added urgency to the drive for Hawaiian annexation after 1894 and figured in discussions of Caribbean expansion later in the decade. One result of such fears was advocacy of a sort of preemptive imperialism, a conviction that the United States should seize desirable areas before a rival power got them.

In addition, the constant example of the European powers in time led many in the United States to take a more positive view of imperialism. Thirsting for national prestige, they saw that colonies were highly valued status symbols in Europe and that colonial empires had already swallowed up most of the non-Western world. Furthermore, if Europeans claimed to spread civilization to unenlightened peoples, did not the United States have a more compelling mission to implant its own superior institutions? Finally, the theorists of the Old World had proclaimed that colonial empires could provide strategic bases, captive markets, raw materials, and investment opportunities—in short, could alleviate the persistent distresses from which the American economy suffered.

IMPERIALISM

By 1895 a small but growing number of American politicians, publicists, naval officers, and businessmen supported a modest expansionist program. This generally included the annexation of Hawaii, the acquisition of one or more base areas in the West Indies, and the construction of an isthmian canal across Central America to facilitate naval and mercantile movement between the eastern United States and the Pacific Ocean. Some also aspired to the peaceable annexation of Canada, while others wished to challenge British political and economic leadership in South America. But virtually all limited their ambitions to the Western Hemisphere, and most to areas traditionally within the sphere of American interests. While this program fell short of a full-fledged scheme of empire, it gave a specific direction to expansionist currents and reinforced the appeal of the imperialist idea.

Many Americans continued to be suspicious of imperialism, but others found that it was increasingly easy to identify imperialism with many aspects of the American tradition. Territorial expansion, a strong sense of national mission, and a dynamic economic growth had been dominant themes of American history. The belief in the inequality of man, which imperialism demanded, offered few problems at a time when the South was even then perfecting a system of segregation and disfranchisement of blacks, the West was in the final stages of suppressing the Indians, and the East fulminated against the inferiority of the new immigrants from southern and eastern Europe. Currently popular theories of social Darwinism held that the various races of man progressed at differing rates according to their place on the evolutionary scale, or failed to progress and fell victim to "natural selection." No one believed more devoutly in progress than Americans, and the presumed duty of carrying progress to backward lands was popularly called "the white man's burden." This combined belief in progress and human inequality, along with boundless self-confidence and a hope of gain, constituted the principal attitudes that underlay imperialism.

Whether the imperialist appeal was chiefly economic, psychological, nationalist, or idealistic, has long been the subject of contention. In fact it was all of these, and perhaps more. The most fundamental explanation of the global imperialism during the nineteenth century was that the Western world, containing a relatively small minority of the world's people, had achieved a virtual monopoly of effective power. The development of the nation-state enabled the effective mobilization of a society's resources, and coincided with the growth of modern science and industrialization. The latter developments created societies of unprecedented wealth and armed them with weapons of unparalleled destructiveness, while the steamship, the railroad, the telegraph, and the oceanic cable greatly diminished the distances that separated the Western peoples from the rest of the world.

The disparity of power between "modern" and preindustrial societies reached its maximum in the nineteenth century, and it was this disparity that was, quite directly, the driving force behind the breakneck colonialism of the period. Conscious of their strength and brought into close contact with weaker peoples, Europeans quickly developed a sense of superiority and discovered desirable goals to seek in vulnerable foreign places. The process soon created its own mystique, which could be shared by almost any member-state in the Western world. While American imperialism had special national characteristics—as did that of England, France, Germany, and other nations—during the 1890's, American imperialism was not essentially different from the parent European variety. Its American disciples believed otherwise, having as firm a faith in their own uniqueness as their European rivals.

Although this new thinking rapidly gained ground during the 1890's, it took the shock of tangible events to bridge the gap between ideas and action. After a revolution in Hawaii, which American officials actively abetted, the proposed annexation of Hawaii in 1893 reawakened the debate over colonial expansion but was blocked by the timely transfer of the presidency from Benjamin Harrison to Grover Cleveland. It was rather the revolt that began in Cuba in 1895 that ultimately mobilized the emotions and ideas of the new expansionism. In 1898 the United States was drawn into a struggle between Cuba and Spain, which had brought mass suffering and wholesale destruction to its very borders. An aggressive national pride, emotional partisanship in favor of the Cubans, and tangible damage to American trade and property—all worked to arouse the public and the press, while the dramatic destruction of the battleship *Maine* acted as a spark to these combustibles. Originally regarded by most Americans as a crusade to free Cuba, the Spanish-American War quickly took on an expansionist thrust. The retention of Puerto Rico, Spain's other Caribbean colony, was soon regarded as a necessary war reparation. Strategically the key to the Pacific, Hawaii was annexed during the war by a joint resolution of Congress. Even the cries to free Cuba gave way to protests that the Cubans needed a period of tutelage before essaying complete self-government.

It was the Philippine Islands, however, that most forcefully brought the imperialist issue to a head. Large, populous, alien, and distant, they neither fell within the traditional geographical scope of American expansionism nor seemed even remotely assimilable to the American federal system. In the United States there had been little thought of acquiring the Philippines before the Spanish-American War, but once war came the American armed forces attacked them because they represented valuable enemy territory that was highly vulnerable. The initial American victories quickly led to a national conviction that the United States now controlled the islands and was responsible for determining their destiny. Expansionists were quick to argue that the nation could not turn the Filipinos back to Spanish misrule, while to let them drift would invite an Anglo-German struggle for their control. On the other hand, American rule could bring enlightenment to the islanders, and their proximity to China might aid American penetration of what was assumed to be one of the great world markets of the future.

Expansionism carried the day, and the peace treaty with Spain provided for American possession of Puerto Rico, the Philippines, and Guam. Hawaii had already been separately annexed, and Cuba was subjected to a three-year military occupation followed by a theoretically sovereign independence in 1902. In fact, however, Cuba became a self-governing protectorate of the United States, with the latter nation retaining important governmental controls and the right of military intervention at its discretion, under the terms of the Platt Amendment of 1901. In the Philippines, meanwhile, an armed independence movement revolted against American rule in 1899, and the ensuing three-year Filipino-American War introduced the Americans to the frustrations and mutual atrocities characteristic of antiguerrilla warfare. While American forces finally succeeded in crushing all resistance, anti-imperialists made the most of the contradictions that were inherent in the spreading of enlightenment at the point of a bayonet. Colonial empire quickly lost its glamor in the United States, while less formal techniques of expansion gained easier acceptance from the relative success of the Cuban protectorate policy. In the twentieth century, American imperialism would be characterized by the extension of influence or control rather than by the outright annexation of territory.

After 1900 the American public quickly lost interest in its new colonies, but the United States continued to expand its power in essentially imperialist ways. This was true principally in the Caribbean region, where the creation of formal and informal protectorates characterized American foreign policy in the period after the Spanish-American War. The war had awakened interest in the building of an isthmian canal, which was to be built as a national project; and following Panama's secession from Colombia in 1903, the project became a reality. The great strategic importance of the Panama Canal—thereafter joined with the considerable American stake in Cuba and its direct sovereignty over Puerto Rico—drew the nation further into Caribbean affairs.

Still fearful of European intervention and solicitous of the growing American economic interest in the area, policymakers in Washington viewed the chronic political instability of the Caribbean and Central American nations as an invitation to foreign penetration and an obstacle to local development. The Roosevelt Corollary to the Monroe Doctrine, enunciated by President Theodore Roosevelt in 1904, claimed for the United States an "international police power," which entailed a general right to intervene and keep order in the Western Hemisphere. Not only Roosevelt but also his successors, William Howard Taft and Woodrow

IMPERIALISM

Wilson, steadily expanded American hegemony in the Caribbean. By World War I, Cuba, Panama, the Dominican Republic, Haiti, and Nicaragua were in some kind of protectorate status, while Puerto Rico remained an outright colony. Actual military interventions occurred in Cuba (1906–1909), Haiti (1915–1934), the Dominican Republic (1916–1924), Nicaragua (1912, 1927–33), and Panama (intermittently and on a lesser scale).

Besides the use of special treaty relationships and military force, the United States attempted to maintain a "monopoly of lending," under which Caribbean governments would borrow money only in the United States; it also established customs receiverships in several countries, which effectively placed their government revenues under control of the United States. Meanwhile private enterprise had permeated the region with American investment and business activity, while the one-crop economies of the Caribbean nations made them heavily dependent upon the American market. Thus the nominally sovereign states of the Caribbean area were subject to American controls, both formal and informal, which made their real status essentially colonial.

After 1898 the United States was also active in the Far East, but its impact was weaker there than in the Caribbean. Faced with a huge and populous China, and competing with most of the other major world powers, American policymakers could not aspire to regional dominance or military solutions. The "dollar diplomacy" of the William Howard Taft administration (1909–1913) attempted to foster American investment in China and to create international financial arrangements, which would impose a Caribbean-style "monopoly of lending" upon the government of China. This attempt to mobilize American economic strength as a diplomatic tool accomplished little in the Far East, however, on account of both the difficulties of the situation itself and the limited interest of the nation's business and financial leaders. The earlier Open Door policy of 1899–1900, therefore, remained the principal basis of policy. It represented little more than an attempt to obtain a general agreement to preserve the existing treaty system of shared control in China, and thus equality of economic opportunity in China for the United States.

The policy was not very effective, and the Chinese market never came near to meeting the inflated expectations of the West. In general, the limited objectives and relative ineffectiveness of American activities in the Far East fell short of real imperialism in this period, although the United States was long a party to the treaty system by which the Western powers jointly had imposed a limited protectorate upon China.

American participation in World War I led to a revulsion against overseas commitments, which reached its peak in the Senate rejection of the Treaty of Versailles (1919) and the new League of Nations. Rising domestic criticism in the 1920's brought about the liquidation of the military government in the Dominican Republic and moderate relaxation of American political controls elsewhere in the Caribbean. At the same time, however, the American government and business community cooperated in pushing American exports and foreign loans, leading some later historians to envision an "open door imperialism" based on American economic influence abroad. An alternate view was that the United States did indeed seek such economic influence, but that most Americans then thought it possible to separate the political and economic aspects of international relations in a manner considered unrealistic by later generations.

The Great Depression brought an even greater emphasis on the economic side of foreign policy and a corresponding decline in interest in other aspects. The Good Neighbor policy of Franklin D. Roosevelt brought the dismantling of Caribbean military interventions and political protectorates, at the same time that Latin America was tied more closely to the American economy by means of reciprocal trade agreements. The Philippine Islands were set on the path to independence in 1934, while the Neutrality Acts of 1935–1938 were designed to minimize economic ties to belligerents in foreign wars. The Monroe Doctrine took on a new theoretical formulation as an association of hemispheric equals for collective security, and the isolationist majority in the United States eschewed any national interest in the world's affairs outside the Western Hemisphere. American imperialism was declared to be dead, never to arise again.

IMPERIALISM

At the end of the 1930's there was a rapid reversal of thinking largely caused by the early victories of Nazi Germany during the new European war, and particularly by the shock created by the fall of France in 1940. Americans quickly became internationalists, the new consensus being that the world's democracies must stand together to check the crimes of "gangster nations" like Germany, Italy, and Japan. It now appeared that peace was indivisible and that the United States must be concerned with events in every corner of the globe. With the Japanese attack on Pearl Harbor late in 1941, the United States went to war in both Europe and Asia. During World War II the United States fought as a member of a coalition that included Great Britain, the Soviet Union, Nationalist China, and many lesser members— a circumstance that drew the United States even further into global affairs. Mobilizing enormous fighting power and productivity, Americans found themselves at the close of the struggle with their armed forces deployed in Europe, Asia, North Africa, the Middle East, Australasia, and Latin America.

World War II humbled or drastically weakened every great power except the United States and the Soviet Union, both of which emerged with greatly enhanced power and prestige. In a world full of power vacuums, this dangerously simplified bipolar balance contributed to a growing rivalry between the two superpowers, as did the strong but mutually contradictory ideas of mission that each possessed. Initially competing for hegemony in Europe, this postwar rivalry soon became global in scope, and American military and political commitments proliferated. At the same time, the preeminent economic position of the United States at the end of World War II much enhanced its influence abroad and gave it great weight in shaping the economic structure of the noncommunist world. Thus American influence over other societies reached a new high and took many different forms. In the Caribbean the United States supported anticommunist military ventures in Guatemala (1954) and Cuba (1961), and in 1965—out of fear that a leftist government would come to power—intervened in the Dominican Republic. In the Far East, South Korea, Taiwan, and, later, South

Vietnam and Cambodia became heavily dependent upon American military aid. Japan grew into an economic giant but retained close economic and military ties to the United States. Other initiatives in the Middle East, Africa, and elsewhere made American activities truly global.

In the economic sphere the United States overwhelmingly became the chief investor and source of credit, as well as principal extractor of raw materials and supplier of new technologies. From the 1940's to the 1960's the American dollar was the keystone of international currency exchanges, while an American-sponsored drive toward freer world trade facilitated American exports of goods and money. The purchase of foreign subsidiaries and the development of multinational corporations gave American business enterprise increased influence abroad, while many foreign nations found their principal export markets in the United States.

The political and economic impact of the United States was accompanied by significant social effects. American-style mass consumption spread its appeal everywhere, as the elite of half the globe rushed to emulate the lifestyles of New York and California. American tourists, motion pictures, and television programs went everywhere, and from all over the world students flocked to American universities to seek advanced training and degrees. Even an economically advanced society like Japan massively assimilated American modes of dress, eating, and amusement, and eagerly accepted bondage to the automobile.

The worldwide distribution of American military bases, security agreements, investments, multinational corporations, foreign-aid programs, and open and undercover political activities gave rise to the charge that American imperialism had not only revived but had expanded over enormous areas. The international vogue of American fashions and consumer products could be viewed as cultural imperialism, while American participation in the Korean War (1950–1953), and especially in the Vietnam War (1963–1973), was perceived by a growing number of critics as crude militaristic expansionism. Some critics described an "open door empire," in which American foreign policy sought to impose everywhere the conditions necessary for the penetration of American exports and enterprise, while keeping underdeveloped nations in a state of perpetual economic colonialism. From this point of view, the term "imperialism" applied to virtually every overseas activity of the United States.

Given the undeniably great impact of the United States in the postwar world, the issue was not whether there had been an American influence on other societies but whether that influence was best described as imperialist. Since the United States annexed no territory during the period in question, the most obvious form of imperialism did not apply: there was no formal empire. Although the global American presence seemed to demand acknowledgment and analysis, the overgeneralized use of any single label posed the dangers of imprecision and inaccuracy. For example, both orthodox Marxists and members of the so-called New Left agreed that imperialism was a phenomenon associated uniquely with capitalist states. They therefore found the term useful in denoting a particular stage of capitalist development, or in distinguishing between capitalist and noncapitalist foreign policies. But after 1945 there was little to validate this distinction, for the Soviet Union created a hegemony in Eastern Europe at least as rigorous as that of the United States in the Caribbean, and embracing far more people. Moscow's economic exploitation of its Eastern bloc was likewise equal to the best that the capitalists could do, while the outright annexation of the Baltic states and portions of Poland and other countries incorporated new minorities into the polyglot Russian empire. No one could call the Soviet Union a capitalist state, yet it had surely practiced imperialism, if the term had any specific content at all. To speak of American imperialism, therefore, might well be legitimate, but in this particular sense it failed to clarify the issues involved.

It was conceptually more useful to return to the notion of a disproportionate difference in power between the strongest societies and the rest. In this case the global activities of the United States and the Soviet Union could equally be classed as imperialism, since the two superpowers approached every nation except each other as grossly unequal in terms of the possession of effective force. Such extreme power disparities generated domination almost as a reflex, and the United States exercised foreign domination in the postwar years as certainly as it had in previous eras. For example, the Dominican Republic found itself the target of an American invasion in 1965, aimed at determining the outcome of an internal political struggle. Afterward the country was governed by Joaquín Belaguer, a president in whose selection and retention in power the United States played an active role. The Dominican Republic knew the machinations of the American Central Intelligence Agency in its domestic affairs, and the country found its chief export market in the United States. This looked very much like imperialism in its broader connotation, if not in the narrower and more precise one.

At the same time, blanket assertions of imperialism went too far. For example, it was doubtful terminology to apply that label to the postwar American record in Europe, in spite of the Marshall Plan, the North Atlantic Treaty Organization, large corporate investments, and the cultural imperialism of Coca-Cola. It is true that the United States threw its considerable postwar influence into an effort to erect a liberal-capitalist system in Western Europe, just as the Soviet Union worked for Marxist-Leninist states in Eastern Europe. Given a virtual power vacuum in one of the vital centers of the world, no less was to be expected of either superpower. It is also true that the Marshall Plan and companion policies were designed not only to aid European economic recovery, but to boost European purchases of American exports. Yet the end result was not merely exploitive, for it helped to recreate in Western Europe one of the great industrial centers of the world, which soon offered stiff competition to the United States itself. Like Japan, West Germany pressed American manufacturers hard in their own markets and often bested them in markets abroad. To call this performance economic imperialism is both misleading and intellectually counterproductive.

Similarly, the North Atlantic Treaty Organization seems to have been a voluntary alliance system, as indicated on the one hand by the major role played by Western Europeans in its initiation, and on the other hand by the virtual withdrawal of France after 1966 and the steadily declining levels of support contributed by most other European members. By the middle 1950's, Western European governments were taking increasingly independent positions on foreign policy—American leadership fading drastically in the 1960's. The United States undoubtedly preferred certain European leaders and political parties to their domestic rivals, as shown by the State Department's support of Italy's Christian Democrats in the Italian general election of 1948. Yet American attempts to influence European internal politics had a limited success after 1949. In short, Western Europe did not become a satellite bloc of the United States, despite the great importance of the American presence there in the years just following World War II.

The American military intervention in Southeast Asia during the 1960's ended in the following decade in humiliating failure and a national reappraisal of the American role abroad. For a time the tide of public opinion ran strongly against further foreign adventures, but the global network of American commitments and interests continued largely intact. American power remained great, and was still widely applied to affect local and regional issues in many areas. It appeared that imperialism was not yet dead, nor would it be so long as a grossly unequal distribution of power and wealth enabled some nations to dominate others. As the strongest and wealthiest nation in the quarter-century following World War II, the United States was responsible for its full share of neoimperialist hegemony. Yet it was simplistic to see imperialism in every manifestation of American power, wealth, or cultural impact. To use the word so loosely would soon result in its retaining no specific meaning at all, while to apply it solely to the United States obscured the fundamental realities of international relations.

BIBLIOGRAPHY

Lloyd C. Gardner, *Economic Aspects of New Deal Diplomacy* (Madison, Wis., 1964), shows that foreign policy of the Franklin D. Roosevelt administration continued to encourage economic expansion abroad, and sees a continuity with earlier Open Door diplomacy. Norman A. Graebner, *Empire on the Pacific: A Study in American Continental Expansion* (New York, 1955), argues that the desire for maritime commerce, rather than land-hunger alone, sparked the drive to acquire the Pacific coast. David Healy, *U. S. Expansionism: The Imperialist Urge in the 1890s* (Madison, Wis., 1970), a multicausal approach, shows the convergence of numerous and dissimilar forces in the movement for overseas empire. Walter LaFeber, *The New Empire: An Interpretation of American Expansion, 1860–1898* (Ithaca, N.Y., 1963), depicts American overseas expansion as creating a commercial empire in order to serve a drive for export markets. Ernest R. May, *Imperial Democracy: The Emergence of America as a Great Power* (New York, 1961), sees the expansionism of 1898 in terms of an eruption of public opinion that swept the nation's leaders before it. A. P. Thornton, *Doctrines of Imperialism* (New York, 1965), is a short but good conceptual study of imperialism. Robert W. Tucker, *The Radical Left and American Foreign Policy* (Baltimore, 1971), is a brief but cogent review of the New Left critique of American foreign policy and economic imperialism. Adam B. Ulam, *The Rivals: America and Russia Since World War II* (New York, 1971), is a view of the two superpowers and their struggle for power in the postwar world, in which the author freely assigns criticism to both sides. Albert K. Weinberg, *Manifest Destiny* (Baltimore, 1935), is still a standard work on the ideology of continental expansion. William A. Williams, *The Tragedy of American Diplomacy* (Cleveland, Ohio, 1959), an influential book, helped launch a revisionist movement in American diplomatic history and popularize an "Open Door School," which held that the economic goals of capitalism were central to the formation of United States foreign policy; and *The Roots of the Modern American Empire: A Study of the Growth and Shaping of Social Consciousness in a Market-place Society* (New York, 1969), is a fuller development of Williams' thesis tying American foreign policy to the effects of a capitalist economy, but giving a larger role to the attempts of farmers to export their surpluses.

[*See also* ANTI-IMPERIALISM; COLONIALISM; DOLLAR DIPLOMACY; ECONOMIC FOREIGN POLICY; INTERVENTION AND NONINTERVENTION; ISOLATIONISM; MANIFEST DESTINY; MILITARISM; THE OPEN DOOR POLICY; PACIFISM; PROTECTORATES AND SPHERES OF INFLUENCE.]

INTELLIGENCE AND COUNTERINTELLIGENCE

Lyman B. Kirkpatrick, Jr.

INTELLIGENCE, the knowledge required by one nation about other nations in order to conduct a successful foreign policy or avoid defeat in war, has been a factor in American government, albeit at times a small one, since the founding of the Republic. For a century and a half, the role of intelligence in the government was a matter left largely to the president and his advisers, and taken for granted by the people. In the latter part of the twentieth century, intelligence activities became an issue of national and public concern.

Counterintelligence, the effort to frustrate the efforts of hostile intelligence services, commenced in colonial days; but not until the twentieth century has it been carried out consistently. The provincial congresses of the colonies attempted to require loyalty oaths and to identify Tories and British spies. Benjamin Church, a prominent Boston physician who enjoyed the respect of the Massachusetts Provincial Congress, was identified as an agent in the pay of General Thomas Gage, commander of the British forces in America.

One British agent whose work remained hidden for many years operated in Paris against representatives of the Continental Congress who had been sent to negotiate a treaty with France and to obtain credit and assistance. When Silas Deane was sent to Paris, Benjamin Franklin suggested that he obtain the assistance of Edward Bancroft, whom Franklin knew through his work as a doctor, scientist, anthropologist, and political historian. Franklin also was impressed by Bancroft's defense of American rights in 1769, when he published *Remarks on the Review of the Controversy Between Great Britain and Her Colonies*. In the summer of 1776 Bancroft made several trips between London and Paris. Deane confided to him all the plans of the Continental Congress and the details of the negotiations. Early in 1777 Bancroft moved to Paris to serve as secretary to both Deane and Franklin, who had arrived to reinforce the former's efforts, and took up residence with them at Passy.

Unknown to the Americans, Bancroft had been recruited for the British Secret Service by Paul Wentworth, a New Hampshire Tory, and reported to Lord Stormont, the British ambassador in Paris. Bancroft placed his letters in a bottle hidden in a hole in the root of a tree on the south terrace of the Tuileries, and every Tuesday evening at half past nine a member of the staff of the British embassy picked up the reports. There was no aspect of the negotiations in Paris that was not known in London within days. The British were not alone in their espionage. The Americans also were under intense surveillance by the many agents of the French foreign minister, Charles Gravier, count of Vergennes.

While the attitude toward counterintelligence may have been casual, the first commander in chief aggressively sought intelligence on British forces and showed a clear appreciation of the necessity for correct evaluation of information. General George Washington looked to his secretary of war, Benjamin Lincoln, as the "fountain of intelligence" but sometimes disagreed with the latter's estimate of the situation, writing on one occasion: "If I may be allowed to ground an opinion upon present appearances, information and past experience, I should think you have greatly overrated our prospects." In 1782 Washington directed General Nathanael Greene to send him a report that should evaluate the "strength, movements, and position of your own army and that of the enemy . . . resources of the country and everything of a military or political nature, which may be interesting to our future plans and operations." Upon assuming the presidency, Washington continued to show intense interest in the information required for the formulation of foreign policy and made a practice of reading the entire diplomatic correspondence of the United States.

The necessity for intelligence also was clear to the men who wrote the Constitution. On 5 March 1788, in the sixty-fourth of the Federalist Papers, Secretary of Foreign Affairs John Jay, writing about the treaty-making power, commented on the necessity for secrecy and speed in negotiating treaties and the wisdom of leaving the management of intelligence to the president. He said:

> There are cases where the most useful intelligence may be obtained, if the persons possessing it can be relieved from apprehensions of discovery. Those apprehensions will operate on those persons whether they are actuated by mercenary or friendly motives, and there doubtless are many of both descriptions, who would rely on the secrecy of the president, but who would not confide in that of the senate, and still less in that of a large popular assembly. The convention has done well therefore in disposing of the power of making treaties, that although the president must in forming them act by the advice and consent of the senate, yet he will be able to manage the business of intelligence in such manner as precedence may suggest . . . so often and so essentially have we heretofore suffered from want of secrecy and dispatch, that the Constitution would have been inexcusably defective if no attention had been paid to those objects.

American presidents experienced no difficulties in obtaining funds from Congress for "secret service," the once popular name for foreign intelligence operations, in the first two decades of the nation. The Eleventh Congress in 1810 acted to establish some form of ac-

counting for such expenditures but provided that the president could avoid reporting an expenditure by using a certificate for it.

On 15 February 1816, a report of the Senate Foreign Relations Committee endorsed the president's use of secrecy in words reminiscent of the Federalist Papers, noting that the chief executive was responsible for relations that frequently required "secrecy and dispatch." As the constitutional representative of the United States with regard to foreign nations, he must necessarily be most competent to determine when, how, and upon what subjects negotiations might be urged with the greatest prospect of success. Furthermore, the report said, the nature of transactions with foreign nations requires caution and unity of design, and success frequently depends on secrecy and dispatch.

In 1846 a resolution of the House of Representatives put the law of 1810 to a test. The resolution requested President James K. Polk to produce all records of expenditures of confidential "secret service funds" during the tenure of Secretary of State Daniel Webster (1841–1843). Webster had served under President William Henry Harrison and President John Tyler, and the latter had signed certificates for the expenditures. Polk refused the demand as a matter of principle. In a reply dated 20 April he argued that there were certain expenditures "for the public safety or the public good" that never should be publicized by sending papers and vouchers to the Treasury. He said:

> In time of war or impending danger the situation of the country may make it necessary to employ individuals for the purpose of obtaining information or rendering other important services who could never be so prevailed upon to act if they entertained the least apprehension that their names or their agency would in any contingency be divulged. . . . But this object might be altogether defeated by the intrigues of other powers if our purposes were to be made known by the exhibition of the original papers and vouchers to the accounting officers of the Treasury. . . .

Although the president had the authority and funds for intelligence operations, no effort was made to establish any regular service. Most of the funds spent were for individuals sent by the president to obtain specific information. As a consequence, improvisation was necessary when the country was at war.

In 1844, when Brigadier General Zachary Taylor was authorized to march an army "corps of observation" to the Rio Grande, the leaders in Washington did not recognize that Mexican public opinion considered the loss of Texas as a matter of national honor and dignity. The consul in Mexico City consistently reported that Mexico would not go to war. The military forces had little knowledge of the terrain or people, let alone the strength and location of the Mexican army. In the advance on Monterrey, Taylor relied extensively on patrols to reconnoiter immediate objectives but made little effort to develop intelligence on the future area of operations. Eventually Colonel Ethan Allen Hitchcock organized the Spy Scout Company, recruiting Manuel Dominquez, a notorious outlaw, and 200 of his band as spies, scouts, and couriers. When Thomas O. Larkin reported from California that the Hudson's Bay Company was offering weapons and money to persons anxious to restore Mexican control over that territory, the government in Washington deputized him as a confidential agent to frustrate that effort.

Little was done between the Mexican War and the Civil War to organize an intelligence service, and once again temporary measures had to suffice. Allan Pinkerton, founder of the detective agency that bears his name, served first as head of a Washington counterintelligence service searching for Confederate spies and later, at the invitation of McClellan, Pinkerton organized a secret service and counterespionage department for the army, which he headed until late 1862. President Abraham Lincoln and the War Department directed the activities of intelligence agents both in the South and in Canada, where Confederate operatives were attempting to disrupt the Union war effort.

The descendants of one of Lincoln's spies brought suit for pay and allowances never paid their ancestor. This resulted in the only opinion of the United States Supreme Court devoted exclusively to intelligence. In *Totten* v. *United States* (92 U.S. 105 [1876]) the Court delivered an opinion on the power of the president to employ secret agents to obtain informa-

tion clandestinely. The Court, after noting that the contract was for a "secret service" to obtain information clandestinely, said: "Both employer and agent must have understood that the lips of the other were to be forever sealed respecting the relation of either to the matter." It concluded that such a condition of employment is implied in all secret efforts of the government in times of war or matters affecting foreign relations, and that public policy forbids a trial that would disclose confidential matters.

After the Civil War the United States Army and Navy started to collect information on foreign military services. In May 1866 Assistant Secretary of the Navy Gustavus V. Fox was sent on a mission to Russia and told to collect details on the navies of Europe. In 1872 the navy posted an officer to London designated as "the naval attaché" to the American minister. In 1875 the chief engineer of the navy was directed by the United States Senate to examine and report on the ships of war and merchant marines of the European nations. Naval observers were sent to the War of the Pacific, fought by Chile against Peru and Bolivia, in 1879–1881, and to the British Tell-el-Kebir campaign in 1882.

It was not until the 1880's that the United States decided to establish formal, permanent intelligence components in the government. The Military Information Division was organized in the Miscellaneous Branch of the Army Adjutant General's Office. It consisted of one officer and one clerk assigned to maintain files on foreign armies. On 23 March 1882 the navy established the Office of Intelligence, which was combined with the Navy Department library and put under the chief of the Bureau of Navigation. It was staffed by four officers.

In 1889 Congress approved a system of military attachés, army and navy officers assigned to United States embassies abroad to gather information openly about foreign armies and navies. Attachés were assigned to Berlin, Vienna, Paris, London, St. Petersburg, and, later, Madrid and Tokyo. Reports from military attachés were to prove of value in the Spanish-American War.

Once again, in World War I there was a temporary expansion of the intelligence services. The Office of Naval Intelligence had a staff of ten officers and ten civilians in 1914. By Armistice Day, 11 November 1918, the organization had grown to 306 reservists and eighteen civil service personnel. In 1920 it was down to forty-two employees. A counterintelligence effort was started by the navy in 1916.

The army experience was similar, but on a larger scale. In the early 1900's the information staff had become a committee of the War College that was responsible for war plans. The Military Intelligence Branch was established in 1917, and by the end of the war it consisted of 282 officers and 1,100 civilians. It was responsible for counterintelligence in the United States.

On 10 June 1917 the War Department established the Cipher Bureau at the War College to serve as the central cryptanalysis and cryptographic agency. Its function was to break foreign codes and ciphers. This bureau was funded jointly by the army and the State Department from 1919 until 1929, after which the latter withdrew its support.

This communications intelligence effort and the small intelligence staffs of the army and navy constituted the entire United States effort between the two world wars. On 10 June 1941 the director of naval intelligence wrote: "We have at present no intelligence network abroad other than naval attachés. When and if the need for agents appears, I believe we can handle the situation. Our plan and organization for combatting espionage and subversive activities at home are progressing continuously."

General Dwight D. Eisenhower said, "A shocking deficiency impeded all constructive planning . . . in the field of intelligence." He ascribed this to American repugnance for anything that "smacks of the spy" and pointed out that no funds had been provided for an intelligence system between the wars.

A landmark ruling by the Supreme Court during the interwar period seemed to imply that the United States had a far-flung network of secret intelligence agents. In the case of *United States* v. *Curtiss Wright Export Corporation* (299 U.S. 304 [1936]), Justice George Sutherland delivered an opinion that upheld the "exclusive" power of the president to conduct the foreign relations of the nation and commented on the role of intelligence:

> Moreover, he [the President], not Congress, has the better opportunity of knowing the condi-

tions which prevail in foreign countries, and especially is this true in time of war. He has his confidential sources of information. He has his agents in the form of diplomatic, consular and other officials. Secrecy in respect of information gathered by them may be highly necessary, and the premature disclosure of it productive of harmful results.

In the period leading up to United States entry into World War II, little was done to expand intelligence collection other than what the army and navy felt necessary; and intelligence generally lagged behind the expansion of the military services. The State Department did benefit when the military services broke the Japanese Purple Code, used for high-level diplomatic and military communications. During his protracted negotiations with Japanese envoys in 1940 and 1941, Secretary of State Cordell Hull was able to read messages from Tokyo ordering Japanese forces into offensive positions and to see the exact instructions sent to the men with whom he was dealing.

Counterintelligence also was playing a role prior to the attack on Pearl Harbor. The Federal Bureau of Investigation was intercepting messages instructing a Japanese agent in Honolulu to report daily on the exact locations and identification of the ships in Pearl Harbor. Ambassador Joseph Grew cabled from Tokyo that there was a rumor of a possible Japanese attack on Pearl Harbor, but it was not given much credence because Americans did not believe the Japanese would be so rash as to attack the strongest defensive position in the Pacific. Despite "danger of war" warnings, the guns were not manned at Pearl Harbor on the morning of 7 December 1941, when the Japanese struck. The result was a naval catastrophe for the United States.

On 11 July 1941 the first step was taken by the United States government to coordinate its intelligence and counterintelligence efforts, which were dispersed in eight departments and agencies, each reporting independently to the president. Franklin D. Roosevelt issued an executive order creating the office of Coordination of Information (COI):

> To collect and analyze all information and data which may bear upon national security, to correlate such information and data and make the same available to the President and to such de-

partments and officials of the Government as the Presidency determines, and to carry out when requested by the President such supplementary activities as may facilitate the securing of information important for national security not now available to the Government.

The new organization was the brainchild of William J. Donovan, an army hero in World War I, a former assistant attorney general of the United States, and a man who had acquired a reputation for correctly assessing international situations, regardless of views contrary to prevailing ones. He had forecast Mussolini's victory in Ethiopia in 1935; predicted that Great Britain would not crumble in 1940 under the German air assault; and correctly estimated that the Mediterranean would become a major war area. Donovan frequently had told President Roosevelt of the need for a coordinated intelligence system and for an organization to conduct unorthodox warfare. The phrase "supplementary activities" in the executive order covered unorthodox warfare: paramilitary activities, propaganda, deception, sabotage, and subversion.

On 13 June 1942 Executive Order 9182 created the Office of Strategic Services (OSS), headed by Donovan, and the Office of War Information, under Elmer Davis. The latter organization absorbed the COI's Foreign Information Service and all overt (or "white") propaganda, while covert (or "black") propaganda was assigned to the OSS along with the intelligence and unorthodox warfare responsibilities. The OSS was placed "under the direction and supervision of the Joint Chiefs of Staff . . . to collect and analyze information, and to plan and operate special services [defined as] all measures . . . taken to enforce our will upon the enemy by means other than military action. . . ."

Although earlier intelligence organizations had been developed by the United States in the heat of war, the OSS was unique in encompassing the entire spectrum of unorthodox warfare, in commencing to plan operations before the country was at war through the COI, and in developing a cadre of experienced personnel. In building the OSS, Donovan and his associates were dependent, at least initially, on the experienced British organizations—the Secret Intelligence Service, the Special Opera-

tions Executive, the Psychological Warfare Executive, and MI-5 (the counterintelligence organization)—as well as on many other intelligence services and resistance groups in Europe and Asia.

Starting with a handful of friends, Donovan built an organization of more than 30,000 men and women with skills as diverse as those in the research and analysis branch, which was widely hailed as the progenitor of area studies programs developed in American universities following the war, and the guerrilla warfare unit, which supported an OSS detachment that harassed the Japanese behind the lines in Burma. Other units engaged in secret intelligence (espionage), counterespionage, sabotage, and morale operations ("black" propaganda and other psychological warfare methods designed to break the enemy's will to fight).

Less spectacular than the operational units but of great value in establishing a base for a peacetime service were such support elements as schools and training, cover and documentation, security, communications, research and development, and a maritime unit.

The OSS was not welcomed by the bureaucracy in Washington. There were established elements in the government that regarded certain area and functional jurisdictions as sacrosanct. The Federal Bureau of Investigation had been given the responsibility for counterintelligence operations in South America, so the OSS was excluded. General Douglas MacArthur had his own intelligence system and would not permit the OSS to send units to his command. Thus the OSS operated primarily in Europe, Africa, and the China-Burma-India theater of war. In the European Theater of Operations an effort was made to place OSS operations under British supervision. Donovan successfully resisted this, and the Joint Chiefs of Staff gave the OSS full and unqualified authority to operate in Europe.

Other bureaucratic battles continued. The army assistant chief of staff, intelligence (G-2), organized his own espionage service because he did not want to depend on the OSS. Some State Department officials were reluctant to provide "cover" for OSS personnel in embassies in neutral nations, even though intelligence of great value could be collected in such capitals as Bern and Stockholm.

Among the greatest achievements of the

OSS were those of Allen Dulles, later the head of the Central Intelligence Agency (CIA), in Switzerland. Dulles crossed the Swiss border from France in 1942, just as the Germans were completing their occupation of southern France, thus ending Allied access to Switzerland. Gradually Dulles developed sources who were to produce intelligence of great value before the end of the war. An anti-Nazi official in the German Foreign Office in Berlin gave Dulles more than 1,600 cables in the year and a half starting in August 1943. A senior German Military Intelligence (*Abwehr*) officer in Switzerland was one of his valuable sources. Dulles arranged the "secret surrender" of the German forces in Italy in advance of the general Nazi capitulation—a surrender that might have taken place two months earlier had it not been for Russian suspicions of the Western Allies.

On 18 November 1944, well before the hostilities ended, Donovan submitted a memorandum to President Roosevelt suggesting a permanent peacetime intelligence service that would report directly to the president but would be guided by an advisory board consisting of the secretaries of state, war, and navy. Donovan's plan placed coordination and centralization at the policy level but left operational intelligence with the existing agencies: the army, the navy and the State Department. The memorandum specified that the proposed agency would have no police or law-enforcement powers; and Donovan urged President Roosevelt to act before the end of the war, so that trained and specialized personnel would not be dispersed.

Donovan's desire to see the Office of Strategic Services become the permanent peacetime service was not completely realized, although his concepts became the basis for the Central Intelligence Agency. After the Japanese surrender, the Bureau of the Budget recommended that the OSS be disbanded, an action implemented on 20 September 1945. Three branches of the organization were preserved. The research and analysis branch was transferred to the Department of State to become the Bureau of Intelligence and Research. The foreign intelligence and counterintelligence branches were placed under an assistant secretary of war, pending a decision on a peacetime service.

With the termination of the OSS, President Harry S. Truman's initial decision was to place the national intelligence effort under the Department of State. Control of the national intelligence effort by the State Department met strong opposition from the military, which argued that a clandestine role for that department would subvert its diplomatic mission. In January 1946 Truman held a series of meetings to examine plans for a centralized intelligence authority. Secretary of State James Byrnes asked for continued control of all intelligence. The army and navy objected, favoring a central organization for national intelligence but with each department still allowed to collect and process the information it needed.

On 20 January 1946 Truman issued an executive order establishing the Central Intelligence Group, supervised by the National Intelligence Authority, which consisted of the secretaries of state, war, and navy and the chief of staff to the president, Admiral William D. Leahy.

The Central Intelligence Group was a temporary organization that was to exist until passage of legislation establishing a permanent intelligence service. It was not until July 1947 that the National Security Act of 1947 (6, stat. 495, 50 U.S.C. 401 or P.L. 80-253) was passed, creating the Central Intelligence Agency, an independent agency in the executive branch that reports to the president through the National Security Council (NSC), which was established by the same legislation. Thus, many of Donovan's concepts were realized.

Under the law the CIA was charged with coordinating the intelligence activities of the federal government; correlating, evaluating, and disseminating intelligence relating to national security; and performing such additional services of common concern and such other functions and duties related to intelligence as the NSC would direct. The act specified that the agency should have no police, subpoena, or law-enforcement powers, nor internal security functions.

The law provides for a director and a deputy director of central intelligence, to be appointed by the president with the advice and consent of the Senate. An amendment to the law of 1949 stipulated that at no time should the two positions be occupied simultaneously by commissioned officers of the armed services, whether active or retired. The act specified that the director of central intelligence was responsible for protecting intelligence sources from unauthorized disclosure. The CIA absorbed the Central Intelligence Group, and the functions of the National Intelligence Authority were taken over by the NSC, which in effect became the supervisory body of the national intelligence effort.

Not long after the passage of the National Security Act, new and unanticipated functions were added to the responsibilities of the CIA. Concerned by the communist takeover in Czechoslovakia and eastern Europe and the successes of the communists in China, advisers to the president urged that the CIA be given authority to engage in covert political warfare. President Truman issued a directive authorizing covert political, psychological, and economic warfare and paramilitary activities when directed by the NSC. The definition of "covert" was that such activities be deniable, that no attribution to the United States government should be possible. Dean Rusk, while secretary of state, described such operations as the "back alley war" against communism. The authority for the presidential directive was based on the clause of the National Security Act authorizing such intelligence-related activities as the NSC may direct.

In 1948 the Supreme Court, in *Civil Aeronautics Board* v. *Waterman S.S. Co.* (333 U.S. 103), again upheld the president's preeminent role in foreign intelligence matters, saying that both as commander in chief and in the conduct of foreign relations, he has available intelligence services whose reports "are not and ought not be published to the world." The opinion held that the very nature of executive decisions on foreign policy ". . . are delicate, complex and involve large elements of prophecy."

The new intelligence structure of the United States was not long in receiving a major test. With the start of the war in Korea in June 1950, the military intelligence services, having been drastically reduced in size during the general demobilization following World War II, were expanded. The CIA was directed to develop a sizable organization to support military

forces in Korea and to intensify its efforts in Europe, where many believed the Russians might take advantage of American preoccupation in Asia.

The priority target for CIA operations throughout the world was communism. Soviet intelligence and political warfare operations were countered by support to individuals and organizations opposed to communism. In some instances organizations were created. The Free Europe Committee, staffed by exiles from the Eastern European countries taken over by the communists, was supported by CIA money and public contributions. Among its activities was Radio Free Europe, which transmitted programs to Eastern Europe. Radio Liberty, a powerful shortwave radio, was set up to broadcast to the Soviet Union in Russian and seventeen other languages. Anticommunist Chinese were supported in Asia, in what proved to be abortive attempts to influence developments in mainland China. The National Students Association received subsidies to support noncommunist student groups and to send delegations to international youth meetings, which frequently were dominated by communists. In short, an effort was made in the 1950's to establish a worldwide counterforce to communism that supported the foreign policy of the United States.

The counterintelligence effort was similar. Revelations of the extent of Soviet espionage against the United States in World War II and the extent of Soviet penetration of the government resulted in intensified security and loyalty programs. Occasional exposures of Russian spies by the Federal Bureau of Investigation produced specific evidence of the intensity of the Soviet effort.

The intelligence system of the government continued to grow. The communications intelligence organizations were integrated into the Armed Forces Security Agency in 1948; the agency was replaced by the National Security Agency in 1952.

In both communications and other areas, the technological revolution was having an impact on intelligence. Advanced methods of high-speed transmission required new methods of coping with an ever-increasing volume of reports, and the intelligence agencies were among the first to adopt computers for automatic storage and retrieval of information.

Technology also had an impact on the CIA's continuing search for new methods of obtaining information. Occasionally its innovations became public knowledge. In the 1950's, faced with inadequate knowledge about the Soviet Union, the CIA developed a new type of aircraft for high-altitude photography. Initially able to fly above the range of radar, intercepter aircraft, and surface-to-air missiles while photographing the Soviet Union, the U-2 became an international issue when one was shot down over Sverdlovsk on 1 May 1960. Soviet Premier Nikita Khrushchev, frustrated by years of being unable to stop the overflights—radar had reached the planes' altitude by the late 1950's—used the downing of the plane to denounce President Dwight D. Eisenhower and the so-called spirit of Camp David. Khrushchev also refused to participate in a four-power summit meeting at Paris until he received a formal apology from the United States. No apology was made and the conference collapsed.

Although it did not become known then, a successor to the U-2 (the A-11) was nearing completion. Now known as the SR-71, this aircraft was developed by the CIA and the air force, and was designed to fly considerably higher than the U-2 at about three times the speed of sound. Both the U-2 and the A-11 used cameras capable of taking precise photographs from distances never before possible.

The advent of the era of photographic intelligence raised new questions of national sovereignty. If the recognized three-mile limit of territorial waters—generally recognized since the sixteenth century, when that was the approximate distance a cannonball could be fired—was applicable, then would not national sovereignty above the earth terminate at the outer limit of defensive weapons (until 1960, approximately ten miles)? With the development of the photographic satellite in the 1960's by both the United States and the Soviet Union, a new dimension to the problem was added: space satellites could collect photographic intelligence from 110 to 150 miles above the earth. A precedent was established by the Strategic Arms Limitation Agreement of 1972, when the United States and the Soviet Union endorsed the photographic satellite as an acceptable means of verification, thus implying that national sovereignty above the earth ended at the upper limits of the atmosphere.

Technological innovation was not confined to activities above the earth. In 1975 it became public knowledge that the CIA had secretly directed the development of a vessel capable of raising objects from a depth of some three miles below the surface of the ocean. A portion of a sunken Soviet submarine, which the Russians had been unable to locate, had been raised from the Pacific for intelligence analysis.

Despite the development of new methods of obtaining information, the most ancient source of all still retained some important attributes. Espionage, the use of paid and controlled agents, could produce information on the intentions of nations that often was impossible to obtain in any other way. While American counterintelligence efforts uncovered Colonel Rudolf Abel operating in the United States in 1957, the Soviet Union apprehended Colonel Oleg Penkovsky, who was working for the CIA in Moscow. Abel was exchanged for the U-2 pilot, Francis Gary Powers, and Penkovsky was executed. The extent of Abel's activities and the degree of his success were never fully revealed; there were clear indications that Penkovsky was of great value to the United States.

Although much intelligence activity remained in the shadows or only partly visible, the responsibility for covert operations raised more issues of foreign policy. In 1953 the CIA staged an operation to overthrow Prime Minister Mohammed Mossadegh of Iran, in order to block the communist-controlled Tudeh party. The following year it supported the coup of Carlos Castillo-Armas that deposed the pro-communist government of Jacobo Arbenz Guzmán in Guatemala. In 1958 the CIA aided the abortive "colonel's revolt" in Indonesia. And in 1961 the CIA directed the disastrous operation, which included the landing of more than 1,400 Cuban exiles at the Bay of Pigs, to overthrow Fidel Castro's government in Cuba.

Of these four "covert" operations only those in Iran and Guatemala could be called successful, if the measure of success was the defeat of a communist government. The Bay of Pigs, an embarrassing failure for the United States, resulted in considerable discussion of the utility

INTELLIGENCE AND COUNTERINTELLIGENCE

of covert operations, but only limited attention to the policy of intervention and the executive use of a secret organization for this purpose.

By the early 1960's the United States intelligence community had become a coordinated group of agencies working under the direction of the United States Intelligence Board, later renamed the Foreign Intelligence Board, a body chaired by the director of central intelligence, who served as the president's personal representative. In addition to the CIA, the State Department Bureau of Intelligence and Research, the National Security Agency, and the FBI, the intelligence community included the army, navy and air force staffs and representatives of the Energy Research and Development Agency, formerly the Atomic Energy Commission. In 1961 the Defense Intelligence Agency was created to provide the top-level intelligence estimates required by the secretary of defense and the Joint Chiefs of Staff. In 1971 representatives of the Treasury Department were added. The United States Intelligence Board, consisting of the directors of all of these organizations, served as a coordinating mechanism for the director of central intelligence, acted as the top managerial body in the intelligence community, and passed on the substance of estimates to the White House.

The intelligence community faced one of its most severe tests in October 1962, when U-2 photography revealed that the Russians were building offensive missile sites in Cuba. In what was perhaps the closest integration of intelligence with policymaking in the history of the nation, President John F. Kennedy established an "ex comm" to ascertain the facts and recommend a course of action. It also was the first instance in which clandestinely collected intelligence was openly used to obtain an international consensus. Photographs of the missile sites were displayed at the United Nations and shown to the heads of state of America's major allies to secure support for United States demands that the Soviet Union remove the missiles.

With the progressive involvement of the United States in Southeast Asia from 1965 until 1972, the intelligence agencies again were active in a major war while maintaining peacetime roles in other parts of the world. The Joint Intelligence Command was established in Saigon to coordinate the efforts of the military intelligence agencies with those of the South Vietnamese. The Army and the CIA mounted operations to destroy the South Vietnamese communists, the Vietcong. Special Forces and the CIA organized the Montagnards (hill people) into paramilitary units for guerrilla warfare. The CIA supported anticommunist forces in Laos with training and equipment, maintaining an army that at times reached 30,000 men, including Thai volunteers, to oppose the communist Pathet Lao and harass the North Vietnamese. Part of the support included the use of Air America, a CIA-subsidized charter service, for aerial supply missions.

Considerable light was shed on the role of American intelligence in Vietnam by the publication of the Pentagon Papers—official documents and studies of the situation in Indochina covering the period from the end of World War II to 1968. Included in the collection were numerous intelligence directives, reports, and estimates. Most revealing was the continually pessimistic view expressed in the national intelligence estimates about the success of the American war effort and the possibility of breaking the will of the North Vietnamese. Publication of National Security Staff Memorandum 1 (*Congressional Record,* 10–11 May 1972, E 4975–5049), a comprehensive review of the Vietnam situation ordered by President Richard M. Nixon in January 1969, provided an even more complete analysis, including the differences of opinion among the intelligence agencies.

Revelations during the investigation of the Watergate affair led to massive exposure of activities of the intelligence and counterintelligence agencies and to analysis of the proper role of such organizations in the American system. Of foremost concern were the extent to which the CIA might have violated its charter by engaging in domestic surveillance of American citizens and whether the FBI had improperly used information obtained in its investigations. Other important issues included the extent and quality of congressional oversight of the intelligence agencies, and whether those organizations had been improperly used by the president. A major foreign policy issue became a public matter with the leak by a member of Congress of top-secret testimony by the director of the CIA on that agency's activities against the government of Salvador Allende in Chile.

Adding fuel to the controversy were books and articles by former intelligence personnel containing allegations of improper activities by the government agencies. One such proposed book led to a government-initiated court case to prevent publication, on the ground that the employee had signed an agreement not to reveal classified information obtained in the course of his employment. This contention was countered with the argument that such an understanding violated the employee's right under the First Amendment. The federal district court upheld the CIA's right to review manuscripts in advance of publication, and the circuit court of appeals issued an opinion that the district court had erred in forcing the government agency to release sensitive material. The Supreme Court refused to hear the case, thus upholding the CIA requirement that manuscripts of its employees, present and past, be submitted for review prior to publication.

The controversy over the intelligence agencies had an impact on foreign relations. Questions were raised in the House of Commons about CIA activities in England. Other nations expressed concern about interference in their internal affairs. The Soviet press used the situation to increase its efforts to discredit American intelligence, an effort that averages better than an article a week on the subject in Russian publications.

In a major reversal Congress in 1974 voted to transfer investigation of the alleged improprieties by the intelligence agencies from the standing committees to a select committee in each house. This change superseded the work of the subcommittees on intelligence of the Senate and House armed services committees, but it did not affect the regular reviews of the budgets conducted by the subcommittees of the appropriations committees. The Senate Foreign Relations Committee also claimed a role in the review process because of the impact of intelligence on the formulation of foreign policy and on the conduct of international relations.

The Senate select hearings, with a full-time staff of about ninety, commenced its investigations into all aspects of the work of the American intelligence and security agencies early in 1975. Committee hearings, both open and in executive session, were reported extensively in the press with the most detailed revelations ever of secret operations. While the basic question was whether the intelligence agencies had exceeded their legal authority, an underlying constitutional issue was the exclusivity of the president's control. Among the subjects investigated were plots for the assassination of foreign leaders, the testing of drugs to influence human behavior, operations against domestic dissidents, interception of electronic communications, counterintelligence operations, and the use of income tax returns.

In the House of Representatives the appointment of the Select Committee on Intelligence was delayed by a dispute over its membership. When the committee commenced its investigations, a controversy with the executive branch over the committee's right to declassify reports halted proceedings until agreement was reached that reports would be released only with the approval of the president. The committee concentrated its attention on the quality of intelligence and on whether accurate predictions had been made on such subjects as the October 1973 war in the Middle East, the Portuguese coup of April 1974, and the Tet offensive in Vietnam in 1968.

Even before the work of the select committees commenced, Congress took steps to tighten control of the intelligence agencies. A subcommittee was created to review the work of the FBI. Legislation was passed requiring that the president personally certify that each covert political action was essential to the national security and that Congress be so advised. And for the first time the authority of each United States ambassador over all activities undertaken in his country of assignment was made a matter of law.

Parallel with the congressional investigations, President Gerald R. Ford established a commission chaired by the vice-president to review all domestic activities by the CIA. Created by Executive Order 11828, dated 4 January 1975, this body, officially the Commission on CIA Activities Within the United States, was charged with reporting to the president within five months anything that exceeded the agency's statutory authority. In a 300-page report the Rockefeller Commission indicated that from 1952 until 1971 the CIA had engaged in surveying mail sent between the United States and the Soviet Union and that in the last year of this program it had examined 2.3 million of the 4.35 million items of mail to the Soviet Union, had photographed 33,000 envelopes, and had opened 8,700. The CIA also had established a special operations group to collect information on domestic dissidents and had infiltrated dissident groups. In addition, the agency had engaged in surveillance of its own personnel, which the commission believed exceeded its authority. In its thirty recommendations the commission urged that the National Security Act of 1947 be amended to make explicit that the CIA's activities must relate to foreign intelligence; that the president prohibit the CIA from collecting intelligence on the domestic activities of U.S. citizens, except those requiring security clearances; and that the president recommend a joint congressional committee on intelligence, appoint a full-time chairman for the President's Foreign Intelligence Advisory Board, and expand that group's responsibility to include oversight. The commission also urged that the president refrain from using the CIA in internal security matters and direct the CIA not to open mail except in wartime. A series of recommendations dealt with clarifying CIA-FBI relations, strengthening the checks on CIA activities, and the use of drugs on unsuspecting persons. In 1976 the Senate established a select committee to exercise oversight of the CIA and the intelligence community.

At issue in all of the investigations was not only the role of intelligence in a free society and its appropriate use as an instrument of foreign policy but also, perhaps even more important, how it is to be controlled.

BIBLIOGRAPHY

Philip Agee, *Inside the Company: CIA Diary* (London, 1975), contains revelations of CIA operations by a former employee. Allen Dulles, *The Craft of Intelligence* (New York, 1963), presents a somewhat philosophical approach by the former head of the CIA. Corey Ford, *Donovan of O.S.S.* (Boston, 1970), was prepared with the use of Donovan's papers. Sherman Kent, *Strategic Intelligence for American World Policy* (Princeton, 1949), is a scholarly analysis of the makeup of intelligence. Lyman Kirkpatrick, *The Real CIA* (New York, 1968), reviews the CIA's early years; and *The U.S. Intelligence Community* (New York, 1973), gives an analysis of impact on policy and controls. Victor Marchetti and John Marks, *The CIA and the Cult of Intelligence* (New York, 1974), contains an attack on the CIA and on the use of the intelligence agencies by the president. Harry Ransom, *The Intelligence Establishment* (Cambridge, Mass., 1970), is a scholarly discussion of pertinent issues. United States Senate, Committee on the Judiciary, "Soviet Intelligence and Security Services, 1964–70, a Selected Bibliography of Soviet Publications" (Washington, D.C., 1972), includes information on Soviet efforts to discredit American intelligence.
[*See also* THE COLD WAR; DECISION-MAKING APPROACHES AND THEORIES; NATIONAL SECURITY; PRESIDENTIAL POWER IN FOREIGN AFFAIRS.]

INTERCULTURAL RELATIONS

Akira Iriye

INTERCULTURAL relations may be defined as interactions, both direct and indirect, among two or more cultures. Direct interactions include physical encounters with people and objects of another culture, as well as mutual influences in philosophy, literature, music, art, and fashion. Indirect relations are more subtle, involving such things as a person's ideas and prejudices about another people, or a government leader's assumptions concerning a foreign country that may form a basis for policy decisions. Intercultural relations are thus simply a sum total of all aspects of relations between countries of diverse cultures. Put more specifically, America's intercultural relations are the country's relations with all other countries except those that belong to the same culture as the United States.

Such a broad definition immediately gives rise to practical difficulty when analyzing the history of American intercultural relations. Which countries belong to the same culture as the United States? How does one define the cultural identity of America? The term "Western civilization" is useful but very loose. One could argue, for instance, that the Soviet Union is no more Western than contemporary Japan or, conversely, that the Ottoman Empire was more Western than the American republics in the nineteenth century. The idea of America as a Western country is also open to question. A key theme of American intellectual history has been the sense of distance from Europe and the assertion of the country's uniqueness in relation to European societies. If we define American culture as both Western and modern, then obviously United States relations with countries that are Western but less than modern (however one defines the term) will have to

be included in the country's intercultural relations. If, as one extreme example, the United States can be identified as a postindustrial society, it may have more in common with Japan and the Soviet Union today than with some European countries. Or, if American culture is to be defined in terms of race, its multiethnicity will as clearly distinguish it from other Western countries as its geography separates it from Europe and Africa.

It may even be argued that all international relations are intercultural relations. America's dealings and contacts with, and the American people's attitudes and policies toward, any foreign country are conditioned by the historical and cultural outlooks of the two countries. Insofar as no two nations are completely identical, any discussion of foreign affairs must start with the assumption that we are analyzing two societies of diverse traditions as well as two entities embodying distinct sets of interests.

Nevertheless, it seems desirable, at least for purposes of analysis, to distinguish different types of foreign relations in order to make some sense of the complex phenomenon. For instance, United States relations with Great Britain would appear to be different from those with China to a greater extent than the differences between American relations with Britain and with France. To be sure, all these relationships can be studied in terms of such conventional factors as military power, security, trade, and national honor. In terms of these aggregate variables, the four nations are interchangeable. Balance-of-power considerations have a logic of their own irrespective of the cultural identity of a given actor, as do commercial interests or national security arrangements. But international relations consist of much more than these macroscopic factors. There are emigration and immigration, tourism, educational exchange, missionary and philanthropic activities overseas, and numerous other instances of individual encounters with other societies. Moods, opinions, and tastes define such encounters. Symbols, words, and gestures reflect a people's thought and behavior patterns, which establish the framework in which more formal decisions are made. It is in these "symbolic" areas that realms of common assumptions shrink further, and the sense of distance and difference grows greater. A feeling of commonality derived from tradition is lacking to a far greater extent when Americans deal with Turks, Chinese, or Indians than would be the case with Spaniards or Russians. Going to Hong Kong is not quite the same thing as going to Paris, and viewing Chinese paintings is a different experience from hearing a Soviet cellist. If they are not different, that fact becomes an important observation about the state of American culture.

For these reasons, it seems feasible to distinguish America's "cultural" relations from its "intercultural" relations and to restrict the latter to the American people's dealings with peoples and societies that do not share the roots from which the majority of Americans are derived, the roots usually characterized as Judeo-Christian or Western. Since these terms are excessively vague, one may arbitrarily say that "Western" here means those parts of the world from which practically all nonblack Americans came before the Civil War. America's "cultural" relations would, on the other hand, have to treat literary, artistic, and educational interchanges between Americans and Europeans, which require a scheme of analysis different from one more appropriate to a discussion of "intercultural" affairs. If such a distinction is too arbitrary, the difficulty it raises may prompt future historians to search for a more satisfactory theory of intercultural relations. At the very least, it is hoped that this essay will suggest conceptual frameworks that may be used for more detailed studies of American relations with other cultures.

From the beginning Americans were interested in peoples in non-Western lands. Writers at the time of the American Revolution were fond of stressing the multiethnic nature of the new republic. In most instances, to be sure, multiethnicity consisted of diverse European nationalities rather than distinctive racial groups. Compared with Western European countries, the United States seemed unique in that no nationality constituted a majority of the nation, even though those of English stock represented nearly half the population. There were Welsh, Irish, Germans, French, Scandinavians, and others whose admixture with, and adoption of the language of, the English-speaking Americans impressed European visitors for decades after the Revolution.

In defining the American nation as multiethnic, few observers at first explicitly stated that non-Europeans would also migrate to the country and turn it into a multiracial society. Yet the idea of racial and ethnic diversity implied something more than a land made up of various European nationalities. The universalism of the concept of the "city on a hill," and the idealized self-perception that the Americans had struggled for the "rights of man," not simply the rights of Englishmen, assumed that others, too, would look to the United States as a land of freedom and opportunity. Conversely, Americans would carry out their mission to spread the blessings of civilization and liberty to the less fortunate in distant countries. If, as so many writers asserted, America was the most progressive land in the world, it was because it was a country without archaic encumberments, where men and women from many countries would come and work together to build a new, ideal community. Anybody, theoretically, could join the undertaking. By the same token, what happened here would be of universal applicability. If various races and groups could join together in the United States to realize an earthly paradise, there was no reason why they could not do so elsewhere in the world. It was in this sense that America was called mankind's best hope.

Such universalism implied a view of other peoples that was monolithic, and an idea of history that was unilinear. Just as divergent groups who came to the United States would create one unified people, so the rest of the world would ultimately tend to that goal. The American dream would be realized globally, and the American experience would become a world experience. America would cease to be unique only when its ideals and institutions were firmly implanted in all parts of the globe. The entire world would become one great America.

This type of revolutionary idealism provided one basic framework in which Americans viewed other peoples. Throughout most of the nineteenth century, it was probably the only way the majority of Americans related themselves to others. Intercultural relations at that level were predominantly a political phenomenon. Arabs, Hindus, or Chinese would be judged in terms of their distance from the American ideals and of their capacity to approximate them—if not immediately, then in the future. It is not surprising that observers of non-European societies frequently argued about whether these societies would ever transform themselves and become more like America. The basic assumption was, of course, that at the moment they lacked most of the ingredients that made the United States so progressive. Native populations in the Middle East, south Asia, or east Asia were almost invariably described as ignorant, indolent, and oppressed by arbitrary despots. They were the exact opposite of the Americans. Joel Barlow, poet and diplomat, described Hassan Pasha, dey of Algiers, as "a man of a most ungovernable temper; passionate, changeable, and unjust to such a degree that there is no calculating his policy from one moment to the next." William Eaton, appointed consul at Tunis by President John Adams, wrote of the "continual altercations, contentions and delays among the Arabs." "Poverty makes them thieves," he reported, "and practice renders them adroit in stealing." Similar expressions can be found at random in American writings on Turks, Chinese, Japanese, and other non-European nationalities throughout the nineteenth century.

A key question, given such an image of non-Europeans, was whether they had some redeeming qualities. On this point American universalism decreed that no people was so inherently depraved as to be totally incapable of reform. The basic credo of American democracy was that any individual had certain abilities that could be developed to their potential if artificial restrictions were removed. Even those suffering under poverty and despotism were not entirely hopeless creatures. Given external stimuli to make them aware of alternative possibilities, and under favorable institutional conditions, they were certain to transform themselves. For, as the *Democratic Review* put it in 1839, "The same nature is common to all men . . . they have equal and sacred claims . . . they have high and holy faculties." It followed that Americans, having developed these faculties and made good their claims to progress, had a unique obligation to the rest of mankind. It was up to them, declared the *Knickerbocker* in 1840, "whether our fellow men shall reach the elevation whereof they are capable, and . . . whether or not [we shall] confer on them the most inestimable of all earthly boons, the boon of civilization."

In such a context, there could not be genuine intercultural relations; Americans would interact with other societies and cultures in the framework of their own ideals and preconceptions. Other peoples would merely be at the receiving end of American civilization without anything to give in return. Such, however, was not altogether the case. Even in the first half of the nineteenth century, when optimism regarding American values was most notable, appreciation of different cultural standards and achievements was not lacking. One has only to recall the great interest in porcelain, silks, paintings, and other objects brought back from China. Curiosity about other societies coexisted with a disdain for despotic institutions or alien religions. Samuel Goodrich's *A History of All Nations,* a popular textbook published in 1851, explained that while Asians on the whole were "slavish . . . superstitious . . . [and] treacherous," their arts compared favorably with those of Europe. "All the efforts of European art and capital," Goodrich wrote, "have been unequal fully to imitate the carpets of Persia, the muslins of India, the porcelain of China, and the lacquered ware of Japan." When the first Japanese embassy arrived at San Francisco in 1860, a correspondent for the *New York Times* recorded, "It makes a white man blush to see how much more simple, tasteful and sensible they were in their uniforms than our grandees were in theirs."

Such observations revealed a fascination with the strange and the exotic that appeared lacking in Western civilization. Some went a step further and found positive significance in things Oriental. No group was more interested in them than the Transcendentalists. As they grew dissatisfied with the Christian religion as it was practiced in the 1830's and the 1840's, they turned to Hinduism and Buddhism with a sense of fresh discovery. Their understanding of these Oriental religions may have been superficial, but they were the first group of Americans who seriously viewed the non-West not as an object of their mission but as a good in itself, as something that might be relevant to their own life. Ralph Waldo Emerson, for instance, was struck by the pantheism of the Hindu religion, which perceived godliness in all beings and all things. The pervading sense of serenity and the absence of a rigid demarcation between self and nature appealed to one who found modern life increasingly distasteful. As he remarked in his celebrated Harvard Divinity School address of 1838, "moral sentiment" had "dwelled always deepest in the minds of men in the devout and contemplative East . . . Europe has always owed to oriental genius its divine impulses."

Only a handful of Americans went as far as the Transcendentalists in embracing the spirit of another civilization, but the appreciation of distinctive values and ways of life sustaining the Orient seems to have produced in many observers an awareness of cultural pluralism in the world. The East was much more than the negation of the West, an object of the latter's contempt or pity, something whose only hope lay in wholesale transformation. For instance, in 1854 the *New York Quarterly* reported the longing of a traveler for the life, manners, and climate of the Orient, which "all our comfort and all our facilities for travelling by steamers and railroads cannot satisfy or dispel." Three years later, dissatisfaction with the "matter-of-fact, work-a-day age" prompted James P. Walker to publish the *Oriental Annual,* an anthology of Eastern folklore and poetry.

Such expressions approach cultural relativism, the feeling that each culture has its own autonomous tradition and inherent characteristics that cannot be artificially changed by external stimuli. In nineteenth-century America, thoroughgoing cultural relativism was a rare phenomenon; but to the extent that some thought about the question, it became inexorably linked with human progress. If a distinct

cultural tradition was a product of centuries of history, could it ever be significantly altered from without? Would it ever be possible to change peoples' ways of life? If they lived in abject poverty and suffered from despotic rule, was it not because they were so conditioned by tradition, and by their collective traits? In short, were they not living as they were simply because they were made to be that way?

These questions were of particular interest to Americans because they had obvious implications for the slavery dispute. Just as they debated among themselves whether the black man was capable of education and progress, and if he would be better off in an industrial than in a plantation economy, Americans discussed colors other than white and black. According to a popular view, mankind was divided into white, black, yellow, brown, and red races, each with distinctive traits that were often considered immutable. Almost invariably, the black man was placed at the bottom of the hierarchy of races. Samuel Morton's *Crania Americana* (1839) asserted that the Caucasian race was characterized by "the highest intellectual endowments" and that the Mongolian race was "ingenious, imitative, and highly susceptible of cultivation," whereas the "Ethiopian" was "joyous, flexible, and indolent—the lowest grade of humanity." The bulk of humanity, being neither white nor black, thus belonged to the gray area between the highest and the lowest categories. It is not surprising that there were considerable ambiguities in American attitudes toward them. They had unique features, some of which could be readily appreciated by Americans, but this did not mean that they were the equal of Westerners.

America's intercultural relations before the Civil War, then, combined the prevailing sense of Western superiority with some appreciation of the strange. Confidence in the universality of certain values was coupled with more rigid racialist thinking. The overwhelmingly European-centered cultural framework was undermined by some individuals who looked to the East as a fascinating alternative. On the whole, however, it would seem that non-Western cultures and peoples had not yet made a strong impact on American society. If there were intercultural relations between them, they were not equal but basically unidirectional.

INTERCULTURAL RELATIONS

The situation did not change drastically after the Civil War, but there was a greater awareness of different civilizations than there had been earlier. Fundamentally this reflected the technological development of the last decades of the nineteenth century, when steam and electricity, as observers were fond of pointing out, narrowed distances between various parts of the world. One could travel far more easily and speedily than before, and news in one corner of the globe could be transmitted almost overnight to most other regions. Great migrations of people started from Asia to the American continent, and from Europe to Africa and South America. One saw more foreigners in one's lifetime than earlier. The opening of more and more Asian ports to Western trade served to introduce commodities from distant lands into the daily life of average Asians and Westerners. In many areas of the non-Western world, the process of reform and transformation began to remake traditional societies in the image of the modern West. But the very experience of modernization caused some hard rethinking about cultural values. Westernization meant a loss of innocence to many a non-Westerner, while the globalization of modern transformation often suggested to Westerners the dilution of their own identity.

These were extremely interesting phenomena, and most of the crucial questions raised then have persisted to this day. It may be said that toward the end of the nineteenth century, world history entered an age of globalization that had cultural, as well as political and economic, implications. Economically, the phenomenon has been referred to as modernization, a neutral term suggesting that any society with certain achievements may opt for change. The most important achievement is commonly taken to be the accumulation of capital to enable a society to industrialize. Since in almost every case local savings in a non-Western country were not sufficient, Western capital had to be introduced; and this inevitably involved the coming of European and American financiers, engineers, and manufacturers who would employ native labor and middlemen to establish their economic institutions. Americans, even though in the aggregate their country was still a net importer of capital from Europe, were already active. They were in-

strumental, for instance, in the construction of the first railroad in China, in the 1870's. They invested in coastal shipping in China and Japan, established syndicates for obtaining railway concessions in Asia and the Middle East, and participated in the development of mines in all these regions. This was intercultural relations in a broad sense. Americans were relating themselves to other peoples through the medium of capitalist enterprises.

Although the profit motive was uppermost, an influx of foreign capital and technology invariably had noneconomic as well as economic effects on the targets of Western expansion. Americans in China, for instance, were never in a sufficient number to involve themselves at all levels of mercantile and industrial activities. They needed local personnel as interpreters, clerks, messengers, business assistants, and even associates, and as "compradors" who acted as liaisons between foreigners and officials. Such diverse contacts were bound to affect Chinese manners and ideas. In fact, among the most "Americanized" Chinese were those who lived in the treaty ports and learned modern capitalist practices. Associations such as local chambers of commerce provided a setting where Americans and Chinese met and conducted social affairs as well as business matters.

Politically, the process of globalization was synonymous with what was then called, and has since been called, imperialism. The world was divided into those who established control over distant territories and those who became objects of such control. A handful of imperialist nations appropriated among themselves the vast lands of Africa, the Middle East, Asia, and the Pacific Ocean as colonies, semicolonies, or spheres of influence. This was a military-political process, since control necessitated that a power structure be imposed upon alien peoples. Without such a regime, it was feared that local instability would create a chaotic condition and threaten the interests of a particular imperialist nation or invite the extension of power by its rivals. It seemed impossible and unwise to leave things as they were. Americans, no less than citizens of other advanced countries, were exhorted to reach out to far corners of the globe to join the forces of imperialist expansion.

Imperialism even in such a narrow sense was

an important chapter in intercultural relations, for the assertion of power over another people entailed both physical and mental contact. The Spanish-American War, for instance, called forth a fierce debate within the United States on the wisdom of acquiring tropical colonies. Americans had never established territorial control over lands in the tropics, and they had to think hard about the implications of the new action. Since they had not given much thought to Filipinos or Puerto Ricans, they turned to what few books were available on these peoples. They read Andrew Clarke and John Foreman, among others—English authorities on the tropical islands. English colonialism provided an intellectual framework within which Americans discussed the new empire. They turned to Charles Dilke, Joseph Chamberlain, Henry Norman, George Curzon, and others to learn how colonies should be governed. Colonial administration seemed a very different matter from the governing of new territories in the continental United States or of the American Indians. The country would have to establish a new colonial service and train men and women fit for work in the tropics. The numerous magazine articles on these subjects during and immediately after the Spanish-American War attest to the impact of the war upon America's intercultural relations. The American people had to learn from scratch what it meant to be masters over an alien race.

This learning took various forms. At the popular level, war stories and novels were written to familiarize the general reader with conditions in the tropics, and children's adventure books sought to impart a sense of patriotic destiny to the younger generation. Quick reference volumes with revealing titles were also published, such as Thomas C. Copeland's *The American Colonial Handbook: A Ready Reference of Facts and Figures, Historical, Geographical, and Commercial, About Cuba, Puerto Rico, the Philippines, Hawaii, and Guam* (1899). Adult education programs such as the Chautauqua Society conducted seminars on the history of the Philippines. As a matter of course the academic community was selected to provide the intellectual leadership needed to deal with imperial problems, and it readily obliged. Universities established courses in colonial administration, imperialism, and tropical geography; and pro-

fessional organizations such as the American Historical Association and the American Economic Association were engaged in turning out data and ideas that would be useful to the government in administering the new empire. The acquisition of overseas territories broadened the horizon for historians, economists, political scientists, sociologists, and anthropologists, who would have to redefine the scope of their respective disciplines to take advantage of the new opportunities. For instance, the *American Anthropologist* noted in December 1898 that students of folklore would find "a rich field awaiting them in our territory." Anthropological studies of the Filipinos provided an intellectual underpinning for the establishment of a colonial regime over the islands.

In all this literature there was a feeling of excitement. Imperialism compelled Americans to encounter, mentally if not physically, a host of alien peoples, whereas earlier their experience had been limited to dealing with Indians and blacks. The result was to reaffirm the sense of America's cultural superiority, which was now much more openly linked to Britain than it had been earlier in the century. It was as if imperialism made the United States akin to Great Britain. The two branches of the Anglo-Saxon race, it appeared, rediscovered their common heritage and vocabulary. They were both expansionists, many writers pointed out, better fitted than any other nation in the world for the administration of less-developed countries. They were to cooperate so that their respective empires would come to stand for enlightenment and efficiency. Elbridge S. Brooks was echoing a widespread sentiment when he told his young readers in *Lawton and Roberts: A Boy's Adventure in the Philippines and the Transvaal* (1900) that "the Stars and Stripes in the Philippines, and the Union Jack in South Africa, are advancing the interests of humanity and civilization. . . . [Untrammeled] liberty to the barbarian is as disastrous a gift as are unquestioning concessions to a republic which has been a republic only in name."

The last sentence reflected self-defensiveness about empire that was just beneath the surface optimism characteristic of the age of imperialism. In extending their control over alien races, Americans could look to the British for experience and guidance; but both of them had to confront the fact that as they advanced to far reaches of the globe, they were causing drastic changes in other societies. The non-Western parts of the world that earlier had been seen as decadent, static, or backward now seemed to be undergoing a period of profound crisis and instability as a result of the impact of Western technology, ideas, and institutions. If the expansionist thrust of the West was an inevitable development of history, then the consequent turmoil, confusion, and even anarchy in many regions of the world would have to be coped with. There were even more serious problems. If non-Western peoples should discard traditional values for new ones, what would happen to their indigenous cultures? Would they ever become thoroughly "Westernized"? What if they were transformed only superficially, and remained basically uncivilized even though the superstructures of their societies were modernized? Would they become pro-Western or anti-Western?

These were some of the most interesting questions in America's intercultural relations during the age of imperialism. That was why so much was written toward the end of the nineteenth century about the nature of Western relations with other cultures. The future destiny of American civilization seemed bound up with the larger question of the evolving relationship between West and non-West. For instance, in June 1897, Benjamin Ide Wheeler, who was soon to become president of the University of California at Berkeley, declared in an article in the *Atlantic Monthly,* entitled "Greece and the Eastern Question," that the real question in the Middle East was "Who is to lead, who is to champion, who is to represent Occidentalism in its antithesis between Occidentalism and Orientalism," an idea expressed in earlier decades but that now seemed an urgent question because of the resurgence of the East. Similarly, the naval strategist and historian Alfred Thayer Mahan discussed the "stirring of the East" and posed the question "whether Eastern or Western civilization is to dominate throughout the earth and to control its physical terms." Observers like Wheeler and Mahan agreed that the West's hope lay in its spiritual superiority to the East; even if the latter should catch up technologically and economically, and even though non-Westerners vastly outnumbered

Westerners, the future of Western civilization was bright because of its unique heritage. Nevertheless, the fear was always present that the East might prove to be a formidable threat precisely because it lacked the West's refinement, humanity, and self-restraint. A modern Orient without the Occident's values might prove to be totally unmanageable. The West should therefore brace itself for what was termed by many "the coming conflict of civilizations" in the twentieth century.

The cultural monism of the earlier decades was thus giving way to self-consciousness and defensiveness in the age of imperialism. Such apprehension, to be sure, was limited to a minority of writers. Most Americans would have agreed with historian John Fiske's optimism, as he expressed it in an article on the new "manifest destiny" in 1885, that "within another century . . . all the elements of military predominance on the earth, including that of simple numerical superiority, will have been gathered into the hands not merely of Europeans generally, but more specifically into the hands of the offspring of the Teutonic tribes who conquered Britain in the fifth century." Yet this type of complacency, reflecting a unilinear view of human (Western) progress, could not entirely accommodate some concurrent developments that had enormous implications for intercultural relations. Most notable among them were the growing fascination with non-Western civilizations and the influx of Asian immigrants.

Americans had always been curious about other peoples and had cherished imports from distant lands. But in the age of globalization there arose serious interest not only in curios and exotica of strange peoples but also in the fine arts, religions, philosophies, and ways of life of other countries, especially in the East. During the 1880's the United States legation in Constantinople was headed by General Lew Wallace and by Samuel S. Cox, both noted for their favorable views of Oriental cultures. Wallace, the author of the popular novel *Ben Hur,* wrote of the "bloodthirsty and treacherous, recklessly brave and exceedingly beautiful" cavalry of the Ottoman Empire. "Even among the meanest of them," he wrote, "you will see noble, well-set heads of the finest mould, testifying to unmixed blood of the most perfect of living races." Cox recounted his experiences in the East in *Orient Sunbeams*. The message he sought to convey to his readers was that they should remove their prejudice toward people of different religions. He wrote of Islam: "Whatever we may think of its founder, however unacceptable may be some of his doctrines . . . yet as a scheme of religion influencing as many, if not more millions of people than Christianity, is it not worthy of being considered by other peoples . . . ?"

This sort of serious interest in what would later be called cultural anthropology was quite visible at the end of the century. The World's Columbian Exposition of 1893, held at Chicago to commemorate the four-hundredth anniversary of Christopher Columbus' voyage, provides a good case in point. Close to 30 million people visited the fair, which was spread over 686 acres of land in south Chicago. Most countries of the world participated, including Japan, which spent millions of dollars to construct buildings specifically for the fair and to present an exhibition of all aspects of traditional and contemporary life. Although this was not the first time that Americans had had an opportunity to examine Japanese artifacts closely—Japan had participated in the 1876 Centennial Exposition at Philadelphia—their observations led to awareness that Japanese culture was much more than a phenomenon to be appreciated in isolation from the rest of that people's life. If the Japanese craftsmen at the Columbian Exposition seemed polite, industrious, and capable of producing refined objects, this had to be related to the totality of Japanese history and values. Japanese civilization could not be understood only within the framework of Western moral standards. Indeed it might be comparable on equal terms with American civilization; and it might be foolish to judge other peoples from the viewpoint of a self-centered value system. "I just made up my mind," said the hero of Carl Western's novel *Adventures of Reuben and Cynthy at the World's Fair* about the exposition, "that if they [the Japanese] were heathens, there were lots of things we could learn from them."

The Japanese were not the only heathens at Chicago. The Columbian Exposition coincided with the World Parliament of Religions, to which many non-Christian leaders were invited. From India came several prominent figures, including Swami Vivekananda, a Hindu leader noted for his belief that all religions contain truth. His arrival aroused much excitement among Americans. He not only attended the parliament but also traveled extensively in the United States. Americans were fascinated by his stress on religious toleration: "I preach nothing against the Great One of Galilee. I only ask the Christians to take in the Great Ones of India along with the Lord Jesus." To groups of ladies in Salem, Massachusetts, or Streator, Illinois, where he gave talks, it must have seemed quite a revelation that a Hindu monk should have so much to offer to contemporary society. Many were rude; in Chicago, Vivekananda recorded in his diary, "A man from behind pulled at my turban. I looked back and saw that he was a very gentlemanly looking man, neatly dressed. I spoke to him, and when he found that I knew English he became very much abashed." But the *Chicago Herald* probably expressed the predominant sentiment of those who heard Vivekananda's lectures when it wrote, "Vivekananda is undoubtedly the greatest figure in the Parliament of Religions. After hearing him, we feel how foolish it is to send missionaries to this learned nation." Far more than an object of curiosity, Indian civilization could be considered an important entity, even an alternative to the modern ways of life.

Perhaps the most logical embodiment of the emerging attitude was that of Ernest Fenollosa, a philosopher and art critic from Salem, Massachusetts. As a lecturer at Tokyo University in the 1890's, he was instrumental both in transmitting Western thought to the Japanese and in discovering the aesthetic value of Japanese art for Westerners. He taught the philosophy of Friedrich Hegel to students in Tokyo while establishing a collection of Japanese prints for a museum in Boston. The two activities were, from his point of view, of equal importance. Whereas earlier Americans had assumed their superiority and gone to non-Western parts of the world as missionaries and educators, he was convinced that West and non-West had a great deal to learn from one another. The two civilizations were of equal significance. Each had its distinctive cultural tradition, and together East and West constituted complementary halves of the harmonious whole that was mankind. The two were like the Chinese dichotomy of *yin* and *yang*, standing for contrasting pairs such as darkness and light, moon and sun, or female and male. The West, as Fenollosa saw it, represented masculinity, strength, and vigor; but it was never whole in itself. Only through a harmonizing relationship with the East, standing for femininity and refinement, could it sustain its existence. No wonder that Fenollosa's favorite analogy was to marriage. As he said in the preface to *East and West* (1893), "The synthesis of two continental civilizations, matured apart through fifteen hundred years, will mark this close of our century as an unique dramatic epoch in human affairs. At the end of a great cycle the two halves of the world come together for the final creation of man."

Not all writers were as sanguine as Fenollosa about the peaceful relationship between East and West. It was at the end of the century that Rudyard Kipling's phrase "East is East, and West is West" became popular. Lafcadio Hearn, a Greek-born American novelist who had long resided in Japan, published his *Kokoro,* a study of the Japanese mentality, in 1896, and stressed that a Westerner could never hope to comprehend the depth of the Japanese mind. In his words, "The more complex feelings of the Oriental have been composed by combinations of experiences, ancestral and individual, which have had no really precise correspondence in Western life, and which we can therefore not fully know. For converse reasons, the Japanese cannot, even though they would, give Europeans their best sympathy." The overwhelming majority of Americans would probably have agreed more with Hearn than with Fenollosa. The popularity of David Belasco's play *Madame Butterfly* (1900) showed, if nothing else, that there was still a very widespread view that West and non-West might meet on a transient basis, but that their encounter produced tragic consequences because of their inability to understand one another fully.

One additional factor in the development of intercultural relations was the coming of Asians to the United States toward the end of the nineteenth century. Chinese laborers had arrived on the west coast during the 1840's, but it was after the Civil War that their immigration

and residence began to create serious social and political problems. And just when, in the 1880's, their influx was checked through treaty arrangements and congressional enactments, the Japanese began to arrive, first in Hawaii and, after the islands' annexation by the United States, in the western states. The bulk of these people were not exactly embodiments of Chinese or Japanese civilization. They were overwhelmingly poor, illiterate or undereducated, and without more than rudimentary skills. Still, they represented the societies from which they came, and to that extent their experiences in the United States constituted part of America's intercultural relations.

This is best seen in the rhetoric of the Oriental exclusionist movement. The exclusionists on the west coast and their supporters elsewhere frequently resorted to the argument that the very fabric of American civilization was at stake. Should Asians be allowed to inundate the country, they said, not only would they compete with native labor because of their low wages, but they would also undermine the American way of life. Unlike European immigrants, they brought alien customs and modes of living and, unless checked, would most certainly orientalize American society. The key to the Chinese immigration dispute, a writer pointed out in 1876, was that the Chinese "never adopts an iota of our civilization. . . . His civilization *displaces* exactly so much of our own; it substitutes Mongolianism." Similar expressions would be heard for many decades. The fundamental issue involved appeared to be the inevitable conflict of civilizations. Americans were called upon to consider whether their country was to remain Occidental or to become Oriental, under Asiatic influence. To those deeply concerned with the problem, it must have seemed axiomatic that East and West could never live together in peace and harmony. Such particularism was a reflection of the growing proximity, physical as well as geographical, of West and non-West in the age of globalization. At this level, then, America's intercultural relations exhibited narrowness and racial prejudice as defensive measures to preserve what were considered unique features of Western civilization.

Not all non-Westerners who came to the United States, however, were poor and illiterate laborers. A small minority of scholars, officials, businessmen, and other members of the elite visited the country, some to stay for a long time. They contributed to America's intercultural relations by associating with their counterparts in the United States and by articulating their views to Americans and to people at home. Some of them came with good classical educations, attracted to an America that was envisioned as a land of the free. For those who were highly educated and politically conscious, but who felt themselves alienated from their own lands for political or cultural reasons, the United States beckoned as a land of freedom, opportunity, and humanism. The image of America as the place to go for education was established in China and Japan by the end of the nineteenth century, as was the image that in the United States one could find a refuge from oppression and persecution in one's own country. Baba Tatsui, a young activist, left Japan for America to pursue his struggle for political rights, and many of his compatriots with socialistic views followed him. Sun Yat-sen engaged in revolutionary activities among Chinese in Hawaii and the United States. Some of China's constitutionalists also visited America, where they founded newspapers and conducted fund-raising campaigns.

What the United States meant to these visiting non-Westerners must be considered an important aspect of the country's intercultural relations. To many of them, this was "the sacred land of liberty," as the Japanese said. But there were others who were shocked by the contrast between that image and the reality. Uchimura Kanzō, the Japanese Christian leader, was repelled by materialistic excesses. Some returned to their homelands to spread certain images of the United States. It can be said that at this time there were non-American as well as American agents of intercultural relations. The United States exerted subtle influences upon other countries not only through its own merchants, travelers, or missionaries, but also through foreigners visiting the country. Often it was through America that the latter first encountered Western civilization, and the importance of this is hard to exaggerate. For better or worse, what they saw in the United States epitomized for them the essence of capitalism, constitutionalism, and Christianity. The experiences of a man like Uchimura, who had been introduced to Christianity through American missionaries in Japan but who came to the United States and discovered the gap between what he called Bible Christianity and American Christianity, are fascinating examples of cross-cultural interactions. It was as if America taught him what Christianity was not.

By 1900, then, there were already complex layers of intercultural relations, some subtle new forces and others that were crude echoes of the past, but all constituting parts of the developing trends toward globalization. These layers continued to evolve after the turn of the century. The history of intercultural relations in the twentieth century is extremely difficult to characterize, since it is an ongoing process. It is possible, however, to examine the period before the outbreak of World War II in terms of two contradictory currents: universalistic and particularistic tendencies. On the one hand, there was every indication that American influence was spreading to other lands; at the same time, there grew self-conscious opposition to American and Western cultural predominance in the world.

By the time of World War I, the United States had established its position as the leading Western power, not only in industrial production, trade, and foreign loans and investments but also in armaments and political influence. While this was not the same thing as cultural hegemony, there is little doubt that the United States came to stand and speak for Western civilization at a time when the European countries were engaged in fratricidal conflicts and disputes. One reason why President Woodrow Wilson wanted to postpone American entry into the war was his fear for the survival of Western civilization. He came to see his country as a guardian of that precious tradition, a sentiment shared by an increasing number of Englishmen. But similar views had also been expressed by Presidents Theodore Roosevelt and William Howard Taft, who had come to take for granted the spread of benign American influence to the rest of the world. Civilization, as Taft never tired of saying, was based on an unlimited interchange of goods and capital, which in turn contributed to international peace, harmony, and understanding. Americans would carry their wares throughout the world and promote economic modernization and political awakening. Because of their superiority in technology, organization, and business practices, Americans were bound to emerge as the most influential group in the new world of enlightened international relations. They would be among the foremost agents of change in the twentieth century. Wilson fully accepted such ideas and elevated them to a vision of internationalism in which American values would reign—valid not as American but as universal values. No wonder that he was eager to promote missionary activities and was captivated by the idea of establishing American mandates in various parts of the world.

Because the European countries lost population, productive capacity, morale, and prestige as a result of the war, the United States was able to replace European power and influence in international affairs. American technology, epitomized by the automobile, dominated the postwar world, as did popular American culture such as jazz, radio, and motion pictures. In Europe one talked of the "decline of the West" after Oswald Spengler's book of that title was published in 1918, but somehow the West that was declining did not seem to include the United States. Observers such as the sociologists Thorstein Veblen and Pitirim Sorokin discussed the ramifications of the emerging mass society; but they implied that this was the way of the future, that developments in the United States portended what was to take place elsewhere. To understand modern society one looked at the United States. Whether one liked it or not, it seemed that Americanization was an inevitable phenomenon of the postwar world.

This was also the way American influence was perceived in non-Western countries. In Turkey, India, China, Japan, and elsewhere the war had caused European prestige to suffer; but the United States appeared more vigorous and resilient than its European cousins. American trade was the most extensive in history, and a growing bulk of it was conducted with non-European countries. Americans appeared in areas where earlier one had seen only Europeans, investing in oil fields and establishing manufacturing plants. John Dewey's instrumentalism became the most popular philosophy in universities throughout Asia, and women in distant societies turned to American

women not only for fashions but also for political ideals. Jazz, baseball, and Charlie Chaplin became just as popular in Japan as in America. "Modern times" was synonymous with American culture for people of the 1920's. Even in the 1930's, it is possible to argue, American influence did not abate; the process of Americanization proceeded unchecked until well into the decade. Visits by American baseball teams were always important news to the Japanese, in overshadowing any feeling of crisis as a result of the latter nation's imperialistic activities on the Asian continent. Charles Lindbergh was as well known across the Pacific as across the Atlantic, and even Japanese martial music had definite traces of American influence. Children and women shed their traditional costumes and started wearing Westernized clothes, and bars and cabarets mushroomed. In many ways Japan on the eve of Pearl Harbor was a society more Americanized than ever before.

While the interwar era, then, was a period of rapid Americanization, it is also true that the 1920's and the 1930's saw self-conscious opposition to, and even rejection of, the West by some non-Western countries. They began to assert their identity, no longer content to remain objects of Western expansion and receptacles of Western influence. This second trend, toward particularism, was already visible at the beginning of the century, when men everywhere noted signs that seemed to indicate the non-West's rise against the West. The Russo-Japanese War, which the Japanese took pains to characterize not as a racial conflict but as one between civilization and barbarism, nevertheless was cheered by non-Westerners from Egypt to China as a victory of a colored nation over a white nation. In the Near East and North Africa, Islam was becoming self-conscious and militant; Islamic spokesmen talked of an Arab renaissance and the coming *jihad* against the Christian West. Mosques began to be built in American cities.

The Young Turks, the Persian nationalists, and the Armenian revolutionaries felt betrayed by the peace settlements after World War I. Asians became disillusioned by the alleged universalism of Wilsonian internationalism when the Western powers failed to adopt a racial equality clause as part of the League of Nations Covenant. The Chinese were bitter toward the United States and Great Britain for their failure to stop Japanese encroachment on Shantung. The Turks viewed the postwar settlement as an imposition by the Western nations at the expense of the Ottoman Empire. For these varied reasons, the international order after 1919 appeared to be an "Anglo-American peace," as Prince Konoye Fumimaro of Japan said.

Nationalism, which had been inspired by the modern Western example, became a force against the West in many non-Western countries during the interwar years. It took on a culturally particularistic meaning as Chinese, Arabs, Indians, and others asserted their distinctive identity as separate from European or American civilization. In China, for instance, nationalism was not only aimed at recovering rights lost to the imperialists; it also revealed itself in a movement to develop native Christian churches and to replace Westerners in administrative posts at colleges and universities. The fascination the Chinese felt for Marxism and Leninism was in part due to the anti-Western messages, explicit or implicit, that they found in these ideologies. Marxist-Leninist thought gave the Chinese a conceptual tool with which to attack Western capitalism as well as Western civilization. The wholesale transformation of the country after the pattern of the West was no longer seriously advocated. Now there were other models and other choices; some sought a Soviet-type revolution, while others visualized a combination of Chinese tradition with modern technology as the best way to save China.

More or less the same phenomenon of self-conscious reassessment of Western values could be observed in Turkey, India, Japan, and other countries. The trend was no doubt encouraged by the literature of pessimism that Europeans were producing in the decade after the war. Many of these writers expressed doubt that Western civilization could survive, and some turned to the East as a source of salvation. As an article in a February 1925 issue of the *Europaische Staats und Wirtschafts Zeitung* put it, "Our Western world is weary; not weary of life, but of strife and hatred. Indeed, our peculiar society and civilization have been found wanting. . . . Men are looking to the East unconsciously, and therefore sincerely. . . . The world of Asia draws us with its promise of something new

and something that will liberate." Eastern philosophers like Rabindranath Tagore and Vasudeo Metta were eager to oblige and to offer this "something" for which Westerners seemed to be looking. Unfortunately, very often their thoughts were utilized in Asia for nationalistic upheavals against pervasive Western influence.

The world crisis of the 1930's that culminated in World War II definitely had a cultural dimension; it may be argued that the major difference between the two world wars was the addition of the cultural factor in the second. World War I was mainly a civil war among Western countries, whereas World War II involved peoples of diverse cultural traditions and ideologies. It was in essence intercultural warfare. This was particularly true of the United States and its relations in Asia and the Pacific. Throughout the 1930's Japan pursued an aggressive foreign policy and gave it an ideological sanction of pan-Asianism. The concept was transparently anti-Western. Asia, according to this view, was to reassert itself against the imperialistic exploitation by the West, which had cultural as well as political and economic aspects. For too long, Japanese nationalists declared, the West had permeated Asian life, subverting traditional values and destroying age-old social customs. Asians had ceased to be Asian; they had either become Westernized or objects of Western influence. They had lost their identities and their souls. If they were to regain these things, they must stand together as Asians and develop a regional system of cultural and economic autonomy. The ideology of Japanese militarism stressed the eradication of Western values from education, mass media, and daily living, and the need to return to the essence of national culture. Apologists for Japanese aggression also viewed pan-Asian regionalism as a viable alternative to both imperialism and particularistic nationalism, two vices that they attributed to the modern West. If Asia were to reject imperialism and yet to avoid repeating the experience of the modern nation-states constantly struggling against one another, it was imperative that Asian countries organize themselves into a regional system.

For the bulk of Americans, these events in distant Asia were of far less importance than their individual struggles for economic survival at home. But there was a genuine cultural dimension in the economic crisis, in that the values of bourgeois mass society seemed less and less relevant to the unemployed, the handicapped, and the racially segregated. Western civilization appeared to be seriously threatened from within, as evidenced by the growth of Italian fascism, German nazism, and Soviet communism. Americans, no longer sure of the eternal validity of middle-class precepts and symbols, often turned to Benito Mussolini or Adolf Hitler or Josef Stalin as possible saviors of civilization. At the same time, many of them embraced isolationism, in the belief that by staying out of war in Europe or Asia, the United States would be able to preserve what was left of civilization and help reconstruct Europe after it had been devastated by war. For a man like Charles Lindbergh, it was nothing short of a crime against Western civilization to enter the fray on the side of either Britain or Germany. Only the uncivilized in other lands would benefit from such fratricide.

In such a context, the war between the United States and Japan could be seen in a cultural context. The irony was that the combatants fought with modern weapons, utilizing all the techniques of scientific warfare. As noted earlier, despite its profession of indigenous values and pan-Asianism, Japan in 1941 was more Westernized than ever before. The decision to establish control in the areas of Asia that were rich in natural resources could also be seen as a device to proceed with further industrialization and economic strengthening. The Japanese dream of an autonomous empire was little different from a Western conception. Cultural particularism did not cloak these ambitions.

The United States, on the other hand, regained the sense of cultural identity and confidence when war came. The self-doubt and crisis-consciousness of the 1930's were replaced by a renewed faith in the essential soundness and goodness of Western values. The faith was expressed in the universalistic rhetoric of the Atlantic Charter, the Declaration of the United Nations, and the communiqués issued by the Big Three at the end of their meetings at Teheran (1943) and Yalta (1945). The language reaffirmed the principles of peace, justice, and human rights, which were seen to be as relevant as ever because the Axis powers were pic-

tured as the would-be architects of a world based on diametrically opposed values. It is true that many Americans saw the Pacific war in more parochial ways, stressing the racial aspect. To cite one extreme example from within the government, Captain Harry L. Pence of the navy reiterated, at meetings of the State Department Advisory Committee on Postwar Foreign Policy, that the war involved the question of "which race was to survive." He favored "the almost total elimination of the Japanese as a race," saying, "Japan should be bombed so that there was little left of its civilization." Moreover, the Japanese "should not be dealt with as civilized human beings. . . . We should kill them before they kill us." Although representative of a current of opinion in wartime America, such views were not part of postwar planning. On the contrary, officials and opinion leaders continued to stress universalistic principles and to search for a new world order in which Japan, no less than other countries, would participate. Japan's surrender thus implied, at the level of cultural affairs, the recognition that particularism had failed and the acceptance by Japan of American ideas as more applicable to its needs.

Intercultural relations after World War II were far more extensive and diverse than earlier. The United States became the virtual inheritor of European civilization, emerging as the strongest and richest country in the world, capable of supporting the arts and financing scholarly and artistic undertakings. European refugees enriched America's cultural life. For the first time it could be said that American art was in the vanguard of modern art, not a pale reflection of European works. The same was true of literature and music. Unlike the period after World War I, however, there was much less self-consciousness about American culture. It was assumed as a matter of course, rather than asserted as a matter of principle, that American artists, novelists, and musicians were engaged in creative work that had relevance to the contemporary world as a whole. Europeans looked to the United States to discern artistic and literary trends. Moreover, American troops stationed in most parts of Europe transmitted American popular culture and life-styles to the Old World. It became important for European intellectuals to study in the United

States if they wished to keep abreast of developments in scholarship.

The impact on the non-Western world was no less great. American influence was transmitted through soldiers, officials, and businessmen who were scattered throughout Africa, the Middle East, and Asia. Consciously or unconsciously, they contributed to a deeper cultural involvement of America in other lands. America came to stand for what was fashionable and up-to-date. At the same time, Americans abroad collectively and individually increased their nation's awareness of other cultures and contributed to a greater appreciation of non-Western traditions. Many who were trained during the war as language specialists and intelligence officers retained their interest in foreign countries, and some of them became leaders in the postwar development of "area studies." American colleges began seriously teaching courses in non-Western civilizations and founded institutes to further research in these areas. There was also a flood of non-Europeans to the United States as war brides, students, and visitors. Through them Americans came into contact with non-Western ways of life.

This flowering of intercultural activities after World War II was viewed for at least two decades through the framework of the model of modernization. The old prejudice against alien civilizations and non-Western peoples was disappearing, but there persisted the idea that all the countries in the world were tending toward a more modern phase. Economic development, political democracy, and social justice appeared to be essential ingredients of modernity; and intellectuals discussed how such an outlook could be encouraged in a traditional society. Appreciation of non-Western civilizations often took the form of discovering elements in them that were potentially "modern." The growing tolerance for cultural pluralism meant not just greater appreciation for Japanese architecture, Chinese food, or Indian philosophy. There was also great expectation of economic, political, and social changes in those countries. The hope was that through such changes, coupled with the new outlook in postwar America, foreigners and Americans would come to a better understanding of one another. They would develop a common vocabulary of mutual respect as they cooperated to bring about a more modern world.

Such optimism could in time be replaced by a radically different outlook. By the 1970's people everywhere had become more aware of the difficulties involved in transforming traditional societies, and even in preserving "modern" societies. The basic resources of food, raw materials, and energy supplies are so unevenly distributed that it seems physically impossible for the underdeveloped nations to reach the level of the United States. And in the United States and other advanced countries, symptoms have been detected that indicate the transition from the industrial to a post-industrial phase. Men everywhere are confronted with the same problems, and it is awareness of these problems, rather than a vision of a rosy future, that unites people throughout the world in their common quest for measures to avoid catastrophe. In the meantime, intercultural relations will take on added significance. In proportion to the growth of the dilemmas of modern industrial civilization, greater tolerance and even admiration for different life-styles and philosophies of living develop. If, in the past, non-Western peoples found solace in their indigenous cultures, that is a significant fact for contemporary Americans who seek a new perspective. Ultimately the cross-fertilization of cultures may prove to be the key to solving the world's problems.

BIBLIOGRAPHY

Intercultural history, defined as the history of relations between American and non-Western cultures, is virtually virgin territory. Quite a number of writers have, however, examined intracultural history (American cultural relations with Britain, France, Italy, and other countries of the West). Although they deal with more familiar problems of tourism, immigration, and intellectual interchanges among peoples who share common cultural roots, these works suggest methodologies and conceptual frameworks that can be applied to the study of intercultural relations as well. Among the best examples of this category are Alexander De Conde, *Half-Bitter, Half-Sweet: An Excursion Into Italian-American History* (New York, 1971); and John P. Diggins, *Mussolini and Fascism: The View From America* (Princeton, 1972).

The best historical treatment of American relations with Middle Eastern countries is James A. Field, *America and the Mediterranean World, 1776–1882* (Princeton, 1969). The literature on American–East Asian relations is enormous, even though only a small minority offers a bicultural treatment.

See, among others, Edwin O. Reischauer, *The United States and Japan,* 3rd ed. (Cambridge, Mass., 1965); John K. Fairbank, *The United States and China,* 3rd ed. (Cambridge, Mass., 1971); and Akira Iriye, *Across the Pacific: An Inner History of American–East Asian Relations* (New York, 1967). Several monographs on American-Japanese cultural relations are included in Akira Iriye, ed., *Mutual Images: Essays in American-Japanese Relations* (Cambridge, Mass., 1975). The Japanese impact on American architecture is analyzed in Clay Lancaster, *Japanese Influence in America* (New York, 1963). American attitudes toward China and India are presented in Harold R. Isaacs, *Scratches on Our Minds: American Images of China and India* (New York, 1958), a classic. On intellectual interchanges between Americans and Asians, a good approach is through individual biographies. Among the most valuable are Lawrence W. Chisolm, *Fenollosa: The*

Far East and American Culture (New Haven, Conn., 1963); and Stephen Hay, *Asian Ideas of East and West: Tagore and His Critics in Japan, China, and India* (Cambridge, Mass., 1970).

Probably the best introduction to the literature on intercultural relations is through reading the works of American anthropologists who have not only described but also raised methodological questions about the study of other cultures. See, for instance, William Graham Sumner, *Folkways* (New York, 1906); Robert E. Park, *Race and Culture* (Glencoe, Ill., 1950); and F. S. C. Northrop and Helen H. Livingston, eds., *Cross-Cultural Understanding: Epistemology in Anthropology* (New York, 1964).

[*See also* COLONIALISM; IMPERIALISM; INTERNATIONALISM; MANIFEST DESTINY; MISSIONARIES; NATIONALISM; PHILANTHROPY.]

INTERNATIONALISM

Warren F. Kuehl

INTERNATIONALISM in United States foreign policy has had different meanings for nearly every generation of citizens and diplomats. It has been associated with all forms of external contacts with the world, the relationships becoming more extensive and political with the passage of time. As a foreign policy, it has usually been discussed as the antithesis of isolationism, and in that sense it has involved a definite commitment or political entanglement through multinational treaties or governmental membership in international organizations. In a broader context, it has encompassed nonpolitical activities as well, both official and nonofficial, in the form of external and direct contacts—economic, social, cultural, and scientific—usually evidenced through affiliation with specialized societies or agencies of global scope. Other individuals have thought in terms of a universal community, a broad brotherhood of people with common concerns, needs, and aspirations that exists as a reality beyond the confines of nation-states. In recent times, internationalism has taken on a new meaning under a doctrine of responsibility, with the United States assuming the burden of "policeman of the world" both unilaterally and multilaterally.

Long before isolationism became an established policy in the nineteenth century, citizens of the American colonies recognized that they could not live apart from the rest of the world. They existed within an imperial system that had involved them in four world wars (Queen Anne's War, King William's War, King George's War, and the French and Indian War) and in many crises related to trade and territories. They found many doctrines of international law applied to them as they sought to discover their relationships toward their neighbors and their mother country. William Penn reflected the cosmopolitan atmosphere when he drafted his *Essay Towards the Present and Future Peace of Europe* (1693), in which he called for a congress of states to promote stability. Evidence of a broad perspective also appeared in a colonial union, the New England Confederation of 1643, and in the suggestion for joint action embodied in the Albany Plan of 1754. Joseph Galloway's proposal for an Anglo-American council in 1774 also expressed a cosmopolitan outlook. Such experiences, as well as an awareness of the league of the "Five Nations" of the Iroquois Indians, may explain why such revolutionary leaders as Benjamin Franklin and Thomas Paine spoke favorably of an international organization; and the establishment of a government under the Articles of Confederation and the Constitution of 1789 revealed a general awareness that separate states could combine to promote their interests.

Events during and after the Revolution related to the treaty of alliance with France, as well as difficulties arising over the neutrality policy pursued during the French Revolutionary Wars and the Napoleonic Wars, encouraged another perspective. A desire for separateness and unilateral freedom of action merged with national pride and a sense of continental safety to foster the policy of isolation. Although the United States maintained diplomatic relations and economic contacts abroad, it sought to restrict these as narrowly as possible, in order to retain its independence. The Department of State continually rejected proposals for joint cooperation, a policy exemplified in the Monroe Doctrine's clearly stated desire for unilateral action. Not until

443

1863 did a United States delegate attend an international conference, and Secretary of State William H. Seward reflected prevailing views by persistently refusing to sign an 1864 multilateral treaty related to the Red Cross; the policy was revised in 1882, when the United States finally subscribed to such a convention. Thereafter, cooperation on economic and social matters seemed acceptable; but political issues, especially those involving Europe, were generally avoided until 1899.

Although most citizens accepted the principle of isolationism, scattered voices throughout the nineteenth century called for a more cooperative and involved stance toward the world. Under the direction of William Ladd, the American Peace Society sponsored essay contests on an international organization in the 1830's, and in 1840 Ladd utilized many of the ideas received in drafting his *Essay on a Congress of Nations.* His proposal for both a political body and a judicial agency gained considerable public notice through petition and educational campaigns in ensuing years. After Ladd's death "The Learned Blacksmith," Elihu Burritt, presented the congress of nations program to European pacifists with such regularity that they referred to it as the "American idea."

The Civil War in America (1861–1865) and conflicts in Europe (1854–1856, 1870–1871) undermined the peace movement, but a developing interest in the law of nations in the last third of the century kept alive the concept of global cooperation. Several societies emerged to promote the codification of international rules of behavior and to encourage the settlement of disputes through arbitration. The resolution of differences by submitting them to a third party and abiding by the decision was centuries old, but leading citizens in many nations seized upon the idea as they tried to persuade their governments to resolve controversies peacefully.

These discussions contributed substantially to the evolution of thought concerning an international organization. As countries signed arbitration accords, men began to think beyond such limited agreements. Agencies would be needed to implement the treaties; laws would have to be codified. As John Westlake, an English professor of law, observed, "When we assert that there is such a thing as International Law, we assert that there is a society of States; when we recognize that there is a society of States, we recognize that there is International Law."

The settlement of the *Alabama* claims in the early 1870's stimulated the signing of many arbitration agreements in the following four decades. Most of these were limited to specified disputes involving monetary and boundary claims and questions arising under treaty clauses; this discouraged pacifists, who hoped to see accords calling for all controversies to be arbitrated. They rallied to promote their goal, gaining public endorsement in the 1890's. The Lake Mohonk (New York) Conference on International Arbitration, which began in 1895 and met annually through 1916, united civic, business, religious, and educational leaders in a quest for treaties involving the United States. Proponents recognized that their government would not subscribe to unlimited agreements, and they suggested that matters involving national honor and vital interests be exempted. Their widespread agitation resulted in the Olney-Pauncefote Treaty with Great Britain in 1897, which called for the arbitration of monetary and territorial differences; but the Senate revised it to exclude disputes affecting national interest and honor, insisted that in each instance it have a voice in approving an issue submitted for settlement, and, after adding other reservations, refused to approve the treaty.

These developments had a lasting impact upon American internationalist thought. First, arbitration accords encouraged the exploration of cooperative methods of resolving disputes and breached barriers that had kept statesmen from previously examining such subjects openly. Discussions about an international society could never have proceeded without such talks. Second, the experience warned thinkers that they would have to be cautious in what they proposed regarding a union of nations. Their government would not assume obligations that would weaken its position in the world or destroy interests deemed vital to its welfare. Finally, the advances in arbitration influenced discussions at the first genuine international assembly of nations, the First Hague Conference of 1899; and agreements there stimulated further effort.

Delegates from the United States at that

gathering supported a convention that created the Permanent Court of Arbitration. Because it was little more than a list of names of persons who could be called upon to hear issues, and clauses exempted matters of national honor or interests, the Senate voiced no real objections in approving this accord. Action was voluntary for those who wished to submit disputes; the treaty met popular desires; and the American delegates had added a proviso that their signing did not mean an abandonment of traditional policies of nonentanglement or of American matters, particularly the Monroe Doctrine.

By 1900 a number of persons had presented plans that would move the world beyond courts of arbitration. Most of these, in calling for a world federation, reflected the experience of the United States. Benjamin F. Trueblood, secretary of the American Peace Society, advanced the idea in *The Federation of the World* (1899), in articles, and in lectures. The interdependence of men and nations, he argued, would lead inevitably to "a complete political union of the world, a great international world state, built up somewhat on the pattern of our union of States, with supreme legislative, judicial and executive functions touching those interests which the nations have in common." Trueblood quickly cautioned that he envisioned no powerful agency. It would operate primarily in a legislative and judicial capacity, without a formal executive, and it would possess no authority to compel its members to maintain peace.

Between 1899 and 1914, a wide variety of proposals appeared, with a few persons devoting extensive thought and time to the subject. Their suggestions and work had considerable impact upon the twentieth-century movement toward an international organization, and their writings reflected a number of basic assumptions. First, they believed that an inexorable evolutionary process was at work. The positive gains in the form of arbitration treaties, the willingness of governments to cooperate in the First Hague Conference, and subsequent discussions about a court of justice seemed to indicate an inevitable trend toward unity. Secretary of State Elihu Root enunciated this viewpoint when he declared in 1907 that the importance of the Hague meeting of 1899 could be found in the fact that it made the next one possible. It appeared that "The world has entered upon an orderly process through which, step by step, in successive conferences, each taking the work of its predecessor as its point of departure, there may be continual progress toward making the practice of civilized nations conform to their peaceful professions."

Raymond Bridgman, a Boston journalist, also expressed this belief in a volume of essays, *World Organization* (1905). He saw continued meetings as the foundation stone for an international body. It could begin with a legislature modeled after that of the United States, then be followed by a court and an executive agency. New York attorney Hayne Davis also reflected this philosophy in many articles published between 1903 and 1912. A "United Nations" would emerge, said Davis in what appears to have been the first use of that term. Just as the United States had been forced to develop a more perfect government after the Revolution and the confederation period, so would the world be compelled to build a better system.

This evolutionary concept appeared in nearly all of the internationalists' proposals. They began by calling for further development of the arbitral network through a series of treaties that would bind nations together. Then states could explore other ways to promote their common needs. Events seemed to confirm such logic. Between 1903 and 1914 governments concluded more than 162 arbitral accords, and the Second Hague Conference occurred in 1907. The United States kept step by negotiating a series of treaties in 1904 and 1905 that fully considered the Senate's concern for American rights, honor, and interests. Even then, in each instance senators insisted on having a voice in whether a dispute should be arbitrated. President Theodore Roosevelt considered this a sham and refused to exchange ratifications, but in 1908 he authorized Root to negotiate others that reflected the Senate's wishes.

President William Howard Taft in 1910 decided to go further and seek agreements to arbitrate all disputes. Two such trial instruments in 1911 inevitably ran afoul of the Senate, which nullified them and restricted the application of the process in such a way that Taft also abandoned the quest. Careful observers should have seen by 1912 that the Senate could be a major obstacle to proposals for a world organization, since it would not approve any instrument that infringed upon the sovereignty of the United States.

This fact may explain why Secretary of State William Jennings Bryan in the Wilson administration took a less controversial course by signing conciliation accords with many governments. Unlike arbitration agreements, these would not obligate the signers to honor the decision of the third party. Bryan introduced another idea, in the form of a "cooling-off" principle, whereby political leaders promised they would not resort to force while a case was pending. This concept was a basic component of suggestions after 1914.

Internationalists soon moved beyond their proposal for an arbitral system and presented a second idea. The world needed a genuine court of justice. Arbitration, they argued, had limitations because there were no fixed principles that could be universally applied. With established laws and impartial judges, nations could entrust their quarrels to a reliable and fair tribunal, and decisions based upon just rules might prompt governments like the United States to reconsider their protective postures and allow cases involving honor and independence to be heard.

The United States officially supported the goal of a court of justice at the Second Hague Conference, but the delegates there could not reach accord on a method of selecting judges. International lawyers and advocates of the evolutionary hypothesis continued to work for some type of judicial agency. The American Society of International Law, established in 1906, and the American Society for Judicial Settlement of International Disputes and the Carnegie Endowment for International Peace, both formed in 1910, concentrated on achieving this objective. Resolutions of peace congresses and other organizations reflected a popular desire for a judicial tribunal. Internationalists hoped that governments might become more amenable to reasonable provisos that would overcome all obstacles. Taft's secretary of state, Philander C. Knox, proposed in 1909 that a maritime prize court discussed at the Second Hague Conference be constituted as an international court of justice; but this and other suggestions failed to lower the barriers that prevented nations from acting.

Thought concerning a tribunal based upon justice inevitably revived interest in the old scheme of a periodic congress. Evolutionists viewed it as a vital "next step"; but even more significantly, the advocates of an international organization based upon law saw it as a major corollary to a court because some agency had to establish the rules upon which the judges would rely. The First Hague Conference had stimulated demands for additional meetings, and the congress theme became increasingly popular after 1900. Bridgman began a successful petition campaign to obtain the endorsement of the Massachusetts legislature, while the American Peace Society embarked upon an extensive propaganda campaign to reach religious and civic bodies. One writer soon called the periodic congress idea "the demand of the hour."

Such agitation prompted action that had a direct bearing upon the call for the Second Hague Conference. In 1904, representatives of the Interparliamentary Union, an association of legislators from congresses within nations, met at St. Louis. Under the leadership of Richard Bartholdt, a congressman from Missouri, they agreed to work for a Second Hague Conference, presented this idea to President Roosevelt, and obtained his promise of support. This led to contacts with European chancelleries that eventually brought action.

Several internationalists moved to influence the discussions at such an assembly. Hayne Davis joined Bartholdt in proposing "that a regular Congress of Nations be created, to meet at stated periods, to discuss international questions and make recommendations to the governments." By April 1906 nearly 200 congressmen who had joined the Interparliamentary Union agreed to endorse Bartholdt's aims. The concept of a periodic congress gained acceptance at The Hague in 1907, in the form of a resolution calling for further meetings; and internationalists hoped that a third session might convene in 1914 or 1915. The outbreak of war, however, frustrated that goal.

As the periodic congress idea gained in popularity, some planners began to explore how an evolving organization would operate and what powers it might have. Most of them concentrated upon a federation modeled after that of the United States, with legislative, judicial, and executive agencies. Such a structure would allow nations to divide their sovereignty by allotting certain responsibilities to the central body while retaining control over those affairs important to themselves. Hamilton Holt, managing editor of *The Independent* magazine, popularized this theme, as did other prominent citizens. Andrew Carnegie endorsed the approach in repeated calls for a "league of peace," and Theodore Roosevelt also may have favored such a method when he proposed a "League of Peace" in 1910.

The most ambitious undertaking came between 1910 and 1912, in the form of the World-Federation League, an organization headed by Holt and Oscar Crosby, a Virginia engineer and inventor. Stimulated by Roosevelt's words, they asked for the creation of a United States commission authorized to "report to Congress . . . a draft of articles of Federation limited to the maintenance of peace, through the establishment of a Court having power to determine by decree all controversies between nations and to enforce execution of its decrees by the arms of the Federation. . . ."

Although Congress did not respond to this proposal, in 1910 it did unanimously pass a resolution that carried the name of Representative William S. Bennet of New York. It called for a commission to explore the possibility of a reduction in armaments and the creation of an international police force comprising the navies of the world. President Taft, however, never acted, despite pressures from pacifists and the federationists.

A few internationalists went beyond federal principles and advocated a world government. Bridgman called for an agency that would coin money, regulate trade, control patents and copyrights, and even supervise global monopolies. Such persons also favored the establishment of an executive agency with considerable authority, and some of them called for the use of arms to maintain peace. Roosevelt suggested the latter in his Nobel address; Holt flirted with the idea at times; and the suggestions of Bartholdt to the Interparliamentary Union in 1905 and the Bennet resolution of 1910 embodied

this principle. Carnegie recognized the need for an international police force, as did Lucia Ames Mead, a Boston reformer and peace advocate. Publisher Edwin Ginn favored an army to maintain order; and Cyrus Street, an eccentric realtor from San Francisco, presented some extreme views. He published a small journal, *The United Nations,* in which he noted the need for a government "with power to make, judge, and execute laws; and to provide for the final disposal of all their armies and navies, and for an army and navy under the sole command of the UNITED NATIONS to *enforce peace* and prevent war from *ever* occurring again." Representative James L. Slayden of Texas added another feature when he introduced House Joint Resolution 72 on 23 April 1913. It called for the nations of the Western Hemisphere to unite in "the mutual guaranty of their sovereignty and territorial integrity. . . ."

Such suggestions represented the views of only a few persons among those who favored the creation of an international organization prior to 1914. The formulas for periodic congresses, a federation with clearly limited powers, and a court of justice appealed to more people. Other persons rejected these options in favor of even more modest approaches. Historian George L. Beer advocated an English-speaking union, while some thinkers believed that the process of internationalism could be accomplished through increased contacts with the world. Throughout the nineteenth century, Americans had participated in a growing number of meetings on an ever-widening variety of topics. These included communications, health and sanitation, weights and measures, patents, copyrights, money, peace, and agriculture. Private citizens attended most of these conferences, but in some instances the government designated representatives. These contacts engendered a growing awareness of the interdependence of the world as the United States developed industrially and thrust outward economically and territorially. Such community thinkers saw the process of unity advancing not through a political process involving an institution created by the nation-state, but through the relationships of people living as a global society.

When war came in 1914, internationalists

despaired for a time. As the legally and politically minded ones rallied, they concluded that their previous ideas had validity; not enough had been done to attain them. A judicial court and a regularly functioning society of states had to be established. The League to Enforce Peace, formed in 1915 to advance that objective, devised a program that fully reflected the prewar faith in procedural machinery that could be used to resolve differences before they erupted in war. It called for a league to compel nations to submit their disputes to various agencies that were to be established. Sanctions, both economic and military, would be applied whenever a party to a dispute refused to follow the procedures, but no effort would be made to uphold the recommendations or decisions.

Smaller groups, endorsing the general principle of a league, argued that no force should be employed by an international organization. The World's Court League called for a judicially centered body with no power either to compel the submission of controversies or to uphold decisions, and this voluntary type of system received the endorsement of many lawyers and pacifists.

The nationally organized League to Enforce Peace campaigned vigorously to promote both its proposal and the idea of a league, and a vast majority of citizens found the general principle attractive by 1919. President Wilson incorporated it into statements of war aims, and he insisted at the Paris Peace Conference that an international organization become an essential part of the settlement. Wilson had opposed the formulation of specific plans during the war, and he did little thinking on his own. He had called for an association of American nations in 1914 and had subsequently endorsed the idea of an organized body of states, but not until late 1918 did he begin to explore the subject. His plans at that time revealed little awareness of prewar developments or thought. He called for an organization with considerable authority, one based upon power politics rather than on judicial principles.

At the Paris Peace Conference, the Covenant of the League of Nations emerged. Because of Wilson's dominant position, it reflected his views as well as prevailing internationalist plans that had concentrated upon procedural ma-

chinery to avert wars before they began. It placed its paramount faith in Articles 10 and 11, which called for a mandatory but undefined response to war or threats of war in order to protect the independence of states and to stabilize the world. Articles 12–15 provided for the peaceful settlement of differences. A court was to be established outside the League, but the Covenant contained few suggestions regarding its jurisdiction or powers. Articles 16 and 17 proposed that economic sanctions, and possibly military force, be used against states that refused to resolve disputes peacefully.

The story of the treaty fight of 1919–1920 has been recounted many times. Conventional interpretations emphasize the clashes over the policies of isolationism and internationalism and between the personalities of Wilson and Henry Cabot Lodge, the chairman of the Senate Foreign Relations Committee. It should be emphasized that differences in ideology also played an important role, because debate in the Senate concentrated not on whether the United States should enter the League, but on the nature of the organization it was asked to join. The fight over reservations reflected an effort by many senators to reduce the responsibilities of membership, while Wilson's intransigence in insisting upon Article 10 revealed a far different perspective. A clear majority of senators favored adherence, but they reached stalemate over whether to accept provisions designed to safeguard the nation's interests. Had the League been more in accord with the judicial and procedural approaches of internationalists and in keeping with developments prior to 1914, the outcome might have been different.

The refusal of the United States to join the League in 1920, followed by Warren G. Harding's victory in the presidential election of 1920 and his subsequent announcement that the result should be considered a mandate against membership, left the official policy of isolation intact. The United States never joined either the League or the Permanent Court of International Justice, organized in 1921. However, scholars do not believe that the voters in 1920 rejected the League; and indicators of popular opinion disclose no "resurgence of isolationism," no immediate renunciation of the internationalist convictions developed between 1915 and 1919. Throughout the 1920's and into the early 1930's, a majority of Americans favored membership both in the League and the World Court. The constitutional requirement for a two-thirds' Senate vote for treaties stood as the obstacle.

Events associated with the World Court reflected that reality. The Advisory Committee of Jurists had met at The Hague in the summer of 1920 to formulate protocols under which the tribunal would operate. The United States had been represented by one of its foremost citizens, Elihu Root; other prominent American legal figures, John Bassett Moore and Charles Evans Hughes, subsequently served as judges. Yet despite such evident legitimacy and the endorsement of every president and the major political parties, the Senate frustrated attempts at membership. It either imposed obstacles in the form of reservations before approval, which nullified membership, or, as in 1935, it mustered a majority but not a sufficient number of votes under the two-thirds' requirement.

The Senate's action in 1920 did not deter internationalists, who continued their quest for League membership for several years. They had seen a world organization created, and they viewed United States participation as vital to its success. Pro-League spokesmen sought the endorsement of their goal in political platforms, a quest that achieved partial success in the early 1920's; and they agitated to inform the people about the League's work in order to maintain popular interest and enthusiasm. The League of Nations Non-Partisan Association, later the League of Nations Association, appeared late in 1922 under the leadership of Hamilton Holt, former Supreme Court Justice John H. Clarke, and George Wickersham, attorney general under Theodore Roosevelt. Women's and religious organizations showed a special loyalty to the League, while pacifist groups and legal bodies endorsed World Court membership. Of the latter, the World Peace Foundation, the Carnegie Endowment for International Peace, and the American Society of International Law led the advocacy.

Because efforts to enter the League failed, internationalists embarked upon two alternative quests. They sought, first, to gain an increasing degree of cooperation with the League and its agencies, and, second, to instill in the people and their government a sense of collective responsibility to help maintain a stable world by supporting those principles in the Covenant that advanced peace. The first program succeeded reasonably well. After a slow start, the United States regularly participated in League commissions dealing with nonpolitical matters, notably health, social, and economic problems. It also cooperated in unsuccessful efforts to discover formulas for disarmament. United States officials generally avoided direct contacts on political issues, yet during the Manchurian crisis of 1931–1932 they were fully involved in discussions at Geneva.

One reason for the success of the internationalists' goal of cooperation with the League stemmed from ties they established at Geneva. American citizens held League administrative posts and promoted contacts between officials in Geneva and in the United States. Arthur Sweetser, a Boston journalist who served in the Information Section, became the focus of such contacts. Internationalists led by Manley Hudson of Harvard University also established study and research centers at Geneva and obtained gifts from Americans to underwrite League programs. The Rockefeller Foundation provided several grants, including $2 million to establish a library at the League's headquarters.

The attempt to generate a sense of collective responsibility to maintain peace in the absence of League membership also succeeded, to a limited degree. Historian James T. Shotwell became the major exponent of this view. He insisted that solidarity had to be achieved against nations that broke treaties or defied the League Covenant. If this could not be done through economic and military pressures, then states should unite in a moral condemnation of such actions. This approach gained support in the form of the Kellogg-Briand Pact (Pact of Paris), under which nations renounced war as an instrument of policy; in the enunciation of the nonrecognition doctrine that Secretary of State Henry L. Stimson first applied against Japan in 1932; and in the neutrality acts of the 1930's, which had highly limited provisions to allow discrimination against aggressors. After war broke out in 1939, the advocates of such measures joined with interventionists who called for the repeal or modification of neutrality legislation and other laws that hindered the free flow of materials to governments fighting the Axis Powers. Through the American Committee to Defend America by Aiding the Allies, they supported moral and economic embargoes and other measures associated with the Franklin D. Roosevelt administration's policy of "all aid short of war."

While most Americans accepted the League and World Court as existing realities throughout the interwar years, some citizens continued to work for older internationalist objectives. The idea of arbitration suffered momentarily after 1920; but through Shotwell's efforts the League in 1924 drafted the Geneva Protocol, which called for the signers to settle their disputes peacefully. The League also established the Arbitration and Security Commission in 1927. Although the United States rejected an invitation to subscribe to the Geneva Protocol, it negotiated twenty-seven arbitral treaties between 1928 and 1931 that excepted traditional policies like the Monroe Doctrine and allowed the Senate considerable voice in making procedural decisions. A few persons who looked longingly at the prewar peace structure spoke hopefully of assembling a third Hague conference late in the 1920's.

Lawyers likewise continued their effort to place the law of nations on a firmer base. The Carnegie Endowment for International Peace in 1923 established and funded the Academy of International Law at The Hague; it also supported efforts to advance codification, especially in the Western Hemisphere. James Brown Scott had encouraged the founding of the American Institute of International Law in 1912, and he worked with that body to prepare conventions for the consideration of delegates to various Pan-American conferences between 1928 and 1939. Such efforts resulted in limited progress.

A few thinkers despaired of the League, especially by the mid-1930's, after aggressors exposed its weaknesses. Such planners returned to earlier proposals for a stronger union. Some citizens endorsed the New Commonwealth movement of Lord David Davies of England, which called for a tribunal with an international air force to uphold its decisions. Oscar Newfang, a New York credit manager, redrafted the League's Covenant to provide for

a federal type of government; and between 1932 and 1935 the World Unity League sought to advance that idea. Another approach appeared in *Union Now* (1939), in which journalist Clarence Streit proposed a federation of leading democracies. Within a few years his book sold more than 300,000 copies, and Streit reached many other citizens with pamphlets and speeches.

Community internationalists also labored to promote a sense of global oneness. Dozens of friendship societies appeared in the 1920's, seeking to foster goodwill and economic development between countries. Other educational agencies worked to create an awareness of the world and its problems. The Institute of International Education had been organized in 1919 to encourage cultural association by facilitating student and faculty exchange programs. The Carnegie Endowment for International Peace, through its Division of Education and Intercourse, sought to achieve Nicholas Murray Butler's "international mind" by creating international relations clubs in high schools and colleges and by building "international alcoves" in hundreds of libraries. The schools provided a convenient channel for such work, and state and national education associations regularly endorsed efforts to provide information on world events. At the college level, efforts led to political science courses on international organization and to the creation of the Harris Foundation at the University of Chicago, the Williams College Institute of Politics, and graduate schools of international relations at Johns Hopkins, Princeton, and other universities. Citizens also organized the American National Committee on International Intellectual Cooperation to combat nationalism through an exchange of ideas and art.

Two influential bodies formed shortly after the war sought to promote global awareness. The Foreign Policy Association embarked upon an extensive publication venture and sponsored summer institutes, lectures, and radio programs on current international problems. The Council on Foreign Relations worked less directly, organizing study groups and presenting their findings.

Other community-oriented citizens warned of nationalistic policies while they proclaimed a doctrine of economic interdependence. In the

INTERNATIONALISM

1920's they sought with considerable success to redraft the reparation clauses of the Treaty of Versailles, and United States citizens played a vital role in conferences that resulted in the Dawes Plan and the Young Plan. Attempts to scale down war debts owed the United States failed, however, despite warnings that those obligations constituted a threat to the economy of the world. Likewise, throughout the 1920's efforts to lower tariff barriers clashed with protective nationalistic attitudes. Some change took place after Cordell Hull became secretary of state in 1933, for he fought vigorously to achieve a trade program based on reciprocity. The Roosevelt administration did not always pursue policies of economic internationalism. The United States sent delegates to a monetary and economic conference held in 1933 under League auspices to seek solutions to the worldwide depression, but Roosevelt decided that domestic recovery programs came first. Globally oriented individuals did see progress under Roosevelt in 1935, when the United States joined the International Labor Organization.

Numerous conferences during the interwar years attracted the support of persons seeking to advance a sense of global community. Many of these gatherings considered social, religious, educational, scientific, humanitarian, and other problems common to mankind; and organizations in the United States became affiliated with most of the worldwide bureaus created to advance particular goals.

The European war in 1939 and the attack on Pearl Harbor in 1941 seemed to confirm what internationalists had been saying for years in their advocacy of League membership and their proposals for collective responsibility. Aggressors had to be faced, and security for the United States would come only after it accepted a full role in maintaining peace. Shotwell and Clark M. Eichelberger, the executive secretary of the League of Nations Association, which in 1943 reorganized as the American Association for the United Nations, assumed the initiative in persuading Americans that they should respond properly to this second chance to create an effective international society. Their Commission to Study the Organization of Peace and the Commission of the Federal Council of Churches to Study the Basis of a Just and Durable Peace led in exploring the problem,

drafting proposals for a new agency and publicizing the need for another world organization. As early as 1941, a public opinion poll showed eighty percent of the people in favor of joining any new body.

At the same time, political leaders sought to avoid the stalemate that had blocked membership in the League. President Franklin D. Roosevelt, Vice-President Henry Wallace, and State Department representatives spoke repeatedly for some type of organization; and Congress revealed a bipartisan spirit in 1943 with resolutions endorsing membership. The House approved these 360 to 29, and the Senate 85 to 5. In the election of 1944 both major parties and their candidates likewise endorsed affiliation with a postwar international organization.

The Department of State, through its Division of Special Research, headed by Leo Pasvolsky, began studies early in 1941; and at various wartime conferences Allied leaders recorded their support for a United Nations. Their representatives met at Washington in the Dumbarton Oaks Conference late in 1944 to formulate provisions for a charter, with subsequent differences resolved at the Yalta Conference in February 1945 and the San Francisco Conference of 25 April–26 June 1945. In July the Senate endorsed membership 89 to 2. It could do so with less concern than in 1919, for no automatic obligation comparable with that of Article 10 existed.

The United Nations Charter reflected much of the structure and many of the operational features of the League Covenant, including a basic reliance upon power politics and a response to crises after a breach of the peace. Like Woodrow Wilson, Franklin Roosevelt believed that an alliance of the major nations, functioning through an organization, could best maintain stability. The United Nations Charter called for no sacrifice of sovereignty, and the provision granting the Security Council "primary responsibility" for peace reflected that outlook. The veto power conferred upon the five permanent members of the Security Council, fully endorsed by the United States, showed that vital interests and national honor would not be sacrificed.

In Articles 92–96, the Charter provided for a new International Court of Justice; and in

1946 the United States accepted the court's statute, although the Senate reflected traditional fears similar to those expressed in the debates over arbitration treaties prior to 1914. The Senate endorsed the Connally amendment, which declared that the court could not consider "disputes with regard to matters which are essentially within the domestic jurisdiction as determined by the United States," as well as issues to go to other tribunals or differences related to multilateral treaties.

Not all citizens accepted the United Nations unquestioningly. Many internationalists had hoped for a more effectively organized agency, especially in the light of atomic bombs and a need to regulate such devastating weapons. Again, most of them called for a world federation. Clarence Streit had continued to promote that idea throughout the war, and bridge authority Ely Culbertson stimulated further interest with his book *Total Peace* (1943). The popularity of this approach appeared after 1943 in the form of societies to promote that objective, including the Student Federalists, the World Citizens Association, and the Institute for World Federal Government. Proponents met in Asheville, North Carolina, in February 1947 to organize the United World Federalists. Several state legislatures approved resolutions endorsing a federation type of agency; and United World Federalists chapters prospered until the Korean War (1950), which revealed that in a politically and ideologically divided world, a stronger type of union was impossible.

Many other suggestions for a stronger United Nations appeared. Chicago philanthropist Anita McCormick Blaine provided $1 million for the Foundation for World Government, but that idea attracted little support. The concept of "peace through law" proved more appealing, as attorney Grenville Clark and Harvard professor Louis B. Sohn discovered after their book *World Peace Through World Law* (1958) appeared. The American Bar Association and the American Society of International Law endorsed this concept, and concerned representatives and senators formed the Members of Congress for Peace Through Law Committee.

Such programs, despite educational campaigns and the endorsements of notable groups, had little effect upon public policies.

Governments ignored repeated calls for conferences to amend the United Nations Charter, and the Connally amendment remained in force even though every president from 1946 to 1974 called for its repeal.

The agencies created in 1945 thus remained inadequate, and the United States turned to other forms of internationalism in an attempt to achieve a better and safer world. It developed alliance systems, a policy of global intervention, and extensive foreign aid programs. These revealed a basic desire for stability, but scholars have disagreed on the motivation behind this new internationalism. Some writers have emphasized the prevailing belief that the United States made a tragic mistake by taking an isolationist posture in the interwar years, which led to the conviction that never again should the American people fail to act against aggressors. Other historians have explained the nation's global commitments as a response to Cold War tensions, while New Left authors suggest that the extensive involvement in world affairs represented an effort to create a climate conducive to American ideas, doctrines, and economic expansion in the form of a new imperialism.

The growth of internationalism after 1945, however, was largely determined by events beyond the control of the American people. The heritage of their colonial experience, the creation of their own union, and a deep faith in principles of justice and right combined with new realities to bring acceptance of the idea of world organization. Technological revolutions in transportation and communication brought Chicago and Moscow closer in time in the middle of the twentieth century than Chicago and St. Louis had been in 1900. Manufacturing, business, and economic interests extended their operations abroad and became increasingly dependent upon trade and overseas investments. This led to more contacts and a growing comprehension of the need for all types of world cooperation.

Such changes, when linked to the feeling of guilt for withdrawal from international problems during the interwar years, resulted in a doctrine of responsibility for maintaining peace that received further impetus from Cold War rivalries and fears. With nuclear arms and increasingly sophisticated delivery systems, the

INTERNATIONALISM

United States had to abandon its isolationist tradition. Internal and external interests and national security could no longer be safeguarded by withdrawal or protective responses; the nation's welfare, tied to events abroad, could be defended only by a full commitment to resolve the problems of the world.

The early internationalists had been correct in their belief that an inevitable evolutionary process would carry their country in the direction of greater cooperation and involvement. The American people recognized the realities of international life and politics in accepting their changed role after 1945, but their conversion was not complete. Remnants of an isolationist philosophy remained in the refusal to relinquish any significant degree of sovereignty to the United Nations, to abandon national honor or vital interests to the International Court of Justice, and to subscribe to the philosophy that laws should determine the relationship of states. The lack of confidence in established international organizations appeared clearly in the allocation of funds to the United Nations. The United States, which at one time underwrote 40 percent of the United Nations' operating budget, gradually reduced that amount; and Congress voted in 1972 to cut its share to 25 percent. This shift reflected a belief that the United Nations should not be too dependent upon one country and also disillusionment stemming from the declining influence of the United States in an organization that had grown from 50 to over 140 members. Despite such changes, public opinion polls consistently showed popular support for the United Nations and even a willingness to grant it additional authority. A survey in 1970 disclosed a 67 percent majority willing to create a United Nations peacekeeping force, but administration and congressional leaders, as in the interwar years, did not respond to the desires of the voters. Appropriations of $60–70 million a year for the regular United Nations budget, in contrast with $70–120 billion annually for defense, revealed the reluctance of officials to move toward a fuller commitment to an international organization.

Even community-oriented internationalists could not erase parochial attitudes associated with isolationism. They noted a population growth rate that would overwhelm limited food supplies; environmentalists proved the existence of global pollution; and economists reported declining natural resources. The rapid growth of private international bureaus and agencies seemed to support the call for a full recognition of the interdependence of the world. Private bureaus had increased from 117 in 1890 to 700 by 1930, to 1,500 by 1960, and to more than 3,100 by 1972. Yet the establishment of such groups did not stimulate a wellspring of brotherly love or a conversion from national to supranational attitudes. The United Nations suggested that by 1975 each developed country should contribute 1 percent of its gross national product to aid underdeveloped lands, but the United States pledged less than one-fourth that amount to relieve global imbalances and meet human needs.

The new internationalism in the form of alliances and a policy of intervention, both multilateral and unilateral, did represent a firm commitment for nearly a quarter of a century. But here, too, involvement in wars in Korea and Southeast Asia stimulated doubts about such extensive and undefined obligations; and Americans began to talk of neo-isolationism. A public opinion survey in 1974 revealed that individuals with "total isolationist" attitudes had increased by 9 percent since 1972, so that 21 percent of the people considered themselves isolationists. At the same time, those who characterized themselves as "total internationalists" fell from 65 percent in 1964 to 56 percent in 1972 and to 41 percent in 1974.

These statistics reflect the fact that the United States has always sought an accommodation between the two extremes of isolationism and internationalism. Despite its membership in the United Nations, its professed willingness to resolve disputes peacefully, its espousal of collective security, its alliances, its doctrine of responsibility to be a policeman for the world, its economic penetration outward (with all of its implications), and its efforts to be a helpful and cooperative neighbor in the community of man, the United States has maintained its freedom of action. No other people have been so active in promoting internationalism yet retained an innate fear of entanglements and commitments. They have searched for, but have not found, a full accommodation between their conflicting desires and fears. Nevertheless, they have moved steadily to recognize the dangers both of standing aloof and of unilaterally applying their power everywhere, and they sense the need for continued and fuller cooperation in an increasingly interdependent world.

BIBLIOGRAPHY

See Selig Adler, *The Isolationist Impulse: Its Twentieth Century Reaction* (New York, 1957), which provides considerable information on the internationalist perspective in the course of an examination of its opposite; Ruhl J. Bartlett, *The League to Enforce Peace* (Chapel Hill, N.C., 1944), excellent on developments between 1914 and 1919; Inis L. Claude, Jr., *Swords Into Plowshares: The Problems and Progress of International Organization,* 4th ed. (New York, 1971), which contains an excellent analysis of ideas and developments; Richard N. Current, "The United States and 'Collective Security': Notes on the History of an Idea," in Alexander De Conde, ed., *Isolation and Security: Ideas and Interests in Twentieth-Century American Foreign Policy* (Durham, N.C., 1957), which traces the evolution of a significant idea; Merle Curti, *Peace or War: The American Struggle, 1630–1936* (New York, 1936), which describes nineteenth-century ideas; Calvin D. Davis, *The United States and the First Hague Peace Conference* (Ithaca, N.Y., 1962), and *The United States and the Second Hague Peace Conference: American Diplomacy and International Organization, 1899–1914* (Durham, N.C., 1975), both of which describe developments between 1899 and 1914; Robert A. Divine, *Second Chance: The Triumph of Internationalism in America During World War II* (New York, 1967), the fullest account of attempts in the United States to re-create a world organization; and Denna F. Fleming, *The United States and the League of Nations, 1918–1920* (New York, 1932), which examines the debate over ratification from the perspective of an ardent internationalist.

Also see Denna F. Fleming, *The United States and World Organization, 1920–1933* (New York, 1938); Sondra Herman, *Eleven Against War: Studies in American Internationalist Thought, 1898–1921* (Stanford, 1969), which develops the position of the community-minded internationalists and their relation to politically oriented thinkers; Harold Josephson, *James T. Shotwell and the Rise of Internationalism in America* (Cranbury, N.J., 1975), which offers insight into the most active proponent of an organized world, 1924–1962; Warren F. Kuehl, *Hamilton Holt: Journalist, Internationalist, Educator* (Gainesville, Fla., 1960), the standard biography of one of the nation's most active internationalists; *Seeking World Order: The United States and International Organization to 1920* (Nashville, Tenn., 1969), which provides the fullest account of early developments; and "The Principle of Responsibility for Peace and National Security," in *Peace and Change,* III (1975), which examines the evolution of that concept; C. Roland Marchand, *The American Peace Movement and Social Reform, 1898–1918* (Princeton, 1972); and David S. Patterson, *Toward a Warless World: The Travail of the American Peace Movement, 1887–1914* (Bloomington, Ind., 1976), both explore the internationalist perspective of peace workers; Max Savelle, *The Origins of American Diplomacy: The International History of Anglo-America, 1492–1763* (New York, 1967), which records the global implications of the colonial experience; Roland N. Stromberg, *Collective Security and American Foreign Policy: From the League of Nations to NATO* (New York, 1963), which contains valuable insights into the evolving belief in sanctions; and Lawrence S. Wittner, *Rebels Against War: The American Peace Movement, 1941–1960* (New York, 1969), which contains the fullest presentation of post-1945 popular attitudes and developments.

[See also ALLIANCES, COALITIONS, AND ENTENTES; ARBITRATION, MEDIATION, AND CONCILIATION; COLLECTIVE SECURITY; EMBARGOES; FOREIGN AID; INTERCULTURAL RELATIONS; INTERNATIONAL LAW; INTERNATIONAL ORGANIZATION; INTERVENTION AND NONINTERVENTION; ISOLATIONISM; PACIFISM; PEACE MOVEMENTS; RECOGNITION POLICY; SANCTIONS.]

INTERNATIONAL LAW

Adda B. Bozeman

UNTIL the middle of the twentieth century, international law was generally accepted in Europe and America as the body of customary and conventional rules that states consider binding in their interactions. Within the context of this broad accord on basic meanings, the United States developed distinctly American understandings of the functions of international law in the conduct of foreign affairs. These can be appreciated on their merits only when the European heritage of the law of nations is borne in mind. In the sixteenth and seventeenth centuries international law evolved in Western Europe as a corollary of certain momentous processes: the eclipse of the authorities of pope and emperor, which had given religious, legal, and political unity to linguistically disparate political entities in medieval times; the rise of the sovereign, territorially bounded state as the ultimate organizational norm; and the consequent emergence of a new political order in which numerous sovereign states were recognized as equals, each officially free to structure its relations with other states according to its own perception of the national interest.

Interstate anarchy appeared inevitable but was kept at bay, albeit often precariously, by well-articulated memories of European unity under pagan and Christian Rome and by the continuing validity, within each state, of certain shared legal and moral norms. Following the example set by the Greeks and Romans, generations of Europeans had never tired of speculating about the proper relations between law and nature, reason, religion, justice, and power or authority. In the course of these intellectual explorations Europeans created concrete legal principles and institutions not found elsewhere.

Several core concepts—all indispensable for the original structuring and, therefore, for the modern understanding of traditional international law—emerge from the records of these endeavors. Foremost is the recognition, duly rendered in the binding language of the law, that the individual is not only an autonomous human being—capable of suffering and inflicting wrongs, of claiming and acquiring rights, and of assuming responsibilities—but also, and in the context of the public order primarily, a legal person free to make contractual commitments under law. This dimension of individualism explains why Europe has traditionally been covered by networks of voluntary associations; why the state could be defined in ancient Rome as a partnership or a bond in law and in eighteenth-century England as a compact between successive generations meant to endure through time; why the meaning of a constitution is rendered as a contract between the governed and the governors; and why the term "legislation" continues to evoke remembrance of a Roman definition, that *lex* is a common engagement of the republic. Diets, synods, curiae, parliaments, *cortes,* and other types of conciliar bodies thus came to characterize the making of decisions in medieval as well as modern European realms.

The ruling convictions upon which common law and civil law systems converged—that the state is a creature of law, whatever its form of government, and that constitutionalism, whether rendered in written characters or implicit in the body of public law, is the most reliable shield for the domestic value system—carried two additional connotations destined to have important norm-setting effects upon international law. These may be described as the

455

commitment to maintain peace and order within each realm and the urge to extend the scope of contractual associations concerned with unity and cooperation between separate realms. Since the structures of contract and constitutionalism were known to promote unity and cooperation by regulating the natural tension always present in relations between the individual and society, they were trusted whenever two or more self-governing communities decided to join their destinies or special interests. Leagues of cities, federations of cantons, commonwealths of abbeys, and concerts of states were formed in Europe—a legacy of associational models without an understanding of which it is impossible to fathom the international organizations that evolved in the nineteenth and twentieth centuries.

The legal and political histories of Continental and English societies suggest strongly that law and order had to exist before representative government could work. Furthermore, they indicate that in Europe, local declarations or pacts to ensure the public peace were customarily written in legal language and that such official proclamations as the "king's peace," the "peace of the city," the "peace of the fair," the "truce of God," and the "peace of God" were allowed to accumulate or merge until they came to constitute general systems of public order, breaches of which could be viewed as violations of criminal or constitutional law. In short, European ideals of peace, order, and unity were organically linked to a complex heritage of law, history, and religious ethics.

This framework of the Christian commonwealth was greatly weakened in the seventeenth century by the ravages of religious and political warfare. However, it was saved from extinction by certain gifted scholars and statesmen who began restructuring the European order by a modified return to the classical and Christian legacies of law and ethics.

The principal draftsman of the new guidelines for the behavior of states was Hugo Grotius, a Dutch jurist and diplomat. His major work, *De jure belli ac pacis* (*On the Law of War and Peace*), published in 1625, during the Thirty Years' War, has come to be regarded as the first basic text of the law of nations. Grotius had only European states in mind when he

sought reliable principles of coexistence and cooperation. Since he was convinced that the efficacy of a new order would be a function of beliefs, values, and conventions upon which preceding generations had agreed, he explored Europe's many cultural legacies. Greeks and Romans, Jews, Essenes and Christians, Goths, Franks, Angles and Saxons are cited in *The Law of War and Peace* as exponents of this heritage. Their judgments of what is just or unjust are abstracted from history, religion, political philosophy, ethics, and law—above all the Roman laws of property and of contract—in order to present concordant answers to the fundamental questions he poses: How might war be conducted justly? How can peace be maintained justly between independent states?

Grotius presents peace as ethically superior to war, but he does not find that war is condemned either by the voluntary law of nations or by the law of nature. This means that states, not unlike individuals, can subjugate each other; that the boundaries of states and cities can be settled by the laws of war; that wars, for the attainment of their objects, must employ force and terror; and that the grounds of war are as numerous as those of judicial actions. "For where the power of law ceases, there war begins." These findings and propositions, which were confirmed in ensuing centuries by the realities of international relations, are presented by Grotius in alliance with two other themes destined to remain dominant in Western civilization: the references to law and to ethics.

The weight of the argument in *The Law of War and Peace* is carried by the thesis that law inheres in each mode of conducting international relations, whether peace, war, truce, or neutrality. Law should thus inform a government of the conditions that make war just and necessary; the privileges and obligations of the victor, the vanquished, and the neutral; how prisoners, inoffensive civilians, and ambassadors are to be treated; and which formalities are requisite if war is to be properly initiated or concluded. Likewise—and here Grotius borrows heavily from the Roman law of property—law prescribes how territorial dominion can be acquired, mortgaged, ceded, or lost, and who should be recognized as the sovereign exercising rightful jurisdiction.

Next, Grotius presents the views that only sovereign states, not their citizens or subjects, are international persons; and that the law of nations is not a jural order above the society of states but, rather, a law regulating relations between consenting states. The express will of states, notably as recorded in multilateral treaties, thus emerges as the single most important source of the new international order. This proposition explains the prominence given not only to treaties but also to the ethical obligation, inherent in the civil law of contract, that pacts must be kept. Treaties are defined in this text, on the authority of Livy, other Roman publicists, and the Roman law of contract, as accords that are made by express authority of sovereign powers. However, being of "the higher order of contracts," they are founded upon good faith and must therefore be considered absolutely binding, even when concluded between hostile states.

Since references to good faith, justice, conscience, moderation, and the Christian "law of charity" pervade *De jure belli ac pacis,* providing the "sinews" for the cultural integrity of the projected jural order, it must be concluded that the first great draft of a law of nations was European in inception and purport.

Post-Grotian generations in Europe and, after the Declaration of Independence, in America, have held steadfastly to the major themes summarized in the seventeenth century. Common legacies of domestic law and government made for a value system that instructed the political representatives of states, as well as their constituencies, to believe that international quarrels ought to be settled if at all possible; that governments and their agents will do so most successfully when they resort to methods of discussion and negotiation customary in domestic constitutional processes; and that intergovernmental accords are best entrusted to the type of document used for registering interpersonal compacts. Thus, the law of treaties that has come to constitute the core of modern international law evolved as an international extension of the Western law of contract.

This cultural consensus, together with the legal and ethical connotations of the idea of peace, also explains why diplomacy was commonly supposed to serve the cause of adjustment or peace rather than of conflict and war; why concerns of statecraft were usually expressed in the language of international law; and why international conferences and councils, modeled upon local legislative assemblies, became the favorite diplomatic forums for discussions of international affairs. Moreover, all trends toward an interpenetration of diplomacy, law, and ethics received support from the growth of the federating instinct in Europe and, later, in America, and from the general acceptance of the balance of power as a fundamental structuring principle of the modern European state system.

Conceived in Renaissance Italy and elaborated after the Napoleonic Wars in the context of the Concert of Europe, the balance of power allowed for fluidity in the interactions between sovereign powers, on the condition that any aspirations to hegemony be held in check through use of alliance diplomacy by the other members of the system. A review of these intricate cultural, legal, and historical records persuaded L. Oppenheim, the most influential authority on international law in the first decades of the twentieth century, that the balance of power was indispensable to the existence of international law. In discussing the second of five "morals" that he deduced from the history of the law of nations, he wrote that if the powers cannot keep one another in check, no rules of law would have any force, since an overly powerful state will naturally try to disobey the law. There is not, and never can be, a central political authority above the sovereign states that can enforce the law of nations; therefore a balance of power must prevent any nation from becoming omnipotent.

This understanding of the relationship between the concept of national sovereignty (which is affirmed explictly) and that of international solidarity (which is considered implicit in the history and coexistence of the Christian nations) has been commonly accepted by theorists and practitioners in foreign policy and international law. That is, it has been openly acknowledged, since the seventeenth century, that states are theoretically free in the management of their domestic and foreign affairs. Nonintervention in each other's jurisdictions is the ruling maxim in international law, even though it is also recognized that interference may be justified if the vital interest of state A is directly affected by the action of state B.

In the logic of these premises, peace, war, and neutrality present equally legitimate options for national decision making. Indeed, since war is recognized in international law as a legal tool of statecraft—and since the older Christian distinction, eloquently advocated by Grotius, among justifiable, persuasive, and unjustifiable causes for war ceased to be plausible after 1800—resort to war is accepted as a question of fact. In short, neither in the seventeenth century nor in the early twentieth century have war and law been viewed as inconsistent with each other.

The situation is different for the actual conduct of war. Here there exists an impressive consensus on the need to fight war lawfully. Treatises on the international law of war are as dense with explanations and definitions of the rights and duties of belligerent and neutral states; the legal effects of war on life, property, and territory; and customary modes of ending war properly, as are most earlier works, including Grotius'. Numerous other concordances or continuities can be cited, but the following propositions deserve particular mention because they gained prominence in the later twentieth century.

Contrary to Eastern systems, in which the territorial nation-state had not emerged as the political norm, generations of Europeans and Americans rallied to the proposition, clearly stated in the law of nations, that war is a violent struggle or an armed contention between states. "Civil war," being an armed contention between domestic rebels and the state, may qualify as "war"—but only when belligerence is recognized in specific ways. Other categories of warfare, notably "guerrilla war," received only passing and indecisive treatment, on the ground that such fighting factions are neither sovereign nor semi-sovereign "states." Besides, legal texts are permeated by the assumption that a state is able to cope effectively with irregular units within its territorial domain.

This supposition is consistent with the fundamental understanding that states, not their inhabitants, are "international persons" under the law of nations. It is also linked to another principle well-established in the modern West: that the condition of peace and the condition of war are polar opposites in life and law, each subject to its own rules of behavior. In the logic of this conceptualization, thresholds between war and peace must be clearly marked; hence the traditional requirement that wars must be officially "declared" and the common expectation that every war must end, preferably with a treaty of peace.

Since the validity of these theorems and practices was impaired in the later twentieth century, when non-Western doctrines of "protracted war," "permanent insurgency," and "no war, no peace" were institutionalized in certain areas of the world, it is well to remember that Grotius had not been as certain about the relationship between war and peace as later diplomats and scholars were. In a significant passage he suggests that it may not always be easy to distinguish clearly between war and peace, or to assert that every war will end, since belligerent powers may agree on "still points" or truces during a war that may last as long as a hundred years. Furthermore, he notes that war may exist even when warlike operations are not being conducted.

Neither of these uncertainties seriously detracted from the European, and later Euro-American, consensus that peace is morally superior to war; but most specialists in international law also held that individual projects seeking eternal and universal peace belonged to the realm of utopian philosophy rather than to that of realistic jural and political thought. It was thus recognized on both sides of the Atlantic that there was not, and in the nature of the international system could not be, an authority superior to the sovereign states that might administer rules of the law of nations, or pass judgments on the actions of states.

This consensus, together with the recognition that war per se was not unlawful, made it illogical to think of an international criminal law in terms of which a state or its governing officials could be held guilty for having waged war. Indeed, even piracy, which relates to unauthorized acts of violence committed on the open sea against persons or goods by a private ship against another ship, or by a mutinous crew against passengers or their own vessel, often gave rise to controversies in legal and diplomatic circles when precise definitions were being sought.

International law, then, was a limited reference for the making of foreign policy between the seventeenth and the early twentieth centuries. Nonetheless, it was an important one, for the records show that its rules were considered binding by the nation-states of Europe. Why this should have been so is best answered by the reminder that the law of nations had evolved in the matrix of a common cultural history that antedates and comprehends the emergence of the European state system, and that it had been tooled to serve the joint interests of politically separate, but culturally unified, states.

The United States entered the Western family of nations as a matter of course. Europeans took it for granted that Americans shared their cultural heritage, however bitter the experience of their severance from the English motherland; and Americans negotiated their claim to independence and to recognition as an independent sovereign state in easy conformity with the precepts of international law. It has often been remarked in retrospective commentaries on this early, assuredly difficult phase in the history of American foreign policy that the country had little experience and no precedents of its own as guides through the tangle of debts, indemnities, commercial restrictions, seizures, impressments, blockades, and rights of privateers in ports of neutral nations. A biographical essay on John Marshall points out that there was no Francis Wharton or John Bassett Moore for immediate reference and consultation—only Grotius, Christian Wolff, Samuel Pufendorf, Emerich de Vattel, and a few known and existing treaties—and that the young nation therefore had to rely on its common sense and spirit of right and justice. This claim is weakened, if not canceled, by the fact that America's early presidents, secretaries of state, and parliamentarians were intelligent and inventive, and that most of them were well schooled in European history, philosophy, and jurisprudence. The list of principles governing neutral conduct that was drawn up during George Washington's administration (issued in 1793) after a close study of European treaties and practices could thus be received as a major contribution to the law of nations. Likewise, John Marshall knew a great deal about international law when he was secretary of state

(1800–1801), being especially well informed of European views about the sovereign equality and independence of states. Indeed, when he was chief justice, Marshall delivered opinions bearing on these subjects, covering such issues in maritime law as the rights of visit, search, and seizure, and on the status of slaves captured by pirates, that established him as a leading authority on international law. In one of his major opinions he held that English precedents involving international law that had been set both before and after the Revolution were to be followed by American courts. Deviations from European patterns were nonetheless clearly apparent. The following are particularly noteworthy because they surfaced frequently in the later history of American foreign policy.

In light of twentieth-century elaborations of the principle of self-determination, it is important to remember that the Americans had not yet formed a state when they claimed power to levy war, conclude peace, contract alliances, establish commerce, and do all that independent states were entitled to do. Furthermore, the Declaration of Independence argued its revolutionary claim not by referring to pragmatic considerations and positive law, nor by analyzing policy problems, but by evoking such moral and philosophical principles as the law of nature and the Lockean theory of social contract as valid precepts for the political organization of humanity in general. As the records of American diplomacy show, this philosophical precedent was often followed when it was necessary to rally public opinion in support of crucial decisions concerning international relations.

Other uniquely American understandings of the relation between foreign policy and international law stem from the Constitution. This document does not contain as many important principles for conceptualizing foreign affairs as does the Declaration of Independence, but does provide mechanisms for distributing functions among the three branches of government. In accordance with the principle of the separation of powers, which was designed to institute checks and balances in order to guard against tyranny, Congress has the power to regulate commerce with foreign nations; to define and punish piracies and felonies committed on the high seas and offenses against the law of nations; to make rules concerning captures on land and water; to grant letters of marque and reprisal; to raise armies and provide a navy. Most important, the Constitution prescribes that Congress declares war and appropriates the funds necessary for the conduct of war. The president, in contrast, is commander in chief of the army and navy. As the highest executive officer of the nation, he is in charge of the conduct of foreign affairs; and in that capacity receives envoys from other countries and nominates ambassadors and consuls. However, the appointment of diplomatic personnel is subject to the consent of the Senate, and the same qualification is stipulated for the ratification of treaties negotiated under the auspices of a president's administration.

These constitutional arrangements, according to some scholars, have at times impeded the formulation of reliable foreign policies. Differences of opinion arose in Washington's administration when Constitution-conscious critics argued that the president's proclamation of neutrality of 1793 was an undue interference with the congressional power to declare war. The most delicate of these jurisdictional uncertainties arose in connection with the distribution of the treaty-making power. While the framers of the Constitution had not expected the United States to conclude many treaties, they had nevertheless provided that treaties negotiated by the federal government and ratified by the Senate are the supreme law of the land. This fact, together with the constitutional recognition that the law of nations is a part and a source of municipal law upon which the courts may draw in determining controversies, has served to give international law a legal importance in the United States that it does not possess elsewhere. It has also encouraged American publicists to give a concrete legal setting to their views, a tendency not usually found in the writings of contemporary continental authorities on international law.

Certain episodes in the nation's relations with the Barbary States of North Africa deserve attention because they provide the first illustration of that uneasy interpenetration of pragmatism and principle, and of ideology and international law, that became markedly discernible in the twentieth century. The issue concerned the capture of American ships and the enslavement of American citizens by Morocco, Algeria, Tunis, and Tripoli—all officially subject to the Ottoman Empire—and the need, felt by American representatives since the end of the revolutionary war, to procure the release of the sailors and stop these acts. Some policymakers felt that only a show of force could change the situation; but the absence of a navy made such a recourse illusory, necessitating instead negotiations under circumstances that seemed humiliating. The corsairs demanded ransom, and the Americans complied by buying treaties. A compact with the Algerians provided an annual tribute payment of $20,000 to the dey in return for the latter's promise to abstain from the piratical acts that constituted his main source of revenue. Another agreement was arranged with Morocco in 1787 through the mediation of the king of Spain, after the sultan had forced the issue in 1784 by capturing the brig *Betsy* and enslaving the crew. However, no concession was instrumental in settling the account with the Barbary powers: relations with them were cited in 1801 by John Marshall as the first in a group of three major problems—the others being American relations with Spain and complaints of American merchants about increased depredations by Great Britain—that would have to preoccupy his successor as secretary of state. A year earlier the United States had declined to cooperate with the governments of Denmark and Sweden when they proposed the use of joint naval forces to protect their commerce from pirates. Marshall's main reason for this response was that existing treaty arrangements should be performed in good faith, however burdensome the terms.

This relaxed attitude toward the North African regimes was not due entirely to absence of military power. Other explanations can be found in prevailing tenets of moral and political philosophy, according to which all human societies are potentially "good" and therefore worthy of recognition even if they have not yet attained statehood or other standards of development considered "normal" in civilized Western societies.

Besides, the young American nation itself had not yet qualified for statehood when it entered into relations of war, peace, and diplomacy with other governments. And the English also engaged in reprehensible maritime practices to the detriment of the Americans, and had signed several "articles of peace and commerce" with the Algerians and their neighbors.

The Anglo-American concordances on policy were first recorded in leading decisions by the High Court of Admiralty, and subsequently in texts on international law. In reply to a legal argument that Algeria was not a state but a mere pirate gang, Sir William Scott said in 1801 that the Barbary powers had long ago acquired the character of established governments, and that Britain was therefore able to have regular treaties with them. Other decisions rendered by the High Court of Admiralty in the same period make allowance for the presence of different cultural traditions in these realms:

> The inhabitants of those countries [i.e. under the protection of the Ottoman Porte] are not professors of exactly the same law of nations with ourselves. In consideration of the peculiarities of their situation and character, the Court has repeatedly expressed a disposition, not to hold them bound to the utmost rigour of that system of public laws, on which *European* states have so long acted, in their intercourse with one another.

To do otherwise, Scott explained, would be to try them by a law not similar to any law or practice of theirs.

Henry Wheaton, a leading nineteenth-century American scholar of international law, acknowledged the propriety of this judicial principle. Reflecting typically American experiences in foreign policy, he also drew attention to mutuality in the interactions between Islamic and Christian systems of law.

> In respect to the mutual intercourse between the Christian and Mohammedan Powers, the former have been sometimes content to take the law from the Mohammedan, and in others to modify the International Law of Christianity in its relation to them. Instances of the first may be found in the ransom of prisoners, the rights of ambassadors, and many others where the milder usages established among Christian nations have not yet been adopted by the Mohammedan Powers.

By and large, then, America and Europe agreed throughout the nineteenth and early twentieth centuries in viewing international law as a Western reference. Non-Western societies were admitted gradually and selectively to the existing family of states—but only when it could be assumed that the state's future international conduct would conform to existing rules or when such a recognition was considered advisable in the interest of foreign policy.

The dominion of the law of nations was thus officially extended to include the Islamic Ottoman Empire and the Buddhist state of Japan. The non-Christian states of Siam, China, Korea, and Persia, and the Christian state of Abyssinia, were long excluded because, at the beginning of the twentieth century, their civilizations were too different from that of the Christian West to assure a continuing consensus on the meaning and purport of international law. Their governments did qualify as "international persons" in the sense that they were deemed capable of concluding treaties; but in all other respects, especially those relating to war, they were rightly placed outside the circle of those observing international law. Yet this exclusion was temporary: it was considered reasonably certain by Oppenheim and Wheaton that the societies in question would mature in time.

American diplomacy encountered some of the difficulties alluded to when it engaged in "opening up" East Asia. On the subject of treaty making, for example, it became increasingly clear that the Chinese and the Japanese cultural traditions did not render the idea of obligation in the contractual terms favored by the West. Indeed, in neither of those civilizations during the last decades of the nineteenth century could analogues be found for any category of Western law, least of all for constitutionalism. The Meiji constitution of Japan (1889) was explicitly described by the nation's scholars as an "authorized," not a contractual, constitution, which, having emerged wholly from the august solicitude of the emperor, could be freely abolished by him. Missing were the norms and predispositions that had accounted for the rise of the law of nations in the West. The same was true of China, where social order was maintained by reliance on Confucian family ethics and on the doctrine, first propounded by the Legalists in the fourth and third centuries B.C., that all effective adminis-

461

tration is dependent upon penal laws of the utmost severity.

Both Confucian ethics and Legalist statecraft had been consistently relayed by Peking's foreign policies. The pivotal notion of the Middle Kingdom's supremacy over other peoples, both near and far, had always been administered either by indirect diplomatic controls (such as the propagation, through rituals and imagery, of trust in the sinocentric universe) or by punitive military expeditions designed to chastise inferior peoples on the periphery of the Middle Kingdom who had misbehaved or were being badly ruled. East Asian and Western diplomatic methods and organizational schemes had thus been incompatible since their inception, and they proved to be so in practice when representatives of later generations recognized in the nineteenth century that they could not decipher each other's "codes" of international communication.

The main factor responsible for these *dialogues des sourds* was the absence in China of any model comparable with international law, and the insistence of American and English diplomats on reading legal definitions of the state and of interstate accords into the culturally alien order they had entered. It was not clearly realized that China's sphere of influence was not a system of equal sovereign states; Peking had long viewed the entire area as the outer fringe of the Middle Kingdom. Each of the component societies was associated with separate characteristics and functions; but there were no neatly defined categories of legal status such as "protectorates," "vassal states," or "colonies." Such classifications did not cover realities in Asia, as the United States Department of State found out toward the close of the nineteenth century when it tried to negotiate a treaty of amity with Korea.

In refusing to deal with Western powers, Korea's spokesmen maintained that their country was "protector of the hedges" for China, that its king was a minister of the emperor, and that "our respective dispositions are mutually dissimilar; our guiding principles are not alike." The Chinese government, which disavowed control over the internal administration of Korea and insisted that the country was not a vassal, was similarly aware of this ambiguity. One of its representatives wondered in 1883 whether the Western states could rightly assume that their international law was the only applicable reference in a part of the world whose system antedated that of the West by thousands of years—a bewilderment echoed by Charles Denby, American minister to China, in a dispatch to Washington:

> Vattel discusses . . . the status of dependent states with reference to foreign powers. This discussion furnishes little information applicable to the peculiar relations existing between China and her dependent states. The text has little application to countries which, in their history, antedate international law of which, also, they never had any knowledge. What unwritten law or tradition controls the relations of China with her dependencies remains unknown.

More than half a century later, when scholars had provided policymakers in the United States and Europe with the missing answers, rigid adherence to the textual formulations of international law continued to control foreign policymaking in this part of the world. The status of Tibet, a vast non-Chinese, non-sinicized realm, was thus not viewed in the light of almost 2,000 years of cultural and political independence under various indigenous governments (neither easily encompassed in Western legal terms) but, rather, in the light cast by Western-type treaties that China's administrations had concluded in more recent times, when they had reason to recognize international law as "a useful defensive weapon" in their relations with the West. This reversal in attitude occurred after the Chinese administrations had successfully invoked certain principles in Wheaton's *Elements of International Law* (translated into Chinese by an American missionary) during a dispute with Prussia.

The United States has been recognized as a Great Power since the late nineteenth century, primarily in virtue of successful expansionist policies on the North American continent and in the Pacific region and, secondarily, by its gradual emancipation from Europe. These developments in the history of American foreign policy induced modifications in the meanings of certain norms and concepts in international law, notably those relating to nonintervention and recognition. They were also responsible for new orientations to war, peace, and the settlement of international disputes.

The Monroe Doctrine (1823) extended the policy of nonintervention, first announced by George Washington and Thomas Jefferson, to Latin America. It asserted that the European political system was essentially different from that of America and that any attempt by a European government to extend the system to any portion of the American hemisphere, or to control the destinies of newly independent Latin American states in some other way, would be viewed as the manifestation of an unfriendly disposition toward the United States. One cannot fault the Monroe Doctrine as a violation of the international legal system, since the latter was so constituted that it authorized each nation to judge its own cause and to act upon its own conclusions in its own way. However, certain inconsistencies in American political thought must be noted, if only because they later assumed normative significance for international law.

Thus, while the American government directed sovereign European states to abstain from certain activities in South and Central America, it declined to consider the doctrine as a self-denying ordinance in its own relations with the neighboring sovereign states. Indeed, as the reach of the policy was extended by presidential interpretations in 1848 and 1870, a Latin American state could not, even with its own consent, come under the dominion of one of the European powers; nor could any of the latter transfer its American possessions to another European state. It must be noted that the United States did not aggrandize itself, except in the case of Mexico, by interfering in the affairs of these societies. Usually it resorted to "protective measures" in the name of the Monroe Doctrine—as when, in 1902, it warded off European creditor nations from Venezuela and when it assumed the fiscal administration of the Dominican Republic in 1905 in order to cope with foreign powers that were pressing for payment of their claims and threatening seizure of local customshouses. There were also numerous armed expeditions and occupations in the Caribbean, especially under the auspices of President Theodore Roosevelt's "corollary"

to the Monroe Doctrine (1904), which announced that "chronic wrongdoing" by some of the region's governments "may in America as elsewhere ultimately require intervention by some civilized nations." Curbing fiscal disorder and "the insurrectionary habit" by the dispatch of marines or the establishment of temporary military governments was an acknowledged policy in the Roosevelt and Woodrow Wilson administrations, especially in Haiti, Nicaragua, the Dominican Republic, Cuba, and Mexico.

This aspect of "protective interventionism" made an issue of the established principle of recognition. As enunciated by Jefferson in 1792, it stated that the United States cannot deny to any nation "that right whereon our own government is founded—that everyone may govern itself according to whatever form it pleases, and change these forms at its own will. . . . The will of the nation is the only thing essential to be regarded." No tests for ascertaining this national will were proposed, however. Until the Civil War it was therefore the American policy in Europe, as well as in South and Central America, to recognize de facto governments. President Franklin Pierce explained in 1856 that the United States would "recognize all governments without question of their source, or organization, or of the means by which the governing persons attain their power. . . ."

But the experience of the Civil War, in which a large segment of the American nation tried to exercise the right of self-determination by secession and gain recognition as a new state or government, undermined the traditional trust in the axiom that nature assumed the independence of all "moral entities," as well as the optimistic expectation that the people know how best to determine their fate. Upon assuming office in 1913, Woodrow Wilson insisted that just government must be based not upon arbitrary or irregular force but upon law—the consent of the governed and public conscience and approval—and that governments established in Latin America by revolution should not be recognized. However, these principles were not uniformly followed. Wilson refused to recognize President Victoriano Huerta of Mexico, on the grounds that Huerta had come into office as the result of murder and

463

that he did not truly represent the people. Yet Wilson reversed his position when he recognized revolutionary changes of government in Peru, Bolivia, and Guatemala.

Fluctuations between these contradictory principles continued to mark America's subsequent diplomatic history. In fact, the ambiguities of the recognition policy—and therefore of avowed commitments to isolationism, nonintervention, and neutrality—became so pronounced after 1914, when the country had to respond to challenges in international affairs it had never faced before, that long-range foreign policy could not be drafted. The new world environment that proved so confusing to the United States was marked by world wars, regional wars, the dismantling of Europe's traditional Great Powers, and local insurrections, civil wars, and coups d'etat in the established states of Latin America and the new states of Asia and Africa, where they invalidated American expectations that the exercise of self-determination and the achievement of independence would lead to the development of republican institutions and democratic processes of government.

Furthermore, American administrations—beginning with that of Wilson—had to contend with the impact throughout the world of communist ideologies and revolutions that attacked the conceptual foundations of Western legal orders and political systems and favored the establishment of a new type of imperial orbit in Eurasian Russia and China, as well as new patterns of totalitarian rule. Two hundred years after the United States had declared its independence, it was clear that the nation had not come to terms with these developments, and that the shortcomings of its foreign policy had brought into question several fundamental norms of the law of nations. The normative uncertainty that followed these interdependent developments is well illustrated by the group of issues connected with the rights and obligations of the sovereign state.

The United States officially identifies itself with humanity in general rather than with Western civilization. In this context it has tended to view itself as the harbinger of a new and better world in which all communities, having expressed the wish for self-determination, are likely to qualify as sovereign states under the existing law of nations. Questions as to whether a given human grouping has a demonstrable will and capacity to approximate the model of the state as set out in international law, or whether the basic concepts of its municipal laws and customs are compatible with those of the law of nations, usually have been bypassed by policymakers, especially since World War II, when policy priorities called for the speedy decolonization of African and Asian peoples then under European imperial administrations. Nor was any heed paid to one of Woodrow Wilson's scholarly strictures on the relationship between self-government and constitutionalism:

Self-government is not a mere form of institutions, to be had when desired, if only proper pains be taken. It is a form of character. It follows upon the long discipline which gives people self-possession, self-mastery, the habit of order and peace and common counsel, and a reverence for law which will not fail when they themselves become the makers of law.

It was President Wilson's political message, eloquently set forth for purposes of peacemaking, that launched the idea of self-determination in world affairs. Confirmed by President Franklin D. Roosevelt in the Atlantic Charter, which proclaimed Allied peace aims during World War II, and recognized as one of the main structuring ideas in the Charter of the United Nations, it has since been endorsed by American administrations, particularly forcefully by President Lyndon Johnson, who announced in his 1966 state of the union message that support for the right of each people to govern themselves and to shape their own institutions was the most important principle in the country's foreign policy.

Neither of the American policy pronouncements contains definitions of self-determination or indicates criteria by which the availability of the right to a given human grouping is to be judged. In fact, means to identify such groups of people are missing. The beneficiaries in the 1919 settlements were certain ethnic, linguistic, and religious minorities in the multinational empires of Central and Eastern Europe and the Ottoman Khalifate; and those singled out after World War II were in the non-self-governing colonies and trust territories administered by the western European empires. The United States acquiesced in these rather arbitrary choices without contributing legally persuasive or logical arguments in support of the policies it espoused. Indeed, the right to self-determination was widely viewed by America as a moral absolute. Enveloped in this aura, it was placed in the legal articles of the United Nations Charter, and in this context it was gradually elaborated as a "human right."

The United States faced other complexities in connection with the principle that represented its birthright. Somehow it was assumed that self-determination could lead only to national independence, and that independence thus achieved under the supervision of an international organization and its law would be final, in the sense that there would be no dissident "people" within the newly established state wishing to secede by invoking the right to self-determination. Yet this is precisely what happened in numerous instances, for many of the new African and Asian states were composed of quite disparate smaller groups and had not met the preconditions for self-government originally laid down by Woodrow Wilson. Revolts and civil wars became commonplace and were put down by force of arms, thus leading to the situation that Secretary of State Robert Lansing had foreseen when he warned President Wilson, during the Versailles peace conference, that his cherished principle would become a rationale for innumerable wars.

The collision between incompatible legal, political, and moral aspects of the principles of statehood, sovereignty, and self-determination that American foreign policy had to administer was most intense and direct in Eastern Europe. Here the United States had to acquiesce in the rise of a totalitarian Soviet empire and to contend with communist policies that led, in the course of a few decades, to the creation of a German satellite state; the extinction of the Baltic states, whose independence an earlier generation of Americans had sponsored; the whittling down of attributes of national sovereignty in Poland, Czechoslovakia, Hungary, and Bulgaria; and the repression, by military intervention, of Eastern European efforts to recover some measure of self-expression.

These developments proved embarrassing for American foreign policy because of pro-nouncements such as that of John F. Kennedy in his inaugural address:

> Let every nation know, whether it wishes us well or ill, that we shall pay any price, bear any burden, meet any hardship, support any friend, oppose any foe to assure the survival and the success of liberty.

They also had negative effects upon the cause of established international law because they contributed to the debasement of the idea of the state and therefore to the erosion of the system of sovereign states in the context of which international law had been devised. The main challenge was the effective institution throughout the Soviet Union's sphere of control of revolutionary ideological and operational codes that declared the state and law to be instruments of exploitation in the capitalist or bourgeois economic order. However, the communist doctrine maintained, since the latter was historically doomed to extinction, the apparatus of the bourgeois law also would be disestablished, provided, of course, that the communist and workers' parties engaged in a relentless class warfare across the boundaries of nation-states so as to stifle opposition among class enemies.

Military intervention by the Soviet Union in the domestic affairs of erring states was explicitly sanctioned by theory, but on grounds not recognized either in existing international law or in the United Nations Charter, which the communist states had signed. For example, the official justification for the measures taken against the government of Czechoslovakia in 1968 states that the sovereignty of each socialist country cannot be opposed to the interests of world socialism; that formal observance of the freedom of self-determination of a nation in the situation that arose in Czechoslovakia would mean freedom of self-determination not of the popular masses, but of their enemies; and that the antisocialist path, "neutrality," to which the people of that country had been pushed, would bring them to the loss of national independence. This doctrine was reinforced in 1976 by the publication of an authoritative article in the Soviet Union maintaining that it is the main military purpose of the Warsaw Pact, signed in 1955, to suppress counter-revolutionary activity in communist countries.

States, then, continue to exist officially; but the normative idea they represent is placed in question either by the absence of a sense of nationhood and the indeterminacy of territorial boundaries (as in many regions of Africa and Asia) or by the presence of empires within the framework of which nominally sovereign states are actually subsumed as dependent, quasi-provincial units. Since common definitions and requirements for the existence of states are missing, it is erroneous to assume that the modern world is accurately perceived as an international system composed of equal sovereign states.

All references in international law and diplomatic discourse to democracy and constitutionalism as universally valid norms of organization have been invalidated by the rise of authoritarian forms of rule. Moreover, internationally relevant political power is no longer uniformly represented by officially functioning governments and traditional political parties. In many areas it emanates also, often exclusively, from international parties, mobile transterritorial military units, and other disguised centers of control that operate in behalf of political designs that are the antithesis of the established order. Last, today's tyrannies and sub rosa organizations are usually described and propagated in the legal value language of the democratic West—a serious distortion of reality with which the United States has not known how to cope in either international law or foreign policy.

In the absence of firm criteria for measuring the quality of states and governments, variable ones have appeared. Thus, whereas the United States has been powerless to correct abuses of human rights in communist dictatorships, it continues to reprimand, at times even to coerce, weak noncommunist authoritarian states, on the ground that they are guilty of violating their own constitutions, international law, the United Nations Charter, or the most favored maxims of the American rule of law. Likewise, since the American government has long been interested in an international accord with the Soviet Union on security and cooperation in Europe, it did not demur when the Final Act of the Helsinki Conference on this subject (1975) was signed not by the official holders of state offices in the Soviet Union, the German Democratic Republic, Czechoslovakia, Bulgaria, Hungary, and Poland but, rather, by the general secretaries of the communist parties in those states. That is, in this situation, as in others in which effective power is actually wielded by political organisms not officially recognized by international law, the United States appears to return to precedents in pragmatism that it had set in its relations with the Barbary pirates.

A historical review of American orientations to laws regulating interactions between different sovereign and quasi-sovereign entities shows a marked consistency in efforts to assure freedom of commerce as well as freedom of the seas. These concerns have been elaborated and extended in recent decades so as to assure freedom, safety, and cooperation in the air and outer space and to provide reliable legal guidelines for the use of the sea's resources and the protection of man's environment. However, it cannot be said that the American commitment, according to Secretary of State Henry Kissinger, "to substitute law for power" in these fields of human life and conduct and to build a "new corpus of the law of nations" capable of benefiting all peoples equally has elicited the desired international consensus.

The second major category of concerns upon which successive American administrations have converged relates to the peaceful settlement of international disputes. The government of the United States had been in existence for only five years when it concluded Jay's Treaty (1794) with England, which provided for three different arbitrations with the mother country—a precedent frequently followed in relations not only with Great Britain but also with France, Spain, Mexico, and other Latin American states. Besides taking an active part in the elaboration of standards for mediation, arbitration, conciliation, and the judicial resolution of conflicts, Americans were active from the late nineteenth century in organizing peace conferences, establishing courts of arbitration and international justice, and submitting such innovative provisions for the adjustment of disputes as those contained in the Taft-Knox treaties of 1911 (abandoned when the Senate added certain amendments) and in some thirty conciliation treaties negotiated by Secretary of State William Jennings Bryan from 1913 onward.

The third area of international law that has consistently preoccupied American statesmen relates to treaty making and all attendant processes of rendering accords and discords, rights and obligations, in the contractual form that has traditionally been trusted within the American and European orders as the best mode of harmonizing diverse interests. Treaties have proliferated in the course of the last two hundred years, particularly between 1917, when it was estimated that the United States was bound by approximately 25,000 official agreements, and 1976, when absolute certainty about the number and nature of the nation's international commitments can probably be reached only with the aid of computers.

The main reasons for the recent explosive growth of treaty relations are the phenomenal increase in the number of states, the intensification of contacts between these states, and the devaluation of other, formerly important sources of international law: custom and the shared classical-Christian inheritance of values, including natural law and common understandings of what is rational and normal. This shift is illustrated by a brief reference to relations with the Soviet Union and other communist societies.

Soviet spokesmen had early notified their friends and adversaries that their country would accept only those international customs that did not contradict the socialist legal conscience, and that only explicit agreements between socialism and capitalism would be recognized as binding. A survey of more than forty years of Soviet treaty theory and policy, made in 1962, explains the Soviet view that treaties are but juridical expressions of the actual correlation of social and economic forces in the world. Being "only" formal legal norms, devoid of intrinsic validity, they can in no way modify "the furious class struggle" in terms of which all foreign relations must be conducted until victory is won. In the context of this conflict system, capitalist or imperialist treaties are by definition unequal, enslaving, and coercive. However, in the Soviet Union and in the People's Republic of China they are nonetheless valued as tactically desirable and necessary tools of statecraft.

Most newly independent states have acceded to this orientation, which achieved note in a presentation by the Soviet jurist G. J. Tunkin, who argued that the emerging African and Asian states should regard customary international law as imposed law because they had never accepted it—a view suggested in 1956 by the Indian diplomat and scholar K. M. Panikkar, who wrote that most of the world does not accept the basic postulates of diplomacy and international law because they had evolved in the West during the nineteenth and early twentieth centuries. These perceptions have been validated by numerous Western scholars, among them Robert L. Friedheim, who concluded from his analysis of negotiating processes between the "satisfied" states and the "non-satisfied" states (mostly Asian, African, Arab, and Latin American caucusing groups and the anticolonial common-interest group) during two United Nations conferences on the law of the sea (1958, 1960) that an all-out assault on law was characteristic of the "dissatisfied" states.

These and related general discords on the relevance and implications of international treaty law have been exacerbated in the last decades by growing uncertainty on two counts: what are the reach and purport of the customary maxim "pacta sunt servanda"? And, more important, precisely what is treaty law today? The norm that every treaty in force is binding upon the parties to it and must be fulfilled by them in good faith matured early in the jurisdictions of the civil law and the common law, in which "contract" has always been the preferred form for registering personal and governmental commitments. That norm has been officially universalized in modern times, but the fact remains that it cannot possibly mean the same thing to non-Western peoples who have developed other, unusually nonlegal, ways of rendering the sense of obligation. This circumstance, together with the memory, in some states, of Western abuses of treaty making and with the appeals of anti-Western ideologies, explains why different types of modern states are apt to make different assessments of which treaties are worthy of respect. That is, at the time when treaties are being acknowledged as the primary source of international law, there is no political, legal, or moral consensus on matters of compliance.

The reactions of recent American administrations to these modern trends have been oblique. For example, when Secretary of State Dean Rusk was asked during hearings on the Nuclear Test Ban Treaty before the Senate Foreign Relations Committee (88th Congress, 1st Session, 1963) whether it would be accurate to observe that nations usually comply with their treaties only so long as those treaties conform to what they regard as their national interest, he answered: "Well, the path of history is littered with broken treaties . . . and in general where vital interests are concerned, a nation by and large felt that it must take care of its vital interests and not give top priority to . . . strictly legal commitments."

However, efforts to channel foreign policy objectives into treaty terms and to stabilize or restructure the law of treaties were intensified in the ensuing years. These efforts climaxed in the Vienna Convention on the law of treaties (1969), which settled many discords even as it introduced new uncertainties. One of the articles embodies the view that a treaty is void if, at the time of its conclusion, it conflicts with a peremptory norm of general international law. Such a "peremptory norm" appears to be one that is accepted and recognized by the international community of states as a norm from which no dissent is permitted and that can be modified only by a subsequent norm of general international law having the same character. The further question—how universally valid norms can be created outside the contexts of both treaties and customs—is unanswered.

The charters of the United Nations and other international organizations that the United States helped to found after World War II were modeled on the American constitution, but subsequent American foreign policies cannot be said to have guarded the integrity of fundamental charter norms from damage by the impact of politicized voting processes, or to have stemmed the tendency, favored by the majority of member states, to attach international law significance to selected "resolutions," "covenants," and "declarations." Indeed, this set of issues confused successive administrations. Presidents, secretaries of state, members of the Senate Foreign Relations Committee, and representatives of scholarly elites have been at odds in their analyses of the subject and also have frequently changed their assessments of the meaning and relevance of such statements as the Universal Declaration of Human Rights (1948), the Declaration on the Granting of Independence to Colonial Countries and Peoples (1960), and the Declaration on the Elimination of All Forms of Racial Discrimination (1963).

For example, in regard to United Nations activities in the field of human rights, President Harry S. Truman openly favored an international bill of rights that "will be as much a part of international life as our own Bill of Rights is part of our Constitution"; and Secretary of State John Foster Dulles asserted that standards in this area should be expressed in terms of law that operates on individuals, not upon states, and that is enforceable by the courts, not by armies. Senator John W. Bricker, of Ohio, and members of the American Bar Association maintained, in contrast, that such moves to extend the rule of international law should properly be viewed as unwarranted attempts to supervise the relation between the state and its citizens; other Americans were convinced that the covenants and declarations of human rights in question were not compatible with provisions of the United Nations Charter that assign these concerns explicitly to the domestic jurisdiction of each sovereign state. No consensus on the international law dimension of the Declaration of Human Rights had been reached in the United States before 1975. Some viewed the document and its affiliates as authoritative statements of the international community or as part of the new customary law of mankind. But Arthur Goldberg, the American ambassador to the United Nations, declared in 1967 that the declaration "is at best a moral obligation," and certainly not "a treaty obligation." This estimate was officially contradicted in 1975 when the human rights provisions of the Helsinki agreement on security and cooperation in Europe were accepted by the administration of President Gerald R. Ford, and again in 1977 when the incoming administration of President James E. Carter decided to link its foreign policies closely to this particular issue.

In the United Nations, where the majority of

member states are ruled by authoritarian governments that do not even pay lip service to civil liberties within their borders, the international bills and declarations of human rights have come to serve partisan political purposes. Having been officially adopted as internationally valid standards in counterpoint to prevalent local norms, they can now be cited readily whenever a majority of states resolves to censure, ostracize, or punish a particular United Nations member that has aroused the ire of one or more voting blocs. In the multicultural environment of 1977, it appears that United States policies have been too shallow and oscillating to protect the core concepts of treaty law, and that this situation has led to the confounding of international law and international organization. Neither of these developments has contributed to the integrity of American foreign policies.

These developments are partly attributable to the nation's federal structure, which does not facilitate unity among the three branches of government when it comes to treaty making. But the main cause of America's failure to formulate and maintain reliable conceptions about the nation's relationships to non-American political systems and cultures is a persistently wavering, fundamentally uncertain national self-view. Isolationism and its corollary, neutrality, have been ardently supported as the main, officially proclaimed ideals of coexistence with other societies, notably the European powers. Yet no period in history comes to mind in which these principles have not been compromised or transposed into their opposites, partisanship and intervention. Lapses from the declared and preferred standards became necessary—for instance, at the beginning of World War I, when the United States lacked power to ensure freedom for neutral shipping. Yet on balance it appears that American administrations elected to be involved in "the broils of Europe" and to be partial to one side in a given conflict, just as, at the turn of the century, they had chosen to take an interest in perfecting the existing European machinery for the peaceful settlement of disputes and in elaborating new ground rules for the application of international law.

What seemed then to be a decisive break with the isolationist tradition was made incon-trovertibly manifest by America's voluntary military participation in the two world wars and the nation's equally sustained efforts, at the end of each conflict, to settle the affairs of Europe and the rest of the world on the basis of principles that represented, to the greatest possible extent, preferred American ideals. These included insistence on the recognition of nationalism and self-determination, the breakup of empires, and the unification of nations in international collective security systems that were expected to ensure world peace because they were based on international law and organized along quasi-federal constitutional lines—on the model of the United States itself. However, the impression of an American commitment to the causes thus espoused in treaty form was destined to be dispelled, most dramatically after Wilson and his delegation had persuaded foes and friends alike to sign the Treaty of Versailles, which included the Covenant of the League of Nations. At that time the nation failed to honor the commitments made in its behalf, in order to withdraw to its trusted isolationist position, leaving those who had reluctantly acquiesced in the American leadership, as well as those who had welcomed the mediating presence of the great non-European power, to cope with the outstanding issues in contexts that were not of their choosing.

The seesaw movement between commitment and withdrawal that remained characteristic of American foreign policy in the later twentieth century was paralleled by equally ambivalent dispositions in matters directly relating to peace and war. Although the nation has been engaged in numerous wars, it has proved unable, in modern times, to accommodate the phenomenon of war either in its own moral, political, and legal systems of norms or in the new codes and structures of international law that it has sponsored.

The country's spokesmen in the early years of this era had been in general accord with John Bassett Moore's view that one must distinguish de facto war from the legal condition called a state of war; that nothing is more misleading than the supposition that a government cannot be said to commit acts of war, or to make war, unless war or a state of war has been declared or otherwise admitted to exist. In other words, war per se was not considered either immoral or illegal. Representatives of earlier generations had tried to prevent disputes from degenerating into armed conflict and to regulate the conduct of war once it had occurred. In fact, these shared perceptions of reality led to circumstances in which Francis Lieber's *Instructions for the Government of Armies of the United States in the Field* (1863) could become the foundation for codifications of the laws of war in 1874, 1899, and 1907.

World War I was the catalyst for a radical transformation of American orientations to war. Not only was that conflict rationalized as a war to end all war; but in agreeing to a peace treaty that held all Germans collectively guilty for having initiated the war, the United States government adopted the view that war could be considered an international crime—a category traditionally reserved for piracy only. The treaty, as well as the Covenant of the League of Nations, was rejected by the Senate. However, the new collective security organization came into being just as it had been designed by its American architects, as a community of power under the rule of international constitutional law that would be fit to displace the balance of power—that "great game now forever discredited"—thus assuring an enduring international peace. Moreover, the notion that war is immoral and must therefore be abolished remained the most active principle in the postwar period. Convinced that there should be laws against war instead of laws regulating war, the United States signed the Kellogg-Briand Pact (1928) "to outlaw war as an instrument of national policy." This was followed in 1932 by the enunciation of the Stimson Doctrine, which declared that the United States would not recognize a situation, treaty, or agreement that had been brought about by means contrary to the covenants and obligations of the Kellogg-Briand Pact.

These pronouncements impressed the historian Thomas A. Bailey as "monuments to illusion." They were indeed solemn moral condemnations, made in the language of international law but not linked to sanctions or other methods of enforcement, and therefore not likely to be persuasive in international relations. As a matter of fact, the opposite became apparent in East Asia, as well as in other regions in which American policymakers were confronted with grave challenges. Commenting on Japan's "Manchuria coup," which had elicited the Stimson Doctrine, the American diplomat Stanley K. Hornbeck concluded from his observations of local reactions to the American initiatives that the Japanese viewed the ideal of peace as an ideal of a few Western states. Even if Japan and other non-Western governments had agreed to this idea officially, the commitment would have remained meaningless, he noted, since their peoples were not "mentally committed" to it. Both China and Japan, Hornbeck continued, were delinquent in their respect for the sanctity of treaties; more important, no Oriental thought that he was under any obligation, moral or legal, in relation to a pledge made under duress. These perceptions were echoed and elaborated a decade later by Japanese Foreign Minister Matsuoka Yōsuke when he remarked that the Western powers had taught the Japanese the game of poker; but, after acquiring most of the chips, they pronounced the game immoral and took up contract bridge. What was called "international law," he mused, was in fact the "family" or "house" law of the great Western nations; and in Japanese eyes this body of norms was discredited by the use to which it had been put.

These reactions, the developments in Asia and Europe, and the record in World War II were unfavorable to the American program of subjugating war to law. But the project was nonetheless realized through the military victory over the Axis Powers; German and Japanese citizens were tried, found guilty, and punished by ad hoc international tribunals that charged them with having begun an unjust war, having violated traditional laws of war, and having committed "crimes against humanity"—a new category of offenses set up by Allied authorities when victory was certain. The notion of the just war was then carried into the charter of the new collective security organization, which had actually been initiated as a military alliance. However, since adequate definitions of what is just and unjust are missing in the United Nations context, it is now the political judgment of the current majority that decides whether the belligerent actions of a given state or group do or do not constitute a righteous resort to arms. These circumstances make it difficult to accept existing Charter provisions and their application either as "treaty law" or as "customary international law," even though they may not offend the new authoritative yet innocuous American definition of international law found in Marjorie Whiteman's *Digest of International Law* (1963):

> International law is the standard of conduct, at a given time, for states and other entities subject thereto. It comprises the rights, privileges, powers, and immunities of states and entities invoking its provisions, as well as the correlative fundamental duties, absence of rights, liabilities, and disabilities. International law is, more or less, in a continual state of change and development. . . .

Present uncertainties about the place of war in international law and policy have multiple causes, including the sudden gathering of different civilizations in a world society based on Western norms and values, and the ensuing difficulty of reconciling disparate, even incompatible, evaluations of war and peace; the gradual erosion of the nation-state as the basic, universally valid organizational norm and the simultaneous rise of other political organisms for which existing international law does not make provision; the spectacular development of military science and technology; the advent of totalitarian ideologies and systems of rule in which total war is an accepted norm; the United Nations Charter, which has officially canceled the law of neutrality, thus inviting the spread of local wars; and the proliferation of guerrilla war, proxy war, insurgency, counterinsurgency, civil war, rebellion, wars of liberation, and the interpenetration of these kinds of violence under the aegis, particularly, of theories affirming the necessity of protracted war or permanent revolution.

These realities of war have been recognized by recent administrations, beginning with that of John F. Kennedy; but it cannot be said that the new perceptions gathered in foreign affairs have been communicated to international law. Kissinger could thus conclude in an address entitled "International Law, World Order, and Human Progress" (11 August 1975) that the modern age has spawned the plagues of aircraft hijacking, international terrorism, and new techniques of warfare, and that these realities, combined with bitter ideological strife, civil warfare, and weakened bonds of social cohesion, have made human conflict more brutal than it had been previously. In regard to international law, he drew attention to the fact that numerous treaties to combat these excesses are on record and that nations already have the legal obligation, recognized by unanimous resolution of the United Nations General Assembly, to refrain from organizing, instigating, assisting, participating in, or acquiescing in terrorist acts. "The law in action," he continued, "has been less impressive than the law on the books"; and the necessary struggle "to restrain violence by law meets one of its severest tests in the law of war."

No exit from the impasse is opened either in this or in other authoritative explanations of the relation between international law and policy. Changes in foreign policy, changes in international law, or changes in the national disposition toward existing international law are nowhere proposed, even though most existing norms and concepts have been found inadequate. Yet, the reasons for this inadequacy—and therefore also for the present discrepancy between theory and practice—emerge clearly from a comparative review of the world's disparate normative systems and ideologies. It is evident that peace is not a shared value, even though it is defined in leading American dictionaries as the "absence of war" or the "normal non-warring condition of a nation, group of nations, or the world." It is also evident that war has remained a morally accepted way of life in most cultural traditions and that international law is at best just one of numerous references in the foreign policies of all non-Western societies. None of these incontrovertible realities seems to have shaken the American commitment to the theory of international law. In fact, the latter is today so closely associated with the desire to free the entire world from war and to serve the cause of human progress that it may well have degenerated into an American ideology. Thus transposed, it cannot serve the national interest in foreign policy.

BIBLIOGRAPHY

See J. Andrassy, *International Law and the Resources of the Sea* (New York, 1970), a leading monograph on the general subject that does not explicitly address problems of United

States foreign policy; Edwin M. Borchard, "The United States as a Factor in the Development of International Relations," in Edmund A. Walsh, ed., *The History and Nature of International Relations* (New York, 1922); Adda B. Bozeman, *The Future of Law in a Multicultural World* (Princeton, N.J., 1971), which traces the origins of constitutional law and international law in the history of Western civilization, presents the major themes that distinguish the public order systems of non-Western cultures, and concludes that international law is not a universally shared reference in foreign affairs; Herbert Butterfield and Martin Wight, eds., *Diplomatic Investigations: Essays in the Theory of International Politics* (London, 1968), which explores whether and in what sense there is an international community, whether there is a distinct Western tradition in international relations, and what meanings inhere in the concepts of the balance of power and international law (several significant comments on United States foreign policy are included); Jerome Alan Cohen, "Chinese Attitudes Toward International Law—and Our Own," in *Proceedings of the American Society of International Law,* 61 (1967); *Digest of United States Practice in International Law* (1973–   ); Robert L. Friedheim, "The 'Satisfied' and 'Dissatisfied' States Negotiate International Law: A Case Study," in *World Politics,* 18 (1965); Wolfgang Friedmann, *The Changing Structure of International Law* (New York, 1964), which reappraises the theoretical foundations of international law as formulated in the West and assesses the changes in certain fundamental concepts that have ensued from the divergence of interests between developed and underdeveloped states and from conflicts of ideologies; Charles Cheney Hyde, *International Law Chiefly as Interpreted and Applied by the United States,* 2nd rev. ed., 3 vols. (Boston, 1945); Henry A. Kissinger, "International Law, World Order and Human Progress," in *U.S. Department of State. Bulletin,* 73, no. 188 (1975).

Also see Louis L. Jaffe, *Judicial Aspects of Foreign Relations—In Particular of the Recognition of Foreign Powers* (Cambridge, Mass., 1933), which deals with the judicial problems arising from the recognition and nonrecognition of foreign nations, and attempts to develop a technique for resolving or determining the nature of the conflict between executive and judicial purposes in recognition cases; Knud Krakau, *Missionsbewusstsein und Völkerrechtsdoktrin in den Vereinigten Staaten von Amerika* (Frankfurt am Main–Berlin, 1967), vol. 14, in the series Abhandlungen der Forschungsstelle fur Völkerrecht und Ausländisches Öffentliches Recht der Universität Hamburg, a historical, legal, and cultural analysis of the relation between the American sense of mission and American doctrines of international law that emphasizes the impact of the interaction between these two factors upon the history of American foreign policy; L. Oppenheim, *International Law: A Treatise,* 2 vols. (New York–Bombay, 1905–1906); Dexter Perkins, *The American Approach to Foreign Policy,* rev. ed. (Cambridge, Mass., 1962); American Law Institute, *Foreign Relations Law of the United States: Second Restatement of the Law, as Adopted by the American Law Institute at Washington, D.C., May 1962* (St. Paul, Minn., 1965); Henry Reiff, *The United States and the Law of the Sea* (Minneapolis, 1959), a succinct presentation of the issues as they existed before their reconsideration in the 1960's; Vernon Van Dyke, *Human Rights, the United States and World-Community* (New York, 1970), which contains several discussions of United States policies and dispositions toward the principle of self-determination and human rights as formulated in the United Nations Charter; Henry Wheaton, *Elements of International Law* (London, 1836), and *History of the Law of Nations in Europe and America* (New York, 1845); and Marjorie M. Whiteman, *Digest of International Law,* 11 vols. (Washington, D.C., 1963–1969), the leading modern American digest.

[See also ARBITRATION, MEDIATION, AND CONCILIATION; BLOCKADES AND QUARANTINES; EMBARGOES; EXTRATERRITORIALITY; FREEDOM OF THE SEAS; INTERVENTION AND NONINTERVENTION; NEUTRALITY; PROTECTION OF AMERICAN CITIZENS ABROAD; PROTECTORATES AND SPHERES OF INFLUENCE; SANCTIONS; TREATIES.]

INTERNATIONAL ORGANIZATION

Inis L. Claude, Jr.

THE international system that began in modern Europe and has only in the twentieth century become global in its membership has always exhibited the fundamental characteristic of decentralization. The concepts of sovereignty and balance of power indicate that it consists of numerous separate, autonomous states, independent producers and managers of power and policy, each dependent for survival and welfare upon its own resources and its shrewdness and skill in manipulating its relationships with other states. The development of international law paralleled the evolution of the system of sovereign states, but the legal system has tended more to reflect and confirm the separateness of the parts than to weld them into a unified whole. The international system has been deficient at both the top and the bottom, having neither a superstructure of authoritative and effective institutions nor a foundation of social consensus. Hence, control over states, protection of states, cooperation among states, and provision of common services for states have been matters for improvisation by states themselves.

International organization is the generic term for the cumulative efforts of states to move beyond purely ad hoc arrangements for obtaining control, protection, cooperation, and services. These efforts have involved the creation of standing structures and procedures, permanent headquarters, and international bureaucracies—in short, the establishment of continuously functioning institutions. To designate these as systematic arrangements made by and for states is to say that international organizations are additions to the international system, elements of a hitherto-missing institutional superstructure. States may be entirely self-interested when they collaborate with others to establish, operate, and maintain forums and facilities for their own use; but in the process they contribute to the reequipment and modernization of the international system, the remedying of its traditional structural deficiency. It is possible, although less certain, that the organizational developments that supply missing institutional components at the top of the system may also contribute to the strengthening of its consensual base. It is clear that both the immediate utility of international organizations and their ultimate systemic significance depend heavily upon their producing such an effect.

International organizations began to appear during the nineteenth century in the predominantly European state system, and a considerable number of separate and limited-purpose agencies had accumulated by the outbreak of World War I. The organization-creating tendency of this period was stimulated primarily by the interdependencies engendered by the industrial revolution; new forms of production and new methods of transport and communication created problems and opportunities that necessitated more elaborate and systematic responses than those traditionally associated with bilateral diplomacy. International organization was an outgrowth of the multilateral consultation that came into vogue. It was a short step, and sometimes an almost imperceptible one, from convening a meeting of the several or many states whose interests were involved in a given problem and whose cooperation was essential to solving it, to establishing permanent machinery for collecting information, preparing studies and proposals, arranging recurrent consultations, and administering schemes agreed upon by the participating states.

The nineteenth-century concern with the challenge of developing rational multilateral responses to the changes wrought by steam and electricity in the economic and social spheres did not exclude concern with either the perennial or the newly developing problems of the "higher" sphere of international relations—war and peace, politics and security, law and order. Indeed, it was clear that changes in the former spheres contributed to difficulties in the latter, and it was hoped that organized collaboration in the first might contribute to improvement in the second. Awareness of the increasing complexity of international politics, anxiety about the problems of preventing and limiting war, concern about the orderly balancing of stability and change, and hope for the strengthening of international law combined to inspire the ideal of applying international organization to the politico-legal realm.

The effort to do this at the end of the Napoleonic Wars had yielded meager results, but the idea of giving firm institutional shape to the Concert of Europe persisted and was supplemented during the nineteenth century by the ideal of developing judicial means for the resolution of international disputes. It remained for the Hague Conferences of 1899 and 1907 to stimulate the hope, and for World War I to demonstrate the necessity, of extending the concept of international organization into the "higher" sphere of international relations. The League of Nations embodied that extension, represented an effort to provide a central focus for the varied organizational activities that had emerged in the preceding century, and accelerated the growth of the organizing process among states. The collapse of the League and the outbreak of World War II gave rise to the establishment of the United Nations and a network of affiliated organizations, and gave impetus as well to the institution-building disposition of statesmen that has produced scores of agencies of almost every conceivable size and concern. If the nineteenth century was the period of the beginning of the movement toward international organization, the twentieth century has been the era of its flourishing. The landscape is now dotted with international agencies—global and regional, single-purpose and multipurpose, technical and political, regulatory and promotional, consultative and operational, modest and ambitious—and the habit of creating new ones and maintaining old ones is well established among statesmen. By any test of quantity and variety, international organization has become a major phenomenon in the twentieth century.

The beginning of the trend toward international organization in the nineteenth century and the flourishing of that trend in the present century have substantially involved the United States. The well-known isolationist tradition of the United States and the fact that it rejected membership in the League of Nations but joined the United Nations at its creation should not be taken as evidence that America is a latecomer, a recent convert, to international organization. On the contrary, American participation in the nineteenth-century organizing process was at least as active as might reasonably have been expected, given the country's geographic remoteness from the European center of the movement and its modest standing among the powers. American initiative contributed to the formation of such multilateral agencies as the Universal Postal Union (1874) and, within the Western Hemisphere, the Pan American Union (1890). Although the determination of the dates of establishment of international organizations and of adherence by particular states is by no means an exact science, one can take it as approximately correct that, by 1900, the United States was a member of ten international bodies and that, by the outbreak of World War I, it participated in twenty-seven—as against twenty-eight for Great Britain and thirty-six for France.

This record would seem to substantiate Henry Reiff's assertion that "The United States . . . is a veteran, if not an inveterate, joiner of unions or leagues of nations," despite its failure to affiliate with the League of Nations and the Permanent Court of International Justice. Indeed, America's record of interest and involvement in international organization made it less surprising that President Woodrow Wilson took the lead in creating the League of Nations than that the United States refrained from joining it. The American rejection of the League, historically considered, was an aberration rather than a continuation of settled policy regarding international organization. Moreover, it did not presage a drastically altered policy. Although the United States never accepted membership, it gradually developed cooperative relationships with the League in many areas of activity and ultimately assumed a formal role in several of its component parts. In the final analysis, the United States became a more active and more useful participant in the operation of the League than many of the states that were officially listed as members. In addition, the United States continued, between the world wars, to join organizations outside the League family—to such an extent that, by 1940, it held a greater number of organizational memberships than did Britain and France, the leading powers in the League. Following World War II, the United States became the world's unchallenged leader in promoting and supporting the development of international organizations of every sort.

The attitude of the United States, however, toward international organization has not been free from ambivalence. Presumably, the United States has gone along with, and has sometimes displayed enthusiasm for, the organizing process for essentially the same reasons that have moved other states: it has recognized the practical necessity, in its own interest, of developing and participating in systematic arrangements for dealing with the complex problems of the modern world; and it has shared the ideal of creating a global mechanism better adapted to promoting and maintaining peace and human welfare. Even when it has been skeptical of the utility or importance of particular multilateral institutions, the United States, like most other states, has generally inclined to the view that it can ill afford to be unrepresented in their functioning, or to give the appearance of being indifferent to the ideals they purport to serve. America's limited and informal engagement in the operation of the League of Nations illustrated the first of these points; this country could bring itself neither to join nor to abstain from the League. Its enthusiastic adherence to the United Nations in 1945 was in part an illustration of the second—a symbolic act of repentance and reversal, a conscious repudiation of the American abandonment of the League.

But America's joining the United Nations was more than a denial of indifference to the high ideals enunciated in the Charter. It was, more positively, a declaration of resolve to accept a position of leadership in world affairs, an affirmation of the intention to play a role that this country had never before assumed in international relations. In this sense, American ratification of the United Nations Charter was a unique act, a dramatization of an event of peculiar significance—the decision of the United States to transform its approach to world affairs. The country's subsequent adherence to the North Atlantic Treaty Organization reaffirmed the same point and even strengthened it, for NATO membership appeared to carry more concrete obligation and more definite commitment than did membership in the United Nations.

In most cases, decisions by the United States to take part in international agencies can be assumed to be motivated in much the same way, and can be assigned essentially the same meaning, as such decisions by other states. Neither in the case of the United States nor in other instances does it make sense to regard acceptance or support of international organizations as, in itself, a demonstration of virtue comparable with the virtue sometimes attributed to the individual because he goes to church and pays his tithe. International agencies are not embodiments of a sacred cause but, rather, instruments of the purposes of their members, susceptible of use to promote both noble and ignoble causes. States join them for mixed reasons, and the mere act of affiliation typically provides no solid information about the constructiveness, the cooperativeness, or the peacefulness of the intentions of the state concerned.

America's inhibitions and reservations concerning international organization are a blend of the typical and the peculiar. Despite the modern vogue of international organization, it is clear that all states maintain some measure of reluctance to become too encompassed, circumscribed, and absorbed by international bodies. It is perhaps unfair to accuse them of harboring the illogical desire to have their cake and eat it too, for in the relations between organization and sovereignty, just as in the relations between national society and individualism, the real question is not which to choose but how much of each to include in the package. In either the domestic or the international case, however, the perennial tension between control and autonomy remains, and becomes especially acute when circumstances require reconsideration of the necessary and proper balance between them. The fact that states need and want international organization does not eliminate their desire to retain as much as possible of the autonomy that the traditionally decentralized international system affords them. The tension between the desire for effective and useful international organization and the urge to continue to enjoy and exploit the free-wheeling possibilities of a simpler era profoundly affects the behavior of states in creating, joining, and operating multilateral agencies.

Although sovereignty may figure as an abstract concept with definable meaning in legal and political scholarship, in the real world of states and peoples it is a symbol and slogan no less powerful for its having indistinct and highly variable meaning. Sovereigntyism as a subjective phenomenon is a more important factor in international relations than sovereignty as an objective fact.

Concern about sovereignty has pervaded America's policy with respect to international institutions, from the earliest days to the present. While it has rarely prevented the joining of organizations, it has always affected American contributions to their design and the style of participation in their functioning. The fear that organizational involvements might cut more deeply into national autonomy than originally intended or agreed has never been far beneath the surface of American politics.

American sovereigntyism was originally linked with isolationism, which was based upon the fact that the new state was substantially isolated from the European cockpit of world affairs; it was distant, separate, and different. Moreover, it was weak and vulnerable to exploitation in any intimate association with European powers. Fixation on sovereignty reflected the conviction that prudence required the fledgling state to go its own way, capitalizing upon its peculiar situation to maintain political distance between itself and the leading states of the day. Isolationist doctrine related to political and military embroilments, not to economic and commercial ties, and for that reason

it did not significantly inhibit American participation in the public international unions that began to emerge in the nineteenth century.

It was when international organization turned political, with the formation of the League of Nations, that jealous regard for sovereignty, nurtured in the era of isolationism, came to the fore as an impediment to American involvement. President Wilson's leading contribution to the formulation of the Covenant made the League largely an American enterprise, but it was nevertheless profoundly un-American in certain fundamental respects. The League promised—or threatened—to involve the United States deeply and systematically in the political and security problems of a world that was still fundamentally Europe-centered. The Covenant prescribed commitments that seemed to restrict America's freedom to keep its distance, to stand aside. By this time, the United States had lost its isolation and the cogency of much of the rationale for isolationism had faded; but Americans continued to value the freedom to decide, unilaterally and ad hoc, whether, when, and how to become involved in the quarrels of other states. The right to be unpredictable constituted a major part of the substance of the American idea of sovereignty, and membership in the League was regarded as involving the drastic curtailment of that right. Wilson lost his battle for American affiliation with the League not to nineteenth-century isolationists who believed that their country was safely moated and ought never to intrude into the politics of Europe, but to proponents of the idea that the United States should continue its recently espoused auxiliary role in world affairs, the central feature of which was untrammeled discretion concerning engagement and disengagement. Wilson's successor, Warren G. Harding, expressed this idea succinctly: "If our people are ever to decide upon war they will choose to decide according to our own national conscience at the time and in the constitutional manner without advance commitment, or the advice and consent of any other power." When the League actually dealt with political and military crises, the United States was sometimes willing and eager to take an active role, but it was never willing to accept an obligation to do so.

Sovereignty, interpreted as the retention of a

free hand, continues to have a major impact upon American policy regarding international organization. World War II convinced most Americans that the advance and well-understood commitment of the United States to throw its weight onto the scales was essential to the preservation of world peace, and the United States made the shift from the policy of the free hand to the policy of commitment that it had rejected when Wilson proposed it. Nevertheless, the urge to keep options open has not been displaced by recognition of the value of clear and credible commitments. The strength of that urge was demonstrated in American insistence upon having the power to veto substantive decisions in the United Nations Security Council, and in the careful hedging of obligations under the various bilateral and multilateral security treaties concluded during the Cold War. The United States has wanted to put the world on notice as to its future policy while retaining the possibility of deciding its policy ad hoc; it has wanted to enjoy the benefits of being committed without paying the price of losing the national freedom to choose its course of action. Since the 1960's, the shift made in 1945 has been largely reversed. Attention has been focused once more upon the dangers of overcommitment and the values of the national right to make foreign policy decisions unfettered by promises to, or participation by, other states. The symbolic significance of American membership in the United Nations has been drastically reduced.

The American conception of sovereignty has traditionally included another element: the right to national privacy, the capacity to fend off external intrusions into domestic affairs. This concern was rooted in the original American sense of separateness and differentiation from Europe; the New World had broken off from the Old World, and maintaining the sharpness of the break was deemed essential to retaining the valued newness of the qualities of American political society. The isolationist tradition combined cautions against being drawn into European affairs and against Europe's poking into American affairs.

The latter concern is typically expressed with reference to international organization by the concept of domestic jurisdiction. Participation in multilateral agencies necessarily involves ex-posure as well as commitment; nothing can be done with the collaboration of, or for the benefit of, a member state without something's being done to that state. American enthusiasm for international organization has always been qualified by fear of expanding the national vulnerability to external interference, a concern that was manifested in the drafting of both the League Covenant and the United Nations Charter by vigorous insistence upon provisions protecting domestic jurisdiction. The campaign that defeated American affiliation with the League concentrated as heavily upon what might be done to this country by and through the organization as upon what the United States might be required to do on behalf of the League. Similarly, misgivings about the United Nations and the specialized agencies have often expressed the belief that the United States has been, or the fear that it might be, improperly penetrated by foreign influences flowing through those institutional channels. "Get the United Nations out of the United States" is not directed exclusively at the existence of the organization's headquarters in New York.

This concern for sovereignty, translated as domestic jurisdiction, is shared by all states. It has received peculiar emphasis in American policy, for reasons that go beyond the attitudes that were initially associated with an isolated position and an isolationist doctrine. It seems probable that the United States has never felt the keen need for international organization, to serve its particular interests as distinguished from its broader interest in a stable and peaceful world, that most other states have felt. As a big country, a continental state, the United States has not required the relief of difficulties posed by cramped territorial area that many other states have felt compelled to seek through international organizations. It has not fully shared the need of European states, now matched by states on other continents with numerous national divisions, for coordinative mechanisms to facilitate interchange across state boundaries; in this respect, the American situation is analogous to that of a great rural landowner, in contrast with that of residents in congested urban areas. The twentieth century finds the United States a powerful, wealthy, and highly developed state, not dependent upon others for protection or for economic and technical assistance. Given these characteristics, it is perhaps understandable that the United States tends to conceive of participation in international agencies as a matter more of giving than of receiving—and that it insists upon limiting both what it gives and what it receives. The United States can afford to resist having undesired things done to it by international organizations because it has little stake in having essential things done for it by those bodies. So far as the impact of multilateral programs and activities upon and within national societies is concerned, the United States accepts the biblical proposition that it is more blessed to give than to receive. America, more than most other states, can plausibly consider its engagement in organized international activities as predominantly a means of contributing to the general welfare of the global body politic, rather than as a means of acquiring particular benefits for itself. Perhaps for this reason, Americans appear especially prone to believe that international organizations are, or should be, expressions of collective idealism and altruism.

Another set of difficulties and inhibitions that affects American participation in international organization might be said to derive from the reverse of the attitude toward national sovereignty discussed above. International organization inevitably cuts into the sovereignty of participating states, in the sense that it requires them to accept commitments, thereby restricting in some measure their freedom to decide what they will and will not do, and in the sense that it enhances their domestic exposure to external impacts, thereby diminishing their sense of national privacy. But one should not conclude from this that the relationship between national sovereignty and international organization is in all respects a competitive one. International agencies are not engaged in a zero-sum game with states, a situation in which the weakening of the latter is the condition of the strengthening of the former. On the contrary, effective international organization requires the participation of broadly competent states—states that are able as well as willing to meet their obligations, that are capable of formulating responsible positions and reaching meaningful decisions, and that can manage their resources, people, and territories

to the degree required for dependable cooperation in multilateral activities. States deficient in these respects are frequently pressed by involvement in international organization to remedy their deficiencies, and the agencies of the United Nations system have in recent years given major attention to building up the capabilities of particularly deficient member states—to increasing, rather than diminishing, the meaningfulness and effectiveness of their sovereignty.

America's engagement in international organization has always been handicapped by limited possession of the kind of national sovereignty essential for effective and reliable participation, and its collaboration in multilateral enterprises has been restrained by reluctance to bend to pressure for strengthening the national capabilities in question. When Americans worry about the implications of membership in international bodies, they are at least as likely to exhibit concern about the enlargement as about the diminution of the sovereign competence of the United States government.

The essence of the matter is that the United States is a political society dedicated to the ideal of constitutional democracy, a state whose central government is designed to operate within a framework of limitations derived from the principles of democracy and constitutionalism. Democracy implies that government must be responsive to the majority will more than—and, in case of conflict, instead of—to the exigencies of the international situation, the rules or decisions or pressures of the organs of international agencies, or the obligations prescribed either by general international law or by treaties. The problem posed by the tension between international commitment to order and domestic commitment to democracy is a real one for the United States; and the more the country becomes involved in multilateral agencies and activities the more intense it becomes.

Unfortunately for international organization, the democratic principle is not exhausted by the proposition that national commitment requires popular consent. Consent theory implies the right of a nation to change its mind and the obligation of a government to accept the implications of the withdrawal of popular consent. The international legal sanctity of national commitments is challenged by the democratic legitimacy of popularly inspired decisions to violate or repudiate such commitments. The government of the United States came face to face with this problem in the 1960's and 1970's, when the popular consensus that had supported the acceptance of commitments in the two preceding decades began to dissolve. So long as the United States undertakes to combine international responsibility with domestic democracy, its leaders will confront serious dilemmas—and uncertainty will prevail in international organizations as to what can be expected from the United States. Democracy coexists uncomfortably with international law and organization.

Constitutionalism, no less than democracy, creates difficulties for the United States as a participant in international agencies. The president's responsibility for the conduct of American foreign relations, including the management of American participation in international organizations, is not fully matched by his legal authority or his political power to exercise this responsibility. He must compete and cooperate with the Congress, which shares in the control of foreign policy. The division of powers associated with American federalism limits the capacity of the federal government to accept and carry out obligations, or to engage in cooperative arrangements, under the auspices of international bodies. The national commitments to preserve a significant degree of autonomy for the private sector of the economy, to maintain the freedom of a press that zealously guards the right to self-definition of its responsibility, and to respect individual rights enshrined in a written constitution and interpreted by an independent judiciary establish further limitations upon the capacity of those who speak and act officially for the United States to engage the country fully and reliably in the work of international organizations.

To say that the United States is a constitutional democracy is to say that the body politic has not conferred upon its central government the full powers, usually associated with the concept of sovereignty, that may be required for loyal and effective performance in international organizations. To say that the American public is dedicated to the preservation of the system of constitutional democracy is to em-

phasize its reluctance to enlarge, or to countenance the enlargement of, governmental capacities relevant to involvement in multilateral enterprises—capacities to make and carry out commitments, to act decisively, and to exercise the degree of control over a variety of internal matters that may be entailed by acceptance of international schemes of regulation or cooperation.

There is a constitutional doctrine, derived from the Supreme Court opinion in *Missouri* v. *Holland* (1920), supporting the view that the valid acceptance of international obligations carries with it the enhancement of federal powers to the extent required for meeting those obligations. Moreover, early enthusiasm for membership in the United Nations was reflected in a widespread tendency to acquiesce in a broad interpretation of executive authority to act as might be required for effective collaboration with the organization. This acquiescence proved to be short-lived. In the 1950's the Bricker amendment campaign revealed that the doctrine of *Missouri* v. *Holland* was more generally feared, as a threat to the integrity of the American constitutional system, than valued, as a promise of the adaptability of that system to the requirements of the age of international organization. The formal constitutional renunciation of the doctrine was obviated by assurances that it would not be exploited. Less than two decades later, there emerged a political mood dominated by insistence that the competence of the president to commit the country in international affairs should be significantly reduced. Generally, it appears that Americans are more concerned about preventing involvement in international organization from impinging upon the distribution of authority within their political system than about preventing the peculiarities of their domestic arrangements from handicapping the nation's performance in international organization. The dominance of this concern had a great deal to do with American rejection of the League of Nations. Acceptance of the United Nations clearly has not eliminated this element from the American attitude toward involvement in world affairs.

Nineteenth-century isolationist doctrine, with its emphasis upon aloofness from European political entanglements and intrigues, expressed not only a pragmatic judgment concerning the best way for the United States to survive in a dangerous world but also a moral aspiration, an ideal of national virtue defined as innocent abstention from the evils of power politics. This heritage of moral distaste for international politics colored early American thinking about international organization to promote world peace and order. Nineteenth-century Americans, ranging from spokesmen for the various peace societies that sprang up after 1815 to leaders in government, tended to conceive organization for peace in essentially apolitical terms, emphasizing legal formulas and arbitral or judicial settlement of disputes. World courts figured more prominently than diplomatic forums or international armies in favored formulations, and the ground was prepared for the perennial popularity of the "rule of law" in American internationalist thought. In particular, the vision of the future did not include the involvement of the United States in the international political arena or the burdening of the United States with weighty political responsibilities—and certainly not its obligation to participate in military sanctions against disturbers of the peace. America was not to be contaminated by being dragged into power politics; rather, the world was to be purified by being persuaded to rise above politics, to the realm of law. Global salvation was to be achieved by formula and gadget—not by American commitment to share in the hard, dangerous, and dirty work of an organized political system.

The scheme set forth during World War I by the League to Enforce Peace and by similar organizations in Europe, then formulated in the Covenant of the League of Nations under the leadership of President Wilson, was not in accord with this American vision. Calling for an essentially political approach to world order supported ultimately by national obligation to engage in military sanctions, it violated the basic tenets of the traditional American creed. It offered a painful, not a painless, solution to the problem of order. The American peace movement had hoped for the appointment of a judge; it was confronted by the demand that the United States serve as a policeman. The League promised not reliance upon predictable legal process but involvement in the uncertain-

ties of political and military activity. True, the new machinery included the World Court, and there was massive American support throughout the life of the League for membership in that body. The movement to join the court was ultimately frustrated, however, by the fear of involvement in the political League through adherence to its judicial annex. The American legalistic tradition demanded acceptance of a court, but it did not permit acceptance of that particular court.

The role of the United States in creating, supporting, and operating the United Nations reflects the official abandonment of preoccupation with legal system-building and of aversion to engagement in the political and military aspects of international affairs. Nevertheless, the postwar record contains numerous indications of the survival of these sentiments. The mood engendered by the Vietnam War is characterized by the revival of the tendency to conceive national virtue in terms of innocence rather than of responsibility. Fighting for peace, the central motif of the twentieth-century ideal of collective security, tends now to be regarded not as paradoxical but as inconsistent at best and hypocritical at worst. Self-critical Americans are inclined to interpret the performance of the United States in the early years of the United Nations as a record of shameful manipulation and abuse of the organization, not of constructive leadership and loyal support; the image of the responsible defender of international order has been overshadowed by the image of the irresponsible adventurer and imperialist. In the eyes of self-pitying Americans, the national image is that of an overloaded and insufficiently appreciated bearer of international burdens. Those who put the matter as the abdication of a discredited tyrant and those who put it as the retirement of a weary servant are advocating the same thing: the diminution of the American role in world affairs. The appeal of this prescription is strengthened by the rise to dominance in the United Nations of political forces and factions that the United States can neither lead nor control; America's opportunity to exercise leadership has declined as much as its inclination to do so.

Traditional American misgivings about involvement in international political organization have been confirmed. Discounting the excesses of guilt and self-pity, we must nevertheless conclude that participation in the United Nations entails the disappointment of national hopes, the frustration of national efforts, and the dirtying of national hands. It requires that the luxury of pure adherence to principle be sacrificed in favor of the more ambiguous, and less satisfying, morality of responsibility. The glamour of sharing in the formulation of a grand design gives way to the never-finished work of international housekeeping and the never-solved problem of managing the affairs of an almost unmanageable international system. It is not surprising that the United States has failed to find this work inspiring or pleasant. What is important is that the United States should continue to recognize that it is necessary.

BIBLIOGRAPHY

Ruhl J. Bartlett, *The League to Enforce Peace* (Chapel Hill, N.C., 1944), is an account of the rise and fall of the movement for American membership in the League of Nations. Lincoln P. Bloomfield, *The United Nations and U.S. Foreign Policy*, rev. ed. (Boston, 1967), examines the way in which the United States has used, and been affected by, the United Nations. Merle E. Curti, *The American Peace Crusade, 1815–1860* (Durham, N.C., 1929), is a valuable source for understanding traditional American pacifism and its legalistic overtones. Denna F. Fleming, *The United States and World Organization, 1920–1933* (New York, 1938), is a treatise on American cooperation, and the lack thereof, with the League—informed by a strong pro-League bias. Hamilton Foley, *Woodrow Wilson's Case for the League of Nations* (Princeton, N.J., 1923), is a useful compilation of materials illustrating Wilson's view of the League and his arguments for American membership. Ursula Phalla Hubbard, "The Cooperation of the United States With the League of Nations, 1931–1936," in *International Conciliation*, no. 329 (Apr. 1937), presents a careful study of the period of closest American collaboration with the League, particularly valuable for its treatment of political questions. *League of Nations, International Labour Organisation and the United States*, Geneva Studies Series, 10, no. 1 (Geneva, 1939), is an excellent account of the development of American relations with the major international agencies of the interwar period. Henry Reiff, "The United States and International Administrative Unions: Some Historical Aspects," in *International Conciliation*, no. 332 (Sept. 1937), gives a brief survey of American participation in limited-purpose international agencies before World War II. Ruth B. Russell and Jeannette E. Muther, *A History of the United Nations Charter: The Role of the United States, 1940–1945* (Washington, D.C., 1958), is the definitive history of the creation of the United Nations, containing invaluable information on the role of the United States. Laurence F. Schmeckebier, *International Organizations in Which the United States Participates* (Washington, D.C., 1935), presents an indispensable compilation of information concerning American involvement in international agencies up to 1935. William A. Scott and Stephen B. Withey, *The United States and the United Nations: The Public View, 1945–1955* (New York, 1958), presents and analyses survey data regarding American public opinion about the United Nations, to the end of the first decade of its operation. Michael Wallace and J. David Singer, "Intergovernmental Organization in the Global System, 1815–1964: A Quantitative Description," in *International Organization*, 24 (1970), is a statistical study including useful data on American membership in multilateral bodies.

[*See also* ARBITRATION, MEDIATION, AND CONCILIATION; COLLECTIVE SECURITY; INTERNATIONALISM; INTERNATIONAL LAW; ISOLATIONISM; PACIFISM; PEACE MOVEMENTS; PRESIDENTIAL POWER IN FOREIGN AFFAIRS; REALISM AND IDEALISM; SANCTIONS.]

INTERVENTION
AND NONINTERVENTION

Doris A. Graber

ANALYSIS of the intervention and nonintervention policy of the United States requires examination of three distinct policy aspects: law, action, and doctrine.

THE LAW

Basically, intervention is unsolicited interference by one state in the affairs of another; nonintervention is the avoidance of such interference. Intervention may be directed against a single state or factions within it, or it may involve interference with the interactions among a group of states. It may take the form of military action or economic or political pressures. These pressures force states to act in a manner prescribed or foreordained by the intervening state. Alternatively, the intervening state may use its own agents to carry out the policies that it desires. States yield because they fear military coercion or punitive action or because they cannot stop the intervening state's agents or activities.

Although the elements of intervention can be readily outlined, they are hard to identify in specific political situations. Most relations among states contain elements of coercion since interacting parties feel constrained to make some concessions to each others' wishes. It is difficult to determine at what point pressure becomes coercive enough to be deemed intervention. Normal intercourse among states merges almost imperceptibly into interventionary practices. In a community of nations that is comprised of states of varying powers

and degrees of interdependence, nations lacking in economic and political resources are most likely to experience interventionary pressures. The world community has not yet agreed on the borderline between the right of the stronger power to insist on its terms, and the right of the weaker power to conduct its affairs free from coercion. At the other end of the spectrum of coercion, it has at times been difficult to determine when intervention becomes outright warfare.

A second problem arises from the interdependence of nations in the community of nations, which makes the complete independence envisaged by the concept of sovereignty a legal fiction, rather than a viable reality. In a community of interdependent nations the domestic or foreign policies of state A frequently have a direct effect on the affairs of state B. There is disagreement about whether intervention has taken place when the actions of A—and even inactions—seriously affect B but have not been primarily designed to affect B. If, as many international lawyers contend, intent to intervene is essential to establish the fact of intervention, the difficulty of proving intent seriously impedes accurate findings. For instance, the United States stopped the exportation of scrap metal to Japan prior to World War II, giving national defense needs as the reason. Japan claimed that the measure was intended to force a change in its military policies. It was difficult to prove at the time which claim was correct.

A third problem is tied to the question of responsibility of a state for the actions of its nationals. Citizens of country A, enraged about the treatment of religious minorities, revolutionaries, or foreign business establishments in country B, may openly or covertly interfere in the politics of country B to change policies that they think are offensive. It remains unsettled whether and under what circumstances their government becomes implicated by their activities.

The problem of accurate identification of interventionary actions was of minor significance in the eighteenth and nineteenth centuries because intervention in the affairs of other states was deemed permissible under international law. In fact, rulers in Europe considered intervention a moral duty to uphold their common culture and to protect the political status quo. When the status quo was threatened by the French Revolution, the major European powers pledged support of interventions that would uphold the existing balance of power and maintain established governments. Numerous interventions took place for these causes. For example, Prussia, Austria, and Russia intervened in Spain, Naples, and Piedmont in 1820 to suppress revolution against the established governments. Similarly, from 1827 to 1832, during the Greek war of independence Britain, France, and Russia repeatedly intervened in the internal affairs of Greece and Turkey to maintain the balance of power in the Middle East. Other interventions aimed to protect religious groups and minorities. At the time the United States appeared on the world scene as an independent nation, international law and practice thus sanctioned a broad right of intervention to protect the interests of nations strong enough to exercise this right.

International developments soon changed the concept of unquestioned legality of all interventions; this raised the problem of defining the nature of legal and illegal interventions. The decline of autocratic monarchies and the rise of democratically controlled nations in the wake of the French Revolution had weakened the idea of a community of nations. Democratic and autocratic governments had little in common except a reciprocal fear that one was determined to destroy the other. They did not share the sense of kinship and personal moral obligation that had united the crowned heads of Europe. Nor did they agree about the most advantageous policies for Europe and the aims

worthy of individual or collective intervention.

Fearing each other, European states wanted to make sure that they would be able to conduct their affairs independently. They therefore looked to the theory of state sovereignty and to claims of an inherent freedom of self-determination as foundations for legal restraints that would protect them from unbridled interventionism. Gradually, the efforts of small nations, supported by larger countries opposed to interventions to sustain absolute governments in Europe, undermined the concept of an unlimited right of intervention. The notion of a duty of intervention was replaced by the concept of a duty of nonintervention.

By the middle of the twentieth century, changing legal philosophies, buttressed by a number of specific resolutions and multilateral treaties, including the Montevideo Convention on the Rights and Duties of States (1933) and the United Nations Charter (1942), had made it a general rule of international law that states may not interfere in matters customarily deemed to be the exclusive purview of another state. A state's internal affairs and its relations with third parties are inviolable. While nonintervention is the general rule, it is still apparently limited by a right of intervention in cases where the current or imminent actions of one state endanger vital concerns of another state or of the community of nations. The clamor of small states for a total prohibition of all interventions has never been heeded.

The general rule that states may intervene in the affairs of other states to protect their own vital interests has been difficult to apply because there is no agreement on the definition of "vital interests." Are the interests that may be protected limited to matters of military security, or do they include major economic and social stakes? Must the danger be imminent or is there a right of preventive intervention? Is it a vital right to protect the property of one's citizens from physical harm in states where effective government has collapsed? Who determines that vital interests are endangered and that intervention is needed to protect them? What is an equitable balance between the safeguarding of vital interests of the intervening state and those of the subject of intervention? If a state violates the human or political rights of individuals within its borders, or if its actions endanger international peace, do members of the international community have the right to interfere to enforce the norms of the international community? May they intervene on behalf of established governments under attack by revolutionary forces within their own borders? The answers to these questions remain moot.

These problems are further clouded by vociferous statements of political activists who claim that interventions on behalf of "good" causes, as they define them, are legal and a moral duty, while interventions for "bad" causes are illegal. Such causes range from aiding persecuted individuals to the duty to provide peoples with good governments, to the obligation to stop civil wars or bring about the victory of the right side.

A second area of controversy concerns the means of intervention. There is substantial consensus that illegal intervention has occurred when a state dispatches armed forces to the territory of another. The Kellogg-Briand Pact, the Covenant of the League of Nations, and the United Nations Charter are examples of international agreements outlawing such armed interventions. There is far less agreement about the legality of the vast array of nonmilitary pressures by which states can affect the affairs of other states. These include economic pressures, such as an offer or withdrawal of loans, trade, or aid, including military supplies; political pressures, such as granting recognition to an acceptable government to bolster its power, and the withholding of recognition from an unacceptable government in hopes of toppling it; and psychological pressures, such as expressing support for one side in a revolution, denouncing the policies of another state, or excluding it from international meetings. There is a good deal of disagreement about which of such economic, political, and psychological pressures are legitimate exercises of a state's right to conduct its affairs with others as it pleases, or undue interferences in the affairs of another state.

A third area of dispute involves the validity of consent to intervention. Many legal experts contend that intervention is legal if it is carried out pursuant to treaty rights or in response to an invitation by an incumbent government. Others dispute the legality of such interventions because treaties granting the right to in-

tervention and requests for intervention frequently spring from duress or are initiated by unrepresentative governments, eager to keep themselves in power. Whether these factors invalidate the consent expressed in the treaty or invitation is a controversial legal question.

A related problem involves the right of collective intervention. For example, because member states of the United Nations have agreed in principle to collective interventions, is this tantamount to automatic approval of all interventions by the United Nations? Can a nonmember of the United Nations validly argue that collective intervention directed against it is illegal because it has not given prior consent?

The official position of the United States on legality and illegality has generally leaned toward a fairly broad construction of the right of intervention. Presidents and secretaries of state have argued since the end of World War I that international law permits states to retain the right to determine which of their national interests may be protected through intervention and the occasions when intervention is required. Likewise, states retain the right to intervene individually when collective intervention machinery fails to operate efficiently. At the same time, the United States has, over the years, narrowed the scope of American interests defined as vital enough to justify protection through intervention. Examples of circumstances claimed as justifying intervention include the establishment of Soviet missile sites in Cuba and aid to noncommunist parties in Italy when communist parties attempted to seize power with Soviet help.

The determination of what constitutes legal intervention has been further complicated by the fact that it is derogatory to charge a government with the practice of intervention. In popular parlance intervention has become equated with the policy of the bully and oppressor, while nonintervention is the hallmark of the virtuous nation. These evaluative connotations cause governments to avoid the label of "intervention" for lawful interventions and to use deceptive names instead, such as "interposition" or "police action." Likewise, illegal interventions are disguised as legal activities by using deceptive names or spurious legal justifications. Actions that do not constitute intervention, or which are legal intervention, are given the false taint of illegality by attaching the intervention label to them. Such misuses of political terms make it difficult to ascertain prevailing views within the community of nations on the precise nature of intervention and the criteria by which one can judge whether intervention has occurred and is legal or illegal.

THE POLICY

If one were to draw a curve charting the number of American interventions over a two-hundred-year span, it would begin and end at a fairly low point, reach a peak roughly at the center, and show several lesser fluctuations during the years of ascent and descent. The major rationale for this ebb and flow of interventionism is the recurring view that the United States is in danger if its hegemony in the Western Hemisphere is not clearly assured. The United States has intervened in the affairs of other nations, or seriously considered intervening, to prevent or foil attempts by powers on other continents to gain a foothold in the Western Hemisphere from which they might mount an attack on the United States; to maintain balances among powers in Europe and Asia so that no single power might become strong enough in these regions to launch an assault on the Western Hemisphere from abroad; and occasionally to establish American strategic and economic bases abroad in order to protect its vital connecting routes to other parts of the world.

When challenges to hegemony were deemed minor, or when interventions were urged for goals not clearly involving the protection of hegemonial interests, the United States has generally ruled out intervention. A major exception has been the policy of intervening on behalf of American citizens abroad whenever their lives and property were threatened by political events in a weak foreign country. American statesmen have generally viewed the protective aspects of such actions as paramount and the interventionary aspects as strictly subordinate. Protective interventions, if limited to that purpose, were ordinarily not counted in the record of interventions, at least not by American officials. The target country often viewed the matter differently.

While the question of protection of the security of the nation has been the major criterion by which the United States has determined whether interventions should be considered as policy options, additional considerations have influenced specific policy decisions. Foremost, particularly in the early years of the country, was the question of capability to undertake effective intervention. Intervention usually requires substantial military, economic, and political resources. When the United States lacked such resources or was already using them to their fullest extent, it could not spare them for interventions.

The balance between political gains and disadvantages derived from the intervention is also important. Intervention by one state may spur counterintervention by another. It may alienate the government and people of the state against which it is undertaken. It may antagonize other members of the community of nations. The chances that it will accomplish the objectives for which it was undertaken may be slim. All these factors are weighed in determining whether a particular intervention is advisable.

Policies of intervention, like other foreign policies, also tend to become entangled with events on the domestic political scene. Political competition for the allocation of human and material resources for various goals may lead to strong opposition to the expending of resources for a particular intervention. In the years before the Civil War, many interventions were appraised within the context of the pro-slavery-antislavery dispute. Later the policy became entangled in the debate over the merits of imperialist expansion. Differences in the appraisal of individual situations also are important. Political leaders often disagreed about whether hegemonial interests were really involved in a particular situation and whether intervention was likely to produce the anticipated results. Political partisanship played a part in opposing or supporting particular interventions. The policy of intervention and nonintervention, however, has never carried a party label. Periods of plentiful and of scarce interventions have been unrelated to the partisan orientation of the government.

Public attitudes within the United States have also had a discernible impact on foreign policy choices. When the public mood leaned toward isolationism and concentration on domestic problems, interventions were chosen less frequently than when the public mood was expansionist or imbued with the idea that the United States, as a world power, must involve itself fully with external affairs.

The history of intervention and nonintervention policies can be divided into three periods. The first, in which the stress on nonintervention was greatest, encompasses roughly the first century of the nation's existence. Then followed an interlude of unabashed interventionism during the closing decades of the nineteenth century and the beginning of the twentieth century. This period ended with the depression years of the 1930's. Finally, there have been the frustrating decades since the 1930's when hopes for meeting dangers to the national interest through collective interventions have turned to dust. Despite a desire to abandon unilateral interventions, the United States has felt compelled to intervene repeatedly to safeguard its national security when American leaders have deemed it endangered by events in various parts of the world.

The First Century. During the first century of the nation's history, intervention was undertaken to consolidate control over the American mainland and adjacent regions. Territories held by European powers or in danger of being taken over by European powers were acquired or kept from passing under the control of a European rival or changing hands from a weaker to a stronger sovereign. Several major interventions to acquire Spanish Florida, and minor meddling in Texas and California, are examples. However, while the country was still weak compared to strong European powers, and during the turmoil of the Civil War and Reconstruction, interventions were undertaken only if the outcome seemed highly promising and few dire consequences appeared in the offing. For instance, intervention to acquire Canada was ruled out because of fear that it might bring war with Britain. Diplomatic activities to acquire Cuba were kept short of intervention lest they embroil the country in war with Spain and its allies. Likewise, intervention to annex the Dominican Republic was scotched by Congress. Intervention was also considered repeatedly during this period in order to keep European powers from intervening in the affairs of

Western Hemisphere states. Again, internal weakness kept the United States from pursuing its policies through intervention on a number of occasions when, at a later period, it would have intervened. For instance, the United States did not stop interventions by France in Mexico and Haiti to collect debts, nor did it halt incursions by Britain into Guatemala, Nicaragua, and Argentina. Verbal protests were made repeatedly, including objections against French intervention in Mexico to support a monarchy, Spain's intervention in Peru and annexation of the Dominican Republic, and Britain's acquisition of parts of Honduras. The United States also attempted to strengthen American influence in areas threatened by European intervention by expressing a strong interest in the fate of these regions. But the United States could do little more. Powerful influences in Congress and among the public opposed preventive interventions that various presidents had suggested to restore public order in Mexico and the Caribbean area or overturn military dictatorships and thereby prevent corrective measures by European powers. The United States even kept largely aloof from the efforts of European colonies in the Western Hemisphere to free themselves from control by their mother countries. Interventions by the United States in revolutions outside the Western Hemisphere were also kept to a minimum, although many revolutions were taking place in Europe to replace absolute monarchies with democratic governments. Later, the support of democratic factions and countries against absolute governments of a different sort would be deemed sound reason for intervention by the United States, but that time had not yet arrived.

The United States did intervene in China, Japan, and Korea beginning with Caleb Cushing's trade mission in 1844, to coerce them to grant trade privileges to American merchants. At the time this was the usual practice of foreign nations that wanted to trade with Asian countries. The eagerness of the United States to have its citizens participate in the spoils of trade in the Far East was explained as much by strategic as by economic considerations. American leaders feared that the European powers would divide the Far East, particularly China, into spheres of influence from which other powers would be excluded. Land bases in China would give them control over the shipping lanes of the Pacific Ocean. The United States, unless it supported retention of control by the weak Asiatic powers or secured spheres of interest of its own, would be deprived of Pacific outposts to protect its access routes to Asia. The United States therefore pursued a two-pronged policy in the area; it protested against increased domination by European powers, and it intervened to acquire trade privileges and to lay the foundations for ultimate acquisition of a number of naval bases in the Pacific.

The Imperial Period. The heady philosophy of the interventionist phase of American foreign policy is epitomized by Secretary of State Richard Olney's claim in 1895 that the United States had become master of the American continent "practically invulnerable as against any or all other powers." Consequently, "its fiat is law upon the subjects to which it confines its interposition." Within the next decade the United States would satisfy all its remaining territorial ambitions, largely through interventions and war with Spain. Puerto Rico, the Philippines, and Guam came under its control, as well as Hawaii and Samoa. Nonetheless, even during this period, reluctance to intervene did not disappear entirely. For instance, the Grover Cleveland administration resisted pleas for intervention in Cuba although intermittent civil strife on the island was deemed hazardous to American security.

From the standpoint of intervention policy, the most crucial territorial acquisition during this period was the Panama Canal Zone. It was acquired through interventionary policies that assured that the Panama region would break away successfully from Colombia and would grant ample concessions to the United States for construction and protection of an isthmian canal. The United States regarded the canal as a lifeline permitting its naval units to shuttle rapidly between the East and West coasts to guard against dangers emanating from Europe or Asia. To protect this vital route, the United States appointed itself policeman of the Western Hemisphere who must and did intervene frequently to restore political order in the small countries near the canal. American political leaders assumed that unrest automatically spelled danger to the canal area, warranting in-

tervention. No specific proof was required in a particular situation that an attack on the canal was imminent. In a number of Caribbean countries, the United States even secured treaty rights of automatic intervention in case of unrest. The most famous advance authorization for intervention was the Platt Amendment to the Cuban constitution, which was in force for more than thirty years.

In areas farther from the canal, interventions were undertaken with more restraint. During this period, Mexico was a source of great concern to American policymakers because of constant internal turmoil, a succession of brutal dictatorial governments, and serious attacks on American citizens and their property in Mexico. The United States used a number of interventionary pressures, particularly economic sanctions and arms embargoes, to control unrest in Mexico, but refrained from full-scale military intervention despite domestic pressures.

During the interventionary period the United States protested more strongly than ever before against European incursions into the affairs of the hemisphere. Boundary difficulties between Venezuela and Britain provide a good example. The United States intervened in the dispute contending that it had a general right to interpose in any conflict in which the political or territorial integrity of an American state was threatened by a non-American power. It claimed that it could insist on arbitration and the enforcement of the arbitration award, even if one of the parties opposed the award.

By nonrecognition of an undesirable government, the United States also intervened repeatedly, although not consistently, to overthrow authoritarian regimes, particularly military dictatorships that had come to power in Latin America. Regimes that had ascended through unconstitutional means and represented authoritarian philosophies were deemed potential sources of instability. They might produce internal unrest, encouraging foreign intervention that would threaten the hegemonial interests of the United States. It was hoped that nonrecognition would make it so difficult for the unrecognized government to conduct its political and economic affairs that it would be weakened and overthrown by democratic forces. While potential danger to the security of the Western Hemisphere usually was the motivating force for nonrecognition, at times the policy was used on purely ideological grounds. Several instances occurred during the Woodrow Wilson administration because President Wilson was loathe to recognize governments that had come to power by force or ruled undemocratically.

Major challenges to the international balance of power continued in Asia during this period. European nations and Japan were establishing spheres of interest at the expense of China. More assiduously than before, the United States aimed to prevent this by means of an open-door policy for China. This involved securing pledges by European nations and Japan to refrain from closing any part of China to access by other powers. The United States protested whenever other powers violated the policy, which it regarded as a guarantee of China's territorial integrity and independence. When protests failed, the United States did not usually attempt stronger pressures for fear that they might lead to war.

The United States did intervene in the Russo-Japanese War (1904–1905) to prevent Russia and Japan from encroaching on China's sovereignty. Later it refused to recognize damaging concessions extorted by Japan from China in the vain hope that this would produce a policy change on Japan's part. The United States also continued to engage in intervention designed to strengthen China economically and politically and to assure an American presence in the area to checkmate European power plays.

The peak of interventionism, if one judges by the frequency of interventions and the number of countries involved, was reached during the first two decades of the twentieth century. Besides numerous interventions in the Western Hemisphere and Asia, this phase included American intervention in World War I on behalf of the anti-German coalition. Ultimately, intervention led to full-scale American participation in the war.

In the postwar years there was a decline in the number of interventions. The weakness of European powers after World War I was one major factor. They no longer presented a real threat to the hegemony of the United States in the Western Hemisphere. No European power was strong enough to assume control over Europe or the tottering Chinese empire. Another major factor was the realization that many goals that the United States had tried to accomplish in the course of interventions in the Western Hemisphere could not be achieved through intervention. For instance, it had been impossible to lay the groundwork for politically stable, economically sound, and democratically governed states in the Caribbean area, despite lengthy American military interventions. Attempts to establish economic influence abroad and to use it for political purposes (known as dollar diplomacy) had also largely failed.

Lastly, interventions had aroused a great deal of opposition from other countries, particularly the nations of the Western Hemisphere, and from groups within the United States. The policy was attacked on legal, moral, and practical grounds as improper coercion of the weak by the strong for the selfish aims of the strong. Behind such charges lay a changing climate of world opinion that placed greater emphasis on the sovereign rights of small nations and condemned coercive diplomacy, particularly the use of military force, to achieve national objectives.

The Collective Security Phase. The dominant feature of American intervention and nonintervention policies after the end of the openly interventionist years was the desire to make interventions—particularly those involving the use of military force—collective enterprises of the world community or regional groupings. Dangers to the vital interests of the international community that would justify protection through intervention were to be carefully defined in advance. The United States hoped that they would encompass all the circumstances that had hitherto tempted it into individual interventions. Additionally, the United States expected to influence the policies of other countries through conditions attached to its economic and military aid policies. It did not consider such conditions interventionary. Rather, they were deemed the right of the donor to dictate the terms of a grant. Unfortunately, the goals set for collective intervention and conditional aid policies were not achieved.

Prolonged negotiations over many years made it possible to organize a collective intervention system in the Western Hemisphere.

INTERVENTION AND NONINTERVENTION

Spurred on by the United States and its supporters, the system was activated repeatedly to curb Axis and communist influence in Latin America. Strong objections by countries such as pro-Axis Argentina and Chile, and procommunist Cuba, Guatemala, and their supporters were overruled. On the international level, the League of Nations Covenant first, and the United Nations Charter and interpretive resolutions thereafter, also contained provisions for collective intervention to protect the vital interests of members of the community of nations. But agreement could never be reached on the kinds of menaces to which this machinery should respond. Nor was there agreement on identifying certain types of dangers, such as threats to world peace.

The weaknesses of the collective intervention machinery encouraged the United States to continue to determine unilaterally whether its security was menaced by particular international developments. When protective interventions seemed necessary, it would then try to initiate collective action. If this failed, or if the collective machinery could not be put into operation quickly and decisively enough to halt the danger, the United States claimed and continued to exercise a right of unilateral intervention.

Two major dangers, similar in nature, roused the United States to a large number of verbal, economic, political, and military interventions during this period. The first was the attempt of right-wing authoritarian regimes in Europe, and later in the Far East as well, to destroy the balance of power in Europe and Asia and to establish their own hegemony. The United States first intervened in World War II in Europe and Asia by verbal attacks and warnings directed against the dictators. It tried to engender and support policies of neutral powers that would be harmful to the dictators' aims, and it gave economic and military aid to their enemies. Along with other American countries, it interfered with the rights of belligerent powers to conduct hostilities on the high seas surrounding the Western Hemisphere in a band 300 to 1,000 miles wide. To protect the hemisphere from Axis footholds, the territorial status of European possessions in the Americas was declared frozen in 1940. Inter-American machinery was established to administer the possessions of subjugated European countries. Ultimately, when verbal, political, and economic intervention failed to halt Axis advances, the United States entered the war.

The victory of the Allied powers in World War II ended the menace to American security created by rightist totalitarian imperialism. New challenges to hemispheric safety soon arose from the attempts of the Soviet Union and other communist powers to spread their ideology and political and even territorial control over a widening circle of countries in Europe, Asia, and other parts of the world. American leaders believed that the United States had a legal right to intervene to halt communist advances because its own survival as a democratic country was deemed at stake. Every addition to the communist coalition diminished the potential of the United States to defend itself successfully against communist subversion and military aggression.

Interventions by the United States to halt or prevent the spread of communist control throughout the world explain most of its far-flung interventionary operations during the latter two-thirds of the twentieth century. In almost every case in which the United States had identified a situation as potential or actual communist intervention, it tried to work through collective action. These efforts failed frequently because other countries disagreed that communist intervention was imminent or because they feared the consequences of the spread of communism less. Moreover, struggles by national liberation movements to free their countries from foreign control or domestic tyranny and corruption had often become so entwined with insurgency by pro-communist forces that it was hard to fight communism without destroying liberation and reform movements. When the United States intervened unilaterally, claiming to act in the name of collectively approved principles to maintain established governments in power, its reputation as a champion of popular, honest government often suffered serious damage at home and abroad.

The United States intervened to prevent the ascendancy of communist governments in Eastern Europe by means of a policy of nonrecognition and economic pressures. It tried to checkmate Soviet influence in places like Iran, Turkey, and Greece. It aided anticommunist nations in the Middle East, particularly the new state of Israel, and pro-Western Jordan and Lebanon in their struggles against covert and overt attacks by Soviet-supported Arab nations. The United States sent aid and rescue missions to assist anticommunist forces in the Congo and, to a lesser extent, Angola. It used a number of interventionary tactics to bring about black majority rule in Rhodesia, South Africa, and Namibia, in hopes of preventing racial warfare in southern Africa which might provide a cover for further expansion of Soviet influence in the area. It also used interventionary tactics to keep Soviet influence in the Mediterranean and the Persian Gulf at bay. To strengthen noncommunist governments faced with strong domestic opposition from communist parties, and to support governments fighting against communist insurgents, the United States intervened in widely scattered parts of the globe, such as Central and Western Europe, the Far East, and Latin America.

In the Far East, intervention was used to prevent the expansion of communist control over much of Southeast Asia, particularly South Vietnam, Laos, Cambodia, and Thailand, and over South Korea. In Korea the United States intervened unilaterally in 1950 until a United Nations force could take over. The bulk of military power that was made available to the United Nations for collective intervention had to be furnished by the United States because other powers gave only verbal support. The Korean intervention and other interventions undertaken to stop the advances of communism made it clear that gains won on the battlefield could not be maintained without permanently stationing noncommunist forces in areas coveted by communist powers.

The most protracted and costly intervention to halt the advance of communist-controlled forces occurred in Vietnam. There the United States and a number of its allies attempted to support noncommunist governments against attacks by procommunist forces eager to reunite North and South Vietnam under a communist government. The fierce controversy over the legality and wisdom of the Vietnam intervention led to serious political cleavages within the United States and within the international community. Opponents of the inter-

vention claimed that the situation involved a domestic struggle between procommunist and anticommunist Vietnamese that did not seriously involve American security interests. The United States finally withdrew its military forces in 1973. Economic and military aid to the South Vietnamese government was discontinued in 1975 when communist forces had assumed full control and further resistance to the spread of communism in Southeast Asia appeared hopeless.

In many instances it is easy to refute charges of illegal interventionism by the United States because American policymakers based their actions on treaty rights providing for joint defense against communist attacks or on requests for help by anticommunist governments in various nations. But, as indicated earlier, the moral and even legal validity of many of these arrangements often is challenged when the agreements were concluded under circumstances that made it practically impossible for one party to decline or when the moral authority of the government to agree to intervention is questionable. Another, possibly more solid, legal defense for anticommunist interventions is the claim to a right of counterintervention. The United States acted in most instances in response to proved, presumed, or anticipated interventions by communist forces that were intervening around the world to guide politics to their advantage. It can be argued that, akin to the right of self-defense, there exists a right of preventive or curative counterintervention.

While it may seem at first glance that the United States missed no opportunity to intervene against the spread of communism, this was not the case. Many possibilities for intervention were bypassed because the threat of advancing communist influence was comparatively limited, because the costs of intervention seemed too high, or because the United States realized that it could not muster sufficient strength in faraway places to engage in effective intervention. A situation involving all three of these contingencies occurred on mainland China. The United States had initially given some aid to the forces of General Chiang Kai-shek to assist him in wresting control over China from the communists. When it became clear that only massive military involvement would save the Chinese mainland from communist control, United States policymakers in the period following World War II, in a highly contested policy judgment, decided against such a major commitment. Limited aid to Chiang Kai-shek, who had retreated to the island of Formosa, continued, however. Similarly, despite explicit declarations and implicit threats, interventions on behalf of noncommunist factions in Eastern European countries to help them shed communist control never materialized. Insurgents in East Germany in 1953, Poland and Hungary in 1956, and Czechoslovakia in 1968 received no official help.

Nor did the United States intervene in most instances when left- or right-wing dictatorships came to power in Latin America in the period after World War II, or when governments expropriated the assets of large American businesses without adequate compensation. Major exceptions to this hands-off policy occurred generally only in areas close to the American mainland and the access routes to the Panama Canal. For instance, the United States intervened to topple a left-wing anti-American government in Guatemala in 1954 by aiding exile forces attempting military invasion of their homeland.

To overthrow the communist government of Premier Fidel Castro in Cuba, the United States helped to plan and execute an invasion by anti-Castro Cuban refugees in 1961. The attack failed and the tactics of the United States were widely condemned as illegal. Few such charges were made a year later when the United States intervened in Cuban-Soviet relations by demanding removal of Soviet missiles stationed in Cuba. In the Cuban missile crisis, most Latin American states and most noncommunist members of the world community concurred that the security of the United States was sufficiently endangered by Soviet missiles ninety miles from its territory to justify intervention. Subsequently, the inter-American community acted jointly to exclude Cuba from the inter-American system and to embargo the shipment of arms and other goods to Cuba. This fell short of the collective break in diplomatic relations favored by the United States in response to Cuba's publicized plans to subvert other Latin American governments, if necessary by guerrilla violence and civil war. Venezuela, Colombia, and Bolivia had been singled out as primary targets. When the dominance of the United States over hemispheric relations declined in the 1970's, restrictions against Cuba were lifted one by one.

Another major intervention against a Latin American government was the attempt to forestall a leftist takeover in the Dominican Republic. More than 30,000 American troops were dispatched in 1965 to stop fighting between procommunist and anticommunist Dominicans in a manner that ultimately led to the defeat of the procommunist forces. Although the United States managed to involve the inter-American collective intervention machinery, participation by the Organization of American States did little to erase the bitterness within the United States, Latin America, and other parts of the globe about the initial failure of the United States to abide by its pledge to abstain from unilateral military intervention. Many observers doubted that the Dominican situation had presented a sufficiently serious threat to the security of the United States to warrant major preventive measures.

After costly, often fruitless interventions had soured American policymakers on benefits to be reaped from intervention, a renewed retreat from overt interventionism began in 1969. It was hastened by a policy of détente and bargaining between the United States, the Soviet Union, and mainland China that helped to reduce the climate of mutual fear that had spawned interventions earlier. The ascent of communist-controlled or communist-influenced governments was no longer deemed an ipso facto threat to the security of the noncommunist world. The United States reduced its interventions and military commitments in Asia. It tried to lessen occasions for intervention in the Middle East by pacifying the area and resuming more normal relations with countries that had drawn their support from the Soviet Union. It also took a more aloof stance toward the tumultuous politics of Latin America. Moreover, to avoid the onus of charges of interventionism, a number of interventions were conducted as covert enterprises. The activities of the Central Intelligence Agency, which contributed to the overthrow of the Marxist government of President Salvador Allende Gossens in Chile in 1973, are examples of the types of actions that were undertaken to weaken governments and policies deemed hostile and dangerous to the United States.

However, increased reluctance to engage in interventions and decreased concern about the dangers posed by the ascendancy of Marxist governments in various parts of the world should not be construed as a complete retreat from the use of collective or unilateral intervention to protect the worldwide security interests of the United States. Additionally, the more restrained approach to interventionism on behalf of security interests may be counterbalanced by increased interventionism on behalf of humanitarian and civil rights causes. President James Earl Carter, following policies reminiscent of the Woodrow Wilson presidency, proclaimed in 1977 that the United States would intervene on behalf of persecuted peoples in various parts of the world where states were denying human or civil rights to their citizens on account of race, religion, or political persuasion.

THE NONINTERVENTION DOCTRINE

How does this record of numerous American interventions during two hundred years of national history agree with the claim that the United States has always upheld the principle of nonintervention? How does it accord with the frequent declarations that nonintervention is the official policy of the United States? The answers require putting intervention policies into the perspective of available options, and also discussing the role that political doctrines play in the conduct of foreign affairs.

Countries, like individuals, rarely act with total consistency. Champions of peace do go to war; a preference for free trade may yield to protectionism when circumstances make protectionism highly advantageous. One generally characterizes a country's policies by prevailing trends within the policy and within the international community. In the case of American intervention policies, the large numbers of interventions are matched by an even larger number of occasions when intervention was eschewed, although it was a viable policy alternative. This was particularly true during the first century of the nation's existence when it first

proclaimed that nonintervention would be its preferred policy. It may again become true in the latter part of the twentieth century. During the interposing years, whenever intervention rather than nonintervention was the prevailing practice, it was deemed inexpedient to acknowledge this change openly because the nonintervention doctrine was a valuable policy instrument. Discrepancies between action and doctrine have created a good deal of confusion about the thrust of American intervention policy.

The American nonintervention doctrine has served three major purposes throughout the years, aside from its use as a guideline for policy. First, it was meant to indicate to other nations that the United States would object to interventions by other powers because it considered nonintervention as the normal rule to be applied by the world community. It was hoped that this declaration would deter European interventions directed against the United States and its neighbors.

Second, the doctrine was intended to inform the American people that pressures on their government for a policy of intervention were likely to be rejected on principle. Expectations were that this would deter interventions that the country could ill afford to undertake.

Third, once the principle had become venerable and established as right and moral conduct, it became useful as a psychological tool of politics. Many undesirable international activities could be readily condemned by labeling them as "intervention." Desired interventions could be excused by claiming that intervention was not involved, or that a particular intervention was within the scope of interventions permitted under the hallowed nonintervention doctrine. Putting policies within a framework of "moral" and "immoral" actions is particularly important for a democratic country where political leaders depend on the support of elected government officials and public opinion. Support can be more readily secured when policies can be defended as moral principles, rather than as complex bargaining schemes or maneuvers in political power games.

All three purposes, envisaged when formulators of American foreign policy from President George Washington onward advocated nonintervention, appeared to be particularly well served during the early years of the nation. When the country was most vulnerable to foreign intervention and ill equipped to intervene individually or collectively in faraway Europe, the doctrine was credited with keeping European powers from intervening in the affairs of the United States as a reward for American nonintervention in Europe's liberation struggles. The doctrine permitted American leaders to refuse most requests for humanitarian interventions and to defeat a large number of political interventions proposed by various political factions. The successes claimed for the doctrine strengthened faith in its value.

At first, the doctrine was generally expressed in absolute terms to give it the strongest possible impact. This formulation was never viewed as a renunciation of the presumably inalienable right of intervention to protect vital interests. Rather, it was adopted for its practical usefulness for American policy needs. That the nonintervention doctrine involved legal and political considerations was not stressed until 1842 when Secretary of State Daniel Webster alluded to its grounding in the legal doctrine of sovereign rights.

Because the absolute formulation of the doctrine was literally interpreted by many people, it grew embarrassing when the United States engaged in numerous interventions in the Western Hemisphere. Therefore American statesmen reformulated the doctrine so that it would specify the exceptional conditions under which intervention would be permitted. The ebb and flow of efforts to spell out the limits of nonintervention, without abandoning the nonintervention doctrine as a general principle, constitute the major aspects of doctrinal developments over the ensuing decades.

President James Buchanan's inaugural address in 1857 is an early example of reformulation. He declared it to be the nation's policy never to interfere in the domestic concerns of other nations "unless this shall be imperatively required by the great law of self-preservation." He did not specify the occasions when the law of self-preservation might apply and the ways in which such occasions could be identified. Buchanan also contended that the nonintervention doctrine did not preclude the duty of preventive intervention. When, as happened in Mexico in 1859, an American country was

afflicted by internal unrest which spilled over its borders, it was the duty of the United States to intervene to stop the unrest and thereby prevent intervention by other powers. Congress did not accept this argument at that time. But when it was revived and amplified during the closing decades of the nineteenth century, it became an accepted clarification of the scope of the nonintervention doctrine.

Officially, a number of major clarifications were labeled corollaries to the Monroe Doctrine. This served to maintain the aura that the nonintervention doctrine remained absolute. For example, the Olney Corollary of 1895 asserted the right of the United States to intervene in any conflict between an American and non-American power that endangered the security of the United States. Under the Roosevelt Corollary of 1904, the United States claimed an even broader right and duty to act as policeman of the Western Hemisphere. If any nation in the hemisphere permitted conditions on its territory that might invite intervention by another country, then it was incumbent on the United States to intervene to remedy these conditions and forestall intervention by others. The United States must assume this obligation because the Monroe Doctrine prevented other powers from exercising their right of intervention.

Many American political leaders were dissatisfied with the doctrinal and practical consequences of the Roosevelt Corollary. In an attempt to adhere more closely to the spirit of nonintervention, President William Howard Taft sought to control internal political affairs in other nations through economic, rather than military, pressures. Since the nonintervention doctrine did not prohibit intervention for the protection of nationals, his administration encouraged American business interests to settle in potentially unstable neighboring countries. If unrest occurred, despite their presence, the United States could then send protective missions as part of its right to protect citizens abroad. In this manner it could control the politics of unstable countries without violating restraints commanded by the nonintervention doctrine.

During the presidency of Woodrow Wilson, the nonintervention doctrine received yet another interpretation. Wilson's claim that the

United States must discourage dictatorships or unconstitutional governments in Latin America by refusing to recognize them was accompanied by strong professions that such interventions accorded with the principles embodied in the established doctrine of nonintervention. Destruction of unpopular governments, Wilson argued, freed foreign nations from undue restraints on their sovereign right to opt for democratic rulers. Intervention thus became a tool to enable nations to exercise their will, rather than a tool for coercing them into unwanted action.

While Wilson expanded the scope of the right of intervention on one hand, he also laid the groundwork for subsequent contractions of the right. His stress on the sovereign rights of states to determine their own fate, regardless of size, led to a series of international agreements that proclaimed the nonintervention principle as a prescription of international law except for individual or collective self-defense. Such agreements became part of the Covenant of the League of Nations and later the United Nations Charter.

Nations of the Western Hemisphere went even further than the rest of the international community. Through a series of agreements and declarations springing from successive inter-American conferences in the 1930's, Western Hemisphere countries, including the United States, adopted a principle of absolute nonintervention by individual countries within the Western Hemisphere. Aside from the right of individual countries to protect the personal security of their citizens, only collective intervention would remain lawful.

The United States was willing to bind itself to such absolute declarations because it believed that the collective intervention arrangements made in the Western Hemisphere and on the broader international scene provided a partial substitute for intervention by individual countries. At the same time, through a series of presidential declarations, it made it clearer than it had done in the early years that nonintervention pledges did not mean an abandonment of the right of self-defense in the absence of effective collective action. Whenever possible, the United States also tried to conclude mutual defense and economic assistance trea-

ties to provide a legal basis for aiding selected countries in resisting communist takeover.

Additionally, the United States explicitly asserted a right of counterintervention against illegal interventions by other powers. Secretary of State Cordell Hull declared that the nonintervention principle applied only to nations that respected the rights of others. As a powerful member of the community of nations the United States had a right and duty to intervene in order to prevent or correct illegal interventions occurring in countries that lacked the power or will to resist such interventions.

The dangers that would give rise to interventions were identified explicitly but broadly. In the 1930's and 1940's, American political leaders believed that world peace was menaced by efforts of the Axis Powers to expand their control over Europe and Asia. With variable success they sought to have these perceptions incorporated into multinational declarations that would take their place beside formal pledges of nonintervention. Suggestions that mutual nonintervention pledges by the United States and the Axis powers might be a better way to protect the United States were rejected by the administration of Franklin D. Roosevelt.

After the defeat of the Axis Powers, communism was viewed as the main danger to the national integrity and security of the United States and the world. In the Truman Doctrine, proclaimed in 1947, the United States declared broadly that unilateral or collective intervention was justified to protect any country in the world against communist rule. The peace and security of the United States and the world were at stake. The Eisenhower Doctrine, proclaimed in 1957, pinpointed some of the areas where intervention might be expected. Specifically, the integrity of Middle Eastern nations was declared to be vital to world peace and American interests. If nations in the Middle East were threatened by overt armed aggression by communist forces, the United States would come to their aid if they requested help.

The Truman and Eisenhower doctrines did not specify the conditions that might bring about interventions. Rather, like the nonintervention principle amplified by these doctrines, they were tailored primarily for psychological effectiveness. They were intended to give moral support to nations fearing communist attacks while deterring their potential attackers. It was hoped that policy pronouncements would take the place of remedial action. If action became necessary, pronouncements would serve as prior warnings to legitimize subsequent actions.

The retrenchment in overt interventions against communist expansion that took place in the 1970's made it appropriate once more to redefine the scope of the nonintervention doctrine to conform to the prevailing official interpretation. The Nixon Doctrine of 1970 expressed the principle that the United States did not consider it an obligation to protect other countries against communist intervention unless it had determined, in specific cases, that American security interests were involved. Even then, intervention was not the sole duty of the United States but was an obligation shared by all countries opposed to the overthrow of noncommunist governments by communist contenders.

Thus, the nonintervention doctrine has come almost full circle in its two-hundred-year history. It has gone from an absolute expression, tempered by the implicit exception that interventions for vital purposes were not precluded, to an emphasis on a broad range of exceptions to the doctrine, which left it little more than an empty shell. Then it has been reformulated in absolute terms, tempered by statements of exceptions stressing that collective or unilateral intervention will still be used by the United States to protect vital security interests. The policy implications of the current doctrine are that the United States, like all sovereign states, claims the right to protect its security by all means within its power—including intervention—whenever its leaders believe that this security is seriously endangered. Despite American capacity to intervene freely in the politics of most small nations, however, intervention will be a last resort, used only when danger is great and all other means have failed. The pledges of nonintervention made in the twentieth century indicate the policy preferences that will guide the United States in its choice of policy options.

BIBLIOGRAPHY

The most complete history of American intervention policies and the nonintervention doctrine prior to 1959 is D. A. Graber, *Crisis Diplomacy: A History of the U.S. Intervention Policies and Practices* (Washington, D.C., 1959). The most complete analysis of the legal basis for American interventions is Ann Van Wynen Thomas and A. J. Thomas, Jr., *Non-Intervention: The Law and Its Import in the Americas* (Dallas, Tex., 1956). A more recent brief history with a Latin American focus is William Everett Kane, *Civil Strife in Latin America: A Legal History of U.S. Involvement* (Baltimore, Md., 1972). Disparate viewpoints on the law and policy of intervention and nonintervention in the post–World War II period, particularly with respect to American involvement in the war in Vietnam, are presented in Richard A. Falk, ed., *Legal Order in a Violent World*, pt. 2 (Princeton, 1968), and *The Vietnam War and International Law*, 3 vols. (Princeton, 1968–1972). Brief yet comprehensive accounts of the most salient aspects of the law and politics of intervention and nonintervention in the contemporary world are Louis G. M. Jaquet, ed., *Intervention In International Politics* (The Hague, 1971); and Robin Higham, ed., *Intervention or Abstention: The Dilemma of American Foreign Policy* (Lexington, Ky., 1975).
[*See also* ANTI-IMPERIALISM; BALANCE OF POWER; THE COLD WAR; COLLECTIVE SECURITY; CONTAINMENT; DOLLAR DIPLOMACY; THE EISENHOWER DOCTRINE; IMPERIALISM; ISOLATIONISM; THE MONROE DOCTRINE; THE NIXON DOCTRINE; THE OPEN DOOR POLICY; RECOGNITION POLICY; THE TRUMAN DOCTRINE.]

ISOLATIONISM

Manfred Jonas

THE TERM "isolationism" has been used— most frequently by their opponents—to designate the attitudes and policies of those Americans who have urged the continued adherence in the twentieth century to what they conceived to have been the key element of American foreign policy in the nineteenth century, that is, the avoidance of political and military commitments to or alliances with foreign powers, particularly those of Europe.

The term itself is of relatively recent origin. Its first known application to the foreign policies of the United States was by Edward Price Bell, the London correspondent of the *Chicago Daily News*. In an article entitled "America and Peace" (*Nineteenth Century* [November 1922]), Bell was critical of what he called the essentially negative attitude of the United States toward international cooperation, but noted that the country was nevertheless in the process of moving gradually "from isolation into partnership." Pointing out that the United States had, despite strong misgivings, ultimately declared war on Germany in 1917, he concluded: "Her isolationism, such as it was, discovered that the strain of a formidable advance against freedom was more than it could bear."

The word "isolationist" was listed for the first time in the 1901 edition of the *Oxford English Dictionary*, although without any indication as to when or where it had been used in its political sense. Standard American dictionaries did not incorporate the word until 1922, and the 1933 supplement to the *Oxford English Dictionary* cites no political use of it before 21 April 1921, when it appeared in the *Glasgow Herald*. Mitford M. Matthews, in *A Dictionary of Americanisms on Historical Principles* (Chicago, 1951), makes a logical but erroneous inference from the listing in the *Oxford English Dictionary* (1901) and traces "isolationist" in a political sense to an article in the *Philadelphia Press* of 25 March 1899. This article, however, uses the word in a medical sense in connection with a smallpox epidemic in Laredo, Texas. The 1970 reprinting of the 1933 *Oxford English Dictionary* repeats the 1901 entry verbatim, including the misleading *Philadelphia Press* reference.

The scholarly literature on the subject of isolationism began in 1924 with the essay by J. Fred Rippy and Angie Debo, entitled "The Historical Background of the American Policy of Isolation" (*Smith College Studies in History*, 9), but the term itself was not prominently used until 1935, when a provocative and still too often neglected interpretation of it was offered by Albert K. Weinberg in *Manifest Destiny*. The major impetus for the serious study of isolationism, however, was provided by World War II and its immediate aftermath, when the United States for the first time genuinely assumed the mantle of a major power. American policy during the interwar years, which frequently had been described as isolationist, came then to be regarded as an anomalous one that required explanation and analysis. Isolation, it was argued, had generally been imposed on major powers only against their will, as in the case of France after the Franco-Prussian War (1870–1871) or of Great Britain in the 1890's. Although the speech by George Eulas Foster in the Canadian House of Commons on 16 January 1896 had led to a flurry of oratory concerning Britain's "splendid isolation," it was clear that the term had been used ironically more often than not and that British policy had been designed to help the empire emerge from that apparently undesirable state. Voluntary

496

ISOLATIONISM

isolation had been sought only by some smaller nations, such as Switzerland, as a way to avoid falling victim to more powerful neighbors, and by culturally threatened ones, such as China and Japan, as a defense against Western incursions.

The United States was the only major Western industrialized nation that had apparently displayed a positive interest in some form of isolation, and that phenomenon attracted the attention of scholars in the late 1940's, and with increasing frequency in the two decades that followed. Ray Allen Billington sought to give isolationism a geographic base in his "The Origins of Middle Western Isolationism" (*Political Science Quarterly* [March 1945]); Henry Nash Smith examined its relationship to "the myth of the garden" (*Virgin Land* [1950]); Samuel Lubell exposed what he took to be its "ethnic and emotional roots" (*The Future of American Politics* [1952]); and Wayne S. Cole explained it as an expression of the "needs, desires, and value systems" of American agricultural society (*Senator Gerald P. Nye and American Foreign Policy* [1962]). Extended analyses of isolationism were also published by Robert E. Osgood, who defined it as a form of "passive egoism" in his *Ideals and Self-Interest in American Foreign Relations* (1953); by Selig Adler, who stressed economic self-sufficiency, the illusion of security, and ethnic prejudices as causative factors (*The Isolationist Impulse* [1957]); by Arthur A. Ekirch, Jr., who explained isolationism as a policy designed to assure de facto independence after the American Revolution had been won (*Ideas, Ideals, and American Diplomacy* [1966]); and by Manfred Jonas, whose *Isolationism in America, 1935–1941* (1966) analyzed the assumptions underlying the isolationist position prior to World War II, and suggested that these indicated a survival of unilateralism bolstered by a fear of war. John Milton Cooper, Jr., has more recently made the claim that isolationism was "a political position with programmatic and ideological dimensions" somewhat akin to a political movement (*The Vanity of Power* [1969]), and a host of other scholars, including Edward McNall Burns, William G. Carleton, Alexander DeConde, Justus D. Doenecke, Bernard Fensterwald, Jr., Norman A. Graebner, Richard Leopold, Charles O. Lerche, Jr., Robert James Maddox, Jeannette P. Nichols, Leroy N. Riesel-

bach, Bruce Russett, Ralph H. Smuckler, Cushing Strout, Kenneth W. Thompson, Robert P. Wilkins, and William Appleman Williams have investigated the subject from the viewpoint of their respective disciplines.

While there continues to be considerable controversy about the precise meaning of the term "isolationism," about the relative importance of various factors in explaining the phenomenon, and about the overall importance and prospects of the isolationist position, certain areas of at least general agreement have emerged from the research. For example, it is clear that isolationists regarded themselves as traditionalists in foreign policy and regularly invoked the Founding Fathers, particularly George Washington and Thomas Jefferson, in support of their position.

Washington was the father of the first American neutrality act (1794), which incorporated both the principle of his Proclamation of Neutrality (1793) that the United States should pursue "a conduct friendly and impartial towards the Belligerent Powers" and the subsequently developed Rules Governing Belligerents. The neutral stance of the United States was noteworthy primarily because of its apparent incompatibility with the French alliance that had been concluded despite strong misgivings in 1778. Since France chose not to invoke the alliance in the 1790's, American neutrality remained unchallenged, and it developed into a tradition that was reasserted, at least initially, with respect to every major international conflict before World War II.

In his Farewell Address in 1796, Washington supplied the rationale for this policy and urged its continuance. He pointed out that "Europe has a set of primary interests which to us have none or a very remote relation," and advised his countrymen "to steer clear of permanent Alliances" and involvement "by artificial ties in the ordinary vicissitudes of her politics and the ordinary combinations and collisions of her friendships and enmities." Less than five years later, Jefferson put this advice in even more enduring phraseology in his first inaugural address. He insisted that American policy should continue to be based on the principle of "peace, commerce and honest friendship with all nations, entangling alliances with none."

Neither Washington nor Jefferson saw

themselves as advocates of a policy of isolation, and indeed that word had not yet migrated to the English language from the French at the time they expressed their views. Both men, in fact, sought to expand American contacts with the outside world. Washington vigorously espoused the expansion of foreign trade and promoted a series of commercial agreements on the model of the one negotiated with Prussia in 1785. Jefferson, although he ideally would have preferred the United States "to practise neither commerce nor navigation, but to stand, with respect to Europe, precisely on the footing of China," clearly recognized after he had become president the necessity of fostering commerce. Both presidents welcomed continued immigration and the influx of European ideas and culture.

Washington and Jefferson did not even rule out alliances categorically. Washington indicated in his Farewell Address that the new nation might "safely trust to temporary alliances for extraordinary emergencies." Jefferson advised President James Monroe in 1823 to accept Foreign Secretary George Canning's invitation to joint action with Great Britain against the threat posed to Latin America by the Holy Alliance. While reasserting that the "first and fundamental maxim [of the United States] should be never to entangle ourselves in the broils of Europe" and the second maxim, "never to suffer Europe to meddle with cis-Atlantic affairs," Jefferson nevertheless concluded that "the war in which the present proposition might engage us, should that be its consequence, is not her war, but ours," and that if "we can effect a division in the body of the European powers, and draw over to our side its most powerful member, surely we should do it."

The basic aim of both Washington and Jefferson was to safeguard the independence of a new and not yet powerful nation by avoiding, whenever possible, involvement in the military and political affairs of the major powers while, at the same time, expanding trade and commerce as a means of fostering national development. Although it is highly questionable that economic and political matters can be separated as neatly as was suggested by both Washington and Jefferson—and evidence to that effect was not lacking even in the early years of the new

nation—both presidents were carrying out the logic of the era of the American Revolution. Thomas Paine had pointed out in *Common Sense* (1776) that one of the advantages of breaking the connection with Great Britain lay in the possibility of assuming a position of neutrality with respect to a Europe "too thickly planted with Kingdoms to be long at peace" and thus promoting and protecting trade with all nations even in wartime. John Adams had urged the Continental Congress to enter only into treaties of commerce and "to lay it down, as a first principle and a maxim never to be forgotten, to maintain an entire neutrality in all future European wars. . . ." Were the fledgling United States to do otherwise, Adams feared, "we should be little better than puppets, danced on the wires of the cabinets of Europe."

Since the foreign policy of Washington and Jefferson proved serviceable, it was followed with reasonable consistency until the end of the nineteenth century. During this period the United States developed its trade and commercial relations to an extraordinary degree, absorbed European immigrants in unparalleled numbers, and engaged freely in the process of cultural exchange. The United States also displayed considerable interest in political and military matters outside its borders. It encouraged the revolutions in Spain's American colonies and with the Monroe Doctrine sought to protect the newly won independence of the colonies. The United States fought Great Britain and attempted to conquer Canada in 1812, and vied with the British for control of the Oregon territory in the 1840's. It followed the Greek Revolution and the European revolutions of 1830 and 1848 with sympathetic interest, and treated at least one of their leaders, the Hungarian Louis Kossuth, to a hero's welcome. The United States was also instrumental in bringing Japan, a truly isolated country, into contact with the world; and it acquired large amounts of territory from other nations, either by purchase or by conquest.

The United States sought consistently to avoid "entanglements," however, by either acting alone or, when that was not possible, refraining from action. Thus it took part in the Napoleonic Wars without entering into an alliance with France, and never made certain of the support of the British fleet by formal treaty, even though that fleet was essential to the effectiveness of the Monroe Doctrine. Despite some strong sentiments to the contrary, the United States consistently refused to commit itself to the active support of the European revolutionaries, and limited its treaty making during the entire nineteenth century to the settlement of specific disputes concerning boundaries, immigration, and fishing and sealing rights. The only treaty to carry even the suggestion of joint action with another power, the Clayton-Bulwer Treaty (1850) with Great Britain, which limited action by the United States with regard to the building of a transisthmian canal, has been called by historian Thomas A. Bailey "the most persistently unpopular pact ever concluded by the United States."

By the middle of the nineteenth century, this unilateralism had become so firmly established that it was above serious challenge. In rejecting, on 11 May 1863, an invitation to join with France, Great Britain, and Austria in an attempt to persuade Czar Alexander II to modify his Polish designs, Secretary of State William H. Seward cited Washington's Farewell Address as the basis for this policy, and applauded the hitherto successful resistance to "seductions from what, superficially viewed, seemed a course of isolation and indifference." It was the first known official use of the term "isolation" with reference to American policy, and it was used, of course, only to be rejected as inapplicable. "Our policy of nonintervention, straight, absolute, and peculiar as it may seem to other nations," concluded Seward, "has . . . become a traditional one, which could not be abandoned without the most urgent occasion, amounting to manifest necessity."

What made this policy peculiar to the United States was not the motivation behind it, but only the circumstances that allowed it to work. Americans, to be sure, had deliberately shaken off their major tie with Europe during the American Revolution and understandably had little interest in replacing it with other ties. Moreover, in 1776 Americans had acted partly out of a sense of uniqueness and of superiority to the Old World and its institutions, and they regarded it as essential to the success of the mission of the United States that its policies remain uncontaminated and free from foreign influence. The development of the traditional American foreign policy was also coeval with the first flowering of an assertive American nationalism. Nevertheless, the freedom of action that the United States sought to exercise during the nineteenth century is the ideal of all nation-states. Alliances, however desirable or even necessary under certain circumstances, inevitably circumscribe that freedom. The avoidance of alliances and the maintenance of neutrality in the quarrels of others is, therefore, a universally appealing policy.

For most nations, however, the policy is also self-defeating and dangerous since it is often incompatible with the continuance and further development of commercial and cultural ties, largely rules out assistance from others when that may be necessary, and invites attack by stronger neighbors. For the United States in the early nineteenth century, as a country of little economic and no military importance, without strong neighbors, protected by wide expanses of ocean and the polar icecap, and favored by a world balance of power that tended in most instances to safeguard its interest, the policy was not only appealing, however, but also practicable. Unallied and uncommitted, threatened neither by invasion nor loss of territory, and possessed of a vast, rich, and sparsely developed hinterland, the United States was able to act independently and at its own discretion in those rare cases in which events elsewhere in the world seemed to affect the nation's interests.

As long as this policy was regarded as natural and obvious, it provided no basis for factional disputes and required, therefore, neither ideological nor programmatic definition nor a specific label. Isolationism emerged as a distinctive and definable political position only when the foreign policy consensus derived from the teachings of Washington and Jefferson began to break down, a development that found its basis in the conditions of the late nineteenth century but full expression only in the period of World War I.

By the end of the nineteenth century, virtually all of the circumstances that had made the traditional policy of the United States possible had either disappeared or been greatly modified. With rapid industrialization and the opening of vast new lands to agriculture, the

United States had become a serious factor in the world economy, and was in the process of converting from an importer into an exporter of capital. The need for the protection of trade and investments, as well as the chauvinistic search for the sinews and symbols of power that infected all Western nations in these years, caused the United States to build a large navy and thus also to make itself into a military factor. At the same time, advances in technology and communications began to shrink the oceans, and the nineteenth-century balance of power—which, for all the abuse that had been heaped on it by American statesmen, had served the country well—was upset by the simultaneous rise to international prominence of Germany and Japan.

The United States responded to these changes with a more active foreign policy, which included the war with Spain, the acquisition of colonial possessions, and the enunciation of the Open Door policy. It did so, however, on the assumption that such actions were fully compatible with the foreign policy of the Founding Fathers, and the traditional consensus thus remained largely intact. Even the anti-imperialists at the turn of the century made surprisingly little of the fact that the acquisition of colonies would almost inevitably lead to involvement in the great power rivalries against which Washington had warned, and that the Open Door policy would have the same effect if attempts were made to enforce it. When the Senate ratified the Algeciras Agreement (1906) and the Hague Convention (1908), it could in good conscience add the proviso that agreeing to them was "without purpose to depart from the traditional American foreign policy."

Less than three months before the outbreak of World War I, the traditional policy was reasserted by Woodrow Wilson, who still insisted that "we need not and we should not form alliances with any nation in the world. Those who are right, those who study their consciences in determining their policies, those who hold their honor higher than their advantages, do not need alliances." The onset of hostilities automatically produced the traditional American response: a declaration of neutrality, and a reassertion of the policy of friendship with all and entanglements with none which, as an editorial in the magazine *World's Work* put it, "was made for us by wise men a hundred years ago. . . ."

World War I nevertheless proved to be the first clear indicator that the United States, by virtue of its new power position, would find it difficult, and perhaps also undesirable, to remain unentangled. Since the conflict pitted many ideological friends and major trading partners of the United States against a group of European autocracies—most particularly after the March Revolution (1917) in Russia—it proved extraordinarily difficult to heed Wilson's admonition to be "impartial in thought as well as in action." The wartime increase in trade flowed naturally into previously developed channels, and loans and credits largely followed the route of established business connections, thus not only favoring one set of belligerents and arousing the ire of the other but giving this country a tangible stake in the outcome of the war. Even aside from such specific considerations, the possibility that nations with political systems and economic aims different from those of the United States might dominate the world after the war could be ignored only with difficulty. For all of his genuine devotion to neutrality, Wilson himself was moved to his desire for a negotiated "peace without victory" at least in part because he found one of the other alternatives—the victory of the Central Powers—to be wholly incompatible with American interests.

The situation of the United States during World War I brought respectability for the first time to the proposition that, given the changed world position of the United States, the country might best protect its interests by more active cooperation with other nations, even if such a course led to commitments and alliances not in keeping with the traditional policy. Wilson's own entertainment of such ideas led him in time to espouse a League of Nations, in which he envisioned full-fledged American participation in a system of collective security. Others with similar views joined together in June 1915 to found the League to Enforce Peace, an American counterpart to the Netherlands-based Organisation Centrale pour une Paix Durable. Among the leaders of the new organization were former President William Howard Taft, President A. Lawrence Lowell of Harvard, and Hamilton Holt, the influential editor of the *Independent*.

This initial articulation of an approach to foreign policy, which contrasted to the traditional one, produced, in its turn, the defensive position that is generally called isolationism. In the context of the time, it amounted to an assertion, implicit or explicit, that changed world conditions had not made a departure from traditional policies either necessary or desirable and that entanglement in what continued to be regarded as the affairs of other nations was more dangerous to the United States than any conceivable result of continued noninvolvement. Among the early isolationists, in this sense, were Secretary of State William Jennings Bryan, Senators William E. Borah of Idaho and George W. Norris of Nebraska, and the pacifist-intellectual Randolph S. Bourne. On a popular level, such sentiments found support in the Hearst press beginning in early 1917.

Although the occasion for this development of an isolationist position was the debate over American entry into World War I, the actual declaration of war did not prove to be the really divisive issue. If the United States entered the war on its own volition and in defense of its own interests, such a step did not necessarily violate traditional policy. Accordingly, a number of confirmed isolationists in the Senate, for example, voted for war. Among them were not only Democrats like Charles S. Thomas of Colorado and Thomas P. Gore of Oklahoma, who might be considered to have put partisanship ahead of conviction, but also Republicans Joseph I. France of Maryland, Hiram Johnson of California, and Borah.

The issue of American entry into the League of Nations, by contrast, provided less ambiguity, and thus a better opportunity for the development of a consistent isolationist stance. Clearly the League was an alliance, an open-ended commitment of the very sort against which the Founding Fathers had warned. Wilson in fact promoted American participation in the international organization as "an entirely new course of action" made necessary by the fact that the isolation of the United States was at an end "not because we chose to go into the politics of the world, but because by the sheer genius of this people and the growth of our power we have become a determining factor in the history of mankind and after you have become a determining factor you cannot remain isolated, whether you want to or not." The isolationists generally agreed with the contention that isolation was no longer a realistic aim, if indeed it had ever been, but took sharp issue with the proposed policy reversal. "We may set aside all this empty talk about isolation," Henry Cabot Lodge of Massachusetts told his Senate colleagues in 1919. "Nobody expects to isolate the United States or make it a hermit Nation, which is sheer absurdity." But he warned at the same time against the injury the United States would do itself by "meddling in all the differences which may arise among any portion or fragment of humankind" and urged continued adherence to "the policy of Washington and Hamilton, of Jefferson and Monroe, under which we have risen to our present greatness and prosperity."

The rejection of the Treaty of Versailles by the Senate and the overwhelming ratification of that action in the election of 1920 can be regarded as a triumph of American isolationism. It was not, as has sometimes been argued, a return to an earlier policy, since that policy had never really been abandoned, but simply a reassertion of it in the face of the first real challenge it had faced. The isolationism of the 1920's was real, despite the continuing commercial expansion of the United States and despite the greater influence on world affairs that the country enjoyed. The traditional policy that lay at the heart of isolationism had always, after all, emphasized trade and commerce even while shrinking from political commitments, and American influence and the desire for it had traditionally been a component of the "mission" of the United States.

Nevertheless, the American position during the 1920's was in some ways an ambiguous one. The experience of World War I had increased the potential role of the United States as an economic, political, and even military factor in world affairs, and made some degree of coordination with other nations all the more important. At the same time, the war had served as an object lesson on the danger of international commitments. American intervention had clearly failed to make the world safe for democracy and thus apparently demonstrated the wisdom of the contention that meddling in the affairs of others was useless and self-defeating. The fact that this intervention had almost led to a total abandonment of the policy of the Founding Fathers only served as a further warning.

On the basis of such perceptions, the United States set out on a course that can best be described as one of cooperation without commitment, a course in no way incompatible with isolationism but operating on its periphery. The United States played a role in negotiations on disarmament and attempted to place the Open Door policy on a more formal basis. When the latter objective led in 1921 to the Four-Power Treaty calling for consultation in case of controversy, the Senate was quick to add the standard disclaimer: "The United States understands that under the statement in the preamble or under the terms of this treaty there is no commitment to armed force, no alliance, no obligation to join in any defense." During these years the most heralded diplomatic achievement by the United States, the Kellogg-Briand Pact (1928), although regarded as a positive contribution to world peace, formally committed the United States to no action of any kind and was strongly supported by leading isolationists, including the chairman of the Senate Foreign Relations Committee, Senator Borah. The isolationist consensus was restated by President Herbert Hoover as late as 1931. Although recognizing a greater interdependence among nations in the modern world, Hoover nonetheless distinguished between the path of the United States and that of other nations. He told his cabinet, "We should cooperate with the rest of the world; we should do so as long as that cooperation remains in the field of moral pressures. . . . But that is the limit." There were few dissenters.

During the 1930's the isolationist consensus was once again threatened, fatally undermined, and ultimately destroyed. It was also the time in which this position was most clearly defined and most ardently defended.

The threat to American isolationism emanated clearly from a world situation in which the totalitarian states—most notably Germany, Japan, and Italy—challenged the status quo, and with it the power position and ultimately the security of the United States. The traditional American foreign policy had always rested, at least in part, on the assumption that the United States was safe from attack and that American trade and ideas would continue to find acceptance regardless of developments in other parts of the world. By the end of the decade, however, it proved difficult for most Americans to counter effectively the rhetorical question raised by the formerly isolationist *Progressive* of Madison, Wisconsin: "If Hitler defeats England and the British fleet is destroyed, what becomes of our splendid isolation, with Hitler on the Atlantic side and Japan and Russia on the Pacific side?"

While world events thus undermined the premises on which the isolationist position had traditionally rested, the Great Depression provided a new and, for a time, persuasive rationale for it. Confronted by urgent domestic problems, the immediate impulse of the United States was to turn inward and to regard events outside its borders as distractions tending to impede the solution of problems at home. The depression also deflated confidence in the strength of the United States and in its ability to influence events elsewhere. Faced with evidence that much was wrong at home, many Americans abandoned the traditional belief that American institutions should serve as a model for the rest of the world. Others reasoned that the economic crisis had so sapped the nation's strength that it would be futile to intervene in international affairs. Both lines of thought led to essentially isolationist conclusions. Finally, the depression increased popular distrust of bankers and businessmen and thus the willingness to sacrifice even trade and commerce, if necessary, to maintain political and military noninvolvement. Because the reputation of the American businessman reached its nadir in the 1930's, the attempt was made to resolve the increasingly apparent dichotomy between "commerce and honest friendship with all nations" and "entangling alliances with none" not by increasing American political involvement but by circumscribing the then suspect commercial contacts.

Paradoxically, therefore, the years from 1934 to 1937, during which the nonserviceability of the traditional foreign policy was most clearly demonstrated, were the high-water mark of American isolationism. Beginning with the Johnson Act, which prohibited loans to countries in default on previous debts, and continuing with the establishment of the Senate's Nye Committee to investigate the munitions industry and the passage of the neutrality acts of 1935, 1936, and 1937, the United States sought to insulate itself from increasingly threatening world events. The rationale behind this policy offers the clearest expression of isolationist assumptions.

The purpose of the legislation of the mid-1930's was to make possible in the twentieth century the stance first adopted by the United States in 1794. Although the recognition that such legislation was necessary implied an acknowledgment that the world had changed since the eighteenth century, it also suggested that the United States might accommodate itself to these changes and maintain its traditional position of neutrality by simply taking certain relatively minor precautions. This assumption required a continuing belief that the vital interests of the United States were not substantially affected by events elsewhere; that Europe still had a set of interests "which to us have none or a very remote relation"; and that the country had become involved in other international quarrels, particularly in World War I, for reasons having little to do with genuine national interest.

The last of these beliefs was given powerful support not only by the conclusions of the Nye Committee, but also by the work of so-called revisionist historians who, at least since the appearance of Harry Elmer Barnes's *The Genesis of the World War* (1926), had been hammering away at the theme that the entry of the United States into war in 1917 had been brought about, contrary to the true interests of the United States, by direct and indirect Allied pressure, and by the machinations of bankers, brokers, and businessmen who had unwisely tied American prosperity to the cause of Great Britain and France. In the mid-1930's, Charles A. Beard and Charles C. Tansill were the most prominent of the historians who repeated this theme and implicitly or explicitly pointed out a "deadly parallel" to the situation that existed twenty years earlier. Walter Millis repeated the same arguments in his best selling *Road to War* (1935).

The neutrality legislation of the 1930's clearly reflected the isolationist contention that the United States went to war in 1917, and might do so again, not because its interests were threatened, but merely because its activities, particularly those relating to trade, produced incidents that blurred judgment and inflamed passions. By prohibiting loans and the trade in arms, by keeping Americans off belligerent vessels, and by insisting that title to all war matériel had passed to the purchaser and that such matériel be carried only in non-American ships, the United States expected to avoid such incidents and thereby involvement in war.

In its application the neutrality legislation demonstrated the degree to which these isolationist beliefs no longer reflected the realities of the world situation. The United States had acquired a far greater stake in the international power balance and exerted far more influence on it than the isolationists were prepared to admit. Neutrality legislation did not reduce this American influence, but simply redirected it, not necessarily into desirable channels. In general, the American policy gave aid and comfort to would-be aggressors since it offered tacit assurance that this country would not actively oppose their actions as long as they did not directly threaten the United States. More specifically, the neutrality legislation in effect aided Benito Mussolini when applied to the Italo-Ethiopian War and Francisco Franco when applied to the Spanish Civil War. The legislation also tended, at least in the first of these cases, to undercut possible peacekeeping actions by the League of Nations.

Since even most isolationists agreed that the victories of the Italian and Spanish fascists were less desirable from the American viewpoint than were other possible outcomes, the wisdom of a policy that contributed to such a result came increasingly to be questioned. "In the long run," Norman Thomas, a staunch isolationist and proponent of neutrality legislation, told President Roosevelt in December 1936, "it is not peace for the world, even for America which will be served by applying to the Spanish rebellion a general principle which should be asserted more rigorously than is yet the case in Congressional legislation concerning neutrality in international law." As a socialist who supported the elected government of Spain and

ISOLATIONISM

abhorred Franco, Thomas was caught in a dilemma that could not be resolved in isolationist terms.

The two events that finally destroyed the rationale for American isolationism altogether were the fall of France in June 1940 and the attack on Pearl Harbor in December of the following year. The first event created a profound sense of insecurity in the United States by raising fears not only of an Axis victory, but also of a direct attack on this country in the event the British fleet were either destroyed or captured. The rise of the Committee to Defend America by Aiding the Allies, the first influential interventionist organization, was a direct result of this fear, and the success of that organization produced, in turn, the establishment of the America First Committee, the last stronghold of the embattled and now outnumbered isolationists. The attack on Pearl Harbor demonstrated how vulnerable American territory had become to actual attack. Under these circumstances cooperation and even alliance with others to forestall further danger seemed dictated by prudence and common sense. "In my own mind," one of the most outspoken and influential of the congressional isolationists, Senator Arthur H. Vandenberg of Michigan, confided in his diary some time after the event, "my convictions regarding international cooperation and collective security for peace took firm form on the afternoon of the Pearl Harbor attack. That day ended isolationism for any realist."

Vandenberg was essentially right. Both the traditional American foreign policy, based on the precepts of Washington and Jefferson, and isolationism, which meant a continuance of that policy in the twentieth century, had rested on the assumption that Europe's interests were sufficiently different from those of the United States and that the United States was sufficiently safe from attack to make political or military involvement with Europe unnecessary. If unnecessary, such involvement was undesirable by definition, since it could only limit the country's freedom of action and thereby its sovereignty without bringing any compensating benefits. Although these assumptions had been challenged by world events since the end of the nineteenth century, they had never before

been clearly disproved. When the assumptions were disproved, the isolationist structure was no longer a viable one, and the United States moved rapidly not only into tacit alliance with Great Britain and into war as a formal ally of the anti-Axis powers, but also into plans for and participation in the United Nations and a host of postwar military alliances, capped by the North Atlantic Treaty Organization in 1949.

What had been destroyed, of course, had only been the practicality of the isolationist position. Its emotional appeal remained largely intact, as it had in nations for whom isolationism had never been a realistic position. Isolationist rhetoric, therefore, continued to be used by some opponents of American postwar policies. In the debate over military aid to Europe, which began late in 1950, Joseph P. Kennedy, the isolationist former ambassador to Great Britain, spoke of "unwise commitments" in Berlin and Korea and scoffed at the idea that the United States had any interest in or responsibility for the defense of Western Europe. Herbert Hoover argued that the Americas were still "surrounded by a great moat," and referred once again to "the eternal malign forces of Europe" with which this country should have as little as possible to do. Senator Robert A. Taft of Ohio, a leading prewar isolationist, minimized the danger that this country faced from the Soviet Union in terms virtually identical to those in which he had discussed the threat emanating from Nazi Germany.

Although some observers promptly labeled this outburst "the new isolationism," it bore little practical relation to true isolationism. Hoover, in fact, strongly favored an American commitment to the defense of a "Western Hemisphere Gibraltar," the bastions of which were Great Britain, Japan, Taiwan, the Philippines, and, possibly, Australia and New Zealand. Taft recognized that an effective international organization would give the best assurance of world peace and, therefore, of American peace, and stated flatly that "nobody is an isolationist today." The whole discussion revolved largely about the extent of American military and economic aid to other nations, and not about the necessity for such assistance. It turned on the question of how the cooperation

504

among allies of the United States might best be secured, not how American alliances could be terminated most rapidly.

Isolationism was simply no longer viable in a world in which neutrality for the United States was impossible, if for no other reason than that the Soviet Union regarded the United States as its primary foe; in which the United States could clearly not be indifferent to wars in Europe or Asia that affected the world power balance; and in which the development of nuclear weapons and intercontinental missiles had eliminated the margin of safety that geography had once provided. In short, isolationism was made practically impossible when the United States emerged as the dominant world power in an unstable world. Just as "splendid isolation" had had emotional appeal but dangerous practical implications for Great Britain at the close of the nineteenth century, so isolation in any form posed a threat to the position of the United States in the postwar world.

As the commitments of the United States multiplied and American foreign policy, particularly in Southeast Asia, proved ineffective and far too costly, the postwar foreign policy of the United States was subjected to increasing criticism. Because many critics urged that American commitments be reduced, that there were limits to American power, and that the United States should withdraw from some of its more exposed positions, including Vietnam, they were referred to as "neo-isolationists," and sometimes they even applied that label to themselves. Yet spokesmen for this point of view, such as former Senators Wayne Morse of Oregon, Ernest Gruening of Alaska, and J. William Fulbright of Arkansas, Senator George McGovern of South Dakota, columnist Walter Lippmann, and former State Department counselor George F. Kennan, did not fall, in any meaningful sense, within the isolationist tradition. All favored increasing the role of the United Nations, the maintenance of key alliances of the United States, and new negotiations and agreements with such countries as the Soviet Union and the People's Republic of China. None suggested, even remotely, that the cure for current problems might be found in a return to the foreign policy of the Founding Fathers.

Isolationism may thus be regarded as a phase in the development of American foreign policy, a phase which has now been superseded and into which reentry is no longer possible. Born of the universal aspiration for unrestricted national sovereignty and the peculiar relation of the United States to the rest of the world in the nineteenth century, it was staunchly defended and raised to the level of dogma when world events in the twentieth century threatened the consensus that had developed around it. In an ever-shrinking world and for a country with a dominating position in that world, however, it has lost the possibility of practical application.

BIBLIOGRAPHY

Selig Adler, *The Isolationist Impulse: Its Twentieth-Century Reaction* (New York, 1957), is the most comprehensive treatment of twentieth-century isolationism. Wayne S. Cole, *America First: The Battle Against Intervention, 1940–1941* (Madison, Wis., 1953), is the only full-scale study of an isolationist organization. John Milton Cooper, Jr., *The Vanity of Power: American Isolationism and the First World War, 1914–1917* (Westport, Conn., 1969), describes the emergence of an isolationist position before World War I. Alexander DeConde, ed., *Isolation and Security* (Durham, N.C., 1957), brings together a number of stimulating and perceptive essays. Justus D. Doenecke, *The Literature of Isolationism: A Guide to Non-Interventionist Scholarship, 1930–1972* (Colorado Springs, Colo., 1972), is the best bibliographic guide to isolationism. Bernard Fensterwald, Jr., "The Anatomy of American 'Isolationism' and Expansionism," in *Journal of Conflict Resolution*, 2 (1958), offers the best psychological explanation for the American isolationist phenomenon. Norman A. Graebner, *The New Isolationism: A Study in Politics and Foreign Policy Since 1950* (New York, 1956), is the most comprehensive effort to define a postwar "isolationism." Manfred Jonas, *Isolationism in America, 1935–1941* (Ithaca, N.Y., 1966), is the most detailed analysis of the actions and arguments of the isolationists prior to World War II. Samuel Lubell, *The Future of American Politics*, 2nd rev. ed. (Garden City, N.Y., 1956), is a lively and perceptive presentation of the "ethnic" explanation for isolationism. Robert E. Osgood, *Ideals and Self-Interest in American Foreign Relations: The Great Transformation of the Twentieth Century* (Chicago, 1953), treats isolationism as one aspect of an ongoing shift in the American foreign policy framework. Leroy N. Rieselbach, *The Roots of Isolationism: Congressional Voting and Presidential Leadership in Foreign Policy* (Indianapolis, 1966), gives the most ambitious behavioral analysis of congressional isolationism. Bruce M. Russett, "Demography, Salience, and Isolationist Behavior," in *Public Opinion Quarterly*, 24 (1960), offers the most serious challenge to ethnic and geographical explanations for isolationism. Albert K. Weinberg, "The Historical

Meaning of the American Doctrine of Isolationism," in *American Political Science Review,* 34 (1940), is the classic brief statement of what traditional American foreign policy was and what it was not. William A. Williams, "The Legend of Isolationism in the 1920's," in *Science and Society,* 18 (1954), argues that the absence of economic isolationism demonstrates the mythical nature of the whole concept.

[*See also* ALLIANCES, COALITIONS, AND ENTENTES; CONGRESS AND FOREIGN POLICY; INTERNATIONALISM; INTERVENTION AND NONINTERVENTION; NATIONAL SECURITY; NEUTRALITY.]

JOURNALISTS AND
FOREIGN POLICY

James Boylan

THE GROWTH of the United States foreign policy apparatus and the expansion of the mass media have brought about increasingly varied relationships between journalists and policymakers. Historians often used to write as if the press fulfilled only two relatively simple foreign policy functions: transmitting information about policy to the public and, through editorials, transmitting public opinion to the policymakers. Partly as a result of the accumulating body of research on public opinion and the effects of mass media, most students now view even past relationships as considerably more complicated. For example, in 1963 historian Frederick Merk expressed doubt that even the most popular American newspapers of the mid-nineteenth century published opinions that were widely shared by their readers.

Recent scholarship has attempted to offer more adequate explanations of the roles journalists and journalism play in the development of foreign policy. In 1950 Gabriel A. Almond, a political scientist, challenged the idea that the press serves only as a medium to transmit information between officials and the general public. Rather, he suggested, the press addresses not only a general audience but also the much smaller "attentive public" that keeps informed on foreign affairs. Moreover, he viewed the press influence on foreign policy less as the reflection of public opinion than as the voice of an elite pressure group.

More than a decade later (1963) another political scientist, Bernard C. Cohen, provided a more elaborate differentiation. He divided journalists' roles into "neutral" and "partici-patory" categories. Among the neutral functions he listed the most commonly recognized roles of the journalist as public informer-educator and as nonpartisan interpreter of policy; he added the less frequently acknowledged role of the journalist as an instrument of government—that is, the use of journalism by officials to carry out policy. In journalists' participatory roles, Cohen found functions analogous to those usually ascribed to interest groups, although in most cases journalists would claim to speak on behalf of the public or to express public opinion rather than a particular interest. Among the participatory roles, Cohen included the journalist as a critic, as an advocate of particular policies, and as an outright policymaker. By extension, of course, these functions can be viewed as roles not only of individual journalists but also of the institutions of journalism. There is plentiful evidence that journalism in each of these roles has played a part in United States foreign policy.

THE JOURNALIST AS INFORMER-EDUCATOR

In its role as informer-educator or transmitter of "straight" news, the press in America offers two kinds of information affecting foreign policy—reports of policy, policymaking, or reaction at home and correspondence from abroad. The latter is among the oldest functions of American newspapers, which came into being in colonial seaport cities largely to publish news off incoming ships. Similarly, the first news agencies of the early nineteenth century were formed to speed "harbor news." In the twentieth century, the volume and extent of international reporting have been enormously broadened with the growth of worldwide news agencies, instantaneous transoceanic transmission of words and pictures, and the development of media capable of offering overseas news to virtually entire populations simultaneously.

Such reporting from abroad, even when it does not deal directly with American actions, affects American foreign policy, for the very act of dissemination is likely to place a given foreign development on the agendas of interested publics and officials. As W. Phillips Davison has observed: "The mass media can divert a top official from matters he considers most important and force him to deal with a controversy he regards as minor; they can also make him face up to the important issues he might prefer to ignore. . . ."

While some reporting on policy and policymaking comes from overseas, most of it focuses on Washington, and on the White House and Department of State in particular. Although the increasingly important role of the president in foreign relations has turned White House correspondents willy-nilly into reporters of foreign policy, the specialists—the "diplomatic reporters"—are generally assigned to the State Department. So recent is the development of this specialty that only in the twentieth century has the department regularized its output to the press and its dealings with journalists. In 1909 Secretary of State Philander C. Knox created the Division of Information; in 1921 Secretary Charles Evans Hughes established its successor, the Division of Current Information, headed for many years (1927–1944) by Michael J. McDermott. After World War II, that division was succeeded by the more elaborate Bureau of Public Affairs, headed by an assistant secretary. Also since the early twentieth century, secretaries of state have given increasing attention to reporters, with regular news conferences initiated in 1915 by Robert Lansing. However, the accessibility of the secretaries to reporters, and the openness of their dealings, have varied greatly.

Routine reporting on foreign policy is usually a product of considerable cooperation between correspondents and officials. So close is this relationship, and to such great mutual advantage, that Davison has described officials and reporters as actors in a single "diplomatic reporting network"—that is, officials want friendly, informed reporting; reporters want friendly, open sources. So considerable is the mutual trust that journalists receive much information on a confidential basis; for example, in the late 1950's New York Times columnist James Reston kept the secret of the U-2 "spy plane" flights over Russia for more than a year.

But reporters sometimes want more than officials are willing to offer. As must be the case in a system that depends on an unofficial, independent press, there are clashes over the availability of information. The government's position has generally been defensive. Elaborate classification systems have been developed to keep foreign policy and defense information secret for years. In times of crisis, the press has been urged or forced to withhold information officially designated as affecting national security. Even in peacetime, there is constant tension between the "competing demands of diplomacy and democracy," as Cohen put it—the need for confidentiality in negotiations and the need for an informed public.

The press frequently has been able to breach diplomatic privacy, usually with the aid of disaffected insiders. As early as 1795, the *Philadelphia Aurora* received and published extracts from the still-secret text of Jay's Treaty, which it opposed. Similarly, the *New York Herald* in 1848 published the Treaty of Guadalupe Hidalgo, concluding the Mexican War, while the terms were still secret, pending Mexico's approval. In the twentieth century, the roster of such "leaks" has grown. Among the most notable was Reston's exclusive reporting in the *New York Times* of details of closed sessions at the Dumbarton Oaks Conference (1944), called to plan the postwar United Nations organization; Reston's source was the Chinese delegation.

However, the most imposing leak of official documents—on so grand a scale as to exceed the category—was the publication by the *New York Times* and other newspapers in 1971 of the Pentagon Papers. These papers, which constituted a secret documentary study of the development of American policy in Vietnam, were given to the press by one of the study's partici-

JOURNALISTS AND FOREIGN POLICY

pants, Daniel Ellsberg. Although the study did not describe policies then current, the Nixon administration sought to halt publication through court action—the first instance in peacetime of an official attempt to impose prior restraint on the press. The Supreme Court decided, 6 to 3, to permit publication to continue, although it did not sanction publication of classified information in every instance. The government's attempt to try Ellsberg failed on a technicality.

Such incidents are outcroppings of a contest that has continued with increasing intensity. Even in seeking to carry out the supposedly neutral function of transmitting information, journalists have frequently chosen the role of adversary. Moreover, the information itself, even when it is not presented in a partisan manner, has inevitably had a political impact. In this sense, hardly any journalism can be called strictly neutral.

THE JOURNALIST AS A TOOL OF GOVERNMENT

The day-by-day work of a journalist unavoidably makes him a tool of the government, serving policymakers' purposes to an extent; an important part of the job is to give the public an accurate summary of official statements and actions. To a degree, Reston wrote in 1967, the reporter "delivers the news as the post office delivers the mail." The steadily increasing flow of official information, combined with the necessity for filling news columns and broadcast time, enhances this tendency; Davison has concluded that "the backing the government usually receives on foreign policy issues is due [in part] to the fact that the government view may be the only one that receives extensive mass media coverage."

Frequently, even reporting that does not deal with official actions nonetheless dovetails with policy objectives. The marathon network radio broadcasts of the Munich crisis of 1938 are credited with alerting the American public to the dangers of isolationism; Edward R. Murrow's radio reports from London during the Battle of Britain helped create support for the administration's policy of aiding Britain. With only minimal official encouragement, moreover, many journalists joined in helping to

change the American view of the Soviet Union in World War II to that of worthy, democratic ally; afterward, with the coming of the Cold War, they helped erase the image.

Sometimes the policy use of journalism is more specific. A "cover story" can be issued to reporters to conceal developments the government wants to keep secret. In 1960 the State Department, vainly hoping to obscure the nature of the U-2 surveillance flights over the Soviet Union, issued a story, soon shown to be false, that the Russians had shot down a weather plane. In October 1962 reporters were asked to write that President John F. Kennedy had a cold, when actually he was returning to Washington from Chicago because of the missile crisis in Cuba. These and other misleading statements issued at that time led to the notorious defense by Arthur Sylvester, Pentagon press secretary, of the government's "right to lie" in a crisis.

Another policy use of the mass media is called "signaling." That is, one side in a dispute can send, via news stories, information that it does not care to state officially. Such channels, used by both sides, prepared the way in 1949 for easing the Soviet blockade of Berlin. Similar signals were passed in the crises over China's offshore islands in 1958, over Laos in 1961, and in the Cuban missile crisis. Negotiations to end the Vietnam War began in 1968 after a long, irregular sequence of such messages. Such practices place journalists in a quandary, for they may not know whether, as James Reston put it in 1967, an official "is speaking to them as reporters or seeking to use them as instruments of psychological warfare. . . ."

Occasionally officials choose to bypass journalists altogether by addressing the public directly. The president and members of his official family have enjoyed the prerogative, authorized in custom rather than law, of requisitioning radio or television time. Franklin D. Roosevelt was the first president to use such opportunity extensively, and subsequent presidents have continued the practice. In the first three years of his administration, Richard M. Nixon preempted television time on three networks twelve times for foreign policy speeches. With the filming of presidential news conferences during the administration of Dwight D.

509

Eisenhower and the initiation of live conferences by John F. Kennedy, a further weapon was added to the official arsenal. However, government officials have complained bitterly about journalists' efforts to place such presentations in a news setting through such devices as post-speech analyses.

The government also has attempted to offer officially approved materials as independent journalism. One such case was the placement in the periodical *Foreign Affairs* (1966) of an article on the Vietcong that had originated with the Central Intelligence Agency (CIA), which also had secretly subsidized publication of books on foreign policy matters reflecting official views. Of a somewhat different character was the revelation in 1976 that the CIA had created false news stories, which it had offered to foreign news agencies; some of these ultimately found their way into the American press. In addition, the CIA placed a few American correspondents overseas on its payroll, but little is known of the extent to which their reports were affected.

Not all propagandizing by American news media has been done on behalf of Washington. Agents for foreign powers have long fed material to the American press: while negotiating the Treaty of Washington (1871), the British minister entertained and propagandized reporters. Much of the coverage by New York newspapers of the Cuban crisis of the 1890's was originated (or fabricated) by a rebel propaganda bureau in New York. During World War I, many American newspapers served, usually unwittingly, as outlets for British propaganda, in part because much American reporting from Europe was subjected to British censorship. The newspapers belonging to William Randolph Hearst, on the other hand, were penetrated by propagandists for the Central Powers.

Very rarely, foreign interests have controlled American news media. German interests acquired the *New York Evening Mail* for a time during World War I. Before World War II, the *North American Review* received official Japanese underwriting. In the postwar era, both the Mutual Broadcasting System and International News Service disseminated "news" paid for by the government of Rafael Trujillo in the Dominican Republic. In recent years, foreign governments have increasingly designated American public-relations concerns to supply material to the American press; such firms are required to register officially as foreign agents.

Thus, both the United States government and, less often, foreign powers have been able to circumvent or nullify the supposed independence of American journalists. If these instances seem inconsistent with the theory of a free press, the inconsistency must nevertheless be recognized as inherent in a functioning news system, for no institution in a society exists free of the pressures of other institutions.

THE JOURNALIST AS A FOREIGN POLICY CRITIC

The line between criticism and advocacy of foreign policy is narrow, and the role a particular journalist or newspaper may play can vary from one to the other. However, the critical journalist can usually be distinguished as not speaking for a particular or original policy, but as pointing out flaws in policy as formulated or executed. In recent decades, this function has been carried out by commentators and columnists with a national audience.

Such critics first gained large readerships with the growth of national feature syndicates early in the twentieth century and later with the development of radio networks. A columnist with 100 newspapers or a commentator with 100 stations was able to address the public more regularly and freely than any one official, even the president. Some commentators became celebrities; many Americans in the 1930's could more readily identify such radio personalities as H. V. Kaltenborn, Dorothy Thompson (who also published articles), and Fulton Lewis than they could cabinet members.

Among newspaper columnists, one stood by himself in sustained influence on United States foreign policy. As a young editor of the *New Republic*, Walter Lippmann had participated in the planning for peace done by the administration of Woodrow Wilson. As chief editorial writer for the *New York World* in the 1920's, he had written penetratingly on foreign policy. But not until the *World* closed in 1931 and Lippmann began a syndicated column, "Today and Tomorrow," from Washington did he have sustained impact. He concentrated on domestic issues in the early 1930's, but shifted his attention as the international crisis worsened. During World War II, he commanded an even broader audience by contributing significant articles to *Life* magazine and writing two widely read books, *U.S. Foreign Policy: Shield of the Republic* (1943) and *U.S. War Aims* (1944). In the postwar years he became the dean of American journalists, working without pause until his semiretirement in 1967.

Lippmann's long-standing influence can be attributed both to his intellectual gifts and to the particular role he played in policy formation. In his writing he combined qualities of thinker and of publicist (in the classical sense of that word), and was able to translate complicated policy problems into the language of a general audience. In regard to policymakers, he placed himself at just the right distance, so that officials might not agree with what he said but had to take it into account nonetheless. Tributes to his efficacy in this role abound: Joseph M. Jones wrote of his contribution; ". . . on foreign policy he is more often right than wrong, and whether right or wrong he thinks ahead publicly in policy terms and concepts that are a steady challenge to official leadership."

His positions over the years displayed a rare consistency—a realism concerning foreign policy that lacked the belligerence sometimes identified with the realist school. Barton J. Bernstein has summarized his positions succinctly:

> In criticizing American policy, he deplored Wilsonian diplomacy, opposed national self-righteousness, distrusted ideological crusades for democracy and capitalism, emphasized the limitations of American power, eschewed isolationism and pacifism, and rejected a peace based upon the United Nations. Instead he offered the counsel of realism: the use of power to serve the national interest.

Even so, Lippmann advocated restraint in the use of power, and his plea for restraint in Vietnam led to a clash, late in his career, with President Lyndon B. Johnson.

Although Lippmann had no real peers or successors, other writers have had periods of influence. Dorothy Thompson's was an important, if shrill, voice in urging opposition to na-

zism before World War II. Joseph Alsop viewed the world with alarm and advocated the use of American military power to set things right. James Reston emulated Lippmann's detachment, but did not consistently reach his intellectual level. In recent years the prominence and influence of the Washington-based columnists appear to have declined—in part, Reston believes, because public comment (and, by implication, public opinion) have played a diminishing part in the formation of policy.

In addition, a part of the critical function may have passed to correspondents in the field. The flaws in American policy in Vietnam were exposed more by reporters based in Saigon than by commentators in the capital. Notable among these were David Halberstam of the *New York Times* (whom President Kennedy asked the newspaper to recall); Neil Sheehan of United Press International and, later, the *Times;* and Malcolm Browne, who worked in Vietnam for the Associated Press. These correspondents—as well as Harrison Salisbury of the *Times,* who reported briefly from Hanoi at the end of 1966—were charged by officials and colleagues with disloyalty. Of them, Theodore Draper in 1968 wrote: "The wonder is not that much of the press was uncritical and covered up for official policy, but that a good part refused to do so."

THE JOURNALIST AS ADVOCATE

The role of advocate, urging particular policies upon the nation, has been played less by individual journalists than by newspaper editorial writers. Divisions of opinion in the Republic's early years generally took place along party lines—as in the controversies of the 1790's over policy toward Britain and France—because newspapers were commonly established by parties or factions. In the nineteenth century, a few newspapers became independent voices under the direction of such editorial giants as Horace Greeley of the *New York Tribune* and William Cullen Bryant of the *New York Evening Post.* For years they contributed forceful opinions to national policy debates; because they lived in an era of primarily domestic crisis, however, their contribution to foreign policy was limited. Twentieth-century editorial writers have been offered greater scope for discussion of foreign policy, but their effect has remained problematical; most practitioners, like Reston, have concluded that news is far more influential than institutional opinion.

Nonetheless, many of the impresarios of popular journalism have made strenuous efforts to impose their views by evoking the sentiments or prejudices of the mass audience. Merk acutely identified flamboyant policy positions of such publishers in the 1840's as simply another form of the sensationalism that was their stock in trade. Of James Gordon Bennett, founder of the *New York Herald* and one of the creators of the popular "penny press," Merk observed: "Bennett supported causes that paid, was inclined to be flippant, irresponsible, chauvinistic." The penny press seized enthusiastically on the doctrine of "manifest destiny" set forth by an influential Democratic journalist, John L. O'Sullivan, and advocated the absorption of all Mexico after the Mexican War. Fortunately, popular support for such editorial policies proved as shallow as the prejudices to which they appealed.

Hearst, commanding a fortune and media resources far greater than Bennett's, for half a century championed a nationalist, even nativist, foreign policy. Speaking not only through his editorial pages (and his brilliantly amoral editorialist, Arthur Brisbane), but also through gaudy headlines and pictures, Hearst employed all the devices of the "new journalism" of the late nineteenth century to arouse popular excitement. His greatest coup was in helping to foment what he called, in his *New York Morning Journal,* "the *Journal*'s war"—the conflict between the United States and Spain. Through sensational coverage and even concoction of incidents inflaming the Spanish-American dispute over Cuba, Hearst stirred popular indignation that made a peaceful settlement all but impossible. He dragged into his maelstrom much of the rest of the American press, including his chief rival, Joseph Pulitzer of the *New York World.*

Hearst's later efforts were of a piece with his Cuban adventure. His newspapers cultivated anti-oriental sentiment and even advocated war with Japan; they urged annexation of Canada; they opposed steps for disarmament between the world wars; they tried to foment intervention in Mexico (where Hearst had substantial landholdings) by publication of forged documents; and in the 1930's they appeared from time to time to be cultivating the Nazis. Until Hearst's death in 1951, his publications, as Thomas A. Bailey put it, "waxed fat on the carrion of public ignorance."

Just as determined in his opinions was Colonel Robert R. McCormick, proprietor from 1919 to 1955 of the largest paper in the Middle West, the *Chicago Tribune.* As with Hearst, his opinions were reflected throughout his newspaper; in his day the *Tribune* was persistently anglophobiac, jingoistic, and isolationist, especially in the period preceding United States entrance into World War II. Twice the newspaper risked government retaliation in that era—first by printing, three days before the Pearl Harbor attack, a secret plan for war mobilization and, later, by publishing a story indicating that the United States Navy had broken the secret Japanese naval code.

The magazine field has produced one entrepreneur of comparable influence. The opinions of Henry R. Luce were offered through a news magazine, *Time* (founded in 1923), and a pictorial magazine, *Life* (founded in 1936). Where Hearst and McCormick had leaned toward isolationism, Luce, while equally nationalistic, propounded intervention. In his publications' most notable statement on foreign policy, "The American Century" (*Life* [18 February 1941]), Luce asserted the duty of the United States "to exert upon the world the full impact of our influence, for such purposes as we see fit and by such means as we see fit." Luce, born in China, of American missionary parents, also firmly supported the Chinese Nationalists of Chiang Kai-shek during and after World War II, as well as the aggressive Asian policy advocated during the Korean War by General Douglas MacArthur. Since his death in 1967, the Luce publications, like their Hearst and McCormick counterparts, have taken less unequivocal positions.

Individual journalists who have sought to become advocates generally have had to step outside their customary professional roles. A number did so, for example, during the debate over American policy before Pearl Harbor. The well-known editor of the *Emporia* (Kansas) *Gazette,* William Allen White, organized the

JOURNALISTS AND FOREIGN POLICY

Committee to Defend America by Aiding the Allies. The parallel Fight for Freedom Committee attracted such notable journalists as Joseph Alsop, Herbert Agar, and Ulric Bell of the *Louisville Courier-Journal,* Geoffrey Parsons of the *New York Herald Tribune,* and the radio commentator Elmer Davis.

The record of the twentieth century shows that even the most strident journalistic advocacy may be of little effect if it runs directly counter to official policy, especially if that policy is enunciated by the president. Such advocacy has been considerably more effective in supporting a developing consensus. For example, during the Vietnam War editorial dissent appeared to count for little until such events as the Tet offensive of 1968 began to produce a reassessment of official policy. However, students of the effects of mass media are inclined to conclude that although advocacy of particular positions may count for little in public opinion, the media have long-term effects on underlying public attitudes. The ultimate effects of the policy positions advocated by Hearst, McCormick, and others may be less visible in diplomacy than in the long-term trends of American public opinion about the rest of the world.

THE JOURNALIST AS A POLICYMAKER

Individual journalists have rarely had an opportunity to take a direct hand in creating foreign policy, and usually do so only by dropping their journalistic roles. On occasion, the government has employed journalists, but usually less for their knowledge of foreign policy than for their journalistic expertise, either in dealing with former colleagues or in heading the quasi-news operations of official propaganda agencies. One such instance was the appointment in 1961 of Edward R. Murrow to head the United States Information Agency.

There are exceptions. Lippmann was named secretary of The Inquiry, designated by President Wilson in the fall of 1917 to prepare peace plans. Anne O'Hare McCormick of the *New York Times* secretly became a member of the State Department's Committee on Post-War Foreign Policy early in World War II. John

Scali, a television reporter, was named American representative to the United Nations during the administration of Richard M. Nixon.

As Bernard Cohen (1963) notes, most policymaking by journalists has been carried on less formally. Reporters can offer confidential advice to officials or can work with sympathetic members of Congress, as did the columnist Drew Pearson.

JOURNALISTIC IMPACT ON FOREIGN POLICY

Relationships between official policy, public opinion, and journalism thus have been varied and complex. Yet there is an essential validity in the original idea that the press is the two-way path between government and public. Although officials may seek ways to circumvent the news apparatus, both to address the public more directly and, through opinion surveys, to weigh public opinion, the day-to-day flow still depends primarily on the news media.

Journalism's chief effect accumulates through this daily process. A frequently cited example is the alleged impact of Vietnam War scenes, viewed by the American public on television network news for several years. The reporting function is the chief daily business of journalism and remains journalists' most important foreign policy activity, outweighing both criticism and advocacy.

It can be seen, nonetheless, that at times of crisis journalists have tended to step into more outspoken roles. At such times journalists—like others in foreign policy elites—have wanted to exert their influence to the utmost. Such exertion can take the form of support of official policy or dissent that invites official retaliation.

Relationships between journalists and policymakers have grown more turbulent in recent years. The sense of trust in the government's good faith has declined among journalists; reporting more frequently seeks to challenge the premises of American foreign policy and to uncover information that contradicts those premises. In this sense at least, journalism has become less an accessory of government and more an independent "fourth branch." As such, although its members may outlast presidents and administrations, they are not always a force for continuity or stability, for they feed on the change that is embodied in the concept of news.

BIBLIOGRAPHY

Gabriel A. Almond, *The American People and Foreign Policy* (New York, 1950), discusses the mass media as one of the elite groups shaping foreign policy; Thomas A. Bailey, *The Man in the Street: The Impact of American Public Opinion on Foreign Policy* (New York, 1948), contains a chapter dealing with the press. Richard J. Barnet, *Roots of War* (New York, 1972), has a section on mass media and foreign policy in the 1960's. Barton J. Bernstein, "Walter Lippmann and the Early Cold War," in Thomas G. Patterson, ed., *Cold War Critics: Alternatives to American Foreign Policy in the Truman Years* (Chicago, 1971), 18–48, is a useful appreciation. William O. Chittick, *State Department, Press, and Pressure Groups: A Role Analysis* (New York, 1970), contains historical background on State Department press relations. Bernard C. Cohen, *The Press and Foreign Policy* (Princeton, N.J., 1963), now dated, is still the only scholarly work devoted to the subject. W. Phillips Davison, *Mass Communication and Conflict Resolution: The Role of the Information Media in the Advancement of International Understanding* (New York, 1974), contains valuable observations by a media sociologist on the role of media in policy formation; and "Diplomatic Reporting: Rules of the Game," in *Journal of Communication,* 25 (1975), describes the mutual aid system of diplomats and correspondents. Theodore Draper, *Abuse of Power* (New York, 1968), appraises news coverage in Vietnam. Michael C. Emery, "The Munich Crisis Broadcasts: Radio News Comes of Age," in *Journalism Quarterly,* 42 (1965). John Hohenberg, *Foreign Correspondence: The Great Reporters and Their Times* (New York, 1964), gives exploits of British and American journalists. Frederick Merk, *Manifest Destiny and Mission in American History: A Reinterpretation* (New York, 1963), is an original study of the expansionist press and politicians of the 1840's. Newton N. Minow, John Bartlow Martin, and Lee M. Mitchell, *Presidential Television* (New York, 1973), describes official use of broadcast facilities. James Reston, *The Artillery of the Press: Its Influence on American Foreign Policy* (New York, 1967), provides valuable insights by a leading journalist. Joseph E. Wisan, *The Cuban Crisis as Reflected in the New York Press* (New York, 1934), is a detailed study of yellow journalism. David Wise, *The Politics of Lying: Government Deception, Secrecy, and Power* (New York, 1973), is a Washington journalist's account of recent issues.

[*See also* MANIFEST DESTINY; PUBLIC OPINION.]

THE KING COTTON THEORY

Gordon H. Warren

THE ANTEBELLUM South was a land of cotton where great fields stretched from South Carolina to Texas and slaves toiled from "day clean to first dark" to support the region's agricultural society. At the prewar height of production, in 1859, planters sent more than 4,000,000 bales to New England and European textile mills—a far cry from the day in 1784 when Liverpool customs agents had seized eight bags (about three bales) from an American ship, on the ground that so much cotton could not have been grown in the United States. Eli Whitney's invention of the cotton gin in 1793 had revolutionized an almost insignificant industry by enabling quick separation of short fiber from seeds. Eight years later cotton production had increased tenfold to 100,000 bales, to a million in 1835, to 2 million in 1842, and to 4.5 million on the eve of secession. By 1860 cotton shipments accounted for 60 percent of the value of all American exports. Proud of their success, Southerners developed a special relationship with their major cash crop, a kind of ethnocentric nature worship that evoked odes to cotton blossoms:

> First day white, next day red,
> Third day from my birth I'm dead;
> Though I am of short duration,
> Yet withal I clothe the nation.

Industrial centers all over the world relied upon Southern cotton to fuel their mills. Chief among them was Great Britain, whose largest industry, cotton manufacture, occupied 2,650 factories and many subsidiary establishments, employed 900,000 workers, and received 80 percent of its cotton from the South. Four million people, a fifth of the population of the British Isles, directly or indirectly depended on the industry. Although other European nations, especially France, operated fewer mills, they, too, bought almost entirely from the United States; the remaining cotton supply, of low quality and high cost, came from the East Indies and West Indies, Egypt, India, and Brazil. In the United States the Northern cotton textile industry, the nation's largest and most profitable manufacturing operation, acquired all of its supply from the South. Throughout much of the transatlantic world, cotton—Southern cotton—clothed, fed, and employed millions of people, constituted the bulk of manufactured goods, dominated exports, and duly enriched national treasuries.

Gradually, and perhaps inevitably, Southerners came to exaggerate cotton's importance. Although lacking sufficient industry, a merchant marine, and capital reserves, the South could always "point to that little attenuated cotton thread, which a child can break, but which nevertheless *can hang the world*." For twenty years prior to the Civil War, Southerners watched Britain futilely attempt to end reliance on American cotton by encouraging its cultivation in India. Innumerable gloomy reports and speeches by British leaders convinced planters that Europe's industrial fate was inextricably linked to the American South. As sectional crises buffeted the United States throughout the 1850's, Southerners developed a deep conviction that with cotton controlling American, British, and French destinies, their side would triumph.

Southern boosters never lost an opportunity to praise their region, illuminate flaws in Northern society, and stress European subservience. Their contentions gained support in the mid-1850's with publication of David Christy's

Cotton Is King, which, while lacking new ideas, carefully and ably summed up conventional beliefs about the world's dependence on cotton. Christy twitted Northerners and Britishers who criticized slavery and pronounced them hypocrites, since they were profiting from the manufacture of raw cotton into finished goods. "COTTON IS KING," Christy declared, "and his enemies are vanquished." The catchphrase dramatized sectional egotism and encouraged the South's leading financial journal, *DeBow's Review,* to abandon its cautious opinion that cotton could not be king without commerce as its queen. The *Review* soon enjoined readers "to teach our children to hold the cotton plant in one hand and a sword in the other, ever ready to defend it as the source of commercial power abroad and through that, of independence at home."

It fell to Senator James H. Hammond of South Carolina to transform a sectional shibboleth into a challenge to the federal union. After William H. Seward of New York had prophesied slavery's extinction during the Kansas debates of March 1858, Hammond retorted that the South and its peculiar institution would be around for a long time. Southerners did not need Northern vessels to carry produce. If the federal government would only remove tariffs, the "whole world will come to us to trade." The South need never go to war. No sane nation would make war on cotton, he said, because "without firing a gun, without drawing a sword . . . we could bring the whole world to our feet." If planters chose not to export cotton for three years, England and the civilized world would fall. The South Carolina senator then threw down the gauntlet to all critics of the South's cotton culture: "No, you do not dare to make war on cotton. No power on earth dares to make war upon it. Cotton *is* King."

Events moved rapidly toward a climax. Many Southerners viewed Abraham Lincoln as the Northern embodiment of antislavery doctrine, and Lincoln's election to the presidency convinced them that life under Republican rule would be unbearable. During the winter of 1860–1861, South Carolina seceded from the federal union; and by February the rest of the states of the lower South had followed. At the Washington Peace Conference—a meeting of Northern and Southern leaders who attempted to reconcile the sections with a compromise proposal on the future admission of slave and free states—Southern delegates seemed possessed by the power of cotton. The South, they told anyone who would listen, "neither wished nor intended to be more prosperous now, or to produce anything but cotton." After the conference's failure there remained only the firing of the first shot at Fort Sumter in April 1861 before the upper South left the Union. The American Civil War had begun.

Prospects at the outset appeared grim for the self-styled Confederate States of America, for in comparison with the resources of the North, those of the South were scanty—an inferior transportation network, a smaller white population, little industry, few skilled workers, and no navy. Despite these shortcomings euphoria prevailed. The war correspondent for the *Times* (London), William H. Russell, found South Carolinians scornful of Yankee martial skills and confident that Britain would intervene by autumn. John Bull, Russell was told, would "make a great fuss about non-interference, but when he begins to want cotton he'll come off his perch." England had to recognize Confederate independence lest the cotton supply be shut off and the working classes revolt. "Look out there," one merchant said, pointing to a wharf piled high with bales, "there's the key will open all our ports, and put us into John Bull's strong box as well." Everyone knew the watchword: "Cotton at 12 cents a pound and we don't fear the world." The South, Russell concluded, saw the world through parapets of cotton bales and rice bags.

Thus, in 1861 the King Cotton theory was set out by publicists and popular notion: the cotton industry employed more workers and brought greater returns than any other business in the United States, Britain, and France; without a steady supply, economic ruin would follow and governments, lacking income from taxes, would be unable to control the ensuing social chaos; the South would not have to win independence on the battlefield because, even if Europe did not recognize the Confederate government, a sudden termination of cotton exports would compel intervention; European warships and Confederate armies together would break the Northern naval blockade, vanquish Union armies, and achieve nationhood for the South; if events developed according to this scenario, the war would end in six months or less. Cotton, as an instrument of national policy, seemed invincible.

The South held a curious attitude toward the purpose of a naval embargo, which in the nineteenth century constituted a form of reprisal or retaliation, one state coercing another into ceasing a harmful practice. The Confederate policy, however, aimed not at eliminating a detrimental practice but at producing a beneficial one. It was a measure of Southern optimism that officials chose the method least likely to force compliance of world powers that in the past had capitulated only to severe physical pressure, and then rarely. The cotton embargo, calling as it did for initiative by European governments, had almost no chance of success. This subtlety eluded Southerners.

Economic coercion had been a favorite weapon of the United States since the days of Thomas Jefferson, when the government first tried to gain the rewards of war by peaceful means. Designed to discourage British and French violations of American neutrality, the embargo of 1807–1809 on all exports was about 75 percent effective. The cessation of American cotton shipments at that time provided a temporary windfall for British and French manufacturers, who profited from the sudden increase in the value of their stocks. The working classes suffered in both countries but, of course, lacked the political power to change official policy. The failure of this first embargo apparently did not affect the thinking of Southerners fifty years later. Perhaps Confederate leaders had forgotten the disastrous Jeffersonian gambit, or they may have felt that during the intervening years Britain had grown too dependent on Southern cotton to survive an embargo. It was an interesting theory but, like its predecessor, it rested on the shaky hypothesis that the British government would allow itself to be blackmailed.

The obsession with King Cotton so deeply permeated every facet of Southern society that the historian Clement Eaton has compared it with "the belief of the French people prior to World War II in the impregnability of the Maginot Line." Ranking Confederate officials, who should have known better, subscribed to its tenets. President Jefferson Davis and his ad-

visers believed cotton so powerful that "foreign recognition was looked forward to as an assumed fact."

In its instructions to commissioners abroad, the Confederate State Department repeated a familiar theme: Britain and France were so dependent on Southern cotton that terrible consequences would result if they permitted the Union blockade to stand. As early as March 1861, Secretary of State Robert Toombs suggested to the Confederacy's first diplomatic agents that they make "a delicate allusion to the probability of such an occurrence."

For a special reason the British had no intention of violating the blockade. The American government, having long protested overbearing belligerent practices, particularly proclamation of a blockade manned by insufficient warships, had made elimination of "paper blockades" a national goal since the Revolution. The United States, however, had not been a party to the Declaration of Paris (1856), which declared them illegal. Five years later Lincoln inaugurated a paper blockade—forty-two vessels guarding 3,500 miles of Southern coast—which bore greater resemblance to a sieve than a stone wall. Nevertheless, the London government appreciated the precedent that the Lincoln administration was setting and later, during the period of America's neutrality in World War I (1914–1917), used it as precedent to meet American complaints against its blockade of Germany.

Southern public opinion overwhelmingly supported the nonexportation of cotton as a means to force recognition of Confederate independence. As early as March 1860 the *Charleston Mercury* had advocated withholding cotton from the market "to control the conduct of the people of the North and of foreign nations, to secure a peaceful result for our deliverance." Sentiment for a total embargo on cotton built rapidly until, by April 1861, talk of selling the crop verged on treason. Southerners had no intention of allowing Britain and France to lay in a cotton surplus and avoid intervention. The South would make the Union blockade so effective, induce such a cotton famine, that Europe would be rocked to its foundations. Planters permitted no cotton to leave their plantations; cotton exporters refused consignments; citizens' committees prevented British blockade-runners from loading cotton. The embargo, the historian Frank Owsley observed, was "as near air-tight as human effort could make it." The Confederate congress, however, never made the embargo official. Members often debated the subject, yet prohibited only exports to the North. They stopped short of enacting a complete embargo because President Davis, feeling it would alienate Europe, preferred to brandish it as a threat, the trump card to be played when all else failed.

Southerners did not confine restrictive activity to withholding cotton; they also burned it or curtailed its production. Newspapers and government officials urged planters to raise less cotton, and cultivate more corn to feed Confederate soldiers. "Plant Corn and Be Free," a Georgia paper warned, "or plant cotton and be whipped." Farmers who did not decrease cotton acreage or plow under a planted crop were publicly condemned; sometimes neighbors destroyed the cotton for them. State legislatures taxed seed cotton and set acreage limits; planting in excess of the limit was punishable by a fine. To pressure Britain and France, the Confederate congress passed a joint resolution recommending that no cotton be planted in 1862. The crop for that year was one-third the size of the 1861 harvest, and the 1863 crop only one-ninth. A more dramatic demonstration of Southern unity was an 1862 act of congress that allowed military forces to destroy all valuable property in imminent danger of capture. Zealots, interpreting the law liberally, sent millions of bales up in flames. Richmond authorities carefully notified foreign consuls.

Ironically, the less cotton was exported, the more binding the blockade appeared. In London the popular mood, which had once been pro-South, began to show a disturbing lack of sympathy with Confederate protests about the blockade's ineffectiveness. *Punch,* the weekly humor magazine noted for caustic political wit, deviated from its normal practice of mocking Union misfortunes and foibles to run a devastating cartoon entitled "King Cotton Bound; or, the Modern Prometheus." Looking for all the world like an angry cotton scarecrow, the helpless monarch lies manacled to a rock, straining to break the chains of the blockade, while the American eagle, talons digging into

his leg, rips out great shreds of stuffing. The caricature of the Greek legend suggested no other parallels; there would be no miraculous rejuvenation of vital parts, no savior to break the chains. King Cotton's fate was sealed.

The success of Confederate diplomacy turned on the appearance of a cotton famine in Europe by the autumn of 1861 or, at least, the winter of early 1862. Unfortunately, the South had created conditions that worked against an early shortage. The years 1859–1860 had produced two bumper crops, totaling more than 8 million bales. Before proclamation of the Northern blockade, about 3.5 million bales of the 1860 crop had been exported, chiefly to Britain. A surplus of several hundred thousand bales crammed British warehouses as late as December 1861, even after some reshipment across the Atlantic to Northern factories. Moreover, quantities of manufactured cotton goods had accumulated in Britain as a result of overproduction, competition from linen and wool, and fewer American orders. The Civil War temporarily rescued British speculators and small manufacturers from impending bankruptcy, but their counterparts in France experienced harder times. French cotton reserves, never large, had declined so precipitously by September 1861 that the Foreign Ministry began to explore the possibility of joint Anglo-French recognition of the Confederacy and breaking of the blockade.

The cotton manufacturing districts in England—mainly Lancashire, Cheshire, and Derbyshire—did not begin to feel the full force of the embargo until April 1862, by which time production in the mills had fallen to half the rate for 1860. Over the preceding six months, cotton imports had dropped to less than 1 percent of the same period a year before. British reserves had plunged drastically by June 1862. With only a three-week supply (about 100,000 bales) on hand in September, cabinet officers in London discussed recognizing Confederate independence, upon the condition that General Robert E. Lee's invasion of Maryland was successful. But then Lee was repulsed at Antietam, and the British government held back.

During the winter of 1862–1863, the cotton famine rose to its peak; the mills did not close, however, since some cotton—admittedly not

THE KING COTTON THEORY

much—remained for manufacture, and inferior varieties from India, China, Brazil, and Egypt passed through British customs. American cotton also continued to arrive. With cotton selling at four times its previous average price, Southern merchants, speculators, planters, government agents, and thieves vied for the trade. Even the Confederate War Department exchanged staple goods for essential supplies from the North. Blockade-runners took 1.25 million bales to Europe, and almost another million was shipped North through Union lines at New Orleans and Memphis. The embargo had failed. "It is an error to say that 'Cotton is King,'" a Confederate diplomat declared on return from Europe. "It is not. It is a great and influential power in commerce, but not its dictator."

Richmond officials turned to new tactics. They had decided in the spring of 1862 to authorize their agent in Paris, John Slidell, to offer enormous amounts of cotton—more than 100,000 bales—to Emperor Napoleon III if he would break the blockade. It amounted to a bribe, a slight improvement over the previous tactic of extortion. Rejecting the proposal, the French foreign minister, Édouard Thouvenel, declared that his government would act only in accord with Britain. Since London would not move without Russian support, the French soon lost interest in intervention.

Extortion and bribery having failed to win the desired results, Southern officials turned belatedly to more practical measures. In December 1862 the Confederacy offered Britain the chance to conclude a massive barter agreement: to exchange $300 million in naval stores, cotton, tobacco, and other crops for a vast array of manufactured goods—upon conclusion of a peace treaty. Otherwise, Secretary of State Judah P. Benjamin declared, Confederate military authorities might have to destroy crops in order to prevent their capture, a policy that, of course, had already been implemented. An additional factor deserved consideration, he said. In the postwar period Northern merchants would swarm over the South, acquiring commodities and selling New England manufactured goods. Trade with Europe would remain "tributary to an intermediary," and the United States would reap all the profits. To

avoid this predicament, neutral businessmen could purchase products in advance from the South and leave them "in depot till the ports are opened."

The British foreign secretary, Lord John Russell, was not interested. Thinking more of the empire's future glory than short-term economic benefits, he made it clear to even the most obdurate Confederate official that Britain would not intervene in the American Civil War unless critical national interests made it necessary. Thoroughly irritated by the counterproductive tactic of coercion, Russell remarked privately that it rubbed him the wrong way.

In desperation the Confederacy initiated its last cotton project. Following months of debate, the Confederate congress in January 1863 decided to put "the sacred King Cotton in hock" by selling an issue of cotton bonds worth $15 million to overseas investors. The issue had a double purpose: income from the bonds would purchase war matériel; and Europeans would acquire a small, though psychologically important, stake in Confederate fortunes. The sale netted more than $8.5 million for the Confederacy. Despite the success of the so-called Erlanger loan, the need for greater amounts of capital caused the Confederate government in 1864 to pressure blockade-runners to carry large amounts of cotton. Southerners had finally realized that if Europe would not come to cotton, cotton must go to Europe.

What had gone wrong? The fantasy of King Cotton reordering world politics had turned into a nightmare. Reflecting on the sad end of their dream, many Southerners sought to explain defeat by reverting to the persecution complex so characteristic of the antebellum psyche. An international antislavery conspiracy, orchestrated by Northern extremists, had prevented recognition, had enforced respect for the blockade, and had given moral support to the Union. The argument contained some truth but, like the King Cotton theory, was simplistic.

The embargo had failed to achieve its objectives. Although contemporary opinion blamed the distress of the cotton mills on a shortage of fiber, sufficient amounts were available at high prices that, according to Eugene Brady, resulted from *"expectations* of a future import shortage." The price of raw cotton climbed beyond reach of many British mills, and speculators actually increased reexports of cotton to France. Meanwhile, mills suffered at the outset of the Civil War from overproduction of cotton goods, which depressed prices and made manufacturing at the previous tempo a losing venture. High-priced cotton and low-priced manufactured goods brought misery to the mill districts. As predicted, discontent did mount among British and French mill operatives, who held protest meetings and signed petitions; but they had little political influence and could not force intervention, a fact apparently not appreciated by the Confederacy.

Seeking explanations for King Cotton's failure, historians have cited supplementary sources of cotton; profits in trade of noncotton textiles, munitions, commerce, and shipbuilding; economic ties to the North; and Confederate military defeats. Undoubtedly a combination of factors deterred European intervention. But one thing is clear: Confederate political and economic theorists erred in assuming that European prosperity rested on cotton. The British minister to the United States, Lord Richard B. P. Lyons, was struck by this misapprehension in 1860. "It is true that cotton is almost a necessity to us," he observed, "but it is still more necessary for them to sell it than it is for us to buy it."

The discrediting of the King Cotton theory reaffirmed the inherent difficulties of any nation seeking to achieve a political objective by economic means. Having based their ill-founded venture in foreign policy on the theory that a cotton embargo or cotton bribe could force Europe to recognize Southern sovereignty or break the North's blockade of the South, Confederate officials persisted in their course long after its futility became obvious. Once again the chimera of omnipotent economic coercion had led American statesmen to disaster. Rather than exporting cotton to establish international credit and to finance mili-

tary and naval purchases, the leaders of the Confederacy had accepted the illusory notion held by so many Southerners that European dependence on the crop would bring intervention. That fundamental miscalculation surely contributed much to the failure of the South to achieve independence. Under the right circumstances—a Confederate victory at Antietam, the providential destruction of foreign cotton by insects—the King Cotton theory might have worked. But Providence did not smile on the Confederate States of America. Southerners who had placed so much faith in the "little attenuated cotton thread" that supposedly could hang the world discovered too late that they had fashioned a noose for themselves.

BIBLIOGRAPHY

Ephraim D. Adams, *Great Britain and the American Civil War,* 2 vols. (New York, 1925), the premier work on Anglo-American relations during this period, places Southern cotton in perspective. Eugene A. Brady, "A Reconsideration of the Lancashire 'Cotton Famine,' " in *Agricultural History,* 37 (1963), discusses wartime prosperity in Britain and demonstrates that the country's suffering did not result from a cotton scarcity. Mary Ellison, *Support for Secession: Lancashire and the American Civil War* (Chicago, 1972), questions the alleged passivity of the working classes and argues that many operatives sympathized with the South. Judith Fenner Gentry, "A Confederate Success in Europe: The Erlanger Loan," in *Journal of Southern History,* 36 (1970), reveals the profitability of a much-misunderstood financial venture. Frenise Logan, "India—Britain's Substitute for American Cotton, 1861–1865," *ibid.,* 26 (1958), deals with alternative cotton sources and their disadvantages. Frank L. Owsley, *King Cotton Diplomacy* (Chicago, 1959), is, despite its Southern bias and some misperceptions, the standard treatment of the role played by cotton in Confederate policymaking at home and abroad. Harold D. Woodman, *King Cotton and His Retainers: Financing and Marketing the Cotton Crop of the South, 1800–1925* (Lexington, Ky., 1968), examines the background of cotton culture, its place in world commerce, and the Southerners' frantic scramble to sell the fiber during the war's closing days.

[*See also* BLOCKADES AND QUARANTINES; ECONOMIC FOREIGN POLICY; EMBARGOES; IDEOLOGY AND FOREIGN POLICY; INTERNATIONAL LAW; INTERVENTION AND NONINTERVENTION; NEUTRALITY; REALISM AND IDEALISM; RECOGNITION POLICY; TRADE AND COMMERCE.]

MANDATES AND TRUSTEESHIPS

Edward M. Bennett

PRESIDENT Woodrow Wilson presented the text of the Covenant of the League of Nations to the Paris Peace Conference on 14 February 1919. He explained to his colleagues that they would find incorporated in the document an old principle intended for more universal use and development—the reference was to mandates for former colonies. In this fashion the mandate system became a part of the new world that Wilson imagined would emerge from the deliberations in Paris. Mandates developed historically from the practice of Great Power supervision of buffer zones; acceptance of British, French, and American conceptions of the rule of law and colonial freedom and self-government; Edmund Burke's suggestion of the trusteeship principle in administering British colonies in the interest of the inhabitants, taken to heart and subsequently expanded by Parliament after the American Revolution; and the Concert of Europe concept and its application to Africa and Turkey. While the principle may have been old, Wilson's perception of it was new because he wished to universalize it.

Although the British and French delegations at Paris did not oppose the mandate system, they were not in the forefront of those demanding it. Nor were they particularly eager to accept Wilson's freewheeling interpretation of the general mandate system as applying to any and all former enemy colonies. The Japanese and Italian representatives were even less enthusiastic about mandates that might restrict their control of former German colonies. They preferred a division of territory. The Americans were insistent that former enemy colonies would not be treated as spoils of war. In a meeting of the Council of Ten on 28 January 1919,

the mandatory principle was discussed. Vittorio Orlando of Italy asked how the former colonies should be divided, what provisions should be made for government, and what should be said about independence. Baron Shinken Makino of Japan asked whether mandates had been accepted, and Georges Clemenceau of France responded that the question was to be taken up later. Wilson would not permit the subject to be buried, so the British prime minister, David Lloyd George, presented a proposal for defining mandates on 30 January 1919, suggesting a division into three types—ultimately defined as A, B, and C mandates. Without citing specific locations, it is sufficient to observe that most of Africa, part of the Middle East, and most of the Pacific island groups were considered to be in one of the categories: A—mandates quickly able to be prepared for independence; B—mandates needing tutelage for some time before being considered for independence; and C—mandates that probably would never be ready for independence.

Wilson's associates at Paris hoped for United States participation in the postwar enforcement of the Versailles settlement and did not feel they could strongly oppose him on the mandate issue. Many members of the conference sincerely believed that the mandate system might work, but that it had to draw on existing experience in the colonies and should not promise too much to peoples who could not in the foreseeable future be prepared for nationhood and full citizenship rights. Wilson agreed that in some cases this would be true, but he was less restrictive in the number of former colonies he would place in this category than were some of his colleagues.

There was a tendency at the peace conference to identify someone else's mandates as ready to be placed in the category reasonably close to independence with minimum preparation rather than one's own. Lloyd George, for example, saw most of the colonies being assigned to Great Britain and British Commonwealth nations as more suitable for either direct annexation or deferral. South-West Africa, he argued, should be annexed to South Africa because it was not likely to proceed to independence; and South Africa would be better able to care for the people of South-West Africa under South African laws and tax structure. Papua might better be classed as an area that would never be self-governing, and therefore should be permanently assigned to Australia. He could visualize French mandates in northern Africa being prepared for independence. Clemenceau, however, was more inclined to see British mandates as nearing preparation for independence. In effect, then, the mandate system would only be as good as the determination of the powers in the League to carry it out.

Woodrow Wilson was the master planner for the mandate system, but the man responsible for laying out the detailed plans of the process was General Jan Christian Smuts of South Africa. The process began with Wilson's Fourteen Points, drawn up by the journalists Walter Lippmann and Frank Cobb under the general supervision of Colonel Edward House. They read through the president's statements of war aims and compacted them into the program that Wilson set forth in an address to Congress on 8 January 1918. Point 5 called for "A free, open-minded, and absolutely impartial adjustment of all colonial claims, based upon a strict observance of the principle that in determining all such questions of sovereignty the interests of the populations concerned must have equal weight with the equitable claims of the government whose title is to be determined." It was made clear in the Council of Ten discussions at Paris, partly because of British fears concerning the Irish and Indian independence claims, that colonial questions would be restricted to colonies belonging to Germany or coming into being as a result of the war. In practical terms this meant that mandates applied only to the German African and Far Eastern holdings and the non-Turkish parts of the former Ottoman Empire.

Secret treaties signed before or during the war had divided these territories among the victorious powers except the United States, which was not a party to them. Wilson went to Paris determined to set aside these treaties and for that purpose had formulated Point 1 of the Fourteen Points, which called for "open covenants of peace, openly arrived at, after which there shall be no private international understandings of any kind but diplomacy shall proceed always frankly and in the public view."

General Smuts set to work to carry out the mandates charge embodied, at Wilson's insistence, in Article 22 of the League Covenant. The article made it clear that certain of the Turkish territories were ready for nationhood almost immediately, that central African peoples needed mandatory powers that would guarantee their human rights and political and moral tutelage, and that the open door to trade would apply in all mandates. It also determined that South-West Africa and certain of the Pacific islands, because of the sparseness of population, isolation, size, and other circumstances, could best be administered under the laws of the mandatory and as integral portions of its territory, with safeguards for the well-being of the inhabitants supervised by the Mandates Commission. The Permanent Mandates Commission, the later official title of the Mandates Commission, was to receive annual reports from mandatory powers and complaints relative to the treatment of inhabitants. The reports and complaints were to be sent to the League Council for deliberation.

Wilson met his first defeat on the mandate issue when his allies refused to consider turning mandates over to the administration of small neutral nations. The distribution followed the pattern of the secret treaties, with some other powers added to the list. Motives concerning the possession of mandates were mixed. Some Japanese saw mandates as preludes to annexation or as convenient means to establish secure military and market areas, while others saw them as symbolic of Great Power status and the promise of a stronger position in the future whether the system worked or not. The open door to trade and the defense of colonial peoples, plus democratization of the world, were the primary American objectives. British, French, and Belgian motives shaded to a greater or lesser degree along the lines of

Japanese thinking. "Little England" advocates, who supported reduction in the size of the British Empire and a refocusing on trade expansion, were relieved to see the lessening of colonial responsibilities, while the imperial advocates were alarmed but convinced that the empire could hold together and peace could be secured while the United States participated in the peace-keeping system. France and Belgium were pleased to see the diminution of German power and could live with mandates if that were the result.

Japan proved a special case because it had emerged as a Great Power at a time when the main symbol of such status—empire—was on the decline. Japanese ambitions in China were set in the old imperial structure. During the war Japan secured a position as a major force in colonial exploitation of China as a result of the Twenty-one Demands presented to China, only to encounter demands for surrender of these privileges at the end of the war. Lloyd George and Clemenceau sided with Japan. This, combined with Japan's threat not to join the League, forced Wilson to accept the assignment of German rights in Shantung to the Japanese—but with a pledge to return the province to full Chinese sovereignty with only the former German economic privileges remaining to them; Japan was also given the right to establish a settlement at Tsingtao. Thus Wilson's hopes for an anticolonial postwar structure were already on shaky ground.

Some scholars have argued that the Allies were not sincere in adopting the mandate process and intended to use it as a subterfuge for expanding colonial control. While in some instances this proved to be true, generally the mandates were administered in the interest of the people concerned and a large percentage of the Class A mandates were moved into independence. Most of these were in the former Ottoman Empire, such as Trans-Jordan, Syria, Palestine, and Lebanon. Wilson's charge to the peace conference in the plenary session of 14 February 1919 was only partially observed; but his expectations on mandates were more fulfilled than in most other areas of the Fourteen Points. Wilson told the conference members that they were "done with annexation of helpless peoples," and henceforth nations would consider it their responsibility to protect and promote the interests of people under their tutelage before their own interests. It would remain for the United Nations, not the League, to carry out this promise.

Often overlooked in judging Wilson's objectives are the underlying premise and promise that he undertook to deliver as a result of American participation in the war—making the world safe for democracy. Success meant the elimination of the monarchical and colonial systems. Wilson envisioned the states that were to emerge from the mandate system as democratic republics.

The United States entered the era following World War II with the same idea and again faced opposition from its allies. President Franklin D. Roosevelt attempted in the Atlantic Charter to reestablish the framework for bringing the colonial peoples of the world to free government. The ramifications of this were not lost on British Prime Minister Winston Churchill, who at one point, in a fit of pique, told Roosevelt that he did not become his majesty's first minister in order to preside over the disintegration of the British Empire. Soviet Premier Josef Stalin, on the other hand, was ready with his own interpretation of what free government meant; it included only the right to be a communist state, insofar as the Soviet Union had the military power to ensure such determination of national sovereignty.

The concept of trusteeship appeared first in discussions of the Big Three at Yalta in 1945 but was also discussed in general form in the Department of State during the war. It was agreed at Yalta that trusts would be set up under United Nations auspices, with decisions being made on the general procedure by the five powers having permanent seats on the Security Council. (Trusts were substituted for mandates in order not to have any carry-over from the moribund League of Nations and because they were to have a broader definition.) Trusteeships would apply only to territories still under mandate in 1939, areas detached from the defeated enemies, or territories voluntarily placed under the system, with the specific geographic areas to be determined later.

John Foster Dulles represented the United States on the Fourth Committee at the twenty-seventh plenary meeting of the United Nations, which was charged with developing the trusteeship system. Dulles followed Wilson in his challenge to the colonial system, proclaiming that the committee was determined to assume the responsibility for boldly addressing the whole colonial problem, which involved hundreds of millions of people, not just the 15 million who might come under trusteeship. He presented a clarion call for the destruction of colonialism. The anticolonial thrust initiated by Dulles in the name of the committee became a part of the United Nations trusteeship system and continued over the next thirty years, implementing Wilson's dreams beyond his expectations and with results not imagined in his time. There emerged such a myriad of states in Africa, the Near East, and Asia, with differing national objectives and systems, as to boggle the minds of those who originated the mandate system and its objectives.

Chapter 4 of the report of the United Nations Preparatory Commission ordered the Fourth Committee to deal with trusteeships in the interest of the trust peoples. Accordingly, the committee outlined the rules and procedures, including creation of the Trusteeship Council. While this looked very good to the creators of the trust system, reservations appeared immediately, including objections from United States Army and Navy spokesmen, who urged outright annexation of the strategic Pacific islands taken from the Japanese. The president and the Department of State proposed a compromise based on the anticolonial position in Articles 82 and 83 of the charter. As primary sponsor of the trusteeships, the United States could scarcely reserve certain areas for annexation. Article 76 sets forth the provisions and restrictions applying to trustee powers and includes procedures leading to independence, representative government, and economic development. It was overridden at the San Francisco conference establishing the United Nations, however, by insertion of articles 82 and 83 of the charter. These articles provide that areas within trust territories might be set aside as "strategic areas" under the direct control of the trustee, which is answerable to the Security Council, where the veto power applies, instead of to the General Assembly, where it does not apply. In this fashion Micronesia—comprising the Marshall, Caroline, and Mariana islands; but not the Gilbert, Nauru, and Ocean Islands administered by Australia and the United Kingdom—became the strategic area of the Pacific under United States supervision.

The trust principle seems to work more effectively for the objectives established in the Charter of the United Nations than did the mandate system under the League, because the Trusteeship Council is composed of those determined to carry it through and because it is under constant public scrutiny. Regular and voluminous reports from the Trusteeship Council had dwindled to pamphlet size by 1972. By 1975 the last two trust territories, Papua New Guinea and Micronesia, were determining their course toward independence or other disposition. The Trusteeship Council report in the July 1974 issue of the *UN Monthly Chronicle* noted the council's concern as discussions between the United States and the Micronesian congress continued to be oriented toward the choice of free association for five districts represented in the congress, while the sixth, comprising the northern Marianas, engaged in separate negotiations concerning commonwealth status under United States sovereignty. Reported discussions between representatives of the Marshall Islands and the United States also disturbed the council, which wondered how they would affect the inhabitants of the Carolines. Micronesia's landmass is only about 700 square miles, comprising more than 2,000 islands in the three major archipelagoes and spanning some 3 million square miles of ocean. The northern Marianas' apparent movement toward becoming the first territory acquired by the United States since the purchase of the Virgin Islands in 1917 was considered by the Trusteeship Council to be a literal violation of the trust arrangement intended to keep Micronesia together as an integral unit.

Members of the Trusteeship Council insisted that the United States should not proceed with incorporation of the area unless satisfactory arrangements were made with the Micronesian congress. The congress agreed to separate discussions, and a commonwealth agreement was signed on Saipan in February 1975, climaxing two years of formal negotiations; it was then to go to the sixteen-member Marianas district legislature for approval. In June 1975 the agreement was submitted to a United Nations–administered plebiscite, which was overseen by a committee of the Trusteeship Council. The Council reported that it was properly conducted and that the results, which favored joining the northern Mariana Islands to the United States by commonwealth status, represented the will of the people. The islands were to be self-governing and when all steps were carried out to accomplish this, the Trusteeship Agreement would be terminated for the entire Trust Territory as well as for the northern Marianas. The United States agreed to encourage the northern Marianas to maintain close and friendly contacts with the rest of the Trust Territory.

Micronesia and Papua New Guinea were the last of eleven original trusteeships assigned to the council. The other nine had been Nauru, Ruanda-Urundi, French Cameroons, French Togoland, Italian Somaliland, Western Samoa, British Cameroons, British Togoland, and Tanganyika. From the trusteeships or released territories ten nations had emerged in 1947, several in the 1950's, fourteen in 1960, and others later. Very often the result has not been satisfying, for the virulent nationalism exhibited by the new states has mirrored the worst traits of their older counterparts. Many celebrated nationhood by immediately sinking into anarchy or by trying to annex neighbors in wars of "liberation."

If success for the mandates and trusteeships is measured in terms of achieving independence, the trusteeship system obviously has been more successful. If it is measured in terms of achieving economic, political, and cultural development before nationhood, perhaps the more cautious approach of the mandate system has provided better results. In any case, the net result was that colonialism of the old order, with direct control of territory and people, and with no pretense of self-government, was dead by the end of 1975.

The objective of creating a nation-state system of democratic republics operating on a constitutional structure with governments of, by, and for the people—Woodrow Wilson's dream—is far from achievement. The most orderly and stable transitions came in the states that emerged from territories formerly under British control, where the population was generally educated for self-rule. Trust territories where there was literally no preparation for self-rule and independence emerged with bloody struggles for power and unstable systems of government. In a considerable measure

this result arose from the failure of mandate and trusteeship powers to take seriously their charge to use all deliberate speed to prepare the populations for independence. All too often, however, the period of preparation was too short; and in some instances the viability of the states created might be questioned in terms of their ability to become economically self-sufficient. For better or for worse the states now exist, and the next problem for them is to learn some degree of tolerance for one another and to curb the excesses of nationalism thus far exhibited.

BIBLIOGRAPHY

Hessel Duncan Hall, *Mandates, Dependencies and Trusteeships* (Washington, D.C., 1948), is the most comprehensive study of the background, origins, and development of the mandate system. Earl Spencer Pomeroy, *Pacific Outpost: American Strategy in Guam and Micronesia* (Stanford, Calif., 1951), is an excellent account of the American concern for strategic position in the Pacific region; it treats the single exception to the general trust system. Ruth B. Russell and Jeanne E. Mather, *A History of the United Nations Charter: The Role of the United States, 1940–1945* (Washington, D.C., 1958), is useful in tracing the background of the trusteeship principle. H. W. V. Temperley, *A History of the Peace Conference of Paris*, 6 vols. (London, 1920–1924), provides considerable insight on the discussions and development of the mandate question. United Nations, Office of Public Information, *Everyman's United Nations*, 8th ed. (New York, 1968), provides extensive information on the development and implementation of the trusteeship system. United States Department of State, *The Foreign Relations of the United States: The Paris Peace Conference*, 13 vols. (Washington, D.C., 1942–1945), gives the best information on Woodrow Wilson's perspective on mandates. Campbell L. Upthegrove, *Empire by Mandate: A History of the Relations of Great Britain With the Permanent Mandates Commission of the League of Nations* (New York, 1954), is the most comprehensive work tracing the British adjustment to the mandate concept and the British government's dealings with the Mandates Commission. For the individual interested in finding general information and observations on mandates and trusteeships, political science texts dealing with foreign relations and international organization are the most accessible sources. Historians of American foreign relations have devoted very little attention to these subjects since World War II. Numerous monographs have been written on specific mandate or trusteeship areas, but no recent studies have been made of the mandate and trusteeship systems or their operation except in the general context of international relations or international organization.
[*See also* ANTI-IMPERIALISM; COLONIALISM; THE FOURTEEN POINTS; IMPERIALISM; NATIONAL SELF-DETERMINATION; PROTECTORATES AND SPHERES OF INFLUENCE.]

MANIFEST DESTINY

David M. Pletcher

THE EPITHET "manifest destiny" is both a symbol and a convenient short name for American territorial expansionism, especially in the nineteenth century. The idea of predestined expansion permeated early American thought and writings, but the term seems to have originated in two editorials by John L. O'Sullivan published in the *United States Magazine and Democratic Review* for July–August 1845 and the *New York Morning News* for 27 December 1845. These editorials dealt respectively with the proposed annexation of the Texas Republic and of the Oregon territory. In the earlier editorial, O'Sullivan accused European nations of interfering in the Texas question "for the avowed object of . . . checking the fulfilment of our manifest destiny to overspread the continent allotted by Providence for the free development of our yearly multiplying millions." In the *Morning News,* O'Sullivan defined American virtues explicitly; this editorial has been more widely quoted:

> Away, away with all these cobweb tissues of rights of discovery, exploration, settlement, continuity, etc. . . . Were the respective cases and arguments of the two parties, as to all these points of history and law, reversed—had England all ours, and we nothing but hers—our claim to Oregon would still be best and strongest. And that claim is by the right of our manifest destiny to overspread and to possess the whole of the continent which Providence has given us for the development of the great experiment of Liberty and federated self-government entrusted to us.

Out of all possible arguments justifying territorial expansion, such as geographical nearness, economic need, or similarity of peoples, O'Sullivan applied his term to only three—the irresistible growth of the American population, the superiority of American political institutions, and the blessing of God (or Providence) on both. But it was usually impossible to dissociate ideas of natural law and natural boundaries from O'Sullivan's arguments; and, as time passed, manifest destiny came to signify virtually the whole range of American expansionist rationalizations. In 1935 Albert K. Weinberg firmly established this broader definition with the publication of *Manifest Destiny: A Study of Nationalist Expansionism in American History.* The purpose of this book was to separate and analyze the "motley body of justificatory doctrines." Weinberg acknowledged O'Sullivan and recognized that the term "manifest destiny" was unknown in its literal form until the 1840's, but the felicitous title of Weinberg's book and its lengthy exposition of arguments completed the obscuring of Sullivan's limited definition. Indeed, by the mid-1930's the term "manifest destiny" was also being used to mean not only nineteenth-century expansionist arguments but also annexations, in expressions such as "the era of manifest destiny," meaning the 1840's and 1850's.

From its first appearance, the term always carried strong moral overtones, and after 1845 opponents of annexation and the Mexican War accused its users of hypocrisy. In 1963 the historian Frederick Merk, in *Manifest Destiny and Mission in American History: A Reinterpretation,* sought to perpetuate a simplified moral distinction with a study of expansionism devoted largely to the 1840's. Both manifest destiny and mission, he argued, were aspects of the profound American desire to spread its people, rule, and institutions over as much of the continent as possible. In manifest destiny he saw the baser, more materialist side of American expansionism; he equated it with imperialism and called both "traps into which the nation was led in 1846 and 1899." Mission, however, he defined as "a truer expression of the national spirit . . . idealistic, self-denying, hopeful of divine favor for national aspirations, though not sure of it . . . a force that fought to curb expansionism of the aggressive variety." Merk blurred his arbitrary distinction by admitting that "zealots of Manifest Destiny" had their own form of mission. A decade after the publication of his book, his use of the term had not replaced the definitions of either O'Sullivan or Weinberg.

Under any definition manifest destiny has deep roots in early American history. The central idea of O'Sullivan's editorials—the linking of divine favor with superior political institutions and expanding population—appeared in British thought and writings even before the founding of the first English colonies in North America. In the sixteenth century, the writings of Richard Hakluyt and others set forth the idea that, like the earlier Romans, Englishmen were predestined (although not always for religious reasons) to take over, colonize, and develop the New World; no other people were capable of such a gigantic task. In the charters of the London and Plymouth companies an ostensibly religiopolitical purpose of the proposed colonies was prominently set forth—they were intended to convert the Indians and bring them "to a settled and quiet government." The Massachusetts Bay Company charter of 1629 joined religion and polity even more closely in the express hope that "our said people, Inhabitantes there, maie be soe religiously, peaciblie and civilly governed . . . [as to] wynn and incite the Natives of the Country to the knowledg and obedience of the onlie true God and Savior of Mankinde, and the Christian fayth." In 1630, during the voyage of the first Massachusetts Bay colonizers across the Atlantic, their leader, John Winthrop, compared their project in well-known words to a "Citty upon a hill" intended by the Lord to furnish an example of religious (and governmental) purity to the world. As the Lord's "chosen people" the New England colonies expanded at the expense of the Indians, and the will of God was used to rationalize conquest in place of conver-

sion. For example, Increase Mather defended Indian wars as just, and Cotton Mather linked Indians and French Canadians: "Who is for Jesus against Satan, and who is for the true Christian, Protestant religion against Popery and Paganism? . . . Take your choice, my dear countrymen; but there is no room to be indifferent."

The colonial wars between Britain and France naturally multiplied these arguments. In the midst of Queen Anne's War (1702–1713), for example, the prosperous merchant Samuel Vetch advocated the acquisition of Canada not only for its supplies of fish, furs, and naval stores but also because this would free settlers and Indians from the dominion of priests and a debauching monarch "and make Canada a noble Colony, exactly calculate for the Constitutions and genius of the most Northern of the North Brittains." The wars of the 1750's and 1760's seemed to some British and colonial writers to be the decisive struggle between "despotic Tyranny" and "Heaven-born Freedom." William Smith, first provost of the College, Academy, and Charitable School of Philadelphia, predicted that victory over French Catholicism would open the way to extend "our empire far over this continent" along with Christianity and the sciences. England had long insisted on the doctrine of effective occupation to counter extensive Spanish and French claims in North America and elsewhere; now the growth of the British people was used to reinforce this argument. In his essay "Observations Concerning the Increase of Mankind" (1755), Benjamin Franklin predicted that with free land to the west, the British population in North America would double every twenty years, while that of Europe remained stationary. A decade later he told the Scottish philosopher Henry Home, Lord Kames, that in a century the territory from the St. Lawrence to the Mississippi would be filled with British people and that eventually "the future grandeur and stability of the British empire [would] lie in America," where the foundations were "broad and strong enough to support the greatest political structure human wisdom ever erected."

Destiny could be used just as easily to support American independence as to rationalize British imperial expansion, and revolutionary thought in the colonies was filled with echoes of the "city on a hill" and the "American Israel," blessed by Providence. Thomas Paine's statement in *Common Sense* (1776) that the Americans were fighting "the cause of all mankind" was only the most famous of many such declarations. While the struggle for independence occupied most of American energies and skill at disputation, some of both was directed toward the inclusion of Canada in the Union, primarily as a measure of security and despite the traditional enmity between French Canadians and the antipapist New Englanders. Even after the Montgomery-Arnold expedition (1775–1776) had failed to kindle enthusiasm among the Canadians, Samuel Adams insisted that "Nature designs we should have" Canada and Nova Scotia; and from 1778 to 1782 Franklin made repeated vain efforts to obtain Canada from Britain on the grounds that since the United States would inevitably acquire it anyway, Britain should thereby prevent future clashes.

The achievement of independence caused active expansionism to subside for nearly a generation, but national idealism and pride continued to grow, nourished by editorials, pamphlets, and Fourth of July addresses such as that of the writer and diplomat Joel Barlow in 1789, which proclaimed every American "the legislator of half mankind." In London, Michel-Guillaume Jean de Crèvecoeur celebrated American virtues in his *Letters From an American Farmer* (1782; reprinted through the 1780's); and Thomas Jefferson proposed that the Great Seal of the United States should depict the children of Israel following a pillar of light. When the explorer-author John Filson sought to attract immigrants to Kentucky, he called it "the central part of the extensive American empire . . . an asylum in the wilderness for the distressed of mankind" (1784). In his *American Geography* (1789), Jedidiah Morse predicted that the United States would humanize mankind and establish its natural rights in "the largest empire that ever existed." But as yet many believed with Jefferson that although Americans might occupy other parts of the continent, they would form independent daughter nations; in his inaugural address of 1801 he stated that the United States possessed "a chosen country, with room enough for our descendants to the thousandth and thousandth generation."

Jefferson proved a bad prophet. Years before he became president the question of Westerners' rights to navigate the lower Mississippi River through Spanish territory had begun to revive the latent expansionism. Their supporters argued national security and the essential unity of the Mississippi valley. For example, the *New York Evening Post* (1803) declared that the valley "belongs *of right* to the United States to regulate the future destiny of *North America.*" In the Mississippi question the superiority of American political institutions did not play as positive a role as usual; indeed, one of the few objections to the Louisiana Purchase (1803) was that it would give votes and power to people unprepared for democracy. As the Federalist Josiah Quincy declared, it was bad enough to admit Kentuckians to Congress; now the country would be governed by "buffaloes from the head of the Missouri and alligators from the Red River."

Jefferson soon resolved his early doubts about the constitutionality of the Louisiana Purchase. He still believed in a compact republic; but in 1809 he wrote to James Madison that the added territory would make possible "such an empire for liberty as [the world] has never surveyed since the creation; and I am persuaded no constitution was ever before so well calculated as ours for extensive empire and self-government." In 1804, a Fourth of July orator, the journalist Joseph R. Chandler, called Louisiana "the commencement of our anticipating hopes" and looked for the day when "our boundaries shall be those which Nature has formed for a great, powerful, and free State." The Floridas, occupying the Gulf coast, provided an obviously natural boundary. About 1803 Gouverneur Morris declared them "joined to us by the hand of the Almighty"; and in a later newspaper it was declared: "They as naturally belong to us as the county of Cornwall does to England." Jefferson even suggested extending the "natural boundary" of American territorial waters eastward to the Gulf Stream.

Divine destiny and natural boundaries also figured prominently in the American desire for

Canada before and during the War of 1812. One member of the House of Representatives declared that "the great Disposer of Human Events intended [the St. Lawrence and the Mississippi valleys] . . . should belong to the same people"; during the 1811–1812 congressional session, another member went even further: "To me, sir, it appears that the Author of Nature has marked our limits in the south, by the Gulf of Mexico; and on the north, by the regions of eternal frost." At the same time General William Henry Harrison was pushing the Indian frontier westward by force and guile; for justification, he asked: "Is one of the fairest portions of the globe to remain in a state of nature, the haunt of a few wretched savages, when it seems destined by the Creator to give support to a large population and to be the seat of civilization, of science, and of true religion?"

The most distinguished and consistent forerunner of O'Sullivan was John Quincy Adams, who, unlike Jefferson, seems to have embraced continentalism at least as early as the Louisiana Purchase and preached it without qualifications until he became an active abolitionist during the 1830's. Adams wrote to his father in 1811 that "the whole continent of North America appears to be destined by Divine Providence to be peopled by one *nation*, speaking one language, professing one general system of religious and political principles, and accustomed to one general tenor of social usages and customs." At a cabinet meeting in 1819, Adams declared that this continental dominion "was as much a law of nature . . . as that the Mississippi should flow to the sea"; to disavow American ambitions would be hypocrisy. In 1823 he called Cuba and Puerto Rico "natural appendages" to North America; Cuba, in particular, he thought "indispensable to the continuance and integrity of the Union itself" and likely to fall naturally to the United States, like a ripe apple, by the law of political gravitation. The historian Samuel Flagg Bemis has written that the Monroe Doctrine was "the voice of Manifest Destiny," being "inseparable from the continental expansion of the United States." If James Monroe and his cabinet consciously intended to reserve territory for future expansion, the inspiration probably came from Secretary of State Adams. After he became an

abolitionist, Adams ceased to support the annexation of Texas—indeed, in 1843 he threatened Northern secession to prevent it—but he continued to defend the American right to the Oregon territory. In 1846, only a little over two years before his death, he justified its acquisition (on the floor of the House) by citing God's command to man: "Be fruitful and multiply, and replenish the earth and subdue it. . . ." It was the American destiny, he went on, to ". . . make a great nation [in Oregon] instead of hunting grounds, for the buffaloes, braves, and savages of the desert."

As publicists discussed the Texas and Oregon questions during the 1820's, 1830's, and early 1840's, they honed and polished the component parts of O'Sullivan's manifest destiny, lacking only the unforgettable name. In 1819, when the Adams-Onís Treaty with Spain surrendered the wispy American claim to Texas, Representative David Trimble of Kentucky lamented that the government had "bartered away" a natural boundary (the Rio Grande), which "the great Engineer of the Universe" had fixed for the United States. In discussions of 1823 concerning Oregon, Senator Thomas Hart Benton placed a metaphorical statue of the god Terminus on the Rocky Mountains, but in the House Francis Baylies declared: "The swelling tide of our population must and will roll on until that mighty ocean [the Pacific] interposes its waters and limits our territorial empire." A depression beginning in 1837 increased migrations to Oregon. John C. Calhoun told Congress that this rapid advance of population "greatly strengthened" the American claim and urged a policy of "masterly inactivity" to await the inevitable outcome. The argument of natural boundaries reinforced by the spreading population reached the level of partly facetious hyperbole in an address by the irrepressible Major Auguste Davezac to the New Jersey state convention of 1844:

Land enough—land enough! Make way, I say, for the young American Buffalo—he has not yet got land enough. . . . I tell you, we will give him Oregon for his summer shade, and the region of Texas for his winter pasture. [Applause.] Like all of his race, he wants salt too. Well, he shall have the use of two oceans—the mighty Pacific and turbulent Atlantic shall be his. . . . He shall not stop his career until he slakes his thirst in the frozen ocean. [Cheers.]

The other part of O'Sullivan's rationalization—the superiority of American institutions—received an enormous stimulus with the publication of Alexis de Tocqueville's *Democracy in America* (1835–1840); he too predicted American dominion over the whole continent down to the tropics. In 1843 Andrew Jackson, not particularly known as a phrasemaker, seems to have first coined an expression, "the extension of the area of freedom," which concisely expressed Tocqueville's salient theme. Among many other statements of the theme, two of this period are notable. One was buried in an encyclopedic "open letter" (1844) by Senator Robert J. Walker of Mississippi, setting forth every conceivable practical argument for the annexation of Texas; near the end he linked expansionism and democracy on a quantitative basis: "The greater the extent of territory, the more enlarged is the power, and the more augmented the blessings of such a government." The other statement appeared in the *Democratic Review* (November 1839) under the title "The Great Nation of Futurity." It was probably written by O'Sullivan himself, and it gathered together previous encomiums of American greatness in terms as bombastic as those of Davezac, although without the major's appealing frontier metaphor:

> The far-reaching, the boundless future will be the era of American greatness. In its magnificent domain of space and time, the nation of many nations is destined to manifest to mankind the excellence of divine principles; to establish on earth the noblest temple ever dedicated to the worship of the Most High—the Sacred and the True. Its floor shall be a hemisphere—its roof the firmament of the star-studded heavens, and its congregation a Union of many Republics, comprising hundreds of happy millions, calling, owning no man master, but governed by God's natural and moral law of equality—of "peace and good will amongst men."

When O'Sullivan introduced the term "manifest destiny" to the American lexicon in 1845, his supporting arguments were already widely accepted as axiomatic. A few months after his

editorials appeared, the United States entered a war with Mexico, which offered almost limitless opportunity for repetitions and variations. Some defended the occupation of California with the argument earlier used against Indians in the Middle West: "Shall this garden of beauty be suffered to lie dormant in its wild and useless luxuriance?" As American armies advanced into northern and central Mexico, publicists began to think of regenerating these areas too, as "a part of our destiny to civilize that beautiful country and enable its inhabitants to appreciate some of the many advantages and blessings they enjoy" (from the *New York Herald*, a leading expansionist organ). Some also believed that if the United States rejected this task, England would occupy Mexico and thereby threaten American security.

In October 1847, after news of the capture of Mexico City had arrived in the United States, expansionist orators and newspapers burst forth in a flood of arguments to justify annexing all of Mexico: the "finger of providence uplifted for the salvation of a people" (Moses Y. Beach in the *New York Sun*); "the religious execution of our country's glorious mission . . . to civilize and christianize" (the *Washington Daily Union*, the organ of the Polk administration); and "the redemption of 7,000,000 of souls from all the vices that infest the human race" (the *New York Journal of Commerce*). Even Walt Whitman felt that the prospect for beneficent use of Mexican land created "a law superior to parchments and dry diplomatic rules." Just as the expansionist hysteria reached its peak, in January 1848, the New York State Democratic Convention promised: "We would hold it [Mexico], not for our use, but for the use of man." Even after the more limited gains of the peace treaty had cooled the passions of most expansionists, Ashbel Smith (who, as an official of Texas, had once resisted annexation to the United States) declared the Mexican War the beginning of "our destiny, our mission to Americanize this continent. . . . The sword is the great civilizer, it clears the way for commerce, education, religion and all the harmonizing influences of morality and humanity" (1848).

If supporters of manifest destiny sometimes confused force and morality, its many opponents were also inconsistent in their arguments.

A large group of Northerners saw in the Mexican War only a slaveholders' conspiracy; as one speaker put it, "Our boundaries are already wide enough for our safety and our permanence; . . . For the acquisition of slave-territory we are now engaged in a wicked war . . . in resistance of His commands" (1847). Others exhaled racism, as when the *Richmond Whig* asked (1846): "Are we prepared to place on a perfect equality with us, in social and political position, the half-breeds and mongrels of Mexico?" Many opponents of expansionism fought back with sarcasm and slashing accusations of hypocrisy. Representative Robert C. Winthrop of Massachusetts parodied the expansionist case for annexing Oregon by pronouncing that the Rocky Mountains were "mere molehills," and he observed dryly that "the finger of God never points in a direction contrary to the extension of the glory of the republic" (1845). Reading O'Sullivan's editorial of 1845, Winthrop presumed that "the right of a manifest destiny to spread will not be admitted to exist in any nation except the universal Yankee nation!"

The most poignant and ironic antiexpansionism of the 1840's sprang from the same roots as manifest destiny itself—reverence for the ideals of self-government and individual liberty on which the United States was founded. In the pro-Calhoun newspaper, the *Charleston Mercury* (1846), a writer pleaded: "Let us not cast away the precious jewel of our freedom, for the lust of plunder and the pride of conquest." Perhaps the best expression of this ideological opposition to the war appeared in three articles by the aged Albert Gallatin, published in late 1847. He reproached the United States because it had betrayed its divine mandate for the first time:

> Your mission was, to be a model to all governments and for all other less favored nations, to adhere to the most elevated principles of political morality, . . . and by your example, to exert a moral influence most beneficial to mankind at large. Instead of this, an appeal has been made to your worst passions: to cupidity, to the thirst of unjust aggrandizement by brutal force; to the love of military fame and of false glory. . . . Is it compatible with the principle of democracy, which rejects every hereditary claim of individuals to admit an hereditary superiority of races?

But the next dozen years carried manifest destiny to new extremes of covetousness and race prejudice. In 1851 Raphael Semmes, a Navy lieutenant, pronounced the war "but the first step in that great movement southward, which forms a part of our destiny" and compared Americans to "the northern hordes of the Alani" spreading their new, energetic civilization over "an inferior people." At about the same time, *DeBow's Review* (1850) proclaimed America's manifest destiny to cover the whole hemisphere, the Hawaiian Islands, and parts of the Far East and Europe itself: "The eagle of the republic shall poise itself over the field of Waterloo, . . . and a successor of Washington ascend the chair of universal empire! . . . The people stand ready to hail tomorrow . . . a collision with the proudest and the mightiest empire on earth." Most expansionists were a little more modest and focused their ambitions on Canada, Mexico, Cuba, or Central America. As before, they emphasized the inevitability of expansion. For example, in 1854 the writer Parke Godwin predicted: "The fruit will fall into our hands when it is ripe, without an officious shaking of the tree." In 1859 a Senate report agreed: "The law of our national existence is growth. We cannot, if we would, disobey it." In 1860 William Walker, nicknamed "the grey-eyed man of destiny," denied that his filibustering was "the offspring of hasty passion of ill-regulated desire; it is the fruit of the sure, unerring instincts which act in accordance with laws as old as creation. . . . The history of the world presents no such Utopian vision as that of an inferior race yielding meekly and peacefully to the controlling influence of a superior people."

Rationalizations such as this further discredited the already suspect manifest destiny. Meanwhile, on account of other writings of the 1850's, manifest destiny was beginning to be directed away from territorial gains and toward economic expansion. The growth of California, Pacific and South American trade, and the opening of the Far East emphasized communication with noncontiguous areas over the occupation of nearby fertile lands. In 1846 Asa Whitney, the father of the transcontinental railroad, declared that it would "revolutionize the entire commerce of the world; placing us directly in the centre of all . . . all must be tributary to us, and, in a moral point of view, it will be the means of civilizing and Christianizing all mankind." With similar language men such as the hydrographer Matthew F. Maury and the promoter Perry M. Collins set forth plans for ocean travel along the "great circle" route and for railroad and telegraph connections with the Far East.

William H. Seward, who, after John Quincy Adams, was the secretary of state most influenced by manifest destiny, clearly reflected the changing orientation. Sometimes, like Adams, he envisioned an American continental empire, including Central America, the Caribbean islands, and Hawaii. At St. Paul, Minnesota, in 1860, Seward delivered a remarkable panegyric about an eventual North American union of white peoples and added: "Providence set aside this continent for the work." But he differed from most manifest destiny eulogists of the 1850's by deferring his dream to the indefinite future (until the slavery problem had been solved) and by opposing the use of force to achieve it. Instead, like Whitney and Collins he urged railroads as "indispensable agencies in perfecting the integrity of the Nation and in attaining its destiny" (1849). Seward sought Alaska as a way station to the Far East (by 1867 he was pronouncing Puget Sound "a base of future empire") and the Danish West Indies as commercial stepping stones to South America and the Pacific coast.

For several decades after Seward's retirement in 1869, manifest destiny sentiments continued to fluctuate between territorial ambitions and the desire for more general economic and social influence abroad. During the Ulysses S. Grant administration, Cuba, Santo Domingo, and Canada were frequently compared to ripening fruit, destined for ingestion by the American Union. But one writer on Cuba balked at "the immediate debts, . . . corruptions and demoralizations that will come with the island"; in 1873 he suggested that it had a "manifest destiny" to achieve its own independence. This antiannexationist sentiment was reinforced by Secretary of State Hamilton Fish's cautious diplomacy during the Ten Years' War in Cuba, Grant's own botched effort to buy Santo Domingo, and growing nationalism in the new dominion of Canada. The most influential writers of the 1880's shifted their emphasis from annexation to a more general but equally predestined racial or cultural expansion, using to good effect Charles Darwin's newly popular doctrine of natural selection, translated by Herbert Spencer as "the survival of the fittest." Thus Josiah Strong, a Congregational clergyman, predicted in 1885 that the civilizing forces of the United States, especially its civil liberty and "a pure, *spiritual* Christianity," would enable the American people to replace inferior races throughout the hemisphere and Africa. In the same year, the American historian John Fiske outlined in *Harper's New Monthly Magazine* the "stupendous future of the English race," destined in two or three centuries to cover Africa and Australia with "populous cities and flourishing farms, with railroads and telegraphs and free schools and other devices of civilization as yet undreamed of." To this process the United States would contribute its federal governmental system, its burgeoning economy, and its peaceful orientation.

During the 1890's a short-lived campaign for a "new manifest destiny" revived the mid-century territorial expansionism and its rationalization of inevitable compulsion. In 1897 the naval strategist Alfred T. Mahan called on Americans to "look outward" and reassured them that their country's growth had come about through "no premeditated contrivance" of their own but was "natural, necessary, irrepressible." According to the *Philadelphia Press*, the nation stood "on the threshold of a new policy as surely as it did in 1803, when Jefferson annexed Louisiana." Senator Henry Cabot Lodge disavowed territorial ambitions to the south, except for the construction of the Nicaragua canal, but in 1895 he added: ". . . from the Rio Grande to the Arctic Ocean there should be but one flag and one country." When Hawaiians, led by American descendants, overthrew the native government and petitioned for annexation in 1893, it was declared in the highly articulate expansionist American press that the United States must yield to "the hand of destiny." "The ripe apple falls into our hands, and we should be very foolish if we should throw it away." Five years later these sentiments prevailed, but meanwhile the chronic Cuban problem brought on the Spanish-American War. Henry Watterson, editor of the

Louisville Courier Journal, justified the war by citing "the law of man, the law of God . . . our own inspiration, our own destiny." And in an article of 1898, significantly entitled "War as a Suggestion of Manifest Destiny," the economist H. H. Powers wrote that forcible expansionism came from a natural human instinct for growth: "There is not a people living which would not, if pressure were removed, populate the earth."

Despite the expansionists, Congress declared that the United States would not annex Cuba, so the postwar battle over annexations was fought largely over the Philippine Islands, many inhabitants of which forcibly resisted American rule. Again expansionists rehearsed manifest destiny arguments. "The inherent tendencies of a race are its highest law," said Senator Albert J. Beveridge in 1899. "The Republic could not retreat if it would; whatever its destiny, it must proceed. . . . Race movements are not to be stayed by the hand of man. They are mighty answers to divine commands." In the same year Charles Denby, one-time minister to China, agreed: "Call it destiny, call it the will of God, call it the overruling result of circumstances, . . . there was no other outcome or outlook [but the cession of the islands]." As in the period of the Mexican War, however, such arguments stirred the opposition to challenge manifest destiny again. In 1893 Carl Schurz had warned that the acquisition of tropical territory would rapidly erode American character and institutions. Five years later he intensified his attack on colonialism with words reminiscent of Gallatin's in 1847:

> I believe that this Republic . . . can endure so long as it remains true to the principles upon which it was founded, but that it will morally decay if it abandons them. I believe that this democracy . . . is not fitted for a colonial policy, which means conquest by force . . . and arbitrary rule over subject populations. I believe that, if it attempts such a policy on a large scale, its inevitable degeneracy will hurt the progress of civilization more than it can possibly further that progress by planting its flag upon foreign soil on which its fundamental principles of government cannot live.

After the war and the defeat of the Philippine insurrection, Senator George F. Hoar concluded sadly in 1902, "We crushed the only republic in Asia. We made war on the only Christian people in the East. . . . We vulgarized the American flag."

A central idea of manifest destiny—the divine mandate to spread American institutions—appeared during the twentieth century in many forms: "missionary diplomacy" in the Caribbean, the crusade to "make the world safe for democracy" in World War I, and the antifascism and anticommunism of World War II and the Cold War, to name only the most obvious examples. But the term itself practically disappeared in its application to contemporary policy.

Why did Americans relegate the literal phrase "manifest destiny" to history books? A number of interacting reasons come to mind. In the first place, publicists of manifest destiny overstated their case during the 1850's and again in the 1890's, producing a revulsion against what many thought their hypocrisy and greed. Moderates who would accept the peaceful annexation of California and later Hawaii recoiled at the prospect of engulfing all Mexico and Cuba or stamping out the Philippine independence movement. Antiexpansionists seized upon this reaction and convinced many that the conquest of alien peoples was no divine inspiration but a denial of basic American political traditions of popular self-rule. Secondly, the incorporation of faraway lands and alien cultures seemed to threaten American unity and security. The rough Westerners in the backwaters of the Louisiana Purchase, whom Josiah Quincy had scornfully called "buffaloes" and "alligators," proved easy enough to assimilate, especially after the government had driven the Indians westward; but later skeptics more reasonably wondered how the United States could apply democratic principles to settled populations of Mexicans, Cubans, or Filipinos without being itself radically changed in the process.

Lastly, the arguments collected under the general term "manifest destiny" related primarily to territorial expansion and extension of political control. Seward and some other publicists tried to adapt these arguments to the spread of trade and communications, but manifest destiny was never well suited to economic expansionism. Perhaps a Bible-taught people

felt instinctively that foreign trade and investments belonged to the realm of mammon, not
God. Eventually, during the Cold War of the
1940's and 1950's, Americans came to regard
capitalism with quasi-religious fervor, in their
struggle against the communist antichrist. But
even then the divine basis of capitalism was
more implicit than explicit; and the rhetoric of
manifest destiny seemed too outmoded and
simplistic for the complex modern world of international politics and finance.

Both before and after O'Sullivan coined the
phrase "manifest destiny," the assumptions and
arguments comprised in the term contained
basic inconsistencies that make it difficult to understand, let alone accept. On the one hand,
with due respect to Merk, manifest destiny has
expressed enlightened humanitarianism in the
desire to uplift mankind through the spread of
free political institutions which—through good
fortune, nature, or Providence—had seemed to
find rooting in the young United States. On the
other hand, it has rationalized the subtle or
gross appropriation of neighboring territory
and sometimes the exploitation of neighboring
peoples. Even more confusing, manifest destiny is a basically irreconcilable mixture of determinism and free will. Concepts such as destiny, divine purpose, and political gravitation
(the ripened fruit falling from the tree) suggest
that American expansion was foreordained
from the beginning of time. Yet the case for
manifest destiny commonly became most urgent at moments of decision: whether to seek
New Orleans from France, to invite Texas into
the Union, to fight Mexico until complete victory, or to demand Cuba or the Philippines
from Spain. If a destiny is manifest, does it
allow a choice? Americans were never sure.

Students of world history will point out that
the component parts of manifest destiny and
even, to some extent, the inconsistencies mentioned above have characterized the nationalist-
imperialist ideologies of other nations: "the
white man's burden," "Nordic supremacy," "la
mission civilatrice," "sacro egoismo," and the rest.

Was manifest destiny, therefore, merely part of
a global pattern? The answer to this question
probably lies in what one believes about American history in general. If the United States and
its institutions are no more than extensions of
European states and cultures, there would
seem to be no reason to distinguish one expansionist ideology sharply from another. But if
the United States is "the last, best hope of mankind," as some have maintained, or if the
"American experiment" has any sort of special
meaning for the world, then perhaps the aspirations and problems of manifest destiny were
unique.

BIBLIOGRAPHY

Norman Graebner, ed., *Manifest Destiny,* American Heritage Series, Leonard W. Levy and Alfred Young, eds. (Indianapolis, Ind., 1968), is a useful survey of "manifest destiny" articles, preceded by an analytical essay. Frederick
Merk, *Manifest Destiny and Mission in American History: A
Reinterpretation* (New York, 1963), written with Lois Banni-
ster Merk, is a revisionist, generally disapproving survey of
manifest destiny from the 1840's to the end of the nineteenth century. Julius W. Pratt, *Expansionists of 1898: The
Acquisition of Hawaii and the Spanish Islands* (Chicago, 1936;
repr., 1964), emphasizes ideology and propaganda; "John
L. O'Sullivan and Manifest Destiny," in *New York History,* 14
(1933), gives the best account of the origin of the phrase
"manifest destiny"; and "The Ideology of American Expansion," in Avery Craven, ed., *Essays in Honor of William E.
Dodd* (Chicago, 1935), is a brief survey of nineteenth-century expansionist sentiments. Richard W. Van Alstyne,
Genesis of American Nationalism (Waltham, Mass., 1970),
presents a survey of expansionist ideology in the colonial
and revolutionary periods; and *The Rising American Empire*
(Chicago, 1960; repr., 1965), surveys American imperialism
through World War I, with considerable attention to ideology. Charles Vevier, "American Continentalism: An Idea
of Expansion, 1845–1910," in *American Historical Review,* 65
(1960), gives a summary of the ideas of Seward, Whitney,
and their contemporaries and the effect of these ideas on
fin de siècle imperialism. Albert K. Weinberg, *Manifest Destiny: A Study of Nationalist Expansionism in American History*
(Chicago, 1935; repr., 1963), is still the standard work on
the subject, a voluminous compendium of expansionist
statements, roughly classified in chapters by general
themes.
[See also COLONIALISM; IDEOLOGY AND FOREIGN POLICY; IM-
PERIALISM; NATIONALISM; PUBLIC OPINION.]

THE MARSHALL PLAN

Gaddis Smith

THE MARSHALL PLAN is the informal, popular name of the European Recovery Program (1948–1952), a major undertaking initiated and financed by the United States and implemented by eighteen European nations for the economic recovery of Western Europe from the devastation of World War II. The basic idea for a comprehensive, coordinated recovery program on a regional basis was publicly proposed by Secretary of State George C. Marshall in a speech at the Harvard University commencement on 5 June 1947. The idea and eventual program acquired his name. The Marshall Plan is widely considered the most successful and imaginative development of American foreign policy in the years of the Cold War.

The decisions of President Harry S. Truman and the United States Congress to launch the most extensive peacetime foreign aid program in American history flowed from three overlapping concerns. First, how could the war-ravaged economy of Europe be restored in order to prevent dire human suffering and economic dislocations that would be worldwide in their ramifications? Second, how could the expansion of the Soviet Union and its brand of communism, perceived to thrive on suffering and economic instability, be contained? Third, how could the United States and Europe avoid repeating the mistakes of the aftermath of World War I, which had contributed to the failure of peace in the 1920's and 1930's and had perhaps brought on World War II? In short, the Marshall Plan aimed to restore a decent standard of living for the people of Europe, stop the Soviet Union, and ultimately prevent a third world war.

World War II lasted for six years (1939–1945) and left European economic life in a shambles. A rain of bombs and the passage of contending armies to and fro had destroyed cities, railroads, and highways. Industrial and transportation equipment were ruined. Millions of people were without adequate clothing, food, or shelter. Wartime deaths, both military and civilian, were approximately 10 percent of the population of Europe. Farmers could not produce enough food for the urban population. Their tools were gone, their livestock dead or dying for want of feed, their soil unproductive for want of fertilizer. The food that was grown could not bring a satisfactory return to the farmers because of the shortage of manufactured goods to be acquired in return. Furthermore, the collapse of transportation systems prevented food from reaching the consumer. The basic source of power was coal, which was as important in the 1940's as petroleum became in the 1970's. But coal mines were producing only a fraction of their prewar output. Mining equipment was lacking, the miners were undernourished, and, again, the transportation problem was an obstacle to the delivery of what coal was brought to the surface. The lack of coal meant that factories could not run. Offices and homes were unheated and barely illuminated. Steam locomotives and electric railways were without sufficient fuel.

While World War II was still being fought, the United States agreed to finance relief for the devastated areas through the United Nations Relief and Rehabilitation Administration (UNRRA). This international organization was established in 1943 and lasted until the end of 1946. UNRRA staff members came from many countries, but the funds were primarily American. UNRRA was never popular with the United States Congress, many members of which believed that the United States should have direct control over and receive credit for the aid that it distributed. UNRRA became even more unpopular in 1946 with the intensifying political conflict between the United States and the Soviet Union. Critics saw the United States supplying aid and comfort, through UNRRA, to potential enemies. President Truman and Secretary of State James F. Byrnes agreed with the congressional critics. The United States ended its financial support. UNRRA died. During 1945 and 1946 the United States also contributed to European relief through a variety of poorly coordinated grants and loans and carried heavy expenses for relief in its zone of occupied Germany.

By the beginning of 1947, although the fighting had been over for more than eighteen months, Europe's economic prospects were grim and getting worse. The impact of a $3.75 billion loan to Great Britain had been negligible. The worst winter weather in generations was paralyzing what feeble production did exist. Germany's potential contribution to European economic revival was hamstrung by profound disagreements among the four occupying powers: the United States, Great Britain, the Soviet Union, and France.

The wartime alliance between the United States and Great Britain on the one hand and the Soviet Union on the other had begun to unravel even before the surrender of Germany. In 1946 there were bitter accusations on both sides and a series of ominous crises: over the prolonged presence of Soviet troops in Iran, over the inability of the two sides to agree on international control of atomic weapons, over Soviet pressure on Turkey for military bases, and over the treatment of Germany. Communist party membership in Italy and France was growing, and American officials feared communist political victories in these countries if the economic situation continued to deteriorate. Once ruler of the oceans and organizer of the world's largest empire, Great Britain was now a power of second rank unable to maintain its former worldwide economic and military burdens.

During 1946 President Truman and his principal advisers concluded that the Soviet Union under Josef Stalin aimed to dominate the world. Only the economic and military power of the United States and American moral leadership could contain Soviet expansion and prevent a third world war. The presentation of this conclusion by the Truman administration to the Congress and the American people was but a matter of time and opportune circumstance. The circumstance was provided by a British decision in February 1947 to end support for the conservative government of Greece embattled in a civil war against left-wing insurgents. Communists were the predominant element in the insurgent movement, and they were receiving material support from communist Yugoslavia and some encouragement from the Soviet Union. The Truman administration believed that insurgent triumph in Greece would be a victory for the Soviet Union. Neighboring Turkey might succumb to Russian pressure. The strategic stability of the Middle East would be endangered. The will to resist communism in Italy and France would be undermined. If Greece fell, all of Europe would be endangered.

Accordingly, on 12 March 1947 President Truman proclaimed in a message to Congress that "totalitarian regimes imposed upon free peoples, by direct or indirect aggression, undermine the foundations of international peace and hence the security of the United States. . . . I believe that it must be the policy of the United States to support free peoples who are resisting attempted subjugation by armed minorities or by outside pressures." This was the Truman Doctrine. To carry out this new policy the president requested, and the Congress granted, $400 million for military aid to Greece and Turkey.

American leaders in the mid-1940's were animated by a determination to avoid the supposed mistakes of the era of World War I. According to a view of history enshrined in innumerable political speeches, newspaper editorials, and textbooks, the United States had bungled an opportunity to retain the leadership of the world, create stable economic growth and prosperity, and ensure lasting peace. By repudiating collective security through the League of Nations from 1919 to 1920, by pursuing selfish economic policies in the 1920's, and by refusing to build up the military power necessary to give pause to totalitarian aggressors in the 1930's, the United States had contributed to the coming of World War II. Now the United States had an opportunity seldom accorded to an individual much less to an entire nation: a second chance to make amends for past mistakes. This second chance had three aspects: first, support for the United Nations; second, maintenance of military strength and political leadership among friendly nations; third, a comprehensive, multilateral approach to world economic problems. The root causes of war, many Americans believed, were economic. When nations pursued selfish, aggressive economic policies the overall level of world trade declined. With the decline of world trade, unemployment rose. Unemployment led to human suffering and political instability. Spiritually akin to Nazi totalitarianism, communism fed on suffering and instability. Totalitarian regimes were inherently warlike and also threatened the basic values of American and Western European civilization. The expansion of communism made war, or defeat of the West without war, inevitable.

Another "lesson" from the experience after World War I related to Germany. In the 1920's the French and British had imposed upon Germany heavy and politically humiliating demands for the payment of reparations. The United States had criticized the harshness of Allied treatment of Germany but had not forgiven the Allies for the debts that they owed to the United States. The tangle of reparations and war debts left a bitter legacy. American investors indirectly financed reparations by buying German bonds, and resented money lost in the process. German humiliation gave Hitler an opportunity to win converts to the Nazi party and ultimately seize power.

Although virtually all Americans agreed that the post-World War I treatment of Germany had been incorrect, they could not agree on policy for post-World War II. Some believed, with President Franklin D. Roosevelt's secretary of the treasury, Henry Morgenthau, Jr., that Germany should be severely punished for its aggression and that the German economy should be forcibly held to a low level. German resources should be used for the rehabilitation of Germany's former enemies. Relatively little sympathy should be shown for Germans themselves. Other Americans, whose views became more influential during 1946, argued that drastic treatment of the German economy would simply impose a heavy burden of relief and occupation costs on the United States. Furthermore, with its skilled working population, Germany was the most advanced industrial state in Europe. German talent and industrial potential could be channeled into peaceful lines. To suppress the German economy would be to make European recovery as a whole almost impossible.

The Soviet Union and France, for different reasons, were obstacles to the revival of the German economy. Ideological differences between the Soviet Union and the West led to the economic isolation of the Soviet zone of occupation in the eastern third of Germany. By the spring of 1947 the United States government had given up hope of reaching agreement with the Soviet Union on economic policies for Germany as a whole. On the other hand, the French government was understandably obsessed by fear of and hatred for Germany, which had invaded French territory three times within the memory of men yet living. The French consistently opposed American proposals to stimulate the German economy while pressing their own futile dream of detaching the Saar, the Rhineland, and the Ruhr from Germany and assuring permanent French industrial superiority in Western Europe.

The treatment of Germany was controversial within the American government and among the occupying powers. The State Department emphasized the goal of restoring France as a major power and thus was unwilling to force the French to retreat from their noncooperative and punitive policy toward Germany. The department found it easier and politically more effective to blame the Soviet Union for all difficulties in Germany. On the other hand, the American army carried the burden of administration of the American zone of Germany. The army wanted rapid economic rehabilitation so that Germany could become self-supporting and its population content, thus easing the burden of occupation. The army enlisted former president Herbert Hoover to its cause. With close ties to the Republican leadership in Congress, Hoover prepared a vigorous report calling for German economic recovery as the key to European recovery. The State Department was appalled by the bluntness of the Hoover approach and saw it endangering the American understanding with France. A German revival would have to be engineered in a way that would reward and thus mollify France. Here, as John Gimbel has shown in his *The Origins of the Marshall Plan* (1976), was a principal source for American policy.

In January 1947 General Marshall succeeded Byrnes as secretary of state. During World War II, Marshall had served as chief of staff of the army, the senior officer in charge of American military strategy. In 1945 and 1946 he was on a special mission to China in an effort to prevent civil war between the Chinese Nationalists and the communists. There was no one more trusted and respected by President Truman than Marshall. The general's greatest strength was his ability to inspire subordinates to "avoid trivia," examine all the ramifications of a problem, and seek a solution in the most comprehensive way. Under Marshall's direction the State Department began a series of broad studies of American foreign aid. Marshall also established a new institution within the State Department: the Policy Planning Staff with George F. Kennan as first director. The Policy Planning Staff was freed from the burden of day-to-day administrative duties and was charged with the responsibility for long-range planning.

Marshall's second in command in the State Department was Under Secretary of State Dean Acheson, who possessed a powerful intellect and a deep conviction that the United States had inherited Great Britain's role as world leader. Acheson had little faith in the United Nations, but he did believe that the United States had the power to stimulate the economic recovery, the military strength, and the political will of Western Europe in the face of Soviet expansion. Since joining the State Department in 1941, he had been involved primarily with international economic questions. Acheson shared a belief with many others in the State Department that the Truman Doctrine approach was too limited, too ad hoc, and not sufficiently directed toward fundamental problems.

Secretary Marshall was in Moscow in March and April 1947 attending a conference of Big Four foreign ministers (the United States, Great Britain, the Soviet Union, and France). Germany was the main item on the agenda. As expected, Marshall failed to reach agreement with the Soviet Union or France, although he and Ernest Bevin, his British counterpart, made plans for removing restrictions on German production in the American and British zones. Marshall was worried, however, about how to carry out Anglo-American plans without antagonizing France. Later he claimed that the Marshall Plan originated in his own mind when he was at the Moscow meeting. As he reported in a radio address to the American people on his return in late April: "The recovery of Europe has been far slower than had been expected. . . . The patient is sinking while the doctors deliberate . . . action cannot await compromise through exhaustion." Marshall wanted action, and got action.

The State Department under Marshall's orders took the lead in consulting the War and Navy departments and the Bureau of the Budget. The Bureau of the Budget stressed the desire of Congress "to see the whole picture at once," and to be presented with some idea of "the overall pattern of U.S. foreign assistance" in order to set legislative priorities. In April the State-War-Navy Coordinating Committee (SWNCC) produced a broad discussion of American purposes behind a comprehensive aid program. It said "a program of assistance to foreign countries should enable the United States to take positive, forehanded, and preventative action" to promote American security. The United States should "support economic stability and orderly political processes throughout the world and oppose the spread of chaos and extremism." For "chaos and extremism" read "communism." The State-War-Navy Coordinating Committee said the United States should give highest priority to nations or areas that are vital to its national security. By providing timely, well-directed support the determination of other nations to maintain their own freedom will be stiffened, but failure will cause other nations to "lose faith in the leadership of the United States." SWNCC emphasized the physical and material foundation of security: "It is important to maintain in friendly hands areas which contain or protect sources of metals, oil and other national re-

THE MARSHALL PLAN

sources which contain strategic objectives, or areas strategically located, which contain a substantial industrial potential, which possess manpower and organized military forces."

The State-War-Navy Coordinating Committee was strongly ideological and anticommunist. The new Policy Planning Staff and its director, George F. Kennan, took a broader view. Kennan said that "the present crisis results in large part from the disruptive effect of the war on the economic, political and social structure of Europe and from the profound exhaustion of physical plant and spiritual vigor." The American effort should be directed at a "restoration of hope and confidence in West Europe" and not toward combatting communism per se. Kennan suggested that any program of American aid should have several fundamental characteristics. It should supplement "intramural economic collaboration among the Western European countries." The United States could fill vital needs and meet specific shortages, but the fundamental work of recovery would have to be carried out by the European countries themselves. There should be a four- or five-year master program; there must be no limping along on a hand-to-mouth, year-to-year basis. The United States should reach some agreement in advance with Great Britain. There should be guarantees in the program to "preclude Communist sabotage." And the program should encourage "some form of regional political association of Western European states."

Another major contributor to preliminary planning was William Lockhart Clayton, the assistant secretary of state for economic affairs. In private life Clayton was a cotton broker from Texas with a lifetime experience in international trade. With Europe steadily deteriorating, Clayton said in May 1947 that if things get worse "there will be revolution." He stressed the economic disaster that would befall the United States after European collapse: "Markets for our surplus production gone, unemployment, depression, a heavily unbalanced budget on the background of a mountainous war debt." Clayton said the United States had the capacity to avert disaster; what was needed was the will. It was essential to take the American people into the complete confidence of the administration, tell them all the facts, and develop a sound and workable plan. He stressed

the importance of using American aid to break down existing trade barriers that clogged the natural flow of Europe's trade and established uneconomic patterns for reconstruction. He believed that Europe should emulate the United States in establishing a large free market for goods and services.

Some historians maintain that the fundamental motivation of the Marshall Plan and of American foreign policy as a whole was a drive to secure an "open door" for American exports. They often cite the words of Clayton and other advocates of the Marshall Plan to sustain this thesis. Undoubtedly, American leaders saw some advantages in the Marshall Plan for the American economy. Naturally they stressed and even exaggerated those advantages when seeking support of business groups. But one should not confuse a convenient argument with the basic purpose of stimulating changes in Europe in order to prevent a third world war. Of course, this objective would benefit American business, but that is a consequence more than an aim.

By the end of May 1947 Secretary of State Marshall had decided to announce in a major speech the readiness of the American government to consider a comprehensive program for European recovery. One important question remained to be answered: How should the United States treat the Soviet Union and the countries of Eastern Europe under Soviet influence? The United States could propose a program vehemently and explicitly anticommunist; such an emphasis would appeal to the increasingly militant anti-Soviet mood of Congress. Or, as Kennan and the Policy Planning Staff recommended, the program could emphasize the alleviation of suffering and the improvement of the human condition generally. If the Soviet Union were willing to abide by the conditions of American aid, it should not be excluded. Marshall accepted Kennan's recommendation to "play it straight" and take a "calculated risk."

Thus, in Cambridge, Massachusetts, on 5 June 1947, Secretary Marshall said, "The United States should do whatever it is able to do to assist in the return of normal economic health in the world, without which there can be no political stability and no assured peace. Our policy is directed not against any country or

THE MARSHALL PLAN

doctrine, but against poverty, desperation, and chaos. . . . Any government that is willing to assist in the task of recovery will find full cooperation, I am sure, on the part of the United States Government. Any government which maneuvers to block the recovery of other countries cannot expect help from us." In other words, the Soviet Union was welcome to participate on American terms: disclosure of economic information, the merging of recovery needs with the rest of Europe, and the subordination of purely national objectives to a European regional approach. No American leader entertained any illusion that the Soviet Union would accept. To do so would be to abandon the closed society and the Soviet system of secrecy fundamental to Soviet behavior.

Another important unresolved question at this stage was the extent of American control. A complaint against the United Nations Relief and Rehabilitation Administration had been the absence of total American control over aid. But the Policy Planning Staff had pointed out the importance of encouraging the European nations to take responsibility for planning their own recovery, especially for integrating and coordinating their needs on a regional basis. Again, Marshall followed Kennan's advice and said: "It would be neither fitting nor efficacious for this Government to undertake to draw up unilaterally a program designed to place Europe on its feet economically. This is the business of the Europeans. The initiative, I think, must come from Europe. The role of this country should consist of friendly aid in the drafting of the European program and of later support of such a program so far as it may be practical for us to do so. The program should be a joint one, agreed to by a number, if not all, European nations."

Marshall had issued an invitation to nations of Europe to produce a proposal. There was, as yet, no "plan." British Foreign Minister Bevin and French Foreign Minister Georges Bidault reacted quickly to Marshall's invitation. They conferred in Paris and invited Soviet Foreign Minister Vyacheslav Molotov to join them, thus pursuing the "calculated risk" suggested earlier by Kennan. Bevin and Bidault believed that the Soviet Union would refuse to participate in a recovery program, but they, like the Americans, wanted to put the burden of refusal on

the Russians. Molotov came to Paris, but left within a few days. The Russians then began a sustained attack on the Marshall Plan as an instrument of American imperialism designed to enslave the economies of the European nations in order to save the United States from economic collapse.

After Molotov's departure, Bevin and Bidault invited twenty-two other European nations to participate in a major conference on a recovery plan. The nations of Eastern Europe that were firmly under Soviet control declined to attend. Czechoslovakia initially accepted, but then declined under heavy, even brutal pressure from the Soviet Union. While the large conference was assembling, the Soviet Union retaliated with a system of special trade agreements that bound the satellite states of Eastern Europe together and significantly reduced their trade with the West. This system is sometimes called the "Molotov Plan." This sharp break between the American and Soviet camps was a relief to American leaders. Walter Bedell Smith, the American ambassador in Moscow, had warned that Molotov's participation would be "for destructive rather than constructive purposes" because an "intelligent and well implemented plan for economical recovery would militate against the present Soviet political objectives." Now Marshall cabled to Bevin and Bidault, "At least the Soviet attitude in these questions has been clarified at this stage and will not continue to represent an uncertainty."

The Conference on European Economic Cooperation convened in Paris on 12 July 1947. Participating countries were Austria, Belgium, Denmark, France, Greece, Iceland, Ireland, Italy, Luxembourg, the Netherlands, Norway, Portugal, Sweden, Switzerland, Turkey, and the United Kingdom. Subsequently the Western occupation zones of Germany were included and, with the end of occupation in 1949, the government of the Federal Republic represented Germany directly. Yugoslavia became a participant in 1949 after Moscow expelled that country from the communist camp. The Anglo-American zone of the Free City of Trieste was also admitted in 1949. Congress showed some interest in adding Spain, but was persuaded by the administration that Spain under Francisco Franco was deemed so objectionable by the other European countries that its participation would jeopardize the entire program.

From the beginning of the conference there was tension between the idea that the European countries should assume full responsibility for proposing a plan and the contrary idea that the United States had to provide firm guidance in order to ensure that a plan was both practical and acceptable to Congress, for, after all, the American people would have to pay the bill. As the conference continued through the summer and into the fall, American guidance became ever more insistent, even dictatorial. This approach risked giving validity to Soviet charges that the Marshall Plan meant American control. The alternative, as seen in Washington, was failure. American leaders believed that unless the European countries were told what to do they would come up with little more than a shopping list of the separate requests of the participants, and not an integrated plan for Western European recovery as a whole.

The status of Western Germany in the recovery plan was crucial from the American point of view. A plan that made maximum use of the productive potential of all of Europe required maximum German economic revival. The French were opposed as always, but the United States insisted. The State Department by now was willing to accept French discontent in order to achieve the larger objective. This shift within the American government was of the utmost importance. For the next generation, American policy toward Europe would be oriented more toward Germany than France. As Kennan commented, "There is a serious gap between what is required of Germany for European recovery and what is being produced there today. Unless this gap can be overcome no European recovery program will be realistic."

The United States also told the conference that its preliminary figure of $29.2 billion for a four-year program was much too high; furthermore, the conference must state unequivocally that the completion of the recovery program would eliminate the need for further external assistance. Those nations with overseas colonial empires inquired of the United States if aid could be applied to colonies. The American answer was ambiguous. Aid would be forthcoming for European recovery, not for the governing of colonies. On the other hand, the European and world economies would obviously benefit by the increase in the production of raw materials in the colonial areas.

Meanwhile the Truman administration was preparing the ground for public and congressional approval of a large aid program. The president appointed three special committees. One, chaired by Secretary of the Interior Julius A. Krug, prepared a report on the relationship of American natural resources to European recovery. The second committee, chaired by the chairman of the Council of Economic Advisers, Edwin G. Nourse, reported on the impact of large-scale aid on the American economy. The third committee was the most important. It was headed by Secretary of Commerce W. Averell Harriman and was composed largely of prominent industrialists (7), bankers (2), labor leaders (2), academic administrators (7), and one former senator. The Harriman report was issued on 7 November 1947. It contained impressively detailed analyses of Europe's needs on a regional and commodity basis, not country by country. Germany, however, was the key: "This Committee wishes to state emphatically that the overwhelming interest of the United States is to prevent the resurgence of an aggressive Germany. The fears of neighboring nations are thoroughly understandable. On the other hand, . . . the revival of Ruhr coal output, along with the increase in British coal output, is the crux of the problem of getting Western Europe back on its feet. Apparent savings to the American taxpayer, accomplished by spending too little money on Germany, have thus far been more than offset by the consequent deterioration of the general European economic situation."

The Truman administration consulted closely with Congress, especially with the Republican chairman of the Senate Foreign Relations Committee, Arthur H. Vandenberg. Ordinarily the House of Representatives does not become intimately involved at a preliminary stage in foreign policy issues. But in this case, because a large appropriation would soon be requested, the House organized a select committee. Under the leadership of Christian A. Herter (subsequently secretary of state at the end of the Dwight D. Eisenhower administration), a group of congressmen conducted extensive investigations and interviews in Europe.

The drawing of plans and the conduct of investigations took time. At best Congress would not be able to act on a comprehensive program until the early spring of 1948. But another winter was at hand. The State Department concluded that some countries, "particularly Italy and France, are without adequate food and fuel supplies for the fall and winter, without sufficient dollars with which to buy them." Without emergency aid they could not survive. Any hope for a grand plan would then collapse. Accordingly, the administration requested and Congress granted emergency interim aid.

President Truman sent the administration's proposal for a $17 billion European Recovery Program to Congress on 19 December 1947. After extensive hearings and debate, Congress passed the Economic Cooperation Act of 1948. In the process the anti-Soviet attributes of the Marshall Plan received ever more emphasis both by administration witnesses and members of Congress. Gone was the fine talk of a program directed against no nation or political system but against human suffering. The Soviet Union stimulated this trend by word and deed, above all by supporting the communist takeover of Czechoslovakia in February 1948. The most influential speech in support of the act was delivered by Senator Vandenberg in characteristic high-flown rhetoric. "This legislation," he said, "aims to preserve the victory against aggression and dictatorship which we thought we won in World War II. It strives to help stop World War III before it starts. It fights the economic chaos which would precipitate far-flung disintegration. It sustains Western civilization. It means to take Western Europe completely off the American dole at the end of the adventure."

The legislation authorized an appropriation of $4.3 billion for the first year. The vote was 69–17 in the Senate, and 329–74 in the House. The opposition came from the right and left—from a few old-line "isolationists" who feared any American entanglement with Europe and begrudged every dollar spent abroad; and from an even smaller number of ultraliberals who saw the Marshall Plan as unnecessarily provocative of the Soviet Union (some called it the

"Martial Plan"). The latter position was best represented by Henry A. Wallace, fired by President Truman from the cabinet in 1946 for criticizing the anti-Soviet direction of American policy. With the president's signature, the law took effect on 3 April 1948.

During the congressional debates on the Marshall Plan, there had been considerable discussion of the most effective form of administration for the aid program. Congressional leaders showed little enthusiasm for assigning the State Department administrative responsibility. They preferred a new autonomous aid administration under the leadership of experienced business executives. The Harriman committee also recommended a new, autonomous agency. The State Department for its part did not want to undertake detailed operating responsibility. Accordingly, Congress established the separate Economic Cooperation Administration (ECA). President Truman wanted to appoint Under Secretary of State Acheson to head the organization. Congress, however, preferred a businessman. The appointment went instead to Paul G. Hoffman, president of the Studebaker Corporation and a member of the Harriman committee. Harriman accepted the position of special representative for the Marshall Plan in Europe. Harriman's office in Paris became, in effect, a second headquarters for the Economic Cooperation Administration. On the European side the participants in the planning conference created a permanent Organization for European Economic Cooperation (OEEC). The United States also established individual "country missions" to each of the participating nations.

The retrospective euphoria, which colors most accounts of the Marshall Plan "miracle," hides the persistent dissatisfaction of American leaders at the time with European performance. Americans were self-righteously superior in boasting of their own federal system and continental free market. They were impatient with the Europeans for failing to cast off overnight the constraints of nationalism and follow the American example. Specifically the United States was persistently critical of Europe's failure to endow the OEEC with prestige and extensive supranational authority. The British government was a particular object of American criticism. Great Britain found it psychologically difficult to adjust to the reality of diminished power. Britain still dreamed of empire (now called "the Commonwealth") and refused to consider itself a "European" nation like France. The British sought rather poignantly to invoke the "special relationship" with the United States, to be treated as an equal partner, not as simply another client. Americans found this all rather irritating.

In practice it is difficult to separate the three "R's" of relief, recovery, and reform. The objective of the Marshall Plan was recovery. But in the first year of the plan there were still millions of Europeans close to starvation. Relief had to come first. Thus, a large portion of the aid during the first year was spent on food. There was also heavy emphasis on agricultural equipment, fertilizers, and feed. In the second year Europe was closer to being self-sustaining in food. The emphasis shifted then to machinery, vehicles, and materials for the manufacturing sector. The objective throughout was to identify needs that would have the broadest impact and stimulate the greatest production. For example, the relatively small investment in machine tools could revive an entire industry. Locomotives, railroad cars, and ships could move existing products to places where they were needed. The staff of the Economic Cooperation Administration and country missions expended considerable effort on reform of management practices, accounting procedures, and methods of currency exchange and international payments.

In the first fifteen months of Marshall Plan aid, from April 1948 to July 1949, dollars were spent almost exclusively on nonmilitary items. But in the second half of 1949 a transition began, which, by the end of 1952, would convert American aid almost entirely to military purposes. American and West European leaders reasoned that economic recovery would be meaningless unless the military power existed to defend Europe against direct Soviet attack. The political expression of this thinking was the North Atlantic Treaty signed in April 1949 and binding the United States, Canada, and most of the recipients of Marshall Plan aid in a military alliance. The United States soon supplied military aid to its partners in the North Atlantic Treaty Organization (NATO). The successful detonation of an atomic bomb by the Soviet Union in August 1949 made military strength seem all the more important.

The outbreak of the Korean War in June 1950 was understood in Washington as signifying the readiness of the Soviet Union to use war as an instrument for the attainment of its ends. Military aid was accelerated. The United States pressed for the incorporation of West Germany in a European defense system, supplied a military commander (General Dwight D. Eisenhower) for NATO forces, and sent more divisions to Europe. In the final year of the Marshall Plan, ending 30 June 1952, military security had supplanted recovery as the overriding purpose of American aid. The emphasis on military aid retarded fundamental economic recovery. Labor and resources were diverted to nonproductive military purposes. Military demands strained scarce resources and contributed to inflation. Nevertheless, the momentum of recovery attained in the first years carried on and enabled Europe to produce both guns and butter.

The United States contributed over $13 billion to the European recovery program, less than one-half the amount which the European participants believed initially they would require. The following table indicates the amounts received by each country (there are some minor miscellaneous, administrative allocations not included):

MARSHALL PLAN AID IN MILLIONS OF
DOLLARS

Great Britain	3,176
France	2,706
Italy	1,474
West Germany	1,389
Netherlands	1,079
Greece	694
Austria	677
Belgium and Luxembourg	556
Denmark	271
Norway	254
Turkey	221
Ireland	146
Yugoslavia	109
Sweden	107
Portugal	50
Trieste	32
Iceland	29

THE MARSHALL PLAN

Approximately 70 percent of Marshall Plan aid was spent to purchase goods in the United States. Almost 12 percent was spent in Canada, mostly on food. The rest was spent in the participating countries themselves and in other nations. The following table indicates the distribution of aid by commodities:

ALLOCATION OF MARSHALL PLAN AID TO COMMODITY GROUPS

Raw materials and semifinished products	33%
Food, feed, fertilizer	29%
Machinery and vehicles	17%
Fuel	16%
Other	5%

American aid constituted less than 5 percent of the gross national products of the participating countries during the period of the Marshall Plan. But this 5 percent was crucial. It provided for essential needs, linked disconnected parts of a productive system, and provided incentives for the Europeans to adopt efficient methods on a regional basis.

On the political side, the Marshall Plan reflected and intensified the division of Europe between East and West, began the peaceful incorporation of West Germany into the European community, and stimulated the regional approach to Europe's problems.

The Marshall Plan did not fulfill all the hopes entertained for it. But it did attain a basic objective of recovery. In 1947 European industrial and agricultural production was hovering around 70 percent of prewar levels. In order to survive, Europe had to import $16 billion of food, fuel, and manufactured items from the United States, but had only half that amount in dollar reserves to pay for imports. By the end of the Marshall Plan, industrial production was 35 percent above prewar levels, and agricultural production 10 percent above. The dollar deficit had declined to $1 billion a year. Trade among the Marshall Plan countries was up 70 percent. The old European system of trade quotas, tariff barriers, and special discriminations was being dissolved—not as fast as Americans wanted, perhaps, but a trend had been started that would produce the European Common Market by the end of the 1950's. Europeans responded well to the American emphasis on productivity. Ultimately many European industries, especially in Germany, would be more productive than their American counterparts.

In the three decades since the idea of the Marshall Plan was born, countless politicians and publicists have called for "Marshall Plans" for Asia, Latin America, the Third World, and even for American cities. There have been other aid programs, but none with the scope or results of the Marshall Plan. Other programs lacked Europe's foundation of a skilled and experienced population, high productive potential, common culture and political outlook, and willingness of leaders to work together.

BIBLIOGRAPHY

Hadley Arkes, *Bureaucracy, the Marshall Plan, and the National Interest* (Princeton, 1972), examines the maneuvering of men and institutions within the American government. John Gimbel, *The Origins of the Marshall Plan* (Stanford, Calif., 1976), contends persuasively that the key to the Marshall Plan is to be found in the American desire to restore the German economy. Thomas G. Patterson, *Soviet-American Confrontation: Postwar Reconstruction and the Origins of the Cold War* (Baltimore, Md., 1973), stresses American hostility toward the Soviet Union. Harry B. Price, *The Marshall Plan and Its Meaning* (Ithaca, N.Y., 1955), is a semiofficial narrative containing basic facts and figures. Daniel Yergin, *Shattered Peace: The Origins of the Cold War and the National Security State* (Boston, 1977), is a detailed and original study of the thrust of American foreign policy in the years 1945–1948.
[*See also* THE COLD WAR; CONTAINMENT; ECONOMIC FOREIGN POLICY; FOREIGN AID; IDEOLOGY AND FOREIGN POLICY; THE TRUMAN DOCTRINE.]

MILITARISM

William Kamman

NEAR the turn of the twentieth century, Secretary of War Elihu Root told a Chicago audience: "We are a peaceful, not a military people, but we are made of fighting fiber and whenever fighting is by hard necessity the business of the hour we always do it as becomes the children of great, warlike races." Theodore Roosevelt's admonition, "Speak softly and carry a big stick," says it more succinctly, and the great seal of the United States with an eagle clutching both an olive branch and thirteen arrows expresses the idea symbolically. The history of the United States offers many examples of the nation at peace and war, speaking softly while carrying a big stick. But does one characteristic dominate?

Although the nation's rise to imperial size and world power during the twentieth century may suggest military influence, historians do not agree among themselves. Samuel Flagg Bemis, a distinguished diplomatic historian, described manifest destiny as a popular conviction that the nation would expand peacefully and by republican example; it was not, in his view, predicated on militarism. During the expansionist period (excepting the Civil War) the army and navy were small and there was no conscription. Dexter Perkins, another distinguished historian of the same generation, would agree with this interpretation. The United States completed its continental domain, he said, with less violence than usually accompanies such expansion. Perkins believes that Americans have only reluctantly recognized the role of power in international affairs and that they desire a reduction of armaments compatible with national security. Undoubtedly influenced by Cold War events, particularly intervention in Vietnam, many writers have challenged such interpretations. Dissenters such as J. William Fulbright, chairman of the Senate Committee on Foreign Relations, saw a trend toward militarism in foreign policy arising after 1945, when extreme emphasis on defense and anticommunism led to a national security state with huge military budgets, increased executive power, and greater commitments abroad. Others maintain that militarism emerged at the beginning of the twentieth century when—according to historian Gabriel Kolko—Presidents William McKinley, Theodore Roosevelt, and Woodrow Wilson "scaled the objectives of American foreign policy to the capacity of American power to extend into the world"; and still others, who discern imperialism broadly defined as a goal of American policy from the very beginning, suggest that recent military events are the logical culmination of trends over two centuries.

Militarism, like its frequent handmaiden imperialism, is an avowedly distasteful phenomenon to Americans. The term can be broadly or narrowly defined and may be tailored to circumstances. Webster defines militarism as predominance of the military class or prevalence of their ideals; the spirit that exalts military virtues and ideals; the policy of aggressive military preparedness. In his history of militarism, Alfred Vagts distinguishes between militarism and the military way, the latter referring to the legitimate use of men and matériel to prepare for and fight a war decided on by the civilian powers of a state. Militarism does not necessarily seek war and therefore is not the opposite of pacifism; in its spirit, ideals, and values it pairs more precisely with civilianism.

Although most nations offer examples of militarism, the attitude is most often associated in the American mind with Prussia and Wilhelmian Germany. Expressions of militarism and policies reflecting it were clearly discernible in the Germany of that time. The writings of historian Heinrich von Treitschke and General Friedrich von Bernhardi seemed representative of a general view that war was natural and right; and Otto von Bismarck, called to lead the Prussian king's struggle for army reform without parliamentary interference, emphasized power at the expense of liberalism, once telling the parliamentary budget commission that iron and blood, not speeches and majority decisions, settled the great questions of the day. For a time the Prussian nobility regarded the army as their almost exclusive opportunity for power and rank and sought to discourage the rise of bourgeois elements in the officer corps. Loyalty was to their noble class for the maintenance of its privileges. With his swashbuckling manner, Kaiser Wilhelm II epitomized German militarism for Americans, and the 1914 invasion of Belgium—despite a treaty guaranteeing that nation's neutrality ("just a scrap of paper" and "necessity knows no law" said Berlin)—represented the immorality of German militarism and its refusal to accept any constraints.

In the American experience some of the traditional marks of militarism are lacking. There has been no aristocratic class, except perhaps in the antebellum South, which regarded military values highly and the army as a career preferable to business and civilian professions. There have been few challenges to civilian dominance over the military and little disagreement during most of American history about a small standing army. In the United States, any militarism must exist alongside democratic, liberal, civilian traditions and sometimes even have their support. Generally this support has not been lacking when achievement of foreign policy goals (continental expansion, defense of the Monroe Doctrine, neutral rights, preservation of the European or world balance of power) has seemed to require military power. With that support the evidence of militarism in the United States increases as the nation accepts greater foreign policy commitments.

Late eighteenth- and nineteenth-century American history shows few signs of militarism. Americans were not militaristic because there was no rationale for it. Yet these were not years of unbroken peace, for as Root said, Americans were willing to fight when need was apparent. American fortune allowed war preparations after the crisis developed and permitted rapid demobilization when it was past, or as historian Daniel J. Boorstin, referring to the American Revolution and later American wars, has said, ". . . the end of the war and the end of the army were substantially . . . the same." Strong pressures for militarism in the United States came mainly after a long development of antimilitaristic sentiment.

American military efforts in the Revolution and the successful preservation of independence brought no changes in colonial antipathy (learned from the English cousins) to standing armies. For colonists the British army might provide needed defense, but it should do so with few demands on colonial life or pocketbook. After 1763, when England kept several thousand troops in America, there was distrust in the colonies; on the eve of the Revolution, the Continental Congress memorialized the king with their grievances about the standing army in their midst and the commander in chief's assertion of authority over civil governments in America. In the Declaration of Independence, the Founding Fathers repeated these charges. Many Americans were convinced that the army was not needed and colonial wars of past years—referred to by the names of the British monarchs—were of little interest to them. This attitude reflects the isolation of the colonies and illustrates its effect on military thinking. Thomas Paine emphasized it when he urged separation from Britain. Britain fought for its own interests, he said, not for any attachment to Americans: ". . . she did not protect us from our enemies on our account; but from her enemies on her own account. . . ." Independence would demonstrate America's isolation and lessen the need for a professional military establishment.

More important in colonial experience was the armed citizen, the embattled farmer who was ready at a minute's notice to defend family and community. Most of the able free male inhabitants of an English settlement were armed because dispersed settlement made it necessary. They were accustomed to the rigors of hard life and were familiar with firearms. Although

MILITARISM

most of them served in the militia, the drills and reviews offered little instruction; the men were little inclined to military training or subordination. These plain citizens with arms were the military men; their presence made civilian control over the army a reality well before adoption of a constitution in which that principle was firmly embedded. During the Revolution many of these armed men served in the Continental Army, the militia, or in some irregular capacity. They have been variously described as ragged, dirty, sickly, and ill-disciplined, unused to service, impatient of command, and destitute of resources. One foreign observer, however, believed the whole nation had much natural talent for war and military life. All descriptions were apt for the citizen soldiers for whom General George Washington sometimes despaired, but with favorable geography and foreign aid, without which success would have been difficult, they won. The victory amid political and economic confusion did not emphasize the military prowess of the Continental Army or of the militiamen, and fortunately, too, for the civilian tradition, the man who commanded those victorious arms did not have the seeming messianic impulse of Napoleon, Charles de Gaulle, or Douglas MacArthur.

Washington reinforced civilian dominance at the time the nation was formed and precedents were set. He understood that the Revolution needed the support of public opinion as well as successful military efforts; he emphasized to his civilian soldiers their own interests (not those of some king) in the conflict; and he remained subordinate to Congress. At the end of the war, when soldiers were grumbling about back pay and unkept promises of future reward, Washington counseled patience and obedience. It was a time when politicians were scheming with discontented officers and there was imminent danger of military interference in political matters, but Washington's position prevailed. In June 1783 the army disbanded and the following December the Virginia planter-turned-general resigned his commission and went home. Never again in American history would the army be so close to open defiance of civilian authority. The disbanded troops met general public opposition to their demands for further pay; many received little or nothing. Civilian

suspicion of military men was also revealed in public reaction to the Society of Cincinnati, a social and charitable organization of officers with membership passing through primogeniture. Opposition focused on the aristocratic trappings and possible military pressure on government. It was a natural civilian and democratic reaction from the likes of Thomas Jefferson, John Adams, and John Jay.

Over the years and after other wars, veterans' organizations developed to promote patriotism and economic self-interest and preserve wartime camaraderie. Some, as the Aztec Club after the Mexican War and the Military Order of the Loyal Legion of the United States after the Civil War, which were modeled on the Cincinnati, had little impact. The Grand Army of the Republic and the American Legion were of greater importance. Their influence has probably been more effective on veterans' benefits and patriotic observance than their sometimes divided opinions on foreign and military policies. As historian Mary Dearing has noted, the G.A.R was so busy with patriotic exercises, textbooks with a loyal Northern bias, and military instruction in schools (denounced by writers, peace groups, and some labor unions as militaristic) that it had little time for "jingoistic fulminations against other countries." Nonetheless the patriotic exuberance may have encouraged public sentiment for war in 1898, and when war came the G.A.R. leadership supported it and the territorial expansion that followed.

The American Legion has advocated similar programs of preparedness and universal military training. The legion supported the idea of a naval disarmament conference in Washington in 1921–1922 but did not want to sacrifice an adequate navy for maintaining the position of the United States as a world power; nor did the legion want its support of the Kellogg-Briand Pact (1928) outlawing war as an instrument of national policy to imply any support for reduction in the nation's military establishment. Whether the American Legion influences public opinion or merely reflects it is uncertain. In the great foreign policy debate before Pearl Harbor, the organization had its own divisions on internationalism and isolationism; and, as for many Americans, the legion's general anticommunist stance gave way before the realities of World War II, returned with the Cold War, and has seemed to adjust to détente. The size and organization of the American Legion have made it a more powerful lobby than its first antecedent, the Cincinnati; but public suspicion and criticism have persisted, reflecting perhaps the American civilian's distrust of military influence.

The colonial heritage, experience in the Revolution, and constitutional constraints influenced the military policy of the new nation. The Constitution firmly established civilian dominance, although it did not prohibit a standing army. The president was commander in chief of the armed forces of the United States, including state militiamen called into the nation's service; Congress had the power to provide and support an army and navy but no appropriations for the army would be for more than two years; and Congress had the power to declare war. Under Congress' suspicious eye, the army remained small throughout the nineteenth century, except for bulges during the century's four major wars. Liberal sentiment—a heritage of the Enlightenment as accepted by Americans and passed on through the Declaration of Independence—emphasized tolerance, progress, and the individual; these traits allowed only restricted acceptance of military development, especially in the absence of any great threat and as American expansion moved apace with little opposition. Alexander Hamilton might call for substantial military preparations in 1797–1798 and support creation of a United States military academy (a proposal attacked as aristocratic and militaristic, but nonetheless implemented in 1802), Secretary of War John C. Calhoun might in 1820 make a well-reasoned plea for the standing army against economy cuts, or Henry Clay might argue for greater defense in the face of an alleged European threat during the Latin American revolutions—but they failed to alter substantially the American mood for a small army. Diplomatic efforts of John Adams preserving peace in the late 1790's, or of Thomas Jefferson and John Quincy Adams extending the nation's boundaries, or unilateral pronouncements such as the no-transfer resolution and the Monroe Doctrine all seemed to provide at little expense what Americans wanted.

When diplomacy faltered, the United States did turn to war. There were more armed conflicts in nineteenth-century American history than students may remember if they ignore the numerous army engagements with the Indians—estimated between 1,200 and 1,500—lasting until 1898. Some of these wars were aggressive, fought by a young, nationalistic, and expansionist people, but throughout the century the nation remained wedded to a civilian tradition. Even during wartime there was vocal and, in the case of the Mexican War, heavy opposition to armed conflict, marked notably by Henry David Thoreau's call for civil disobedience, more a challenge to the extension of slavery than to the war itself.

Slavery provided the moral setting for the greatest threat to the Union and the most severe test of the civilian-military relationship in the nineteenth century. The occasion was a civil rather than a foreign war, and for that reason the internal threat seemed more imminent and restrictions on civil liberties more justified. President Abraham Lincoln was not happy about some measures taken nor the exuberance of some officers in carrying out regulations, but he thought preservation of the Union required adequate measures, even including suspending the writ of habeas corpus, detaining thousands of persons for disloyalty, sending hundreds of provost marshals into the country to oversee conscription and internal security, and using military officers and men in political campaigns to ensure election of administration supporters. Few people today would question Lincoln's motives, although his means are debatable. Yet national elections were not canceled (Lincoln defeated a general he had earlier removed from command) and the restrictions were not permanent although military governments were established in the South, some occupation troops remaining until 1877. Noteworthy, too, is the civilian control of the restrictive militaristic policies—a condition, according to some historians, not dissimilar to the civilian aspect of present-day militarism. In foreign relations the Civil War demonstrated the nation's relative immunity to foreign dangers even at a time of great internal peril—what better argument to challenge calls for greater military preparedness after the war? Also significant was Lincoln's broad interpretation of presidential powers during wartime, a legacy enlarged by future chief executives whose actions have fed much of the debate on militarism and imperialism in recent American history.

When the guns fell silent after Appomattox, more than a million men went home and the fleet of almost 700 ships declined to fewer than 200, many unseaworthy. Public attitude was the usual postwar aversion to things military, although the war had its heroes and the people elected General Ulysses S. Grant president as earlier they had chosen George Washington, Andrew Jackson, William Henry Harrison, and Zachary Taylor. Old dogmas of civilian dominance over the military and a small army and navy prevailed, but there were changes affecting the economy and foreign policy that would alter the traditional civilian-military relationship over the next decades. In the thirty-five years following the war, the nation's population more than doubled; by the end of the century American manufacturers had made the United States the world's industrial giant; American exports during the latter half of the 1890's exceeded a billion dollars annually. Few people could doubt America's claim to the status of a world power: there remained only the emulation of European imperialism to give formal recognition of that fact, and that came with the Spanish-American War of 1898. Whether America's fin de siècle imperialism was a great aberration, part of a search for markets, a continuation of earlier expansionism, an expression of manifest destiny, or simply a duplication of European practices, United States policy would not be the same again and there were in the formulation of that foreign policy unmistakable signs of militaristic thinking.

As early as the 1840's General Dennis Hart Mahan, father of the naval officer and historian Alfred Thayer Mahan, had urged creation of a more effective regular army to carry America's influence to the world. Mahan believed that the United States was probably the least military of the civilized nations, "though not behind the foremost as a warlike one." "To be warlike," he went on, "does not render a nation formidable to its neighbors. They may dread to attack it, but have no apprehensions from its offensive demonstrations." The Mexican War had demonstrated the military potential of the United States, and however slow Americans were in profiting from the lesson,

the rest of the world recognized it. General Mahan's vision of military glory went far beyond defense of the nation to an extension of its power outside the continent. Despite Mahan's vision and the arguments of such generals as Emory Upton, who deplored civilian control over strictly military matters and overdependence on armed citizenry in war, there was little change in American opinion. While the navy experienced the same reluctance to abandon traditional military policies and became embroiled in politics and spoils, it was free of some of the public's extreme suspicion of a standing army and benefited immensely from that apostle of navalism and imperialism, Alfred Thayer Mahan, and two of his sometimes overlooked contemporaries, Rear Admiral Stephen B. Luce, founder of the Naval War College where Mahan expounded his ideas, and Benjamin Harrison's secretary of the navy, Benjamin F. Tracy, advocate of a battleship fleet. The naval building program also spawned lobbyists and vested interests in the industries providing the new matériel and equipment. Wanting to avoid overdependence on foreign suppliers, Congress in 1886 required navy shipbuilders to use only matériel of domestic manufacture. The following year the Bethlehem Iron Company agreed to supply the first American-made armor plate and in 1888 began production of the first steel propeller shafts for American warships.

Like his father, Alfred T. Mahan had a vision of America's world position—a vision, perceived through study of British naval history, not confined to defensive preparations. The younger Mahan's message emphasized seapower as a source of national greatness: the building of a battleship fleet to protect American interests, if not to reach distant countries at least to keep clear the main approaches to America. The sea is a highway, he said, and ships providing access to the world's wealth and traveling on that highway must have secure ports and must, as far as possible, have "the protection of their country throughout the voyage." The United States with safe frontiers and plentiful internal resources might live off itself indefinitely in "our little corner" but, suggested Mahan with a tone more of warning than speculation, "should that little corner be invaded by a new commercial route through the Isthmus, the United States in her turn might have the rude awakening of those who have abandoned their share in the common birthright of all people, the sea. The canal—a great commercial path—would bring the great nations of Europe closer to our shores than ever before and it will not be so easy as heretofore to stand aloof from international complications." He saw in Americans an instinct for commerce, preferably in their own ships, a possibility for colonies, and a need to control an isthmian canal. For him war was sometimes necessary just as the policeman's work was necessary; through such organized force the world progressed.

As many Americans accepted Mahan's strategic proposals to give a historical validity to their imperialist, militarist policies, so many also adopted Charles Darwin's theory of biological development to lend scientific support for survival of the fittest in international relations. In his study of social Darwinism, historian Richard Hofstadter has remarked that although Americans did not have to wait for Darwin to justify racism, militarism, or imperialism—all present in American history before 1859—Darwinism was a convenient handle to explain their beliefs in Anglo-Saxon superiority, meaning pacific and belligerent expansion.

Few people typify the spirit of Mahan in the milieu of Darwinism as well as Theodore Roosevelt, a strong exponent of the "large policy" designed to make the United States a world power and possessor of colonies to provide bases and encourage trade. As Roughrider, public official, or historian, Roosevelt admired strength, pursued power, was sometimes a demagogue, sometimes chauvinistic, his ardent nationalism easily becoming militaristic. Roosevelt's call for a strenuous life revealed much that could be ominously dangerous. "We do not admire the man of timid peace. We admire the man who embodies victorious effort; the man who never wrongs his neighbor, who is prompt to help a friend, but who has those virile qualities necessary to win in the stern strife of actual life." He did not want to avoid war simply to save lives or money; the cause was what mattered. "If we," he said, "are to be a great people, we must strive in good faith to play a great part in the world. . . . The timid man, the lazy man, the man who distrusts his

country, the over-civilized man, who has lost the great fighting, masterful virtues, the ignorant man of dull mind, whose soul is incapable of feeling the mighty lift that thrills 'stern men with empires in their brains' "—thus he characterized people unwilling to undertake the duties of empire by supporting an adequate army and navy. He urged Americans to read the *Congressional Record* to identify those opposed to appropriations for new ships, or the purchase of armor, or other military preparations. These men, Roosevelt declared, worked to bring disaster on the country; they had no share in the glory of Manila; "they did ill for the national honor." He feared the nation would become a weak giant like China. That tragedy could be avoided through a life of strenuous endeavor. Every man, woman, and child had duties: the man, to do man's work; the woman, to be homemaker and "fearless mother of many healthy children"; and the child, to be taught not to shirk difficulties. Roosevelt had little patience for the timidity of those who opposed empire or their canting about liberty and consent of the governed "in order to excuse themselves for their unwillingness to play the part of men." Not many Americans had Roosevelt's eloquence or his platform, but many shared his sentiments.

Nationalism, an effort to exert greater influence beyond the country's borders, and a willingness to threaten or use force, while not new in United States foreign policy, seemed more apparent as the country moved into the twentieth century. Several episodes of American foreign and military policy highlight this trend.

Deficiencies of the American army in the Spanish war necessitated a revamping of the military organization. Using European precedents, Secretary of War Elihu Root proposed several changes, including creation of the Army War College and a general staff. Much opposition came from entrenched interests in the army and the state militias, but through compromise Root's proposals passed. America's participation in World War I was more effective because of these changes. For some people development of the general staff raised a specter of militarism. Walter Millis, a student of militarism, writing in 1956 commented on Root's contribution and mused that without it American participation in the Great War might not have occurred. "But Root, like all large figures," Millis said, "was only a reflection of his times. There were many other architects of the great disaster of militarism which was to supervene in 1914–18."

The new navy was begun under the administration of James A. Garfield and Chester A. Arthur. In 1883 Congress approved four steel vessels, and the building program continued through subsequent administrations, especially the Mahan-influenced presidency of Theodore Roosevelt, when emphasis was on battleship construction. A major turn came after war broke out in Europe. Since Roosevelt's presidency, American naval policy had called for a navy second only to Great Britain. In 1915 policy proclaimed a navy second to none. The naval appropriations act of 1916 had no precedent for its naval construction plans. A strong opponent, House majority leader Claude Kitchin, argued futilely that approval would make the United States "the greatest military-naval Nation the world has ever seen." The act reveals an interesting dichotomy, showing the uneasy American attitude toward military measures by combining large appropriations for warships with a renunciation of armed aggression, and an endorsement, in principle, of disarmament. Wilson's support for a strong navy shows his realization of the interaction of military power and diplomacy. The navy would allow the United States to meet existing challenges and to perform the international tasks it expected after the war.

In Latin American policy and in implementation of the Monroe Doctrine, Americans showed a new assertiveness resulting, particularly in the twentieth century, in frequent military interventions, intervention to remain a standard response to political instability until the 1930's. In 1896 Secretary of State Richard Olney and President Grover Cleveland confronted the British with "the United States is practically sovereign on this continent, and its fiat is law upon the subjects to which it confines its interposition." A few years later Theodore Roosevelt, fearful of European intervention (perhaps a German naval base in the debt-ridden Dominican Republic), accepted for the United States the role of international policeman in the Caribbean. From the Roosevelt Corollary, the Platt Amendment with Cuba, the re-

sponsibilities of dollar diplomacy, and the 1903 canal treaty with Panama, whose independence Roosevelt assured by timely naval maneuvers, there emerged a Caribbean foreign policy often characterized by the big stick. American troops and tutelage countered political and economic chaos. Clashes were bound to occur: in 1912 American forces in the Caribbean for the first time went into battle to suppress revolutionaries, this time in Nicaragua. In ensuing years the Dominican Republic, Haiti, Mexico, and Nicaragua experienced extensive interventions, often with violence and with a full-scale guerrilla war in Nicaragua in the 1920's and early 1930's. Guerrilla opposition was not new to Americans, who had faced it in the Philippines after the Spanish-American War.

If broad interpretation of the Monroe Doctrine in areas near the Panama Canal and if growing interests in Far Eastern affairs born of the Open Door and the search for that vast Asian market cast the United States in a role of greater involvement calling for more reliance on military solutions, this was not accompanied by surrender of traditional attitudes toward military matters. Compromises were always necessary: even entering the war in 1917 was put in the perspective of fighting German militarism, of fighting a war to end war. While most Americans might applaud a combative nationalism that had Roosevelt proclaiming, "Perdicaris alive or Raisuli dead,"—when Raisuli, a Moroccan bandit, abducted an alleged American citizen near Tangier—or while pacifist Jane Addams might lose much of her popularity during World War I and have her speeches considered dangerous, or while Eugene Debs might be sent to jail in 1918 for a speech condemning war, these and similar events were more a result of exuberant patriotism of the times than a widespread tendency toward militarism. In the postwar years there is substantial evidence that Americans wished to return to policies less likely to involve force. Much of the opposition to the League of Nations came from those who thought Article X of the Covenant deprived Congress of a free hand in deciding on war. These men did not want to guarantee the "territorial integrity and existing political independence of all members of the League," for that might lead to a war not in America's interest. The disarmament conferences and the

MILITARISM

Kellogg-Briand Pact to outlaw war as an instrument of national policy did not usher in a long era of peace, but they were symptomatic of peaceful desire. Weary of the Nicaraguan embroglio, President Herbert Hoover and Secretary of State Henry L. Stimson concluded that marine interventions were too costly and should end. Revelations of war profiteering, exposés of the armament industry, and the revisionist historical literature on American entry into the Great War brought disillusionment and a determination that it should not happen again. Presidential power in foreign policy was suspect, the neutrality laws of the 1930's tried to close all loopholes that might lead to war, and there were restraints on presidential flexibility in foreign policy. One proposal, the Ludlow Resolution (1935), even indicated distrust of Congress on the matter of war by urging that declarations of war should be by national referendum. These questions became more pressing as world crises multiplied. During the debate on American foreign policy in the late 1930's and early 1940's, each side proclaimed its approach as the true road to peace while the opponent's was sure to involve the United States in war.

Among isolationists in the interwar period there was fear of militarism. Historian Charles A. Beard felt the military interests seeking a larger navy would, if left to themselves, "extend America's 'strategic frontiers' to the moon." If Americans rejected the policy encouraged by Alfred T. Mahan, Theodore Roosevelt, John Hay, and Henry Cabot Lodge and if by plan, will, and effort they provided "a high standard of life and security for the American people," using to the fullest the national resources, technical arts, and managerial skills in the United States, there would be no need for large military forces. Defense policy should be based on "security of life for the American people in their present geographical home"; the army and navy should not be huckstering and drumming agencies for profit seekers, promoters, and speculators nor defenders of every dollar invested abroad. Guided by such a clarification of policy, Beard said, military authorities could make calculations adapted to clearly defined ends; until then they "will demand every gun and ship they can get." Beard saw military leaders com-

mitting themselves to a policy of trade promotion and defense all over the world. Sometimes, he believed, they took dangerous chances and then tried to convince the people that national interest or points of honor were at stake. As long as naval strategists demanded more ships, men, and financial support, by using "the kind of propaganda they have been employing," they were more a danger to American security than a guarantee of it.

Senator Robert A. Taft also urged restraint on interventionist policies because he opposed war. He did not trust President Roosevelt; he thought there was little the United States could do about democracy abroad; and he felt war would expand the power of the federal government to the detriment of democracy at home.

Not all isolationists would agree with this reasoning, especially since German and Japanese aims appeared more aggressive. Senator George Norris came to believe by the late 1930's that despite the dangers of militarism the United States must rearm.

The first four decades of the twentieth century witnessed no marked trend toward militarism in the United States. Yet more than ever before in the nation's history, Americans were having to come to terms with world power, having to think about international relationships that had been far from their minds in earlier times. Many Americans believed that the old truths of civil-military relations were still valid, although they realized that some concessions were necessary for adequate defense in a world not free of war. The big question then and still today centers on how much is adequate. In the interwar years, the army was seldom above 200,000 men and most often below 150,000; there was rejection of conscription until 1940 and much debate on the advisability of compulsory ROTC in colleges. The navy also suffered postwar neglect, and many officers regretted naval weakness in the Pacific, where they considered Japan the enemy. A change came with Franklin D. Roosevelt's support of naval expansion and more jobs in the shipbuilding industry.

A majority of Americans came to accept Roosevelt's policy of gradually increasing both aid to the Allies and military preparation at home. When war erupted most people were still unaware that the free security from which they had unknowingly benefited for so long was gone forever. Many Americans believed that when the war was over national life would return to the prewar style. As Samuel A. Stouffer and others noted in their sociopsychological study *The American Soldier* (first two volumes of *Studies in Social Psychology in World War II* [Princeton, 1949]), there was little feeling of personal commitment to war after the early sense of national peril had disappeared. The war was simply a detour that must be taken before one could return to the main, or civilian, road. At war's end the soldier had no desire to reform the United States or the world; he was interested in himself and his family. Cessation of hostilities brought not-surprising demands for rapid release of fathers, sons, and husbands; by 1946 the number of men on active duty had fallen from over 12 million to little more than 3 million, which was reduced by half the following year. In his plans for the postwar world, Roosevelt had sensed the public mood and anticipated a small armed force. At Teheran, when Stalin suggested that Roosevelt's idea of four policemen to preserve world peace might require sending American troops to Europe, Roosevelt envisaged the United States providing ships and planes while Britain and the Soviet Union provided the land armies. And at Yalta the president doubted if United States support for future peace would include "maintenance of an appreciable American force in Europe." Clearly the United States accepted an international role and would not make the mistake of rejecting membership in the new world organization, but Americans expected to fit their participation into a familiar mold requiring only limited military effort. This paralleled Wilson's first hopes in 1917 that the American contribution to the war would come mainly from the navy and industrial production, and Roosevelt's hopes in 1940 and 1941 that nonbelligerency would prevent defeat of Germany's enemies while keeping the United States out of war. These hopes were lost in events.

With the destruction of Western Europe and the decline of Great Britain as a balancer of European power, the door to American retreat in the face of any new totalitarian threat closed. The challenge seemed to come from the Soviet Union, and this challenge as perceived by Americans has largely determined American foreign and military policies since 1945. Wartime cooperation with the Soviet Union had always been a marriage of convenience, although some hoped the social, economic, and political differences could be smoothed over to allow a peaceful working relationship after the war. Disagreements over Poland and Germany soon revealed the incompatibility of American and Russian postwar goals. By 1947 the administration of Harry S. Truman was convinced that the world was polarized between the United States and the Soviet Union, and to protect itself the United States must preserve the balance of power against Soviet expansion. Truman came forth in broad rhetoric to tell the American people that the United States would support "free peoples who are resisting attempted subjugation by armed minorities or by outside pressures." Not long after, diplomat George F. Kennan in his "X" article in *Foreign Affairs* provided an analysis of Russian behavior and prescribed a response in the form of "a long-term patient but firm and vigilant containment of Russian expansive tendencies." On these appraisals the American government based its foreign and military policies and over the years perhaps went far beyond what Truman and Kennan had intended. In his *Memoirs* Kennan regretted his failure to make clear that he was not talking about "containment by military means of a military threat" and his failure to "distinguish between various geographic areas." Later reference to "containment" to explain American involvement in Vietnam disturbed Kennan. Certain areas of the world were more important to the United States, he said, and the world situation had changed since 1947; there was no longer only one center of communist power.

Although the major change in American defense policy came with the Korean War (1950–1953), there was even before that conflict much of the temper of the war years. Despite rapid demobilization of American forces after World War II, they were still larger than during any peacetime in American history; the military budget was many times the 1940 level; President Truman was pushing for universal military training; and the United States was heavily armed, with a monopoly on the atomic bomb.

Nonetheless Truman was reluctant to raise defense spending above $15 billion, much to the concern of military leaders and Secretary of Defense James Forrestal. On the eve of the Korean War, a committee of State and Defense Department officials described in a plan (NSC-68) the potentially rapid economic and military growth of the Soviet Union and emphasized the need for strength if there were to be any successful negotiations with the Soviet Union or any agreement on arms regulation. According to Paul Hammond, it was a program calling Americans to rise to the occasion by giving more effort and resources to prevent further deterioration of the strategic situation of the United States. The Korean War provided the impetus for the administration and public to accept the call: the national security budget shortly went above $40 billion and the number of military personnel on active duty more than doubled.

Events occurring and attitudes established during the five years after the end of World War II set a pattern for response to subsequent challenges to American foreign and military policies. Supporters argued that reliance on well-prepared armed forces supplied with the latest weaponry and stationed around the globe was a deterrent to war, while critics perceived it as an example of militarism little related to the defense needs of the United States and, as in Vietnam, sometimes disastrous.

Many conditions acceptable for achieving victory during World War II have been denounced as militarism in the postwar era. Believing that the war was essential for the achievement of legitimate national goals, most Americans accepted industrial mobilization, strong and sometimes secretive executive leadership, large armed forces, large military budgets, and the use of whatever weapons were available. From the beginning of the Cold War, however, there have been many dissenters who doubt any international danger and question the military and foreign policies designed to counter communist aggression.

Probably the most cited example of militarism in American life is the military-industrial complex—an alliance between the military establishment and the companies supplying weapons and matériel used by the armed forces. The relationship was not new during World War II, but huge postwar defense bud-

gets and great dependence of some companies on government orders brought lobbying activities to new heights and saw substantial increases in the number of former military men on corporation payrolls. Add to this intellectual, political, labor, and geographic interests in various research projects or companies whose operations represented thousands of jobs, and there emerges a vast constituency to influence defense decisions. In his farewell address of 1961 President Dwight D. Eisenhower warned against unwarranted influence from the industrial-military complex. Generally critics of the military-industrial complex disagree with much of American foreign and defense policy since 1945 and fail to see any challenge requiring a large military response. Sociologist C. Wright Mills saw a greater penetration of military men in the corporate economy, which seemingly had become a permanent war economy, while Gabriel Kolko argues that the military establishment is only an instrument of civilian business leaders who seek strategic and economic objectives. Many of the critics reveal the old animosity toward munitions makers who peddle their wares that soon become obsolete and necessitate a new round of even more sophisticated and destructive weapons. Modern weapons are many times greater than needed to destroy an enemy, but the nation's security is less than ever before. Failure to achieve international control over weapons, for which some critics blame the United States' lack of suitable initiative when it had a monopoly of the atomic bomb, continues the wasteful arms race and increases chances for their use—an unthinkable event, or so it seemed until Herman Kahn's *Thinking About the Unthinkable* (1969).

Opponents of postwar policies frequently center their attacks on the president and his almost exclusive direction of foreign policy and his broad use of powers as commander in chief. According to critics, presidents have exaggerated foreign dangers and secretly committed the United States to other countries, entangling the nation in war in violation of the Constitution. Broad use of presidential power from Washington's declaration of neutrality, through James K. Polk's occupation of disputed territory, Lincoln's reinforcement of Fort Sumter, and Franklin D. Roosevelt's destroyer-base deal appears often in American history. The American people and their historians generally praise and admire (at least in historical perspective) the strong, active executive, but the Vietnam War and Watergate revelations have caused a reexamination of recent presidential use of power. Some writers who supported presidential prerogative but became disillusioned in the later years of the Vietnam War have been at pains to distinguish which presidents faced real emergencies and were justified in wielding their authority. The distinction is difficult.

Critics also note Defense Department influence in foreign policy decisions as another example of militarism. During the John F. Kennedy administration, the Joint Chiefs of Staff at first opposed a comprehensive test ban treaty because it might reduce American vigilance, and finally gave support only with extensive safeguards. During the Cuban missile crisis, the Joint Chiefs advised an air strike against Cuba, and earlier they had seemed at least tacitly to support American participation in military operations against Castro. Often cited are the optimistic and frequently misleading military reports of progress in Vietnam, reports that suggested victory was within reach with a little more effort. Acceptance of the idea that only the military people had the facts made effective challenging of Pentagon estimates difficult even for the sometimes skeptical President Kennedy. According to reporter David Halberstam, Kennedy's failure to match his growing inner doubts with his public statements would have made his successor's task extremely difficult even if President Lyndon B. Johnson had been less accepting and admiring of his military advisers.

No one can deny the widespread emphasis on military preparedness, the evident abuse of power by agencies created to improve American defense, the questionable American presence in Southeast Asia, and myriad other examples of militarism in American life. Nonetheless the traditional American attitude toward civil-military relations is still present if not exactly in its pre-1940 form. Reluctance to maintain a large standing army has given way before international realities that no longer allow the United States that free security described by historian C. Vann Woodward. There have been attempts to maintain civilian control, and the Korean War is a case in point. The controversy between Harry Truman and General Douglas MacArthur over limiting the conflict to the Korean peninsula ended in victory for the president. While the people might wildly welcome MacArthur home and while they might be bemused by the concept of a limited war, they wanted little of his plan to broaden the war; nor were there many ready to accept MacArthur's belief that military men owe primary allegiance to the country and the Constitution rather than those "who temporarily exercise the authority of the Executive Branch." General MacArthur won a brief, emotional victory—his New York ticker-tape parade bested Charles Lindbergh's almost two to one in paper tonnage—but it was General Eisenhower, with his promise to go to Korea to seek an early and honorable end to the war, who won the votes and became the soldier-hero president. His willingness to please the fiscally conservative Robert A. Taft wing of the Republican party and his search for a strong military policy compatible with a sound, growing economy—a concern not new with Eisenhower—was no surrender to militaristic thinking. In fact he feared that a prolonged military program might lead to a garrison state, and he wished "to keep our boys at our side instead of on a foreign shore," even though some American troops remained abroad. At times Secretary of State John Foster Dulles engaged in militaristic rhetoric, but policy remained generally cautious, although "massive retaliation," "going to the brink," and "liberation" were added to the slogans "containment" and "aiding free peoples everywhere"—slogans that undoubtedly affected popular thinking and allowed people to accept policies or actions without serious considerations. Involvement in Vietnam, where these policies and actions merged and gradually escalated, had no willing hand or perceptive mind to limit it until the commitment was very large. It was a self-perpetuating and self-deluding conflict without clear purpose, entangled in personal and national pride. Yet popular sentiment and journalistic and historical accounts of the war reveal a lively antimilitaristic sentiment that challenged authority and induced eventual withdrawal.

For some Americans the end of the Vietnam War dispelled fears of militarism. Others suggest only abandonment of American economic expansionist goals as seen in the open-door, or open-world policies would reverse conditions feeding militarism. For still others,

MILITARISM

greater congressional supervision of foreign and defense policies, limiting executive initiative, is needed. All these views are speculative. Finally any control of militarism rests with the people and their traditions. Democracy is not always reliable, for a warfare economy has many constituents and overzealous patriotism may lead to uncustomary actions. American tradition is firmly on the civilian side. Americans have not easily accepted the martial virtues emphasizing authority and subordination, and, at least in theory, they have accepted beliefs in freedom and the pursuit of happiness.

Historian Howard K. Beale believed that Theodore Roosevelt's more ominous predilections were restrained by democratic tradition, respect for public opinion, fear of political defeat in elections, concern for the nation's wellbeing, acceptance of a cautious middle-of-the-road approach to problems, and a sense of the worth and dignity of the individual. These traits continue to have support from an American consensus. When American policy seems to veer too far from democratic traditions, opposition grows, particularly if there is no clear relation between policy and national security and, in the case of Vietnam, if there are continuing demands for men and matériel. Withdrawal from Vietnam did not alter the general trend of American foreign and defense policy, and the militarism that critics see as part of it remains. Yet experiences like the Bay of Pigs, the Dominican intervention in 1965, and the Vietnam War have been sobering. Americans also seem to have become more cautious in foreign and military policies—the War Powers Act of 1973, the Nixon Doctrine for a lower profile in the Far East, and senatorial refusal to support covert aid to Angola—than they were in the heyday of the Cold War. American policy probably will not change quickly as long as most Americans see a challenge to their national security and as long as there are sufficient resources to contain domestic problems. With these considerations the major difficulty in the limitation of militarism will involve provision for adequate defense with minimum waste.

BIBLIOGRAPHY

See Alfred Vagts, *A History of Militarism, Civilian and Military*, rev. ed. (New York, 1959); Albert T. Lauterbach, "Militarism in the Western World: A Comparative Study," in *Journal of the History of Ideas*, 5 (1944); and Hans Speier, "Militarism in the Eighteenth Century," in *Social Research: An International Quarterly of Political and Social Science*, 3 (1936). These titles concentrate on the European experience, with some reference to the United States. Dexter Perkins, *The American Approach to Foreign Policy*, rev. ed. (New York, 1968), suggests that Americans on the whole have not been imperialistic and have not surrendered their essential liberties and democratic customs to demands of war. Arthur A. Ekirch, Jr., *The Civilian and the Military* (New York, 1956), notes the importance of antimilitarism in American history but sees the penetration of militarism through the technological implications of modern warfare and perpetual mobilization in the post-1945 world. The Cold War has attracted interest in the American military establishment and militarism. C. Wright Mills, *The Power Elite* (New York, 1956), sees a unity of the power elite based on the coincidence of interests among economic, political, and military organizations. Gabriel Kolko emphasizes that the growing military establishment is a result of political policy, not its cause, in *The Roots of American Foreign Policy* (Boston, 1969). For a description of the influence of the military in nonmilitary areas, see Adam Yarmolinsky, *The Military Establishment: Its Impact on American Society* (New York, 1971). Jerome Slater and Terry Nardin, "The 'Military-Industrial Complex' Muddle," in *The Yale Review*, 65 (1975), analyzes the literature on the topic and concludes that there is an exaggeration of the unity and coherence among groups and their effectiveness in controlling policy. Tristram Coffin, *The Armed Society: Militarism in Modern America* (Baltimore, 1964), recounts the growing military influence; and James A. Donovan, *Militarism, U.S.A.* (New York, 1970), suggests a cut in military manpower and reduction in defense appropriations as the best means for controlling militarism. Erwin Knoll and Judith Nies McFadden, eds., *American Militarism 1970* (New York, 1969), is a dialogue among politicians and intellectuals who bemoan current trends in military and foreign policies and doubt if they are defending the basic values of American society. For a coverage of American military history, see Walter Millis, *Arms and Men: A Study of American Military History* (New York, 1958), and *American Military Thought* (Indianapolis, 1966), an anthology; Harold Sprout and Margaret Sprout, *The Rise of American Naval Power, 1776–1918* (Princeton, 1969); and Russell F. Weigley, *Towards an American Army: Military Thought From Washington to Marshall* (New York, 1962).
[See also AMERICAN ATTITUDES TOWARD WAR; THE COLD WAR; CONTAINMENT; DISARMAMENT; IMPERIALISM; INTERVENTION AND NONINTERVENTION; THE MILITARY-INDUSTRIAL COMPLEX; NATIONALISM; NAVAL DIPLOMACY; NUCLEAR WEAPONS AND DIPLOMACY; PACIFISM; PEACE MOVEMENTS.]

THE MILITARY-INDUSTRIAL COMPLEX

David F. Trask

ON 17 JANUARY 1961 President Dwight D. Eisenhower made a farewell address to the nation, hoping to illuminate certain sound principles and various unresolved problems. The speech is remembered primarily because of its reference to a "military-industrial complex"—a "conjunction of an immense military establishment and a large arms industry." Eisenhower noted that it stemmed from circumstances unique in the national experience. No permanent arms industry had developed in the United States until World War II, but unprecedented threats to national security since then had forced the nation to build huge arms industries and to support a defense establishment of 3.5 million people. For this reason the military-industrial complex played a crucial role— "economic, political, even spiritual— . . . in every city, every state house, every office of the federal government." Although this situation could not be avoided, Eisenhower urged the American people to consider carefully its serious import. "Our toil, our resources, and livelihood are all involved; so is the very structure of our society." Then came a solemn warning:

> In the councils of Government, we must guard against the acquisition of unwarranted influence, whether sought or unsought, by the industrial-military complex. The potential for the disastrous rise of misplaced power still exists.
>
> We must never let the weight of this combination endanger our liberties or democratic process. We should take nothing for granted. Only an alert and knowledgeable citizenry can compel the proper meshing of the huge industrial and military machinery of defense with our peaceful methods and goals so that security and liberty may prosper together.

In passing, Eisenhower mentioned a related concern. Because many academicians and intellectuals conducted defense-connected research, the possibility existed that government might eventually dominate learning; but Americans "must also be alert to the equal and opposite danger that public policy could itself become the captive of a scientific-technological elite." The antidote to the dangers of the military-industrial complex was not to dismantle it; statesmen had the responsibility "to mold, to balance, and to integrate these and other forces, new and old, within the principles of our democratic system—ever aiming toward the supreme goals of our free society."

These striking remarks did not at first arouse great interest; but when the United States later enmeshed itself in an unpopular war in Southeast Asia, discussion of the military-industrial complex became widespread. During 1968–1969 a sustained debate took place on this issue, much of it associated with efforts of the Department of Defense to obtain legislative authority for two controversial and costly weapon systems—the TFX fighter-bomber (F-111) and the Safeguard antiballistic missile system. Publicists and scholars poured out a river of commentary—mostly polemical attacks on the military-industrial complex and those who allegedly composed it. Various terms to denote the complex became common currency: "the garrison state," "Pentagon capital-

THE MILITARY-INDUSTRIAL COMPLEX

ism," "the warfare state," "the weapons culture," "the national security state," and "armed society."

Historians have not yet devoted much study to the military-industrial complex. It has surfaced as a concept and concern only in very recent times. Moreover, well-developed bodies of theory and data are not readily available. The editors of the *Journal of International Affairs* have aptly summarized the situation:

> Of all the political ideas that gained popular currency in the 1960s, the military-industrial complex is the concept perhaps most gravely deformed by public mastication. The debate of 1968 and 1969 over the influence of the military establishment in the United States proved, with few exceptions, consistently unsatisfying. After all was said, the concept of the military-industrial complex remained muddled and its attendant questions of international and domestic political influence were still unanswered.

What follows is an attempt not to present a point of view on the military-industrial complex but, rather, to summarize the extant information about it as a point of departure for future historical study. Students of the subject have advanced conflicting views on its origins, characteristics, membership, activities, and legitimacy.

Many commentators have joined President Eisenhower in tracing the rise of the military-industrial complex to unprecedented problems of national security that appeared during and after World War II. Following all of its previous conflicts the nation had disarmed immediately and drastically, but the onset of severe Soviet-American rivalry in 1945–1947 precluded repetition of this practice. The needs of the military during the Korean War and the Vietnam War also helped to sustain large expenditures on armaments. Throughout the postwar period the United States took the position that the deterrence or containment of the communist bloc of nations demanded powerful military forces. Associated with this strategy was a continuing effort to develop new, more effective weapons systems, including those required to wage nuclear war. This requirement fostered extensive collaboration between military and industrial leaders. General David M. Shoup, a former commandant of the United States Marine Corps, warned against

"our militaristic culture" and stated this general view of the origins of the complex. "Both the philosophy and the institutions of militarism," he wrote, "grew during these years because of the momentum of their own dynamism, the vigor of their ideas, their large size and scope, and because of the concentration of the emergent military leaders upon their doctrinal objectives." Other motivations also existed: "The dynamism of the defense establishment and its culture is . . . inspired and stimulated by vast amounts of money, by the new creations of military research and matériel development, and by the concepts of the Defense Department-supported 'think factories.' " Shoup concluded that "the basic appeals of anti-Communism, national defense, and patriotism provide the foundation for a powerful creed upon which the defense establishment can build, grow, and justify its cost."

It was true, of course, that in the past suspicions had arisen of alliances between military and industrial leaders, usually as manifestations of lively antimilitary and antibusiness traditions. Many Americans attributed the aggressive behavior of Germany at the time of World War I to an unholy nexus of the Krupps and the military classes of Prussia. A similar thesis enjoyed popularity during the 1930's as an explanation of American entrance into the struggle of 1914–1918. The Nye Committee popularized the belief that arms manufacturers—"merchants of death"—had conspired to bring about American intervention. This kind of analysis is not new. Americans have frequently ascribed sudden and mysterious national setbacks to conspiracies and have embarked upon witch hunts to extirpate the conspirators. Former Secretary of State Dean Acheson explained recent criticism of the military establishment as a modern manifestation of this tendency:

> One of our failings as a people I think is a preoccupation with witches. For some among us it is hard to get accustomed to the new circumstances. The temptation is to take the old situation as normal, to regard the huge expenses and unremitting danger as aberrant, and to blame malign or heedless forces within our own establishment. Identify them, expose their machinations, cut down their powers, and lo the difficulties will be abated.

THE MILITARY-INDUSTRIAL COMPLEX

Increasingly, however, scholars seeking the origins of the military-industrial complex find its roots in the Progressive era of American history (1900–1920). At that time the nation embraced two concepts of great significance for the future, strong executive leadership and extensive governmental participation in economic life. These ideas provided a broad theoretical basis for cooperation between the armed forces and business during World War I. That conflict confirmed the necessity of a powerful industrial base for the successful conduct of modern war, as well as the importance of prewar planning to tap industrial capabilities in wartime. Paul A. C. Koistinen, one of the few historians to study the origins of the military-industrial complex, has assembled considerable evidence to support his view that the modern military-industrial complex "is an outgrowth of economic mobilization for World War I, of interwar planning by armed forces and the business community for future emergencies, and of defense spending during the 1920s and 1930s." The course of World War II confirmed the trend. When Soviet-American antagonism during the postwar period stimulated support for a huge defense establishment in peacetime, considerable prior experience provided a model for cooperation between the armed forces and defense-related industry to ensure national security.

Marxist or para-Marxist scholars advance another line of interpretation, holding that the military-industrial complex derives from the imperatives of the class struggle in history. The contradictions of capitalism give rise to monopoly and militarism, among other phenomena, as means of perpetuating the power of the bourgeoisie. The complex is considered a specific type of exploitative organization designed to concentrate the fruits of labor in the hands of the privileged class.

In order to describe and analyze the military-industrial complex, non-Marxist students draw upon two well-established sociological traditions. One of these, the Machiavellian thought associated with Gaetano Mosca and Vilfredo Pareto, finds expression in the work of C. Wright Mills. The other, which emphasizes the power of bureaucracies, derives from Max Weber; its most influential exponent in recent years has been John Kenneth Galbraith. In *The*

Power Elite (1956), Mills provides an appealing theoretical structure for the study of leadership in modern society. He argues that a narrow elite—composed of corporate, political, and military leadership—rose to preeminence in postwar America and that it operates with considerable freedom of action despite democratic institutions designed to locate power in the whole people. In *The New Industrial State* (1967) Galbraith develops the concept of the "technostructure" rather than management as the source of power in modern industrial contexts. It embraces "all who bring specialized knowledge, talent or experience to group decision-making. This, not the management, is the guiding intelligence—the brain—of the enterprise." This approach leads to a pluralist view of the exercise of power; many individuals and groups possessing diverse and frequently conflicting interests influence public policy.

According to Charles C. Moskos, Jr., the pluralist and elitist perspectives constitute opposite ends of a spectrum that covers the range of possible approaches to the study of the military-industrial complex. "At one end," he argues, "are those who see the military-industrial complex as one of many institutional linkages occurring in our society and which was engendered primarily by quite real external threats. Conversely, others see the military-industrial complex as a self-generating structure which is a force for repression at home and abroad."

Galbraith has applied his own analysis to the "national security state" in *How to Control the Military* (1969). In accounting for the emergence of the military-industrial complex, he draws attention to the general bureaucratization of modern life. In the case of the bureaucracy associated with defense, secrecy was required; therefore only a few insiders had full knowledge of Soviet weaponry and American responses. Outsiders thus found it difficult to raise questions about weapons acquisition. Dissidents often remained silent because of possible persecution by political figures such as Sen. Joseph R. McCarthy of Wisconsin. Another factor that limited criticism of the military-industrial complex was the failure of widespread domestic discontent to develop in postwar America until the 1960's. Only then did reform projects at home begin to compete energetically with national security for the largest share of the federal budget, a situation that finally fostered extensive discussion of the military-industrial complex. Galbraith treats the complex as a natural societal derivation from the pluralistic circumstances of modern life, one that presumably can be kept under control by various devices.

In contrast with Galbraith, economist Walter Adams specifically rejects the notion that the military-industrial complex evolved, without conscious direction and control, in connection with the general tendency to bureaucratic organization. He believes that industrial concentration results from "unwise, man-made, discriminatory, privilege-creating governmental action." Government has consciously fostered the military-industrial complex that defies "public control." Adams uses the term "private socialism" to describe the complex. This line of reasoning appeals to those who believe that the complex can, and should, be destroyed.

Pluralistic views of the military-industrial complex often stress countervailing power as the means of controlling possible excesses. Charles J. Hitch, who served as comptroller of the Department of Defense during the 1960's, sees not one giant complex but a "whole array . . . each promoting its own service or branch of the service, its favored weapon, and its own firm, each cheerfully attempting to cut down all the competing little military-industrial complexes. The mutual backscratching that goes on among them is more likely to be outdone by the backstabbing." He concludes that "the safety of the general interest lies in large part in the fierce competition among the many special interests that comprise the supposedly monolithic military-industrial complex."

Elitist approaches frequently lead to malign interpretations of the military-industrial complex. Harold L. Nieburg claims that defense-industry relationships originally called forth because of an emergency have been "normalized through a cabal of vested interests." For him the complex becomes "a fact of contemporary public life that is eating the heart out of our society, reducing potential for real economic and social growth and eroding the foundation of economic pluralism." One of the most extreme interpretations comes from Juan Bosch, former president of the Dominican Republic, who writes of what he calls "Pentagonism." No longer do advanced capitalist nations send out their military to conquer and exploit colonies. Foreign warfare or the threat of warfare provides "access to the generous economic resources being mobilized for industrial war production. What is being sought are profits where arms are manufactured, not where they are employed, and these profits are obtained in, and bring money in from, the place where the center of pentagonist power lies." In short, the domestic population is exploited now as colonies were in the past.

The most thoroughgoing indictment of the military-industrial complex comes from radicals, frequently of Marxist or para-Marxist persuasion, who deny the presence of countervailing power in American society. Marc Pilisuk and Thomas Hayden, who state views broadly representative of those held by radicals in organizations of the 1960's such as Students for a Democratic Society, see all of American society as a military-industrial complex. "It can accommodate a wide range of factional interests from those concerned with the production or utilization of a particular weapon to those enraptured with the mystique of optimal global strategies." It can accommodate practitioners of brinksmanship and advocates of arms control and disarmament. "What it cannot accommodate," they conclude, "is the type of radical departures needed to produce enduring peace."

Of particular interest to historians is the analysis of Seymour Melman, one of the more active critics of the military-industrial complex, who argues in *Pentagon Capitalism* (1970) that the military-industrial complex underwent a transformation during the 1960's. The complex to which Eisenhower directed his attention was "a loose, informally defined collection of firms producing military products, senior military officers, and members of the executive and legislative branches of the federal government—all of them united by the market relations of the military products network and having a common ideology as to the importance of maintaining or enlarging the armed forces of the United States and their role in American politics." During the tenure of Robert S. McNamara as secretary of defense under President John F. Kennedy and President Lyndon B. Johnson, the "loose collaboration" gave way to a clearly structured and formally organized system of "state-management." The Pentagon has become a central management office to administer the military-industrial complex. The managerial context, rather than the marketplace, constitutes the arena within which the components of the military-industrial complex come together. Melman concludes portentously: "A normal thrust for more managerial power within the largest management in the United States gives the new state-management an unprecedented ability and opportunity for building a military-industry empire at home and for using this as an instrument for building an empire abroad. This is the new imperialism."

McNamara himself wrote that he attempted to make important changes in the management of the Department of Defense, but he gave reasons for this activity different from those Melman attributes to him. He began with the assumption that the United States possessed sufficient wealth to spend whatever proved necessary to ensure its defense, but he also believed that strict standards of effectiveness and efficiency should govern expenditures. He installed the "systems analysis" approach in the Pentagon in order to arrive at the most cost-effective solutions to defense problems. During his long tenure, McNamara concentrated on three tasks: improvement of strategic retaliatory forces; development of nonnuclear forces; and increase in the competence of the Department of Defense. He concluded that on all but a few occasions his administrative reforms prevented the military-industrial complex from forcing decisions contrary to sound principles of ethics, management, and economy.

This brief recital of various views suggests that Carroll W. Pursell, Jr., is correct in isolating relationships among special interests as critical to the debate over the nature of the military-industrial complex. Do contending subgroups within the complex reinforce or countervail each other? "[D]oes the traditional American political reliance on the balance of special interests really work in this case to check tyranny, or has this special interest coalesced to a point where it can, to a dangerous degree, operate free of effective constraint from other interests?"

Who are the people who make up the mili-

tary-industrial complex? Almost all authorities identify three groups of participants—leading political figures in the executive and legislative branches of government, senior military commanders, and executives of large defense-related businesses. Several other groups are mentioned less frequently. Because research and development play a central role in the process of procuring weapons systems, both the military and private enterprise have turned for assistance to individual scholars and educational institutions. Many academicians, such as the physicist Edward Teller, have become a part of the military-industrial complex. Linkages exist with large universities, such as the Massachusetts Institute of Technology, and with private research organizations, among them the RAND Corporation and the Institute for Defense Analysis in Washington, D.C. Leaders of organized labor also participate because of their desire to foster employment for their members. Finally, various organizations enter into the equation. Among them are those providing liaison between industry and the defense establishment, such as the American Ordnance Association; others, like the Navy League, represent military personnel; and some of a less active nature occasionally agitate in favor of defense—veterans' organizations, trade associations, chambers of commerce, and certain fundamentalist religions. Journalist Jack Raymond summarizes the membership broadly as including "all those elements of American society—economic, political, and professional—that have a material or philosophic stake in a large defense establishment . . . in short, all who for reasons of 'pork or patriotism' support the Armed Forces' requirements." Those observers who favor the complex see its members as responding intelligently to real external dangers. Those who oppose it stress the desires for profits and power as motivating factors.

In a recent examination of the literature treating the military-industrial complex, Jerome Slater and Terry Nardin point to some serious deficiencies. They question the tendency of some analysts to rely on conspiracy theories as causal explanations. They also note a proclivity to simplistic economic determinism. Authorities prove inconsistent in specifying the constituent elements of the complex. Finally,

THE MILITARY-INDUSTRIAL COMPLEX

some theorists are open to the charge that they use implausible assumptions about the degree of power ascribed to the complex. These concerns reflect a general desire apparent among scholars to develop a more satisfactory body of theory regarding the nature and function of the complex.

Discussion of the military-industrial complex has centered not only on its general description and analysis, but also on a number of specific issues. Critics have charged that it is responsible for a bloated defense budget; excess profits in defense-related industry; improper defense contracting procedures; failure to bring about arms control and disarmament; collusion through the employment of retired officers in defense-related companies; corruption of educators and scholars; and a number of dangerous or questionable practices, including support of the international arms traffic, unnecessary stockpiling, and assignment of defense patents to private holders.

No aspect of the debate over the military-industrial complex has been more heated than that concerning its effects on the federal budget. Critics argue that the defense budget is larger than necessary to insure national security and that its size precludes adequate appropriations for such pressing domestic needs as housing, health care, welfare, education, and transportation. Spending priorities therefore encourage aggressive adventurism overseas rather than reform at home. Charles J. Hitch cites two reasons why the defense share of the

federal government has been so large in comparison with the share for nondefense purposes: perceived threats to national security and increasing costs of modern military technology. More hostile writers stress the lack of effective opposition to the demands of the Department of Defense and assiduous lobbying by the military-industrial complex. Statistical information reveals that the defense budget as a percentage of gross national product and as a percentage of the overall federal budget has been holding relatively steady in recent years, although the dollar amount has been increasing as the nation's economy has grown.

Those who wish to increase nondefense spending argue that dangers to international security have declined and that increasing domestic requirements justify such policy. In 1973 the outgoing secretary of defense, Melvin R. Laird, maintained that defense costs could not be lowered appreciably without courting great danger. He objected to charges that the size of the defense budget accounted for deficiencies in other categories. While costs could be cut to some extent by improving management procedures, he strongly opposed arbitrary cuts in defense spending to meet needs of other programs.

Critics of the military-industrial complex regularly present statistical information to show that defense contractors make swollen profits, but just as often other students produce data demonstrating that nondefense industries typically achieve even higher profits. No develop-

DEFENSE EXPENDITURES AND THE FEDERAL BUDGET 1939–1970 (IN 1954 DOLLARS)

Year	GNP	Federal Budget ($ billion)	Defense Budget as Percent of GNP	Nondefense Budget as Percent of GNP	Defense Budget as Percent of Federal Budget
1939	87.6	8.8	1.3	8.8	13.2
1943	177.5	78.9	35.5	8.9	80.0
1947	219.8	36.5	6.3	10.5	37.4
1952	337.2	68.0	12.3	7.9	60.2
1957	431.3	76.7	9.3	8.9	52.4
1962	542.1	106.8	8.9	11.3	44.2
1964	612.2	118.6	8.3	11.5	41.8
1966	720.7	134.7	7.7	11.5	40.0
1968	822.6	178.9	9.5	12.8	42.5
1970	960.0	192.9	8.3	12.4	40.3

ment causes more discussion than cost overruns on various expensive weapons systems. Some investigators argue that unexpected increases in costs derive from pressure for excess profits exerted by the military-industrial complex. Robert Art's research on this issue points in somewhat different directions. He believes that cost overruns develop as a result of five phenomena: "goldplating"—including expensive and unnecessary items in weapon systems; "bidding-and-lying"—entering bids known to be short of costs, on the assumption that the government will make up the shortfall; "profits for inefficiency"—basing profits on costs when making defense contracts; "managers without power"—failure to give project managers sufficient power to protect against cost increase; and "concurrency"—beginning production of weapon systems before completing research and development. The implication is that inadequate procedures and inefficiency, rather than the profit motive, cause cost overruns.

A related controversy, the question of contract procedures in the Department of Defense, perhaps attracts more attention than any other aspect of the debate over the military-industrial complex. Critics point out that the leading 100 defense contractors remain relatively constant over time and that they receive a disproportionate percentage of contracts in terms of dollar volume. Between 1957 and 1968, for example, the top 100 contractors' share of dollar volume varied between 64.0 percent and 74.2 percent of the total. Critics also demonstrate considerable overlap between the 100 largest contractors and the 500 largest industrial corporations. In 1968, twenty-nine of the largest military contractors ranked among the fifty largest corporations. Other charges are that defense contracts tend to go to firms concentrated in certain states and cities—for example, Texas and California, Dallas and Pasadena—and that the economic effects are therefore inequitable. The policy of awarding contracts through negotiation on a cost-plus basis that guarantees a given profit is constantly criticized because it tends to circumvent competition that presumably produces efficiency and economy. Also, the Defense Department occasionally advocates letting of "follow-on" contracts to companies that have completed previous contracts in order to keep them in business. It also calls at

times for "bailout" subsidies or loans for companies in serious fiscal difficulties, such as the Lockheed Corporation. Many critics believe that the Department of Defense should institute "fly-before-you buy" procedures—that is, contracting arrangements that require producers to deliver and test products before receiving compensation.

Supporters of present contracting practices respond to these allegations in various ways. Some simply maintain that the government follows normal and necessary business practices that are in no way irregular or unsound. Others hold that reforms should be, and are being, made to correct abuses, but that contracting procedures in general are appropriate. John S. Baumgartner, a businessman who is one of the few thoroughgoing champions of the military-industrial complex in its present form, argues that some problems arise because no management is completely free of error. Secretary McNamara once claimed that the Department of Defense in his time made remarkably few contracting mistakes—probably in not more than 2 percent of the cases. Recent research, notably that of Stephen Cobb and Charles Wolf, Jr., demonstrates that votes of senators and congressmen show little or no correlation with the amount of defense contracts awarded in their states or districts.

One of the most serious charges leveled against the military-industrial complex is that it campaigns actively and effectively against arms control and disarmament, and exerts a controlling influence on the shaping of foreign policy. Those who traffic in military procurement have a vested interest in an unstable international environment. According to proponents of this view, the profits and power of the complex would decline catastrophically if real progress were made in limiting strategic nuclear weaponry and conventional weapons systems. For this reason, it is claimed, advocates of huge arms expenditures use all available means of shaping public attitudes and governmental behavior to perpetuate an illusion of great international danger emanating particularly from the communist bloc of nations. Modern "merchants of death" pursue selfish interests in complete disregard of humanitarian considerations.

Two types of responses come from those

who reject these charges. Some affirm that defense spending has been essential to the preservation of security and freedom. Congressman L. Mendel Rivers, for many years chairman of the House Armed Services Committee, asserted in 1969 that without a huge industrial plant the military would be unable to perform its functions; then "our only hope would be that the Russians and Chinese would take a benign attitude toward our country. . . . We have got to get over the national guilt complex at having kept the world free. This is what we have done with our military might." Others insist that progress toward arms control and disarmament is slow, not because of the machinations of arms producers but because of the sheer complexity of the issues associated with restrictions on armaments and because of continuing instability manifest in world politics.

Senator William Proxmire associated himself with a popular complaint against the military-industrial complex in 1969 when he drew attention to what he considered to be a large number of retired military officers in the employ of defense-related industries. By his count 2,072 officers who had held the rank of colonel, naval captain, or above worked for the leading 100 defense contractors, an average of twenty-one per firm. Of this group 1,065 worked for the top ten contractors, an average of 110 per firm. Ten years previously, in 1959, a similar survey showed that the leading 100 firms employed only 721 retired officers, an average of slightly more than seven per company. The large numbers noted in 1969 and the substantial increase over 1959 engendered great concern because the flow of retired military officers into defense-related business constituted a linkage that might well work against the public interest.

This line of argument found an opponent in Senator Barry Goldwater, who pointed out that Proxmire's figures appeared imposing only if dealt with outside their proper context. The group of 2,072 retired officers made up only a small percentage of the people in the employ of the leading contractors or of the total body of retired military personnel. Some 36,800 officers with the rank of colonel, naval captain, or above had been retired since World War II. The pool in 1959 had been much smaller, a factor making for lower numbers in defense in-

dustry at that time. Other observers noted that Proxmire had not distinguished between full-time and part-time employees or between those holding policymaking positions and those without influence on defense contracts. Mere numbers do not demonstrate dangerous linkages; the key question was whether retired officers were in a position to exercise improper influence. Some critics conceded this point, but noted that a mere handful of well-placed retired officers could provide many useful services to the military-industrial complex.

Survey material showed that retired military officers tended to congregate in such areas as Washington, D.C., San Antonio, and San Diego, a circumstance that might affect the local political atmosphere. In response to this allegation, others claimed that many people living in these areas already were involved in defense enterprises and that the numbers of retired military officers in the community amounted to a very small percentage of total population—not enough to exercise significant influence. Moreover, because military men on active duty moved frequently and habitually embraced a nonpolitical attitude in the tradition of General George C. Marshall and most other distinguished career officers of the past, they neither developed significant political influence nor wished to exert it.

Some detractors of the military-industrial complex commented worriedly about its effect on academic institutions and personalities. The opening for intellectual participation in the complex materialized because of the need for extensive research and development and deployment of weapons systems. Scientists and engineers fashioned second careers as consultants and contractors for the Department of Defense and other agencies. Certain educational institutions, including several of the most prestigious universities in the nation, became extraordinarily dependent on government contracts for financial support. All this tended to realign educational priorities away from the traditional functions of educators and intellectuals—independent thought and instruction. Senator J. William Fulbright, a former professor and university president, lamented the fact that "universities might have formed an effective counterweight to the military-industrial complex by strengthening their emphasis on

THE MILITARY-INDUSTRIAL COMPLEX

the traditional values of our democracy, but many of our leading universities have instead joined the monolith, adding greatly to its power and influence." He was not surprised at this development. "No less than businessmen, workers, and politicians," Fulbright observed, "professors like money and influence. Having traditionally been deprived of both, they have welcomed the contracts and consultantships offered by the Military Establishment." In answer to comments of this nature, defenders of academic contributions to the military-industrial complex argued that federal funds made possible a varied program of instruction in many schools. They also insisted that mere participation as consultants or contractors did not in itself prove the existence of problems such as those cited by Fulbright.

A miscellany of other, less general charges against the military-industrial complex includes the following:

1. The Department of Defense has encouraged a brisk sale of arms and munitions throughout the world. Presumably, development of such markets overseas creates demand for military hardware produced in the United States. The arms traffic feeds international tensions and establishes government priorities that work against international peace. Those who reject this argument say that the arms traffic is really not extensive and that purchasers would buy elsewhere if the United States market did not exist.

2. Some economists have drawn attention to the practice of stockpiling strategic materials, supposedly a means of insuring an adequate supply in the event of war. For example, Walter Adams believes that the real purpose of stockpiling is to benefit certain mining interests, since it provides a vehicle for supporting the prices of various minerals.

3. Contracts for research and development frequently permit assignment of patent rights for inventions to the defense contractors. Critics hold that since public moneys are used to finance research and development, resulting patents should be retained by the government. The conventional response to this observation is that the privilege of retaining patents constitutes a sound incentive for contractors and also represents appropriate compensation for services rendered.

What should be done about the military-industrial complex? If it does not constitute a serious danger, say its champions, it should be praised and protected rather than scorned and abused. Harvard political scientist Samuel P. Huntington argues that if antimilitary opposition continues, it "is likely to make the military-industrial complex more like what the opposition claimed it was. . . . When defense goes on the defensive, defense firms are more likely to see common interests in collaboration among themselves against an external threat." If the military-industrial complex is considered necessary but in need of more effective controls than presently exist, then it follows that it should undergo reform designed to eliminate inadequate or dangerous performance. Charles J. Hitch recommends that competition based on price should play a significant part in the contracting process; that former personnel of the Department of Defense should be discouraged from accepting employment in firms they dealt with during procurement negotiations; that strong civilian control of the military establishment should continue; and that budget decisions should be made on the basis of systems analysis in order to eliminate special pleading by interest groups. Finally, if the military-industrial complex is deemed unnecessary or dangerous, it presumably should be dismantled. One proponent of this view, Sidney Lens, provides a list of measures to destroy it. Military assistance to foreign governments should cease immediately, and economic assistance to nations in need should be funneled through the United Nations in much increased amounts. The government should buy out American firms operating overseas. Disarmament should take place, preferably as a consequence of multilateral agreement but, if necessary, on a unilateral basis. At home a varied program of legislation should be developed to ameliorate many social ills that trouble the country.

BIBLIOGRAPHY

Richard J. Barnet, *The Economy of Death* (New York, 1969), is an all-out attack on the military-industrial complex. John Stanley Baumgartner, *The Lonely Warriors: Case for the Military-Industrial Complex* (Los Angeles, 1970), is a thoroughgoing defense. Congressional Quarterly, *The Power of the Pentagon* (Washington, D.C., 1972), is a compendium of information. Alain C. Enthoven and K. Wayne

THE MILITARY-INDUSTRIAL COMPLEX

Smith, *How Much Is Enough? Shaping the Defense Program, 1961–1969* (New York, 1971), explicates the systems approach of the McNamara era in the Department of Defense. John K. Galbraith, *How to Control the Military* (New York, 1969), gives prescriptions for limiting undue military influence in policymaking; and *The New Industrial State,* 2nd rev. ed. (Boston, 1971), presents a theory of bureaucratic influence that guides much of the writing on the military-industrial complex. John Francis Gorgol, *The Military-Industrial Firm: A Practical Theory and Model* (New York, 1972), presents technical discussion; Seymour Melman provides an introduction. Paul A. C. Koistinen, "The 'Industrial-Military Complex' in Historical Perspective: The Inter-War Years," in *Journal of American History,* 56 (1970), is a unique investigation by a historian on the origins of the military-industrial complex. Ralph E. Lapp, *The Weapons Culture* (New York, 1968), is a powerful assault on the military-industrial complex by a well-known scientist. C. Wright Mills, *The Power Elite* (New York, 1956), is an influential sociological analysis of elite power in American life often used as the theoretical basis for criticism of the military-industrial leadership. Seymour Melman, *Pentagon Capitalism* (New York, 1970), by a veteran opponent of militarization, traces transformation of the military-industrial complex into a system

of "state-management" during the 1960's. Victor Perlo, *Militarism and Industry: Arms Profiteering in the Missile Age* (New York, 1963), reflects Marxian viewpoints. Carroll W. Pursell, Jr., *The Military-Industrial Complex* (New York, 1972), is a reader for students that presents a collection of information from many viewpoints on the military-industrial complex. Steven Rosen, ed., *Testing the Theory of the Military-Industrial Complex* (Lexington, Mass.–Toronto–London, 1973), includes excellent scholarly analyses from various viewpoints and is most useful. Sam C. Sarkesian, ed., *The Military-Industrial Complex: A Reassessment* (Beverly Hills, Calif.–London, 1972), reports results of a conference; very helpful. Herbert I. Schiller and Joseph D. Phillips, eds., *Super-State: Readings in the Military-Industrial Complex* (Urbana, Ill., 1970), is a collection of views largely from the debate on the military-industrial complex that took place during the late 1960's. Adam Yarmolinsky, *The Military Establishment: Its Impacts on American Society* (New York, 1970), is an influential report of a survey commissioned by the Twentieth-Century Fund.

[*See also* AMERICAN ATTITUDES TOWARD WAR; ANTI-IMPERIALISM; THE COLD WAR; DISARMAMENT; ELITISM AND FOREIGN POLICY; IMPERIALISM; MILITARISM; NATIONAL SECURITY; NUCLEAR WEAPONS AND DIPLOMACY.]

MISSIONARIES

Paul A. Varg

THE PRESENCE of thousands of American missionaries in Asia, Africa, the Middle East, and in other parts of the world constituted a major facet of foreign relations. The motivation was essentially religious, but their presence abroad had significant political implications. Missionaries gained entry to foreign countries by means of treaties guaranteeing their right to residence. In some countries, particularly in China, the native population viewed them with deep hostility and did their best to oust them. In turn the United States, like other Western governments, demanded protection and, when injury had been done, indemnity. Consequently, throughout the nineteenth century, legations in countries where missionaries were present devoted a large part of their time to missionaries' pleas to uphold the treaties. In many countries the missionaries could never have carried on their work without the protection provided by their home government. Both missionaries and advocates of missions at home sought to influence foreign policy. A close link between diplomacy and the overseas efforts of churches developed.

In the United States the dynamism of the missionary movement during the early nineteenth century had its source in the revival movement in the American churches. The urgency to convert individual souls and to save them from damnation became a dominant theme in most denominations. A literal interpretation of the Bible and acceptance of the Bible as the infallible word of God and the final authority on all subjects was a primary article of faith. During the same years Protestantism embraced the eschatological belief that the end of the world was impending and that immediate action must be taken to prepare the way for the

heavenly kingdom. Preparing the way came to mean revivalism—mass meetings where evangelical preachers implored sinners to confess and to accept divine grace. From the first frontier camp meetings in the early nineteenth century until the revivals led by Dwight L. Moody in the last three decades, revivalism simplified all Christian teaching into a vigorous effort to bring salvation to the unsaved before the approaching Judgment Day.

Divine sanction for rescuing the heathen in non-Christian lands rested upon the Biblical injunction: "Go ye into all the world, and preach the gospel to every creature" (Mark 16:15). All men were sinners, at home and abroad, all equally precious in the eyes of God, and the creator intended his grace for all.

Developments in the secular world abetted the religious impulse. Improvements in ocean transportation, the rapid expansion of commerce, and the intense competition of nation-states with their concomitant imperialism increased public interest in faraway places not only among merchants but also among church leaders and scholars. On some occasions, indeed, the merchants and the missionaries were allies and, in the case of China and the Near East, some of these merchants helped finance missionaries and contributed to the building of schools and hospitals.

Interest in foreign missions in the United States began during the second decade of the nineteenth century and centered in Andover Theological Seminary. The major denominations organized boards to raise funds, appoint missionaries, and to supervise the overseas work. The first and most prominent was the American Board of Commissioners for Foreign Missions, a society representing Congrega-

MISSIONARIES

tionalists, Presbyterians, and both the Dutch and German Reformed churches, which was organized in 1810. The Missionary Society of the Methodist Episcopal Church came into being in 1819. Two years later the Episcopalians established the Domestic and Foreign Missionary Society. These were the most prominent among the scores that came into being during the first half of the century. By 1830 American missionaries carried on work in the far corners of the world. American missionaries first went to India in 1813 and to Turkey in 1820. The first two to go to China, Elijah C. Bridgman and David Abeel, sailed on 14 October 1829. China itself was closed to missionaries, and they carried on their work among Chinese in countries to the south.

The primary goal was conversion. The message rang with the authority of divine revelation and spelled out conditions of salvation as precise and uncompromising as a legal contract. The saving of souls was the missionary's one and only assignment, and there was to be no toning down of the doctrine of an arbitrary God. One of the early missionaries to China wrote: "In this field the work to be done is to 'preach the gospel.' Men are rebels to be brought into allegiance; sinners to be saved. There is only one authority competent to settle the terms, and this authority has settled them. The business of his ambassadors is to proclaim those terms."

This aim was all encompassing; only the strategies for achieving the aim varied. The first efforts concentrated on the translation of the Scriptures into the native language and the preparation of tracts. Religious services were first conducted by the missionary in his home, and the native servants were required to attend. Street preaching attracted crowds of curious onlookers. When conditions permitted, street chapels and churches were constructed for services. Many mission stations established day schools and boarding schools that provided elementary education and religious studies aiming at conversion. Boards at home frequently questioned the usefulness of medical work as a way of winning converts, but doctors and hospitals were a significant part of the overseas enterprise. As soon as possible, natives were employed as distributors of tracts and as preachers. It was by means of these native helpers that

most early converts were made. There was almost invariably greater success among the lower classes and in rural areas.

Native resistance to foreigners and to the foreign religion posed what the pious missionary termed "a peculiar trial of faith." It was not until nine years after the arrival of the first missionary in Fu-chou, China, and after some thirty-five missionaries had served for a shorter or longer period of time, that the Congregationalists baptized their first convert. Many shared the feelings of the missionary who wrote home in 1852, "at other times my weak faith leads me almost to despondency." Not only in China but everywhere the resistance to Christianity defied the earnestness of its apostles. The strangeness of the message, its incongruity with native views of both the world and the nature of man, as well as the fact that converts suffered cruel and almost intolerable social ostracism, explain the snaillike pace of Christianizing. Christians exhibited a different attitude toward women, demonstrated a freedom from native superstitions, and challenged both political and religious beliefs, which the native leaders rightly saw as a threat to tear apart the traditional social fabric and undermine the venerated values.

Resistance did not end with the rejection of the missionary's message. Hostility met the missionaries at every turn. In no place was this more true than in China. Efforts to lease land and to build chapels and hospitals set off riots and inspired unequaled ingenuity in contriving legal obstacles directed at denying the missionaries locations for chapels, hospitals, and places to reside. Throughout the nineteenth century the foreigners met with angry epithets, physical attack, scenes of mob violence, and hostility from local officials. In China the gentry appear to have inspired much of the violence, but the common populace were most certainly willing accessories. Appeals to the authorities in Peking to enforce treaty provisions granting rights of residence and preaching frequently led the Peking government to issue orders to local officials, who, in turn, with almost equal frequency excused themselves on the ground that they could not control popular feelings. Riots were regular occurrences and reached their peak in the early 1890's, with two of the most serious taking place in 1891 along the

Grand Canal and at Wu-hu, some 300 miles up the Yangtze River.

A close relationship developed between missions and government in the United States. President John Quincy Adams agreed that the extension of Christianity was in the national interest. In a letter written in 1829 Adams took the position that the extension of education and "the true religion" was "the best and only means, by which the prosperity and happiness of nations can be advanced and continued. . . ." Protection of missionaries in foreign countries became government policy, and it was carried out with consistency. The government of the United States thus made itself a party to the propagation of Christianity.

In the Middle East, more particularly Turkey, diplomatic and navy representatives did not hesitate to use their influence to convince native governments that the doors should be open to missionary work nor were they hesitant in filing protests when missionaries found themselves in difficulty. During the earlier period, roughly 1810 to 1845, the leading missionary societies were inclined to prefer independence of the government and eschewed the support of government officials, an attitude reflecting their firm advocacy of separation of church and state in domestic affairs. This did not prevent missionaries from welcoming the support of the British political and naval agencies that were prominent in the area, and the British government took for granted that official support was a legitimate exercise of political authority. By 1843 the British precedent was fully accepted by American mission boards, and throughout the remainder of the century the federal government and the missionary enterprise were allies. American legations and consulates in the major mission fields invariably extended protection to missionaries. Behind the diplomatic agencies lay the threat of force, and in both the Middle East and in China the presence of warships served to warn hostile native populations that attacks on the foreigner would not be tolerated.

The ties to the home government were not limited to protection. Owing to their facility for language and knowledge of a particular foreign country, missionaries often became participants in diplomacy. This took place more often in China, but it was not limited to that country.

The very first treaty with China, Cushing's Treaty (1844), also known as the Treaty of Wanghia, was largely the work of three missionaries: Samuel Wells Williams, Peter Parker, and Elijah Bridgman. Williams and Parker occupied diplomatic posts in the years ahead. When Parker accepted appointment in 1844 as assistant to the American commissioner to China, the secretary of the American Board, Rufus Anderson, terminated his support, but Anderson's opposition to ties to the government was only a passing phenomenon.

Foreign missions entered a new stage in the 1890's. From 1890 to 1914 there was a tremendous expansion of foreign missions. Three major changes took place: Asia, particularly China, became the major focus of missionary efforts; the emphasis on snatching the heathen from the jaws of hell gave way to humanitarian appeals; and the movement, earlier limited to a small segment of the churchgoing public, reached proportions of a popular crusade.

The missionary cause in the United States enjoyed its broadest base of support during the first two decades of the twentieth century. In addition to the denominational missionary societies there were interdenominational organizations. The major recruiting agency, the Student Volunteer Movement for Foreign Missions, organized in 1887, had branches on virtually every American college campus. Every four years the organization held a national convention featuring addresses by young candidates about to go abroad for the first time, returned missionaries, and national leaders. The volunteers published outlines and textbooks for classes conducted by them. By 1914 more than forty thousand volunteers were enrolled in the classes. By that same year almost six thousand volunteers had gone out as missionaries. Women in the churches were equally active in raising money and in promoting societies for various age groups. In 1902 the Young People's Missionary Movement was organized, and six years later more than one hundred thousand were enrolled in its mission study courses.

There were also periodic national conventions of clergy and laymen to promote interest and at one of these, in 1906, the Laymen's Missionary Movement was organized. During the next several years the new society did much to change the image of the missionary movement from that of an other-worldly pietistic and esoteric undertaking to that of a respectable, statesmanlike campaign to help the disadvantaged people in non-Christian areas. Additional respectability flowed from the fact that every president from Benjamin Harrison to Woodrow Wilson endorsed missionary work and made support a matter of civic duty and pride.

After 1890 the missionary task was taken up by denominations not previously involved. By the 1920's virtually every Protestant denomination recruited missionaries and supported mission stations abroad. The widespread participation and the energetic promotion campaigns resulted in an increase in contributions from about $8 million in 1905 to almost $19 million ten years later.

The emphasis on China accorded with the sharp increase of interest in Asia on the part of publicists, scholars, and government officials after the Sino-Japanese War (1894–1895). The economic crisis of the early 1890's raised a cry for foreign markets as a solution to the surplus goods turned out by the vast industrial complex of the United States. Intellectuals, like Brooks Adams and Alfred Thayer Mahan, pointed to a changing configuration of world powers and saw the question of future control of Asia as central in determining whether Western civilization or a crude authoritarianism stripped of Anglo-Saxon values would triumph. Politicians of the persuasion of Senators Henry Cabot Lodge and Albert J. Beveridge, advocates of the "large policy," held that the United States was now a first-class power and it must act like one or suffer shame. The churches joined in the crusade believing now that missionary work was a part of the outward reach of an advanced civilization to extend the blessings of Christian humanitarianism, science, education, and technology to the half of the world that remained in darkness.

The publication of James S. Dennis' three-volume *Christian Missions and Social Progress: A Sociological Study of Foreign Missions* (1897–1906) marked a shift from evangelization to humanitarian goals. The aim, wrote Dennis, was to elevate human society, eradicate traditional evils, and introduce new ideals. Almost nothing was said in board reports, missionary letters, or the many books and articles written by missionaries about the future destiny of the non-Christian peoples. By 1910 Robert E. Speer, along with

John R. Mott and James Barton, the most prominent leaders of the missionary movement in the United States, charged that saving the heathen from damnation had never been the goal.

The report of Commission VI at the World Foreign Mission Conference held in Edinburgh in 1910 included the results of a questionnaire sent to several hundred missionaries inquiring as to their motives. The testimony received showed that conversion of individuals remained a major motive. What was new was the desire to participate in the building of a new world society based on Christian teachings. The report stated: "While the old motive may have been primarily to prepare men for the life after death, the present-day motive lays emphasis rather upon saving the individual, the community, the nation, for life here upon earth until this world shall be transformed into the likeness of heaven. . . ." The optimism was a reflection of an age that found it easy to believe in progress, but by 1910 missionary leaders of the front rank had also learned much from experience and a great deal from the new social sciences of anthropology and sociology.

Living according to Christian teaching in the setting of a non-Western society was essentially to seek to abide by codes of behavior, attitudes, and ethical beliefs in a society bound together by radically different folkways and mores. These differences set up barriers to the winning of converts, and the alienation from his native society that the convert experienced posed the greatest obstacle to the missionary's success. Once experience provided this insight, the conclusion that almost inevitably followed was that the native societies must be transformed. In this respect the missionary movement was dedicated to a revolutionary message. The new point of view was incorporated in the conclusions of the World Missionary Conference of 1910:

The Protestant Missionary Societies of Christendom through their representatives in this Conference, have for the first time given themselves to the careful and comprehensive study of the problem of the evangelization of the entire non-Christian world. In round numbers 1,000,000,000 of the human race are yet to accept the message of salvation through Jesus Christ. Among these vast populations it is our task to establish, not only the Christian Church, but those institutions of Christianity by which the Church shall be perpetuated.

The new emphases were on schools, medical work, and the introduction of Western ideals. These goals were closely related to the new thinking concerning foreign policy and the increasing popularity of the view that the United States must play a large part in world affairs. Woodrow Wilson's conviction that the United States had a duty to lead the world in the ways of peace and righteousness was the secular counterpart of the church's advocacy of a new world order tied to Christianity.

This new approach harmonized with the changes taking place in China and in other non-Western countries. The old societies fell upon evil days as Western commerce, new forms of communication, and the threats posed by Western imperialism undermined traditional institutions. The younger generation looked to the West and sought to carve out a future career by means of acquiring Western education. Consequently, there was a great demand for schools. By 1917 there were eleven American-supported Christian colleges in China and thirteen in the Middle East. Schools and colleges controlled by missionaries, however, were often staffed by teachers who saw their function as proselytization, who stressed religious instruction, and who taught courses the subject matter of which was Western oriented. This resulted in sharp criticism by American academic leaders who were called upon from time to time, beginning in 1910, to study these schools. Yet, prior to World War I, while the schools suffered shortcomings, they were often the only ones available.

The numbers of schools at all levels increased rapidly. By 1925—including all Protestant schools supported by both European, Canadian, and American missionary societies—there were 46,580 elementary schools and 1,512 high and middle schools conducted by missionaries. More than 7,000 of these elementary schools and 333 of the high and middle schools were in China. There were 101 missionary-supported colleges and universities, including 24 in China, 37 in India, 6 in Turkey, 3 in Egypt. This vast educational enterprise, after World War I, became a costly burden.

From 1890 to the close of World War I, the missionary movement put forth its strongest bid to shape American foreign policy. China was the lodestar of the idealistic missionary volunteers, and the crusade of the student volunteers with their slogan, "The Evangelization of the World in This Generation," helped to create among American churchgoers a special interest in China. Home on furlough every seven years, missionaries traveled from church to church across the United States seeking to build support for the cause of missions, but they also gave to their listeners a vision of China marked by an emphasis on the mysteries of the Orient, the qualities of the Chinese as people, and the prospect of a modernized and Christianized China. The result was a paternalistic but sympathetic view of China that provided a backdrop for relations between the two countries.

Aside from the compulsion to protect missionaries in China, the American government was guided by wholly secular considerations in making decisions concerning the policy to be followed in Asia. Despite all the protestations that the United States was guided by philanthropic considerations and the resulting myth that Secretary of State John Hay had by enunciation of the Open Door policy saved China from partition at the turn of the century, government actions followed a course dictated by national interests. The policy was superficially friendly and did not offend China's friends in the American churches, but it also stopped far short of accepting commitments to protect China from the inroads of imperialism. In the missionary movement itself, following the Boxer Rebellion of 1900, missionaries in China and leaders of the movement at home made a sharp turn from the ethnocentrism characteristic of the nineteenth century, turned their backs on demands for indemnities, and heartily approved of the rise of Chinese nationalism after 1905. Goodwill toward China became the watchword, and the North American Conference of Foreign Missions, the interdenominational agency of mission boards, hailed the birth of the Republic of China in 1912. In that same year Woodrow Wilson, the enthusiastic advocate of missions, was elected president. With many of his close friends, Wilson shared the idealism of a new generation of missionaries inspired by humanitarianism.

Missionary organizations had assurance that President Wilson was an ardent believer in their work. In spite of his goodwill, however, Wilson took their advice only during the first two months of his administration. The missionary spokesmen were critical of the international consortium of bankers whom they held responsible for the failure of the preceding Taft administration to grant recognition to the recently established Republic of China. Wilson withdrew his support of the consortium and promptly established diplomatic relations with the republic. The president certainly professed deep interest in China and hoped that the country would be free to modernize and establish its own sovereignty, but his initial gestures of friendship gave way to expediency when confronted by powerful opposition. Bishop James W. Bashford, former president of Ohio Wesleyan University, and the first Methodist bishop of China, vigorously sought to gain Wilson's support for China in 1915 when Japan presented China with the Twenty-one Demands; but both Wilson and Secretary of State William Jennings Bryan limited their opposition to Japan to inquiries and the doctrine of nonrecognition. Again, in 1919, in spite of strong feelings on the part of missionaries in China, and after pleading at the Paris Peace Conference that Japan should surrender the rights it had taken over from Germany in the province of Shantung, Wilson dismissed further opposition to Japan as futile given Japan's secret treaties with its European allies.

At no one moment of missionary history was there a closer liaison between the government and missionary leaders than during the Paris Peace Conference. The Middle East, the first extensive field of American missionary endeavor, had led to an interest in that part of the world, an interest symbolized by the establishment of a number of colleges and schools in Turkey and elsewhere. The missions among the Armenians and Nestorians gave rise to a thriving nationalism that created political problems for the Ottoman Empire. The resulting persecution by the Turks reached a peak during World War I when both Armenians and Nestorians fell victim to Turkish military campaigns. This development led to large-scale relief efforts under the leadership of missionaries and to huge fund-raising drives at home, which stressed the widespread suffering of the Armenians and Nestorians and the brutality of the Turks. Armenian relief became the major

philanthropic enterprise. Minorites in the Near East came to be viewed as a ward of the American public. Missionaries, in turn, were leaders in administering the relief. The relief effort promptly became a part of a far-reaching political program aimed at converting a large part of the Middle East into a League of Nations mandate to be under American control.

A remarkable group of prestigious leaders, who had entrée into the highest offices in government, constituted an effective lobby with influence far surpassing that of the missionaries from any other area. James Barton, president of the American Board of Commissioners for Foreign Missions, was a close associate of Cleveland Dodge, President Wilson's closest friend. Wilson and Dodge shared a common heritage of pious evangelical outlook; both drew upon Protestant teaching of high principles and morals in determining what was good for their own country and the world. A wealthy philanthropist, Dodge was a generous supporter of missions and relief work in the Middle East. Members of Dodge's family were important missionary educators in the area. With the full support of Dodge, Barton masterminded the campaign from 1918 to 1920 to create a body of public opinion as a base for political action. He enlisted both scholars and journalists to promote the cause and thus successfully mobilized broad public support for the proposed mandate. In addition to Barton there were the missionary educators—effective spokesmen such as Alexander MacLachlon, president of the International College in Smyrna; John Merrill, president of Central Turkey College; Mary M. Patrick, president of Istanbul Woman's College; and Caleb F. Gates, president of Robert College, Istanbul. It was contended that a mandate would protect the American missionary institutions, create stability in the area, and prevent international rivalry that would lead to a second world war.

Some wished an American mandate over all of Turkey; others pleaded for a mandate over Armenia. The motivating force was the conviction that minority people had to be freed from both Turkish control and European imperialism, and liberated by education to proceed with modernization and creation of a society guided by American Christian ideals. Self-righteousness and paternalism permitted an unwarranted optimism that led to heavy responsibilities and trouble. Behind the optimism of rhetoric was a brashness that failed to take into account political realities. The efforts to establish one or more American mandates failed. Wilson never withdrew his support, but he placed highest priority on the United States joining the League of Nations; and fearing that to push for a mandate would strengthen the opposition, he delayed. By 1920 the public was in no mood to take on responsibilities anywhere beyond the three-mile limit and the missionaries of the Middle East retreated from the political scene.

The period of public prestige and acclaim came to a close in the 1920's. Changes in American society contributed to the decline of the missionary movement. The Protestant churches faced challenges to the authority they once enjoyed. Within the churches, controversy raged over issues of theology and previously unquestioned assumptions. The Modernist-Fundamentalist strife reached down to basic questions of faith in revealed religion and to the validity of philosophical humanism. Relativism, the most fashionable intellectual current, reduced traditional biblical authority in all matters to an anachronism. More injurious than the direct challenge of the validity of the church's teaching was the inroad made by the automobile, motion pictures, and radio. The church as a center of social life lost out to these more exciting diversionary activities. The change taking place resulted in a sharp decline of financial support and a dramatic drop in the number of recruits.

The rapid rise of nationalism in the countries where a large portion of missionary work had been centered created other difficulties. The rise of Kemal Atatürk in Turkey and the nationalist revolution in China generated sharp hostility to all forms of Western intrusion and particularly to the paternalism inherent in missionary activity. Schools and hospitals in China faced strikes, and many closed. In the eyes of patriotic Chinese these enterprises created feelings of dependence and friendly attitudes toward the West, thereby attenuating the vitality of Chinese nationalism.

In China the difficulties of the missionaries escalated because of the unequal treaties under which the foreigner enjoyed special privileges.

A Chinese member of the National Christian Council wrote: "The Protestant Church in China has been established for one hundred and twenty-one years, yet it is still not deeply rooted in the mind and the heart of the Chinese." It had, she said, "neither been adapted to the needs of the common people or to the civilization of China." An idealistic young Congregational missionary in Tientsin told of "wholesale criticism." The Chinese asked: "Why do missionaries spend so much on themselves? Why do they live in such luxury? Outsiders ask, wasn't Christ a poor man?" Missionaries, probably a majority of them, acknowledged that to continue their work they must free themselves of the obloquy of being tied to the treaties, and they favored treaty revision. After 1924 many young missionaries, sympathetic with Chinese aspirations and feeling unwanted, left China.

The decline of the 1920's culminated in the Laymen's Inquiry. The study was chaired by William Ernest Hocking, a professor of philosophy at Harvard University. The findings of fact were published in a series of seven volumes, and the final conclusions, in *Re-Thinking Missions* (1932). Teams of qualified investigators visited the major mission fields. The critical report reflected in considerable part the philosophical persuasion of its authors, who rejected revealed religion and advocated that Christianity give up its claim to superiority and join with leaders of other religions in finding some common basis for strengthening spiritual values. While phrased in polite language and interspersed with friendly evaluations of both personnel and various missionary undertakings, the report was overridingly harsh in its judgment. Conservatives in the Protestant churches looked upon the findings as nothing short of blasphemy, but the findings were greeted with general approval. The Laymen's Inquiry confirmed that the missionary movement as a national expression of philanthropy and religious conviction had succumbed to the secularism of a new age, the increasing distrust of Western nations by countries emerging from colonial and subcolonial status, and to the vibrant nationalism characteristic of newly established nations.

The missionary movement suffered serious and permanent setbacks but did not die. In fact by the late 1930's there were signs of recovery, but the movement was increasingly dominated by conservative denominations and Fundamentalist churches; among these, revealed religion and the authority of the Bible were not questioned and the salvation of the non-Christians continued to be viewed as a divine duty.

American Roman Catholics, who did not enter upon foreign missionary work until 1911, also maintained steady but slow growth after World War I. The Catholic Foreign Mission Society, popularly known as Maryknoll, sent its first missionary to China in 1918. In the years between the wars the society concentrated its attention on China and Korea. After the close of World War II, the work shifted to Japan, South and Central America, and Africa. The major emphasis was on conversion, but mission stations also carried on educational and medical programs. By 1936 the society had 204 priests, 2 bishops, 90 seminarians, 74 brothers, and 500 nuns.

The success of foreign missions, whether measured in terms of converts or cultural diffusion, is difficult to estimate in any precise way. In China there were approximately three million Chinese Christians, two million Catholics, and one million Protestants; but these figures would not bear scholarly scrutiny. The role of the missionary in the conveyance of Western attitudes, educational and medical practices, and a modern approach to problems was undoubtedly significant; but the Western intrusion was only in small part the work of the churches. Traditional societies broke down under the impact of commerce, colonialism, and other forms of economic penetration.

BIBLIOGRAPHY

James A. Field, Jr., *America and the Mediterranean World* (Princeton, N.J., 1969), is a well-written account that deals with missionary enterprise throughout the entire Mediterranean area. Field is a sympathetic observer and draws upon thorough research. Joseph C. Grabill, *Protestant Diplomacy and the Near East Missionary Influence on American Policy, 1810–1927* (Minneapolis, Minn., 1971), a detailed account of the missionary's impact on Turkey, is especially valuable for the student who is interested in Woodrow Wilson and the Near Eastern question. Kenneth Scott Latourette, in *The Great Century in the Americas, Austro-Asia, and Africa,* and vol. VI, *The Great Century in Northern Africa and Asia* (New York, 1944), has written encyclopedia volumes on the entire history of Christian missions throughout the world. He was at one time a missionary and writes from the missionary point of view. Orville A. Petty, ed., *Laymen's Missions Inquiry Fact Finders Reports* (New York, 1933), is an invaluable survey of the missionary enterprise throughout the world as it existed in the late 1920's. Paul A. Varg, *Missionaries, Chinese, and Diplomats* (Princeton, N.J., 1958), seeks to examine the history of American Protestant missions in China and to do so as a critical scholar.

[*See also* COLONIALISM; IDEOLOGY AND FOREIGN POLICY; INTERCULTURAL RELATIONS; MANIFEST DESTINY; THE OPEN DOOR POLICY; PHILANTHROPY.]

MISSIONARY DIPLOMACY

Roger R. Trask

MISSIONARY diplomacy is a descriptive label often applied to the policies and practices of the United States in Mexico, Central America, and the Caribbean during the presidency of Woodrow Wilson. According to Arthur S. Link, "[Secretary of State William Jennings] Bryan and Wilson were both fundamentally missionaries of democracy, driven by inner compulsions to give other peoples the blessings of democracy and inspired by the confidence that they knew better how to promote the peace and well-being of other countries than did the leaders of those countries themselves." Both missionary diplomacy and his domestic program, the New Freedom, were related to President Wilson's personal concepts of morality and democratic government. Despite Wilson's admirable ideas and objectives, missionary diplomacy was a disaster. Perhaps many of the historians who have placed Wilson high in the presidential pantheon have not given enough consideration to the failure of missionary diplomacy.

Woodrow Wilson came to the presidency with little knowledge of or interest in foreign affairs. His well-known remark to a Princeton friend, "It would be the irony of fate if my administration had to deal chiefly with foreign affairs," emphasized his concentration on domestic questions. But from the start of his term, Wilson saw close relationships between domestic and foreign policies. The New Freedom envisaged a return to free competition in the United States. The monopolistic interests had to be destroyed at home and their influence in foreign policy dispelled. Thus Wilson's initial rejection of "dollar diplomacy." Although he was not unqualifiedly hostile to business interests, he believed that their activities

ought to serve, rather than dominate, the public interest.

Wilson's ethical and religious beliefs also profoundly influenced his foreign policy. Nations, like individuals, should adhere to high ethical and moral standards. Democracy, Wilson was convinced, was the most Christian of governmental systems, suitable for all peoples. The democratic United States thus had a moral mandate for world leadership. At the end of World War I, the president saw the League of Nations as an instrumentality for the application of Wilsonian democracy on an international scale.

When Wilson took office in March 1913, the immediate problems he faced in Mexico, Central America, and the Caribbean gave him opportunities to apply these concepts to Latin American policy. A week after his inauguration, Wilson presented a draft policy statement to his cabinet. Most of the cabinet thought Wilson's proposal radical and hasty; it had not been discussed with Secretary Bryan or other advisers, nor with Latin American diplomats in Washington. But Wilson held firm, arguing that the change in administration in Washington could not be the occasion for a wave of irresponsible revolutions in Latin America. Wilson's statement, essentially as he had drafted it, appeared in the press on 12 March 1913.

Wilson said that his administration desired the "most cordial understanding and cooperation" with Latin America. "As friends . . . we shall prefer those who act in the interest of peace and honor, who protect private rights, and respect the restraints of constitutional provision." Wilson concluded by extending "the hand of genuine disinterested friendship." The statement was a curious mixture of Wilson's

575

commitment to democracy and constitutionalism, a profession of neighborly friendship, and a threat against revolutionists. He put forward a significant change in United States recognition policy: de facto governments would have to be constitutionally legitimate in order to gain recognition. Otherwise, Wilson's statement did not really change Latin American policy.

Wilson's address to the Southern Commercial Congress at Mobile, Alabama, on 27 October 1913, presumably did. "The future," according to Wilson, ". . . is going to be very different for this hemisphere from the past. These States lying to the south of us . . . will now be drawn closer to us by innumerable ties, and, I hope, chief of all, by the tie of a common understanding of each other." Referring to the Panama Canal, then under construction, he noted that "while we physically cut two continents asunder, we spiritually unite them. It is a spiritual union which we seek." The canal would "open the world to a commerce . . . of intelligence, of thought and sympathy between North and South." Wilson deplored the exploitative nature of foreign concessions in Latin American nations. "I rejoice in nothing so much as in the prospect that they will now be emancipated from these conditions, and we ought to be the first to take part in assisting that emancipation." The United States must be a friend on terms of "equality and honor."

In conclusion, Wilson emphasized his commitment to "constitutional liberty" and promised that the United States would never again seek even one additional foot of territory by conquest. But as Wilson's first term progressed, the promise of the Mobile address disintegrated. United States intervention in Latin America escalated to heights perhaps beyond the comprehension of earlier practitioners of "Big Stick" diplomacy and dollar diplomacy. Missionary diplomacy created seemingly permanent hostility between the United States and its southern neighbors. This was especially true in Mexico, Nicaragua, Haiti, and the Dominican Republic, which experienced Wilsonian interventionism in its most virulent forms.

Events occurring in Mexico as Wilson became president gave him his first opportunity to test his Latin American policy. In February 1913 Mexico entered a new stage in the epic revolution that had begun in 1910 against Porfirio Díaz. Francisco Madero, the leader of the rebels, was a moderate revolutionist who eventually aroused the ire of radicals like Emiliano Zapata, who demanded redistribution of land to peasants, and others like Francisco (Pancho) Villa, Pascual Orozco, and Felix Díaz, nephew of the deposed dictator.

President William Howard Taft, although unenthusiastic, recognized Madero as president of Mexico in November 1911. United States ambassador Henry Lane Wilson, concerned about threats to American business interests in Mexico, maintained only cool relations with the Madero government. In the "Pact of the Embassy," 19 February 1913, Ambassador Wilson joined with Victoriano Huerta, Madero's top general, and Felix Díaz in a plan to replace Madero. Huerta would become provisional president, and Díaz would be a candidate in a later presidential election. Huerta assumed the presidency after pressuring Madero and Vice-President José María Pino Suárez to resign. Although assured of safe conduct, Madero and Pino Suárez were assassinated on 22 February, apparently by some of Huerta's men.

Taft left the problem of recognition of Huerta to the incoming Wilson administration. Wilson believed that Huerta had gained power by undemocratic and unconstitutional means, and the Madero-Pino Suárez murders shocked him. Furthermore, the president had deep suspicions about Ambassador Wilson, who flooded Washington with dispatches lauding Huerta and asserting that the new Mexican leader would cooperate with United States interests. President Wilson, however, applied the tough tests of constitutional legitimacy to the Mexican regime.

The president sent a friend, the journalist William Bayard Hale, to Mexico in June 1913, to get firsthand information. Hale was unenthusiastic about Huerta, describing him as "an ape-like old man" who "may almost be said to subsist on alcohol." With Hale's views in mind, President Wilson continued to shun the new Mexican government, even though Ambassador Wilson virtually insisted that Huerta be recognized. Acting on the president's orders, Bryan recalled Wilson and accepted his resignation.

In August 1913 President Wilson sent another personal representative, John Lind, to Mexico. Lind, a former congressman and former governor of Minnesota, had no diplomatic experience. His instructions put forth terms for a Mexican settlement: an immediate cease-fire, an early and free election, a promise from Huerta not to be a candidate, and pledges that all Mexican factions would respect the election results. Huerta's government flatly rejected these proposals, as well as a subsequent offer of a large private loan if Huerta would agree to an election in which he was not a candidate. On 27 August, Wilson told a joint session of Congress that the United States would wait patiently until the Mexican civil strife had run its course, meanwhile embargoing arms sales to all sides. Unfortunately, Wilson did not consistently adhere to this policy of "watchful waiting."

In the fall of 1913, the constitutionalist party leader Venustiano Carranza, Huerta's main opponent, announced that his group would boycott the presidential election scheduled for 26 October. After Huerta arrested more than 100 opposition deputies in the Mexican congress, Wilson announced that the United States would ignore the election results. After an inconclusive election, Mexico's congress reappointed Huerta provisional president until balloting scheduled for July 1914. Wilson now abandoned "watchful waiting." As Secretary Bryan wrote to United States diplomats in Latin America, President Wilson considered "it is his immediate duty to require Huerta's retirement," and that the United States would "proceed to employ such means as may be necessary to secure this result." At this point, Wilson sympathized with the Carranza group. The president's struggle with Huerta had become personal as well as national.

Wilson, feeling that England's role was crucial, put special pressure on London to repudiate Huerta. Although the British fleet depended somewhat on Mexican oil, England's problems in Europe dictated rapprochement with the United States. England withdrew recognition of Huerta in mid-1914, after negotiations with the United States that included a satisfactory settlement of the controversy over a United States law providing discriminatory tolls on the Panama Canal.

In February 1914, in a further attempt to strengthen Carranza and the constitutionalists, Wilson lifted the embargo on arms to Mexico; but Huerta continued to hold out. A new crisis in United States-Mexican relations developed on 9 April 1914, when eight American sailors were mistakenly arrested at Tampico. Within an hour, Huerta's commanding general in the port released the men and apologized to Rear Admiral Henry T. Mayo, the commander of the American squadron at Tampico. Mayo gave Huerta twenty-four hours to make a more formal apology, punish the arresting officer, and fire a twenty-one-gun salute. Wilson backed Mayo and ordered an increase in United States forces in Mexican waters. Congress gave him permission to take punitive action against Mexico. These acts, presumably, were on behalf of constitutionality and democracy.

Before these plans could be implemented, the United States consul at Veracruz reported the imminent arrival of the German steamer *Ypiranga* with a cargo of guns and ammunition for Huerta's forces. Wilson decided to seize the customhouse at Veracruz and impound the cargo. When this was done on 21 April, the Mexicans resisted, precipitating a battle in which 126 Mexicans died and 200 were wounded. Huerta severed diplomatic relations after United States forces occupied the city.

President Wilson, not expecting Mexican resistance, was appalled by the bloodshed. Thus he welcomed the offer of Argentina, Brazil, and Chile to mediate; and Huerta also accepted. Wilson intended to use the mediation conference, which began in Niagara Falls, Canada, on 20 May 1914, to get rid of Huerta and bring the constitutionalists to power. But Carranza, who had denounced the American aggression at Veracruz, instructed his delegation—which never really participated in the mediation conference—to refuse a cease-fire and to deny the right of the mediators to discuss the Mexican situation. The conference adjourned on 2 July without practical results. But the United States intervention and heightened conflict with his enemies forced Huerta to resign on 15 July. Venustiano Carranza soon entered Mexico City. Although earlier an advocate of Carranza, Wilson now rejected him and initiated negotiations with Carranza's chief rival in northern Mexico, Pancho Villa, who had a favorable image in the United States.

Carranza, who retained the support of Alvaro Obregón and other leading generals, refused to give in to Villa. As the months passed, Wilson's policy became more threatening; but Carranza insisted that he would fight until victory over his opponents.

At this juncture, Wilson proposed a meeting of the United States and six Latin American nations (Argentina, Brazil, Chile, Bolivia, Uruguay, and Guatemala), anticipating joint intervention to remove Carranza; but by the time the conference convened at Washington in August 1915, Wilson had changed his mind. Secretary of State Robert Lansing, worried about German activity in the hemisphere, thought it necessary to improve relations with Mexico in the face of this external threat. Although the conferees offered to act as mediators in Mexico, Wilson ignored them and extended de facto recognition to Carranza on 19 October 1915.

Even if Wilson wished to concentrate on problems other than Mexico, Pancho Villa was unwilling to let him. Unable to defeat Carranza with his army, Villa apparently decided to provoke United States intervention as an alternative way to achieve his goal. On 10 January 1916 Villa forces murdered sixteen American mining engineers and technicians in Chihuahua. On 7 March the United States Congress responded with a resolution advocating armed intervention. Two days later, Villa raided the border town of Columbus, New Mexico, killing seventeen Americans. Wilson immediately ordered troops into Mexico, initiating an intervention reminiscent of that at Veracruz two years earlier. General John J. Pershing's force never caught Villa, but frequently fought Carranza's army. Unsuccessful in his efforts to extort concessions from Carranza, and embroiled in a serious crisis with Germany, Wilson withdrew the troops from Mexico in February 1917.

Mexican-American relations followed a less spectacular course for the rest of Wilson's presidency. The Mexican constitution of 1917 contained several provisions threatening to foreign concessionaires, but Wilson extended de jure recognition to Carranza in August 1917 after assurances that such interests would be respected. A potentially serious dispute developed in 1918, after Mexico decreed taxes on oil property, rents, royalties, and production based on contracts effective before 1 May 1917. American oil companies refused to register their land titles, arguing that to do so would be a recognition of Mexican claims to subsurface deposits. Carranza ignored State Department protests; but he did not enforce the decrees until June 1919, when Mexican troops moved into the oil fields to halt unapproved drilling operations. Secretary of State Lansing, backed by the Association for the Protection of American Rights in Mexico, urged Wilson to be more aggressive. But in January 1920 Wilson wisely rejected Lansing's recommendations, and the oil producers arranged a satisfactory modus vivendi with Carranza. After Obregón ousted Carranza in May 1920, a Senate subcommittee recommended that the United States delay recognition until American citizens were exempted from certain articles of the Mexican constitution. Wilson and Secretary of State Bainbridge Colby favored this approach, but negotiations failed and Obregón was not recognized until 1923.

Whenever missionary diplomacy was used elsewhere, it led to the same legacy of failure and ill will as in Mexico. In Nicaragua, Wilson inherited from the Taft administration a military intervention and an extensive effort at dollar diplomacy. Taft broke relations in 1909 with Nicaraguan President José Zelaya and encouraged the latter's enemies to revolt when he menaced the nearby Central American nations, threatened the ouster of United States financial interests, and mortgaged his country to European interests. When his successor, Adolfo Díaz, faced a revolt in 1912, Taft sent marines who were still there when Wilson became president. In 1911 the two countries signed the Knox-Castrillo Convention, providing for a large loan from United States bankers to refund the Nicaraguan debt and American administration of the customs services. The United States Senate rejected this plan; but a new treaty signed early in 1913 gave the United States an option on a canal route, naval base rights on the Gulf of Fonseca, and leases on the Corn Islands in the Caribbean, in return for a payment of $3 million. Bryan favored this glaring example of dollar diplomacy and persuaded President Wilson to accept it.

The Senate demurred, partly because of an

amendment (patterned after the 1901 Platt Amendment for Cuba) allowing the United States to intervene to maintain internal order. Bryan then suggested to Wilson that the United States should be a "modern example of the Good Samaritan"—the government should make direct loans to Latin American nations by issuing bonds at 3 percent and lending the proceeds at 4.5 percent, with the profit used for debt retirement. Wilson rejected the proposal, leaving private loans the only alternative. In October 1913 the American firms of Brown Brothers and J. and W. Seligman, by buying stock in the Pacific Railroad and the National Bank of Nicaragua, purchasing Treasury bills, and lending money to the railroad, provided Nicaragua with more than $2.5 million. Bryan consulted Wilson before approving this formal act of dollar diplomacy.

In August 1914 the United States and Nicaragua signed the Bryan-Chamorro Treaty, a restatement of the 1913 proposals without Platt Amendment provisions. Because of questions about the role of American business interests in Nicaragua, charges that the United States was dealing with a puppet regime, and protests from several Central American countries, the Senate delayed approval of the treaty until February 1916. El Salvador, Honduras, and Costa Rica, by raising critical questions about United States motives, exposed the bankruptcy of missionary diplomacy. Costa Rica argued that the canal concession violated its rights in the area; El Salvador and Honduras claimed that their equal rights in the Gulf of Fonseca would be violated by establishment of a naval base. In 1916 Costa Rica and El Salvador brought charges against Nicaragua in the Central American Court of Justice. Both the United States and Nicaragua argued that the court had no jurisdiction, and refused to accept its decisions in favor of Costa Rica and El Salvador. This reaction made it clear that the court, which the United States had helped to establish in 1907, was useful only when it did not tread on the toes of the United States. Impotent to enforce its decisions, the court soon ceased to exist.

After ratification of the Bryan-Chamorro Treaty, the United States moved to control Nicaraguan politics and finance. Political and economic pressures and a naval demonstration helped to ensure the election of the conservative Emiliano Chamorro as president in 1916. The United States also dictated the disbursal of the $3 million Bryan-Chamorro fund, handed over after adoption of the "Financial Plan of 1917." The plan limited the monthly budget of Nicaragua, provided for a high commission dominated by American citizens to monitor government spending, and established a schedule for payment of the Nicaraguan debt to British bondholders and American bankers. Another financial plan in 1920 increased the government's monthly allowance, but the presence of United States Marines and continued financial and political control tainted this progress.

As in Nicaragua, the Wilson administration inherited a difficult situation in the Dominican Republic. Political instability and nonpayment of debts threatened American business interests and invited European intervention in the country as early as 1904. These problems influenced President Theodore Roosevelt to announce a corollary to the Monroe Doctrine that assumed a unilateral right for the United States to intervene in Latin America. After the administration of William Howard Taft intervened in a civil war in the Dominican Republic in 1912, Archbishop Adolfo A. Nouel became president; he resigned in late March 1913, however, giving up the almost impossible task of pacifying the various political factions.

The Dominican situation demanded astute action by the Wilson administration; but Secretary of State Bryan replaced a competent minister, William W. Russell, with James M. Sulllivan. Sullivan was associated with New York financiers who controlled the National Bank of Santo Domingo, an institution hoping to become the depository of funds collected by the receiver general of the Dominican customs. Sullivan was later forced to resign after a State Department investigation disclosed his deficiencies. Another bad appointment was that of Walter C. Vick as receiver general. Bryan's choices inevitably led to inaccurate, biased reports from the Dominican Republic.

In September 1913, when a new revolt broke out against the provisional government in Santo Domingo, Bryan announced that the United States would not recognize any revolutionary regime, thus invoking Wilsonian constitutional legitimacy. After an armistice the United States supervised elections for a constituent assembly in December 1913, even though the Dominican government resented the outside pressure. With less than gentle prodding by Minister Sullivan, President José Bordas Valdés agreed to the appointment, in June 1914, of Charles W. Johnston as financial expert, with power to control Dominican expenditures. Following an American electoral plan, a presidential election was held in late 1914. The candidates, Juan Isidro Jiménez and Horacio Vásquez, represented the two strongest political factions in the country. Jiménez won and was inaugurated on 5 December 1914; the United States immediately pressed for more financial control and intervention privileges. Jiménez resisted these demands, but he could not overcome the continued opposition of his rivals, including Desiderio Arias, whom he dismissed as minister of war in May 1916. After Arias' forces took the city of Santo Domingo and Jiménez resigned, the United States intervened. Admiral William B. Caperton occupied the city after demanding that Arias withdraw. Fearing that Arias would come to power, President Wilson proclaimed full military occupation of the Dominican Republic on 26 November 1916. He cited political and fiscal disorder and the Dominican government's refusal to reform as reasons for the intervention. Undoubtedly another factor was State Department concern about possible war with Germany and the influence of pro-German elements in the Dominican Republic.

Until 1924 an American military government ruled the Dominican Republic. Although there were noticeable improvements—highway construction, establishment of the constabulary, expansion of the schools, and a better system for the collection of internal revenue—the opposition to United States domination steadily increased. When the troops finally left late in 1924, a new treaty continued American financial control.

Events in Haiti followed a familiar path. When Wilson became president, political and economic instability and threats of foreign intervention existed there. American citizens owned perhaps 40 percent of the stock in the

National Bank of Haiti, half the stock in the national railroad, and a smaller portion of the German-dominated Central Railroad. Loans from foreign sources contributed to the financial crisis and increased the threat of intervention. By 1915, Haiti's public debt stood at $32 million.

In January 1914 a revolution brought Oreste Zamor to power. The United States recognized him as president on 1 March 1914, even though he declined to accept a customs receivership and to pledge that no foreign power other than the United States would secure a naval station at Môle St. Nicholas. President Zamor later rejected a similar proposal, strengthened perhaps by German and French demands to share in the customs receivership; President Wilson objected, in effect invoking the Monroe Doctrine.

In October 1914, when Davilmar Theodore ousted Zamor, Secretary of State Bryan notified him that recognition would be extended only after agreement on a customs convention, settlement of disputes between the government and the railroads and the national bank, and guarantees against leases of coaling or naval stations to any European country. Theodore rejected these demands. Domestically he became involved in a serious controversy with the national bank. Theodore's government printed a large quantity of paper currency and seized $65,000 of the bank's gold supply. To prevent further raids, the bank transferred $500,000 in gold to New York aboard the U.S.S. *Machias*. Although Bryan denied Haitian claims that armed intervention on behalf of United States business interests had taken place, American investment in the national bank was extensive.

Theodore resigned in February 1915, and General Vilbrun Guillaume Sam assumed the presidency. Wilson sent a special agent to Haiti to press a treaty upon Sam's government as a condition for recognition. Failing to achieve his mission, the agent suggested that marines be used to impose a settlement. Although the State Department did not overtly accept this recommendation, the revolutionary situation in Haiti made its implementation possible. President Sam apparently ordered the murder of 167 political opponents at the prison in Port-au-Prince on 27 July. Although he took asylum in the French legation, he was dragged out by a mob that dismembered him in the streets. As these events occurred, the U.S.S. *Washington,* under Admiral Caperton, landed forces in Port-au-Prince. Caperton proceeded to occupy the major coastal towns and take charge of customs collections.

After some confusion, the Haitian congress designated Caperton's choice, Sudre Dartiguenave, as the new president. The State Department soon presented Dartiguenave with a draft treaty providing for United States control of Haiti's finances, creation of an American-officered constabulary, appointment of American engineers to supervise sanitation and public improvement, a pledge not to transfer territory to any power other than the United States, and an article giving the United States the right to intervene to enforce the treaty and preserve Haitian independence. Dartiguenave's government signed the treaty after the United States refused to discuss substantive changes and threatened to establish a full military government. To implement the pact, five treaty services were set up—a customs receivership, the financial adviser, the public works service, the public health service, and the constabulary. Although each except customs was subordinate to the Haitian government, the top officials, at first naval officers, were nominated by the president of the United States.

Late in 1917 the State Department proposed a draft constitution for Haiti. (This was the document that Assistant Secretary of the Navy Franklin D. Rooosevelt later claimed he had written.) The Haitian congress resisted, but President Dartiguenave proclaimed it after a plebiscite (with a low vote and opponents abstaining) endorsed it. The constitution incorporated the 1915 treaty and validated acts of the military government. As in the Dominican Republic, there were improvements in Haiti under American occupation. The constabulary, a well-trained force, maintained peace in the country; prisons were improved; and the road-building program greatly extended the internal transportation and communications system. The courts and public schools did not receive the attention they deserved, however, and Haiti's financial problems remained unsolved.

When President Wilson left office, resentment against continued military occupation and the financial adviser's complete control of government expenditures was high.

This account of missionary diplomacy suggests that there was no significant change from earlier (1898–1913) United States policy in Latin America. If anything, missionary diplomacy meant "missionaries" (United States diplomats, military and naval officers, and businessmen) working in distasteful and ill-conceived ways, certainly not destined to insure the voluntary "conversion" of the flock. Woodrow Wilson's objectives for Latin America, emphasizing democracy and constitutionalism, were admirable in the abstract; but they did not accord with reality in the nations affected. Furthermore, Wilson's methods were paradoxical: he did not use democratic and constitutional means to achieve his objectives. As on many other occasions during his service in higher education and government, Wilson was consumed by personal combat; his struggles with Huerta, Carranza, and Villa ultimately became tests of personal strength and honor. On such occasions he lost his sense of perspective and the ability to see varieties of opinion and alternative approaches.

Missionary diplomacy was not devoid of positive effects. The negotiation of a treaty with Colombia in 1914 to resolve the deep resentment over that nation's loss of Panama in 1903 is a case in point. In the treaty, the United States expressed "sincere regret that anything should have occurred to interrupt or to mar the relations of cordial friendship that had so long subsisted between the two nations" and proposed to pay Colombia $25 million. Partly because of opposition from Theodore Roosevelt, the Senate ignored the treaty while Wilson was president, but approved it in 1921 after removing the expression of regret. Wilson's support for the settlement appears to have been based on a conviction that American actions in 1903 were wrong, that the whole affair had contributed substantially to Yankeephobia, and that an apology and reparations were long overdue. But Wilson could take this stand because the Colombian treaty did not interfere with his basic objectives for Latin America.

Some observers have pointed to Wilson's

support for a "Pan American Pact" in 1914–1916 as another effort to put United States-Latin American relations on the basis of "equality and honor," as promised in the Mobile address. The draft pact was a multilateral agreement to guarantee territorial integrity, political independence, republican government, arbitration of disputes, and arms control. Presumably the United States would forgo the unilateral right of intervention in Latin America. Colonel Edward M. House, who did much of the planning for the proposal, saw it as a way to promote hemispheric peace, just as Wilson later envisaged the League of Nations' world role. Efforts to secure agreement on the pact failed. Some of the larger countries, such as Chile, rejected the idea of guaranteeing territorial integrity before the settlement of existing boundary disputes; and, given the contemporary United States interventions, it was difficult to see the pact as anything other than a cloak for established policy. In fact, neither Wilson nor his advisers were willing to renounce the practice of intervention.

How, in the final analysis, can missionary diplomacy be explained? What were Wilson's motives and objectives? No single explanation will suffice, although there were unquestionably occasions when one consideration carried more weight than others. First, Wilson's concern about democracy and constitutionalism was genuine, and this was probably the main component of his Latin American policy when his administration began. What makes acceptance of this point so difficult is that from the beginning Wilson apparently assumed that the United States might have to use a heavy hand, to act undemocratically to install democracy. It was hard to see his commitment to constitutionalism in the midst of the bombardment of Veracruz or the marines' occupation of Santo Domingo, but it was there. Revolutions were unconstitutional and had to be prevented; illegitimate governments could not be recognized.

There is a second explanation for Wilson's policy that became clearer as World War I progressed—concern about the security of the hemisphere. Potential enemies, such as Germany, became of increasing concern. State Department documents illustrate the point clearly. What more startling example than the 1917

Zimmerman telegram, in which the German foreign minister invited Mexico to ally with Germany against the United States in the event of a German-American war? Security considerations were not always the primary explanation for missionary diplomacy; but they were constant concerns for Wilson, the State Department, and diplomats in the field. With a world war being fought during most of the Wilson presidency, and with the United States a belligerent by 1917, the situation was understandable.

There are also economic explanations for missionary diplomacy. As had long been the case, American entrepreneurs hoped to increase trade, find new markets and raw materials, and expand investment fields. Clearly these goals were applicable to Latin America during the Wilson administration. The available evidence does not prove that Wilson's central objective, as some scholars insist, was to advance American economic interests. But facilitating the work of these interests, and giving them diplomatic protection, was important to Wilson and the State Department. Some diplomats, such as Henry Lane Wilson in Mexico and James Sullivan in the Dominican Republic, were dominated by their personal economic interests.

Missionary diplomacy contributed enormously to the Yankeephobia that had been building steadily in Latin America since the late nineteenth century. The task of the interwar presidents and the State Department was to dispel this aura of hostility. Considerable progress was made by what came to be known as the "Good Neighbor" policy, which reached its peak in the late 1930's. Whether the Good Neighbor policy represented substantive change or merely a shift in rhetoric and tactics is debatable. Whatever the case, Woodrow Wilson, the practitioner of missionary diplomacy, made a good neighbor policy, or something similar, a necessity.

BIBLIOGRAPHY

For an exhaustive list of documents, articles, and books, see David F. Trask, Michael C. Meyer, and Roger R. Trask, eds., *A Bibliography of United States-Latin American Relations*

Since 1810: A Selected List of Eleven Thousand Published References (Lincoln, Neb., 1968).

Secondary works that are useful sources of information on missionary diplomacy include Peter Calvert, *The Mexican Revolution, 1910–1914: The Diplomacy of Anglo-American Conflict* (Cambridge, 1968), an excellent work with emphasis on England's role in the United States-Mexican conflict through the first two years of the Wilson administration; Alberto María Carreño, *La diplomacia extraordinaria entre México y los Estados Unidos, 1789–1947*, 2 vols. (Mexico City, 1951), a comprehensive study from the Mexican point of view, strongly anti-United States; Clarence C. Clendenen, *The United States and Pancho Villa: A Study in Unconventional Diplomacy* (Ithaca, N.Y., 1961), a detailed account of Wilson's relationships with Villa, climaxing with the Pershing expedition of 1916–1917; Howard F. Cline, *The United States and Mexico*, rev. ed. (New York, 1965), a classic study with emphasis on the twentieth century, as well as a comprehensive general history of Mexico; N. Gordon Levin, Jr., *Woodrow Wilson and World Politics: America's Response to War and Revolution* (New York, 1968), a tightly argued analysis of Wilsonian foreign policy, emphasizing economic motives; Arthur S. Link, *Wilson: The New Freedom; Wilson: The Struggle for Neutrality, 1914–1915; Wilson: Confusion and Crises, 1915–1916; Wilson: Campaigns for Progressivism and Peace, 1916–1917* (Princeton, N.J., 1956–1965), volumes II–V in Link's monumental biography of Wilson, in which the story of missionary diplomacy can be traced in detail—Link presents a favorable portrait of Wilson but is critical of missionary diplomacy; Dana G. Munro, *Intervention and Dollar Diplomacy in the Caribbean, 1900–1921* (Princeton, N.J., 1964), a valuable, detailed account of relations with the Caribbean nations and one of the few works dealing with the Caribbean aspects of missionary diplomacy—Munro deemphasizes the economic motives and stresses the strategic-political; Robert E. Quirk, *An Affair of Honor: Woodrow Wilson and the Occupation of Veracruz* (New York, 1967), an excellent study based on both American and Mexican archival sources that concludes that Wilson acted hastily at Tampico and Veracruz, without proper information and without anticipating violence; Hans Schmidt, *The United States Occupation of Haiti, 1915–1934* (New Brunswick, N.J., 1971), a well-researched book that concludes that Wilson's policy was ill-conceived and economically motivated; George M. Stephenson, *John Lind of Minnesota* (Minneapolis, Minn., 1935), an old work, but still essential in understanding Lind's role as a practitioner of missionary diplomacy in Mexico; and Luis G. Zorrilla, *Historia de las relaciones entre México y los Estados Unidos de América, 1800–1958*, 2 vols. (Mexico City, 1965), a well-balanced survey, less critical of United States policy than the Carreño volumes.

[*See also* DOLLAR DIPLOMACY; ECONOMIC FOREIGN POLICY; EXECUTIVE AGENTS; IMPERIALISM; INTERVENTION AND NONINTERVENTION; THE MONROE DOCTRINE; NAVAL DIPLOMACY; PAN-AMERICANISM; PROTECTORATES AND SPHERES OF INFLUENCE; RECOGNITION POLICY; REVOLUTION AND FOREIGN POLICY.]

THE MONROE DOCTRINE

Richard W. Van Alstyne

MONROE'S doctrine (the apostrophe appeared in the original) was the phrase picked by a convention of Democratic party delegates in December 1843 as a slogan to be used against their opponents, the Whigs. Daniel Webster, the Whig secretary of state, was rumored to be seeking British support in a move to induce Mexico to relinquish California—or at least enough of it to include San Francisco Bay. The *quid pro quo* for Great Britain would be all of the Pacific Northwest (Oregon, as it was then called) north of the Columbia River. The scheme was attractive to American merchants and seafarers of the eastern seaboard: they believed San Francisco was the port of the future, destined to provide them with a direct rail and ship connection to Hawaii and the Orient. But it went against the grain of an established ideology, best put into words by President James Monroe in his message to Congress just twenty years previously. Warning that the plan was "dangerous to peace and a repudiation of Monroe's doctrine that the American continents are closed to European colonization," the Democrats already had the battle half-won. Their Whig opponent, the incumbent President John Tyler, not only beat a hasty retreat but joined in the cry for the whole of Oregon, meaning all of the Pacific Northwest up to 54° 40′ N., the treaty line of 1824 with Russia.

Monroe, it should be noted, had put the matter in a negative way: the American continents were *not* open to future colonization from Europe. But in 1845, while the controversy was still warming up, a writer in the *United States Magazine and Democratic Review* suggested a positive approach stating it was the manifest destiny of the United States to annex all of North America.

This phrase too caught on: a group of militant Democrats who called themselves Young America adopted it as their watchword, and to this day historians employ it as a convenient copybook phrase for expressing the continental aspirations of the United States. Young America ultimately found their spokesman in Franklin Pierce, whose administration (1853–1857) attempted various annexations outside of the continent, notably Cuba, Santo Domingo, and Hawaii. Thus manifest destiny was stretched to include outlying territories, but it began to take on other meanings that are recognizable as attributes of the American national mission. John L. O'Sullivan, the originator of the phrase, gave it a religious overtone by insisting that Providence had allotted this task to the United States.

The Monroe Doctrine also carried religious overtones, and to the same end. Commodore Thomas ap Catesby Jones, commanding the Pacific squadron, seized the port of Monterey from Mexico in 1842, acting under the impression that his British counterpart was planning to anticipate him. Jones acted on a hunch, but the British admiral had done nothing to justify his action. Reading his reports of the incident, however, one is struck with the strength of Jones's conviction that he was doing right. Monroe's "celebrated message" was tantamount to a command: It was "our bounden duty to possess ourselves at every point and port in California which we could take and defend." "I never till now," declared Senator George Mc-Duffie of South Carolina in 1844, "fully realized the truth and justice of Mr. Monroe's declaration. . . . We are called on to counteract [British diplomacy] by every consideration of wisdom, prudence, and patriotism. . . . No European power must ever be permitted to establish a colony on this continent."

Since Monroe's declaration was now a doctrine, it contained the elements of church dogma transferred into the field of national politics. By definition a doctrine is a belief, a precept, or a principle made binding upon the faithful, who in this case were the citizens or patriots. Monroe was their master teacher, and his word was law. This view becomes the more clear when we notice the verbs with which the doctrine is invariably associated: "infringe," "violate," "defy," "enforce." Historically the United States claims the sole right to define the Monroe Doctrine; and if foreign nations disregard it, they have "violated" it. Dexter Perkins, whose books are seminal upon the subject, habitually falls into this usage. The Monroe Doctrine is like canon law, and the United States resembles the medieval papacy reserving to itself the claim of infallibility. Theoretically, according to Perkins, the British "violated" the doctrine in 1833, when they occupied the Falkland Islands in the South Atlantic. Allegedly these islands "belonged" to Argentina, and hence were a part of "this hemisphere" as designated by Monroe. But realistically they were centers of the rich sealing and whaling industries, exploited by American and British seafarers; thus their association with the Monroe principle borders on the absurd. But, as we shall see, the Monroe Doctrine was like Joseph's coat: despite its apparent consistency, not to say simplicity, it was an ideological garment of many colors.

Here it seems appropriate to say a word about the works of Perkins, whose principal books are cited in the bibliography. Many of the quotations in this essay come from them. Standing by themselves, these books are of the very essence of the Monroe Doctrine. Without them one would be lost in the maze of variations in meanings and in the multitude of details involving the doctrine both directly and indirectly. Perkins is almost like James Monroe in the flesh, the alter ego who puts a hundred years of history into the doctrine. Not foreign policy alone, "but the development of Ameri-

can political thought, of American nationalism, and of American ideology" is involved.

Perkins admits the affinity of the doctrine to manifest destiny; but one is tempted to say that, like Monroe, he has his principles. He insists that the Monroe Doctrine has a distinct set of ideas all its own. Always, however, during nearly a century and a half of usage it is, he says, "the great American shibboleth" that "has frequently clouded thought, and substituted loose generalities for sustained and practical analysis." The human mind seldom, if at all, puts ideas into separate cages, least of all shibboleths as complex and long-lived as the Monroe Doctrine. Trying to follow it through history is much like trying to keep on a trail leading through a dense forest and across streams. Other shibboleths and other stereotypes cross the trail. Manifest destiny and Monroeism crisscross constantly, so that the same people, be they politicians, statesmen, or writers, walk both trails, often without knowing it. One trail vanishes while the other reappears.

In the presidential message of December 1823 that gave him his title to immortality, James Monroe set forth three propositions:

1. "That the American continents, by the free and independent condition which they have assumed and maintain, are henceforth not to be considered as subjects for future colonization by any European power."

2. "The political system of the [European] powers is essentially different . . . from that of America. . . . We owe it, therefore, to candor and to the amicable relations existing between the United States and those powers to declare that we should consider any attempt on their part to extend their system to any portion of this hemisphere as dangerous to our peace and safety. . . . We could not view any interposition [in this hemisphere] by any European power in any other light than as the manifestation of an unfriendly disposition toward the United States."

3. "Our policy in regard to Europe . . . is not to interfere in the internal concerns of any of its powers. . . ."

The first of these propositions was the special province of John Quincy Adams, the secretary of state. Indeed, he was the probable author of the whole paragraph in which the passage occurs. The content of the paragraph sums up the diplomatic negotiations that Adams was currently conducting with Russia and Britain concerning the Pacific Northwest, a region he believed was destined to become exclusively American.

Historians, including Perkins, tend to read the paragraph containing the first proposition in context with a ukase issued by the czar two years previously. All the coastal waters from Baja California north to Bering Strait were hunting grounds for the sea otter, but the best hunting was in Russian waters far to the north. The ukase warned intruders away from these waters; but the business was international and intensely competitive, the Americans far in the lead. Not surprisingly, a Russian monopoly over such a wide expanse of ocean (100 miles out from the coast north of the fifty-first parallel) proved to be impracticable: a single warship on patrol could hardly be effective, and Adams found the czar's minister in Washington agreeable to a negotiation. By April 1824 a treaty was concluded whereby the waters were reopened and a boundary on the coast set at 54°40'.

Colonization is incorrectly used when applied to these maritime activities, nor were the Russians attempting to colonize. The slaughter of the sea otter went on, and Adams was interested in keeping it competitive in favor of the Americans. But he believed the stakes to be much bigger. The Pacific Northwest was highly strategic from several standpoints, and the moment was opportune for making a claim that could be covered by the broad term "colonization." As far back as 1783, Thomas Jefferson had drawn attention to the possibility of an all-American route to Asia via the Columbia River. Jefferson was credited with originating the idea of the "North American road to India" and what it would do in diverting the trade of the Orient to the United States. The route would pass through St. Louis on its way to the Columbia, and would ultimately bring about a revolution in the world's trade routes.

Behind this dream of an enormous accretion of wealth in American hands was the still older idea that North America belonged only to Americans. It was a legacy handed down from the Elizabethan English, such as Sir Walter Raleigh, who did not question their ability to crowd the Spanish and French from the New World. By "the New World" Raleigh and his contemporaries meant both North America and South America, and Raleigh developed a theory of war aimed at driving out the Spanish. His naïve supposition that Spain did not have the capacity to colonize was proved wrong; but it survived in a curious way in nineteenth-century America, which became receptive to ideas and schemes for dominating the countries to the south.

Meanwhile, English colonization concentrated on North America, where it met stiff competition from the French. The no-colonization formula was first directed against the latter for trespassing on lands granted the colonies by the king. Calling upon the crown to come to the aid of Virginia, Lewis Burwell, an influential planter, denied the right of the French to appropriate the Mississippi hinterland. "It is the Seating & cultivating the soil & not the bare travelling through a Territory that constitutes Right," he said. In the same year (1751), Benjamin Franklin pressed the argument in a more positive sense by pointing to the rapid growth of the American population, which was doubling every twenty years and was certain to overspread the continent. Jefferson and others of the Revolutionary War generation were indoctrinated with these ideas and accepted them without question. North America—all of it—was "our continent"; but it was in danger of being lost to a company of Scots, the Nor'-Westers of Montreal, who were forging a route west toward the Pacific. Jefferson fretted over this as early as 1783, but he was somewhat reassured some twenty years later, after Lewis and Clark had found an alternate all-American route.

Thus the dogma of North America for Americans was an accepted eighteenth-century creed, which Adams and Monroe merely reiterated. Adams could put it positively: "The world shall be familiarized with the idea of considering our proper dominion to be the continent of North America" (1819) or negatively: "It is not imaginable that *any* European Nation should entertain the project of settling a *Colony* on the Northwest Coast of America. . . ." (1823). He then tried persuading the British foreign secretary, George Canning, to allow the United States all of the coast up to the fifty-first parallel, a line that would leave all of the inhabitable land and all of the good ports and harbors to the United States. But the British were too well entrenched and too well informed of the inestimable value of this region to entertain such a proposition, so Adams had to fall back on the agreement made in 1818 to leave the future of the Northwest to the forces of competition between the two countries.

Since Britain was the only strong competitor, in terms of either trade or settlement, it would seem convincing that the no-colonization fiat was directed at Britain rather than Russia. When the Democratic politicians of the next generation demanded the whole of Oregon and used "Monroe's doctrine" as their justification, they were merely reviving an old ambition; but after clamorous calls for "Fifty-four forty or fight!" they acceded to a compromise treaty division of the territory at the forty-ninth parallel. It was a compromise much in the American favor, but it was also a setback to Monroeism. Small colonies formed in this region—on Vancouver Island and on the mainland, where there was valuable harbor frontage. These eventually consolidated to form the province of British Columbia, which in 1871 joined the new Canadian federation. Canada thus became a transcontinental nation, barring the United States from further expansion northward.

The ideology of the Monroe Doctrine is, of course, much more sweeping than the continental ambitions of the United States. It put negatively what precursors of Monroe and Adams had expressed positively. When Jefferson exclaimed in 1807, "I had rather have war against Spain than not . . . ," he was taking the words from the mouth of Daniel Defoe, who had argued vigorously almost a century before for the conquest of the Spanish dominions in the New World. Jefferson had eyes on Mexico and Cuba, whether as direct objects of conquest or as revolutionary countries that would help "to exclude all European influence from this hemisphere." A revolution did subsequently occur in Mexico, leading to independence from Spain and recognition by the United States (1822), but there was none in Cuba. Nor was it wanted. Cuba was the "ripening apple" that, to quote Adams again, "cannot choose but fall to the ground." As an appen-

dage to the Florida coast, Cuba was marked for annexation; but a possible Cuban insurrection in 1823 was something to be discouraged lest France or Britain take advantage. When Monroe wrote of "the free and independent condition" of the American continents, he could pass over the island of Cuba in silence.

Monroe's allusion to "this hemisphere" in the second proposition of 1823 had tradition behind it, but not geography. The seventeenth-century colonists conceived of themselves as arriving in a new sphere, a new world where life was sweeter, a new heaven on earth. The idea of traveling west to reach a better world was as old as the ancient Greeks. To them the Elysian Fields lay in the west; to the Renaissance English, England was "the seat of kings"; to the Massachusetts Puritans, Boston was the "new Jerusalem"; to the American patriots, America was the "land of liberty." Emerson called it "the home of man," a refuge from a sodden and tyrant-ridden Europe. Jefferson's blend of a mundane imperialism and a lofty idealism was summed up in his characterization of the United States as an "empire for liberty." The American empire would spread over North America and take in both Cuba and Mexico; it would exert its influence over the remainder of its "hemisphere." Jefferson had been attracted as far back as 1787 to the possibility of revolutions in Latin America, and to the gains in prestige that they would bring to the United States.

Whether Jefferson was aware of it or not, substantial aid, chiefly in the form of filibustering raids and privateering, flowed from New Orleans for the benefit of the Mexican revolutionaries. But nothing illustrates the doctrinaire bent of Jefferson's mind so well as a letter he wrote in 1813 to his friend Alexander von Humboldt, the German geographer who had supplied him with much information about Mexico. Latin American regimes gave him doubts, but ". . . in whatever governments they end they will be *American* governments, no longer to be involved in the never-ceasing broils of Europe. The European nations constitute a separate division of the globe; . . . they have a set of interests of their own in which it is our business never to engage ourselves. America has a hemisphere to itself. It must have its separate system of interests, which must not be subordinated to those of Europe. . . ."

All of this is good eighteenth-century doctrine, the credo of the American Revolution that makes Monroe's message read like scripture. But when he speaks of "this hemisphere," he is in the realm of pure fiction. There are only two definable hemispheres on the globe, the northern and the southern, divided by the equator. The "western hemisphere" is an imaginary area, a figure of speech used, as Monroe used it, to identify the two American continents. But this is of course a geographical absurdity, a conventional expression symbolizing an idea that grew out of the seventeenth-century illusion of the two spheres. To be sure, any cartographer can depict any hemisphere and give it any label that he wishes; but when we reflect that a scientifically drawn "western hemisphere" depends upon fictitious boundaries and that these boundaries can be changed at will, the concept opens itself to ridicule. Iceland, in the remote North Atlantic, was never inside the Monroe zone; but in 1941, as a means of securing the sea-lanes to Britain, the United States Navy occupied that island and, to justify the step, the administration of Franklin D. Roosevelt calmly moved the "boundary" of the "western hemisphere" east to longitude 26°W.

In 1823 Monroe restated the revolutionary tradition of republican America in such a way as to make it appear that the United States was the self-appointed guardian of all the other American republics. He raised the prestige of America in its own eyes, but did not have to face the practical threat from Europe that Roosevelt faced from Nazi Germany in 1941. Both Monroe and Roosevelt talked in terms of two spheres and of two different political systems, the one needing protection against the other. But, relying upon the strength of Britain, Monroe ran no risk, whereas in 1941 the risk was taken in the virtual certainty that it would lead to war.

Monroe's third proposition—that the United States would not interfere in the internal concerns of the European powers—called for no practical application then or at any time after 1900; but the change in status that occurred at the turn of the twentieth century created an ironic situation. Having realized its ambition to become not only a continental, but also a world, power, the United States was forced to repudiate this portion of Monroeism in favor of a different ideology. Monroeism is isolationism—it presumes an anti-Europe bias. The ideology of the two spheres, however, had always been in conflict with a much older ideology—the idea of the West, which since Homeric times has assumed almost countless forms and countless modes of expression. At the present stage of history this is the dominant idea.

In the age of Monroe, however, the dominant idea was American hegemony: annexation of North America and of its island dependency, Cuba; absorption of at least portions of Mexico; and the extension of American influence southward to include Argentina and Chile. Monroe "prohibited" European intrusion, but stopped with words. In 1826 Henry Clay expressed himself in terms of "intercontinental law"; but the American envoy to Mexico, Joel R. Poinsett, was rebuffed in his attempts to direct Mexican internal affairs. To thwart the United States, the Mexicans wanted more support from Britain than the latter was willing to give. Shrill demands for Texas and Oregon, coming mainly from the Jacksonian Democrats, brought responses from Britain and France—by no means disinterested parties to these issues, especially when the annexation of California appeared imminent. The Democrats fortified their cause with the Monroe Doctrine; and their new president, James K. Polk, in December 1845 raised the warning finger of Monroe against the European powers interfering with the doctrine.

The *Times* of London gave the British response in a lengthy editorial exposing the geographical fallacy of the two spheres, or two worlds, and offering a critical analysis of the political implications of the Monroe Doctrine. In Paris, François Guizot, the French premier, decided that the issues were too important to be allowed to go unanswered. His speech in the French Chamber of Deputies in January 1846 was the equivalent of Polk's message to Congress. Guizot turned the Monroe Doctrine inside out by denying that the United States was "the only nation of North America." There were "other independent nations," notably Mexico, with equal sovereign rights and political connections with Europe. Domination by a single power over a whole continent was dangerous, as European experience had demonstrated. "What was not good for Europe under the form of universal monarchy would not be good for America under the form of universal republicanism." The French, like the British, urged a "balance of interests" in America as a check upon United States hegemony. Basic to this argument was the thought that, wedged between America to the west and Russia to the east, Europe would ultimately lose its own independence. Like the United States, Russia was on the march. The brilliant commentator on American society, Alexis de Tocqueville, had already conceived of a shift in power away from Europe; and in 1845 the influential Paris daily, the *Journal des débats,* expressed the fear quite openly.

From then on, the Monroe Doctrine penetrated more and more into the American mentality—how deeply, it would be hazardous to estimate. Treating it in context with the acquisitive policy being pursued toward Cuba in the Caribbean and toward Hawaii as a stepping-stone to China in the Pacific, British minister to the United States John F. Crampton in 1853 commented on how the Monroe Doctrine was being inculcated and exploited domestically in order to generate a war spirit among the masses. "By eternal repetition this so called doctrine is gradually becoming in the minds of the Democracy here one of those habitual maxims which are no longer reasoned upon but felt. . . ." James Gadsden, responsible for the Gadsden Purchase (1853), which acquired more territory from Mexico, said as much. To him "Monroe's manifesto" was "the Bible and sacred oracle of expansion."

The principal proponents of the Monroe Doctrine, all high in the Democratic party, were Caleb Cushing, who, among other related activities, busied himself in the affairs of Argentina (1846); President Polk, who used Monroe to justify a scheme for detaching Yucatán from Mexico (1847); Lewis Cass and James Buchanan, who made a convenient target of the Clayton-Bulwer Treaty, which the Whig administration of Zachary Taylor had signed with Britain in 1850; and Stephen A. Douglas, the "Little Giant" from Illinois who spoke for Young America. These five and many other Democrats were ardent advocates of ousting

Spain from Cuba; and while he was minister to Britain (1853–1856), Buchanan made it his special province to try to induce the British to reinterpret the Clayton-Bulwer Treaty in such a way as to leave the United States a free hand in Central America.

During the 1850's, filibustering expeditions, privately organized but well publicized, launched attacks on various weak spots in Mexico, Cuba, and Central America. The most notorious of these aggressions was one of several led by William Walker, who made himself the ruler of Nicaragua and was rewarded with official recognition by the administration of Franklin Pierce. Trying to distinguish between the slogans of manifest destiny and the "Europe go home" formula of the Monroe Doctrine would be a curious exercise in historical semantics.

The dual nature of this compulsion is best illustrated by the situation that unfolded in Mexico: "the battleground for the maintenance of American supremacy in America; the theater for the practical illustration of the value and virtue of the Monroe Doctrine," as John Forsyth, a former secretary of state and in 1857 minister to Mexico, so well put it. The inevitable European reaction was put into words by French minister to Mexico de Gabriac: "Only Europe can save Mexico . . . the avowed object of the conquering ambition of the United States. If it finishes by falling into their hands, it would be difficult to arrest the march of their domination in the New World. Masters of this immense territory, will they not be able to lay down the law to Europe?"

A victim of unstable dictatorships and in danger of falling to pieces, Mexico stimulated both American and French greed. Speculative interests in both countries, aided and abetted by their respective governments, schemed to gain control of various parts of Mexico: Sonora for its mines, the other northern Mexican states for railroad concessions, Tehuantepec as a transisthmian route. Unpaid debts and a plenitude of complaints against Mexicans filed by resident foreign nations furnished ground for intervention by the United States and by at least three European nations acting in concert or separately: Britain, France, and Spain. As a reward for supporting the republican regime of Benito Juárez, the Buchanan administration obtained by treaty (1859) concessions that would give the United States a stranglehold over Mexico. Except for the imminence of civil war in the United States, this diplomacy might have ended in success; a similar negotiation consummated two years later under the auspices of Abraham Lincoln's administration was likewise aborted.

In Europe, France was the natural leader for bringing order to Mexico and putting a checkrein upon the United States. What Guizot had said in a speech, Emperor Napoleon III prepared to put into action: a Mexican throne, for which Napoleon chose Austrian Archduke Ferdinand Maximilian as occupant, and restoration of the rights and privileges of the Catholic Church, whose lands the Juárez government had confiscated. Once established in Mexico, a Catholic monarchy would set an example for the rest of Latin America and contain American Protestant republicanism inside United States boundaries. Mexican political refugees in Paris worked assiduously to this end. French bankers bent on collecting badly inflated loans, and speculators in various mining and railway schemes, were willing advocates of an all-out effort. Napoleon's envoy to Mexico, the comte Dubois de Saligny, personified this complex of interests and outlined the master plan for armed intervention: occupation of the ports and confinement of the revolution to the interior, after which the forces of conservatism in Mexico would rally to the cause of monarchy. (The expectations of the French, their plan of operations, and their ultimate failure in Mexico bear a striking resemblance to American "containment" ambitions in Southeast Asia a century later.)

Of the other two powers, Spain was a half-hearted accomplice of France, politically motivated but sour toward accepting a French puppet. Spanish intervention was short-lived and barren of results. The British studiously avoided even the appearance of political involvement, and hastily backed away from even their debt-collecting intentions. Still, the British role seems equivocal. They did not care to yield to "the extravagant pretensions implied by what is called the Monroe Doctrine" (Foreign Secretary Earl Russell's words); but when, in October 1864, the French army seemed to have Mexico under its thumb and to have rendered

Maximilian's throne reasonably secure, they accorded him recognition. Although skeptical from the outset of his success, the British were willing to gamble: a Mexican monarchy would thwart American ambitions and, what was equally important, would hamper France in Europe "for some years to come" (Prime Minister Lord Palmerston's words).

French military successes in Mexico in 1863–1864 were deceptive; an army of 40,000 men was required to do the job—far in excess of the original estimate. The attitude of the United States was well understood in advance; and even if the Union split apart, it was foreseen that the Confederacy would adopt a Monroe Doctrine policy. Napoleon III met with stiff opposition at home, and Maximilian was advised not to fall into the trap. But both the emperor of the French and the impressionable young archduke lived in a dream world, obsessed—in a sense even hoodwinked—into believing they could save Mexico, and ultimately South America, for Europe (as against the United States). Dexter Perkins' phrase "a clash of systems" seems appropriate, and Mexican preference for a monarchy capable of uniting the country and of standing off the United States was taken on faith.

Disappointments followed: except for the clericals and ultraconservatives, the Mexicans demonstrated against alien rule; guerrillas, armed and supplied from the United States, continued to harass the French forces; heavy casualties, worsened by the ravages of yellow fever, and mounting costs with no end in sight added to the discontent in France and emboldened the emperor's critics to speak out the more loudly. Privately, Napoleon III confessed (November 1863) that he had boxed himself in; but, like the American presidents who set up and supported puppet dictators in South Vietnam a century later, he refused to turn about. Still professing his belief that the war could be "Mexicanized," Napoleon agreed with Maximilian (April 1864) on a withdrawal of French troops over a period of three years. Maximilian was filled with good intentions; he and his attractive consort Carlotta traveled around the country, hoping to befriend the population. Mexican officials failed to respond, however, and Mexican soldiers had to be paid from funds controlled by the French commander. By

THE MONROE DOCTRINE

December 1864 even Carlotta knew that she and her husband were in a blind alley. Only an open-ended commitment from France could save them, and Napoleon III never intended to provide it.

Meanwhile, in war-torn America, speeches, congressional resolutions, and pamphlet literature on the Monroe Doctrine failed to obtain wide distribution until 1863, by which time a French force was well on its way to Mexico City. Democrats and abolitionists, dissatisfied for different reasons with Lincoln's conduct of the war against the South, seized on the doctrine as an "axiomatic truth," the established law in North America that it was Lincoln's duty to enforce. Popery and monarchy were enemies to be squelched; and France, now depicted as the great rival of the United States in the coming struggle for control of a trans-Pacific route to China, must not be allowed to control a country regarded as "the key to a continent." By the end of 1863 Mexico and the Monroe Doctrine formed a synthesis in the public mind; and in April 1864, when a resolution sponsored by the Republican chairman of the House Committee on Foreign Affairs passed unanimously, the term originally devised by the Democrats for party purposes was demonstrably palatable to their opponents. Prominent Republicans joined in eulogizing Monroe; warlike posturing and intrigues to get North and South to make common war on France reached a climax in 1865, when General Ulysses S. Grant put an army of 50,000 men on the Rio Grande; the next step, according to Grant, was to infiltrate 10,000 "immigrants" into Mexico. Reckless leadership of this type, gambling on a French surrender, could eventuate in a republican countercrusade against monarchy, with Mexico as the pawn.

The Monroe Doctrine was now "the idol of patriotism" with the American masses, according to the marquis de Montholon, the French minister in Washington, who was working hard in the summer of 1865 to lower a war fever. An experienced diplomat, he knew how to meet the situation: convince moderate opinion in the United States that France really meant to withdraw from Mexico. Barring some hasty act in the name of Monroe, time was on his side. Montholon's best ally was William H. Seward, the American secretary of state, also experi-

enced and correctly informed by his advisers in Europe of French intentions. Seward stopped Grant from invading Mexico and risking a battle with the French army; and he kept a restraining hand on Andrew Johnson, Lincoln's unexpected successor, who had indulged in some heated campaign oratory.

One of Seward's best advisers was John Bigelow, consul general in Paris, and Seward made him head of the legation. Maximilian was being ridiculed in Europe as "the archdupe," and the emperor was searching for an escape. But Europe had no patience with the pretensions of the Monroe Doctrine. Seward should steer around it, avoid the language of rivalry with France, and stress the common interest of the two countries in leaving Mexico to the Mexicans. In January 1865 Seward had positive intelligence from Bigelow that Napoleon III would withdraw, and the withdrawal actually did commence in October. Using the president's annual message as his medium, Seward avoided the ideological challenge to Europe sought by Monroe Doctrine advocates and stressed the practical side of the settlement. Napoleon III lost face; Maximilian lost his throne and his life; and the Mexicans, by their actions, showed that an alien monarchy really was "disallowable and impracticable" (the strongest words Seward permitted himself in a diplomatic dispatch after he knew the evacuation had started). But the Monroe Doctrine became a legend in the United States. It had scored a great victory over Europe. All the complications and nuances involved in the ill-starred French intervention were matters of indifference to the American public, and the doctrine was henceforth the national shibboleth.

Suppression of the South's rebellion brought the United States to the threshold of world power, the first step on which was the acquisition of Alaska. The Monroe Doctrine was now "the club of Hercules," the "jihad to which all the faithful must give heed"; and although successive administrations did not allude to it by name, they used it as an ever-broadening frame of reference. Congressmen, editorial writers, pamphleteers, and others felt no comparable restraints in their frequent expressions of alarm and jealousy over any incident that seemed to threaten the paramountcy of the United States in the "western hemisphere." A resolution proposed in the Senate denounced the Dominion of Canada (1867) as a "violation."

It is instructive to observe how these American jealousies kept pace with the growing great-power rivalries in Europe. In fact, it is not possible to evaluate the psychological power of the Monroe Doctrine unless the United States is viewed as a participant in the system of *Weltpolitik*. Since Germany under Bismarck had made clear its intentions to establish its hegemony in Europe, the American government reacted nervously to recurrent rumors of a German desire for the Virgin Islands. The United States itself, through Seward, had made the opening bid to Denmark for these islands; and it had schemed for a protectorate over the Dominican Republic. Since these projects had fallen through, it stood ready to protest the advent of any new European power in Caribbean waters. Three times Secretary of State Hamilton Fish, a kindred spirit to the now deceased Seward, questioned Copenhagen and Berlin, getting little satisfaction.

The ultimate expression of American distrust of Germany in the Caribbean was stated in 1902, when a German naval blockade of Venezuela (shared by Britain and Italy) was interpreted as a first step in taking control over that country. Mutual recrimination broke out in the press of both Germany and the United States over this and other points of friction, and the Monroe Doctrine came to the front of the stage as the pace of this ideological warfare increased. "An extraordinary piece of insolence," Bismarck once said of it. Opposite this sentiment was Theodore Roosevelt's wish to drive every European power "off this continent." Having had prior warning of "the truly hysterical irritation" aroused in the United States whenever the Monroe Doctrine was criticized, and of the "incalculable consequences" that might follow its "violation," the German government in 1903 behaved cautiously and the Monroe Doctrine, it was agreed even in Germany, was victorious.

Nothing better illustrates the Monroe spirit of "America for the Americans" than the spontaneous chorus of disapproval that greeted the proposal of Ferdinand de Lesseps, the builder of the Suez Canal, to duplicate his achievement in Panama. Law and logic were on de Lesseps'

side: the Clayton-Bulwer Treaty (1850) had authorized an international waterway to be built by private enterprise and be open to the ships of all nations on equal terms; and the French engineer proposed (1879) to attract capital from international sources, including American. He journeyed to New York expressly for this purpose, only to receive a thorough rebuff. A flood of speeches, congressional resolutions, editorials, and magazine articles ensued on the theme of the Monroe Doctrine, America for Americans, and the necessity of keeping European governments out of any isthmian canal project. The irony of this is that no European government showed any interest in participating. Nevertheless, de Lesseps stirred up great reaction; the national psychology was all against him, for the Monroe Doctrine represented "a deep, ineradicable, and most formidable instinct in the character of the American people."

The American government entered the lists (1880–1881) with a statement by President Rutherford B. Hayes that an isthmian canal was "part of the coast line of the United States"; this was followed by an argument addressed to the British government that it was time to discard the Clayton-Bulwer Treaty. When that failed, the United States signed a separate canal treaty with Nicaragua (1884) giving the United States exclusive rights, in open repudiation of the Clayton-Bulwer Treaty. By this time the excitement seems to have died down; the Nicaraguan treaty obtained a majority vote in the Senate, but not a two-thirds majority. Nevertheless, the fat was in the fire, for when the issue of an American-controlled canal became really pressing in 1900, the argument grew so heated that Britain was literally forced to yield (Hay-Pauncefote Treaty, 1901). The British concession was part of the play of world politics, Britain recognizing the shift in power resulting from the Spanish-American War. James Monroe was more alive than ever.

Only rarely during the nineteenth century did Latin American republics appeal to the Monroe Doctrine for help against Europe. The Juárez regime in Mexico played on the doctrine with notable success in 1864, but this was a special case. Invoking the no-colonization fiat, Venezuela launched a series of complaints against the British government for permitting encroachments from British Guiana on lands claimed by Venezuela. Venezuela was rebuffed by the State Department, but suddenly in 1894 the situation changed dramatically in its favor. A former American diplomat, William L. Scruggs, lit the fire with a pamphlet entitled *British Aggressions in Venezuela, or the Monroe Doctrine on Trial.* Scruggs, a Republican, had been relieved of his post in Caracas by the Democrats, whereupon Venezuela hired him to influence public opinion in the United States.

The pamphlet brought into play all the various elements of jealousy and national self-assertiveness that had been gathering force in the United States since the Civil War. Similar forces, accentuating great-power rivalries and inflated national pride, were at work throughout the world. Sentiment in the United States demanded that "the supremacy of the Monroe Doctrine . . . be established and at once"; and President Grover Cleveland and his secretary of state, Richard Olney, rose to the occasion. "Today," Olney informed the British government, "the United States is practically sovereign on this continent, and its fiat is law upon the subjects to which it confines its interposition." Some shadow boxing ensued, with the British prime minister, Lord Salisbury, keeping his head and declining to answer in kind. The upshot of this controversy was the appointment of an arbitral tribunal presided over by a Russian jurist; the court awarded the land to Great Britain. Venezuela, the original plaintiff, received scant attention during the argument; and the tribunal dismissed its claims as virtually without merit. Meanwhile, since the United States had made its position clear, distrust and rejection of the Monroe Doctrine was expressed in countries as remote as Chile. Mexico had the most to fear; and its capable ruler, Porfirio Díaz, issued a masterpiece of tactful disagreement while editorials wrote of "the suffocating pressure of the Colossus," "the inundating overflow of the Anglo-Saxon race and its anxiety to found a single colossal state extending from the North to the South Pole."

Considering that the ink was hardly dry on the Venezuela arbitration, fears expressed by the American delegation to the First Hague Conference (1899) that the convention signed there for the pacific settlement of international disputes would "infringe" upon the Monroe Doctrine seem amusing. The delegation took the position that an arbitral court composed partly of European jurists must not be allowed to arbitrate a dispute involving any American republic, even though the other party to the dispute was a European state. To avoid embarrassing questions, the American delegation put through a reservation to the effect that the convention did not "require any abandonment of the traditional attitude of the United States towards questions purely American." This insistence that the Monroe Doctrine (or its euphemism, "traditional policy") be immunized against international treatment remained a staple of American diplomacy for many years, reiterated in some form whenever an arbitration treaty or its equivalent involving Europe arose. Thus, in the hope of saving the League of Nations Covenant from defeat in 1919, a clause specifically exempting the Monroe Doctrine was inserted (Article 21). But Woodrow Wilson's unique description of the doctrine as a "regional understanding" was contrary to fact, and met with a chorus of dissent in both the United States and Latin America. The Mexicans attacked it as a system of "forced tutelage," and Mexico continued to refute the doctrine whenever the occasion demanded. In the United Nations Charter (1945) the doctrine was protected from ridicule (Article 52) by a vague reference to "regional arrangements" being kept apart from United Nations jurisdiction.

As a system of compulsory tutelage the Monroe Doctrine was made practice in the Caribbean region. The starting point was the Platt Amendment of 1903, which pertained to Cuba and gave the United States the right to intervene at will in the affairs of that country. In drafting this amendment to the Cuban constitution, Secretary of War Elihu Root declared his intention to draw up a bill of particulars regarding the Monroe Doctrine. Cuba thus became a protectorate. To Root and to Theodore Roosevelt the test of the Monroe Doctrine was the ability of the United States to keep the Latin American republics on their best behavior. Defaulting on debts owed to European banks and chronic revolutions spelled trouble from Europe; and the way to head this off was for the United States to take over, impose a collector of customs who would allocate the funds and pay off foreign creditors, set up a puppet dictator who would follow the advice of the American minister, and garrison the protectorate with enough marines to ensure order. The small republics of Central America and the islands were managed with comparative ease; but in 1914, when Woodrow Wilson attempted to bring Mexico to terms, he ran into trouble. Mexico was too large and the issues too complex to be controlled in the simple manner applied to Nicaragua or Haiti.

To Philander C. Knox, William Howard Taft's secretary of state, the Monroe Doctrine was "providential wisdom" confirmed by honest customs collection and debt servicing in the Dominican Republic and elsewhere; to Woodrow Wilson the doctrine meant a refusal to allow any European country a share in the financing of any Latin American republic and, in addition, it meant, for the sake of the safety and interests of the United States, "the establishment and maintenance of republican constitutional government in all American states. . . ." Stretched to South America, the latter was too tall an order even to be tried. In contrast with this ambitious program of benevolent despotism, the Wilson rhetoric included a proposal (1917) that all nations "with one accord adopt the doctrine of President Monroe as the doctrine of the world." Characteristically, Wilson was oblivious to the running fire of denunciation the Monroe Doctrine was drawing from Latin America: it was not a guarantee of their independence, but was "regarded as a menace to their very existence." Ironically, although the doctrine was still rigidly anti-Europe in its bias, the stream of protest came not from Europe, torn apart by its own troubles, but from Latin America, which emphatically rejected its supposed benefits.

Since the Latin Americans, from Mexico to Argentina, had made clear their aversion to the Monroe Doctrine, and since at the same time the sacred shibboleth was so imbedded in the national consciousness of Americans as to make renunciation impossible, it behooved the American government, or so it thought, to try to wipe away the bad name the doctrine had acquired. A verbal redefinition came the more easily since the United States, not Europe, was Latin America's banker—made so by the changes of World War I. Moreover, the policy

of playing teacher-policeman to the Caribbean republics was obviously falling short of success. Official redefinitions (1923 and 1929) had the effect of Alice's Cheshire cat: "I wish you wouldn't keep appearing and vanishing so suddenly," said Alice, "you make one quite giddy!" On both occasions the State Department (1) asserted that the Monroe Doctrine and the right of intervention were separate but nevertheless kept them both; (2) denied that the United States was seeking overlordship; and (3) declared that the doctrine was a statement of the right of self-defense, in the exercise of which the United States "must have an unhampered discretion." The 1929 definition in particular catered to the pronounced anti-Europe bias of that decade, as exemplified by high tariff walls, recriminations over "war debts," and opposition to joining the League of Nations. "The Doctrine states a case of the United States vs. Europe, and not of the United States vs. Latin America." So the myth of the doctrine was revived, while "ending with the grin, which remained some time after the rest had gone." In 1929 there was no "threat" from Europe. The definition placated American national sentiment—the doctrine was "purely unilateral" —but it had little, if any, effect on Latin America. Argentina and Mexico announced that, so far as they were concerned, the doctrine was "nonexistent."

The surge of Nazi Germany, commencing in 1933, began an entirely new act in the intercontinental relations of the United States. For the first time in its history, American diplomacy faced a real challenge emanating from Europe—not the challenge of an invading army, but the challenge of subversion, of ideological warfare, of severe economic competition, and of political sympathies and alliances. The scene of the contest was South America, in many countries of which large German communities resided and where, as we have observed, there existed a long-standing anti-American tradition. Keeping the Monroe Doctrine and its well-known implications hidden from view, the administration of Franklin D. Roosevelt found a winning slogan in its Good Neighbor policy, which smacked of Pan-Americanism. It subscribed to a formal agreement (1936) declaring intervention "inadmissible"; but in 1940, facing possible German occupation of the French and Dutch possessions in the West Indies, it retained a discretionary right to occupy those islands in case of need. The high point of this achievement was reached in 1942, when the Latin American republics subscribed to the sentiment that an attack by a "non-American" state on any one of the American republics, including the United States, was an attack on all of them. So, without bringing in the Monroe Doctrine at all and in the face of considerable sniping from Argentina and Chile, the diplomacy of "the good neighbor" achieved a fairly united front against the Axis Powers.

Wooing the "good neighbors" through the years of World War II took all the professional skill that the State Department could muster, however; and the wartime marriage that few of the South American countries were willing to consummate began breaking up even before the conflict in Europe was over. High-sounding phrases like "intercontinental solidarity" continued to be sprinkled throughout press releases and official documents, and in 1947 the United States made another valiant effort to put substance into them. The good neighbors agreed to set up an organ of consultation that they professed to believe would act unanimously in the event of an armed attack from outside the hemisphere upon any one of them. The atmosphere was already electric with the new challenge from Europe: as early as 1943, Soviet communism had begun filling the vacuum left in Latin America by the departing Nazis. But the challenge was political rather than military, and the real effect of communist infiltration was seen in the stepping up of factional warfare in sundry Latin American republics.

The ersatz nature of the inter-American system emerged into the full light in 1954, when Secretary of State John Foster Dulles pleaded in vain with the Latin Americans to help him overthrow the communist government of Guatemala, which had been in power in that country for more than three years. An invading force from Honduras, supplied with arms from the United States, did the deed; but the Latin Americans refused to agree that Guatemala under communism constituted an attack on the hemisphere. So, after years of studied avoidance of the name of Monroe, the United

States suddenly resurrected him. The American ambassador in Guatemala openly helped in the coup d'etat; and Lyndon B. Johnson, then a senator, promoted a resolution to the effect that under the Monroe Doctrine, Soviet interference in the Western Hemisphere could not be tolerated.

With the advent of Fidel Castro in Cuba and his open alliance with the Soviet Union, the administration of Dwight D. Eisenhower spoke out bravely. The president affirmed "in the most emphatic terms" that the United States would not tolerate a regime dominated by "international communism"; and in a formal statement the Department of State intoned the familiar phrases of 1823, declaring them as valid in 1960 as when first written. Subsequently an ill-assorted band of Americans and Cuban exiles mobilized under official American auspices in Guatemala, and in the spring of 1961 they set sail on American vessels for the Bay of Pigs. Like the filibusterers of the 1850's, the expedition expected to overthrow the Cuban government. The administration of John F. Kennedy was optimistic that it would succeed, but failed to understand that Castro had the Cuban masses behind him. The invasion was easily routed, and the American government suffered a further humiliation when Castro asked for and obtained help from the Soviet Union. Another joint resolution in support of Monroe emerged from Congress in September 1962, but a war scare suddenly arose with the discovery of Soviet missile bases in Cuba. During the crisis of October 1962, the Soviets agreed to dismantle their bases and the Americans agreed not to sponsor another attempt to overthrow Castro. The immediate danger of war was resolved; but Russian economic aid continued to flow into Cuba, and American diplomacy failed in its attempt to make Castro an international outlaw.

Like Scripture, the Monroe Doctrine can be quoted to any purpose. It is ideological rather than substantive, emotional rather than practical. It is central to the creed of American nationalism, definable only in terms of national self-interest. Whenever Congress or the executive branch has invoked it with reference to some particular policy, it has always insisted that the doctrine is unilateral. Tempers are aroused when other nations step onto this forbidden ground, especially if they utter an un-palatable truth. Lord Salisbury's cool analysis (1895) made Grover Cleveland "mad clean through," to quote the president. Nikita Khrushchev's rude dismissal of the doctrine (1960) elicited a tart response, but the name of Monroe wrought no magic on the Cuban link with Russia. In his final book (1955), Dexter Perkins sagely advised that the doctrine be discarded: the very words "convey a definite impression of hegemony, of supercilious arrogance, of interference." The doctrine is so vulnerable, so far removed from realities, that it becomes an easy target for ridicule or contempt.

The moment of supreme irony arrived in the midst of the Cuban crisis (5 October 1962), when President Adolfo López Mateos of Mexico, averring that Cuba was not "a threat to the hemisphere's peace," went on to say that no Latin American nation was "obligated" to help the United States "enforce" the Monroe Doctrine. Coming from "a friend and neighbor," this paraphrase of the American tradition ought perhaps to be taken as the cruelest blow of all. Verily, Mr. Monroe has had a great fall.

BIBLIOGRAPHY

Alfred J. and Kathryn A. Hanna, *Napoleon III and Mexico* (Chapel Hill, N.C., 1971), is a narrative of the rise and fall of Napoleon's "Grand Design." Dexter Perkins, *The Monroe Doctrine 1823–1826* (Cambridge, Mass., 1927), is an early work by the recognized authority on the subject; also see his *A History of the Monroe Doctrine* (Boston–Toronto, 1955), *The Monroe Doctrine 1826–1867* (Gloucester, Mass., 1965), and *The Monroe Doctrine 1867–1907* (Gloucester, Mass., 1966). R. W. Van Alstyne, *The Rising American Empire* (Oxford–New York, 1960), is an analysis of the origins and emergence of the United States as a national state; also see his *American Diplomacy in Action* (Gloucester, Mass., 1968), especially the introduction to part I, which analyzes the Monroe Doctrine as an attribute of American nationalism, and *Genesis of American Nationalism* (Waltham, Mass., 1970), which treats the Monroe Doctrine in context with inherited ideas of American nationalism and its mythology. [*See also* IDEOLOGY AND FOREIGN POLICY; IMPERIALISM; ISOLATIONISM; MANIFEST DESTINY; NATIONALISM; PAN-AMERICANISM.]

THE MORGENTHAU PLAN

Warren F. Kimball

WARTIME emotions have frequently engendered radical programs for postwar treatment of a defeated enemy, but none envisaged more extensive changes for a nation than the plan for defeated Nazi Germany offered in September 1944 by American Secretary of the Treasury Henry Morgenthau, Jr. Horrified by the inhumanity of the Nazis, Morgenthau had assumed that harsh postwar punishment for war criminals would be accompanied by broad reforms of German society that would eliminate that nation's ability and willingness to wage war.

But Morgenthau's assumption proved mistaken. By the summer of 1943, the State Department and War Department had each developed distinct proposals for postwar Germany. Secretary of State Cordell Hull and most of his advisers posited their plans on two beliefs: first, that the Treaty of Versailles following World War I had been unnecessarily harsh and had actually made Germans receptive to Hitler's militant nationalism; second, that an economically sound and self-supporting Germany was essential to both European and American prosperity. Arguing for a neomercantilist international economy, State Department officials hoped to eliminate all trade barriers and establish a totally interdependent world economic system under American leadership.

The War Department program dealt almost exclusively with short-term questions of occupation policy, since responsibility for the immediate administration of Germany after the war fell upon the army. Although concern for law, order, and efficiency dominated the military's planning, the solutions to those problems soon resulted in such suggestions as using wartime German bureaucrats and quickly converting German industry to peacetime production. Both the State Department and the War Department supported plans for demilitarization and denazification of Germany, but the long-term implications of their political-economic plans demanded the restoration of German industrial power.

At the meeting in Teheran, Iran, in November–December 1943, American President Franklin D. Roosevelt, British Prime Minister Winston Churchill, and Soviet Premier Josef Stalin gave attention to the question of postwar Germany but did not reach a final resolution. The three leaders agreed to try German war criminals at the location where the crime had been committed, a clear indication of the consensus for harsh punishment. Stalin and Roosevelt also expressed support for some sort of deindustrialization of Germany after the war —a key element in the program later proposed by Morgenthau. They discussed the dismemberment of Germany, but could not agree on whether to divide Germany into a few or many separate states.

The distrust and tension that had developed between the three great powers prevented the Big Three from reaching a final decision on Germany during the Teheran Conference. Roosevelt, wedded to a policy of creating an atmosphere of trust and cooperation that would survive in the postwar era, sided with Stalin so frequently that some British advisers claimed the Americans viewed England as the villain of the piece, even though most Anglo-American quarrels represented family arguments rather than fundamental differences. Roosevelt supported Russian proposals for the partitioning of Germany, for example, but quickly recommended that they be referred to a study committee when the British offered strong objections.

Still, one thing was clear after Teheran. Franklin Roosevelt personally inclined toward a harsh and punitive peace settlement with Germany. Suggestions by both the Soviet Union and Britain that the announced policy of "unconditional surrender" be modified so as not to prolong German resistance met with vehement opposition from the president. In a cable to Churchill, Roosevelt condemned "Nazism and Prussian militarism and the fantastic and disastrous notion that they constitute the 'Master Race.'" Although unconditional surrender was at least partly designed to reassure the Soviet Union of Anglo-American intentions prior to the opening of a second front in France, it also stemmed from Roosevelt's own interpretation of how World War II began. As the president saw it, Prussian militarism and general German acceptance of Nazi expansionism had brought about a national consensus for aggressive war. Hence, Roosevelt believed that only a complete discrediting of the entire German political-military establishment could prevent a redevelopment of such ultranationalism.

Throughout all the discussions of postwar plans for Germany, two outside factors constantly arose. First came the question of Anglo-American images of a postwar confrontation with the Soviet Union; second was the dispute over postwar zones of military occupation in Germany. Fears of Soviet expansion led British and American planners to oppose the unification of Germany because they feared a united Germany might fall under Soviet domination. Ironically, the evidence indicates that Stalin felt the precise opposite would happen if Germany stayed together. Thus the tension between the Soviet Union and the West effectively eliminated any chance that Germany would survive the war as a unified state, and made negotiations over zonal boundaries a matter of specifics rather than principles. In fact, the primary dispute over those boundaries was between the United States and Britain. Roosevelt, fearful of revolution and chaos in postwar France, believed the English hoped to involve the United States in the reconstruction of France by assigning the Americans a zone in southern Germany. He demanded the zone in northwest Germany, despite British protests

that the buildup for the Normandy invasion had assumed that American troops would invade on the southern flank and then proceed into southern Germany. Not until Roosevelt later became convinced that the occupation of Germany would be brief did he accept the southern zone.

Throughout the first half of 1944, Roosevelt assumed that the Teheran Conference had provided sufficient guidance to those making plans for postwar Germany. Moreover, as he told Churchill, he did not want to make hard, specific plans. Not only did such planning have to await the outcome of military actions, but Roosevelt also believed that the Russians should be present at all major postwar planning sessions. Postwar cooperation with the Soviet Union remained a high priority in the president's thinking, and he realized that the Russians were intensely concerned about Germany's postwar makeup. But the planners in the State Department and War Department could not read Roosevelt's mind, and the programs they drew up continued to reflect the long-term concerns of their own departments.

By the summer of 1944, State Department personnel had drawn up comprehensive guidelines for the occupation and reconstruction of Germany. Although they called for stern punishment of war criminals and a program of denazification and disarmament, State Department officials rejected the notion that long-term limits on German industrial capabilities could prevent a rebirth of militarism. Instead, their plan called for the integration of Germany into the postwar liberal-capitalist world system. Convinced that the adoption of American political, economic, and social principles would effectively prevent any development of German militarism, State Department planners sought to integrate Germany into their new world order—that *novus ordo seculorum* about which the Founding Fathers wrote.

In the course of a routine "inspection" trip to Europe in August 1944, Treasury Secretary Morgenthau read a copy of the State Department plan. His reaction was immediate and intense. Convinced that the diplomats were willing to forget the horrors of German and Nazi aggression in order to implement their grand plan, Morgenthau immediately confronted Roosevelt with the State Department plan as well as an occupation handbook drawn up by Allied military planners in London. The president's reaction was crude but clear. He told Morgenthau: "We have got to be tough with Germany and I mean the German people, not just the Nazis. You either have to castrate the German people or you have got to treat them in such a manner so they can't just go on reproducing people who want to continue the way they have in the past." Roosevelt angrily demanded that the War Department withdraw the "Handbook for Military Government for Germany" from circulation, commenting that he saw no reason for starting any major relief programs in Germany, as envisaged by the guide. At that point, Morgenthau decided to offer his own alternative.

The Morgenthau Plan for Germany, written by Treasury Department officials under the direct guidance of Morgenthau and his primary adviser, Harry Dexter White, was presented to Roosevelt early in September 1944. It called for dismemberment of Germany into three states, in accordance with Roosevelt's position during the Teheran Conference; for harsh punishment of war criminals; for denazification; and, most importantly, for the deindustrialization of Germany.

The main elements of such deindustrialization were the elimination of all industry and mining in the Ruhr industrial complex and in the Saar Basin, international control of the Ruhr, and a prohibition against long-term reparations—the last provision aimed at defeating arguments that German industry should be restored in order to pay such reparations. The Morgenthau Plan forbade any economic policy-making action by military occupation authorities lest the army, in its concern for law, order, and efficiency, take steps to restore German industry. The war crimes sections were harsh but clear and straightforward, calling for the summary execution of certain "arch-criminals" and the mandatory death penalty for any person who had caused the death of another in reprisal for the actions of others, in violation of the rules of war, or because of that person's race, nationality, or political beliefs.

Although there were few real reforms suggested in the Morgenthau Plan beyond the confiscation of all Junker (Prussian landed aristocracy) estates and their redistribution among the peasants, the proposal was aimed at the complete reconstruction of the German economic, social, and political orders. Like many New Dealers (though like few New Deal policies), Morgenthau believed that grand plans could solve problems. His grand plan called for the elimination of aggressive nationalism and militarism from the German national character by returning the Germans to a life of simple farming. Morgenthau rejected later accusations that his plan would have caused starvation, since farmers could grow enough food for themselves. His goal was simple: Germany had to become like Denmark, "where the people, through small-scale farming, were in intimate association with the land and were peace-loving and without aggressive designs upon others." Morgenthau's acceptance of the agrarian myth implied his belief in the Jeffersonian argument that urban-industrial life corrupts men. Although Morgenthau later argued that Europe did not need German industry in order to recover, that Great Britain would benefit by the elimination of German competition, and that a hard line in Germany would improve Russo-American relations, punishment and reform for Germany were his real goals.

Franklin Roosevelt's reaction to the Morgenthau Plan reflected the president's belief that Germany had become "Prussianized" and that all the German people were responsible for Hitler's crimes. Shortly after Morgenthau unveiled his formal proposal, Roosevelt told his foreign policy advisers that he liked the plan and favored the creation of an agrarian Germany. Although Secretary of War Henry L. Stimson protested emphatically, the president, on 11 September 1944, left for his meeting with Churchill at Quebec still committed to the principles of the Morgenthau Plan. Despite later insinuations that Roosevelt's failing health had contributed to his decision, it is clear that the harsh proposals of the Treasury Department's program fit in with his previous condemnations of the Germans. Although Roosevelt placed more emphasis upon dismemberment than upon deindustrialization, the Morgenthau Plan promised to make the former more effective without any requirement for a long-term American military presence in Germany. Since Roosevelt believed that domestic public opinion would force him to bring all troops home from Europe between six and twenty-four months after the German surrender, the Morgenthau Plan seemed to present a practical means of guaranteeing the partitioning of Germany. Moreover, the breakup of the German state was apparently a Russian policy aim; hence the plan could also serve the president's goal of improved Soviet-American relations. As the clinching argument, Morgenthau pointed out that the elimination of German manufactured goods from the European market would measurably increase British export sales. Since Roosevelt greatly feared a British economic collapse after the war, that premise decided the issue.

Shortly after arriving at Quebec, Roosevelt requested that Morgenthau attend the conference. At the president's instruction, he presented an outline of the plan to Churchill. Despite Morgenthau's emphasis on the economic benefits to England, Churchill expressed angry contempt for the proposal. However, by the next day Morgenthau and F. A. Lindemann (Lord Cherwell), one of Churchill's advisers, had convinced the prime minister that the economic benefits were real, not imagined. Moreover, the Americans and the Russians seemed in agreement, so why argue just to save the Germans? Whether or not Churchill hoped to gain in his negotiations with Morgenthau for postwar economic assistance is not clear, though it is certain that Roosevelt had made up his mind to help the British without reference to the German question. Once converted to belief in the Morgenthau Plan, Churchill became its ardent advocate, and even strengthened the language of the joint memorandum he and Roosevelt signed by inserting the phrase that called for changing Germany into a "pastoral" state. A few weeks later, when he met with Stalin at the TOLSTOY conference in Moscow, Churchill enthusiastically outlined the plan to the premier.

Even while Churchill was presenting the Morgenthau Plan to Stalin, Roosevelt was backing away from it. Under heavy pressure from both Stimson and Secretary of State Cordell Hull to repudiate the Quebec memorandum, the president claimed the Morgenthau Plan was only an alternative and that policy had not yet been decided. When the State Department

shrewdly mounted a campaign in the press against the plan, Roosevelt backed off even further. The president disliked open disputes and, confronted with strong opposition from his two senior cabinet officials, decided that the question of postwar Germany should await resolution at the peace conference. He maintained that position until his death.

But the planners in the Civil Affairs Division of the United States Army could not wait. Assigned the task of drawing up occupation policies as guidance for military authorities, those planners came up with an interim occupation directive that received the number JCS (Joint Chiefs of Staff) 1067. Although it contained escape clauses that were later used by the military to reconstruct German industry, the basic concern of JCS 1067 lay with establishing law and order while avoiding any long-term responsibility for economic or social problems. Aware that he could no longer hope to obtain Roosevelt's support for all of his plan, Morgenthau supported the army in its fight against the State Department, since the military did not openly call for the rebuilding of the German industrial plant.

By the time of the Yalta Conference in February 1945, the postwar German question was as far from settlement as it had been in 1943. Roosevelt had the same options open to him that had existed since the German question had become pressing. He could firmly endorse the Morgenthau Plan, with or without modifications; he could embark on a new course by accepting the State Department proposals, which called for integrating German industrial production into an interdependent world market; or he could continue to procrastinate, thus leaving the initiative with the War Department and its corps of occupation experts. A fourth option, that of turning Germany into a bastion against the Soviet Union, was never seriously considered by Roosevelt.

Churchill arrived at Yalta with a vastly different attitude toward Germany from the one he had adopted at Quebec. Convinced by Foreign Secretary Anthony Eden that the Allies would never persevere in anything like the Morgenthau Plan, Churchill also realized that Roosevelt had backed away from the plan. To the British the most crucial issue at Yalta concerned the future political makeup of Europe; hence Churchill opposed any final decisions on Germany while awaiting a clearer indication of Russian policy elsewhere.

Stalin appeared surprised by the Anglo-American uncertainty over Germany. Thinking the question had essentially been resolved at Teheran, the Soviet premier apparently expected Churchill and Roosevelt still to support the dismemberment and deindustrialization of Germany. Stalin firmly endorsed the partitioning of Germany but settled for Roosevelt's prophetic suggestion that the zones of occupation, which had been agreed upon almost a year earlier, could well serve as the starting point for a permanent division of the German state.

The Morgenthau Plan disappeared as an alternative under discussion at Yalta largely because of the problem of reparations. Roosevelt treated the German question as something that should serve the greater cause of improved relations with the Soviet Union, and he supported the Russian demands for extensive reparations. Ever mindful of American experiences after World War I, the president adamantly opposed the creation of any new war debts problem, yet he feared that the sort of long-term reparations required by the Russians might have to be financed by the United States unless Germany's industry were at least partially reconstructed. Although Henry Morgenthau had anticipated that problem and had proposed extending a $10 billion credit to Russia in lieu of reparations, the State Department had expressed strong opposition, preferring a program that made economic aid dependent upon political concessions. Roosevelt, uncertain of the effect of either policy, refused to make a choice.

Thus, the Yalta Conference only postponed the time of final decision for Germany, although the outlines of the eventual settlement had emerged. Occupation zones and minor boundary adjustments (Alsace-Lorraine to France, East Prussia split between Russia and Poland) became a substitute for dismemberment. The establishment of a standard of living no better than that in the Allied nations displaced the notion of deindustrialization. Establishment of the Central Control Commission implied a centralized authority and a degree of Allied responsibility for Germany's economy. Even though the denazification and war crimes sections of the Yalta agreements breathed the spirit of the Morgenthau Plan, the basic notion of reform by turning back the clock to a pre-industrial age was gone.

With Franklin Roosevelt's death on 12 April 1945, the Morgenthau Plan disappeared completely as a viable proposal. Even though the president had moved away from the plan, he did believe in the collective guilt of all Germans; and that belief gave Morgenthau a lever to use against those who supported the complete rebuilding of German industry. Moreover, Roosevelt had steadfastly opposed moves that would engender unnecessary Russian suspicion, a policy that had served to restrain those in the State Department who wanted to make Germany a barrier against Soviet expansion. Roosevelt's successor, Harry S. Truman, proved far more susceptible to such State Department arguments; and American policy soon reflected that shift. By the late 1940's, West Germany had become part of the Western alliance and the Soviet Union had begun to rebuild East German military and industrial strength.

The long-term effect of the Morgenthau Plan is vague, for it was an alternative that was rejected. Some have argued that the spirit of the plan lived on among many army planners and administrators in Germany, but such a view equates revenge and harshness with Morgenthau's proposals. Although punishment was integral to his plan, the ultimate goal was reform, not revenge. The Morgenthau Plan, for all of its anachronistic appeal to a simple pastoral world that could no longer exist in industrial Germany, did offer a political answer to a problem that Europe has yet to solve. The creation of a unified German state in the mid-nineteenth century had stimulated a series of wars, culminating in World War II. The division into two states lessened, but did not eliminate, the problem. The Morgenthau Plan, even with only partial implementation of deindustrialization, would have created a neutralized Germany, thus significantly changing the structure of Cold War confrontation. By the time statesmen like George F. Kennan and Adam Rapacki proposed such neutralization during the 1950's, it was too late. "If" history is a dangerous practice; but if the Morgenthau Plan had been adopted—with some practical modifications—true coexistence would be much more possible.

BIBLIOGRAPHY

The documentary story of the Morgenthau Plan can be found in the series published by the United States Department of State entitled Foreign Relations of the United States (Washington, D.C., 1862–   ), particularly the volume *Conference at Quebec, 1944* (1972). A great deal of additional documentary evidence is found in United States Senate, Subcommittee to Investigate the Administration of the Internal Security Act and Other Internal Security Laws of the Committee on the Judiciary, 90th Cong., 1st Sess., *Morgenthau Diary (Germany)*, 2 vols. (Washington, D.C., 1967). Henry Morgenthau, Jr., defended his plan in *Germany Is Our Problem* (New York, 1945). Additional information based on the Morgenthau papers and diaries is in John M. Blum, *From the Morgenthau Diaries: Years of War, 1941–1945* (Boston, 1967).

Three secondary sources contain the latest scholarship as well as excellent bibliographies: Paul Y. Hammond, "Directives for the Occupation of Germany: The Washington Controversy," in Harold Stein, ed., *American Civil-Military Decisions* (Birmingham, Ala., 1963); Warren F. Kimball, *Swords or Ploughshares?: The Morgenthau Plan for Defeated Nazi Germany, 1943–1946* (Philadelphia, 1976); and Bruce Kuklick, *American Policy and the Division of Germany: The Clash With Russia Over Reparations* (Ithaca, N.Y., 1972).
[*See also* THE COLD WAR; DECISION-MAKING APPROACHES AND THEORIES; REPARATIONS; SUMMIT CONFERENCES.]

THE MOST-FAVORED-NATION PRINCIPLE

Justus D. Doenecke

WHEN commerce first began among nations, the trader—particularly if a foreigner—faced suspicion and even hostility. Such powers as Egypt, Athens, Carthage, and Rome exacted trading rights from each other as spoils of war. For example, when the Hebrew king Ahab won a victory over the Arameans at Aphek, he forced the Syrian king Ben-hadad to permit Israelite traders to conduct bazaars in Damascus (I Kings 20:34). During the Middle Ages commerce continued to be unsure, subject to local taxes and regulations.

In the twelfth century, Genoa, Pisa, Venice, and other Italian city-states began to make formal commercial treaties with each other. Although such treaties covered a variety of topics ranging from protection of patents to rights of burial, most general commercial treaties soon fell into three categories: consular rights, concerning the privileges of diplomatic agents; national treatment, usually guaranteeing equal treatment to citizens of each nation; and the most-favored-nation, usually granting citizens and goods of another state the same privileges already granted to a third state. Under most-favored-nation status, any favor or immunity that either of the two contracting parties grants to a third state would be granted automatically to each other.

Despite the language of the term, the clause was not intended to make any single nation "more favored" commercially than any other. On the contrary, it sought equal treatment for all nations. As the historian and State Department official Stanley K. Hornbeck noted in 1910, "The object centered on uniform treatment without discrimination." Each state would be assured that it would always be treated as favorably as the state "most favored." The clause, in fact, could more accurately be called the "equally-favored-nation" clause.

Since it affords a convenient form of negotiation, the most-favored-nation principle has long been the most common single rule of conduct in international trade. Because a country extends new privileges to one state, it need not renegotiate all its treaties. Instead, by ensuring past and future concessions to all contracting states, the clause interjects a convenient multilateralism into otherwise bilateral agreements. The most-favored-nation pledge, however, is not a free-trade device. A country may still set its tariffs as high as possible and in no way violate uniformly applied most-favored-nation terms.

The clause can be applied in several ways: (1) single transfer, granting a privilege without reciprocity or condition (a practice once often imposed on non-Western nations); (2) specialized reciprocal, applying only to certain goods; (3) simple reciprocal, by which blanket favors granted to any other state would be granted to the grantee; (4) the unconditional form, by which all favors granted to any state would immediately, and without qualification, become common to all third parties; and (5) the conditional form, which would grant privileges to third parties only if they, in turn, would make special compensations.

The crucial distinction between conditional and unconditional deserves further elaboration, and can best be explained by the following example. Assume that the United States affords France conditional most-favored-nation status. The United States later signs a trade treaty with the United Kingdom providing for a reduced American tariff on British worsteds. Although France has been accorded most-favored-nation status, it will not necessarily find its own worsteds permitted to enter the United States at the new reduced rate. For the French to receive the same privileges as the British, they would have to make a concession of the same magnitude—admitting an American product (say typewriters) at a lower rate. If the most-favored-nation clause between France and the United States had been unconditional, however, France would receive the lower United States rate on worsteds without being required to make any further concession.

Countries have used other devices in order to weaken most-favored-nation commitments —for example, by making such minute distinctions among products in their tariff schedules that one state is obviously favored over another. Such provisions certainly weaken the spirit of a most-favored-nation clause, and can violate the letter. For example, in 1902 Germany made such exact specifications for cattle imports ("reared at a spot at least 300 meters above sea-level . . . belonging to the long headed variety, especially to the races of Alpine cattle") that only cattle from Switzerland or the Austrian Tyrol could be admitted. Other devices include discriminatory sanitary regulations, restrictions on quantity (quotas), and voluntary restraint agreements entered into by exporters with the insistence of importing nations.

The first known use of the most-favored-nation practice dates back to 1226. At that time Emperor Frederick II conceded to the city of Marseilles privileges previously granted to citizens of Pisa and Genoa. Although the granting of reciprocal forms existed much earlier, not until the seventeenth century did the most-favored-nation clause itself appear. England and Holland were competing with Spain and Portugal, France and Scandinavia with the Hanseatic League and the Italian Republics. With private monopolies giving way to state trading, each state sought a guarantee of the greatest possible commercial advantages. In order to gain advantages, a country had to give

concessions and hence include the most-favored-nation clause in its treaties.

From the very beginnings of the United States, the most-favored-nation proviso has been a cardinal point of its diplomacy. In the Model Treaty, or Plan of 1776, drafted for the Continental Congress by John Adams, Benjamin Franklin, John Dickinson, Benjamin Harrison, and Robert Morris, the American negotiators were instructed (if direct reciprocity could not be obtained) to bargain with the French for most-favored-nation privileges. In the alliance made between the United States and France on 6 February 1778, and negotiated by Benjamin Franklin, Silas Deane, and Arthur Lee, the parties included a most-favored-nation clause. Article II read:

> The most Christian King and the United States engage mutually not to grant any particular favour to other nations, in respect to commerce and navigation, which shall not immediately become common to the other party, who shall enjoy the same favour freely if the concession was freely made, or on allowing the same compensation if the concession was conditional.

Such French ports as were open to any foreign ship were therefore open to the ships and cargoes of the United States. However, the treaty in effect included the conditional form of the most-favored-nation principle. Although the conditional form had been of French—not American—origin, it immediately became the basis of United States policy.

The Model Treaty of 1776 and the terms of the French alliance can best be seen in a wider framework. Most states then perceived commercial conventions as sources of friction. Such treaties were seen as instruments of power politics, with political alliances reinforced by commercial preferences. Americans, however, believed the opposite: a free and equal trade system would eliminate political conflict. Hence, the new republic sought as great a commercial freedom as possible. Such freedom did not imply "free trade" without tariffs, although the United States retained a relatively low tariff until 1816. Rather, through such devices as most-favored-nation clauses, it meant preventing nations from levying discriminatory duties against the new state. With abundant natural resources for export and a growing market for

European manufactures, the United States was able to exchange relatively easy access to its growing domestic market for the removal of unequal foreign restrictions. The United States was attempting to project its own commercial system upon the rest of the world scene, acting in the belief that its policy of "a fair field and no favor" was bound to benefit an increasingly interdependent globe.

The American rationale for commercial prosperity, however, differed markedly from that of most other countries; and this was most apparent in the fervor with which the United States insisted upon the conditional version of the most-favored-nation principle. In opting for the conditional form, America showed how anxious it was to combat harsh discrimination while increasingly making efforts to protect its own infant industries. The British, on the other hand, had little fear of being undersold and promoted free trade in order to better sell their manufactured goods. Since they had no tariff with which to bargain, they favored the unconditional form. The unconditional principle is usually proposed by strong industrial nations that want to secure markets for a broad range of their manufactures. Only such great powers could risk injury to some of their industries in order to obtain far larger markets. In practice, few countries—other than the United States— have used the conditional form as a basis for withholding privileges to which, under the unconditional form, countries would have been entitled.

By the end of the eighteenth century, America had entered into a series of commercial treaties, each containing the most-favored-nation principle: with France in 1778, the Netherlands in 1782, Sweden in 1783, Prussia in 1785 and 1799, Morocco in 1787, Spain in 1795, and Tunis and Tripoli in 1797. The principle was written into Jay's Treaty of 1794, an agreement placing the United States on a most-favored-nation basis with regard to the British Isles and the British East Indies, but not the extremely important British West Indies. Even shaky political relations with France did not alter commercial privileges. In the Convention of 1800, ending the undeclared naval war between the two countries, the most-favored-nation proviso was retained. Similarly the treaty of 1803, for the sale of Louisiana, stipulated that the ships of France and of Spain should "forever" be treated "upon the footing of the most-favored-nation" in the ports of the ceded territory. Perhaps through oversight, neither treaty attached any conditions whatsoever to most-favored-nation treatment. Since the two treaties were not commercial ones, they did not contain the usual conditional clause.

In all such agreements, the United States held contracting parties to the conditional form, even when it was not clearly specified in the relevant treaty. In 1787 John Jay, secretary of foreign affairs, recognized that the Netherlands treaty of 1782 did not specifically include the conditional form. Yet Jay declared that it was inconsistent with "reason and equity," as well as with "the most obvious principles of justice and fair construction," to demand that the United States grant unconditional privileges. If "France purchases, at a great price, a privilege of the United States," the Dutch—Jay said— could not "immediately insist, on having the like privileges without [paying] any price at all."

Controversy over American insistence on the conditional form continued. Shortly after the War of 1812 had ended, the United States and Great Britain made a reciprocal agreement. Dated 3 July 1815, the treaty gave British ships privileges in American harbors not allowed ships of France. The French government insisted upon the literal interpretation of the most-favored-nation clause. Refusing to grant concessions to the United States, France claimed that it had given America an "equivalent" at the time of the Louisiana Purchase. Secretary of State John Quincy Adams asserted in 1817 that "the condition, though not expressed in the article, is inherent in the advantage claimed under it." Only when the French reduced their duties on wines in 1831, acceding to a request from Secretary of State Martin Van Buren, did the United States grant France permanent commercial privileges in Louisiana.

The United States interpretation was occasionally modified. When Britain later claimed that the United States Tariff of 1824 discriminated against certain British cotton exporters, a joint arbitration commission decided in favor of the British. The 1815 treaty, the commission held, entitled British imports to as favorable a treatment as was granted gratuitously to imports from any other country.

THE MOST-FAVORED-NATION PRINCIPLE

The most-favored-nation principle was strongly stressed in American treaties, and could be said to have served as an ancestor of the Open Door policy. In 1833 Edmund Roberts, a large shipowner and an agent of President Andrew Jackson, made treaties with Muscat and Siam, opening both areas to United States trade on most-favored-nation terms. At the end of the Opium War in 1842, the Manchu negotiators—of their own accord—applied the principle of equal treatment for all "barbarians" in China. They sought to prevent the victorious British from getting the credit for admitting Americans to these privileges. Instead, they hoped that the United States would feel indebted to the Chinese emperor. Two years later Caleb Cushing, a plenipotentiary of President John Tyler, negotiated the Treaty of Wanghia (near Macao), providing for national guarantees in five treaty ports. The Treaties of Tientsin, made in 1858, ended the joint French-British war against China and gave the United States most-favored-nation privileges in eleven new treaty ports.

Historian John King Fairbank shows that the most-favored-nation clause was an instrument of Western commercial exploitation, a means by which China could be placed in "semi-colonial status." Although the Chinese had hoped to play off the Western nations against each other, they only succeeded in uniting the West. The clause was part of a "one-way street," by which any concession gained by one power accrued immediately to all. Since China could never reverse the tide, the treaty privileges were extended to Chinese travel and immigration rights. In 1868 Anson Burlingame, acting as envoy of the Chinese Empire to all the Western powers, negotiated eight additional articles to the American Treaty of Tientsin. One article gave China most-favored-nation privileges in regard to visit, travel, and residence in the United States, thereby opening the country to Chinese immigrants. In 1880 China permitted modification of the 1868 treaty by agreeing to recognize America's right to "regulate, limit, or suspend" (but not prohibit) the immigration of Chinese laborers in return for receiving guaranteed most-favored-nation treatment for Chinese already established in the United States. The Boxer Protocol of September 1901 incorporated the most-favored-nation clause,

and, in a commercial treaty concluded in 1903, China specified that American citizens and businesses might engage "on equal terms with those granted to the subjects of any foreign power."

United States–Japanese relations also revolved about the most-favored-nation concept. Commodore Matthew C. Perry's treaty of friendship, made in 1854, granted trading concessions for two minor Japanese ports, Hakodate and Shimoda. More important, it permitted the United States to receive any concessions that might be granted other powers in the future. Three years later Townsend Harris, arriving in Shimoda as the first American consul, signed a treaty that recognized in writing the extraterritorial and trade privileges already accrued to the United States by Perry's negotiations. In 1894 a treaty of commerce and navigation with Japan abolished extraterritorial courts and settlements, but continued to apply most-favored-nation clauses to all commercial matters. When, in October 1906, the San Francisco school board ordered that all Japanese schoolchildren attend a segregated school, Japan protested that the act violated most-favored-nation treatment. Theodore Roosevelt, recognizing the justice of this protest, persuaded the school board to rescind its action. (In 1907 he made the Gentlemen's Agreement with Japan, by which Japan voluntarily restricted immigration to the United States.)

The United States did not always adhere to the conditional interpretation. In treaties with the Orange Free State (1871) and with Serbia (1881), it clearly provided for unconditional most-favored-nation treatment. In 1909 it gratuitously extended a reduction to Spanish wines. Spain had made a commercial agreement with the United States in 1906, and in 1908 sought wine privileges given in that year to France. In 1911 the United States permitted Canadian pulp and paper to enter the country free of duty. A number of European countries claimed that they too—under most-favored-nation agreements—were entitled to the same privilege. The United States Court of Customs Appeals recognized the validity of these claims; the privilege extended to Canada, it said, had been granted freely and without receipt of compensation. The Canadian case, however, is more evidence of oversights in American drafting than of acceptance of the unconditional form.

The United States–Prussia Commercial Treaty of 1828 probably caused the most controversy of any such trade treaty. The Germans singled out a clause of the treaty that suggested the unconditional form, while ignoring another proviso that specifically denoted reciprocity and conditional stipulations. In 1878 Germany called attention to special privileges the United States granted Hawaii as a result of a convention signed in 1875, although it soon admitted that "extraordinary circumstances" made the preferential between Hawaii and the United States warrantable. In referring to "certain relations of proximity," the United States had admitted free a list of Hawaiian commodities—of which sugar was the most important—in return for free admission to Hawaii of many American manufactured articles, grains, and breadstuffs. (Under an 1851 treaty with Hawaii, Great Britain was legally entitled to any concessions granted the United States in 1875. The American government, however, refused to let Hawaii honor its obligation to Britain.)

Germany protested, with more effect, against special commercial benefits that the United States accorded Switzerland in 1898. In that year the Swiss had demanded that the United States yield to them the same concessions granted the French earlier in the year. Since an American treaty of 1850 with Switzerland had deliberately provided for most-favored-nation treatment in terms "absolutely unconditional," the United States declared that "both justice and honor" involved meeting the Swiss claims. After Germany claimed the same treatment, the United States in 1899 renounced the most-favored-nation provisions in the Swiss treaty.

Supreme Court cases added to foreign anger. In *Bartram* v. *Robertson* (1887), the court ruled that sugar from St. Croix, one of the Danish Virgin Islands, could be charged a higher duty than sugar from Hawaii. The court denied that there was anything in the 1826 conditional treaty with Denmark that would entitle it to receive without compensation privileges granted to Hawaii for compensation. *Whitney* v. *Robertson* (1888) concerned New York merchants who claimed that, under a most-favored-nation treaty of 1867, sugar from

Santo Domingo should be admitted on the same terms—free of duty—as sugar from Hawaii. The court, again upholding the Hawaiian privilege, asserted that such treaties as the one with Santo Domingo were "never designed to prevent special concessions." With skilled sophistry, the court noted the absence of any specific conditional clause, but ruled that "It would require the clearest language to justify a conclusion that our government intended to preclude itself from such engagements with other countries, which might in the future be of the highest importance to its interests."

Not many years after these decisions were rendered, the State Department—negotiating with Russia in 1895—claimed that the United States should gratuitously share concessions that Russia had granted to other countries for compensation. Yet, within a few months after America had made such a claim, it denied that Russia, under the same pledge, could share gratuitously in the American concessions to Hawaii. The United States also acted in a discriminatory manner toward Great Britain. Under Section 3 of the Dingley Tariff Act of 1897, the United States gave special reductions in duty to several European countries in return for minor concessions from their high tariffs. It withheld these concessions from Great Britain, for Britain had no concessions to make and was already admitting most American products free of duty.

On the whole, the United States use of the conditional "most-favored-nation" clause backfired. After 1890, America could not obtain as favorable a tariff treatment from continental Europe as Great Britain could with its use of the unconditional clause. In fact, in the period 1890–1920, the United States was the one important commercial nation not reasonably certain of being granted equal tariff treatment by the rest of the Western world. Ironically, instead of operating to gain special advantages for American commerce, the conditional clause could not even secure mere equality of treatment.

The reason for America's misfortune lay in changing trade patterns. In the early years of the Republic, American exports consisted predominantly of agricultural products and raw materials. Since foreign countries often depended upon the United States for such

607

supplies, they were not likely to apply discriminatory duties. The United States also purchased many European manufactured products, and hence had the power to retaliate effectively against hostile legislation. In the last decades of the nineteenth century, the United States increasingly exported manufactured products while importing more foodstuffs and raw materials. American goods now competed with European exports, and Europe soon showed its anger with America's conditional policy and extremely high tariffs. It began to denounce most-favored-nation treaties with the United States, to make all tariff arrangements on a temporary basis, and to discriminate in customs legislation against American products.

After World War I, the United States changed to an unconditional policy. Woodrow Wilson included a demand for "equality of trade conditions" as the third of his Fourteen Points, but only in the Fordney-McCumber Tariff Act of 1922 did the United States change to the unconditional form. The 1922 tariff consisted of a single column of tariff rates applicable to all nations without discrimination.

Secretary of State Charles Evans Hughes, justifying the American change to unconditional practice in a note to the Senate Committee on Foreign Relations, admitted that the conditional form did not gain America the desired equality of treatment, and claimed that what might constitute equivalent compensation was "found to be difficult or impracticable." "Reciprocal commercial arrangements," declared the secretary, "were but temporary makeshifts; they caused constant negotiation and created uncertainty." In instructions to American diplomatic officers, Hughes was quite blunt concerning the reason for the new commercial offensive levied against a discriminatory bilateral system of trade blocs: "The enlarged productive capacity of the United States developed during the World War has increased the need for assured equality of treatment in foreign markets."

The new practice was soon instituted. The American government refrained from renewing its request for the preferential tariff treatment of Brazil and drew up a model for a new series of commercial treaties couched in unconditional form. The new policy was first ratified by the Senate in 1925, when a commercial treaty was made with Germany. When Congress passed the Reciprocal Trade Agreements Act in 1934, it instructed the tariff commission to incorporate the principle of unconditional most-favored-nation treatment in each trade treaty. However, the Reciprocal Trade Agreements Act tended in practice to work against unconditional most-favored-nation treatment, for the United States would withhold a reciprocal concession until it could be made with a chief supplier and in return for an equivalent grant.

During World War II, the United States discovered important defects in the Reciprocal Trade Agreements Act. Sometimes foreign governments were hesitant to give the United States concessions because they wanted to keep some bargaining power in reserve for other countries. At other times, foreign governments that had granted major concessions to the United States found that they had little with which to bargain with other governments. American officials began to favor simultaneous multilateral negotiations, by which each government could evaluate its gains, decide what concessions to offer, and discover what privileges it had been receiving "free" through most-favored-nation treatment.

In 1948 the United States took advantage of its postwar dominance of the international economy and led the leading Western commercial nations in establishing the General Agreement on Tariffs and Trade (GATT). The most vital part of the GATT commercial code lies in the most-favored-nation clause: "Any advantage, favour, privilege or immunity granted by any contracting party to any product originating in or destined for the territories of all other contracting parties."

Most-favored-nation principles throughout the world have recently been weakened. Mother countries have made exceptions in order to meet the special needs of former colonies and less-developed countries (LDC's). Specifically, generalized systems of preferences have been instituted, giving manufactured goods exported from LDC's preferred treatment over similar goods exported from developed countries. Such preference systems have been adopted by the European Community (1971), Japan (1971), and the United States (1975).

The United States may be reverting to a con-

THE MOST-FAVORED-NATION PRINCIPLE

ditional form of the most-favored-nation principle. The Trade Act of 1974 requires the president, at the conclusion of any negotiations, to certify that concessions granted by the United States to industrial nations are balanced by concessions of the trading partner. If a nation is getting a "free ride," the president is required to withdraw concessions. The effect of this new provision is yet to be measured. Applied on a massive scale, it could mean the end of pure, unconditional most-favored-nation practice.

Future prospects are unclear. Surely the old model of a single, worldwide group of trading nations, all on the same footing, is over. Systematic preference is given to LDC-manufactured exports. Yet at present, the most-favored-nation principle still forms the basis of trading relationships between developed nations. It remains a status very much sought after by countries not having it, in particular most nations of the Eastern bloc. Only Poland and Rumania have so far achieved this status. In the abortive commercial negotiations of 1974 with the Soviet Union, the United States promised most-favored-nation treatment (and credits from the Export-Import Bank) if the Soviet Union would permit its citizens to emigrate. The Russians turned down the proposal.

BIBLIOGRAPHY

W. S. Culbertson, "Commercial Treaties," in *Encyclopaedia of the Social Sciences* (New York, 1934), puts "most-favored-nation" principles in a wide historical and economic context. John King Fairbank, *Trade and Diplomacy on the China Coast, 1842–1854*, 2 vols. (Cambridge, Mass., 1953), shows how the most-favored-nation clause became an instrument of Western exploitation. Felix Gilbert, *To the Farewell Address: Ideas in Early American Foreign Policy* (Princeton, N.J., 1961), reveals the commercial philosophy behind the Model Treaty and the French alliance of 1778. Wendell C. Gordon, *International Trade* (New York, 1965), offers excellent examples of conditional and unconditional agreements. Stanley Kuhl Hornbeck, *The Most-Favored-Nation Clause in Commercial Treaties* (Madison, Wis., 1910), is a thorough study containing a defense of American conditional practice. League of Nations, Committee on Experts for Progressive Codification of International Law, "Report on the Most-Favored-Nation Clause," in *American Journal of International Law*, Supplement, 20 (1928), is a summary of "most-favored-nation" practice, with an abundance of historical material. Raymond F. Midesell, "International Trade Controls: Trade Agreements," in *International Encyclopedia of the Social Sciences* (New York, 1968), although not as helpful on this topic as the older Culbertson essay, shows why the "most-favored-nation" doctrine was in trouble in the 1960's. John Bassett Moore, "Most-Favored-Nation Clauses," in *Digest of International Law*, 5 (Washington, D.C., 1906), is an account containing much raw material for the historian willing to dig. Sidney Ratner, *The Tariff in American History* (New York, 1972), is particularly helpful on the reciprocal trade agreements of the 1930's and GATT. Jacob Viner, "The Most-Favored-Nation Clause in American Commercial Treaties," in *Journal of Political Economy*, 32 (1924), is a learned polemic against the American conditional practice, with much information of value to the historian. The author is indebted to Ray A. Meyer, international economist with the Trade Agreements Division of the Department of State, for information on current trends.

[See also Economic Foreign Policy; Freedom of the Seas; The Open Door Policy; Reciprocity; Trade and Commerce; Treaties.]

NATIONALISM

Lawrence S. Kaplan

NATIONALISM suffers from confusion both over the meaning of the term and over its role in the modern world. Its antecedents may be found in the fifteenth and sixteenth centuries, with the rise of the nation-state under dynastic rule, but its ideology and vitality are no older than the late eighteenth century, the period of the American and French revolutions. Nationalism represents a political creed in which the people offer their supreme allegiance to a nation-state. It underlies the cohesion of modern societies and legitimizes a nation's assertions of authority over the lives of its inhabitants.

The earliest manifestation of nationalism, as opposed to mere patriotic impulses, was the rejection of an ancien régime and the transfer of sovereignty from monarch to people. There is in this event a note of liberation of the nation from oppression, either internal or external. As Hans Kohn pointed out in 1957, "Nationalism is inconceivable without the ideas of popular sovereignty preceding." In the words of Carlton Hayes, it is a state of mind, "a modern emotional fusion of two very old phenomena—nationality and patriotism." If freedom to realize one's individual potential can be realized only in the nation-state, then nationalism becomes the antithesis of tyranny and oppression.

But this is not necessarily the totality of the nationalist experience. When the nation demands the supreme loyalty of its citizens, the freedom of the individual may be sacrificed to the welfare of the state. In this elevation of the state there is the concomitant denigration of the outsider and the temptation to advance the nation at the expense of other nations. As nationalism evolved in the nineteenth century, it assumed the ugly forms of imperialism, racism, and totalitarianism; it helped to stimulate world wars in the twentieth century.

It is these pejorative qualities that have led some American critics of nationalism to separate the American experience from the nationalism of Europe. Paul Nagel, an intellectual historian at the University of Missouri, refused even to use the term in dealing with American nationality. For him, "'Nationalism' regularly has implied a doctrine or a specific form of consciousness conveying superiority or prestige." Such glorification of country, he felt, should not be part of American loyalties because of the essentially different view of their land and themselves that distinguished Americans from other nationalities. Despite disquieting links between manifest destiny and European imperialism, most American critics find a qualitative difference in American nationalism.

Conventional definitions do not apply. One of the fundaments of nationalism is the sense of folk, of a kinship derived from a common ancestry. Where this bond is lacking or is of secondary importance, a common religion serves as a unifying force. Usually a people united in race and religion also have a clearly defined territory with which they are identified, either in the present or in the past. None of these attributes fits American history. Although England was the primary supplier of settlers, colonial Americans were also fully conscious of their Scottish and German roots at the time of the Revolution. An attenuated Calvinist heritage was as close to common religion as could be found in the eighteenth century, and this was vitiated by the fact that where there were established churches, they were more likely to be Anglican than Calvinist. It was a secularized religious spirit that was found in

610

America. A specific territorial claim evoking national emotions was lacking among a people for whom territorial concerns were equated with an expanding frontier. America was more an idea than a geographical entity.

The "invention of America," as Mexican historian Edmundo O'Gorman has happily phrased it, marks a major departure from the experience of more organically developed nations. The mythic roots of Italian or Japanese peoples are nourished by a prehistory that tells of special strengths an Aeneas brought to Rome from Troy, or special considerations conferred on Japan by virtue of divine descent. It is difficult to locate these qualities in a nation whose beginnings followed the invention of the printing press in Western Europe by little more than a generation. The words and deeds of founding fathers could be checked and countered as John Smith's tales about Virginia were examined by contemporaries who kept modern records.

Granted that every nation is a mixture of races with synoptic religious values, America is one of the very few nations the distinguishing features of which may be traced directly to the needs of other peoples at a particular period. The courage to embark on an American adventure, as well as the knowledge and skills necessary to discover and settle the New World, stemmed from a Renaissance belief in the capacity of man to achieve a new life. Such a conception was beyond the grasp of the medieval mind. The Reformation's pursuit of individual salvation outside the claims of established religions provided a moral imperative to much of the colonizing experience. Boston became a new Jerusalem when older Zions in Rome, London, and even Geneva had failed. Above all, the potential existence of vast quantities of precious metal in the New World gave a powerful impetus to the discovery and exploitation of American resources. The road to a transformation of life in a secular world, opened by the information of Crusaders about the Levant and the Orient, led to Europe's colonizing of the Western Hemisphere. American nationalism was touched by all these forces.

The first problem, then, in defining American nationalism is to identify it. An automatic expression of nationalism did not accompany the establishment of the United States. The emotions of the Revolution were attached to state rather than to nation, and the search for a substitute for a historic memory or a common church or a unifying ruling elite required forty years before it could bind the loyalties of Americans. It was an issue that absorbed the energies of the fathers of the new republic, and achieved a tentative resolution only after the War of 1812. By that time the focus of nationalist sentiment was on the special conditions of liberty protected by a new and superior government that had no counterpart elsewhere.

The development of a national identity proceeded throughout the nineteenth century, and continued to be a preoccupation of Americans in the twentieth century. The effort to find suitable symbols to display loyalty was a lengthy process. As late as the Civil War there was more than one design of the national flag. Not until 1942 was the ritual for its display on buildings or on platforms completed, and the pledge of allegiance was made obligatory in many schools only a generation earlier. The insertion of "under God" in the pledge of allegiance was a product of the pieties of the post–World War II era. Even the national anthem, "The Star-Spangled Banner," was not so designated until 1931. The insecurity over identification of nationalism is equally apparent in the sensitivity over the meanings of "Americanism" and "un-Americanism."

A second, and overlapping, element in nationalism is the peculiar relationship between state and federal governments. The question had its roots in the making of the Constitution, as did the term "federal" used by its framers. It was a euphemism designed to secure support for a new basic law that implied the supremacy of a strong central government. An open affirmation of this purpose in 1787 would have meant the failure of the Constitutional Convention in a country where primary loyalties still belonged to the states, and where the word "federal" suggested a fair sharing of power. The struggle between state and nation, begun with the failure of a genuine federal system under the Confederation, was a persistent theme in American life for three-quarters of a century. Although it was present in the Jeffersonian challenge to Hamilton in the 1790's and in Federalist disaffection from the Jeffersonian conflict with England in the next decade and a

611

half, its dominance over American life coincided with Southern sectionalism culminating in the Civil War. That conflict ended not only in the triumph of the North but also in the vesting of new mystical powers in the Union and the Constitution. Nationalism after 1865 would always be equated with a nation, "one and indivisible," with the "unum" in "e pluribus unum" superior to the "pluribus."

A third strand in American nationalism, which is also as old as the Republic, is the special destiny of America. The hand of Providence as well as of man is involved. If America is a "new world," its rise must have a divine meaning; and that meaning was always translated into some form of sharing the blessings of liberty with less-favored peoples. The religious quality inherent in the image of a "chosen people" was enhanced by the secular opportunities open to Americans. Vast, empty, rich lands held insecurely by European imperialists seemed manifestly destined for American occupation. Movement into Texas and California was a fulfillment of a destiny not only to occupy the entire continent but also to help the rest of humanity see how that occupation would spread the principles of free speech, free religion, self-government, and boundless economic opportunities that were denied to the Old World. Here was a sense of mission that sharpened in clashes with Britain or with Spain. But it was a mission that was susceptible to foreign influence. The unique character of a civilization serving as a beacon to others, a model to be copied, could be (and was) compromised by the change in status from a small, vulnerable republic to a continental empire with overseas ambitions. The altruism of an earlier time was thoroughly mixed, at the end of the nineteenth century, with prevailing influences of social Darwinism and Anglo-Saxon racism.

Most of the elements making up America's self-image of a divinely favored nation still survive, even though the trauma of a great economic depression in the 1930's, the burdens of world governance in the 1950's, and increasing doubts over social injustice and corruption at home and exploitation abroad have had disillusioning effects upon the meaning of the American mission. Yet with all these doubts, the connection between God's special favor and the American way of life remains part of nationalism. And, for all its flaws, the virtues associated with the record of American nationalism suggest distinctive qualities not found in other national experiences.

The most difficult period to identify in the evolution of nationalism is the time of its inception. The very name of America came comparatively late into the consciousness of the British colonies, and the first awareness of a separate destiny is a matter of continuing speculation. Boyd Shafer found an incipient national loyalty appearing as far back as 1740, during King George's War. Paul Varg of Michigan State University settled on 1759, Britain's *annus mirabile* in the war with France. Richard Merritt, a Yale political scientist, employed quantitative techniques to determine that 1770 was the year when key colonial newspapers cited "America" more frequently than "British colonies" in their columns. Although by the middle of the eighteenth century it was obvious that Americans were becoming something more than transplanted Englishmen, many future revolutionaries were quick to proclaim their British affiliations as the mother country triumphed over France in the French and Indian War. There was genuine pride in membership in a great British empire. As late as 1775 the poet Philip Freneau was convinced that Britain could and should "rule our hearts again," if only the rights of the American part of the empire were respected.

After the Revolution had shattered that empire, no automatic transfer of loyalty from London to the Confederation, with its seat in Philadelphia, took place. To a New Englander or a Georgian, Philadelphia was as distant as London. The differences between North and South, tidewater and piedmont, were potentially as deep as differences between Americans and Englishmen. Culture as well as geography distinguished the Bostonian from the Virginian, and the tidewater Virginian from the Scottish frontiersman of the Blue Ridge. Some of the most fundamental characteristics of the American—freedom from arbitrary government and freedom of speech and religion—were Virginian or Pennsylvanian as well as American. The America of 1776 could have remained as much an abstraction as Europe was then and now. The experience of Latin American revolutions a generation later could have been that of the former British colonies.

The vulnerability of a young republic in a world of hostile monarchies provided a major incentive for the cultivation of an American identity. The strength of nationalism was an inspiration to American statesmen aware of the temptations that quarreling American states offered to Europeans awaiting the demise of the American experiment. An anxious neighbor like Spain to the west and south, and an angry neighbor like Britain to the north, looked forward to exploiting the divisions among the former colonies. Even the ally France observed American weakness with complacence, knowing that it would bind Americans to their French patron.

The anticipated failure of the republican regime made success all the more important to the Founding Fathers, and this success depended on a strong pride in their achievements. Richard Morris pointed out that an ideology of nationalism could be built on what Europeans regarded as intolerable infirmities: the spectacle of a free people governing themselves under conditions of liberty no other people enjoyed, and managing their affairs in such a way as to be an inspiration to the less fortunate. As Thomas Paine phrased it in his *Crisis,* the United States would be in a position "to make a world happy, to teach mankind the art of being so—to exhibit on the theatre of the universe a character hitherto unknown, and to have, as it were, a new creation intrusted to our hands."

There was an important distinction, however, between pronouncing American superiority on such grounds and building a foundation to support it. Poets, playwrights, and even lexicographers were as sensitive to the importance of building institutions to sustain American achievements as were the diplomats and statesmen. Noah Webster's labors on a dictionary were intended to establish an American language distinct from the English of the mother country. At one and the same time his dictionary would proclaim the differences between the two nations and provide a standard that could be used to deepen those differences in the future. His work was a success, but not quite on the terms he had set. The American language was only partially freed from its inferiority complexes.

Other intellectuals of this period harked back to classical antiquity to assert the American distinctiveness. The American republic was to be accepted, not as a replication of any contemporary European nation but as an improved reincarnation of ancient Greece and Rome. From language to architecture to political imagery, the classical period was invoked. If Rome had its *Aeneid* to glorify its origins, the Connecticut poet Joel Barlow was willing to offer his country *The Columbiad,* which attested to

A work so vast a second world required,
By oceans bourn'd, from elder states retired;
Where, uncontaminated, unconfined,
Free contemplation might expand the mind,
To form, fix, prove the well-adjusted plan
And base and build the commonwealth of man.

Whatever its poetic merits, *The Columbiad* claimed a new world to be even more superior to the Old World than Rome was to its rivals. But, like Rome, the United States was prepared to grant to mankind something better in human relations than it had ever witnessed before.

This language was the stuff of nationalism. It was also braggadocio, inviting the mockery of enemies and condescending friends. If, as Europe observed, America was no Rome, certainly Barlow and Freneau were neither Virgils nor Homers. America's pretensions were fair game for Europeans of all stripes. It was the American abroad whose national sensibilities were most exposed. John Adams, minister to Great Britain under the Confederation, was never more the American than when he was snubbed at the Court of St. James's. Even in France, which came to the aid of the United States in war, Thomas Jefferson, Adams' counterpart at the Bourbon court, was a victim of many of the slights suffered by Adams, although French motives were less hostile.

That America was unlike other nations was not the question. It was the nature of the differences that distressed diplomats in Europe. French enthusiasts of America were frequently as denigratory as open adversaries were. The idealization of Americans as Rousseau's "noble savages" stirred European sympathies for the United States, but the European emphasis upon savagery over nobility stirred resentment among Americans. One of Jefferson's more emotional moments in Europe was his encounter with the pejorative opinions of French intellectuals concerning the American character. His *Notes on the State of Virginia* was a response to those Europeans who shared the views of the naturalist Georges Buffon that animal life in America was inferior in size and strength to that of the Old World. Jefferson's response went beyond a literary effort, Buffon received skins and skeletons of American animals sent to France at Jefferson's behest to prove the equality, if not the superiority, of life in the New World. Even more galling was the charge of the philosophe Abbé Guillaume Raynal that human life degenerated on the American continent. This observation contained aspersions on American virility as well as on American genius. Jefferson countered this assault with a spirited presentation of Indian virtues. He labored valiantly, but under obvious handicaps, in pointing out poets and artists, mathematicians and scientists, to match the products of Europe. Benjamin Franklin and David Rittenhouse were not the equals of Galileo and Newton.

The vigor of American ripostes to perceived insults to their nationality inspired more derision than respect among Europeans of this period. None was more devastating than the Reverend Sydney Smith, a Yorkshire wit who reacted to American claims to being "the greatest, the most enlightened, the most moral people upon earth" by asking rhetorically, "In the four quarters of the globe, who reads an American book? or goes to an American play? or looks at an American picture or statue?" So much for the pretensions of American nationalism. A sense of inferiority in relation to older civilizations seemed to have given rise to a hyperbolic style of self-defense that invited ridicule.

Yet, Smith's famous article in the *Edinburgh Review,* which appeared in 1820, would have been more deflating had it appeared a generation earlier, when Barlow and Freneau were poetizing. Between 1783 and 1815 national pride expanded enormously to encompass a much larger company than a few diplomats abroad and Hartford Wits at home. The nation, having acquired an inland empire and having faced down Britain in war, again shared their exhilaration. The very newness and freedoms of an empty land lacking oppressive government or a cultivated aristocracy, which Eu-

ropeans translated as barbaric and uncultured, were the reasons for American superiority.

The Revolution had not stimulated nationalism among most Americans in the immediate postwar years. National attention was on the disarray—economic and political—that separation from Britain had brought. There was little occasion for self-congratulation. Such loyalty to country as was visible in this period was to the patriarchal figure of George Washington, and even this symbol did not emerge untarnished from the political debates. In the absence of a court, and even of a flag, Washington's services as the unifying father of his country were vital for the rallying of national sentiment. He was the Cincinnatus of America who sacrificed himself to perform services no one else could provide, and then retired rather than retain power. His was a vital function for the growth of nationalism, and yet it was incomplete. He found himself enmeshed, and ultimately damaged, by political controversy in the last years of his presidency. The Fourth of July, Independence Day, was a supplementary unifier, as toasts were drunk and cannons fired in honor of the declaration of independence. But as exciting as the celebrations may have been, they celebrated a victory over the British by Pennsylvanians or New Yorkers, as much as a victory by Americans.

The wave of nationalism that failed to rise in the 1780's and 1790's finally broke over America in the second war with Britain. The Francophilia that had briefly prevailed among Jeffersonians had dissipated in the disillusionment over the policies of the French Republic and in recognition of the dangers of Napoleonic imperialism. Federalist failure to exploit Francophobia fully during the Quasi-War with France in 1798–1800 reflects a deficiency in the quality of nationalism as much as it does the political power of the Jeffersonian opposition. Anglophilia, more enduring among Federalists of the Northeast, ended more gradually. For those who could not forsake British ties for reasons of custom or conviction or commerce, the consequence was isolation from most of their countrymen and, ultimately, extinction of the Federalist party as a political entity. The majority of that party joined Republicans in a nationalism influenced by the trans-Appalachian and trans-Mississippi West. The former had exerted minuscule influence in 1783, and the latter did not come into being until the Louisiana acquisition of 1803.

During the War of 1812, Jonathan Russell, a businessman-politician, was inspired by the *Constitution*'s victory over the British frigate *Guerrière* to burst out in a paean of praise of its commander, Isaac Hull. The event elevated Hull to Washingtonian heights:

> Yes! deathless, oh Hull, shall thy fame live in story
> And cheer, in the battle, our sons on the wave—
> Through ages unborn shall the beams of thy glory,
> Unclouded, illumine the march of the brave.

If such a minor figure as Hull could evoke such emotion from such an unlikely source, it is understandable that the common soldier, who was ignored after the Revolutionary War, would also receive attention. Congress finally granted pensions for Revolutionary War service in 1818.

American identity was no longer a problem on 4 July 1826, when the two great builders of nationalism and independence, Thomas Jefferson and John Adams, died within hours of each other on the fiftieth anniversary of the Declaration of Independence they both helped to write. A generation earlier, when Washington died, the apotheosis of the first president was still a tribute to a single man, no matter how significant the deification was in the fashioning of national unity. On Independence Day of 1826, the passing of the second and third presidents of the United States was the occasion for the nation's apotheosis of itself.

For nationalism to flourish, it was obvious that the United States had to prove its experiment successful. The War of 1812 was one proving ground. More significant than a diplomatic success against Britain was the spectacular rise in the national economy, sparked by population increase, territorial acquisitions, and technological changes in transportation and industry. Speaking of the period after the Treaty of Ghent, Henry Adams observed, "The continent lay before them, like an uncovered ore-bed. They could see and they even could calculate with reasonable accuracy the wealth it could be made to yield." The steady accumulation of power to the central government at the expense of the states was equated with the growth of America. Nationalism implied the denigration of sectionalism and states' rights.

The conflict between central and local governments that accompanied the rise of nationalism was not surprising. The European nation-states experienced the assertion of central power by means of powerful monarchies overcoming the separatism of feudal nobilities. What distinguished the American experience from others was the special nature of the central authority; it was not personified by a president, not even George Washington. The mystical conception of a constitution blessing a union permitted the cherished American liberties to flourish.

The argument for centralizing government during the Confederation had been fought on the assumption that no other government could perform that function. States' rights might rally libertarians worried about the tyranny of rule from afar, but the veterans of the Revolutionary War returning to their farms and villages were more concerned about economic depression and foreclosures on their properties than with the potential evils of a distant national government. Had there been a stronger central authority in the Confederation, Revolutionary War heroes of the order of Ethan Allen in Vermont and George Rogers Clark in Kentucky would have been less tempted to join with the former British enemy and the hostile Spanish neighbor. Where the states individually or collectively as the Confederation had failed to respond to Indian or European threats in the West, the Union drove the Indians out of the Northwest, saved the nation from the British in 1812–1815, and wrested Florida from the Spanish in 1819. As the western territories entered the Union their loyalties were to the nation that welcomed them rather than to any pristine colonial commonwealth. Unlike the original thirteen states, they had been created by acts of the federal Congress.

Still, the centrifugal forces that had always been a part of the American experience had not disappeared. Such "good feeling" as existed after 1815 did not have its premise in the end of sectionalism or even states' consciousness; rather, the "American system" of Henry Clay was built on a common hostility to British economic power that would help to mesh the economies of the North, the West, and the South. If there was temporary harmony at this time, it was largely because each section had unrealistic expectations of special advantage from congressional support of tariffs or of internal improvements.

The slave-oriented South found the Union ultimately a threat both to its economy and to its society, and in the Civil War provided the greatest challenge the Union had to surmount in the nation's history. The war was considered by some as a struggle between two competing nationalisms. In the years preceding this conflict, the Union became the most vital national symbol to the North. Southern challenges on constitutional grounds became increasingly insufferable. The South's interpretations signified more than just a peculiar gloss of the Constitution; the North regarded them as a rending of the instrument of America's sovereignty and the consequent extinction of the American nation. While loyalty to a section greater than loyalty to the nation could be considered patriotism, by 1860 the majority of the country was convinced that an effective American sovereignty could be expressed only in a unified nation.

A generation earlier Alexis de Tocqueville, that astute French visitor, wrote, "The Union is an ideal nation that exists, so to speak, only in the mind." It also existed in the heart. The passions over slavery converted it into something more than a means of achieving effective government. The Union became an object of reverence, the indispensable foundation of national values.

Daniel Webster attempted to exploit this sentiment to deflect sectional rivalry into the popular channel of xenophobia. In a direct insult to Austria in 1849, President Zachary Taylor promised recognition to Hungary if its revolution succeeded and then, after its failure, his successor Millard Fillmore gave its leader a tumultuous welcome to America in 1852. Secretary of State Webster not only rejected Austria's subsequent protest but went out of his way to taunt its minister to the United States, Chevalier J. G. Hülsemann. He lectured the Austrian on Hungary's good sense in imitating the American Revolution. Should the Austrians have any objection, they must reckon with the fact that "The power of this republic, at the present moment, is spread over a region, one of the richest and most fertile on the globe, and of an extent in comparison with which the possessions of the House of Hapsburg are but as a patch on the earth's surface."

This well-publicized letter struck just the chord Webster hoped to reach in Americans. The appeal to chauvinism with hyperbolic rhetoric performed an important function in 1850. It united North and South in opposition to Europe. But the forces of disunion that Webster had hoped to dissipate were stronger than those of nationalism. In even greater desperation a decade later, Secretary of State William H. Seward tried to divert the country from war by urging President Abraham Lincoln to turn over the executive powers to him so that he could save the Union by initiating war against France or Spain, or all of Europe. The president rejected the proposal; but unrealistic as it may have been in 1861 and fantastic as it has sounded to later generations, the spirit behind the plan was the same one that had propelled the "American system" of Henry Clay, the Mexican War maneuvers of President James K. Polk, and Daniel Webster's note to Hülsemann. Antagonism to the Old World was a staple of American nationalism, especially in times of crisis.

The traumas of sectional conflict resulted in the removal of the constitutional question from nationalism. The Union had triumphed, and with it, sentiments of nationalism. The sobriety with which nationalism was expressed in the middle years of the century yielded to a reassertion of the older boisterous spirits. The end of war witnessed a period of even more rapid growth in population, wealth, and power than had been seen fifty years earlier, after the Treaty of Ghent. It also revived—in exaggerated ways, before the century was over—the idea of mission that had been implicit in the American self-image from the beginning: the notion that God had given America a special portion of blessings, and with it a mission to share them with less-favored peoples.

Prior to the Civil War the most vocal articulation of the American mission had accompanied crises with Spain or Britain or France over their possessions in North America. They all violated a divine plan. While the idea of providential occupation of the West antedated the annexation of Texas and the demands for Oregon—and, indeed, may be found in Jeffersonian ruminations in the 1780's—it was John L. O'Sullivan, editor of the *Democratic Review,* who in 1845 specifically charged foreign hostility and jealousy with "limiting our greatness and checking the fulfillment of our manifest destiny to overspread the continent allotted by Providence for the free development of our yearly multiplying millions." Texas, California, and Oregon—and even Upper Canada—represented empty land awaiting the arrival of Americans to bring it under proper cultivation.

Americans did not regard these views or the actions that followed from them as analogous to European imperalism; they were simply the natural spread of free peoples and free institutions into unoccupied space wrongly claimed by others. Although such assertions might have sounded hypocritical to hostile observers, even opponents of the Mexican War could concede that the mission to spread liberty bore marks of idealism. Frederick Merk found in expansionism a spirit that was "idealistic, self-denying, hopeful for divine favor for national aspirations, though not sure of it." So if manifest destiny was connected with the grasping for land, it was also linked to the land's improvement by peopling it with a better society than could have been achieved under its original proprietors. In the midst of the Mexican War, Albert Gallatin defined the American mission as a great experiment in which "a representative democratic republic" had a chance to try out its ideals on a large scale. "If it failed, the last hope of the friends of mankind was lost, or indefinitely postponed; and the eyes of the world were turned towards you. Whenever real or pretended apprehension of the imminent danger of trusting people at large with power were expressed, the answer was 'Look at America. . . .'"

In this spirit the migration of Americans to Texas or California or Oregon signified not exploitation of native peoples, or governance over unwilling subjects, but the sharing of liberties over a wider area. The growing United States had spilled its surplus population into neighboring territories that were providentially empty. When those territories were sufficiently populous, they would enter the Union, ultimately as full and equal partners of the older states. If there was conflict within the United States over their admission, this was a function of the slavery quarrels, not of a desire for imperialist control on the part of the nation.

Yet, it was difficult to deny that the partial dismemberment of Mexico tended to compromise the missionary spirit behind manifest destiny. The opposition of such distinguished figures as John Quincy Adams, an authentic expansionist, and the poet James Russell Lowell helped to arouse a sense of guilt over a war that many abolitionists regarded as an act of aggression by Southern slavery interests. That Mexican and Indian populations, no matter how small, lived in California or New Mexico gave a taste of imperialism to the fruits of American nationalism. Was manifest destiny, then, merely a mask for American conquest of a weak neighbor?

Although a repugnant element can never be expunged from nationalism, extenuating factors refine the annexation of Texas and even the ensuing war with Mexico. Manifest destiny was more than an instrument of Southern interests; the pull of California had attracted New England mercantile ambitions as well. More important, it was a national rather than a sectional impulse, with a powerful England, as in the case of the Oregon quarrel, a major antagonist in 1844. The hope was that the two Canadas would sue for admission to the new and enlarged Union. O'Sullivan speculated that Canada, as easily as California, could be the next "customer."

Arrogant and self-serving as this language sounded in press, pulpit, and schools, its users could unreservedly contrast the freedom of religion and self-government in the territories under American control with the repression of a state church in Mexico and the limitations of political freedom in Canada. When the demands for annexation threatened to get out of hand, as in the pressure for the absorption of all Mexico, opponents stopped the threat effectively. Partisan fears of Mexico parceled into slave states may have been a powerful incentive for opposition, but they were fueled as well by the unpalatable prospect of governing an unassimilable population that would not participate in the American political process.

Although controversy continues to swirl

about the purity of American motives in continental expansion, it does not apply to the display of nationalism in this period. It was genuine and widespread. If any emotion could have overcome the deep divisions within the Union in the middle of the nineteenth century, it was pride in American institutions and in the nation's power to proclaim them to the world. Had it not been for the slavery issue, Thomas Bailey of Stanford University speculated, "Americans would not only have swaggered more in the subsequent years but would have grasped more territories." As it was, the Young America spirit that flourished in the wake of the Mexican War expressed itself in provocations against Europe. The Revolution of 1848 was a suitable occasion for its display. George Bancroft, historian and diplomat, from his post in London expressed America's approval of the revolutions: "Can we show ourselves lukewarm, while the Old World is shaking off its chains and emancipating and enthroning the masses?"

Changes that occurred later in the century provided a different gloss both to the idea of manifest destiny and to the meaning of mission. The new "manifest destiny" of the 1890's involved acquisition and control of an overseas empire. Although the older xenophobia and the civilizing mission remained, they were more strident in their tone and also more derivative from the European experience. The distinctions between European and American imperialism appeared to blur at the turn of the century. It was not that the popular nature of nationalism had altered significantly. The beer-garden simplicity with which the flag was venerated in the 1890's and the gusto with which the Spanish were rebuked for their behavior in Cuba linked Theodore Roosevelt to Davy Crockett. Finley Peter Dunne, the leading press satirist at the time of America's rise to world power, put words into the mouth of his Mr. Dooley that would have been as fitting half a century before: " 'We're a great people,' said Mr. Hennessy earnestly. 'We are,' said Mr. Dooley. 'We are that. An' th' best iv it is, we know that we are.' "

What was different was a respectful interest in European imperialism and a wish by many American leaders to imitate it. As the burgeoning American economy produced enormous wealth, the instant oil, meat-packing, and rail barons sought marriage alliances with the Old World and pursued culture by bringing the French Middle Ages or Tudor England architecturally to their Rhode Island estates or New York City palaces. But they were conscious that they still lacked a sense of ideological security that European aristocrats possessed as a birthright. The spirit of Teutonic, and especially Anglo-Saxon, solidarity filled some of the needs of an insecure upper class. Although England may have remained a commercial and political rival, there was a surge of appreciation for the kinship of the two peoples that would account for the greatness of both.

Scholar-diplomats George Bancroft and John Lothrop Motley had commented earlier on the role that racial stock had in assuring a nation's greatness. Both had been students in Germany. Granting his distaste for some aspects of Prussian militarism, Bancroft claimed that it would be the instrument to win "more rapidly liberty in Europe than all that the Kossuths, Garibaldis, and Mazzinis could effect in half a century." Motley celebrated Teutonic virtues by noting that Holland's struggle with Spain in the sixteenth century "must have particular interest, for it is a portion of the records of the Anglo-Saxon race— essentially the same, whether in Friesland, England, or Massachusetts." Another diplomat, James Russell Lowell, more poet than scholar, brought the good news to England that "The duty which has been laid upon the English-speaking races, so far as we can discover, has been to carry over the great lessons of liberty combined with order. That is the great secret of civilization." In a major disquisition on democracy in 1884, Lowell had spoken of the problems that Americans encountered with the irresponsible masses in the large cities that were composed of peoples of inferior stock. America's success in overcoming these obstacles to become a great democracy could be traced to the fact that "the acorn from which it sprang was ripened on the British oak."

The only trouble with these perorations was the implication of a junior partnership for America in the racial connection. This became increasingly unacceptable to nationalists. A colonial relationship with even the best of the Old World did not fit America's self-image by the time the nineteenth century ended. America would be superior to Britain even in racism. Albert J. Beveridge of Indiana pointed out to the Senate that "God has not been preparing the English-speaking and Teutonic peoples for a thousand years for nothing but vain and idle self-contemplation and self-admiration. . . . And of all our race He has marked the American people as His chosen nation to finally lead in the redemption of the world."

For those who might not heed a divine appeal, the mandate of social Darwinism brought the same message. The transfer of Darwinian principles from a struggle among species for survival to a competition among nations moved the naturalist's theory of evolution from biology to sociology and international relations almost from the moment of its conception. Presumably the laws of nature justified power in the hands of the fittest; and in the late nineteenth century the arena for the display of national superiority lay in carving out colonial empires in Asia and Africa. For the United States to stand by and remove itself from this competition would be an admission of inferiority. Since the American continent was filled, expansion would have to take place overseas. The alternative would be both a sapping of national strength and increasing advantage to European competitors in the Darwinian struggle for greatness.

The naval historian Alfred Thayer Mahan, more than any other figure, tied together the strains of racial pride and Darwinian sanctions with the economic significance of the acquisition of colonies. Such an undertaking would solve the problems of surplus goods flowing from what appeared, after the Panic of 1893, to be an overdeveloped economic plant; of the defense needs of the nation, through a navy protecting routes to new colonies; and of the imperative carrying the blessings of American civilization abroad.

Indeed, the American mission was ultimately the most important rationalization for imperial control. The Reverend Josiah Strong, secretary of the Evangelical Alliance and a powerful publicist for expansion, exhorted Americans to respect their sacred trust by bestowing their privileges upon other sectors of humanity. After all, "They are not proprietors, apportioning their own, but simply *trustees* or managers of God's property. . . . Our plea is not America for America's sake," he wrote in *Our Country* (1885), "but America for the world's sake." It is this eleemosynary spirit that gave meaning to President William McKinley's reluctance to leave the Philippines under Spanish control or under its own governance. In confessing his agony over the decision to annex the islands, he finally realized "There was nothing left for us to do but to take them all, and to educate the Filipinos, and uplift and civilize and Christianize them, and by God's grace do the very best we could by them, as our fellow-men for whom Christ also died."

The gulf between McKinley's understanding of America's mission and those of the French, British, Germans, and Russians was not as wide as the gulf between McKinley's or Theodore Roosevelt's conception of mission and that of Jefferson or John Quincy Adams. The Monroe Doctrine had made it clear that America was to serve as a model for others to emulate, but not as an instrument to involve itself in the afflictions of the less fortunate. America's own system could only be corrupted by such involvement. So Adams concluded when he counseled President James Monroe not to intervene against Turkey on behalf of the admired Greek revolutionaries. But by the end of the century the combination of racial pretensions, Darwinian impulses, and putative economic imperatives had broken one great barrier of isolationism. They affected more than the special interests of navalists, businessmen, or missionaries. Even so sensitive a scholar as Frederick Jackson Turner found virtue in overseas expansion. He "rowed with the tide of the new nationalism," Ralph Gabriel noted in his *Course of American Democratic Thought,* at least for a while, as he pondered the effect of the passing of the frontier upon American democracy. It was hoped that settlement of Hawaii and the Philippines could have the same beneficial results for democracy as the settlement of Ohio and Iowa had had in the past.

For Turner and for most Americans, the new manifest destiny was a mistake, an aberration from American tradition. In the wake of Filipino resistance to American occupation in 1899, William Jennings Bryan observed, " 'Destiny' was not as manifest as it was a few weeks ago." Most American leaders were slower to realize this than Bryan had been. The tide of empire finally receded, but not before it had left a permanent imprint on the fabric of American nationalism, or at least had deepened indentations that had always been there. The country came to recognize the incompatibility between the governance of Iowa and the governance of the Philippines; the former was based on self-government and eventual statehood, the latter, on imperial control over unassimilable peoples. The result was the gradual disengagement from the imperial plans of 1900, and ultimate independence for those islands.

But if nationalism in the twentieth century recoiled from the problems of assimilation abroad, it could not avoid those problems at home. The rise of Anglo-Saxon racism coincided with massive emigration from non-Anglo-Saxon eastern and southern Europe, which raised questions about the dilution not only of the race but also of the institutions of America. Not all the nativist reactions were hostile. Some were patronizing and even melioristic. The Daughters of the American Revolution and other patriotic societies recognized their duty to "Americanize" the foreigner, to teach him proper speech and manners as well as values. The public school would be the instrument, according to Josiah Strong, by which "the strange and dissimilar races which come to us are, in one generation, assimilated and made Americans." American Catholic and Jewish historical societies, accepting the importance of Americanization, were organized in the 1880's and 1890's to show the nation their own ties with the American past. Their objective was to justify themselves as Americans, different in background but sharing in the creation of a new people. The constitution of the American Irish Historical Society expressed the hope that "In the days to come, that lie in the womb of the future, when all the various elements that have gone and are going to make the republic great, are united in the American,—the man who in his person will represent the bravest elements of all the old races of earth,—we declare that the deeds and accomplishment of our element shall be written in the book of the new race, telling what we did and no more; giving us our rightful place by the side of the others."

Such modesty of aspiration on the part of an immigrant group and such generous impulses on the part of the patronizing older stock were balanced by less-edifying side effects of the racist component in nationalism. Ethnic and religious communities vied with each other in claiming credit for contributions to the national history or character, while the Anglo-Saxon elite, under the impact of war and depression in the twentieth century, blamed immigrants for the nation's troubles. The revival of the Ku Klux Klan in the 1920's, with its particularly ugly brand of national exclusiveness, was a manifestation of the Anglo-Saxon tradition translated into a self-conscious white Protestant ascendancy. Immigration restriction rather than immigrant amelioration was a consequence of this mood in the period of disillusionment that followed World War I. The vehement denunciation of the "hyphenated" American indulged in both by Woodrow Wilson and Theodore Roosevelt during the war was another by-product of the new manifest destiny. Both political parties had warned against misplaced loyalties to an ancestral motherland; but they understood that hyphenation applied to the Irish and Germans, not to the British. The latter's heritage was indistinguishable from the American in 1917.

It is ironic that a generation later, in the aftermath of another world war, the followers of Senator Joseph McCarthy, many of them from ethnic backgrounds that could not meet the test of Americanism in the past, led a nationalist assault on the loyalty of the older elite. In the struggle with Soviet communism after World War II, McCarthy's unprincipled attacks on putative American communists numbered among their victims not merely the principles of civil liberties but also the American Eastern "establishment," mostly Anglo-Saxon, which was accused of negligence and worse in the struggle of the nation against external enemies. The emotions of the time evoked the xenophobia of earlier crises, except that the "American" embraced a wider constituency. Nonetheless, the nationalism that was demonstrated in the 1950's, as much as in the 1920's or in the 1890's, was a narrow and self-centered view of the nation's interests.

Despite the many xenophobic impulses released in the name of nationalism, the missionary elements did not disappear in the twentieth century. The retreat from moral uplifting of the natives of the Caribbean or East Asia was short-lived, and was replaced by an attempt to uplift the entire world, not merely those regions under American governance. In both world wars American democracy became the exemplar for the world. Although Woodrow Wilson won a reputation as a supreme internationalist, seeking a new world order that would end national rivalries, his new order would be on American terms. His conception of the American mission was to disseminate those progressive values, both economic and political, that would serve America's own interests in the world. It was nothing less than the remaking of the world according to an American pattern. Wilson himself rejected a narrow distinction between nationalism and internationalism. "The greatest nationalist," he claimed, "is the man who wants his nation to be the greatest nation, and the greatest nation is the nation which penetrates to the heart of its duty and mission among the nations of the world."

In this context the mission of World War II and the Cold War was a continuation of the Wilsonian world view. The United Nations would replicate the League of Nations by serving to help America fulfill its duty to humanity. Both the goals and the methods were clearly outlined. Nations would be freed from fear of conquest, with American military power protecting them from Nazis or communists; they would be freed from want by the application of American technology to their economies; they would be freed from ignorance by American learning spread through a Fulbright scholarship program or a Peace Corps. These were the benign purposes of the Marshall Plan and Point Four. The language in which they were expressed lacked the overt racial biases and self-satisfied smugness that had characterized many early missionary activities. Publisher Henry Luce anticipated an "American century," in which the United States would serve "as the dynamic center of ever-widening spheres of enterprise, . . . as the training center of the skillful servants of mankind, America as the Good Samaritan, really believing again that it is more blessed to give than to receive, and . . . as the powerhouse of the ideals of Freedom and Justice."

In 1967 Ronald Steel claimed that Luce's American century was in fact a Pax Americana, with very few distinctions between its dictates and those of Rome's imperialism. Whether America willed it or not, it built a world empire to serve its own economic needs; it elevated communism into a monster out of all proportion to the threat presented; it arbitrarily divided the world into Manichaean spheres of good and evil; and, in the name of altruism, it helped to turn parts of Southeast Asia into a wasteland. As Americans reflected with disillusion upon the exaggerated promises of the Truman Doctrine, undertaken in the afterglow of successes in World War II, when the United States sought to extend its system throughout the world, they discovered flaws in even the most altruistic postures. Nationalism was a cover for the erosion of civil liberties identified with McCarthyism, for the corruption of government by the accretion of enormous power in the hands of the executive, and for the corresponding diminution of power in the Congress. While the crudities of American imperialism of the Theodore Roosevelt era may have been smoothed, the brutalization of the American character stemming from the anticommunist campaigns in Asia and Latin America was even more distressing.

The result in the post-Vietnam era has been a decline in nationalist spirit. The conscious abuse of the flag by many of the younger generation was a symbolic act of revenge upon a nation that, in the name of liberty, sought conquest of the world for selfish reasons. The very idea of an American mission has been in question, not simply the matter of its betrayal. The result has been a retreat into a neoisolationist stance that has affected both liberals and conservatives. The latter would turn America's attention back to its own problems, rather than waste resources on an ungrateful world. The former urge a less grandiose vision for America's role in the world, blaming American arrogance for troubling the peace of the world.

There is nothing unique about the present low estate of nationalist emotions. It has occurred in the past, and probably will recur in the future. Indeed, skepticism about nationalism is endemic in the American system. Although nationalism is dependent upon an allegiance above all others, the nature of American pluralism militates against a monistic devotion. The nature of the pluralist society makes a state or a religion or an individual a legitimate focus of primary loyalty. The nation must compete for public attention. For all its flaws in the past and the present, the special qualities associated with American nationalism—an open society, a mobile society, and above all a society divinely favored—will remain a force in America as long as the nation-state system of governance prevails among the peoples of the world.

BIBLIOGRAPHY

Karl Deutsch, *Nationalism and Social Communication: An Inquiry Into the Foundations of Nationality* (Cambridge, Mass., 1953), employs the techniques of the social sciences to examine nationalism. Carlton J. H. Hayes, *Essays on Nationalism* (New York, 1926), is a collection of writings by the founding father of American studies in nationalism. Hans Kohn, *American Nationalism: An Interpretive Essay* (New York, 1957), is particularly useful for its insights on the American character and its relationships to nationalism. Walter LaFeber, *The New Empire: An Interpretation of American Expansion, 1860–1898* (Ithaca, N.Y., 1963), presents an economic explanation of the growth of nationalism. N. Gordon Levin, Jr., *Woodrow Wilson and World Politics: America's Response to War and Revolution* (New York, 1968), links American nationalism with Wilsonian internationalism. Ernest R. May, *American Imperialisms: A Speculative Essay* (New York, 1968), offers speculations on reasons why nationalism developed into imperialism at the end of the nineteenth century. Frederick Merk, *Manifest Destiny and Mission in American History: A Reinterpretation* (New York, 1966), gives a favorable view of "manifest destiny" as a link between nationalism and American ideals. Boyd C. Shafer, *Faces of Nationalism: New Realities and Old Myths* (New York, 1972), is the most recent summation of the many approaches to nationalism. Ronald Steel, *Pax Americana* (New York, 1967), treats nationalism and the Cold War. Richard W. Van Alstyne, *Genesis of American Nationalism* (Waltham, Mass., 1970), is an examination of nationalism in the early republic. Albert Weinberg, *Manifest Destiny: A Study of Nationalist Expansionism in American History* (Baltimore, 1935), is a major revisionist statement on nineteenth-century nationalism as expressed in "manifest destiny."

[*See also* ANTI-IMPERIALISM; ELITISM AND FOREIGN POLICY; IMPERIALISM; MANIFEST DESTINY; NATIVISM.]

NATIONAL SECURITY

Gerald E. Wheeler

WHEN we speak of national security, we are talking about national defense or even, in the words of the Preamble to the United States Constitution, "the common defense." To feel secure, the American people have, since the nation's birth, concerned themselves with protection of the Republic "against all dangers, domestic or foreign." As the years passed, the menace of domestic rebellion receded, particularly after the American Civil War proved the viability of the Union. With American national maturity and abandonment of the policy of isolationism, paralleled by the rise of powerful states abroad, the potential, if not actual, danger to the nation increased. The safety of the country—its "national security"—became less sure. As it developed into a highly industrialized, wealthy, and socially complex state, America in the twentieth century also became much more liable to external aggression, or even to such internal disorders that the continuation of the Republic might be called into question.

In the eighteenth and nineteenth centuries, protection against such dangers was the leading function of the armed services and the state militias. Today defense of the nation, or national security, is still largely a military problem; but the problem has been complicated by the very complexity of the nation itself, the expansion of the international state system, and the refusal of many nations to accept the status quo in terms of their own level of development, extent of territory, or uniqueness of political system. Whereas before 1941 Americans sought to protect their national security through reliance upon the military and deliberate isolation from entanglements abroad that could jeopardize the nation's safety, World War

II and the years that followed caused a change in national policy. The military recovery of the Soviet Union from its massive wartime damages, the creation of a cordon of communist satellite nations between the Soviet Union and the Western European democracies, and the victory of the communist forces in China convinced Americans that they and the democracies of the world again were under siege by powers bent on their destruction. National security is now considered by America's leaders to lie in collective defense with other nations willing to pool their military capabilities for an international defense of their territories and a commonly accepted set of political values. Given the nature of the historical process, the meaning of national security has changed steadily with the development of America; and national security has always possessed a certain quality traceable to the changing threats against the nation's safety.

The Founding Fathers based the Constitution of 1787, and its defense provisions, upon the experience of the American colonial and revolutionary eras. The British colonials in North America had learned that their geographical isolation protected them from direct menace by the major European states. While the European wars before 1754 had caused ripples of concern to cross the Atlantic, no meaningful invasion of North America had succeeded because of British naval power. The one great French effort to gain control of the continent, during 1754–1763, had been beaten back by a combination of colonial effort and English reinforcement on land and at sea. Neither the Spanish nor the French colonies had the determination or strength necessary to defeat the British colonials and master the continent. As a revolutionary confederation, supplied and reinforced by the French, the Americans had been able to hold the English at bay until further attempts to suppress the rebellion appeared too costly to continue. Except for the fateful Chesapeake Bay campaign of 1781, North American geography and American resistance had frustrated coordination of British campaigns, despite the capability to land troops at will. By 1787 the oceanic distance from Europe had become a gigantic defensive moat in the thinking of most Americans. This distance, or isolation from Europe, early became America's first line of defense.

In the years before 1787 Americans also developed an appreciation of the menace that might be expected from their neighbors. The Indians about them represented a danger to individuals or isolated communities, but Indian tribal organizations and rivalries normally made it highly unlikely that they could coalesce and confront the colonials with effective military resistance. This inability to organize and confederate meant, in the end, that the native Americans were defeated and pushed ever westward by the advancing Americans. The Spanish to the south and in the trans-Mississippi West and Southwest lacked the numbers to pose a serious threat to the American colonials. The Spanish outposts, in former French Louisiana (ceded in 1763) to the West, were not designed for the conquest of North America, but they early became defensive positions for the rich viceroyalties of New Spain (Mexico) and the regions farther south. The French neighbors on the north were another matter. Weak as it was, the expansion of New France into the Mississippi Valley threatened to pen the British colonials into the Atlantic seaboard region. The British defeat of France in 1763, and the latter's virtual expulsion from North America, left the Americans with a weak British colony to the north—certainly no longer a threat to them. At the close of the American Revolution in 1783, British Canada did not join the new American nation; but neither did it endanger the new nation. In sum, Americans in 1787 did not view the world about them as particularly threatening.

The years before 1787 also had helped to create a unique American attitude toward the military institutions necessary for defense.

Given the nature of the Indian menace, the earliest settlers in Jamestown, Plymouth, and Massachusetts Bay had resorted to the use of militia organizations to defend themselves. Any male capable of bearing arms was expected to equip himself and contribute to "the common defense." With the enemy constantly present, each man was required to defend his homestead and family. The organization, drill, and officering of the local militia units was haphazard at best, but the Indians seldom made more than random attacks. On those occasions when the native Americans did organize, either among themselves or with the French (or later with the British in Canada), the settlers were driven to intracolonial and, in the case of King Philip's War (1675–1676), intercolonial cooperation for defense. Because these Indian attacks could be handled with the use of militia, the British never found it necessary to garrison their North American colonies with the regular army; nor did the colonials find it necessary to support a standing army for defense. While such a force might have been convenient, its cost was unacceptable on either side of the Atlantic.

In a similar manner the colonials learned they did not need a standing army to meet any threats from the Spanish, Dutch, or French settlements. Although a tactic inefficient in the extreme, the British had found before 1754 that they could war against their enemies in North America by using militia, reinforced by expeditionary troops from England. The Seven Years' War (1756–1763) provided the British with a severe lesson about the military unreliability, cost, and political difficulties that came from dependence on colonial militia. The colonials, however, drew a final lesson in 1783 that was different. Though the Seven Years' War and American Revolution had demonstrated the inefficiency of the militia in warfare against regular armies, the absence of any strong enemies in North America caused the new American nation to conclude that the militia would be adequate for the common defense.

Two other concerns of the Founding Fathers concerning military force are traceable to the colonial and revolutionary experience. These were an almost paranoid dislike of "standing armies" and an absolute unwillingness to countenance military conscription. Before the Seven

Years' War, the British colonials had had very little contact with the British regulars. When England found it necessary to send expeditionary forces to the colonies, the inhabitants were required to share in the cost. Later, after the Seven Years' War, the British garrisoned regulars in the North American colonies as a means of controlling them. The costs were borne, reluctantly, by the colonists. Their resentment eventually found its place among the grievances against George III listed in the Declaration of Independence. It was not only the cost, but also the impairment of their civil liberties by the troops, that so deeply offended the colonists. Finally, the whole colonial and Revolutionary War experience had not required the use of military conscription. Militia service had been an adult male obligation in all colonies except Pennsylvania, and even this had seemed onerous to many. Facing defeat after the disastrous campaigns of 1776 and 1777, neither the individual colonies nor the Continental Congress had been able to resort to conscription. Fearing the emergence of a strong and coercive central government more than the loss of the war, the individual states resisted any enlargement of powers for Congress. As a result, the Revolutionary War was fought with militia, volunteers formed into state units, and the short-term-enlistment Continental Army. Throughout the war, in debates in Congress, in the state governments, and in the press, it was constantly stated that all must be alert to any possible attempt to establish a dictatorship, or an overly powerful central government, built on the support of a standing army.

By 1787, when the Constitution was drafted, Americans accepted the following premises concerning how the safety of their new nation would be maintained: neither the Indians nor the existing Spanish and British colonies were a serious threat; national security (safety) would be enhanced by nonparticipation in the quarrels of the European nations and by a policy of nonalliance with any power except France; the Atlantic Ocean to the east and the undeveloped land to the west provided a strong natural defense for America; only a minimum standing army would be necessary to defend the nation; and the national defense would rest with the state militias, available at the call of the president to put down insurrection or repel invasion.

For almost 110 years after the drafting of the Constitution these basic assumptions upon which American national security was founded remained largely intact. To them were added two more, both of which have remained viable: national strength (security) required a vigorous foreign trade and a healthy economy; and the nation would be more secure if the Western Hemisphere were closed to further colonization by European states. From the first addition came eventual recognition that America's commerce would require protection by a navy. Once established, the navy was also considered a valuable adjunct to the passive fortification system constructed to protect the national littoral.

The Treaty of Paris (1783) created an American nation that extended westward beyond the Appalachian Mountains to the Mississippi River, south to the Florida border, and north to the Great Lakes. In 1803 this domain was more than doubled by the purchase of the Louisiana Territory, which in 1800 had been retroceded by Spain to France. If the earlier treaty created an extensive buffer of unsettled land to protect the seaboard states, the 1803 addition provided even more security for the settled areas. Yet land-hungry Americans quickly undermined the buffer quality of the area by pressing settlement westward, creating new states and territories from a region formerly inhabited only by Indians and American trappers and traders except for the major cities of St. Louis and New Orleans.

The most obvious, and expected, resistance came from the Indians. Because these natives were blocking the advance of settlers into the region north of the Ohio River, a series of wars was prosecuted against them during 1789–1796. The small United States Army created by Congress, reinforced by state militias, eventually broke the back of Indian resistance. Again from 1810 to 1817 the combination of regulars, militia, and short-term volunteer levies eliminated Indian resistance in the Old Northwest and in the area south of the Ohio, including Florida. Waging these campaigns with a small regular army that normally numbered between 2,500 and 6,500 soldiers, augmented by militia and volunteers, reinforced the popular conception that a minimum standing army was adequate for the nation's needs. Except for periods of national war (1812–1815, 1846–1848, 1861–1865, 1898, 1898–1902), the regular army usually numbered considerably less than 0.10 percent of the national population and grew proportionately smaller as the national population increased by almost one-third every decade until the 1870's.

The Founding Fathers expected that occasional insurrections would be raised against the states or the national government, but they believed the new nation eventually would win the loyalty of all citizens. They proved correct over the long term, but both political and military measures of a repressive type were taken from time to time against the citizenry. Because it believed public criticism of the Adams Federalists (1797–1801) served the interests of France, with whom the United States was almost at war, the administration of John Adams passed and enforced the Alien and Sedition Acts (1798). Deportation of anti-Federalist aliens and jailing of political dissenters became one approach used by the Federalists to promote national security. Occasional rebellions or conspiracies aimed at promoting insurrection or separatist movements did occur, but they were easily suppressed by the use of state militia or small detachments of the army. Pennsylvania's Whiskey Rebellion (1794), the Wilkinson-Burr conspiracy at the turn of the nineteenth century, and anti-British insurrectionary activity along the Canadian border in the 1830's and 1840's all proved little more than national annoyances. The American Civil War, of course, was a crisis of much greater magnitude. But even in this case, once the rebellion was suppressed, the United States Army was reduced from 1 million (3 percent of the population) in 1865 to 37,000 (0.10 percent) in 1870 and to 28,000 by 1897, a minuscule force in comparison with a population of 72 million. Given the extent of the national territory in 1897, and the size of the American population, it is quite evident that fear of a standing army had resulted in the army's being a "corporal's guard" rather than a meaningful body to "provide for the common defense." Perhaps the leaders of the early years of the Republic were lucky, but their estimate proved correct: major problems concerning the national domain and its boundaries could be settled by honest bargaining.

On the other hand, American commerce, designed to bring financial security to the nation, resulted in armed conflict with France and later with Great Britain. The Federalist dream of liquidating early national indebtedness through foreign trade did not realistically take into account the perils involved. Three years after the new government was launched in 1789, revolutionary France was at war with most of Western Europe. As a declared neutral, desiring the rich trade with both sides, America found its commerce attacked by both France and Great Britain. Unable to obtain respect for its flag at sea, the Federalist administration of John Adams turned against its former ally, raised a navy, and fought a naval war against France between 1798 and 1800. The victories of the new navy, plus France's conclusion that America was a necessary friend, led to a satisfactory settlement of the dispute. The Convention of 1800, which settled various Franco-American issues, terminated the alliance that had bound the two nations since 1778. The Adams administration hoped that America could now steer clear of the maelstrom of European war that threatened to sink the young republic.

With the Francophile Thomas Jefferson in office from 1801, maritime problems with Great Britain partially replaced the troubles with France. In time, during the administration of Jefferson's successor, James Madison, America found it impossible to pursue a neutral course in its maritime trade and decided to force the issue with the British. The War of 1812 proved that the United States Navy could not defend American trade or prevent a British invasion of the United States. But the war also saw a repetition of the strategy of the American Revolution. Unless they wanted to wage war far more aggressively, and at much greater cost, the British could not bring the enormous American nation to heel. The Treaty of Ghent (December 1814) recognized this situation, and both sides settled for the *status quo ante bellum*. The lesson for Americans was obvious: defense of neutrality rights at sea could drag the United States into foreign wars.

Had Americans not suffered humiliation

from another quarter, it is entirely possible that the navy might have been allowed to fall into disuse and decay. However, the harassment of American trade by Mediterranean corsairs from the Barbary States of North Africa resulted in a policy of paying tribute to some of those states from 1789 until 1815. In the latter year, the practice was replaced by increased naval pressure against those states. After the close of the naval war against Tripoli in 1815, Americans were unhampered in their Mediterranean trade, provided a naval squadron remained on that station. Until the end of the century, the United States maintained cruising squadrons in the Mediterranean, Caribbean, eastern Pacific, and Far East.

The United States derived another very important lesson from the War of 1812: with France finally vanquished, Americans saw that the British preferred peace to war in order to pursue their own maritime trade. Between 1812 and 1823 this British desire for maintenance of a peaceful status quo, and their dominance of trade in Latin America, led them to interpose the Royal Navy between Europe and the Western Hemisphere to prevent a reintroduction of French, Spanish, or Russian power into the New World. This meant, of course, that America was protected not only by the expanse of Atlantic waters but also by the presence of British sea power. Secretary of State John Quincy Adams understood this situation and encouraged a public statement of national policy in December 1823, later known as the Monroe Doctrine. This policy merged an earlier principle, that American safety would be best served by abstaining from entanglements in European affairs, with a second principle, that American security would be harmed by further colonization or interference in the Western Hemisphere by European states.

During the half-century after 1823, President James Monroe's approach to national security was buttressed by additional principles that became more viable with a national increase in wealth and population. These principles included such ideas as the following:

1. American security would be best served by engrossing the unoccupied and lightly occupied territories between the Louisiana Purchase and the Pacific coast.

2. American security would not be endangered so long as the nation's continental neighbors to the north and south remained weak states.

3. A chain of fortifications on all coasts, manned by regular troops, with the state militias for reinforcements, could prevent or at least detain an invading force until reinforcements arrived.

4. A cruising navy, operating as squadrons in the Mediterranean, Caribbean, eastern Pacific, and Far East, could protect American commerce and be recalled to defend the coasts when war was imminent.

This approach to promoting American national security was based upon premises that international relations outside the Western Hemisphere would not significantly affect the United States; that there was little danger of harm being visited upon the country so long as the nation did not intrude itself into the affairs of other states; and that the existing defense establishment could handle the situation should aggressive nations seek to invade the country.

By the end of the nineteenth century, the static international situation had begun to change, and so had the national security system that had served the United States since 1823. The unification of Germany and of Italy, the modernization of Japan, the international scramble for markets and colonies, and the generation of a new pugnacious spirit of nationalism in many countries had worked to undermine the years of relative peace since the Congress of Vienna. While there had been no major changes in the size or structure of the United States Army between the Civil War and the Spanish-American War (1898), the same was not true of the navy. By the early 1880's the fleet inherited from the Civil War period was almost useless. Given this situation, Congress in 1883 began a program of renewal based on modern steel-hulled vessels armed with rifled guns.

In the 1890's the nation and the navy began to accept the ideas of Captain Alfred Thayer Mahan concerning proper employment of the new navy. While small squadrons, cruising on distant stations, were deemed useful for protecting commerce and citizens, and for showing the flag, Mahan and his followers (among them

627

Theodore Roosevelt) argued that a nation was best defended by a concentrated fleet capable of seizing "command of the sea" by defeating the navy of an enemy power. Drawing upon his study of maritime warfare, and particularly the historical success of the British navy, Mahan decried the value of commerce raiding and stressed the invulnerability the United States could expect once it had a modern fleet that operated as a single body. A commercial imperialist, the captain believed national greatness could be maintained only by a vigorous foreign trade. This commerce would need a navy to defend it; and such defense required foreign naval bases, preferably within American colonies. Mahan's promotion of naval power, colonies, and foreign trade coincided with the surge in American productivity that followed the modern industrialization of the 1880's and 1890's with its potential surpluses.

The conclusion of the Spanish-American War found the nation with an overseas empire and a new vulnerability. From the 1880's the United States had been competing with Great Britain and Germany for naval bases in Samoa and Hawaii and for the markets of Asia and the Caribbean. By 1899 it owned Puerto Rico, a portion of Samoa, the Hawaiian Islands, Guam, and the Philippine Islands. In four more years the nation would have a lease in perpetuity on the Canal Zone that bisected the new nation of Panama. With the acquisition of this isthmian and insular real estate came responsibility for its defense. Whereas American defense policy previously had been fairly simple, it now became complex. While the United States Navy might be able to defend the coasts against any nation except Great Britain, it was in no position to protect the nation's commerce, island possessions, canal site, and coasts if a challenge came in the Pacific and Atlantic simultaneously. Given the magnitude of the defense tasks, an army of 70,000 in 1904 could be considered little more than a cadre for training purposes. It was evident to many, though distasteful to more isolationistic Americans, that national security now depended upon maintenance of a balance of power in Europe by Great Britain. Fortunately, American security received no serious challenge between 1898 and 1914.

The commencement of World War I in 1914 completed the destruction of the national security system that had protected the United States for a century. Desiring to trade equally with all belligerents, neutral America found itself ground between the upper and nether millstones of British control of the seas and Germany's destructive submarine campaign. With its merchant shipping seriously endangered by German U-boats, and its nationals killed when sailing on belligerent passenger liners, the United States in April 1917 chose to enter the war on the side of Great Britain and its allies. Once again America fought in defense of neutral rights. Though not clearly stated in President Woodrow Wilson's call for war, it is evident that the nation was joining the British in order to prevent a total German victory and its concomitant destruction of the European balance of power. Were England and France to fall—and it seemed possible in 1917—the German navy might control the seas and render the United States vulnerable to invasion. With American entry into the conflict, every premise upon which national security had stood, except continuation of the European balance of power, was negated. The United States now chose to intervene in the affairs of Europe; it sent the enormous American Expeditionary Force to Europe; and it increased the navy to levels never before seriously considered. Finally, though describing itself as an "associated power" in the struggle, America fought as an ally in war against the Central Powers.

Driven by a messianic idealism and a deep international-mindedness, President Wilson between 1918 and 1920 attempted to create a new foundation for American national security. Through the creation of the League of Nations, and American leadership of it, the president hoped to abolish future wars by eliminating or controlling their causes. American national security was to become entwined with international collective security. A League of Nations army and navy, formed by the commitment of the armed forces of the major powers, would keep the peace. But such was not to be. While acceptable to Wilson, the League Covenant did not meet the expectations of the American public. Sensing this fact better than the president did, his political opponents prevented American adherence to the Treaty of Versailles and the League Covenant. The balance had been somewhat restored in Europe;

no threat to American safety could be imagined; and the American nation now chose to return to the old patterns of protecting national security.

Though postwar Americans returned to traditional views concerning defense of the nation, the actual implementation of a national security program became much more complicated from 1919 to 1939 than had been the case before 1916. The prosecution of the war had directly involved the president through his constitutional position as commander in chief of the armed forces. By logical extension of his "war powers" through acts of Congress and presidential fiat, Wilson directly controlled the manpower, industrial resources, agricultural output, and shipping of the country. At his order a great variety of councils, boards, bureaus, and agencies, governed by his appointees, directed the war effort. Though cumbersome, this new structure did prove that America could effectively reinforce its allies in Europe and contribute significantly to the final victory. At the war's end the whole structure was dismantled almost overnight, but the experience was not forgotten.

The National Defense Act of 1920 set the defense pattern for the next two decades. Congress enlarged the regular army and authorized 297,000 officers and men, though funds actually allocated kept its strength around 135,000 until 1940. The National Guard received new stature, but again moneys spent held this second line of defense to about half of its authorized strength. There was to be a third element of manpower, the national militia pool, but congressional unwillingness to conscript men for peacetime training meant that this group remained only a potential one. The air service was limited to approximately 10,000 men until 1926, when with new status as the air corps it grew slowly to 16,000 men and 1,800 aircraft. As with the ground forces, economy-minded presidents and congresses starved the air arm of funds; and thus modern matériel was acquired only slowly. The Naval Construction Act of 1916 became the authorization program for the postwar navy. In 1924, 1927, and 1933 and 1934 additional cruisers, river gunboats, and aircraft carriers were authorized to "round out the fleet"; but the battleship force remained fixed at levels provided

at the Washington Conference (1922) and the London Conference (1930). Only in the late 1930's, once the naval limitation system came to an end, did Congress provide funds for new capital ships. During these years naval personnel was reduced from a wartime high of 225,000 officers and men to an average of 95,000, until expansion after 1937. Navy ships, air corps bombers, and heavy artillery in army coastal fortifications were to be the first and second lines of defense until the army and National Guard could be brought to action. As in 1810, or 1910, the national security depended upon a defensive strategy.

Whereas total mobilization of the nation's resources characterized the war effort of 1917–1918, in the postwar years the nation did not follow a fully integrated program of defense. President Wilson had found it necessary to coordinate the work of the State Department, the War Department, and the Navy Department through his office; but after 1919 each department began to follow its own program, with little contact among them. The army and navy did coordinate their war planning through the Joint Army-Navy Board, but such activities bore little official relationship to what was done at the State Department. When the Joint Army-Navy Board developed assumptions for plans designed to support the nation's foreign policies, the military planners normally worked only with what they believed were official policies. No national intelligence-gathering apparatus existed to provide information about the capabilities of potential enemies. There also was no national Committee on Public Information, similar to that headed by George Creel during the war, to inform the public or other nations about American policies, plans, or hopes. Occasional White House or State Department press releases were the best and only sources of such guidance.

To the casual observer or reader it might appear that America in the 1920's or 1930's was pursuing an approach to national security that differed little from that of a century earlier. Yet there was one striking difference. As a matter of national policy, the nation was attempting to enhance its security by committing itself to naval limitation and what amounted to disarmament of land forces by example. Given the size of the United States Army—approximately the same as that allowed a "disarmed" Germany—America menaced no one. At the 1921–1922 Conference for the Limitation of Armament, and later at the 1932–1933 World Disarmament Conference, American army delegations could be almost disinterested spectators. Between February 1922 and January 1937, the United States Navy was limited in its battleships and aircraft carriers (1922–1930) and in the numbers of all naval units (1930–1936). The naval ratios, established by the Washington Five-Power Naval Treaty (1922) and the London Naval Treaty (1930), were designed to provide defense superiority for each signatory power. America would be supreme in the Western Hemisphere; Japan would control Asian waters; and Great Britain, France, and Italy could each protect their home waters. The British, of course, found themselves unable to defend the United Kingdom and their outlying empire. America likewise forfeited defense of the Philippines, but the system did provide for near invulnerability in the homeland. In the end, this approach to national security broke down because Japan, Germany, and Italy believed they could advance their individual national interests by rearmament and territorial expansion. The interwar defensive system was built on the premise that the status quo would be maintained; but this premise lacked both reality and durability.

The commencement of World War II in Europe in September 1939 found the United States a little better prepared than in 1916 to begin the necessary military buildup that would provide for the nation's defense. Led by President Franklin D. Roosevelt, Congress in 1938 began a program of enlarging the fleet and pressed forward with the "two-ocean Navy" construction act of 1940. The army likewise was authorized steadily to expand the regulars and the National Guard, but real acceleration came only with the establishment of peacetime conscription in August 1940. Simultaneously with the program of national rearmament came industrial mobilization. Experience in national economic planning and control that had been gained in World War I, and sharpened during the New Deal years after 1933, made it possible for the Army and Navy Munitions Board, and later the Office of Production Management, to organize industrial production to meet the needs of the new war plans.

In 1939 the Joint Army-Navy Board accelerated its restudy of national defense plans. Very quickly it decided that Germany was the major menace to national safety. From this premise came the national strategy decision that if the United States were to enter the war, and if Germany were allied with Japan, the total American effort would be directed first toward the defeat of Germany. On the basis of this decision, the president urged supplying military armaments to Great Britain, the Lend-Lease Act of 1941, and eventually American convoying of shipping destined for the British Isles. The "Europe first" decision also established the American policy of trying to limit Japanese expansion in Asia, short of going to war. The resources of Southeast Asia and the British eastern dominions were vital to England's war effort; thus the United States connected its strategy of neutral support to Europe with its Far Eastern activities. Finding itself blocked by the United States, Japan chose war on 7 December 1941.

As in World War I, the president quickly mobilized the nation for the war effort. The Office of War Information told the public of the necessity for a total effort, at home and on the battlefields abroad. From January 1942, with the signing of the Declaration by the United Nations, the war became a great coalition struggle, to be fought to complete victory. If there was any persistent theme presented by the Office of War Information, it was the idea that American security could be guaranteed only by total victory through coalition effort. Because American troops were fighting and stationed in Latin America, Africa, Europe, the southwestern Pacific, India, Southeast Asia, the Philippines, and China, the American public received a total education on global politics and international war. This education, plus the reinforcement provided through Office of War Information efforts, undoubtedly played a part in preparing public opinion to accept American membership in international organizations and to develop faith in collective defense.

World War II ended under conditions that were strikingly different from those when it had begun. Germany and Japan, the principal enemy powers, were devastated and helpless. The cost to the victors was much heavier than imagined; but for the moment, in America and elsewhere, the triumph itself was sufficient to erase any fear of what the future might hold. Yet, for those who had to think about national security in the years ahead, the last year of the war portended the terrible shape of things to come. In its final campaign to terrorize the British, Germany had launched guided missiles, the "buzz bomb" V-1 and the high-trajectory V-2 rocket, at England. It also had commenced operations with a new generation of highly sophisticated submarines that might have changed the course of naval warfare had they been available earlier. The United States, during the last year of the war, had mounted a strategic bombing campaign against Germany and Japan that effectively burned the heart out of each nation. Finally, to convince Japan that further resistance could be nothing less than national suicide, American long-range bombers dropped atom bombs on Hiroshima and Nagasaki. The cremation of the two cities awesomely demonstrated that any future war, using this new generation of weapons, would be international folly at its worst.

Given the total Allied victory, and the lack of physical destruction in the United States, Americans felt both secure and generous at war's end. Owning the preponderance of the world's military armament, and an industrial capacity to meet their every need in weaponry, there was no reason to be insecure. This situation made it possible for the United States to take the lead in supporting the United Nations as it sought to insure future peace. But the very power of America, with its unfettered ability to intimidate, bred in the Soviet Union a desire to protect itself behind a buffer zone of satellite nations. Thus began the communization of Eastern Europe and the onset of the Cold War. Actions taken by the Soviets between 1945 and 1947, when the United States was demobilizing its army and "mothballing" its navy, awakened a national sense of outrage and frustration among Americans. It was in this period, particularly during 1947, that Congress and the executive branch created a new national security structure for the nation.

While the National Security Act of 1947, and its modifications of 1949 and later, established a new organization for control of America's armed forces, it represented only one part of the nation's new approach to maintaining its security. Central to the whole system was acceptance of the idea of collective defense on an international scale. Membership in the United Nations was designed to promote a sense of security for those belonging to it. As the most powerful of the founding nations, and one of the permanent members of the Security Council, the United States helped to enhance the security of others and in return received support from the organization. In 1947 and 1949, through signatory membership in the Rio Pact and the North Atlantic Treaty Organization, both regional defense organizations permitted within the United Nations Charter, America further merged its defense needs with those of like-minded nations. The nation was returning to old concepts for promoting national security: defense of the Western Hemisphere and prevention of domination of Europe by a single power, in this case the Soviet Union. Between 1951 and 1954, in order to create an enormous buffer area in the Pacific Ocean, and to contain any expansionist tendencies that might develop within the newly established People's Republic of China, the United States negotiated bilateral and multilateral defense pacts with Australia and New Zealand (1951), the Republic of the Philippines (1951), Japan (1951), the Republic of Korea (1953), and the Republic of China (1954). In 1954, as a means of thwarting further communist inroads into Indochina, America pressed the establishment of the Southeast Asia Treaty Organization. Through these treaties, and association in 1955 with the military committee of the Central Treaty Organization (Baghdad Pact), the United States tried both to contain anticipated expansionist ambitions of the Soviet Union and the communist Chinese and to enhance American national security through collective defense measures.

America's leaders also recognized, during the years immediately following World War II, that the nation would have to help rebuild the shattered economies in Europe and Asia. The inroads of communist parties in France, Italy, and Greece presented clear evidence that weakened nations might choose political systems other than democracy to solve their national problems. Military and economic assistance to Greece and Turkey began in 1947 under the Truman Doctrine. A year later, Congress authorized the Marshall Plan as a means to begin rebuilding Western Europe. Though an interest was exhibited in assisting China, moneys allocated for that beleaguered nation proved insufficient and much too late. For reasons beyond the control of America, the Nationalist regime of Generalissimo Chiang Kai-shek succumbed to the communist armies. From the "loss" of China to the communists came a new urgency in America to see that no other nations passed under their control. Toward this end, mutual security legislation by Congress made it possible for the United States to provide military and technical assistance, both in personnel and matériel, to nations attempting to maintain their independence. Through such assistance the United States reinforced commitments it had made in the name of collective defense. In 1950, with Point Four economic and technical assistance, and after 1961, with the establishment of the Peace Corps and placement of the Agency for International Development within the State Department, assistance was directed toward nations not necessarily menaced by hostile neighbors or by communist-led minorities within their boundaries. From 1947 to 1961, and down to the present, the national security concept has been simple: America cannot be safe unless it takes an active role in alleviating international misery.

While collective defense treaties and economic assistance programs have been vital to the enhancement of American national security since 1945, the establishment of a sound military defense system has remained the most important focus of national attention. It was obvious to those who led the United States Army, Navy, and Air Force in the war that full coordination and concentration of effort against the enemy had seldom occurred. Through the agency of the Combined Chiefs of Staff, British and American plans were reasonably well focused, but the same was not true among the American armed forces. Despite central direction of the American effort against Japan by the Joint Chiefs of Staff, costly duplication of materials, competition for resources, and se-

vere disagreement concerning planned operations were all too evident in the measures taken by General Douglas MacArthur and Admiral Chester Nimitz in the Pacific. By 1947 it was recognized in Congress, and by the president, that peacetime conditions had not led to any significant changes in the behavior patterns of the services. Given the tense relations that were developing with the Soviet Union, and the fact that inefficient operations by the armed forces could have catastrophic consequences for the nation because of the new weaponry, the call for change through unification became insistent.

The National Security Act of 1947 and of 1949 centralized the military aspects of defense planning and operations under the secretary of defense, who was directly responsible to the president. Actual direction of the armed services remained with the Joint Chiefs of Staff, though orders flowed from the president through the secretary of defense. The secretaries of the army, navy, and air force no longer sat in the cabinet but were responsible for the management of their services. With the enlargement of the Department of Defense after 1949, and expansion of the secretary of defense's authority, there was a sharp return to the historic concept of civilian supremacy. This centralization of control in civilian hands, considered so vital by the Founding Fathers, was further institutionalized in 1947 by the creation of the National Security Council.

From the earliest days of the Republic until 1947, the setting of national goals and the formulating of policies to attain them had been a diffuse operation. In the area of defense (security) policies, the presidents normally made their recommendations in budget messages and hoped for congressional authorization and funding where required. In the process of investigating, setting priorities, and finally legislating, Congress had ample opportunity to create policies of its own and force them on the president. Because of their expertise, superior data, and operational experience, the armed services also participated in the policy process through advice to the president or Congress. Finally, the public had its say, though somewhat indirectly, through the usual channels of communication and by participation in the elective process. Before 1941 this process of policy formulation and implementation was slow and awkward at best, but it was acceptable. Given the complex problems of defense and foreign affairs after 1945, it was clear that policymaking needed to be streamlined if it was to be effective. The National Security Council became the agency for defense policymaking. By statute it consists of the president, vice-president, secretaries of state and defense, and director of the Office of Emergency Preparedness. It is formally advised by the chairman of the Joint Chiefs of Staff, the director of the Central Intelligence Agency, the president's adviser on national security affairs, and others whom the president sees fit to add.

Because of the presence of the president, secretaries of state and defense, and chairman of the Joint Chiefs of Staff, the National Security Council is in the position to create realistic policies to support national security. Its position papers, once adopted by the president, become official guidance to achieve national goals. In theory, because of the membership, realistic goals can be set and policies established that are capable of achieving the desired goals. Implementation of a policy, always a problem, normally rests with a cabinet official or agency closest to the problem. Because the National Security Council is a formal institution, and presidents by definition are creatures of politics, the chief executives since 1947 have relied upon the council to differing degrees. Presidents Harry S. Truman, John F. Kennedy, and Lyndon B. Johnson used it as one of several institutions to create policy; presidents Dwight D. Eisenhower and Richard M. Nixon made it central to the operation of their national security system.

Since World War II, the international activities of the United States have clearly demonstrated the modern and greatly enlarged meaning of the term "national security." The creation and support of the North Atlantic Treaty Organization affirmed the concept that American security was connected intimately to that of Western Europe. Participation in the Korean War (1950–1953) and the extension of military support to Japan, Korea, the Republic of China (Taiwan), the Philippines, and the newly independent nations of what had been French Indochina represented acceptance of the view that the defense perimeter of America extended to the boundaries of the People's Re-

public of China. Behind these advance defense positions in Europe and Asia was erected a deterrence system designed to enhance the security of the United States and its allies. The United States Air Force Strategic Air Command long-range bombers and the intercontinental ballistic missiles in their midwestern silos, plus the navy's globally ranging missile-armed nuclear submarines, are considered the nation's deterrent shield against general nuclear war. Thus shielded, the United States between 1964 and 1973 fought a protracted war in Southeast Asia to demonstrate, in part, the viability of its commitment to assist those the nation had pledged to defend. Though the nuclear weapons shield remained in place, Americans recognized, from the days of the Kennedy administration, that their ultimate safety, and that of all mankind, required the limitation and eventual elimination of nuclear warfare capabilities in all countries. To this end the country has engaged in Strategic Arms Limitation Talks (SALT) with the Soviet Union since 1969, but it is clearly understood that both national and international security require that other nuclear powers join in this endeavor.

By 1975 it was possible to recognize that the national security of the United States rests upon premises strikingly different from those of 1789:

1. A highly complex system of foreign affairs that features established relations with most of the countries of the world and full participation in and leadership of the United Nations.

2. A large number of bilateral and multilateral security treaties for mutual defense, and membership in and commitment to three (Organization of American States, North Atlantic Treaty Organization, Southeast Asia Treaty Organization) regional defense organizations.

3. Support of a large number of nations, through provision of financial aid and military equipment assistance, as a means of tying them to the defense interests of the United States.

4. Maintenance of a large and reasonably well integrated military establishment designed to deter major nuclear warfare and capable of using conventional military force to achieve national ends.

5. A healthy national economy capable of meeting the nation's needs and of generating

enough surplus wealth to assist America's friends and allies.

BIBLIOGRAPHY

C. Joseph Bernardo and Eugene H. Bacon, *American Military Policy: Its Development Since 1775* (Harrisburg, Pa., 1955), one of the few historical studies of the development of American military policy, is documented with a bibliography; the authors hold quite successfully to the focus on the development of policy. Lincoln P. Bloomfield, "Vital Security Interests and Objectives of the United States," in *National War College Forum* (1970), a good analysis of the goals of American security policies, was delivered as a lecture and is not annotated. Bernard Brodie, *Strategy in the Missile Age* (Princeton, 1959), a historic approach to the questions raised by missiles and nuclear weapons, is essentially an interpretive work with light documentation by a preeminent author in the field. Stanley L. Falk and Theodore W. Bauer, *National Security Management: The National Security Structure* (Washington, D.C., 1972), a short but well-annotated study of the national security structure of the United States, has good chapters on the National Security Council, the secretary of defense, and the intelligence community. John Greenwood, comp., *American Defense Policy Since 1945, A Preliminary Bibliography,* Kansas State University Library Bibliography Series, no. 11 (Lawrence, Kans., 1973), is a very comprehensive, but unannotated, classified bibliography with an emphasis on the post-World War II period; a large percentage of the works cited have historical information for the period before 1945. Don Higginbotham, *The War of American Independence: Military Attitudes, Policies and Practice, 1763–1789* (New York, 1971), a well-written study with an excellent bibliography, deals fully with the history of early defense ideas. Harold A. Hovey, *United States Military Assistance: A Study of Policies and Practices* (New York, 1965), a fairly full study, for the time, of American military assistance and the part it plays in the promotion of national security, focuses on individual country and regional programs and is documented with a good bibliography. Senator Henry M. Jackson, ed., *The National Security Council: Jackson Subcommittee Papers on Policy-Making at the Presidential Level* (New York, 1965), is a collection of government hearings, documents, studies, and reports dealing with the operation of the national security structure. Walter Millis, *Arms and Men: A Study of American Military History* (New York, 1956), is a highly interpretive background history for modern national security and strategy questions. Louis Morton, "The Origins of American Military Policy," in *Military Affairs,* 22 (1958), is an excellent, highly interpretive article on defense policy origins in the colonial period; Morton is one of the outstanding writers in the field of military history. Clark G. Reynolds, *Command of the Sea: The History and Strategy of Maritime Empires* (New York, 1974), a broad interpretive study of the development of sea power on an international scale, is very useful for understanding the role of the navy in American national security and has an excellent bibliography. Roland N. Stromberg, *Collective Security and American Foreign Policy: From the League of Nations to NATO* (New York, 1964), a lightly documented interpretive study with a good bibliography, carefully analyzes the United States move from isolationism to collective security; it focuses on the League and United Nations, but not on the post–World War II alliance system. United States Congress, Senate, Committee on Government Operations, Subcommittee on National Policy Machinery, *Organizing for National Security,* 3 vols. (Washington, D.C., 1961), is a collection of government hearings, documents, studies, and reports dealing with the operation of the national security structure. Russell F. Weigley, *History of the United States Army* (New York, 1967), which focuses on the history of the regular army, with full coverage from the colonial period to present, contains excellent research, documentation, bibliography, and writing.

[*See also* ALLIANCES, COALITIONS, AND ENTENTES; THE COLD WAR; COLLECTIVE SECURITY; CONSCRIPTION; CONTAINMENT; THE DEPARTMENT OF STATE; DISARMAMENT; IMPERIALISM; INTERNATIONAL ORGANIZATION; ISOLATIONISM; THE MONROE DOCTRINE; NEUTRALITY; TRADE AND COMMERCE; TREATIES; THE TRUMAN DOCTRINE.]

NATIONAL SELF-DETERMINATION

Betty Miller Unterberger

IT IS generally accepted that the principle of self-determination refers to the right of a people to determine their own political destiny; but beyond this broad definition, no legal criteria determine which groups may legitimately claim this right in particular cases. No universally accepted standards mark the measure of freedom a group of people presumably must enjoy before they can exercise it. Nothing approaching a consensus exists regarding the feasibility of the principle itself. As a concept it cannot be stated in terms applicable to any given context. Consequently it has been both a factor of cohesion and a source of disunity, depending on the circumstances in which the question has arisen.

The term "self-determination" is derived from the German word *Selbstbestimmungsrecht* and was frequently used by German radical philosophers in the middle of the nineteenth century. As a concept, however, it can be traced back to the beginning of government. The right has always been cherished by all peoples, although history has a long record of its denial to the weak by the strong who claimed, and often enjoyed, superiority over them. Both the Greek city-states and the earlier Mesopotamian ones were jealous of their right to self-determination. Yet to the Greeks, non-Greeks were barbarians, born to serve them and the object of conquest if they refused to submit. The development of modern states in Europe and the rise of popular national consciousness enhanced the status of self-determination as a political principle, but it was not until the period of World War I that the right of national independence came to be known as the principle of national self-determination. In general

terms it is simply the belief that each nation has a right to constitute an independent state and to determine its own government.

Actually the principle might best be defined as a theory about the relationship that should prevail between the nation and the state, the latter being understood as any separately governed political community. Historian Alfred Cobban says that not every kind of national revolt can be included under the description of self-determination. The movement for national independence, or self-determination, falls into the same category as utilitarianism, communism, or Jeffersonian democracy. It is a theory, a principle, or an idea; and no simple, unconscious national movement can be identified with it. Struggles like the rising of the French under the inspiration of Joan of Arc or the Hussite Wars are fundamentally different from the national movements of the last two hundred years because of the absence of a theory of national self-determination, which could appear only in the presence of a democratic ideology.

In this context, then, the revolt of the English colonies in North America has been defined as the first assertion of the right of national and democratic self-determination in the history of the world. Resenting domination from across the seas, and especially the imposition of taxes without representation, the American colonists invoked natural law and the natural rights of man, drawing inspiration from the writings of John Locke to support their view. Locke taught that political societies are based upon the consent of the people who compose them, each of whom agrees to submit to the majority. Man has a natural right to life, liberty, and property. Sovereignty belongs to the people and is therefore limited by the necessity to protect the individual members.

Thomas Jefferson, the great leader of the American Revolution, emphasized Locke's theories as American ideals and epitomized the republican spirit of the century. In drafting the Declaration of Independence, which followed a resolution of the Continental Congress on 7 June 1776 that "these United Colonies are and of right ought to be free and independent States," Jefferson stated his fundamental philosophy of government, upon which the modern concept of self-determination rests:

> We hold these Truths to be self-evident, that all Men are created equal, that they are endowed by their Creator with certain unalienable Rights, that among these are Life, Liberty and the Pursuit of Happiness.—That to secure these Rights, Governments are instituted among Men, deriving their just Powers from the Consent of the Governed,—That whenever any Form of Government becomes destructive of these ends, it is the Right of the People to alter or to abolish it, and to institute new Government, laying its foundation on such Principles and organizing its Powers in such Form, as to them shall seem most likely to effect their Safety and Happiness.

In considering the American Revolution as the seminal example of the modern principle of self-determination, it is important to focus attention on both elements of Jefferson's view. He was concerned not only with throwing off the foreign yoke but also with ensuring that the government was that of the people and that their will was supreme.

Since the formation of the American nation, American statesmen have continually expressed sympathy for the basic principle of self-determination. In 1796 President George Washington stated clearly that his "best wishes were irresistibly excited whenever, in any country, he saw an oppressed nation unfurl the banner of freedom." Three years earlier Thomas Jefferson, then the American secretary of state, had said: "We surely cannot deny to any nation that right whereon our own is founded—that every one may govern itself according to whatever form it pleases and change those forms at its own will."

Jefferson's view, supported by his fellow Virginians James Madison and James Monroe, was widely accepted by the American public during the ensuing years although never actually implemented as official policy. However, regardless of its original intent, throughout the nineteenth and twentieth centuries the American Declaration of Independence provided a beacon of hope both to European peoples struggling for independence against autocratic governments and to colonial peoples seeking to advance toward independence. Frequently American idealists threatened to drag the nation into European affairs by demanding that the government underwrite a policy of liberation abroad. For example, when the Greeks staged an abortive independence movement against the Turks in the 1820's, the Monroe administration was assailed by Daniel Webster in Congress and by many others for its apparent indifference to the cause of liberty in other parts of the world. Although realists like John Quincy Adams opposed the expression of sentiments unsupported by action, President James Monroe nonetheless placed on record his public support of the Greek struggle for self-determination in his famous message of December 1823.

Yet it must be noted that while Adams recognized that American history fostered a sympathy for self-determination, that same tradition also had established as a cardinal priority the doctrine of nonintervention so forcefully enunciated by Washington in his Farewell Address. For Adams, concerned with the limits of American power in this period, the doctrine of nonintervention took precedence over the principle of self-determination.

Despite Adams' position, throughout the nineteenth century the American public frequently expressed sympathy for the struggles of oppressed peoples in Europe, such as the Poles, the Hungarians, and the Finns. This feeling was most vigorously demonstrated in relation to the Hungarians upon the failure of their revolution in 1848–1849. In the summer of 1849 the nation had applauded the Hungarian triumphs against Austrian rule and Secretary of State John Clayton had even sent a special agent to Hungary to offer American encouragement. After the Hungarian Revolution had been crushed by Russian troops sent to aid the Austrian emperor, Louis Kossuth, the eloquent Hungarian leader, came to the United States. Arriving in New York City in 1851, he was greeted with the greatest ovation given anyone since the visit of the Marquis de Lafayette twenty-five years earlier.

When the Austrian chargé d'affaires protested to the State Department against the overt public sympathy expressed in favor of Hungary's liberation, Daniel Webster, then secretary of state, responded in a note that has become famous. While explaining America's sympathy for Hungary as a natural expression of the national character, he assured the Austrian government that such popular outbursts constituted no desertion of the established American doctrine of noninterference in the internal affairs of other countries. Nevertheless, while American official policy continued to advocate nonintervention even in the affairs of nations struggling for liberty against autocratic oppressors, many persons in official positions demanded that the United States use its moral and physical power to support the freedom of Hungary. Nor did the government suppress the rights of Congress to pass resolutions expressing the sympathy of the nation for struggling peoples, like the Hungarians, seeking freedom.

But the attitude of the federal government changed at the outset of the Civil War, when the United States found itself in the embarrassing position of using force to suppress the will of a minority of the nation seeking to establish its own independence. Among the interested European observers of the American Civil War there were perhaps as many partisans of the South as of the North. To some it seemed that the Southern states, by fighting for their self-determination as a nation, were striking a blow for political freedom and independence in the spirit of similar revolutionaries and national movements in the Old World. Southerners themselves contended that they were following the example of the American patriots of 1776—a view that appeared reasonable to many Englishmen. To the latter, Secretary of State William H. Seward made it clear that the United States could not regard as friends those who favored or gave aid to the insurrection under any pretext. In taking this position the United States pointed out that it was claiming only what it conceded to all other nations. Thus

the Civil War clearly determined the official policy of the United States toward self-determination. The United States had in effect denied the right of communities within a constituted federal union to determine their allegiance, and that denial had been enforced by military power. Clearly the doctrine of national sovereignty, supported by the principle of nonintervention, had officially and unequivocally taken precedence over the concept of self-determination.

This official view also influenced the policy of the United States in regard to the use of the plebiscite as a means of settling questions of sovereignty and self-determination. For example, Secretary Seward adamantly opposed a plebiscite on the abortive cession of the islands of St. Thomas and St. John in 1868. Again, on 14 August 1897, in response to the Japanese minister's suggestion that a plebiscite be taken regarding the annexation of the Hawaiian Islands, Secretary of State John Sherman drew upon the history of international relations to confirm the impropriety of "appealing from the action of the Government to 'the population'. In international comity and practice the will of a nation is ascertained," said Sherman, through the established and recognized government, and "it is only through it that the nation can speak." The same principle in regard to annexed territories was asserted in the memorandum of the American Peace Commission at the conclusion of the Spanish-American War. Thus, by 1899 the United States had emphatically asserted its adherence to the principle and practice of annexation without the consent of the peoples annexed.

On the fall of the Spanish empire in the Western Hemisphere in 1898, the United States gained colonial control of Guam, Puerto Rico, and the Philippines and enjoyed quasi suzerainty over Cuba, from which it withdrew its military presence in 1902 while reserving certain rights for itself. This put the United States in the anomalous position of having fought a war against Spain at least officially for Cuban self-determination, only to deny that principle to the colonies acquired in the peace settlement. Those who opposed annexation constituted a powerful anti-imperialist movement, headed by many political and intellectual leaders. Deeply concerned over the concept of self-determination, although they did not specifically mention it, they clearly opposed annexation on the ground that it involved the suppression of a conquered people. Although the anti-imperialists could not defeat the peace treaty, they were able to bring the issue of imperialism into the open and to raise considerable national doubt as to whether the treaty was in accord with the direct traditions of self-determination as revealed by the establishment of the nation.

The nation's ambivalence concerning the proper interpretation and appropriate application of the concept of self-determination was exposed again when the American people were called upon to decide the novel questions of whether the Constitution followed the flag across the Pacific, and whether democracy could be preserved at home in its new imperial setting. Anti-imperialists argued against the abandonment of American principles for the ways of the Old World. Imperialists also called upon American traditions to bolster their view of American foreign policy. The imperialists maintained that democracy could be extended only to a people fit to receive it. Self-government depended on a nation's capacity for political action; and if a people were not ready for independence, they must undergo a period of political tutelage and protection. Thus the imperialists joined the American conception of manifest destiny with Rudyard Kipling's call for the Anglo-Saxon nations to take up the white man's burden. In the curious reasoning of an official United States commission to the Philippines, "American sovereignty is only another name for the liberty of the Filipinos." And yet it must be noted that every president since William McKinley extended the prospect of freedom and independence to the Philippines until it was actually granted in 1946.

By 1899, then, the American conflict of principle in regard to self-determination might clearly be seen by examining the two greatest heroes in American history. The popular reputation of George Washington rested less on his great work as the nation's first president than on the successful conduct of a struggle for self-determination, while Lincoln's rested on his success in suppressing such a struggle. Although pursuing diametrically opposite principles, both were adjudged right by posterity—

even, in the main, by the descendants of the defeated sides. Later events have caused the Civil War to be regarded as waged on the issue of slavery, but at the outset Lincoln asserted that it was fought not to abolish slavery but to maintain the Union—that is, to resist the claim of the Southern states to independence. Such a claim or right has its limits; and, to state the matter from the cold standpoint of political philosophy, the national government believed that in this case the claim was not within the limits where the principle properly applied.

Considerations like these induce one to reflect upon the limited nature of principles commonly accepted as universal; upon the conflicts that arise when two inconsistent universal principles come into collision; and how far such conflict may be avoided by recognizing that there are limits, with a debatable region in which neither can be rigorously applied.

World War I and the leadership of President Woodrow Wilson provided the nation an opportunity for a supreme effort to reconcile the principles of self-determination and national sovereignty in a way that might provide a lasting peace. From the moment of his address at Washington on 27 May 1916, before the League to Enforce Peace, when he announced as a fundamental principle "that every people has a right to choose the sovereignty under which they shall live . . . ," Wilson was selected as leader by those who believed that the new frontiers drawn at the peace conference should be based on self-determination. During the following two years, Wilson continued to proclaim vigorously and with passionate conviction his version of the right of national self-determination: "No peace can last or ought to last which does not accept the principle that governments derive all their just powers from the consent of the governed," and "no right anywhere exists to hand peoples about from sovereignty to sovereignty as if they were property." The president's repeated affirmation of an abstract principle of justice that should be universally applied had a profound influence on the subsequent statements of both the Allies and the Central Powers. On 8 January 1918, in a dramatic appearance before Congress, Wilson crystallized his war aims in the famous Fourteen Points address. Although the word "self-determination" was not specifically used, at least six of the Fourteen Points dealt with some interpretation or application of the principle.

As was to be the case in World War II, the Bolsheviks played a decisive role in the specific clarification and implementation of the American concept of self-determination. When the Bolshevik leaders Vladimir Lenin and Leon Trotsky had come to power in November 1917, they had demanded an immediate, general, and democratic peace with the Central Powers, based on no "annexations and contributions with the right of all nations to self-determination." On 3 December the Russians suspended hostilities with Germany and its allies, a state that lasted until 17 December. During this period the Bolsheviks used the concept of self-determination heavily on behalf of peace. After a powerful propaganda campaign they were finally able to convince their opponents to allow more time for the negotiations, so as to permit the Allies to define their war aims and to decide whether they wished to participate. During this period the Bolsheviks published the six points for world peace that they had laid down for the guidance of the peace conference. Five of the six points dealt with self-determination. Although the United States and the Allies failed to perceive it until Trotsky pointed it out to them, the points were directed at them as much as at the Central Powers. Indeed, the Russians had proposed five points that in essence were the same as five of the Fourteen Points of President Wilson, published only a few weeks later.

On 29 December, with six days remaining during which the Entente Powers could exercise their option to participate in the negotiations, Trotsky sent them his longest and most impassioned appeal. The address was clearly an ideological challenge. He pointed out that the Allies could no longer insist on fighting the war for the liberation of Belgium, the northern departments of France, Serbia, and other areas, since Germany and its allies had indicated willingness to evacuate those areas at the conclusion of a universal peace. Some response appeared to be necessary, for not only did Trotsky call for violent proletarian revolution against the Allied governments but he had also shrewdly based his primary argument on Wilson's principle of self-determination. Indeed,

his interpretation was a direct confrontation to the president's view of that principle. Although it appears that he never fully realized it, Wilson was in an ideological corner; either he must accept the Bolshevik conclusion that all peoples in all states, including all colonies, had the right to immediate self-determination, or he must reject it but in its place offer some standard of what constituted an acceptable unit for the application of that principle.

While Wilson had been sympathetic to the principle of self-determination as enunciated by Lenin, he had no illusions concerning the German response to it. By the end of December 1917 it appeared clear that self-determination, as understood by the Germans, justified the severance from Russia of the territories occupied by the German army: Russian Poland, most of the Baltic provinces, and parts of Belorussia (White Russia). Indeed, by the middle of December the State Department was aware that the Ukraine, Finland, and Transcaucasia were in the process of declaring themselves independent under the auspices of Lenin's program of self-determination. Finally, it was apparent that if Petrograd was to have peace according to the German interpretation of self-determination, it was to be purchased at the price of heavy territorial sacrifices. Wilson was clearly opposed to such an interpretation of self-determination. Indeed, on several occasions he had declared his opposition to the dismemberment of empires. If Wilson's concept of self-determination did not anticipate the dismemberment of empires, what did it really mean? Trotsky had made it clear that to demand self-determination for the peoples of enemy states and to refuse self-determination to the peoples within the Allied states or their own colonies would "mean the defense of the most naked, the most cynical imperialism."

In view of the ideological challenge presented by Trotsky's last invitation, an analysis of the American response becomes crucial. Secretary of State Robert Lansing was totally opposed to it. His attack was based on his social conservatism, his personal animosity to Bolshevik ideology, and, most important, on his insight into the logical and political requirements for a meaningful application of the principle of self-determination in foreign policy. His advice to the president betrayed the contradictions

NATIONAL SELF-DETERMINATION

that still existed in his thinking. On the one hand, he argued that the president should meet this challenge from the Bolsheviks by refusing to make any response whatsoever to their appeals. On the other hand, he admitted that Trotsky's logic demanded some answer and that a restatement of American war aims in greater detail might well be expedient.

In his analysis of the Bolsheviks' reasoning, Lansing apparently also sought to convince the president of the undesirability of settling territorial problems by means of self-determination. He pointed out that the current concept of the sovereignty of states in international relations would be destroyed if the "mere expression of popular will" were to become the governing principle in territorial settlements. He reminded Wilson of the nation's decision in regard to popular sovereignty in its own civil war. "We as a nation, are therefore committed to the principle that a national state may by force if necessary prevent a portion of its territory from seceding without its consent especially if it has long exercised sovereignty over it or if its national safety or vital interests would be endangered." The Bolshevik proposal, Lansing warned, would be "utterly destructive of the political fabric of society and would result in constant turmoil and change."

One of the strongest points in Lansing's analysis was his discovery that the whole discussion regarding self-determination up to that point had a major ideological flaw. There was no definition of the "distinguishing characteristic" of the unit to which the principle was to be applied. Trotsky had discussed the right of nationalities without defining what a nationality was. Was it based on blood, habitation of a particular territory, language, or political affinity? Clearly, accurate definition of the word was necessary if the terms proposed were to be properly interpreted; otherwise they were far too vague to be considered intelligently. Lansing added that if the Bolsheviks intended to suggest that every community could determine its own allegiance to a particular state, or to become independent, the political organization of the current world would be shattered. The result, he said, would be the same conditions that prevailed in Russia or international anarchy. Lansing did not provide a definition of "nationalities." He surely must have perceived

that his criticism of the Bolsheviks applied equally to Wilson's position.

President Wilson was now in possession of two totally divergent views on self-determination. Whereas Trotsky had pushed the political logic of the principle to its limits, thereby advocating that all peoples, not just a selected list, be liberated from foreign rule, Secretary Lansing had drawn his sword against Trotsky and negated the usefulness of self-determination in settling world issues. He insisted that if the present political and social order was to be preserved, then the principle of the legal sovereignty of constituted states must take precedence over any consideration of the popular will of minorities.

The president was clearly at odds with the logic of both points of view. At the core of his belief, self-determination meant the moral necessity of government by consent of the governed. Self-determination was to Wilson almost another word for popular sovereignty; *vox populi* was *vox dei*. Rousseau's "general will" was for him no merely ideal will, but the actual will of the people, which had only to be freed from the ill will of autocratic governments for its innate goodness to be manifested. The idealization of democracy was an essential part of Wilsonian ideology. Because he was firmly convinced of the goodness of the people's will, he believed in the possibility of building a new and better international order on the basis of national sovereignty, in which he assumed the democratic will of the people to be embodied.

To put it in another way, Wilson's belief in the goodness and power of world opinion, which might be termed the general will of humanity, and its identity with the general will of every democratic nation, enabled him to hold the view that the self-determination of nations and national sovereignty was a possible basis—indeed, the only basis—of world peace. The president never conceived of these principles as divided or as being applied separately. He had concluded that the primary cause of aggression by one state against another was a desire for territorial and economic security in the absence of international political security. The hallmark of this lack of international security was the bipolar alliance system that operated in an atmosphere of struggle for the elusive balance of power. This being the case, the president reasoned, if national security could be restored to the various states, then the motive for political and economic aggression would be removed from international politics. Wilson believed that an international organization of states, through the common resources of a community of power, would provide the required security. Once states adjusted to operating for the common welfare of mankind, without resorting to the exploitation of one state by another, then the existing inequities regarding points of sovereignty could be resolved by an international organization based on the principle that government must be with the consent of the governed. This was Wilson's long-range view of the application of self-determination. Even before the United States had entered the war, he had come to regard the League of Nations as central to his thought.

Nevertheless, the day after receiving Lansing's letter opposing the Bolsheviks, President Wilson revealed in a conversation with Sir Cecil Spring-Rice, retiring British ambassador, that while he sympathized with the Bolshevik desire to settle the war on the basis of self-determination, he was also deeply influenced by the views of his secretary of state: "In point of logic, of pure logic, this principle which was good in itself would lead to the complete independence of various small nationalities now forming part of various empires. Pushed to its extreme, the principle would mean the disruption of existing governments, to an indefinable degree. . . ." Wilson's introduction to his Fourteen Points speech appeared to be a direct answer to the Brest-Litovsk summons. His deep concern with Russia's plight seems apparent from a reading of the passages concerning that nation, which Colonel Edward House thought constituted "in some respects the most eloquent part of his message." Indeed, Wilson's decisive passage on Russia indicated his full awareness of the nation's prostration before the grim power of Germany. Apparently seeking to impress both the ruler and the ruled, he did not call for the overthrow of Bolshevik power as a condition for renewed cooperation; indeed, he even seemed to hold out the faint hope of American assistance to Russia's legitimate rulers. Moreover, fully resolved to continue the crusade regardless of all suggestions for a negotiated peace, Wilson refused to aban-

don Russia's borderland to the tortured interpretation of self-determination put forth by the Central Powers. Thus the sixth of the Fourteen Points called for an evacuation of all Russian territory and the adoption of diplomacy by all other nations of the world, actions that would permit an unhampered and unembarrassed opportunity for Russia's independent self-determination under institutions of its free choosing.

Even though the United States later, under tremendous pressure from the Allies, participated in expeditions to Siberia and northern Russia, Wilson justified these departures from his clearly enunciated principles on the ground that he was seeking to preserve the territorial integrity of Russia and the ultimate right of self-determination for its people while at the same time "rescuing" the Czech legion presumably trapped in Russia, and preserving the Open Door policy in the Russian Far East and northern Manchuria against suspected Japanese imperialism. But perhaps even more important, he was seeking to retain the goodwill of the Allies, whose support was vital to the success of a League of Nations, the capstone of his Fourteen Points. Thus, in order to block Japan and to further the League, Wilson followed a policy that appeared to be totally at variance not only with the principle of self-determination he had enunciated concerning Russia but also with the principles of his proposed League. Wilson, above all the man of principle, had found himself caught, as had the nation itself many times since its inception, in a debatable situation where, despite deep convictions, none of his principles could be rigorously applied.

Wilson was in a somewhat similar quandary in relation to the tenth point, concerning Austria-Hungary. From the American entry into the war, he had disapproved of the dismemberment of the Dual Monarchy, in the hope of strengthening those elements in Vienna that favored an early negotiated peace. By encouraging the Austrian forces of conciliation, Wilson hoped to drive a wedge between Vienna and Berlin. Although sympathetic to the desires for self-determination of the oppressed nationalities within the empire, he could not accept "the extreme logic of this discontent which would be the dismemberment of Austria-

Hungary." Thus, in the tenth point Wilson stopped short of a clear-cut endorsement of independence by placing his emphasis on providing the peoples of Austria-Hungary with the free opportunity for "autonomous development." Clearly, he saw this as the Aristotelian mean between the preservation of national sovereignty and the secession of the various nationalities from the Hapsburg empire.

Moreover, in January 1918 Wilson had reason to believe that such a policy might still keep open the door to a negotiated peace with Austria-Hungary. However, subsequent events, including his decision to "rescue" the Czechs in Siberia and the vigor of the nationalistic movement itself, pushed him into unqualified support for the self-determination of the national minorities. Nevertheless, it appears that in principle he arrived at this position reluctantly and only after his own secretary of state, who so opposed the principle of self-determination as a general guide for the settlement of the problems of Europe, had decided for reasons of state that German power might best be contained by the creation of a series of independent Danubian states.

Curiously, the first of Wilson's territorial points dealt with the colonial problem. Here the president very cautiously advocated "a free, open-minded, and absolutely impartial adjustment of all colonial claims." Regardless of however broad or narrow the interpretation of what was to be included under "colonial claims," Wilson insisted that their settlement be based upon strict observance of the principle that in determining all such questions of sovereignty, the interests of the populations concerned must have equal weight with the equitable claims of the governments whose title was to be determined. Lansing's caution had surely had an effect. Once again, the president appeared, perhaps without realizing it, to be seeking some reconciliation of the historic conflict of principles.

An examination of the remainder of Wilson's points on self-determination reveals that only in the case of Poland did the president offer an outright and unqualified commitment to independence. The thirteenth point, then, contrasted sharply with Wilson's application of the self-determination principle in the preceding seven points. It must have been evident to

Wilson that the national and language conflicts destined to emerge with the future rebirth of Poland were likely to be intense. It is therefore noteworthy that Poland was given specific political and economic guarantees. First, Wilson publicly proclaimed Poland to be in need of a "free and secure access to the seas." Second, this economic strategic safeguard was further supplemented by Wilson's proposal that Poland's "political and economic independence and territorial integrity should be guaranteed by international covenant." His thirteenth point, which gave an international guarantee for the independence of Poland, might be looked upon as the link to the fourteenth point, which called for the establishment of the League of Nations.

Though millions rallied to the idea of a League of Nations as the essential guarantee for a perpetual peace, it must be noted that Wilson, without even mentioning peace, chartered an association of nations in order to secure "mutual guarantees of political independence and territorial integrity." Peace was the ultimate objective, but the immediate function of the League was the preservation of the territorial arrangements that would emerge from the peace conference. The fourteenth point compensated for the lack of precision with which Wilson treated self-determination in some of his other "plaquered paragraphs." The association of nations was meant to be a sort of midwife to nations about to be born; it would help them pass from the precarious stage of infancy through adolescence, to full maturity—in a new "community of power."

Even the president himself possibly did not realize the full significance of the explosive principle that he had done so much to set in motion. Certainly a fundamental weakness of Wilson's ideas was his failure to realize how indeterminate a criterion nationality might be, and how little assistance it might sometimes give in deciding actual frontiers. Moreover, although he had spoken of self-determination as though it were an absolute principle of international right, from the very beginning he perforce allowed competing principles to influence his decisions and derogate from its claims. Yet, by and large the peace conference of 1918 proceeded on the theory that, insofar as possible, boundaries should be readjusted by balancing the principle of national self-determination against other factors. The new boundaries would then be guaranteed against forcible change. Although it would be easy to mention numerous violations of self-determination—always in the interests of the victorious powers—it must be noted, for whatever it is worth, that by and large self-determination won in Paris. In part this was because of Wilson's espousal of the principle and because of Allied propaganda, but perhaps more importantly because of the spontaneous actions of the nationalities themselves and the progress of the war. In any case, as the historian Thomas Bailey noted, "many more millions of minority groups were released from alien domination than were consigned to alien domination. The result was the closest approximation that modern Europe has ever had to an ethnographic map coinciding with a political map." Whether or not such an order of things was necessarily good, it was what Wilson had sought.

Once a fairly precise settlement in Eastern Europe had been achieved, Britain and the United States paid little further attention to the area. Because, despite Wilson's efforts, the principle of self-determination was not explicitly written into the League of Nations Covenant, many predicted that it would soon be forgotten. Moreover, after the war American officials tended to regard the Slavic states of Europe as politically corrupt, economically unstable, and strategically insignificant. During the interwar years United States concern for the region was limited to occasional statements in behalf of religious freedom and self-determination of peoples. United States officials never formulated any specific policies to achieve such aims, for the simple reason that Eastern Europe lay outside the region of historic American intersts. It was obvious, therefore, that America would not oppose any serious German or Russian challenge to these newly created states. Thus, when Nazi power destroyed Czechoslovakia and Poland in 1939 and overran all of Eastern Europe in 1940, the American people were reluctant to offer anything more than deep sympathy.

However, as events were to demonstrate, the view that self-determination was merely an anomaly of World War I proved to be based on an erroneous estimation. Amid the confusion of World War II, the outline of the future world settlement began to appear and take shape. A brief recapitulation of World War II reveals that Franklin D. Roosevelt was both as challenged and as baffled by the idea of self-determination as Wilson had been. Just as Wilson had believed that an international organization was needed to transform the doctrine of self-determination into political reality, so Roosevelt saw the United Nations, Wilson's grandchild, as trying to play the role in which Wilson had cast it. The United Nations was to accept "the fact of nationalism and the need for internationalism." Just as Wilson had experienced difficulties in interpreting and applying the doctrine of self-determination in the face of Allied objections, the secret treaties, and Bolshevik competition, so did Franklin Roosevelt have similar problems. In the Atlantic Charter of 14 August 1941, he and Prime Minister Winston Churchill of Great Britain joined to make known certain common principles and national policies on which they based their hopes for a better future. Once again the principle of self-determination of peoples was affirmed and the desire expressed "to see no territorial changes that do not accord with the freely expressed wishes of the peoples concerned." Respect was also reaffirmed for "the right of all peoples to choose the form of government under which they will live" and "to see sovereign rights and self government restored to those who have been forcibly deprived of them."

As in World War I, both the meaning and the scope of these abstract principles were open to conflicting interpretations. For example, the Atlantic Charter ignored the burgeoning interests of the Soviet Union in European politics. For Josef Stalin its repudiation of any alteration in the prewar political and territorial status of Eastern Europe—the only region that offered the Soviets any tangible and lasting fruits of victory—rendered it totally unacceptable as a basis of action. That the Soviet Union, unlike both the United States and Britain, suffered incalculable physical destruction and twenty million deaths at the hands of the invading Nazis made inevitable vast disagreements over the applicability of the Atlantic Charter to the territories of Germany and Eastern Europe. While both Britain and the United States recognized that without the continued and unlimited military efforts of the Soviet Union, the West could hardly hope to defeat Germany, the Atlantic Charter assumed that the two Western democracies, even before the United States had formally entered the war, could dominate the postwar settlements in a region that comprised not only the historic territorial objectives of the Russian nation but also the area the Soviet armies might actually occupy.

During the interwar years not only official Washington but also first- and second-generation Americans of East European stock, including more than seven million Polish-Americans, had displayed a negligible interest in the affairs of Eastern Europe. However, when the realization came in 1941 that the future status of Eastern Europe had slipped beyond Western control and hinged on the outcome of the Nazi-Soviet war, a profound revolution occurred in the nation's diplomatic posture, in part a response to the wartime moralism of such men as Roosevelt and Secretary of State Cordell Hull, and in part the product of the growing influence of East European minorities in American politics.

Fighting for their existence, the Russians were in no position to antagonize their Western allies. At the meeting of the Allies in London on 24 September 1941, they accepted the principle of self-determination; but clearly, from its interpretation, the Soviet Union would follow the precepts of the Atlantic Charter only to the extent that they served its security interests. That the immediate military requirements far outweighed the matter of ultimate political intention was illustrated in January 1942, when the Soviet Union and twenty-five other nations signed the United Nations Declaration, the opening paragraph of which accepted the purpose and principles of the Atlantic Charter.

In 1944, as the Allies began to free vast areas of Europe from Nazi control, their political differences could no longer be submerged. As the Russian armies rolled across Eastern Europe, what the United States had denied Stalin earlier by refusing to accede to a spheres of influence agreement now fell to the Soviet Union through rapid military advancement. Yet as late as April 1944 Hull, committed to the Wilsonian vision of self-determination, not only opposed any negotiation of spheres of influ-

ence with the Soviet Union but also promised the American people a postwar world based on the principles of the Atlantic Charter. Whatever security Stalin required along his western boundaries, said Hull, he could obtain through a strong postwar peace organization. When it became clear to Stalin that free governments in such nations as Poland and Rumania would not do his bidding, he employed his military advantage to impose governments friendly to the Soviet Union through the agency of communist puppet regimes. This eliminated the possibility of any serious negotiation on the postwar Soviet frontiers of Eastern Europe. By 1945 the Western powers could no longer assure even limited self-determination for the Slavic peoples of Europe. What remained for the United States was the cruel choice of compromising the principles of the Atlantic Charter or sacrificing the alliance itself.

The principle of self-determination fared considerably better in other areas of the world. In effect, what World War I did for Eastern Europe, World War II accomplished in Asia and Africa. Roosevelt's efforts to implement the concept of self-determination were augmented enormously—indeed, decisively—by the rising tide of nationalism on these continents. Nevertheless, the United States was again beset with the problem of balancing its conflicting interests and its conflicting principles. As Cordell Hull wrote in his memoirs, the prime difficulty generally with regard to Asian colonial possessions was to induce the colonial powers—principally Britain, France, and the Netherlands—to adopt American ideas with regard to dependent peoples. Yet, they could not be pressed too far without jeopardizing the very close cooperation the United States sought with them in Europe. Fortunately for Roosevelt's objectives, the movement for national self-determination in Asia and Africa was greatly accelerated by the quick, total collapse of French resistance to German aggression and the Japanese conquest and "liberation" of European colonial possessions in the Far East.

These events profoundly changed the attitudes of Asian and African masses. Moreover, Roosevelt himself sought to exert a beneficial influence on his allies. For instance, in spite of suggestions that the date for granting full independence in the Philippines should be reconsidered as a consequence of the ravages of war and the cooperation of prominent Filipinos with the Japanese, the United States kept its promise and the islands became independent on 4 July, 1946. Nor did Britain, in its old liberality and realistic wisdom, attempt to restore its Asian empire. From 1947 it brought to fulfillment the work of true liberation that had started throughout the empire even before World War I. France, resenting its humiliation in World War II and seeking to restore old imperial glory, deeply resented Anglo-American accommodation to changing reality. Britain was held responsible for France's loss of Syria and Lebanon, and American greed or innocence— or perhaps a combination of both—was suspected of being behind the national liberation movements in Indochina and North Africa. Yet the American conflict of principles was clearly revealed by the fact that France was able to fight wars in Indochina and Algeria only with the help of American arms and money.

On the other hand, the United Nations Charter reflected both the triumph of Wilson's concept of self-determination and the change in international relations that had occurred during the intervening years. Whereas the Covenant of the League of Nations ultimately deleted all references to the concept of national self-determination, the Charter of the United Nations mentioned it three times. However, the Charter did not insist on independence, but spoke only of self-government. The principle of federation was more promising than that of national independence. What was essential in the democratic traditon—and here the Charter drew largely from Wilsonian thought—was not national independence but self-government, government based upon the consent of the governed, and respect for the equality of the peoples involved.

In the ensuing years, both within and outside the United Nations, the United States continued to face the dilemma of which it became aware during and immediately following World War II. On the one hand, it hesitated to antagonize West European countries whose cooperation was needed in the postwar world. On the other hand, American idealists continued to express their deep-rooted sympathy with any people aspiring to freedom. The problem, however, was exacerbated by the onset of the

Cold War and the American adoption of a policy of containment. Actually, the rationale for the policy developed in the Truman Doctrine drew heavily upon American ideological support of the principle of self-determination. However, the new interpretation changed America's early historic role of merely expressing sympathy to active and official economic and military support of the self-determination of "free peoples" who were "resisting attempted subjugation by armed minorities or by outside pressures." For the first time, President Harry S. Truman officially expressed the view of the necessity of actually assisting "free peoples to work out their own destinies in their own way." Clearly he was advocating an interpretation of international communism as being inimical to the independence of "free peoples" everywhere. From this point on, official American policy held that international communism violated the principle of self-determination and was irreconcilable with the right of each state to develop its own political, economic, and cultural life.

The official pursuit of anticommunism raised pertinent questions concerning the nature and use of America's commitment to self-determination. For example, in the Western Hemisphere the Monroe Doctrine had been used by the United States to bar undesirable outside influence while securing the dominance of its own influence. Within ten years after World War II, the Monroe Doctrine, extended, supplemented, and reinterpreted by the Inter-American Treaty of Reciprocal Assistance (Rio Treaty) in 1947 and the Declaration of Caracas in 1954, gave the United States a claim to keep communism, now clearly accepted as incompatible with the concept of self-determination, out of the American states. In furtherance of this policy the United States intervened in Guatemala in 1954 and was instrumental in unseating the incumbent government. The invasion of Cuba at the Bay of Pigs in 1961 was an abortive attempt to unseat the socialist and populist government of Fidel Castro. When disturbance broke out in the Dominican Republic in 1965, the United States intervened, purportedly to protect its nationals, but later extended its action to include the occupation of the capital, Santo Domingo. President Lyndon Johnson justified such a policy on 2 May 1965 by indicating his view that what had begun as a popular revolution committed to democracy and social justice had fallen into "the hands of a band of communist conspirators."

In Asia, Africa, and the Middle East, the United States adopted a somewhat similar stance. The triumph of communism in China, the Korean War, McCarthyism in the United States, and the moral principles enunciated by John Foster Dulles, Dwight D. Eisenhower's secretary of state, enormously enhanced this position. Thus, the recognition that communism itself was a basic threat to the self-determination of virtually any nation, as well as a threat to the American way of life, led the United States to support almost any "anti-communist regime" or to associate itself with traditional regimes whose days were numbered because they had alienated mass support: Bao Dai and Ngo Dinh Diem in Indochina and King Faisal in Iraq were only three such examples. The fact that these countries' governments were pro-American and anticommunist qualified them in American eyes as "democratic," or at least potentially so; by the same token, the United States opposed internal movements to overthrow them and condemned these as communist or procommunist. Moreover, such policies were implemented and elaborated by the formation of pacts like the Southeast Asia Treaty Organization (SEATO) in 1954 and proposals like the Eisenhower Doctrine in 1957. Such a response was typical of the apparent inability of the United States to understand the unique social and political nature of the struggles for self-determination of Asia and the Middle East. In the attempt to contain communism and thus maintain its new concept of self-determination, the United States became committed to the domestic, social, and political status quo not only in these countries but throughout the world. Thus the United States, in seeking stability and the implementation of its now-distorted concept of self-determination, was paradoxically supporting ramshackle autocracies that were unrepresentative of their peoples' aspirations.

Nowhere did such a policy ultimately come to be regarded by the American public as more bankrupt than in Vietnam. When France was driven from Indochina by the communist forces of Ho Chi Minh in 1954, the United States established a noncommunist regime in South Vietnam in the hope of confining communism to the northern half of Vietnam. The objective was not only to help "free people" maintain their independence but also to save neighboring regimes from communist subversion. It was assumed that if one country fell, all the others in the area would topple in rapid order, like a row of upright dominoes. Communism would dominate all Southeast Asia, and be in a position to threaten the Indian subcontinent. American secretaries of state from John Foster Dulles to William P. Rogers offered the American public this rationalization for American involvement in Vietnam. By 1967 the weakness of the Saigon government and the military success of the Vietcong had led the American government to commit a military force of 550,000 soldiers and a budget of roughly $24 billion. But as President Johnson escalated the war and the costs and casualties mounted, public criticism reached a level that made the Vietnam conflict the most unpopular war in American history. Such criticisms ultimately led to President Johnson's decision to announce a halt in bombing north of the seventeenth parallel and to state that he would not be a candidate in the 1968 presidential election. Among the arguments used to oppose the war was the charge that not only had the United States betrayed its own revolutionary traditions by becoming the aggressor in a civil war between peoples of the same linguistic background who resented foreign interference, but it was also violating the Wilsonian principle of self-determination by conniving at the flouting of the Geneva Agreement of 1954, which had stipulated that general elections to unify the country be held in Vietnam in July 1956 under the supervision of the International Control Commission.

In the 1970's, as criticism of the war continued to mount, and particularly after President Richard Nixon authorized ill-starred incursions into Cambodia and Laos, serious peace negotiations, begun by Secretary of State Henry Kissinger, resulted in the signing of cease-fire agreements on 27 January 1973. The military collapse of South Vietnam in 1975, combined with the serious pursuit of détente with both the Soviet Union and the People's Republic of China by the administrations of both Nixon and Gerald R. Ford, appeared to offer the possibility not only of a redefinition of the American concept of self-determination but also of a modified implementation of the doctrine of intervention as a means of supporting it.

Yet it must be noted that throughout this period, Washington continued to oppose self-determination movements that appeared to favor any communist cause. This could be clearly seen in even the most cursory review of American policies in south Asia, Chile, and southern Africa.

On 9 August 1971, some three weeks after President Nixon had announced his visit to Peking in an effort to normalize relations, the Soviets signed a twenty-year treaty of friendship (and quasi alliance) with India. The Indians feared another crushing onslaught from the bordering Chinese (as in 1962), while the Soviets were evidently eager to clasp hands with India against an increasingly menacing China. Although India and Pakistan had been enemies since the partition of British India in 1947, the United States had been supplying arms to the Pakistanis. Pakistan was an American ally in SEATO and an associate with the United States in the Central Treaty Organization (CENTO), which was designed to "contain" the Soviet Union.

This unpromising Asiatic pot came to a furious boil in March 1971, when populous East Pakistan, separated by more than a thousand miles from West Pakistan, formally rebelled against alleged mistreatment by West Pakistan overlords. The secessionists officially proclaimed the independent state of Bangladesh. The West Pakistan army with alleged genocidal intent undertook to crush the uprising with full scale butchery, rape, and pillage. An estimated nine million destitute refugees began to pour across borders into already over-populated and underfed India. In November 1971, responding to protests from India, Washington cancelled further shipments of arms to Pakistan. Then, early in December, India, after declaring war on Pakistan, proceeded to invade and free Bangladesh in a mercifully short clash of fifteen days. The United States, supporting the losing side, emerged from the episode looking rather foolish. Evidently seeking to counter a reported So-

viet naval presence in the Indian Ocean and to display sympathy for its Pakistani ally, Washington had hastily dispatched a powerful naval task force to the Indian Ocean. The transparent explanation given at the time was the necessity of evacuating a handful of American citizens most of whom had already left Bangladesh. This futile exhibition of old-fashioned "show the flag" gunboat diplomacy, with its "tilt toward Pakistan," probably gratified pro-Pakistan China but pleased neither the Soviets, the Indians, nor even the Pakistanis. Relations with India became frigid, especially after Washington suspended $87.6 million in development loans, charging that India, already the beneficiary of some $9 billion in American aid, was the "main aggressor" in the conflict. Nearly a year later, in November 1972, Pakistan withdrew from the SEATO alliance and in other ways indicated alienation from the United States. Thus, Bangladesh was born—a satellite of India, famine-ridden, and impoverished.

In the meantime, leftist trends in Chile, once a foremost democracy, had become especially worrisome to Washington. A left-wing coalition that accused American copper mining and other interests of "milking" the country won control in 1970 by electing to the presidency Salvador Allende Gossens, a home-grown Marxist. Certainly as the first avowed Marxist to win a free election in the hemisphere, Allende posed an unusual problem to the United States. The dilemma intensified when he nationalized nearly $1 billion of American investment, opened diplomatic relations with the government of Fidel Castro, and signed a trade agreement with the Soviet Union. The United States retaliated by refusing to help Chile with trade or developmental programs. American banks and the Export-Import Bank cut credit. President Nixon secretly ordered the Central Intelligence Agency to follow a "get rougher" policy that encouraged anti-Allende demonstrations by middle-class Chileans. Kissinger wholeheartedly approved, in part because he was afraid that a successful radical left coalition might have contagious effects not only in Latin America but also in France and Italy. It was his own version of the "domino theory."

Allende's inability to stop a rapid economic deterioration brought attacks from both con-

647

servatives and ultraleftists. In the autumn of 1973, a coup by army officers resulted in Allende's death and a new conservative government. The United States quickly reopened its aid program; some property taken from American corporations was returned or paid for; and when the American ambassador protested the army's repression, which included torturing and imprisoning thousands of political opponents, Kissinger angrily told the ambassador "to cut out the political science lectures." By 1975 there was no longer any doubt that the United States had played a role in overthrowing the Allende government in Chile in 1973 and replacing it with a military junta.

For many Americans the most alarming collapse occurred in Vietnam. The Paris accords, which Kissinger negotiated in early 1973 with North Vietnam and South Vietnam, had never worked. The pact promised discussions leading to reunification "without coercion or annexation by either party." However, by late 1973, both sides were engaged in what amounted to a total war. The South Vietnamese lost more soldiers in 1974 than in 1965, 1966, or 1967. At the same time, a depression-ridden United States cut back its aid from over $1 billion to $700 million. By early 1975, President Nguyen Van Thieu, forced to surrender two-thirds of the country, prepared to defend Saigon and called for President Ford to provide the American "full force" promised by President Nixon in 1973. No significant help arrived. In late 1973, Congress had prohibited the reintroduction of any American forces in Vietnam. Nixon's 1973 promise was of no effect for he and Kissinger did not make the promise public, while Congress never acted to make it a national commitment. In April 1974, South Vietnam fell into communist hands. The thirty-year war was over. The war had clearly demonstrated that American efforts to impose self-determination military style in Southeast Asia were confessions of political and economic failure.

American policy in Africa, although not so heavily involved, followed the same pattern. The dominant element since 1946 had been opposition to communism and to the communist powers. As far as Africa was concerned, responsibility for pursuing these objectives was delegated to America's trusted allies—Britain, France, Belgium, and even Portugal—whose policies in the area were therefore broadly supported despite minor disagreements that arose as American business became interested in Africa's potential. Inevitably this placed the United States in opposition to an Africa seeking to win its independence from those same powers; but when political freedom could be achieved peacefully, the United States was able to appear to Africa like a bystander. The United States was therefore able to adjust its policies and accept the new status of African sovereign states without any difficulty. Notwithstanding these adjustments, America continued to look at African affairs largely through anticommunist spectacles and to disregard Africa's different concerns and priorities.

In southern Africa, events did not force any readjustments of American policies during the 1960's, so none were made. Practical support for the status quo continued unabated until after the Portuguese revolution in April 1974. Thus, despite America's verbal criticism of Portuguese colonialism, American arms and equipment were used by Portugal in its military operations in Angola, Guinea-Bissau, and Mozambique. Despite the verbal opposition to apartheid, American trade and investment in South Africa were expanded, and the United States opposed any effective United Nations demonstration of hostility toward the apartheid state. The United States had also fought a hard and largely successful rearguard action against the demands for international intervention against South Africa's occupation of Namibia (South-West Africa). In Rhodesia, the United States had trailed behind British policies, weakened the sanctions policies it had endorsed at the United Nations, and criticized black African regimes for the vehemence of their opposition to the minority Ian Smith regime.

This general approach to African questions, and particularly to southern Africa, culminated in the American government's support for the Frente Nacional de Libertacao de Angola/Uniao Nacional para a Independencia Total de Angola (FNLA/UNITA) forces in the dispute between the Angolan nationalist movements. Throughout the anticolonial war in Angola (1960–1974), the United States had supported

NATIONAL SELF-DETERMINATION

Portugal, not any of the nationalist forces. Supplying the FNLA with money and military and other equipment while decolonization was taking place was thus a rather blatant attempt to place "friends" in political power in the new state. Not surprisingly, it was the least effective of the contending nationalist groups that was open to this kind of purchase; success therefore depended upon the quick collapse of the Movimento Popular de Libertação de Angola (MPLA), which was under assault. But the MPLA did not collapse. Instead, it asked for and received more arms from its supporters to meet the simultaneous South African invasion of Angola (1975). The MPLA also welcomed Cuban troops. When the FNLA demanded more help than the American administration alone would give it, the United States Congress—with the lessons of Vietnam still fresh in its mind—refused its support.

It is not cynicism that attributes the beginning of the "Kissinger initiative" in April 1976 partly to this experience. Nations, like people, sometimes need to be shaken out of habitual modes of thought. Nor was the Angolan debacle the only factor leading toward a reassessment of traditional United States policies in southern Africa. Some Americans had long been urging support for the anticolonial struggle, and American blacks were beginning to take a greater interest in these matters. Further, trade with independent Africa had been growing and now included oil from Nigeria. The possibility that this trade might be jeopardized by pro-South African actions was no longer of merely academic interest to the United States. Moreover, the guerrilla war in Rhodesia was intensified after mid-1975, arousing fears of a repetition of the Angolan experience.

Black Africa welcomed the Lusaka statement by Kissinger that majority rule must precede independence in Rhodesia, and that the United States would give no material or diplomatic support to the Ian Smith regime in its conflict with the African states or the African liberation movements. With some hesitation, Africa also cooperated with the Kissinger "shuttle diplomacy" later in the year. For Africa hoped that "even at that late stage, the use of American power in support of majority rule could enable this to be attained in Rhodesia without further bloodshed."

The "Kissinger initiative" did force Ian Smith to shift his ground, but it did not succeed in its declared objective. Neither did it remove African uncertainty about the depth and the geographical limitations of the new American commitment to change in southern Africa. History cannot be wiped out by one speech and a few months of highly individualistic one-man diplomacy.

With the election of President James E. Carter and a new administration, the need to respect human rights became a focus of public attention and debate. Such a development was clearly a reflection of rising popular expectations, which in some cases had led to a growing tension between governments and the governed. There had been a worldwide trend to assert individual and collective aspirations and to bring about changes in governmental processes at all levels in order to make them more responsive to these aspirations. This trend appeared in many forms—from movements of national independence to devolution and demands for worker codetermination. In the United States, a growing interest in the "human dimension" of world politics was seen by many as a natural and healthy reaction to an overemphasis on great power diplomacy, to elitist cynicism, and to excessive secretiveness during the recent past. The articulate stand adopted by the new administration on the question of human rights implied a distinct departure from the position of the preceding administration. This advocacy of respect for human rights and fundamental freedoms in the widest sense had an important implication for national self-determination. First and foremost, it implied an insistence on effective guarantees to safeguard the position of the individual citizen in the society to which he belongs and particularly to protect him against infringement of basic civil rights and liberties, such as freedom of expression, freedom of assembly, and freedom of movement—liberties that are inscribed in practically all modern constitutions, including those of the Soviet Union and the East European countries. Second, to champion human rights involved supporting a long-established principle of international relations, reconfirmed in the final act of the Conference on Security and Cooperation in Europe (CSCE); this so-called Helsinki Agreement recognizes the collective rights of peoples to self-determination and equal status in the international community.

In the ensuing months the Carter administration demonstrated its commitment to human rights and self-determination by seeking to re-establish normal relations with both Cuba and Vietnam, and withdrawing its opposition to Vietnamese membership in the United Nations. While reiterating a continued deep American commitment to Israel, President Carter also indicated sympathy for the nationalist goals of the Palestine Liberation Organization (PLO), if not for an independent state, at least for a separate homeland, perhaps in Jordan. In one of its first acts, the Carter administration moved to comply with United Nations sanctions against Rhodesia and achieved repeal of the Byrd Amendment, which had placed the United States in violation of those sanctions and thus in violation of international law. At the same time it supported additional diplomatic efforts within the United Nations to promote basic civil and political rights in Namibia and throughout southern Africa. In his inaugural address, President Carter had said, "Because we are free, we can never be indifferent to the fate of freedom elsewhere." At the very least, there was now the hope that the United States would no longer use its power and prestige to hinder movements for national self-determination throughout the world.

BIBLIOGRAPHY

Thomas A. Bailey, *Woodrow Wilson and the Lost Peace* (New York, 1944), contains a scholarly analysis of the implementation of Wilson's concept of self-determination. Walworth Barbour, "The Concept of Self-Determination in American Thought," in *Department of State Bulletin,* 31 (1954), presents an official view. Sir Ernest Barker, *National Character and the Factors in Its Formation* (London, 1948), is a classic work. Paul Birdsall, *Versailles Twenty Years Afterwards* (Hamden, Conn., 1941), presents a "realistic" view of Wilson's efforts to implement the concept of self-determination at the Paris Peace Conference. Alfred Cobban, *The National State and National Self-Determination* (New York, 1969), presents the most nearly definitive history and political analysis of the general concept of national self-determination by means of a pragmatic approach. Paul Diesing, "National Self-Determination and U.S. Foreign Policy," in *Ethics,* 77 (1967), is a provocative ethical analysis. Clyde Eagleton, "The Excesses of Self-Determination," in *Foreign Affairs,* 31 (1953), is an excellent analysis of problems presented by the attempt to apply the concept of self-determination in the post–World War II period. Rupert Emerson, *Self-Determination Revisited in the Era of Decolonization* (Cambridge, Mass., 1964), a good synthesis, contains a fresh examination in a new nation-forming setting. Louis L. Gerson, *The Hyphenate in Recent American Politics and Diplomacy* (Lawrence, Kans., 1964), is especially helpful on the role of East European hyphenates in promoting self-determination during the Wilson and Roosevelt administrations. Philip C. Jessup, "Self-Determination Today in Principle and in Practice," in *Virginia Quarterly Review,* 33 (1957), is an evaluation by a first-rate scholar of international law. Harold S. Johnson, *Self-Determination Within the Community of Nations* (Leiden, Netherlands, 1967), presents a careful analysis of conflicting interpretations of the great powers. Robert Lansing, *The Peace Negotiations: A Personal Narrative* (Boston–New York, 1921), is important for an understanding of Lansing's criticisms of national self-determination. Arthur S. Link, *Wilson the Diplomatist: A Look at His Major Foreign Policies* (Chicago, 1965), is necessary for an appreciation of how Wilson's principles influenced his foreign policy. Arthur J. May, *Contemporary American Opinion of the Mid-Century Revolutions in Central Europe* (Philadelphia, 1927), is essential for the mid-nineteenth-century outlook. Arno J. Mayer, *Politics and Diplomacy of Peace Making, 1918–1919* (New York, 1967), provides vital background for the Wilsonian position. Robert E. Sherwood, *Roosevelt and Hopkins: An Intimate History* (New York, 1950), presents a glimpse of Roosevelt's efforts to secure support for self-determination from both Churchill and Stalin. Muhammad Aziz Shukri, *The Concept of Self-Determination in the United Nations* (Damascus, Syria, 1965), is a scholarly study analyzing attitudes of major powers. Umozurike Oji Umozurike, *Self-Determination in International Law* (Hamden, Conn., 1972), is the most recent scholarly analysis with emphasis on historical background. Sarah Wambaugh, *A Monograph on Plebiscites With a Collection of Official Documents* (New York, 1920), is a classic work with an excellent introductory chapter on self-determination. Sarah Wambaugh, *Plebiscites Since the World War With a Collection of Official Documents* (Washington, D.C., 1933), has a first chapter that presents a historical summary of self-determination covering the years 1914–1933.

[See also ANTI-IMPERIALISM; THE COLD WAR; CONTAINMENT; THE EISENHOWER DOCTRINE; THE FOURTEEN POINTS; IDEOLOGY AND FOREIGN POLICY; INTERNATIONAL ORGANIZATION; INTERVENTION AND NONINTERVENTION; MANIFEST DESTINY; PROTECTORATES AND SPHERES OF INFLUENCE; SANCTIONS; THE TRUMAN DOCTRINE.]

NATIVISM

Geoffrey S. Smith

DEFINED by historian John Higham as "intense opposition to an internal minority on the grounds of its foreign connections," nativism has appeared in three basic forms in American history. The first form, anti-Catholicism, emerged during the colonial period and reflected traditions of Reformation Protestantism, stimulated by American fears of Spanish and French threats in the New World. In the nineteenth and twentieth centuries, anti-Catholic nativism mirrored intricate economic, social, and religious rancor against immigrants. A second form, the fear of alien radicalism, appeared during the 1790's when the wars of the French Revolution embroiled the United States and menaced the republican experiment. A third manifestation developed during the 1840's as citizens celebrated their "manifest destiny" to expand territorially to the Pacific. Strengthened by "scientific" analyses after 1860, the cult of Anglo-Saxon superiority influenced American imperialism and became the major weapon in the drive to restrict immigration.

Historians explain nativism in two ways. One approach, exemplified in the scholarship of Higham, focuses upon actual, face-to-face conflicts and tensions between aliens and native ethnic groups and between early and subsequent immigrants. Emphasizing the newcomers' battle for social and economic advancement in a competitive, individualist, Protestant culture, Higham concentrates on organized nativist movements, the realities behind nativist stereotypes, and the social setting in which nativists have achieved success.

Other intellectual historians argue that such a sociological emphasis tends to reduce nativist bigotry to mechanistic terms, missing the psychological and ideological functions of nativism and its importance as a clue to underlying tensions within American culture. Richard Hofstadter and David Brion Davis define nativism more broadly than Higham. They describe the phenomenon as a state of mind of native-born and naturalized citizens seeking to define their own Americanness by condemning real and alleged alien challenges to national values and institutions. For these historians nativism denotes the ideology of persecuting groups, and minority targets generally are portrayed as victims.

Although manifesting itself primarily in varied forms of domestic intolerance, nativism has affected, and been affected by, American foreign policy. Although hostility toward immigrants and alien influences has diverted attention from national problems and their sources, nativist stereotypes and images have also hindered the effective formulation and implementation of foreign policy. On several occasions nativist attempts to legitimize selfish interests by identifying them with the nation's interests have provoked crises involving the federal government. More important, by encouraging a distaste for the European concept of power politics, nativism has contributed to the provinciality of America's historic self-image of innocence in a decadent world. Therefore, the study of nativist ethnocentrism provides clues that can aid historians in clarifying the interplay between domestic issues and foreign relations. These clues help to explain the persistence of moralism and rigidity in American diplomacy and to assess the degree to which emotional responses by Americans have threatened to subvert the nation's interest at critical junctures.

With the exception of the immigration acts

of 1921 and 1924, optimistic tendencies within American nationalism have usually prevented nativism from becoming federal policy. In several instances, however, nativists have garnered sufficient power to affect the nation's course. The Alien and Sedition Laws sought to stifle Jeffersonian dissent against Federalist foreign policy during the Quasi-War with France (1798–1800); but when President John Adams negotiated for peace, the legislation boomeranged, split the Federalist party, and contributed to Thomas Jefferson's election in 1800. During the 1850's the American, or Know-Nothing, party hastened the disintegration of the national political system by offering citizens a way to avoid confronting the greatest sectional crisis the United States had known. In the late nineteenth century, nativism exacerbated many social and economic problems generated by industrial capitalism. Finally, World War I unleashed a campaign of brutal repression against German-Americans and foreign- and native-born Bolsheviks, socialists, anarchists, and pacifists. Wartime intolerance did not cease with the Treaty of Versailles. Xenophobia persisted through the 1920's, influencing government attitudes toward international cooperation, immigration, and relations with the Soviet Union.

Before independence nativism was informal and cultural, shaped by the identities and attitudes of European settlers, whose roots ran far back into the traditions of Western civilization. The winning of independence confronted Americans with the need to define their own national identity. Conditioned by their experience as British subjects, the Founding Fathers feared centralized power and believed that the ship of state faced the danger of being swamped in a sea of monarchy and despotism. With unity an essential requirement of national survival, many citizens understandably opposed European immigration. Jefferson believed that the United States exhibited "the freest principles of the English Constitution, with others derived from natural right and natural reason." Like many Americans, Jefferson expressed fear lest immigrants "warp and bias" the direction of the nation by rendering it "a heterogeneous, incoherent, distracted mass." Ironically, although his fears were realized during the 1790's, by the end of the decade the

newcomers whom he had suspected had become Jefferson's staunchest allies.

The first organized expression of political nativism occurred in 1798, while the John Adams administration conducted an undeclared naval war against France. The urgency of Federalist hostility toward both France and Jefferson's Democratic-Republicans stemmed from the interaction of foreign and domestic issues following the French Revolution of 1789. The European conflict reverberated in George Washington's cabinet. Influenced by Secretary of the Treasury Alexander Hamilton, an ardent Anglophile, the president rejected any policy that might provoke Britain. Washington's diplomacy aided the British and opened a gap between Hamilton and Secretary of State Jefferson, a partisan of France. This schism reflected a broader political division within the new nation, a divergence that according to leading Federalists threatened to introduce the corruption that had plagued Europe for centuries.

Nevertheless, the fear of immigrants as a source of faction and corruption affected both emerging political parties in the mid-1790's. The Naturalization Act of 1795 was a bipartisan document that required aliens to renounce earlier allegiances and disavow titles of nobility. But Washington's Federalists, men of orthodox social and religious attitudes who were united by their aristocratic demeanor and pessimistic view of human nature, evinced increasing concern that incoming United Irishmen, British radicals, and French émigrés would spread sedition and "Jacobinism" among the populace.

This fear reflected French endeavors to defeat Jay's Treaty in 1794 and to influence the election of 1796 in Jefferson's favor. Moreover, the attachment of many immigrants to the opposition heightened Federalist anxieties. Republican militia units and Democratic-Republican societies in New York and eastern Pennsylvania included recent Irish and Scots-Irish arrivals. These immigrants had participated in the Whiskey Rebellion of 1794 and led opposition to Jay's Treaty. Immigrant opposition to Federalist policies thus appeared to be connected with the intrigue of French agents. Dissent, a symptom of factionalism, had frightened the framers of the Constitution, who considered faction the chief enemy of Republican virtue. Factionalism ostensibly wrecked the Articles of Confederation and now made the nation vulnerable to external enemies.

Washington warned of this possibility in his Farewell Address, but seemingly to no avail. By 1798 national leaders had only to look at the lessons of classical antiquity to feel that the United States had begun to decline. Divisive issues having stimulated the lust for power in Federalists and Democratic-Republicans alike, politics now reflected "a complete distrust of the motives and integrity, the honesty and intentions of one's political opponents."

The notorious XYZ affair and subsequent naval hostilities with France presented the Federalists with an opportunity to utilize their control of foreign policy "to crush internal opposition in the name of national security." Embracing the undeclared war as a means to strengthen their own power, Federalist hawks sought to establish an army and navy, to create arsenals, and to abrogate the treaties of 1778. While the more moderate wing of the Federalist party supported Adams' hope of achieving a diplomatic solution to the crisis, "high" Federalist ambitions soared. Amid reports of a pending French invasion, the hawks called upon Adams to declare war. The president did not accede to this demand; but by linking his political opponents with France, he too contributed to an outburst of nativism that momentarily diverted the Federalists from serving the national interest.

The Quasi-War generated widespread fear within Federalist circles that French spies and their internal collaborators endangered national security. Congressman Harrison Gray Otis railed against "wild Irishmen" and "the turbulent and disorderly of all parts of the world," who came to the United States "with a view to disturb our own tranquility after having succeeded in the overthrow of their own governments." David Tappan, Hollis professor of divinity at Harvard, warned graduating seniors against impending world revolution. Congregationalist minister Jedidiah Morse called attention to the machinations of the "Bavarian Illuminati," a cabal of radical atheists who already had initiated a plan to subvert American schools and churches.

Federalist fears of subversion facilitated con-gressional passage of the Alien and Sedition Laws. According to most historians, this legislation was clearly political, constituting an attempt to destroy the Democratic-Republicans and force internal conformity to Federalist policies. Seeking to quell domestic dissension rather than to repel an external danger, the Alien and Sedition Laws questioned the political role of immigrants in American life. The Naturalization Act (1798) raised from five to fourteen years the period of residency required for citizenship. The Alien Friends Act (1798) empowered Adams to expel aliens suspected of activities deemed "dangerous to the peace and safety of the United States." The Act for the Punishment of Certain Crimes, commonly known as the Sedition Act (1798), provided fines and imprisonment for aliens and citizens who engaged in rioting, unlawful assembly, or hindering the operation of government. The Sedition Act was not directed exclusively against immigrants. Based on the premise that war would be declared, the law would expire on the last day of Adams' term and was intended to gag political criticism.

For the first time, American political leaders had defined the limits of dissent in a representative government. With no tradition of civil liberties to guide them, the Federalists naturally turned to English history to justify themselves. Assuming that government was the master and not the servant of the people, Federalist lawmakers cited the seventeenth-century concept of seditious libel to defend the Sedition Act. Any criticism of government was illegal, they argued, because it subverted the authority and dignity of rulers. Politics was not a popular right; it belonged "to the few, the rich, and the well-born."

Federalists thus identified their administration with government, and government with the Constitution. This analysis led them to conclude that Democratic-Republican criticism constituted an attempt to undermine the Constitution and overturn the government. Jeffersonian editors and publicists soon appreciated this point. With Federalist courts presuming that opposition writers were guilty unless they proved their innocence, published criticism of elected officials became synonymous with conviction. As Jeffersonians steadfastly opposed Adams' call for an accelerated defense program, Federalist judges and juries stepped up their harassment. The Democratic-Republican argument that the Sedition Act allowed the Adams administration to escape accountability for its actions had no immediate effect, other than the indictment of *Philadelphia Aurora* editor William Duane, and the incarceration of Scots pamphleteer James T. Callender, the Irish-born Vermont congressman Matthew Lyon, and Pennsylvania editor Thomas Cooper.

Adams withstood Federalist hawks and dispatched William Vans Murray, the American minister at The Hague, to France, where he signed the Treaty of Mortefontaine ending the naval conflict and abrogating the treaties of 1778. With many "high" Federalists no longer supporting him, the president acted courageously in seeking peace. But Adams' action and the nativist program of 1798, a cornerstone of "high" Federalist foreign policy, split the party irreparably. As Federalists sought evidence of Jacobinism and the Illuminati, the Jeffersonians constructed an efficient political machine.

Democratic-Republican editors continued to attack President Adams. Jefferson and James Madison drafted the Kentucky and Virginia resolutions, condemning the administration's violation of individual and states' rights; and the malevolence toward the Federalist party harbored by immigrant groups became implacable. The immigrant vote may not have been crucial in the election of 1800, but Federalist nativism moved numerous Pennsylvania Germans, New York French, and Irish and Scots-Irish into Jefferson's camp.

Jefferson's victory elevated the First Amendment to the Constitution above the English common-law doctrine of seditious libel. The election of 1800 also signaled the political maturity of American immigrants and underlined the importance of public opinion in the young republic by legitimating dissent. The new president symbolized the people's right "to think freely and to speak and write what they think."

Although the Federalist party was now moribund on the national level, the New England nativist impulse remained strong. During the War of 1812, commercial interests gathered to express dissatisfaction with the economic effects of the conflict. Delegates to the Hartford Convention (1814–1815)—erstwhile protectors

of the nation against French intrigue—now found themselves a nearly powerless minority. Their unhappiness with the direction of national affairs, combined with the desire to recapture the homogeneous culture of an earlier time, figured prominently in the convention's declaration that European monarchs were dumping paupers on American shores, and in its proposed constitutional amendment excluding naturalized citizens from serving in Congress or holding civil office.

The Federalists sought to protect the nation (and their own political fortunes) against revolution by muzzling dissent and eliminating immigrant radicals. During the period before the Civil War, nativism became more complex, drawing its inspiration from a variety of sources. Antebellum xenophobes expressed a need for consensus at a time when rapid, constant, often bewildering change appeared to threaten "the old landmarks of Christendom and the glorious common law of the Fathers." A lack of institutional authorities and standards strengthened the ensuing drive for common ideological unity. The very diversity of the Jacksonian era—with its myriad religious sects, faddist groups, and voluntary organizations —implied divisiveness and generated fears for national unity. Nativists took up the battle against autonomous groups that combined secrecy with a demand for complete loyalty. Such organizations as the Church of Jesus Christ of Latter-Day Saints, the Masonic Order, and the Roman Catholic Church impressed many native Americans as the antithesis of the ideals of Jacksonian democracy. In this era of "Pax Britannica," nativism provided citizens with a series of fabricated crises—moral equivalents of war—that allowed patriots to rebuff undemocratic enemies and thus uphold the just authority and legitimacy of American institutions.

Expressing clearly the transition nativism underwent between Federalist and Jacksonian America, anti-Catholicism transferred the battle for democracy from the level of intellectual combat to parochial politics and mob violence, "where every son of liberty could strike his blow for righteousness." The Adams-Onís Treaty of 1819, concluded between John Quincy Adams and the Spanish minister Luis de Onís, struck such a symbolic blow. In addition to extending American territorial claims to the Pacific, the treaty "liberated" a huge expanse of territory from a Catholic state. In 1823 James Monroe warned the Quadruple Alliance not to intervene in the affairs of the newly emerging Latin American republics. Monroe's "doctrine" was, of course, upheld by British sea power; but some Americans believed that European despots might yet attempt to reassert their power in the Western Hemisphere.

Samuel F. B. Morse, artist and inventor, reflected upon this possibility during a trip to Europe, and in 1834 he wrote of a Catholic plot to undermine democracy. Criticizing the complacency of his fellow citizens, Morse's *Foreign Conspiracy Against the Liberties of the United States* pictured the Leopold Association, a missionary society aiding American bishops in the Mississippi Valley, as the entering wedge through which Metternich, the Austrian statesman, and Nicholas I of Russia would gain control. A year later, fellow New Englander Lyman Beecher published *A Plea for the West.* A prominent minister who had become president of Lane Theological Seminary in Cincinnati, Beecher stressed the mission of the United States to evangelize the American west and emancipate the world. This task carried an awesome responsibility. Either the west would be Christianized in the image of Protestant orthodoxy or the area would be captured by an institution that destroyed freedom of thought, cloaked its atheism behind false symbols of religiosity, produced revolution wherever it appeared, and knew no limits in its quest for power and riches. If Catholicism were not checked, Beecher averred, the republican experiment would expire in a wasteland of infidelity and ignorance.

These warnings carried expansionist connotations, reflecting the concern of native Americans, especially New Englanders, who felt that the orthodox Protestant establishment had begun to deteriorate. Even more alarming was the influx of Irish and other Catholic immigrants that threatened to adulterate Protestant culture and to impede the nation's mission to save both the west and the world. The immigration of the 1830's and 1840's suggested to some Americans that Europe's leaders hoped to extinguish the light whose very brilliance endangered their own despotic regimes. These

tyrants might not be able to launch navies across the Atlantic, but they could send their illiterate, destitute, and criminal elements.

Presumably, anti-Catholicism should have figured prominently in the Mexican War (1846–1848); that it did not underlines the peripheral relationship between nativism and foreign policy at this juncture. For several reasons Protestant nativists proved unable to transform the conflict into a militant elimination of Catholicism. Some southern denominations did warn that unless Mexico was crushed the "yoke of papal oppression would be placed upon every state of the Republic." But the absence of a unified anti-Catholic base was manifest in the existence of numerous Protestant enemies, most notably war and slavery. War, according to a writer in the *Boston Christian Examiner,* would unleash "the worst passions of the human heart and the worst memories of human experience." Many northern Protestants already sensed a threat posed by an aggressive, slave-power conspiracy to extend the peculiar institution into the western territories. Human bondage was a more immediate threat than Rome.

In addition, the very forces of change that had so alarmed Beecher and Morse had softened Protestantism, secularizing it and stretching its basic tenets. Most Americans, in fact, rejected attempts to link Mexico with the Catholic menace. For example, midwestern Protestants harbored few uncertainties about the durability of their civilization. Mexican culture was primitive and impotent, and Mexican armies obviously posed no danger to national security. The historic Catholic culture of the Mississippi Valley would not impede American expansion to the Pacific.

Nativist violence against Catholic immigrants nevertheless checkered the 1830's and 1840's, agitating Boston, Philadelphia, Brooklyn, and numerous other cities. Anti-Catholic hostility centered upon such issues as trusteeship and the correct version of the Bible to be used in public schools, rivalry in the labor market, and the alleged role of immigrants in corrupting politics by serving unscrupulous municipal bosses. These problems were accompanied by the nativist accusation that England was ridding itself of "poor, vicious, and degraded Irishmen," thus creating critical dilemmas of crime control and poor relief, and threatening to destroy national economic foundations.

Anti-Catholicism constituted the dominant theme in antebellum nativism but was not synonymous with it. Nativists also opposed non-Catholic immigrants or native Americans whose religious tenets or sociopolitical affiliations challenged dominant national ideals or established power structures. In addition, numerous immigrant groups, including Scots-Irish Presbyterians in Philadelphia and German radicals in the Ohio Valley, joined the Protestant crusade, as did many native-born Catholics. Then too, Roman Catholic Bishop John J. Hughes of New York excoriated the radicalism of Hungarian patriot Louis Kossuth, while Boston Irish-Catholics denounced German "Forty-eighters" as "red" republicans, anarchists, and defamers of the Sabbath.

The presence of three foreign visitors during the early 1850's sharpened controversy over the relationship between political refugees and the traditional American concept of asylum, especially when each visitor challenged American neutrality and isolation by calling for a policy of intervention to liberate suppressed nationalities in Europe. Not surprisingly, the arrival of Kossuth, "Father" Alessandro Gavazzi, and Monsignor Gaetano Bedini stimulated nativist hostility toward German radicals and Irish nationalists who hoped to engage the United States in freeing their homelands from despotism.

Kossuth had led an abortive uprising against Austria in 1848, and as a guest of the United States Senate had been lionized by many citizens who saw in him an example of America's own revolutionary spirit. The Hungarian nationalist became an issue in politics late in 1851 when he charged that his American opponents, including Bishop Hughes, acted in the service of European tyranny. Then, denying that he opposed all Catholics, Kossuth cautioned against the historical ambition of the Jesuits to rule the world. More important, Kossuth attempted to secure material aid to renew Hungary's battle against the Hapsburg Empire. Ignoring American aversion to European politics, he struck nativists as a revolutionary who might upset the delicate balance between the means and ends of American foreign policy. Democratic party leaders, who might have

aided Kossuth, did not embrace his cause. By 1852 the Whig party had split along sectional lines as a result of the slavery controversy, and Kossuth consequently failed to enlist political support.

Gavazzi and Bedini arrived in the United States in early 1853 and quickly engaged in a contretemps that appeared to transfer the battle over Italian unification to the United States. "Father" Gavazzi, an apostate monk, participated in the Italian uprising of 1848, while Monsignor Bedini, representing the Pope on his American visit, staunchly opposed Italian unification. When the nationalistic Gavazzi accused Bedini of leading papal forces at the Battle of Bologna, what had been a pleasant journey for the papal nuncio turned into a nightmare as hostile crowds greeted him at every stop.

Kossuth's visit and Gavazzi's denunciation of Bedini strengthened the isolationist sentiment in American foreign policy. These episodes, which held out the possibility of American intervention in European affairs, focused renewed attention upon the loyalty of Catholic and radical immigrants, raised questions concerning church-state relations, and stimulated anti-Catholic mob violence, especially by lower-class, nativist workingmen.

The fear of immigrants assumed political overtones during the 1850's as the slavery controversy slowly paralyzed both political parties. In 1854 the secret Order of the Star Spangled Banner transformed itself into the American party. Terming themselves "Know-Nothings" because they claimed to "know nothing" about their organization, members of the group claimed to uphold the asylum concept. All immigrants, except criminals and paupers, were welcome as long as they remained out of politics. The initial strength and subsequent weakness of the Know-Nothings lay in their promise of an issue—the peril of immigration—that avoided the slavery controversy. The party thus utilized nativism less as an end in itself than as a means to achieve national unity.

Although an expression of nationalism, the American party was defined primarily by sectional and local conflicts. In the South, where defensiveness and anxiety approximated the feelings dominating New England in 1814, antagonism centered upon the tendency of most

NATIVISM

immigrants to settle in, and strengthen, the political power of northern states. In New England, Know-Nothingism demonstrated an affinity with reform, especially with the antislavery movement. This contradiction hastened the decline of the American party, which survived only as long as the nation avoided final commitment on the slavery question. Know-Nothing nativism had the ironic effect of retarding the assimilation of Irish immigrants into American society. Caricatured and stereotyped, the Irish continued to be regarded as undesirable, primarily because of their loyalty to the Catholic Church. But by the force of sheer numbers the Irish were slowly winning the battle for urban America against lower-class Protestants. Toward the end of the century, in fact, the Irish would join nativists in defending the United States against the "new" immigration from southern and eastern Europe.

Yet by 1865 nativists had secured no legislation directly restricting the volume of immigration. American religious tolerance survived the socioeconomic conflict and mob violence of the 1830's and 1840's, the Mexican War, and the Know-Nothing movement. Until the 1880's, confidence in the nation's power to assimilate newcomers checked nativism in most regions. Even the radical Irish Fenians discovered that the "free security" of the United States, combined with the presence of a deep strain of Anglophobia in political rhetoric, arrested much resentment against Irish immigrants. Speaking for the majority of his American countrymen, who believed that immigrants had much to offer the nation, Oliver Wendell Holmes lauded Americans as "the Romans of the modern world, the great assimilating people."

For some time it appeared that even the Sinophobia that was especially strong in California during the 1850's would be overcome. The Fourteenth Amendment protected the Chinese, while the Burlingame Treaty of 1868 satisfied nativists by allowing Chinese to enter the country to provide cheap labor, while preventing them from becoming citizens. Changing conditions, however, led to the Chinese Exclusion Act of 1882, which suspended immigration for ten years and marked the first change in the federal government's laissez-faire policy.

The legislation was also important because it affected American attitudes toward the "new" European immigration, underlay the image of a yellow peril, and foreshadowed the national origins laws of the 1920's.

The Chinese Exclusion Act officially sanctioned anti-Orientalism and, with depression and social unrest increasing, Sinophobia swept the Northwest and Rocky Mountain area during the 1880's. Mob violence occurred at Rock Springs, Wyoming Territory, and at Squak Valley, Washington Territory, in 1885. An organized riot sponsored by workingmen disturbed Seattle a year later. The attack forced most of the Chinese from the city and President Grover Cleveland had to utilize military force to restore order. A similar outbreak occurred in Tacoma in 1885, after a local water company hired Chinese to lay pipe despite a high rate of white unemployment. The Chinese quarters were razed, and the Chinese were expelled. This incident—a "glorious victory" to local workingmen—resulted in China receiving an indemnity of $10,000 from the United States.

In 1892, after the Geary Act extended the exclusion law, requiring registration of all resident Chinese and the deportation of nonregistrants, the Chinese government protested that this legislation violated the Burlingame Treaty. A year later, mobs in two California central valley towns attempted to expel Chinese laborers. Meanwhile, citizens in San Francisco and Los Angeles initiated a series of systematic arrests of Orientals. By the end of September 1893, sixty-four Asians had been jailed without bail, pending determination of their appeals to avoid deportation. These difficulties were finally settled in 1894, after Chinese viceroy Li Hung-chang informed the American counsel at Tientsin, William Bowman, that Sino-American relations were near the breaking point. But war with Japan intervened to weaken China's position, and the Gresham-Yang Treaty of 1894 succeeded in placing exclusion and registration laws passed since 1882 on a proper treaty basis.

The intensification of nativism during the 1880's owed much to a nationwide depression beginning in 1882. Economic difficulties and renewed social strife undermined the positive view of immigration held by many citizens. Businessmen and reformers joined labor leaders and workingmen who argued that the contribution of the newcomers was less significant than their role in promoting domestic discord. John Hay and Representative James A. Garfield took the minority view during the 1870's when they linked working-class discontent with immigrant radicalism. But by the mid-1880's this thesis had found new adherents. Chief among these were such critics of the urban-industrial scene as Jacob A. Riis, Richard T. Ely, Edwin L. Godkin, and Josiah Strong, who knew that something had gone awry but proved unable to pinpoint the cause of difficulty. Unable to see that city government lacked the administrative experience needed to cope with the new industrial order, they argued that the capitalist emphasis upon profits and materialism had somehow hardened class lines, produced inequalities, and made socialism a real threat. According to the reformers, immigrants were the major part of the problem. Settling in cities and corrupting American politics, the newcomers transformed the melting pot into a pressure cooker. National immunity from the ills of Europe seemed to have expired.

By stressing the European origins of class conflict, nativists avoided hard questions relating to internal change. Imported radicalism became a scapegoat for property-holding citizens attempting to make sense out of the labor-management strife of the era. The Haymarket Riot of 1886 heralded a decade of industrial warfare and catalyzed within the American mind a dread of foreign conspiracies. Frightened adversaries of "long-haired, wild-eyed, bad-smelling, atheistic, reckless foreign wretches" did not make distinctions between Marxists and anarchists. Instead patriotic Americans parceled together all varieties of immigrant radicalism and left the package in front of the house of labor.

Fears of national decay reached their height during the 1890's, after the panic of 1893 and ensuing depression spread misery across the land. An inarticulate agrarian crusade attacked capitalism and international finance with a cataclysmic rhetoric not designed to reassure jittery Easterners. Labor discontent reached bloody pinnacles during the Homestead and Pullman strikes. While time seemed to be running out, portending the end of opportunity, geography appeared to conspire in the process.

In 1893 Frederick Jackson Turner informed the American Historical Association that "the frontier has gone, and with its closing has closed the first period of American history." Turner's paper implied that the dynamic source of American nationalism, individualism, and democracy had become inoperative. Something new would have to be found to supplant this font of characteristics that made the nation great.

Amid these crises, in 1894, a group of New England Brahmins formed the Immigration Restriction League. Self-avowed champion of Anglo-Saxon civilization, the league set out to restore the virtues of the agrarian past. These New Englanders read with interest the works of John Fiske and John W. Burgess, who applied the precepts of social Darwinism to American history and politics. The restrictionists looked with favor upon the Foran Act of 1885, which outlawed European contract labor. But the restrictionists would go further than this; they would slam shut the gates to the asylum.

Having become self-consciously nationalistic by the late 1880's, nativists began attempts to restrict the entrance of undesirable aliens and to Americanize newcomers already on the scene. In a society that doubted its ability to resolve conflicts, such aggressiveness was understandable. Worry over the apparent lack of stamina in the United States led many citizens to demand evidence of their country's virility.

A positive correlation between nativism, domestic reform, and an active foreign policy permeated the writings of Josiah Strong, who exhibited anxiety about the capacity of Protestant, Anglo-Saxon culture to withstand the pressures of the new immigration. A native of Massachusetts who was active in the home missionary movement, Strong echoed Beecher in expressing dismay at the excesses of industrial capitalism, feeling that communal disruption wrought by voracious materialism threatened the nation's mission to spread Christianity around the globe. In *Our Country* (1885) Strong suggested that immigrants who were not Christianized were not Americanized. A good dose of Protestantism, however, would counteract the "ignorant power" of Catholicism, socialism, intemperance, and political corruption.

Strong's argument for domestic reform,

dominated by hostility toward cultural diversity, emphasized the potential of the United States for overseas expansion. Where Beecher earlier had stressed the urgency of rescuing the West from Rome, Strong envisioned a "Righteous Empire of American Protestantism" expanding throughout the world. *Our Country* and other writings exhibited the racist thesis that civilization would reach its apex when the Anglo-Saxon race extinguished less-vigorous peoples and achieved international hegemony. Strong warned that domestic corruption threatened this divine mission, made all the more imperative by the pending "final competition of races, for which the Anglo-Saxon is being schooled."

A nationalist who advocated the mission of the United States rather than its manifest destiny, Strong saw clearly the providential role of the Anglo-Saxon race. This vision flowed logically from his nativism. Just as Protestant Christianity would cure domestic ills, Anglo-Saxon torchbearers of Protestantism would carry Christianity to the far corners of the earth—not on the end of a sword, but through the persuasive power of example.

The pressure generated by numerous domestic crises did not subside immediately after William McKinley's election to the presidency in 1896, but rather contributed indirectly to the administration's declaration of war against Spain and subsequent acquisition of empire. War in behalf of oppressed Cubans offered Americans a chance to reassert national vigor and virtue, and to discharge safely feelings of hostility and social protest. Thus, in this general sense nativism and jingoism were closely related. Both were negative expressions of nationalism; both were antiforeign movements—one domestic, the other international.

New Left diplomatic historians have stressed the continuing quest by agricultural and commercial interests for overseas markets as the key to understanding the emergence of modern American imperialism. But although William Appleman Williams and Walter LaFeber, among others, have broadened our understanding of the economic impetus behind foreign policy, they fail to account for the bitter political and emotional rivalries that underlay and affected economic aspects of foreign relations. Nor does recent radical historiography

explain why the American people, around 1890, suddenly became sensitive to insignificant issues.

Hofstadter's concept of a "psychic crisis" suggests why the American people were eager for foreign adventure during the early 1890's. Yet despite its apparent utility as a means of correlating domestic affairs and subsequent imperialism, the term lacks historical precision and does not clarify the process of decision making: Why, for example, did the McKinley administration declare war against Spain? Why did the administration reach for empire instead of attempting to resolve national frustrations in other ways? In short, lacking in Hofstadter's stimulating analysis is convincing evidence that would link developments in the domestic social structure to change in foreign affairs.

However problematic as a guide to the ultimate causes of war and empire, the notion of a "psychic crisis" nonetheless underlines the close relationship between the domestic distress of the 1890's, nativism, and a new bellicosity in American diplomacy. During the decade, the United States went to the brink of war with Italy, Chile, and Great Britain over issues that had little to do with national self-interest. Nativism seemed to be a catalyst for these developments, demonstrating the possibility of unifying a divided nation. For example, in 1891 a New Orleans mob lynched eleven Italians suspected of murdering the city's police chief. The lynching occurred after a jury refused to convict the suspects, and the incident quickly grew into a diplomatic crisis. After Secretary of State James G. Blaine rejected Italy's demand for redress, Premier Antonio Starabba Rudini recalled the Italian ambassador. Amid fears of impending war, rumors circulated that Italian criminals were being "dumped" in the United States as part of a fifth-column movement. As volunteers offered their services to Secretary of War Redfield Proctor, restrictionists demanded the exclusion of "murder breeds" from southern Europe, and big-navy men called for an ambitious construction program. The Italian war scare blew over, but many journals noted that in the face of the threat national unity had replaced sectional bickering over the lynchings.

The ebbing of the nativist tide following the Spanish-American War (1898) suggests that xenophobia functioned as a safety valve for domestic discontent. Paradoxically, the war heralded a return of confidence and prosperity that dissipated the sense of crisis and impending disaster that dominated the 1890's. For the moment the restriction movement found itself checked. Immigration standards were tightened, however, after the assassination of McKinley by anarchist Leon F. Czolgosz in 1901. By 1907, in addition to anarchists, immigrant undesirables excluded from American shores included paupers, polygamists, lepers, beggars, prostitutes, epileptics, victims of tuberculosis, persons suspected of "moral turpitude," and imbeciles.

Nativism did not disappear completely during the first decade of the twentieth century. In 1906 San Franciscans wrote an important chapter in the West Coast battle against Orientals, bringing that region's concern for Anglo-Saxon supremacy into symmetry with the national attack upon the new immigration. The San Francisco School Board order excluding Japanese children from public schools demonstrated the ease with which regional prejudice could embroil the federal government. The issue also threatened to upset President Theodore Roosevelt's Far Eastern policy.

Long a site of Sinophobia, California assumed an anti-Japanese stance naturally. The Japanese and Korean Exclusion League, formed in 1905, reiterated charges made previously against the Chinese, arguing that Japanese immigrants would jeopardize the living standards of native laborers and weaken the white race. The school-board order reflected the fear of what many nativists—including Jack London, William Randolph Hearst, and General Homer Lea—termed the yellow peril. Not only had Japan's strong showing in war against Russia heralded her emergence as a world power; her new position menaced both the balance of power in the Far East and the self-image of the United States as a superior, Anglo-Saxon nation. According to the *San Francisco Chronicle,* soldiers discharged from the Japanese military would soon crowd the Golden State with "immoral, intemperate, quarrelsome men bound to labor for a pittance, and [able] to subsist on a [food] supply with which a white man can hardly sustain life."

The school segregation order stung the pride of Japanese nationalists and produced a domestic and international crisis. The directive also placed the federal government in the awkward position of convincing Californians of their obligation to the Union, while at the same time attempting to secure equal treatment for citizens of a foreign power. Roosevelt expressed anger to associates over a matter "so purely local that we never heard of it here in Washington until we got despatches from Tokyo." Uneasy at Japan's new power in Asia and upset by riots in Tokyo protesting the Treaty of Portsmouth, which he helped negotiate, the president sought to reestablish cordial relations with Japan.

Theodore Roosevelt's own racist views did not prevent his quick resolution of the crisis. Despite opposition on economic and racial grounds from residents of the Pacific Coast and Rocky Mountain areas, and despite political protests from southern advocates of states' rights, the president prepared to employ military force, if necessary, and sent a personal emissary to San Francisco. In return for Mayor Eugene Schmitz's revocation of the segregation order, Roosevelt promised to negotiate with Japan to restrict immigration by treaty. At the same time, the chief executive's uncertainty about Japanese intentions led him to augment military and naval strength, and to dispatch the fleet on a dramatic global voyage—after informing Tokyo not to view the move as an unfriendly act.

The "schoolboy crisis" led to negotiation of the Gentlemen's Agreement of 1907, which restricted passage of Japanese laborers from Hawaii to the mainland. This agreement came too late to prevent a war scare in both countries, and was in the long run ineffective. Roosevelt did not bend to nativist opinion in 1906, but after leaving office he came to support West Coast opposition to Oriental immigration, agreeing that cultural and economic conflict was inevitable in relations between Americans and Orientals.

Nativism reached its zenith during and directly after World War I. Just before the United States entered the conflict, immigration restrictionists in Congress overcame President Woodrow Wilson's veto and passed the major recommendation made by the Dillingham Commission six years earlier. The Immigration Act of 1917 excluded illiterate adult immigrants;

established a head tax of eight dollars per person; and barred vagrants, alcoholics, advocates of violent revolution, and "psychopathic inferiors." Another provision created a "barred zone" in the southwest Pacific, thus closing the gates to most Asian immigrants not already excluded by the Chinese Exclusion Act and Gentlemen's Agreement.

The demand for a literacy test dated from prewar days, but its passage in 1917 indicated the extent to which anxieties generated by the conflict strengthened the drive for exclusion. Gone suddenly was the geographical and political isolation that placed foreign policy above controversy, kept immigration attitudes nonpolitical, facilitated assimilation, and upheld the melting pot. Aliens who earlier had solicited American support may have annoyed many citizens, but at no time did Washington policymakers abandon their noninterventionist premises. Even the wars with Spain and Mexico had stressed unity and diverted nationalism from nativist channels. To some extent World War I exerted a similar force: Nativistic themes survived only if they contributed to national unity. As early as 1915, an unprecedented demand for conformity actually shielded immigrants who were neither German nor Irish and who agreed with government policy. Consequently, divisive themes like anti-Catholicism and Teutonic racism disappeared from the nativist lexicon. Anglo-Saxons ceased praising German institutions, and Catholic-baiters realized that Kaiser Wilhelm was a greater menace than the Pope.

World War I, however, transformed nativism into a powerful, sinister force that had much in common with xenophobia during the Quasi-War. With first- and second-generation immigrants constituting approximately one-third of the population, Americans confronted the brute issue of immigrant loyalty. The major expression of American nationalism, "100 percent Americanism" as it became known after the United States entered the war, bore witness to the widespread realization of social and cultural diversity. This discovery had been facilitated by a loss of confidence affecting the Progressive reformers; hence it came as no surprise that the preparedness campaign that developed during the years of neutrality contained a distinct evangelical, service-oriented

tone. Nor was it surprising that German immigrants encountered the brunt of an increasingly militant nativism. Prosperous, well-organized, and self-consciously retaining their Old World mores, the German-American community mobilized shortly after the outbreak of war to prevent the export of munitions to belligerents and to counteract the lurid "Hun" propaganda emanating from British sources. At a meeting in Washington in January 1915, the German-American Alliance demonstrated a great show of unity—and played directly into the hands of American nativists.

This gathering coincided with Kaiser Wilhelm's announcement of submarine warfare against Britain, and with reported German attempts to bomb American vessels and munitions factories. Impressed by what seemed to be a subversive conspiracy, politicians and editors joined the man in the street in decrying "hyphenated" Americanism. Former President Roosevelt vied with Wilson in denouncing German and Irish immigrant disloyalty. Any division of allegiance, according to Roosevelt, was "moral treason." "America for Americans!" he counseled repeatedly. "Our bitter experience should teach us for a generation . . . to crush under our heel every movement that smacks in the smallest degree of playing the German game."

The campaign for preparedness that occupied the nation in 1915 and 1916 intensified nativism by transforming radicals and dissenters, along with German immigrants, into surrogate enemies for patriotic citizens. It did not matter that the United States was not at war, or that German armies were thousands of miles away, or that German-Americans were not spies and saboteurs. Men like Henry Cabot Lodge and Augustus P. Gardner, wealthy New Englanders, moved easily from attacking new immigrants, socialists, and labor unions to emphasizing the terrors of German subversion and the threat of pacifism. Groups like the American Defense Society and the National Security League worked overtime to strengthen the armed forces and to foster unity in all areas of national life.

Attempts by German propagandists to alter American foreign policy created a distrust of immigrants not only in the popular mind, but also within the Wilson administration. Although the German-American Alliance forbade political activity, state and local immigrant organizations contributed to the bitter feelings that emerged during the 1916 election. The president stressed the issue of immigrant loyalty when he denounced "that small alien element among us which puts loyalty to any foreign power before loyalty to the United States." When Wilson's opponent, Republican Charles Evans Hughes, refused to become involved in the hyphenate issue, Democrats quickly portrayed him as "a dupe of the Kaiser in pro-British areas, and as a Roosevelt-dominated jingo spoiling for war with Germany in areas with a large Teutonic population."

With American entrance into the war, the mailed fist of patriotism struck fiercely at the German-American community. As the United States battled to make the world safe for democracy, belligerent nationalists nearly tore up the Bill of Rights. German culture came under attack on all fronts: German language courses disappeared from school curricula; street and building names were changed; the lowly hamburger became "Salisbury steak"; sauerkraut became "liberty cabbage." The Americanization of immigrants, a voluntary process in prewar days, became both a patriotic duty and a coercive experience. Vigilante groups like the American Protective League received unofficial blessings from the Justice Department and ferreted "spies" and "traitors" from within the German-socialist-pacifist-Wobbly-trade unionist monolith.

A celebrated victim of the amateur spy chase was Robert Paul Praeger of Illinois, whose socialism and labor radicalism sufficed to hang him in April 1918. Despite frantic avowals of loyalty to the United States, Praeger was lynched in Collinsville, Illinois, an area previously scarred by labor-management and racial violence. Most opinion makers responded to the incident by saying little in defense of the victim's civil liberties. On the contrary, the hanging demonstrated the inadequacy of federal legislation to suppress sedition. Although the *New Republic* condemned this argument as "a species of sickening cant," editors and politicians who disdained vigilante justice praised the Sedition Act of 1918.

The first American experience with total war left a peacetime legacy. The martial psychology

of 1917–1918 did not immediately subside; if anything, it intensified in the face of significant domestic problems, the apparent menace posed by the Bolshevik revolution, and most important, the absence of national unity and purpose fostered by war. The Germanophobia that had dominated the war years now gave way to a hatred of immigrant and native-born radicals, who were blamed for the inflation, racial violence, and economic recession that accompanied demobilization and reconversion. The crusade against postwar radicalism, spearheaded by Attorney General A. Mitchell Palmer, owed a measure of its impetus to the hostility toward the war displayed by the Industrial Workers of the World and other radical labor organizations. But the red scare also reflected the prominence of immigrant workers in the violent textile and steel strikes of 1919 and the concomitant appearance of new American communist parties, directed by the Moscow Comintern, and also possessing a high proportion of alien membership.

The threat of Bolshevism affected the debate over the Treaty of Versailles and the League of Nations. Republicans and Democrats alike pointed out that the United States could never trust the statesmen of the Old World. This admonition applied especially to the Soviet Union. Wilson argued that the League would halt the expansion of Soviet communism, while Nicholas Murray Butler advanced a view that came to dominate American thinking during the 1920's: Wilsonian internationalism was tainted "red" and the Treaty of Versailles was "unpatriotic and unAmerican," an example of "subtle, half-conscious socialism."

Against a background of domestic turmoil and apparent foreign danger, a series of bombings and violent incidents involving socialist and anarchist groups culminated on 2 June 1919 with a dynamite explosion at Palmer's home, and the dynamiting of public buildings and the homes of leading citizens in eight other cities. At this point Palmer's own anxieties coalesced with political ambition and, utilizing nativist fears, he set out to smash the "reds" and capture the Democratic presidential nomination in 1920. Forsaking the tenets of his Quaker background and his earlier liberal Progressivism, Palmer reorganized the Justice Department, creating a general intelligence division under the direction of J. Edgar Hoover. Hoover's unit soon garnered more than 200,000 cards outlining the composition of radical organizations and publications, and the case histories of more than 60,000 "dangerous radicals."

With Wilson incapacitated by a stroke, and thus unable to restrain patriotic excesses, leadership of the crusade passed to conservative editors and businessmen, the American Legion, and ambitious politicians like Palmer. And within months postwar nativism had left its mark: the Palmer raids, accompanied by the violation of civil rights of suspected immigrant radicals; the deportation of 249 Russian immigrants whose Bolshevism was more imagined than real; the Lusk Committee investigations in New York, resulting in the expulsion of five socialist delegates from the state legislature; the utilization by management of scare propaganda to obscure legitimate grievances of labor; the assertion that communists had fostered the racial violence sweeping the nation; and the charge that Albert Einstein's theory of relativity had Bolshevik origins.

As domestic conditions improved in 1920, the red scare waned. Palmer's errant prediction of widespread violence on May Day made him the laughingstock of editors and politicians who only a short time before had urged him "to do something and do it now, and do it quick, and do it in a way that would bring results." A chief instigator of the red scare, the attorney general became its major victim.

The red scare left an indelible imprint upon the years that followed. Soviet-American relations were corrupted from the outset by judgments and actions conditioned by wartime and postwar xenophobia. The so-called Sisson Report, released by George Creel's Committee on Public Information, purported to show that Bolshevik leaders were in reality German agents, while quasi-diplomat William Boyce of the American Red Cross alienated leaders of the successful November revolution by supporting the Kerensky regime. The long, red line of emotional anticommunism continued to plague Soviet-American relations, preventing American recognition until 1933, provoking distrust during World War II, and fueling the fires of the Cold War.

Xenophobia unleashed during the red scare had other effects. Bipartisan disillusionment with the politics of Europe contributed to the economic nationalism of the 1920's and affected the refusal of the United States to join the World Court. The postwar identification of radicalism with disloyalty tarnished the entire labor movement for more than a decade. In Massachusetts two Italian anarchists were convicted of murder in a trial that arrayed the values of the Brahmin establishment against imported radicalism. The patent unfairness of the proceedings was revealed in presiding judge Webster Thayer's reference to Nicola Sacco and Bartolomeo Vanzetti as "anarchist bastards." Liberals throughout the nation and the world professed outrage and transformed Sacco and Vanzetti into martyrs upon their execution in 1927. But in the eyes of most Americans the Italian immigrants were anarchists and had been punished properly.

Finally, the red scare strengthened the Immigration Restriction League, which now possessed sufficient "evidence" to show that the melting pot endangered American society. The early 1920's witnessed the full flowering of Anglo-Saxon racism, manifested in the popularity of such writers as Lothrop Stoddard and Madison Grant, Irving Babbitt's "new humanism," university quotas and employment restrictions directed against Jews, I.Q. tests, and the notion that a person's genes determined his destiny.

A sharp depression in early 1920, combined with a new wave of European immigration and a national outbreak of crime, led to the renewal of congressional debate on immigration. Proponents of restriction based their arguments primarily upon the need to protect a depressed labor market. Nonetheless, affected by racial considerations, restrictionists did distinguish between "old" and "new" immigrants. Led by Albert Johnson of Washington, an enemy of local Wobblies since 1912, congressional restrictionists overrode President Wilson in early 1921 and passed a law limiting immigration, especially from southern and eastern Europe. This legislation interjected the novel principle of proportional restriction based on nationality: The number of immigrants per year from one country could not exceed 3 percent of the total of that nationality resident in the United States in 1910. The Johnson-Reed Act of 1924 was even more restrictive. It provided that quotas would be based on resident populations of 1890, that immigration would be limited to 150,000 per year after 1927, and that Asians would be excluded. In approving the bill President Calvin Coolidge observed solemnly, "America must be kept American."

Coolidge's remark indicated that nativism remained a strong force in American life. By imposing an artificial unity that did nothing to reconcile fundamental tensions within society, the red scare had prevented the nation from adapting successfully to postwar conditions. Consequently, attempts to restore the values of an earlier time dominated the activities and attitudes of many citizens during the 1920's. Nativist defenders of an idealized gemeinschaft culture attempted to halt the encroachments of urbanism, secularism, modernism, and ethnic heterogeneity.

During the so-called tribal twenties, nativism was more psychic than geographical in character. The nativist impulse of the 1920's expressed a retrospective idealism, at once parochial and nationalistic. It reflected something that Americans had sensed for a long time, but that became indisputable with the 1920 census. For the first time urban residents outnumbered their rural counterparts, and there could be no turning back the clock to a preindustrial epoch. The war had determined the configuration of the future—complex, interdependent, technological. But many citizens did not accept this prognosis. Amid the cultural strain of the 1920's, a large segment of Anglo-Saxon, old America fell back upon religious and racial bigotry as its response to the basic challenge of modern, urban-industrial America—the assimilation of immigrants.

Henry Ford probably best illustrated the paradoxical nature of this rearguard action. The father of mass production of the automobile—itself the most dramatic new force eroding traditional standards of behavior—Ford helped revive ideological anti-Semitism during the 1920's. A scion of the rural Midwest, he organized a "peace ship" in 1915 to halt European hostilities. Three years later, while seeking a Senate seat, he approved Wilson's proposed League of Nations. During the red scare he censured intolerant patriots and looked ahead to an era of harmony between capital and labor. The frustration of these hopes, however, and his personal economic difficulties in 1920 combined to disillusion Ford and set him upon an anti-Semitic path. Soon his *Dearborn Independent* presented readers with details of an alleged Jewish cabal seeking to dominate the world. One of history's most influential forgeries, the "Protocols of the Learned Elders of Zion," provided Ford and other nervous citizens a facile explanation of dismaying cultural trends and a dramatic symbol of the danger to the United States posed by the League of Nations and the World Court.

A similar hostility to internationalism and immigrant mores fed the amazing growth of the Ku Klux Klan, which peaked in 1923 with a membership of two and one-half million persons. The soul of the organization lay in the towns and villages of the nation, the same sites that embraced Ford's anti-Semitism. But units of the Klan also appeared in many cities, especially in the Midwest and Southwest, reflecting demographic changes wrought by World War I. For members of the not-so-invisible order, the seeming inability of government to preserve white, Anglo-Saxon, Victorian civilization made it imperative that patriotic citizens join what Imperial Wizard Hiram W. Evans called "the fight for Americanism." Like Henry Ford, however, the Klan seemed most concerned with the preservation of traditional moral standards. Most of the organization's violence focused not upon the minorities damned in the literature but upon fellow Protestant apostates. The Klan's major task thus consisted of moral regeneration, to be achieved by forcing adherence to "the ancient standards of the community."

The 1920's were checkered with similar examples of rural-minded, defensive "imperialism." Yet as they battled to prevent control of the nation's destiny from passing from Main Street to the metropolis, tribal nativists often proved unwilling to forgo the material benefits of the modernity they so shrilly denounced. This paradox mirrored a similar ambivalence in American foreign relations during the decade: Throughout the 1920's Washington policymakers carefully refrained from commitments that would have involved them in continental politics, though at the same time these same leaders fostered renewed invest-

NATIVISM

ment and the search for markets in Europe, China, the Middle East, and Latin America.

As an organized movement, nativism triumphed with passage of the Johnson-Reed Act in 1924. This legislation produced a drastic decline in the volume of European newcomers and hastened the Americanization of those immigrants already present in the United States. The Great Depression that struck at the end of the decade also facilitated the assimilation process, as economic trauma blurred cultural differences between ethnic groups in the working population, at the same time that it sharpened class feelings. Franklin D. Roosevelt's New Deal also blunted the power of immigrant social and cultural organizations by making immigrants look to government for relief. Immigrant acculturation was further stimulated by new developments in mass communication—Roosevelt's fireside chats, documentary films, and Works Project Administration chronicles and guidebooks—which subjected all Americans to common experiences.

These developments became more important as the United States moved closer to involvement in World War II. Paradoxically, although immigration restrictionists during the 1920's had sought to cleanse the body politic of an alien growth, nativism actually shielded immigrant minorities by sharply restricting fields open to them. With the advent of economic chaos in 1929 the American people directed their hostility at the establishment—white Anglo-Saxon, and Protestant.

World War II failed to generate the vicious nativism that had appeared after 1916. The Japanese attack upon Pearl Harbor imposed unity upon Americans who in the preceding two years engaged in a bitter, divisive debate over national self-interest. Then too, the German-American community harbored memories of the indignities visited against it during World War I, and refused to become involved in the Great Debate. For these and other reasons anti-German feelings focused not upon Americans of German descent but upon Nazi ideology, government, and leaders. Consequently, in reaction to Hitler's treatment of religious minorities and to the Nazi doctrine of Aryan supremacy, anti-Catholicism and racial nativism became anathema to most Americans. Racial nativism remained strong only among

established Roosevelt-haters, who resented the administration's position that civil liberties and minority rights were an integral part of federal policy.

Anyone who championed so-called 100 percent Americanism during the late 1930's, therefore, risked an identification with anti-Semitism and fascism. Yet such champions appeared during the years before Pearl Harbor. The Great Depression catapulted into prominence such mass leaders as Father Charles E. Coughlin, the Michigan radio priest; William Dudley Pelley of the Silver Shirts; and Fritz Kuhn of the German-American Bund. These men purveyed a curiously inverted form of nativism. Father Coughlin did not condemn foreigners at all. Anticipating the strategy and tactics of Senator Joseph R. McCarthy of Wisconsin, the priest denounced treason within government circles, singling out Herbert Hoover, Andrew W. Mellon, government bureaucrats, and, finally, the entire Roosevelt administration. By attacking these "aliens" and linking them together through the image of the subversive "Judeo-Bolshevik," Coughlin pinpointed the enemies controlling the nation's destiny. The priest's careful strategy enabled the traditional targets of America nativists (Irish, Italian, and German Catholics) to turn the tables on their historic adversaries. Kuhn's Bundists, Pelley's Silver Shirts, and numerous other extremist groups joined Coughlinites and members of the American Liberty League in expressing dismay at the social liberalism of the New Deal, and the ethnic heterogeneity of the Democratic political coalition—which by 1936 included blacks, urban laborers, Jews, and a cadre of brain trusters.

The charge that members of the legitimate political order were the real aliens in the United States allowed Coughlin and other mass leaders to secure a large following during the nadir of depression. But in charging that a cabal of Democratic politicians, Anglophiles, international bankers, and Jews controlled the nation, the countersubversives of the 1930's unwittingly allowed the Roosevelt administration to posit the existence of an internal fascist movement, and to link this alleged conspiracy with noninterventionists seeking to prevent American entrance into the European war.

As the United States moved closer to the

665

conflict after 1940, propaganda emanating from nativist ranks hindered responsible non-interventionists from concentrating upon issues of national security. By mid-1941, in fact, non-interventionists and their adversaries were engaged in a symbolic debate in which anti-Semitism assumed critical importance. Ironically, the nativists had hoped to ride the high tide of isolationism while convincing their countrymen that the success of Hitler's battle against communism was imperative to American safety. Instead, the nativists presented non-interventionists an intolerable burden. When Charles A. Lindbergh, the leading orator for the America First Committee, denounced the Jews (along with the British and the Roosevelt administration) for dragging the country into war, the Great Debate on foreign policy was replaced by a public argument on patriotism. After Lindbergh's September speech, the term "isolationism" connoted un-American affiliations. Noninterventionists everywhere found themselves on the defensive. With their attention diverted from Roosevelt's responses to developments in Europe and the Far East, they expended valuable time in attempting to convince liberal interventionists that they were not Nazis.

The major departure from the tolerance that characterized wartime America began shortly after Pearl Harbor, when the federal government fell victim to the Pacific Coast obsession with the yellow peril and accepted Lieutenant General John L. DeWitt's doctrine of "military necessity" to remove Japanese-Americans on the coast to relocation camps scattered throughout the west. Contrary to popular belief, the 110,000 evacuees were not spies and saboteurs; they were a prosperous, hard-working people whose virtues would have pleased Horatio Alger.

The mass relocation was something new in the history of American nativism. The Japanese were not tarred and feathered or made to kneel and kiss the flag. Rather, they were coolly and efficiently shipped off to concentration camps where they sat out the war behind barbed wire, having lost their property, their jobs, and their constitutional and legal rights. Responsibility for this episode of bureaucratic nativism rested less with Californians than the entire nation. The threat of Japanese-American betrayal, upon which relocation was based, received support from President Roosevelt, was approved by Congress, and upheld by the Supreme Court. Curiously, the war relocation camps had the ultimate effect of facilitating Japanese-American movement eastward, and of transforming the community's occupational emphasis from truck farming and gardening to business and varied professional fields.

Eroded foundations of ethnic group loyalty and changes in the basic structure of society hastened the decline of nativism after 1945. Religious affiliation replaced ethnic origin as the primary means of achieving self-identity and promoting group loyalty. Moreover, the onset of the Cold War allowed refugees and immigrants from central and eastern Europe to move within the national consensus. Poles, Hungarians, and Czechs could be as good, or better, Americans than the white, Anglo-Saxon Protestant establishment—especially the perjured "traitor," Alger Hiss, and his principal character witness, Dean Acheson. In its animus against Anglophiles and intellectuals (and its implicit anti-Semitism), McCarthyism intensified the patriotism of these anticommunist Europeans.

During the 1960's, no less than in the 1790's and 1890's, doubt and anxiety concerning America's ability to survive spread throughout the United States. By the end of the 1960's the nation's abortive foreign policy in Vietnam had clearly influenced the decision of a large group of antiwar dissenters and radicals of varied persuasions to become strangers in their own land—"immigrants" by choice. They also became targets of patriotic action ranging from Chicago Mayor Richard J. Daley's police action of 1968; to the Kent State tragedy of 1970; to the Richard M. Nixon administration's duplicity, corruption of language, and unprecedented assaults upon individual dissenters and political institutions.

Washington's continuing failure in foreign policy generated a political crisis of immense proportion. The war in Asia, more than any previous American foreign conflict, was transferred to American shores. By 1972, apparently, triumph in Vietnam had become incidental to winning the more crucial struggle for public opinion on the home front. When that battle began to falter, with most Americans resisting Washington's determination to uphold what it defined as "national honor" in Southeast Asia, Nixon and his advisers stepped up their illegal operations, justifying them on the grounds of national security, and severely compromising numerous political rights of the American people.

Unwilling to admit the honorable intentions of his adversaries, Nixon defended his strategy by making repeated references to a fifth column, financed by alien forces, that posed a definite threat to the safety of the United States. Indeed, Watergate signified the logical denouement of Nixon's political career. In 1946 and 1948, at the height of the Cold War, he had defeated political opponents in California by linking them with the menace of communism. By 1972 he seemed to believe that anyone who opposed him and all he stood for—free-enterprise Americanism—must be subversive. This conclusion justified whatever tactics necessary to protect what his administration perceived to be the national interest. The results of this crusade were not inconsistent with the fate of most nativist movements in American history.

BIBLIOGRAPHY

Gunther Barth, *Bitter Strength: A History of the Chinese in the United States, 1850–1870* (Cambridge, Mass., 1964), notes that Californians engaging in violence against Chinese were not the rabble of society, but men of property and standing whose nativism exhibited a zeal for order. David H. Bennett, *Demagogues in the Depression: American Radicals and the Union Party, 1932–1936* (New Brunswick, N.J., 1969), analyzes the inverted nativists of the 1930's, emphasizing the Union Party campaign of 1936. Stanley Coben, "A Study in Nativism: The American Red Scare of 1919–1920," in *Political Science Quarterly*, 79 (1964), utilizes anthropological theory in comparing the red scare with "revitalization movements" like the Boxer Rebellion in China and American Indian ghost dance cults of the late nineteenth century. Like Richard Hofstadter, David Brion Davis, "Some Themes of Counter-Subversion: An Analysis of Anti-Masonic, Anti-Catholic, and Anti-Mormon Litera-

ture," in *Mississippi Valley Historical Review*, 47 (1960), stresses ideological and psychological functions of nativist literature. Alexander DeConde, *The Quasi-War: The Politics and Diplomacy of the Undeclared War With France, 1797–1801* (New York, 1966), explains how the "Black Cockade Fever" nearly pushed President John Adams into declaring a war that might have destroyed the nation. Thomas F. Gossett, *Race: The History of an Idea in America* (New York, 1965), is rich in illustration and imaginative in its approach to the interplay between nativist racism, expansion, and war. John Higham, *Strangers in the Land: Patterns of American Nativism, 1860–1925* (New York, 1963), remains the indispensable starting point for all students of nativism. Richard Hofstadter, *The Paranoid Style in American Politics and Other Essays* (New York, 1965), analyzes the recurrence of nativist patterns of thought from the late eighteenth century through the McCarthy and Birch eras. Maldwyn A. Jones, *American Immigration* (Chicago, Ill., 1960), presents a reasonable synthesis of recurrent nativist impulses in American life. Ira M. Leonard and Robert D. Parmet, *American Nativism, 1830–1860* (New York, 1971), contains a useful bibliography of primary and secondary sources pertaining to antebellum themes. Lawrence W. Levine, "Progress and Nostalgia: The Self-Image of the 1920's," in Lawrence W. Levine and Robert Middlekauff, eds., *The National Temper: Readings in American Culture and Society* (New York, 1972), stresses the cultural strain of the 1920's as a fertile source for nativism. Stuart C. Miller, *The Unwelcome Immigrant: The American Image of the Chinese, 1785–1882* (Berkeley, Calif., 1969), challenges the notion that Californians generated Sinophobia by demonstrating that anti-Chinese stereotypes were nationwide by 1870. Robert K. Murray, *Red Scare: A Study in National Hysteria, 1919–1920* (Minneapolis, Minn., 1955), remains the standard work on nativism immediately following World War I. Jonathan Schell, *The Time of Illusion* (New York, 1976), describes how the Nixon administration became involved in a global public relations struggle, in which a reverse in any part of the world, no matter how small, could undermine the whole structure of American power. In no other study is the countersubversive and implicitly nativist character of administration policies so skillfully drawn. Geoffrey S. Smith, *To Save a Nation: American Countersubversives, the New Deal, and the Coming of World War II* (New York, 1973), links the activities of the mass leaders of the 1930's to political and diplomatic developments before Pearl Harbor. James Morton Smith, *Freedom's Fetters: The Alien and Sedition Laws and American Civil Liberties* (Ithaca, N.Y., 1956), presents a careful analysis of Federalist attempts to muzzle Jeffersonians during the Quasi-War.

[*See also* AMERICAN ATTITUDES TOWARD WAR; ASYLUM; DISSENT IN WARS; ETHNICITY AND FOREIGN POLICY; IDEOLOGY AND FOREIGN POLICY; IMPERIALISM; ISOLATIONISM; MANIFEST DESTINY; NATIONALISM; PACIFISM.]

NAVAL DIPLOMACY

William R. Braisted

THE HISTORY of American naval diplomacy may be divided into three periods that correspond with technical developments in naval warfare and with the changing situation of the United States in world affairs. During the first century of the nation's history, when the United States enjoyed considerable security provided by the oceans separating it from Europe and Asia, its naval forces were largely directed toward protecting American merchants, missionaries, and government officials in Africa, Asia, and Latin America. This involved showing the flag to induce non-European peoples to treat Americans according to European and American conceptions of civilized practice. During the half-century from 1890 to 1941, the diplomatic role of the navy was revolutionized by the emergence of the United States as one of the great naval powers. To its earlier responsibilities of police and protection, the "new navy" of steam and steel added the strategic objective of defending the Western Hemisphere and a good part of the Pacific against intrusion by the European powers and Japan. Finally, after 1945 the navy joined with the air and land arms to provide the element of force behind American global diplomacy when the great military powers were reduced to two.

To protect Americans as they moved across the seas during the early days of the Republic, the navy eventually followed the example of the British Royal Navy by establishing ships on distant stations in the Mediterranean, the Far East, the Caribbean, the southern Atlantic, the Pacific, and Africa. The ships on each station, rarely more than three to six, were too few to meet all the calls from ministers, consuls, and citizens for a show of force. Only on excep-

tional occasions did the navy organize a squadron for impressive display, such as the Japan expedition of 1853–1854. The station commanders were both itinerant diplomats and administrative officers who kept their ships moving individually from port to port; reported on conditions in their areas; and watched over enlistments, supplies, and ships' fitness. Before the rank of rear admiral was introduced during the Civil War, they usually were accorded the courtesy rank of commodore.

Since the Navy Department was unable to undertake detailed direction of the distant stations before the advent of electrical communications, the station commanders enjoyed broad discretion within their domains. Their instructions were generally to protect American commerce and to heed the appeals from Americans to the best of their ability. Only rarely was a navy man placed under direction of a State Department official. Indeed, in a day when American consuls were commonly merchants—and even foreigners—and when ministers were usually political appointees, naval officers were often the most reliable officials serving the United States abroad. In contrast with the independence of naval men overseas, the Navy Department in Washington was under pressure to follow the State Department's wishes. Introduction of cable and radio by the time of World War I ended most of the autonomy enjoyed by flag officers abroad.

The roots of the distant-stations policy extend to the late eighteenth century, when Americans sailing to the Mediterranean were overhauled by corsairs from Algiers, Tunis, and Tripoli. The Barbary pirates assumed that those outside Islam were subject to capture and enslavement unless they were protected by treaties involving tribute payments. It was in response to Algerine depredations that Congress resorted to naval diplomacy in 1794 by voting to construct six frigates for a navy. Within three years Algiers, Tunis, and Tripoli had agreed to call off their corsairs in return for monetary considerations. Thereafter, however, the navy was diverted from chastising North African potentates by the Quasi-War with France (1798–1800) and by differences with Great Britain that culminated in the War of 1812.

Once peace with Britain was restored in 1815, Congress voted for further war against the Algerine corsairs and Commodore Stephen Decatur quickly forced a treaty on Algiers that ended tribute payments. Decatur's decisive action halted Barbary depredations, and the Navy Department provided against further outbreaks by establishing a permanent squadron in the Mediterranean. Before 1845 its ships were based at Port Mahon, Minorca.

The navy's cruising range in the Mediterranean extended eastward to Turkey, where in 1800 the frigate *George Washington* (captained by William Bainbridge) was the first American warship to call at Constantinople. After the destruction of the Turkish-Egyptian fleet at Navarino during the Greek War of Independence (1827), the Sublime Porte in 1830 finally signed a treaty of commerce with Captain James Biddle and two American commissioners that included a "separate and secret" article providing for American assistance in rebuilding the Turkish navy. Although the Senate rejected the article, President Andrew Jackson overrode the Senate's veto by sending Commodore David Porter, the first resident American representative, to Turkey with instructions to help the Turkish navy.

The Mediterranean Squadron was also a symbol of American sympathy for the liberal movements in Christian Europe. After the revolutions of 1848, American and European liberals jubilated when the steam frigate *Mississippi* conveyed the Hungarian hero Louis Kossuth and fifty other refugees safely to freedom. The squadron, like other distant stations, was practically disbanded during the Civil War. After it was revived in 1865 as the European Squadron, with expanded area, it provided amiable social billets for naval officers as they watched the Mediterranean and Africa fall under an order dominated by Europe.

Although the American China trade dated from the sailing of the *Empress of China* from New York for Canton in 1784, the East India Squadron gradually took shape only during some nine cruises to Asia between 1800 and 1839, six by single ships and three in pairs. Initially, the navy dispatched ships to the East Indies to protect American merchantmen on the high seas and to transport public officials such as Edmund Roberts, who negotiated treaties with Siam and Muscat in 1833. In the conflicts between China and the West that destroyed the traditional Chinese tribute system in East Asian relations, it was the diplomatic mission of the United States Navy to support the claims by Americans to the various rights that Britain, and later France, gained for their nationals by war. During the first Opium War between China and Britain (1839–1842), Commodore Lawrence Kearney on the frigate *Constitution* won from the governor-general at Canton what amounted to a promise of most-favored-nation treatment for Americans in China. This principle, anticipating the American Open Door policy toward China, was written into the Treaty of Wang Hsia (1844) secured by Caleb Cushing with support from the East India Squadron. Once China was opened under the "unequal treaties," the American navy's ships on the renamed Asiatic Station, including the famed Yangtze Patrol, were important props for the vast system of interlocking foreign treaty rights, including extraterritoriality, that Chinese nationalists bitterly resented.

The most spectacular demonstration of American naval diplomacy in the nineteenth century was the expedition led by Commodore Matthew Calbraith Perry to reopen Japan after two centuries of seclusion. Planning his expedition to impress the Japanese with the wealth and power of the United States, Perry first moved up Edo (Tokyo) Bay in July 1853 with a squadron of two steam frigates towing two sloops to present letters from President Millard Fillmore and himself urging the Japanese to modify their closed-country policy. Returning seven months later with a more impressive squadron, he induced the decrepit Tokugawa shogunate to sign the Treaty of Kanagawa, which met American demands for limited intercourse. Quite unwittingly, Perry proved to be the catalyst that unleashed a furious struggle within Japan, within fifteen years bringing the full reopening of the country, the overthrow of the Tokugawa, and the great changes of the Meiji Restoration.

To Commodore Robert W. Shufeldt fell the honor of opening the hermit kingdom of Korea to Americans. Korea was historically a Chinese tributary without desire for other intercourse. The expansionist Shufeldt embarked in 1878 on a much-publicized cruise to the Far East on the U.S.S. *Ticonderoga,* during which he mediated differences between Liberia and its neighbors, investigated sites for coaling stations in Africa, negotiated with the rulers of Madagascar and Johanna (Anjouan), and introduced the American navy to the Persian Gulf. Shufeldt's ultimate objective was to open Korea, which he sought unsuccessfully to do through the good offices of Japan. On a return trip to the Far East, he finally negotiated a Korean treaty with China's leading scholar-official, Li Hung-chang, which the Koreans signed in 1882. Although the treaty established relations between the United States and Korea, it also proved to be a further blow to the Chinese tribute system without winning secure independence for Korea.

The United States Navy established stations embracing waters of the Americas where, in addition to showing the flag in support of trade, it watched for alien intrusions into the hemisphere and occasionally intervened in its troubled lands. The West Indies Station, created in 1821 to run down pirates infesting the area, was expanded to form the Home Station in 1841 (the North Atlantic Station after 1865), when strained relations with Great Britain reminded the navy that American coastal shipping was defenseless against raids from overseas. The navy operated its ships in the Caribbean throughout the nineteenth century in the presence of the more powerful British navy. The Monroe Doctrine of 1823, proclaiming the American continent closed to further colonization, was initially rendered effective by tacit support from the Royal Navy. By the

Clayton-Bulwer Treaty of 1850, the United States won from Great Britain the right to participate on equal terms with the latter in building an isthmian canal at a time when the United States Navy was not yet dominant in the Caribbean.

South of the Caribbean was the Brazil Station, established in 1826 primarily to extend protection to Americans in feuding Brazil, Argentina, and the states of the Rio de la Plata. Usually numbering from two to six ships except during a crisis with Paraguay in 1858, the Brazil Station after 1843 included some 17 million square miles north from Cape Horn to the Amazon, eastward to Cape Negro, and then south along the African coast to the Cape of Good Hope. The station was reconstituted after the Civil War as the South Atlantic Station.

Largest and probably least well defined of the stations was the Pacific Station, dating from 1818. During the early years, the few ships on station tended to cruise between Callao, Peru, and Valparaiso, Chile, with occasional runs to Panama and to the Pacific islands: the Marquesas, Tahiti, Hawaii, and others. After the cession of California by Mexico in 1848, the focus of the station shifted northward, with San Francisco serving as home port. Although it was involved in spectacular crises with Chile in 1891, when Chilean sailors clashed with sailors from the U.S.S. *Baltimore* at Valparaiso, and with Germany over Samoa in 1889 and 1899, after the Civil War the navy's primary concern on the Pacific Station was the fate of the Hawaiian Islands. It habitually kept a ship at Honolulu, gave moral support to white planters against the native monarchy, acquired naval base rights at Pearl Harbor in 1887, and provided protective cover for the movement that led to American annexation of the islands in 1898.

Most lonely of the distant stations was the African Station, created in 1843 after the United States agreed in the Webster-Ashburton Treaty (1842) to cooperate with Britain in suppressing the slave trade. Whereas the Royal Navy seized 594 ships suspected of slave running between 1840 and 1848, however, the few American ships on station captured but nineteen suspected runners between 1843 and 1857. Moreover, since before the Civil War the

NAVAL DIPLOMACY

United States denied British warships even a limited right to visit American merchantmen, the illicit trade found shelter under the American flag.

The "old navy" of wooden ships distributed to distant stations gave way in the late nineteenth century to the "new navy" of steel that operated in a world of great powers competing for empire. Men of the "new navy" strove to build fleets sufficiently powerful to guarantee the United States control of the sea within an American sphere that eventually embraced most of the Western Hemisphere and the Pacific. The half-century from about 1890 to 1941 was also the navy's battleship age, during which most American naval men and many civilians looked to a fleet of battleships (capital ships) as the key instrument for assuring the hegemony of the United States within its sphere and for promoting American diplomacy. From the appearance of his first major volume on sea power in 1890, Alfred Thayer Mahan was preeminently the American naval writer who conceptualized a theory of sea power for the battleship age. Mahan was an economic determinist who held that national power derives from the flow of commerce through key maritime arteries protected by naval power. In emulation of the British Empire, Mahan and his disciples conceived of an American naval line of empire protected by battle fleets and extending from the western Atlantic through the Caribbean and an isthmian canal to the Pacific and west.

Conspicuously absent during the battleship age was formal institutional provision for integrating American naval and diplomatic policies. A president like Theodore Roosevelt might himself serve as a one-man National Security Council, but the Navy Department and the State Department tended to plot their own courses with a minimum of exchange. Important for developing the naval officers' appreciation of their role in the world were such institutions as the Office of Naval Intelligence (1882), the Naval War College (1884), and the General Board (1900). Under the presidency of Admiral George Dewey, the General Board advised the secretary of the navy on a wide range of policies that touched foreign relations. The board's influence, however, gradually declined after the establishment in 1916 of the Office of

Naval Operations, the navy's approach to a naval general staff. A step toward improved cooperation with the army was the creation in 1903 of the Joint Army and Navy Board, the often-ineffectual predecessor of the Joint Chiefs of Staff.

Dewey's May Day victory at the outset of the Spanish-American War (1898) was perhaps inadvertently the navy's most significant act that contributed to American political commitment in the western Pacific. By the peace with Spain, the United States gained possession of the key positions of Puerto Rico, Guam, and the Philippines, as well as control over Cuba. These island territories, together with Hawaii, Samoa, and the Panama Canal Zone (acquired in 1898, 1899, and 1903), included the prime sites for overseas bases that naval men wanted to support their imperial strategy up to 1941.

After the Spanish-American War, the navy followed a modified distant-stations policy in the Americas and the Far East while assembling its battle forces in the Atlantic and on the Asiatic Station. Whereas American naval men feared German aggression in the Caribbean, "the American Mediterranean," they also wanted a fleet in the Far East to support the Open Door in China. In 1906, however, all American battleships were concentrated in a single battle fleet in the Atlantic, the area of the nation's greatest interests and of its vulnerability to German attack. It became a naval axiom that, until the opening of the Panama Canal, the battleship fleet should be concentrated in one ocean so that its divided squadrons could not be defeated separately.

From 1898 to World War I, the navy's Atlantic and Caribbean policies were to build a fortified isthmian canal under exclusive American control, to acquire bases for the canal's protection, and to deny the Western Hemisphere to outside aggressors. By the Hay-Pauncefote Treaty of 1901, Britain released the United States to construct a wholly American canal without restriction as to fortifications. When Colombia failed to reach quick agreement on terms for a canal in its Panama territory, the navy in 1903 afforded cover for a revolt in the isthmus. Within fifteen days a new government of independent Panama accorded the United States a ten-mile-wide canal zone in perpetuity. For Caribbean bases, the General Board by

1903 had settled on two positions: Guantánamo Bay, Cuba, close to the Windward Passage, and a lesser base farther east, probably the island of Culebra, off Puerto Rico. While determined to prevent non-American nations from acquiring bases in the region, the board wanted the United States to take no more than the navy could defend. The navy and the marines also intervened in Haiti, Santo Domingo, Cuba, Nicaragua, and elsewhere in the Caribbean in support of the roles of debt collector and policeman that the United States assumed under the Platt Amendment relating to Cuba (1901) and the Roosevelt Corollary to the Monroe Doctrine (1904), in order to obviate interference by others. During the British and German blockade of Venezuela (1902), the United States concentrated in the Caribbean, under Admiral Dewey's command, the most powerful fleet ever assembled for maneuvers, another potent reminder that other nations must keep out.

In the Far East after 1898, American naval men initially conceived of the United States as one of a half-dozen naval powers competing in China. Their planning assumed that the maritime nations (Britain, the United States, and Japan) were committed to the Open Door in China, in opposition to the continental powers (Russia, France, and Germany). In addition to a main fleet base at Subic Bay in the Philippines, the General Board wanted an advanced base on the China coast, within easy steaming range of the European bases in northern Asiatic waters.

After Japan's triumph in the Russo-Japanese War (1904–1905), the American navy's outlook in the Pacific changed radically as Japan moved from the position of sure friend to that of possible enemy. When Theodore Roosevelt ordered sixteen battleships of the Atlantic Fleet to the Pacific on the first lap of their spectacular world cruise in 1907, he was testing the navy's capacity to concentrate its power in the Pacific and reminding Japan and the world that the Pacific was an area of American naval responsibility. The navy also decided, in 1908–1909, to build its first major overseas Pacific base at Pearl Harbor rather than at Subic Bay, because the army insisted that it would be unable to hold the Philippine base against Japanese attack until the arrival of the battle fleet

from the Atlantic. The navy's most important war plans on the eve of World War I were its Black Plan for defense of the Western Hemisphere against Germany and its Orange Plan for a war against Japan precipitated by the immigration question or by Japanese aggression into China or the Philippines. Although the United States had no formal agreement with Britain, still the world's greatest naval power, there emerged before World War I a wholly informal system of naval power in which Britain built to contain the German navy while the United States strove for naval equality with Germany and decisive superiority over Britain's east Asian ally, Japan.

The advent of Woodrow Wilson to the presidency in 1913 brought to the White House a leader determined to preserve civilian control over the conduct of foreign affairs, yet willing to employ the navy in war and diplomacy with utmost vigor. After the outbreak of World War I in 1914, the Wilson administration was involved in acrimonious debates with Britain and Germany in defense of the cherished American principle of freedom of the seas. The tension of the war also moved the president to support the great Naval Act of 1916 directed toward a navy second to none through the construction of ten battleships and six battle cruisers. This program would provide the United States with a powerful voice in diplomacy, whatever the outcome of the war.

Upon American entry into the war, the navy joined the Allies in a coalition wholly unpremeditated in its Black Plan and Orange Plan or its building programs. Conservatives in the navy, especially on the General Board, were reluctant to halt construction of capital ships so that American shipbuilding facilities could be devoted to building desperately needed antisubmarine and merchant craft. In addition to fearing that the United States might face greatly strengthened German and Japanese navies should the Allies suffer defeat, these naval conservatives apparently were uncertain what policies Britain might adopt should the Allies triumph too completely. It was to allay such anxieties, and thus to promote full American naval participation in the war, that President Wilson's intimate adviser, Colonel Edward M. House, unsuccessfully sought from Britain an option on five British capital ships to meet postwar contingencies. The Navy Department finally halted its capital ship program in order to provide ways for submarine destroyers, and it reached an accord with the Japanese whereby the Imperial Japanese Navy watched the Pacific while the United States Navy concentrated on war in the Atlantic.

The Allied naval jealousies, subdued during the war, surfaced during the Paris Peace Conference in 1919. British leaders saw President Wilson's call for freedom of the seas as a threat to the British Empire, and they strove unsuccessfully to prevent a resumption of building of American capital ships that might relegate the Royal Navy to second place. The naval advisers to the American delegation, on the other hand, opposed any division of the German navy likely to perpetuate British naval supremacy. For the American navy, however, the most significant act by the peace conference was its decision to award Germany's Pacific islands north of the equator to Japan as unfortified mandates of the League of Nations. Unfortified in Japanese hands, the islands would be open to a superior American fleet in a campaign against Japan. At the close of the war, American naval representatives were prominent in the Allied interventions in Russia and at Constantinople during the resurgence of Turkey under Mustafa Kemal.

Britain, the United States, and Japan emerged from World War I as the three great naval powers. Whereas American naval authorities watched for any new evidence that Britain might attempt to retain its naval supremacy, they held as an article of faith that any new naval construction by Britain's ally Japan was directed against the United States. The General Board stated in 1921 that the United States should maintain a navy equal to the British and twice the Japanese. If the Anglo-Japanese alliance remained, however, the board wanted a navy equal to the combined British and Japanese navies. While the navy stationed the most powerful battle forces in the United States Fleet in the Pacific to guard against Orange (Japan), the estimates of naval war planners from 1919 to 1931 also dealt with possible wars against Red (Britain) or against a Red-Orange (Anglo-Japanese) coalition.

In 1921 civilian leaders in the United States, Britain, and Japan were united in their desire to avoid a ruinous naval race and to settle numerous Pacific questions unresolved by the Paris Peace Conference. At the nine-power Washington Conference called by the United States in 1921 to consider these issues, Secretary of State Charles Evans Hughes proposed a naval holiday and a limitation on the American, British, and Japanese navies at just half the levels recommended by the General Board. Hughes's plan was incorporated in the Five-Power Naval Treaty, which limited capital ships and aircraft carriers allowed the United States, Britain, Japan, France, and Italy at a ration of 5:5:3:1.67:1.67. At Japan's insistence, the three great naval powers also undertook, in Article XIX of the treaty, to refrain from building new bases and fortifications from which their fleets could menace each other's vital territories in the Pacific. The United States thus abandoned new naval shore construction west of Hawaii, such as the proposed base on Guam that could serve the fleet in operations against Japan. The Washington naval agreements were part of a package settlement that included the Four-Power Treaty to maintain the status quo in the Pacific, the Nine-Power Treaty relating to China, and the abrogation of the Anglo-Japanese alliance.

The statesmen at Washington sought a new naval order that would provide security for the United States in the Western Hemisphere, the British Empire from the United Kingdom to Singapore, and Japan in the western Pacific. The Five-Power Naval Treaty, however, failed to limit lesser naval categories: cruisers, destroyers, and submarines. The three-power Geneva Naval Conference of 1927 broke down when British and American naval men were unable to agree on cruisers. Japan and Britain, meanwhile, built ships in the unrestricted classes more rapidly than did the United States; and Japanese naval men at the London Naval Conference of 1930 demanded a 10:10:7 ratio rather than a 10:10:6 (5:5:3) ratio in cruisers. As at Washington, the delegations at London overrode vigorous opposition from their services; and the resulting naval treaty in theory preserved the 10:10:6 ratio in heavy cruisers but in substance promised Japan higher ratios in the lesser classes through the life of the naval treaties (1936). The bitterness provoked in the Japanese navy contributed significantly to the collapse of naval limitation after 1931.

The Washington naval system crumbled after Japan occupied Manchuria in 1931–1932. While the American and British governments were unprepared to halt Japan by force, Secretary of State Henry L. Stimson looked to the navy to deter Japanese aggression. After Japanese naval forces landed at Shanghai in 1932, Stimson publicly warned that since the Washington agreements were interdependent, a violation of a political accord, such as the Nine-Power Treaty relating to China, would nullify other Washington agreements, such as the American promise to desist from building bases in the western Pacific. The United States Fleet was concentrated for maneuvers off Hawaii in 1932, and Stimson induced President Hoover thereafter to retain the entire fleet in the Pacific as a caution to Japan.

Stimson's gestures proved futile. The ratio of American and Japanese naval strength in the early 1930's probably approximated 10 to 8, rather than 10 to 6, and the "fleet faction" in the Japanese navy forced the Tokyo government in 1934 to seek a common upper limit (naval parity) with the United States and Britain. The intransigent Japanese stand drove the Americans and the British to unite in defense of the 10:10:6 ratio at the preliminary and main London Naval Conferences called in 1934 and 1935 to review the naval treaties. The Japanese left the second conference, and effective naval limitation ended with the expiration of the treaties in 1936.

During the London conferences British and American naval officers established cordial relations that paved the way for increasing intimacy between their services as they faced the rising threats from Germany and Italy in Europe and the outbreak of the China incident in 1937. Only days after Japanese aircraft sank the U.S.S. *Panay* in December 1937, President Franklin D. Roosevelt sent the navy's war plans director to London for consultations with the Admiralty during which a plan was drawn for possible joint action against Japan by an American fleet operating from Hawaii and a British fleet based in Singapore. This scheme was modified in 1939, when Britain was prevented by the Axis menace in Europe from undertaking powerful action against Japan. Admiral William D. Leahy, American chief of naval

operations, then volunteered that, should a war break out in Europe to which the United States was not a party, the United States Fleet would assemble at Pearl Harbor to deter Japan. Should the United States be associated with Britain in war against the Axis and Japan, Leahy expected the American navy to care for the Pacific while the British navy would be responsible for the Atlantic. When war broke out in Europe in September 1939, the Joint Army and Navy Board had already begun work on five Rainbow Plans for war situations involving the United States and the European democracies against the Axis powers and Japan.

After the fall of France in June 1940, the United States Navy was party to a succession of measures short of war to prevent the collapse of Britain, to prepare for war in two oceans either alone or in association with the British Empire, to deter Japan in the Pacific, and to enlist Canada and the Latin American states in Western Hemisphere defense. In September 1940 Britain and the United States concluded an arrangement by which Britain granted the United States bases in British possessions in the western Atlantic in return for fifty American destroyers to be used against German submarines. This limited American naval assistance to Britain swelled in 1941, after Congress approved the Lend-Lease bill, American navy yards were open to British warships for repair, and the navy began patrolling the western Atlantic against German submarines.

In August 1940 representatives from the Navy Department and the Admiralty entered into urgent consultations on how the navy could best help in the war. After Japan, Germany, and Italy concluded the Berlin Pact in September 1940, the chief of naval operations, Admiral Harold R. Stark, prepared his famous Plan Dog memorandum for a two-ocean war in which British and American forces would seek victory over the Axis in the Atlantic before turning to defeat Japan in the Pacific. This memorandum was the basis for the detailed ABC-1 Plan, drawn up during Anglo-American staff talks at Washington in February and March 1941. In line with this plan, the United States shifted about one-third of its battleships to the Atlantic in order to release British units for service in the Far East.

It was with gravely weakened naval forces in

the Pacific that the Roosevelt administration in July 1941 finally turned to halt Japanese aggression by enlisting Britain and the Netherlands to freeze Japanese assets under their control, thereby terminating Japanese trade with the world outside East Asia. The United States and its associates thus sought to bring Japan to terms by cutting off the flow of oil and other materials vital to the Japanese economy through a distant blockade supported by naval forces divided and inferior to those of the Japanese. Facing the immobilization of their forces as their supplies ran out, Japanese leaders, including those of the Japanese navy, opted for war that closed the battleship age.

During the immediate prewar and war years, Franklin Roosevelt, as had his cousin Theodore, drew the integration of naval and diplomatic policies into his own hands. A State-War-Navy Liaison Committee established in 1938 was largely confined to Latin American affairs and lesser matters. After the president moved the Joint Army and Navy Board into the new executive offices in 1939, the military chiefs participated increasingly in foreign affairs without necessary reference to their service secretaries or even the State Department. Indeed, during World War II the State Department repeatedly bowed to service interests; naval officers and other military men negotiated directly with foreign governments; and the military chiefs accompanied the president to summit meetings to which the secretary of state was not invited. Only a year before the war's end was the State Department restored somewhat to decision making in foreign affairs with the establishment of the State-War-Navy Coordinating Committee (SWNCC) to prepare for peace. In 1942 the chief of naval operations joined with American army and air force chiefs in the Joint Chiefs of Staff, which provided institutional partners for the British chiefs in the Combined Chiefs of Staff, who determined war strategy under the watchful eyes of President Roosevelt and of British Prime Minister Winston Churchill. Cooperation with the British in coalition war was important preparation for naval men when they turned to work for what amounted to a coalition peace.

The thirty years following the end of World War II in 1945 witnessed political, institutional, and technological changes that revolutionized the navy's role in diplomacy. In 1945 American naval officers had not yet devised a strategy geared to the atomic bomb, to a divided world in which the United States was for a time without a naval rival, and to the passing of battleship fleets as a measure of naval and national power. Insofar as they had speculated on the postwar world, they tended to assume a return to a division of responsibility in which the United States Navy would dominate the western Atlantic and the Pacific while the British navy would remain supreme in Eastern Hemisphere waters: the eastern Atlantic, the Mediterranean, and the Indian Ocean. The navy's one clear objective during the war was to secure the Pacific islands that Japan had held since World War I as League of Nations mandates. The navy was soon confronted, however, by the Cold War with the Soviet Union, the Chinese communist victory on the Asian mainland in 1949, and the steady retreat by Britain to Europe that left the United States increasingly alone to deal with the supposed global menace of the Soviet Union and its allies. Moreover, whereas the navy had been the strong arm of American diplomacy through most of the nation's history, the air force emerged at the dawn of the atomic age to claim for the bombers of its Strategic Air Command (SAC) the preponderant responsibility for deterring war.

The period from 1945 to 1950 was a critical one for the navy, during which the service sought meaningful roles in response to claims made by the air force in the course of the movement to organize a single Defense Department. The navy survived the unification struggle as one part of the new national security structure in which the State Department and the Defense Department were institutional equals. Under the National Defense Act of 1947 and amendments of 1949, the chief of naval operations became but one of five members of the Joint Chiefs of Staff, whose chairman conveys the chiefs' collective advice to the president, the secretary of defense, and the National Security Council. When the service secretaries lost their cabinet rank in 1949, the navy was denied separate representation on the National Security Council, the key institution responsible for integrating diplomacy and defense into national security policies. The civilian secretary of defense thereafter sat on the council for the Defense Department, which embraces all the military services. Although the Defense Department and its powerful secretary thus assumed responsibility at the highest levels of strategy-diplomacy, naval officers after 1945 served in unprecedented numbers on politico-military bodies concerned with foreign affairs.

While the navy thus lost its proud position as the leading force behind American diplomacy, it fought for programs of balanced defense against the claims by the air force that the threat of massive retaliation by the Strategic Air Command constituted the most effective deterrent to Soviet aggression. The navy's arguments for a variety of weapons were fully vindicated after the outbreak of the Korean War in 1950 demonstrated the effectiveness of carrier-based air and other capabilities in a limited war unsuited to massive retaliation with atomic bombs. The glamour of massive retaliation faded still more as the Soviet Union successfully tested an atomic device in 1949, achieved a thermonuclear explosion five years later, fired the first intercontinental ballistic missile in 1957, and launched the first man-made satellite (Sputnik) two months later.

To support friends and allies as well as to deter the Soviet Union, naval planners developed a transoceanic naval strategy to project the navy's power over the land and to keep the sea-lanes open. The fleets of the transoceanic navy, like the task forces of World War II, were commonly mixed forces that included two or three carriers, an amphibious marine force, and antisubmarine units. Most spectacular for display were the supercarriers, numbering fifteen in the 1960's and ranging up to 100,000 tons, whose versatile weapons could deal with local outbreaks or convey nuclear destruction to the heart of the Eurasian landmass. Responding to the Soviet Union's missile capability, the navy after 1960 also completed forty-one nuclear-powered submarines armed with Polaris and improved long-range missiles carrying atomic warheads. The navy claimed that its mobile, seaborne forces were far more secure against Soviet attack than the land-based bombers and missiles of the air force.

Together with the army and air force, the transoceanic navy provided the American commitment of force to the multilateral regional pacts, bilateral alliances, and other arrange-ments through which the United States sought to organize the nations of the free world. Since Western Europe seemed the most vital area to save from Soviet domination, the North Atlantic Treaty Organization (NATO), formed in 1949, assumed prime importance in American strategic planning. Through NATO the navy sought to expand its earlier "special relationship" with the British navy into a multilateral association in which the American navy provided important leadership and the largest commitment of force. The NATO supreme commander for the Atlantic (SACLANT) is the commander in chief of the United States Atlantic Fleet, based with his NATO staff at Norfolk, Virginia. The NATO powers preserve independent control of their most important naval forces, from which they contribute elements for NATO maneuvers and for a small standing force.

The most visible American naval contribution to European security is the Sixth Fleet, established in the Mediterranean since 1948. In addition to its earlier role as a major segment in the maritime artery between Europe and Asia, the Mediterranean gained significance after 1945 as a deep inlet into which the United States could move naval power 2,000 miles eastward from the Atlantic, to within striking distance of the Russian homeland. It was also a sea from which the navy could support friends and allies on NATO's southern flank and in the Middle East, as well as a moat separating Europe from Africa. The United States first restored a naval presence in the Mediterranean in 1946–1947, when the Soviet Union pressed Turkey for rights within the Dardanelles and when President Truman extended assistance to Greece under the Truman Doctrine. The Sixth Fleet has commonly numbered more than fifty ships, including two supercarriers organized to meet the needs of a transoceanic navy. Its position in the Mediterranean became increasingly lonely, however, with the withdrawal of British naval power after the Suez Crisis of 1956, the spectacular buildup of Soviet naval forces in the 1960's, and the growing hostility among the Arab states that looked for Soviet aid to counter American support of Israel.

The Seventh Fleet is the navy's Far East counterpart to the Sixth Fleet. At the close of World War II, the navy and the marines helped the Chinese Nationalists receive the

Japanese surrender in eastern China, but American forces withdrew from the Chinese mainland in advance of the communist victory in 1949. In January 1950 Secretary of State Dean Acheson, voicing recommendations from the Joint Chiefs of Staff, outlined an American defense perimeter in the western Pacific, extending from Alaska through Japan, for whose defense the Seventh Fleet would assume major responsibility. Acheson's omission of Korea, Taiwan, and Southeast Asia suggested that the United States was disengaging from the Asian mainland. American participation in the Korean War in 1950, however, demonstrated that the United States government would employ its naval and other forces to counter aggression on the mainland that threatened a key area on the American defense perimeter such as Japan, which after 1949 replaced China as the most important American partner in East Asia.

The Korean War also brought the first public American commitment to the Chinese Nationalists on Taiwan, when President Truman in 1950 ordered the Seventh Fleet to interpose its power between Taiwan and the mainland, to neutralize the Taiwan Strait, and to prevent the Chinese communists and the nationalists from attacking each other across the strait. After the United States and the Chinese Nationalists signed a mutual defense treaty in 1954, the Seventh Fleet provided massive cover in 1954 for the nationalist evacuation from the Tachen Islands and again in 1958 for nationalist logistic operations to sustain their garrisons defending the islands of Quemoy and Matsu against Chinese communist bombardments. During the relatively placid year of 1961, the Seventh Fleet included some 125 ships and 650 aircraft based at Subic Bay, Okinawa, and Japan.

Although the Seventh Fleet's commitments to the Southeast Asia Treaty Organization (SEATO) under the Manila Treaty of 1954 were unclear, the United States in 1962 landed marines in Thailand to deter communist infiltration from neighboring Laos. The fleet also fought in the Vietnam War after Congress, in the Tonkin Gulf Resolution (1964), authorized the president to employ American armed forces in defense of freedom in Southeast Asia. With the winding down of the war after 1969, the Seventh Fleet resumed its station in defense of a western Pacific perimeter.

Between the normal cruising ranges of the Sixth Fleet and the Seventh Fleet, the Indian Ocean area, including the oil-rich Persian Gulf, remained free of a significant American naval presence after 1945. Responding to growing Soviet naval forces in the ocean during the 1960's, however, the navy occasionally dispatched units from the Seventh Fleet to show the flag and to participate in Central Treaty Organization (CENTO) maneuvers. After 1966 the navy also joined with Britain to construct a communications station, landing fields, and other amenities on the British island of Diego Garcia.

Three decades after World War II, the navy was again adjusting to major world changes as the Cold War confrontations gave way to bitter rivalry between the Soviet and Chinese communist camps, détente between the United States and the Soviet Union, and accommodations between Washington and Peking. Even as the United States and the Soviet Union moved to limit their atomic arsenals, including their seaborne missile forces, through accords at the Strategic Arms Limitation Talks (SALT), however, American naval men watched the emergence of the Soviet navy as a contender on the high seas and the spread of Soviet and Chinese influence in the Middle East, Africa, and elsewhere. The modest easing of tensions between the United States and the communist world, therefore, was followed by no lowering of the American naval guard. Indeed, the thaw in the Cold War was overshadowed in many areas of the world by the emergence of strong regional sentiment hostile to the United States and to any American naval presence. While the navy still strove to provide global force sufficient to honor security arrangements negotiated two decades earlier, when conditions were very different, it was increasingly regarded in Africa, Asia, Latin America, and even Europe as an agent of outside interference rather than as a protection.

BIBLIOGRAPHY

Robert G. Albion, "Distant Stations," in *U.S. Naval Institute Proceedings,* 80 (1954), is the most useful brief survey of the distant-stations policy. William R. Braisted, *The United States Navy in the Pacific, 1897–1909* (Austin, Tex., 1958), and *The United States Navy in the Pacific, 1909–1922* (Austin, Tex., 1972), are concerned chiefly with the navy's relation to American diplomacy in eastern Asia from the Spanish-American War through the Washington Conference. Thomas H. Buckley, *The United States and the Washington Conference, 1921–1922* (Knoxville, Tenn., 1970), is the most recent monograph on the major naval conference following World War I. Richard D. Challener, *Admirals, Generals, and American Foreign Policy, 1898–1914* (Princeton, 1973), is a magnificently documented study of the relation of both the army and the navy to American diplomacy from the Spanish-American War to World War I. Vincent Davis, *The Admirals' Lobby* (Chapel Hill, N.C., 1967), deals with institutions, planning, and politics of the navy during the twentieth century. James A. Field, *America and the Mediterranean, 1776–1882* (Princeton, 1969), includes the best treatment of the navy in the Mediterranean during the distant-stations era. Kenneth J. Hagen, *American Gunboat Diplomacy and the Old Navy* (Westport, Conn., 1973), concerns Commodore Shufeldt's cruise on the U.S.S. *Ticonderoga*. Robert E. Johnson, *Thence Round Cape Horn: The Story of United States Naval Forces on Pacific Station, 1818–1923* (Annapolis, Md., 1963), is the best survey of the first century of American naval diplomacy in the eastern Pacific. Raymond G. O'Connor, *Perilous Equilibrium: The United States and the London Disarmament Conference of 1930* (Lawrence, Kans., 1962), the most complete study of the conference, is based on American archival materials. Charles Oscar Paullin, *Diplomatic Negotiations of American Naval Officers, 1778–1883* (Baltimore, 1922), is a pioneer work that has never been completely replaced. Stephen E. Pelz, *Race to Pearl Harbor: The Failure of the Second London Naval Conference and the Onset of World War II* (Cambridge, Mass., 1974), views the naval approach to Pearl Harbor through British, American, and Japanese sources. Harold Sprout and Margaret Sprout, *The Rise of American Naval Power, 1776–1918* (Princeton, 1946), and *Toward a New Order of Sea Power: American Naval Policy and the World Scene, 1918–1922* (Princeton, 1946), are the classic surveys of the navy's history through the Washington Conference, including illuminating comments on naval diplomacy. David F. Trask, *Captains and Cabinets: Anglo-American Naval Relations, 1917–1918* (Columbia, Mo., 1972), is a superb multiarchival study of Anglo-American naval cooperation during World War I. Thaddeus V. Tuleja, *Statesmen and Admirals: Quest for a Far Eastern Policy* (New York, 1963), is a survey of the navy in the Far East from 1931 to 1941. Arthur C. Walworth, *Black Ships off Japan: The Story of Commodore Perry's Expedition* (New York, 1946), is a good-humored account of the navy's most important diplomatic venture in the nineteenth century. Gerald E. Wheeler, *Prelude to Pearl Harbor: The United States Navy and the Far East, 1921–1931* (Columbia, Mo., 1963), is the standard study of the navy in eastern Asia during the decade before the Manchurian incident.

[*See also* BLOCKADES AND QUARANTINES; THE COLD WAR; EXTRATERRITORIALITY; FREEDOM OF THE SEAS; IMPERIALISM; THE MONROE DOCTRINE; THE OPEN DOOR POLICY; PROTECTORATES AND SPHERES OF INFLUENCE.]

NEUTRALITY

Ruhl J. Bartlett

THE TERM "neutrality" is generally used to designate the legal status under international law of a sovereign state that wishes to avoid military involvement in a conflict between belligerent states and expects to enjoy its rights as well as to perform its duties as a neutral. A neutral nation, therefore, has the right to remain at peace, the right to prohibit acts of sovereignty by belligerents within its jurisdiction, and the duty to treat belligerents in an impartial fashion. The interpretation of such rights and duties rests on customary international law, the interpretation of treaties, and relevant domestic legislation. A nation's sovereignty extends to its territory, its ships on the high seas, and the air space above it. In recent years, particularly after World War II, unsolved problems have arisen concerning the extent of territorial seas and the upper boundaries of national air space. Since a neutral may engage in all legal international intercourse, neutrality does not mean isolation, nor should it be confused with neutralism or nonalignment, terms that refer to peacetime foreign policies of nations that desire to remain detached from conflicting interests of other nations or power groups.

This concept of neutrality had no foundation among the ancient empires of the Middle East or in the Roman Empire, only limited recognition among the city-states of ancient Greece, and no part in the feudal system of the Middle Ages. Its evolution took place in western Europe after the rise of independent sovereign states following the Peace of Westphalia at the close of the Thirty Years' War in 1648. Even then the idea of neutrality developed slowly because, to a significant degree during the seventeenth and eighteenth centuries,

Europe was in a state of anarchy as far as international relations were concerned and the rights of neutral nations were limited to what belligerents would accept. What advancement occurred was largely the result of rivalry among states for trade and empire in the New World. The attempt of the Iberian nations to divide the New World between themselves, to establish a monopoly of trade and colonization there, and to close to other nations the seas leading thereto was soon challenged and their alleged rights were discredited by early writers on international law. Hugo Grotius laid down the doctrine in 1608 that since the seas could not be occupied, they could not become the property of any person or nation and were, like the air, the common property of all men. This doctrine, reluctantly accepted by Spain and Portugal, was firmly established by the end of the seventeenth century and the way was opened for the concept of neutrality.

For the most part the restraints on neutral trade revolved around the laws of blockade, the definition of contraband of war, the idea that "free ships give freedom to goods," and the right of neutrals to trade between the ports of belligerents. In all these matters the restraints on neutrals resulted from the obvious desire of belligerents to prevent their enemies from receiving war materials or other goods useful in war. The law of blockade grew out of the law of siege in land warfare. It was accepted practice that a city or a place effectively besieged could be legally cut off from all outside assistance. When this principle was applied to ports, it was agreed that a blockade must be effective in order to be legal; but it was difficult, particularly in the days of sail, to seal off a port completely. No precise definition of effectiveness was ever found, although an attempt was made by stipulating in some commercial treaties that a blockaded port must be sufficiently guarded as to render a ship "in imminent danger of capture" if it attempted to run the blockade.

The laws of contraband of war had a long history. Under a late medieval code, *Consolato del Mare,* all goods destined for an enemy, in belligerent or other ships, were subject to seizure. Early in the seventeenth century, commercial treaties began to distinguish between contraband and noncontraband, the earliest example being the Anglo-Dutch Treaty of Southampton (1625). Usually such treaties contained lists of goods under both categories, but there was no uniformity in such lists save that obvious materials of war were always considered contraband. The term "free ships give freedom to goods" was related to the problem of contraband. It meant that the nationality of a ship determined the status of its cargo, and that enemy goods on a neutral ship, excepting contraband, would not be subject to capture on the high seas.

Thus, by the time of the American Revolution there existed a considerable body of customary law relative to the rights of neutrals, derived from European commercial treaties and the writings of jurists. The law was quite nebulous because it lacked uniformity in the practices of European nations or any means of enforcement. Nevertheless, it provided the basis for American policy.

Among the fundamental causes of the American Revolution was the conviction that the English colonies in America had been the victim of the British mercantile system; and it was virtually inevitable that when the Continental Congress decided on independence, it would decide at the same time to formulate a plan for commercial treaties that would allow the new nation the greatest possible freedom in foreign trade and would embrace the most liberal principles of the rights of neutrals. The committee of the Congress that formulated the Treaty Plan of 1776 studied the commercial treaties of Europe and drew from them the provisions on neutral rights most likely to be accepted by European nations in their commercial relations with the United States. The commercial treaty with France of 1778 resulted from this effort. It was stipulated in the treaty

that "free Ships shall also give Freedom to Goods," contraband excepted, and that this provision applied to persons unless they were soldiers in actual service of an enemy. Neutral ships could sail with "Liberty and Security" to enemy ports and between enemy ports, as well as from enemy ports to other neutral places. The treaty provided lists of contraband and noncontraband, with the addition that "all other goods" should be free unless they had been worked into an "Instrument or Thing" prepared for war, an exception later enlarged and called "conditional contraband." All neutral goods on enemy ships on the high seas could, however, be seized, and neutrals were obliged to observe the law of blockade. It was not stated in the treaty, but probably was implicit, that a neutral had the obligation to treat belligerents impartially and to prevent its territory from being used for belligerent purposes.

The United States hoped to make similar agreements with other European states, and was encouraged when Catherine II of Russia issued a declaration of the rights of neutrals in 1780 and suggested the formation of a League of Armed Neutrality to maintain such rights. Although the principles of the declaration were accepted by Spain and Holland and by various neutral nations of Europe, the United States during the revolutionary war was able to make a treaty embracing the principles only with Holland. After the Treaty of Paris (1783), commercial treaties containing the principles of neutral rights were made with Sweden and Prussia, but the new nation failed to make similar arrangements with Spain and Britain, with which relatively unrestricted commercial intercourse in both trade and shipping would have been greatly to the advantage of the new nation. Nevertheless, American trade revived during the general peace in Europe, and no serious problem existed concerning neutral rights until the outbreak of the war between France and Britain in 1793.

In addition to the desire for the establishment of liberal principles of neutral rights, it was a basic principle of early American foreign policy to remain free from European conflicts. This doctrine was almost as old as the history of the English colonies in America. It had been asserted indirectly by the Massachusetts Bay Colony in 1644, and had been known as the

Doctrine of the Two Spheres. It had two aspects. One was that a European nation might restrict the trade of its colonial citizens to the mother country although it allowed commerce between its metropolitan citizens and other metropolitan areas. The other aspect was that wars in Europe between the colonial powers would not extend to their colonies and, conversely, that conflicts between their colonies would not spread to Europe. The doctrine failed in practice during the stresses of colonial wars; but the Doctrine of the Two Spheres— the belief that the United States could have a destiny separate from that of Europe— remained and was asserted in the debates in the Continental Congress over independence. As long as the colonies were attached to Britain, it was said, they would be involved in Britain's wars.

The desire to remain free from European affairs and to remain neutral in European wars was connected with the determination to protect American neutral rights. If the United States became involved in a conflict over the protection of these rights, it would be an American war for an American cause. One of the important reasons for the establishment of a stronger central government in 1789 was the desire for retaliation against British restrictions on American trade, and this desire increased when Britain began the seizure of enemy goods carried on American vessels and the impressment of alleged British subjects serving on American ships. Both policies violated the principle that "free ships give freedom to goods"— or, more precisely, that a nation's sovereignty extends to its ships on the high seas. The nationality of an impressed seaman was not relevant. The virtual certainty that Congress would take retaliatory measures against Great Britain alarmed those who feared involvement in the war, possibly on the side of France.

A further danger to neutrality existed in the terms of the treaties of commerce and alliance with France (1778). These treaties were made under the stress of necessity during the revolutionary war and were contradictory to the Doctrine of the Two Spheres and to the principle that a neutral was obligated to treat belligerents with impartiality. Under the Treaty of Alliance, the United States guaranteed to France its possessions in America, a guarantee that might be

invoked if French possessions were attacked. The Treaty of Commerce allowed French warships and privateers to enter American ports and sell their prizes, a privilege denied to the enemies of France. France interpreted this as implying that it could fit out privateers in American ports. In these circumstances President George Washington decided on 22 April 1793 to issue a proclamation designed to inform belligerents of his intention to maintain a neutral stance and to warn American citizens against committing acts contrary to the law of nations. Although the federal courts already had jurisdiction, under an act of 24 September 1789, to deal with cases involving international law, Congress passed the Neutrality Act of 5 June 1794, giving the courts additional authority. At the same time, President Washington moved to reduce the danger of conflict with Britain by sending a special mission to London that resulted in a treaty of commerce and navigation, commonly known as Jay's Treaty (19 November 1794). While this treaty removed various items of conflict between the two nations, it was controversial in other respects because it failed to mention impressments and conceded to Britain the right to capture enemy goods on American ships—in direct contradiction of the principle that free ships give freedom to goods.

Jay's Treaty initiated serious problems with France involving neutral rights and duties. France decided, in June 1796 and in March 1797, to treat American ships carrying goods to Britain in the same manner that Jay's Treaty permitted Britain to treat American ships carrying goods to France, a policy in clear violation of the Treaty of Commerce of 1778. Whatever may have been the logic of its position, the United States held that its commercial arrangements with Britain did not affect its treaty agreements with France, and in May and June of 1798 Congress authorized President John Adams to employ the navy to protect American merchant ships from French spoliation in the Atlantic. In addition, American merchant ships were allowed to arm for defensive purposes and to take French armed vessels as prizes if attacked. The Quasi-War with France lasted until 1801, and the American navy ranged farther than the Atlantic. Meanwhile, President Adams took advantage of the new government in

France, which wished to avoid a possible Anglo-American alliance and negotiated the Convention of 1800. The convention abrogated the troublesome alliance of 1778 but retained in general terms the commercial provisions and the liberal definition of neutral rights characteristic of the earlier commercial treaty. This agreement, together with the Treaty of Amiens (1802) between Britain and France, ended for a time the struggle of the United States to pursue an independent course from the European conflict and at the same time to maintain its neutral rights. Under the Convention of 1800 the interdiction on American trade regarding all countries except Great Britain and France was removed, and the president was authorized to permit trade with them if they should cease to violate the neutral commerce of the United States.

Whether the concessions to Britain in Jay's Treaty made the War of 1812 inevitable cannot be determined. It is true, however, that when the Treaty of Amiens ended with the formation in 1805 of the third coalition against France and a renewal of war between France and Britain, the United States was again confronted with violations of its neutral rights. A series of acts and retaliatory measures by both belligerents, although aimed primarily at each other, impinged on American rights and endangered all American commerce with Europe. After futile protests the United States responded with the extreme remedy of prohibiting (22 December 1807) the departure of any American ship "bound to any foreign port or place." This policy was noble in purpose, as a substitute for war in defense of national dignity and human rights; but it was based on not fully valid assumptions of its enforcement and continuance, European conditions of trade, and tolerance of hardship in the United States. It did not quickly bring about respect for American neutral rights, and was replaced in 1809 by an act less restrictive on American trade but equally futile.

American resentment was greater against Britain than against France. This was because France made some alleged concessions to American interests and because British restrictions against American commerce were more effective and British impressment of American seamen more intolerable. While there were other causes for the War of 1812, impressment was the final casus belli. The war ended with a stalemate as far as either belligerent's achieving its expressed purpose. Yet the establishment of peace and the conclusion with the United States of a treaty of commerce, as well as an agreement to limit naval armaments on the Great Lakes and to settle disputes over boundaries and fisheries, possibly implied a decision by Great Britain to abandon its policy of impressment. At any rate, the Treaty of Ghent (1814) and the end of the Napoleonic Wars in Europe (1815) concluded an epoch in the American struggle for neutral rights.

A new phase in the American policy of neutrality was brought about by the revolutions of the Spanish colonies in America. The United States took no official part in these and did not greatly concern itself about them until it decided that some of the resulting governments had established themselves permanently and should be recognized as independent states. When it appeared in 1823, however, that one or more European states might help Spain to recover its American empire, the United States became more concerned and President James Monroe issued a message to Congress that included what became known as the Monroe Doctrine. In essence it was a reaffirmation of the Doctrine of the Two Spheres but announced that while the United States would continue to refrain from involvement in European political matters, it would consider its own security endangered if European states attempted further colonization in the Western Hemisphere or tried to extend their political systems to American states or interfere in their internal affairs. Congress did not confirm the doctrine and no occasion developed immediately to test or implement it, but it became the most cherished and most permanent element in American foreign policy.

From the announcement of the Monroe Doctrine until the American Civil War, the United States had no serious problems regarding neutrality. It maintained a neutral position during the Texas war for independence and during an uprising in Canada in 1837, and was able to establish an effective, and therefore legal, blockade of Mexican ports during the Mexican War. When the Crimean War broke out in 1854, Britain and France agreed to a set of principles later codified and proclaimed by the principal powers of Europe as the Declaration of Paris (1856). This declaration adopted the long-standing American position that free ships give freedom to goods and that a legal blockade must be effective. It added the principles that noncontraband goods on enemy ships should be free from capture and that privateers should not be commissioned. The United States did not adhere to the declaration because it was unwilling to surrender the right to commission privateers and possibly hoped to secure the further agreement that all private property save contraband would be free. After the outbreak of the Civil War, the United States offered to adhere to the declaration if its signatories would apply its provisions to the Confederacy. This retroactive proposal was refused.

At the beginning of the Civil War, the United States found itself in an anomalous situation as far as its legal position on neutrality was concerned. It did not declare war against the Confederacy or accord it belligerent status and considered military operations to be police action against rebellious citizens. Under this interpretation of the conflict, the blockade of Confederate ports, proclaimed by President Abraham Lincoln on 19 April 1861, was an act under domestic law and did not have to be effective in order to be legal. Britain, however, proclaimed its neutrality on 13 May 1861, thus indirectly granting the Confederacy belligerent status—which implied, among other things, that Great Britain would consider a blockade of Confederate ports as subject to customary rules of international law. The United States did not have sufficient naval power to make the blockade effective, if effectiveness meant that ships attempting to enter Confederate ports would be in imminent danger of capture. The Confederacy hoped, therefore, that European nations would challenge the legality of the blockade. This did not happen, primarily because Great Britain decided that its long-range interests would be advanced by accepting the American interpretation of effectiveness. Well before the Civil War was over, the United States brought European commerce with the Confederacy virtually to an end by means of increased naval strength and the capture of major Confederate ports.

In addition to its position on blockade, the United States adopted the doctrine of continuous voyage, a principle taken from British prize law: a ship carrying contraband goods for a belligerent could be captured on the high seas in voyage from a neutral port to another neutral port whenever such a port was only a way station and not the ultimate destination of the cargo. The adoption and use of this doctrine by the United States established a precedent in American policy that was useful to Great Britain and the Allies in their conflict with the Central Powers when the United States was a neutral prior to its entrance into World War I.

The major conflict over neutral rights and duties during the Civil War concerned the construction of warships for the Confederacy in a neutral country. This issue was significant primarily in the relations of the United States with Great Britain, whose laws permitted—as did international law—the sale of merchant ships to belligerents but prohibited the sale of warships. The Confederacy attempted to circumvent this prohibition by having vessels built ostensibly as merchant ships, but so constructed as to be easily converted into warships either at sea or in a Confederate port. The most famous case, although not the only one, was that of the Confederate cruiser *Alabama,* whose history conformed to the pattern. The United States contended that Great Britain had failed to perform its obligations as a neutral in allowing the *Alabama* to leave British waters. The British government held that the *Alabama* was a merchant ship until it was structurally altered and equipped with naval armament in a Confederate port. This controversy continued during the Civil War and became more acrimonious until it was settled by the Treaty of Washington of 1871. The significance of the treaty was in the concession by Great Britain that a neutral had an obligation to use "due diligence" in preventing a ship from being built "in whole or in part" as a warship for a belligerent. The treaty bound only its signatories, but the principle was incorporated in a convention on the rights and duties of neutrals at the Second Hague Conference (1907), with the difference that the imprecise rule of "due diligence" was changed to the obligation of a neutral to use the "means at its disposal" for the object in question.

During the period between the American

Civil War and the outbreak of World War I, the United States had no serious problems concerning its neutral rights. In one instance, however—during the revolution of Panama against Colombia in 1903—the United States failed in the strict performance of its neutral duties as well as in adherence to its treaty obligations. It departed from a position as a neutral by preventing the landing in Panama of Colombian troops intended to aid in suppressing the revolution, and in the same action violated its obligations under a treaty (1846) with Colombia (then the republic of New Granada), under which the United States guaranteed "the rights of sovereignty and property" of Colombia over the Isthmus of Panama. The United States compensated Colombia for the loss of Panama in 1921.

At the Second Hague Conference, the United States hoped to secure an agreement on the rights and duties of neutrals that included the principle, advocated by the United States since 1784, of exempting neutral private property, save contraband, from capture. The conference adopted a convention on neutral rights; but so many significant issues, including that of private property, remained unsettled that the major maritime powers organized a separate meeting to consider such matters. It met in London in 1908 and issued the Declaration of London the following year. This declaration provided the most complete and, as far as neutrals were concerned, the most liberal rules governing neutral trade in time of war that had ever been made. They did not prohibit the capture of private property, but enumerated an extensive free list and limited the principle of continuous voyage to absolute contraband. Universal acceptance of the declaration would have benefited neutral trade with belligerents and assisted belligerents who would have profited from such trade, but would have restricted other belligerents in the exercise of rights hitherto sanctioned under the generally accepted rules of international law. For this reason Great Britain rejected the declaration; and since it did not secure universal approval, the United States withheld ratification even though the Senate had given its consent.

When World War I began, the United States issued a proclamation of neutrality and there-after endeavored to treat the belligerents impartially under the conventional rules of international law and to maintain fully its neutral rights. Conflicts over neutral rights were mainly with Great Britain and Germany. Great Britain did not attempt to establish a traditional close blockade of German ports. Instead, it gradually expanded the contraband list to include goods that could be used in manufacture of war materials or would be of significant value to the German war effort, and made extensive use of the doctrine of continuous voyage. Although the United States protested, vigorously at times, against some British maritime acts, Britain had substantial bases in international law for its policies. No precise lists of contraband had ever been universally adopted. The idea that some materials normally on free lists might become contraband had been a feature of treaties since the seventeenth century, and during the Civil War the United States had added naval stores and "articles of like character with those specifically enumerated" to the contraband list. The doctrine of continuous voyage was also firmly based in international practice and had been sanctioned by the United States during the Civil War. Even under the Declaration of London, in which the principle of continuous voyage was limited to absolute contraband, the legal extension of such contraband was admitted. The United States might protest the extremes to which Britain carried its maritime policies; but it had no solid basis in international law to deny their validity, nor did it grant to the Allies rights prohibited to the Central Powers.

The conflict between the United States and Germany was confined almost exclusively to the issue of unrestricted submarine warfare. The United States did not oppose a German blockade of Allied ports if the blockade were proclaimed and effective, nor did it deny the right of Germany to stop neutral ships on the high seas to determine their cargo and to seize both the cargo and the ship if it carried contraband. The conflict between the two nations grew out of the German proclamation of 4 February 1915, declaring the waters around Great Britain, including the whole of the English Channel, a war zone in which all merchant ships, even those of neutrals, would be sunk without warning or provisions for the safety of their

NEUTRALITY

passengers and crews. The United States replied to this policy on 10 March 1915 by stating that if American ships were destroyed in the manner stated or American lives lost, it would consider this "an indefensible violation of neutral rights" and would "take any steps it might be necessary to take to safeguard American lives and property."

During the following two years, President Woodrow Wilson endeavored to foster a peace settlement between the belligerents, and used great restraint when an American ship, *Gulflight,* was torpedoed on the high seas with loss of life. British maritime policies were kept within a defensible position under international law, and for a time Germany abandoned its unrestricted submarine warfare. When, however, Germany failed to achieve victory during the summer of 1916, it decided to renew unrestricted submarine warfare, with the full knowledge this would result in war with the United States.

By the end of the war, President Wilson had concluded, and the major statesmen of the world agreed, that in the interests of humanity as well as of national security, a new approach to world peace should be attempted. The Covenant of the League of Nations was the result of this decision. Its signatories agreed "to preserve as against external aggression the territorial integrity and existing political independence of all Members of the League," and agreed that if a member of the League resorted to war in disregard of its obligations under the Covenant, the members of the League would prohibit all trade and financial relations and all intercourse between their nationals and the nationals of the Covenant-breaking state, and that nonmembers of the League would be required to abide by these sanctions. Thus the traditional rights of neutrals to trade with belligerents would be prohibited. When, however, Japan (1931) and Italy (1935) violated the Covenant, the League failed to impose sanctions at all in the first case and only partially and ineffectively in the second, and the whole League system of security collapsed. To what extent the refusal of the United States to join the League and the possibility that it would refuse to abide by economic sanctions against an aggressor caused the failure of the League cannot be determined.

During the twenty years that followed World War I, the United States rejected the League of Nations, pursued nationalistic economic policies, promoted naval arms limitation as a panacea for peace, and signed feeble and useless pacts; at the same time it gave vehement attention to its domestic affairs and displayed apparent indifference to the moral and political disintegration of world order. And when the ominous specter of a new world war appeared, it sought seclusion and safety in the complete abandonment of its once-cherished policies of neutral rights, characteristic of its entire national history and for which it had fought two foreign wars. American neutrality had never meant simply noninvolvement in world affairs; it meant the determination to support the rights of its people under rules of international law that, in turn, would contribute to the civilized conduct of nations.

This reversal of policy was accomplished through a series of congressional measures that began in 1935 and reached their most complete form in the Neutrality Act of 1937. Under this act, if the president found "a state of war" to exist among two or more foreign states, American citizens were prohibited from exporting arms, munitions, or implements of war, as enumerated by the president, to the belligerents or to neutrals for transshipment to them, or to a state where civil strife existed. The selling of securities or making loans to belligerents was forbidden, as was travel on belligerent ships; and American merchant ships were not permitted to be armed or to carry prohibited materials of war. Nonprohibited goods could be sold to belligerents, provided the title to them was transferred before transportation abroad. Presumably, therefore, by renouncing its neutral rights the United States would avoid involvement in a foreign war.

Coincident with this "new neutrality" policy, the United States moved to strengthen its ties with the nations of Latin America. The Neutrality Act of 1937 specifically exempted Latin American states from its application in case of war between one or more of them and a non-American state. In a series of conferences between the United States and Latin America, beginning at Buenos Aires in 1936, the American republics agreed to safeguard their neutrality and to act in concert if any danger to their safety or independence occurred. When, however, war broke out in Europe and the United States began to change its neutrality policies, it acted independently of its Latin American neighbors. During World War II some Latin American states that remained neutral referred to their status as "non-belligerency," a term without precise meaning in international law, but in practice signifying the extension of commercial rights to the United States not accorded to other belligerents.

The "new neutrality" failed in its avowed purposes for many reasons, but above all because the United States was unwilling to stand aside while the aggressor nations that eventually signed the Berlin Pact threatened to dominate the world. The new policy was progressively eroded first by presidential acts and later by Congress. The president failed to find that a war existed between Japan and China or between Russia and Finland, sold or traded warships to Britain, and extended the Monroe Doctrine to the mid-Atlantic, while Congress in 1939 repealed the arms embargo provisions of the Neutrality Act of 1937, curtailed trade with Japan, and eventually passed the Lend-Lease Act in 1941, which in effect made the United States an ally of the nations opposing the Axis Powers. By the end of October 1941 a state of war existed between the United States and Germany, and American lives had been lost more than a month before the Japanese attack on Pearl Harbor. As soon as this attack occurred and war broke out between the two nations, the United States began unrestricted submarine warfare against Japan, a policy almost unnoticed by the American people.

Before World War II was fully over, the United States completed its second reversal of policy since 1920 by assisting in the creation of the Charter of the United Nations. While this differed significantly from the Covenant of the League of Nations, its effect on the concept of neutrality was virtually the same. The Security Council was given the primary responsibility for world peace and for authority to take action against a state deemed to have endangered world peace. This action could be in the form of economic sanctions that abridged the historical rights of neutrals.

In the military conflicts that have occurred since World War II, the historical concept of neutrality has not been significant. Although a state of war existed in these instances and diplomatic relations between one or more of the conflicting parties and other nations were sometimes severed, none of the conflicts was a formally declared war. In the Korean conflict most nations accepted the theory that it was a police action against North Korea under authority of the United Nations, and the nations that rejected this interpretation did not base their assistance to North Korea on the doctrine of neutral rights. Nor were such rights invoked by any nation during the conflicts in Indonesia. During the hostilities that took place in Indochina, the subcontinent of India, and the Middle East, commerce with noninvolved nations either was not curtailed or was interrupted only temporarily.

The view may not be justified that the concept of neturality has come full circle since the Treaty of Westphalia and the historical rights of neutrals under international law no longer exist. A war could conceivably take place in which the United Nations would not interfere and belligerents and neutrals would assert their traditional rights. In the circumstances of the modern world and the increase among nations of nuclear war capabilities this does not seem likely to happen.

BIBLIOGRAPHY

Albert Hall Bowman, *The Struggle for Neutrality: Franco-American Diplomacy During the Federalist Era* (Knoxville, Tenn., 1974), is the best account of the early difficulties over neutral rights in American relations with France. Alexander DeConde, *Entangling Alliance: Politics and Diplomacy Under George Washington* (Durham, N.C., 1958), is a thorough treatment of European-American conflicts over neutrality after the revolutionary war. Robert A. Divine, *The Illusion of Neutrality* (Chicago, 1962), is a scholarly survey of the origins and consequences of the Neutrality Acts of 1935–1939. Charles G. Fenwick, *International Law, 4th ed.* (New York, 1965), is one of the best general surveys of the principles of international law. Philip C. Jessup *et al.*, *Neutrality, Its History, Economics, and Law*, 4 vols. (New York, 1936), is the most extensive work on the history of neutrality to the time of its publication. Arthur S. Link, *Wilson: The Struggle for Neutrality, 1914–1915* (Princeton, 1960), is vol. III of Link's authoritative study of Woodrow Wilson; Wilson's policies on neutral rights are considered here and in vols. IV and V. J. Lloyd Mecham, *The United States and Inter-American Security, 1889–1960* (Austin, Tex., 1961), includes accounts of efforts by the United States to secure unity of neutrality policy with Latin America and hemispheric security prior to and during World War II. Bradford Perkins, *Castlereagh and Adams: England and the United States, 1812–1823* (Berkeley, Calif., 1964), continues the study of British-American conflicts over neutral rights that Perkins began in his *Prologue to War: England and the United States, 1805–1812* (Berkeley, Calif., 1961). Max Savelle, *The Origins of American Diplomacy: The International History of Angloamerica, 1492–1763* (New York, 1967), is the most detailed examination of European treaties and agreements that influenced early American diplomacy relative to the Doctrine of the Two Spheres. Hans L. Trefousse, *Germany and American Neutrality, 1939–1941* (New York, 1951), is an indispensable study of the response of Germany to American policies on neutral rights prior to World War II.

[*See also* ALLIANCES, COALITIONS, AND ENTENTES; ARMED NEUTRALITIES; BLOCKADES AND QUARANTINES; COLLECTIVE SECURITY; THE CONTINENTAL SYSTEM; EMBARGOES; FREEDOM OF THE SEAS; INTERNATIONAL LAW; INTERNATIONAL ORGANIZATION; ISOLATIONISM; THE MONROE DOCTRINE; PAN-AMERICANISM; SANCTIONS; TRADE AND COMMERCE; TREATIES.]

THE NIXON DOCTRINE

Thomas H. Etzold

RICHARD M. NIXON became the thirty-seventh president of the United States at a time of great change in international relations. A man with a strong sense of history, he strove to assess that change, understand its implications for American foreign relations, and, if necessary, alter the course of those relations. Within a few months he announced a reorientation of policy perhaps intended to win him a lasting place in the lexicon of American foreign affairs, a formula that was named the Nixon Doctrine soon after its enunciation at a press briefing on Guam, 25 July 1969, only six months after his inauguration.

Several features of the new international order particularly impressed Nixon in contrast with former circumstances. At the outset of the Cold War, he said, the United States had been the only major country to have escaped the social and economic destruction of World War II. Consequently, friends and former enemies alike had depended on America for aid in recovery. The years after the war were marked by the successes of nationalist movements as the old colonial powers of Europe proved too weak to maintain their empires. In the troubled times of the early Cold War, new nations such as India and Egypt had turned to the United States for assistance in development as well as for defense against communist penetration. All the while the United States had faced a communist foe: most of Eastern Europe, the vast and resource-rich Soviet Union, and even more populous China.

By 1969 it seemed to Nixon that this postwar world was no more. The first postwar era, the Cold War, had ended; a new epoch had opened. Former European recipients of American recovery aid had become strong. Once dependent on the United States for protection, they were now capable of contributing more to their own defense. The weak nations of the late 1940's had become independent, proud, and jealous of their sovereignty. They were no longer the easy marks for communist agitators they once had been, and so required less American help and protection. Fragmentation of the communist bloc eased fears earlier raised by the specter of monolithic communism. The monolith had distintegrated. The Soviet Union used its military power not against enemies in the Western democratic camp but against its own allies in East Germany in 1953, Hungary in 1956, and Czechoslovakia in 1968. The Soviet Union and China, formerly friends, had become adversaries.

Nixon interpreted the changes of previous years as auspicious for a new diplomacy. Perhaps deliberately, perhaps unwittingly, he ignored the fragile nature of the West European-American monetary economy and put off dealing with what his successor in the White House, Gerald Ford, would nominate public enemy number one: inflation. He drastically underestimated the extent to which America's European friends had been alienated during the Vietnam years, as well as the widening divergence between European and American interests and strategies in relation to the Soviet Union, Eastern Europe, and the Middle East.

Nixon therefore proclaimed that new international circumstances held out both challenges and opportunities to Americans: challenges to make peace durable, opportunities to "get at the causes of crises" and to "take a longer view." Under the new circumstances he believed that the three pillars of enduring peace were partnership, strength, and willingness to negotiate. These supports of peace under-girded the realities of the time, which, according to the president, were "that a major American role remains indispensable; that other nations can and should assume greater responsibilities, for their sake as well as ours; that the change in the strategic relationships calls for new doctrines; that the emerging polycentrism of the Communist world presents different challenges and new opportunities."

The Nixon Doctrine was vague enough to require repeated and lengthy explanation. Nixon attempted to describe it more precisely in an address to the nation of 3 November 1969, in which he said that "the United States will keep all of its treaty commitments. . . . Second, we shall provide a shield if a nuclear power threatens the freedom of a nation allied with us or of a nation whose survival we consider vital to our security. . . . Third, in cases involving other types of aggression we shall furnish military and economic assistance when requested in accordance with our treaty commitments. But we shall look to the nation directly threatened to assume the primary responsibility of providing the manpower for its defense."

The doctrine especially needed to be explained to America's allies. Everyone had realized that it portended changes in policy, but hardly anyone was certain what the new orientation would mean in practice. According to the president, it meant that the United States was going to bring policy into line with national interests, not just national commitments. The United States would take on or renew commitments only as they accorded with national interests under the changed circumstances of world affairs. To avoid upsetting the delicate workings of international affairs, the administration promised to move carefully and slowly in altering the American role abroad, taking time to educate the American people and foreign leaders alike to the new relation between American capabilities and goals. Nixon and his adviser for national security affairs (and later secretary of state), Henry A. Kissinger, spoke carefully of "gradualism."

Confusion remained. The doctrine's geographical confines were unclear. Did it apply to Europe? Government officials persistently, if vaguely, linked the Nixon Doctrine with the

principles of peace—partnership, strength, and negotiation. Finally the European implications got through to America's North Atlantic Treaty Organization allies. It became clear that the Soviet Union was Nixon's leading partner in the building of peace; that strength was expensive, and might bankrupt the staggering economies of Western Europe; that negotiation, even on questions of vital importance to European nations, would go forward between the United States and the Soviet Union without consultation of the NATO allies.

Certainly the doctrine applied to Asia—to Vietnam, most of all. Referring to point three of the doctrine as stated in the November 1969 speech, Nixon promised to hasten the program of Vietnamization begun under President Lyndon B. Johnson, in which improvement of South Vietnamese forces permitted progressive withdrawal of American troops long before a negotiated end to the conflict was in sight. It remained unclear, at least officially, whether Vietnamization was a new policy or a euphemism for the failure of intervention. Elsewhere in the Far East the administration reduced American troop contingents in South Korea, Japan, Okinawa, Thailand, and the Philippines.

The Nixon Doctrine, then, opened a new era in American foreign policy. Or did it? Critics of the Nixon-Kissinger diplomacy have divided over the novelty, meaning, and effect of the doctrine in American affairs, so that contradictory evaluations have to be examined, if not reconciled. Some writers have considered the Nixon Doctrine an attempt to hold fast to outmoded goals rather than to redefine them. According to this view, the doctrine still depended on the assumption that it was necessary and possible to prevent communist victory in Vietnam, at least for a time. Indeed, the Nixon Doctrine represented no departure from willingness to commit troops to prevent communist victories elsewhere in the world or, for that matter, even in Southeast Asia. For instance, in 1970 the Nixon administration sponsored an attack on the "Cambodian sanctuaries" of the North Vietnamese.

The doctrine, so critics wrote, rested on "flaccid generalizations" about the changing world of international affairs, generalizations that remained unproved because they could not be proved and that only deceived those who propounded them. The assumptions and policies of the administration, so the president's opponents said, added up to a simple but wrongheaded analysis: With an era of negotiation replacing one of confrontation, America's allies would be able to meet communist threats with their own resources, and in any event such threats were less likely than in the recent past. The defect of the Nixon analysis, so wrote the disbelievers, was that it avoided the more difficult question of how to stave off the communists without falling into another Vietnam-style intervention. Even worse, the government was not considering the validity of such earlier goals as resisting communism at home or in foreign countries.

In contrast, supporters hailed the Nixon Doctrine and the diplomacy of Kissinger as new, remarkable, and a genuine alternative to the bitter contentions of the first postwar years. In the domestic as well as the international circumstances of the latter 1960's, massive intervention of the sort that had punctuated the postwar era was no longer possible. Supporters pointed out that Nixon and Kissinger had turned to a diplomacy that was novel for Americans, based on the principles of the balance of power. Although Kissinger repeatedly objected to comparisons between the conditions of nineteenth-century and twentieth-century international politics, he often resorted to the language of balancing when he described what he and the president were trying to do. Equilibrium and interest were the watchwords of the new era, as they had been in the days of Lord Castlereagh and Prince Metternich. Writers who believed the new outweighed the old in the policies of the Nixon years hailed Kissinger as an American Metternich, an image supported by his scholarly writing on that master of the European balance, by his German accent, and by his personal skill at negotiation.

Were Nixon and Kissinger proponents of a new diplomacy? The difference between the old and the new seemed striking when statements of the Nixon era were juxtaposed with those of only a few years earlier. Nixon had said in 1969 that the United States could no longer do it all—that is, provide all the plans, programs, decisions, and defense for the free world; in the future, America would help only where "it makes a real difference and is considered in our interest." A mere eight years earlier, President John F. Kennedy had bravely promised to "pay any price, bear any burden, meet any hardship, support any friend, oppose any foe to assure the survival and success of liberty." That, clearly, had been too much of a promise.

In sum, perhaps the Nixon Doctrine was not a new diplomacy, or at least not to the extent its supporters claimed. Some of the assumptions of the Cold War assuredly were passing from American policy by 1969, such as the belief in American omnipotence, the inflexibility with which communism had to be contained, and vague ideas about what constituted a threat to American national interests, including a dangerous vagueness even as to what those interests were. Détente with the Soviet Union and rapprochement with China seemed signs of a new policy, hopeful auguries for the new era just opening. But there were other signs. The new China policy violated almost all the promises of openness, frankness, and publicly measured calculation remarked by the Nixon Doctrine. Planned in secret, without consultation with allies, the president's approach to Peking burst on a surprised world and sent tremors through the governments of many nations. At the same time the United States was Vietnamizing the war in Southeast Asia, it was secretly opposing and subverting a left-wing government in Chile that it had publicly dismissed as no threat to American interests. The administration secretly took sides in the Indo-Pakistani War of 1971 and was found out. It supported Israel in the Arab-Israeli Yom Kippur War (1973), but without any public debate over the issue. After that war it gave a combination of open and secret aid to Israel worth nearly $5 billion. None of these measures seemed to be a retreat from overcommitment.

The Nixon Doctrine, then, may have been no more than a reasonable attempt to bring American policy into line with capabilities, to draw back definitions of interest to correspond with what America could afford to do and could hope to accomplish, a necessary corrective after a generation of Cold War in which American activities constantly expanded, in which Americans shouldered burden after burden, only to learn in the latter 1960's that they had overreached their resources. It was less than fundamental reform, for the realities of the new age, those of the external world and those of American policy, remained much the same.

BIBLIOGRAPHY

Michael J. Brenner, "The Problem of Innovation and the Nixon-Kissinger Foreign Policy," in *International Studies Quarterly,* 17, no. 3 (1973), is one of the most thorough and negative critiques of Nixon-Kissinger policy to have appeared. Richard M. Nixon, *U.S. Foreign Policy for the 1970's: A New Strategy for Peace* (Washington, D.C., 1970), and *U.S. Foreign Policy for the 1970's: Building for Peace* (Washington, D.C., 1971), two of the president's annual reports to Congress on foreign policy, are the most accessible official statements on the Nixon Doctrine and contain comprehensive descriptions of its origins, principles, and applications. Earl Ravenal, "The Nixon Doctrine and Our Asian Allies," in *Foreign Affairs,* 49 (1971), established Ravenal as one of the earliest serious critics of the doctrine; it asks many of the questions raised by the announcement of new, but insufficiently explicit, policy for Asia. Michael Roskin, "An American Metternich: Henry Kissinger and the Global Balance of Power," in Frank J. Merli and Theodore A. Wilson, eds., *Makers of American Diplomacy* (New York, 1974), contains an appraisal of the Nixon-Kissinger diplomacy that, though qualified, is more favorable than those of Brenner and Ravenal.

[*See also* ALLIANCES, COALITIONS, AND ENTENTES; BALANCE OF POWER; THE COLD WAR; CONTAINMENT; DÉTENTE; THE DOMINO THEORY; INTERVENTION AND NONINTERVENTION.]

NUCLEAR WEAPONS
AND DIPLOMACY

Kenneth J. Hagan

ON 6 August 1945 a single atomic bomb dropped from an American B-29 bomber, named "Enola Gay" after the pilot's mother, virtually destroyed the Japanese city of Hiroshima. Three days later a second bomb demolished most of Nagasaki, and Japan immediately sued for peace. World War II had ended in the convulsive birth of the atomic age.

President Harry S. Truman justified his use of the revolutionary weapon on the grounds of military necessity. By the middle of 1945 the United States had dismembered Japan's overseas empire, blockaded its home islands, and leveled parts of its major cities with explosive and incendiary bombs. Still Japan refused to surrender unconditionally. An American invasion of the Japanese homeland seemed inescapable, but General George C. Marshall warned Truman that casualties might total 500,000 in any such assault. Truman chose to seek a cheaper victory through the shock of atomic bombing.

Historians initially agreed that ending World War II dominated the president's thinking in the summer of 1945. However, in recent years revisionists have argued that Truman's desire to practice what historian Gar Alperovitz aptly calls "atomic diplomacy" strongly affected his decision to authorize the nuclear attack on Japan. According to this thesis, Truman sought to influence Soviet policy by dramatically proving that the United States possessed an unprecedentedly destructive weapon that American leaders were willing to use against an enemy. With one awesome stroke Truman could show his mettle as a tough warrior, end the war, de-

preciate the Soviet Union's claim to share in the occupation of Japan, and discourage Soviet communism's expansion into Europe and Asia.

In a radio address delivered the day Nagasaki was bombed, Truman elaborated the fundamental tenet of his postwar nuclear policy. Because the atomic bomb "is too dangerous to be loose in a lawless world," he warned, "Great Britain and the United States, who have the secret of its production, do not intend to reveal the secret until means have been found to control the bomb so as to protect ourselves and the rest of the world from the danger of total destruction." It soon became obvious that in the minds of American policymakers, "control" connoted some kind of global inspection system.

At first, prospects for negotiating the international regulation of atomic weapons appeared deceptively bright. In December 1945 the foreign ministers of the United States, Great Britain, and the Soviet Union met in Moscow. They jointly proposed the creation of an atomic energy commission responsible to the United Nations Security Council, where the veto precluded any action abhorrent to one of the five permanent members. The Soviets insisted upon this procedure to compensate for the Anglo-American preponderance in the General Assembly. However, the guidelines of the proposed commission also included the inspections demanded by President Truman.

On 24 January 1946 the General Assembly voted unanimously to form an Atomic Energy Commission precisely as envisioned by the three foreign ministers. In June the commission met to forge the machinery for controlling atomic weapons. The American delegate, Bernard Baruch, immediately derailed the negotiations by introducing the concept of an International Atomic Development Authority that would operate independently of the Security Council. This autonomous body would have the power to punish, possibly by atomic attack, any nation that violated its pledge not to construct nuclear weapons. In a single sentence that broke the Moscow agreement, Baruch tersely explained the American rejection of the Security Council as the ultimate punitive agency of the United Nations: "There must be no veto to protect those who violate their solemn agreements not to develop or use atomic energy for destructive purposes."

Baruch's stringency reflected the views of a president deeply worried by the deterioration of American relations with the Soviet Union. During the spring of 1946 the Soviet Union and the United States had failed to agree about the admission of Soviet satellite states to the United Nations, the composition of the Security Council's military arm, and the future of Germany. Moreover, Truman was upset by Soviet penetration of Iran and Manchuria, the latter an area of historic interest to the United States. According to the official historians of the United States Atomic Energy Commission, the president recalled the Manchurian crisis of 1931 and 1932, reasoning that if Secretary of State Henry L. Stimson had been able to threaten the use of force at that time, World War II would have been avoided. For all of these reasons, Truman decided that the veto rendered the Security Council impotent against any transgression by the Soviet Union.

By the middle of 1946, the Soviet Union had also shifted its position on the international regulation of nuclear weapons. Five days after Baruch spoke, the Soviet delegate, Andrei Gromyko, addressed the United Nations Atomic Energy Commission. Ignoring the American's remarks, Gromyko proposed a multilateral treaty binding the signatories to destroy "all stocks of atomic weapons whether in a finished or unfinished condition" within three months. The Russian made no provision for inspections to insure compliance, thus rendering his proposal utterly unacceptable to an American president who refused to "throw away our gun until we are sure the rest of the world can't arm against us."

As hope for the international control of atomic weapons waned at the United Nations, the Truman administration began to shape a coherent nationalistic nuclear policy. The domestic political impediments were formidable, with the public and Congress demanding sharply reduced postwar military expenditures and rapid demobilization of all branches of the armed forces. The army, for example, shrank from more than 8 million men to fewer than 2 million in nine months. In this environment Truman won approval only for the creation of the Strategic Air Command (SAC) in March 1946 and a test of the effectiveness of atomic weapons against ships at Bikini atoll later in the year.

Watchful waiting characterized American foreign policy immediately after the failure of the Baruch plan. Then, beginning in February 1947, a series of crises swept the non-Communist world. England's announcement of inability to continue to sustain anticommunist forces in Greece and Turkey elicited an immediate promise of aid from President Truman, the first formal step toward the policy of containment. For sixteen months international tension mounted, until in June 1948 it reached a peak with a Soviet blockade of land routes to West Berlin.

American nuclear diplomacy during that year and a half focused on England more directly than on the Soviet Union. In highly secret wartime agreements, Prime Minister Winston S. Churchill and President Franklin D. Roosevelt had apportioned the rich Belgian Congo (Zaire) uranium ore reserves, with the approval of the Belgian government-in-exile, to Britain and the United States on an equal basis. At Quebec, in 1943, they also had agreed that neither nation would use atomic weapons in war without the consent of the other. By the middle of 1947, policymakers in Washington viewed these two agreements as detrimental to the United States. In order to enlarge its nuclear arsenal, the United States needed more than half of the annual supply of Belgian Congo ore. In order to exercise full control over its own foreign and military policies, Washington had to eliminate London's voice in the use of atomic weapons. Britain finally agreed to these American demands in December 1947, receiving in exchange the promise of technical aid in the search for peaceful uses for atomic energy.

The military facet of Anglo-American nuclear interdependence manifested itself in the early weeks of the Berlin blockade, when the British permitted the newly autonomous United States Air Force to deploy to England three squadrons of B-29 heavy bombers modified to carry atomic bombs. This deployment was the first forward staging of American strategic air power since World War II. It complemented the growing emphasis on military aviation within the United States, as evidenced by appointment of the aggressive General Curtis LeMay to head SAC, accelerated development of very-long-range bombers, and agitation in Congress and the new Department of Defense for a seventy-combat-group air force. Moreover, the American search for overseas air bases to encircle the Soviet Union and threaten it with nuclear attack began in earnest with the creation of the North Atlantic Treaty Organization (NATO) in 1949.

In August 1949, the Soviet Union successfully detonated an atomic bomb, thereby ending the American nuclear monopoly. Secretary of State Dean Acheson, Secretary of Defense Louis Johnson, and members of the powerful Congressional Joint Committee on Atomic Energy pleaded with President Truman to counter the Soviet advance by building a hydrogen bomb. The outgoing chairman of the Atomic Energy Commission (AEC), David Lilienthal, openly expressed the fear of such scientists as J. Robert Oppenheimer that it was morally wrong for the United States to base its foreign policy on "a weapon of genocide." But other equally prominent scientists, notably the nuclear physicists Ernest O. Lawrence and Edward Teller, carried the day by arguing that the Soviet Union would surely try to outflank the American preponderance in fission weapons by developing the much more powerful fusion bomb as quickly as possible. The only way for the United States to retain overall predominance in nuclear weapons technology was through creation of the hydrogen bomb, which Truman ordered in January 1950.

At the same time, in response to requests from the State Department and the National Security Council (NSC), Truman ordered a thoroughgoing reassessment of American foreign and military policy by representatives from the State Department, the NSC, and the Pentagon. In April they presented a paper entitled NSC-68, a blueprint for the future that he soon approved.

NSC-68 is a stark document whose authors attributed to Moscow a "fundamental design" of completely subverting or forcibly destroying the governments and societies of the non-Soviet world and replacing them with "an apparatus and structure subservient to and controlled from the Kremlin." Only the United States had the potential to thwart Russian expansionism and ultimately "foster a fundamental change in the nature of the Soviet system." But successful containment would require that America increase all facets of its political, economic, and military power and aid its allies in strengthening themselves. To ensure maximum American strength, NSC-68 discouraged seeking a negotiated control of atomic energy because agreement "would result in a relatively greater disarmament of the United States than of the Soviet Union." Looking ahead to 1954, when the Soviet Union presumably would possess a substantial atomic stockpile of its own, NSC-68 postulated a time of maximum danger during which the Soviet Union could lay waste the British Isles, destroy the communications centers of Western Europe, or devastate "certain vital centers of the United States and Canada."

This suspicious and belligerent attitude permeated the highest levels of the executive branch when the advent of war in Korea loosened congressional restraints on massive military expenditures. President Truman immediately sought and obtained supplemental appropriations for the defense budget. By 1952 he had nearly quadrupled annual military spending, which had averaged about $15 billion since 1946. Although the president allocated a great deal of the vastly expanded sum to Korea and the buildup of conventional forces for NATO, the increase also made possible an exponential enlargement of the American capacity to wage nuclear war.

Truman moved on several fronts. First, he accelerated development of a hydrogen bomb, which the Atomic Energy Commission successfully tested on 1 November 1952. The second most important item on the atomic agenda was multiplication of fission weapons. Discovery of rich uranium deposits in the American southwest and construction of several plutonium-producing reactors contributed to this atomic proliferation, but the big breakthrough in sources came with the determination in 1951 that the amount of fissionable material required for a bomb could be cut in half by surrounding the nuclear core with a neutron shield.

The new abundance of fissionable substances permitted a third advance, the creation of tactical nuclear weapons. General Omar Bradley, chairman of the Joint Chiefs of Staff, had publicly advocated this step in October 1949. Speaking as a soldier challenging the congressional popularity of the Strategic Air Command, Bradley argued that wars were won on battlefields, not by destruction of cities and factories. If Russian armies massed to invade Western Europe, tactical nuclear weapons could devastate them. Only in that manner could the thin divisions of NATO defeat a numerically superior foe.

Bradley won increasing support from nuclear physicists and congressmen. By the fall of 1951 Representative Henry Jackson of Washington, a member of the Joint Committee on Atomic Energy, was urging an annual expenditure of $6 billion to $10 billion for tactical nuclear weapons. Under this pressure, the Atomic Energy Commission moved energetically. In March 1953 it exploded a fifteen-kiloton device amid simulated battlefield conditions. Two months earlier, at President Dwight D. Eisenhower's inaugural parade, the army had displayed a cannon allegedly capable of firing nuclear projectiles.

The Truman administration and Congress had also created sophisticated delivery systems for new weapons. The long-range, very-high-altitude, all-jet B-52 bomber took shape as the principal strategic aircraft of the future. As an interim measure, Truman acquired bases from America's allies for the intermediate-range B-47 jet. Congress finally allotted funds to the navy for the first aircraft carrier capable of launching jet-propelled nuclear bombers, the *Forrestal* class supership with a flight deck nearly 1,000 feet long. The Atomic Energy Commission and Westinghouse undertook design of a reactor to propel the new aircraft carriers in 1952, but nuclear propulsion of submarines had the navy's highest priority thanks to the unrelenting vigor of one naval officer, Admiral Hyman G. Rickover. By mid-1952 reactors for two submarines designed to attack other submarines and surface vessels with torpedoes were under construction. President Truman himself laid the keel for one of them, the *Nautilus,* in June of that year. Eventually, a submarine of this class would be redesigned to accommodate the intermediate-range Polaris ballistic missile.

Truman did not intend these weapons for limited war. His solitary threat to use them in Korea was apparently inadvertent. On 30 November 1950, as Chinese troops swept the Americans south from the Yalu River, he held a press conference. In response to a question about possibly dropping the atomic bomb in Korea, he said, "There has always been active consideration of its use." He immediately added, "I don't want to see it used." But the alarm had been sounded. A thoroughly aroused House of Commons dispatched Prime Minister Clement Attlee to Washington to determine exactly what Truman intended. At an extended series of high-level meetings in December, the president and his advisers assured the British that so long as General Douglas MacArthur retained a toehold on the Korean Peninsula the United States would not use atomic weapons.

Commentators have subsequently concluded that Truman refrained from atomic warfare mainly out of belief that Korea was a Soviet feint and that the real communist attack would come in Europe, in which case the United States would need all the nuclear warheads it could muster. Moreover, American use of atomic weapons in Korea could spark a North Korean retaliation against Pusan or other South Korean cities with Soviet-supplied atomic bombs. Of some importance in restraining Truman were British disapproval and the racist implications inherent in again employing the ultimate weapon against an Asian people. Finally, the military impetus was lacking because American field commanders professed to find no suitable targets in Korea, so imbued had they become with the idea that existing nuclear bombs were usable only against cities. Thus, Truman accepted stalemate in conventional warfare in Korea while simultaneously fathering what Atomic Energy Commission chairman Gordon Dean described in September 1952 as "a complete 'family' of atomic weapons, for use not only by strategic bombers, but also by ground support aircraft, armies, and navies."

Dwight D. Eisenhower, who succeeded Truman in January 1953, warmly embraced this monstrous "family." The new president's conservative economic advisers demanded a balanced budget, and reduction of swollen defense expenditures was an obvious step in that direction. Complementing this fiscal orthodoxy was Eisenhower's conviction that Soviet leaders hoped their military challenge would force the United States into what he called "an unbearable security burden leading to economic disaster. . . . Communist guns, in this sense, have been aiming at an economic target no less than a military target." Thus he abandoned NSC-68's conception of a time of maximum danger and began planning a less costly strategy for the "long haul."

Throughout both his terms, Eisenhower limited annual defense spending to about $40 billion. He sought to deter communist aggression with an array of nuclear weapons rather than an enlarged army. His strategic mainstay was SAC, supplemented by the navy's carrier-based atomic bombers. By the late 1950's, SAC was flying some 1,700 intermediate-range B-47's from domestic and foreign air bases, and during the decade hundreds of intercontinental B-52's became operational. If deterrence failed and the Red Army attacked Western Europe or the Soviet air force dropped atomic bombs on the United States, Eisenhower intended to use his strategic airpower to destroy the Soviet Union.

Until 1956, when the Soviet Union demonstrated its technologically advanced strike capacity by successfully launching an intercontinental ballistic missile (ICBM) and the Sputnik satellites, American policymakers generally considered a Soviet ground attack upon Western Europe the most likely form of overt aggression. In order to convince the Soviets that the United States would respond with a huge nuclear counterattack, Secretary of State John Foster Dulles on 12 January 1954

made his famous speech promising "massive retaliation." This public pronouncement completed an intensive high-level review of American strategy begun the previous May. As early as October 1953, Eisenhower had approved NSC-162/2, a paper attempting to reconcile deterrence with reduced defense spending. The solution was to use tactical nuclear weapons as a relatively inexpensive "trip-wire" that would ensure escalation to full-scale American nuclear attack on the Soviet Union if the Red Army marched west.

For Truman, the only "trip-wire" had been American troops stationed in Europe, and they were expensive to sustain. Eisenhower hoped to limit their numbers and cost by arming them with tactical nuclear weapons. By early 1954 he had equipped them with huge atomic cannons and short-range, air-breathing missiles carrying nuclear warheads. In February he induced Congress to amend the Atomic Energy Act to permit sharing information about operational characteristics of American nuclear weapons with NATO allies. By December 1954 he had persuaded NATO strategists to assume that tactical nuclear weapons would be used in any future conflict with the Red Army. A year later, in January 1956, General Lauris Norstad, NATO's supreme commander, succinctly summarized the new strategy. The threat to use tactical nuclear weapons would "link the lowest and highest levels of violence and reinforce the credibility of the Western deterrent."

Although the rhetoric of massive retaliation usually did not discriminate between geographic areas, Eisenhower did have a different plan to meet aggression beyond Europe and the Western Hemisphere. If a noncommunist Asian nation were attacked, he intended to place the primary burden of defense upon that country's ground troops. American nuclear airpower might be brought to bear, but only selectively. As Secretary of State Dulles said in a news conference on 18 July 1956, "In the case of a brush-fire war, we need not drop atomic bombs over vast populated areas." It might suffice merely to vaporize key military and industrial installations.

Abstract bombast about massive retaliation notwithstanding, in only three instances did Eisenhower actually warn other governments that the United States was prepared to launch a nuclear attack if its demands were not met. In April 1953 the Korean armistice talks between the Communist Chinese and Americans had bogged down over the question of exchanging prisoners of war. At Dulles' behest, neutral India cautioned China that if peace did not come soon, the United States would resort to nuclear warfare. The two sides quickly agreed on international supervision of repatriation. Shortly thereafter, as the French position in Indochina disintegrated, Washington warned Peking that direct military intervention in support of the Vietminh would be met with an American atomic attack on China. Finally, on 20 March 1955, as the Communist Chinese bombarded the Nationalist-held islands of Quemoy and Matsu, Dulles publicly speculated about possible American use of "new and powerful weapons of precision, which can utterly destroy military targets without endangering unrelated civilian centers." This statement sent shivers around the world, and Eisenhower began to realize that even in Asia he could not rattle the nuclear sword without arousing global apprehension.

The Soviets were also providing a strong stimulus for American reconsideration of the doctrine of limited nuclear warfare. They had detonated a hydrogen bomb in August 1953, unveiled the intercontinental turboprop Bear bomber in 1954, and displayed the all-jet, long-range Bison bomber in 1955. Eisenhower's response had been to build an extensive radar network and multiply the air force's interceptor wings. But the successful Soviet test of an intercontinental ballistic missile in the summer of 1957, coupled with the launching of Sputniks I and II in the fall, made these defenses prematurely obsolete. The United States was suddenly exposed to a thermonuclear threat against which every countermeasure was helpless. For the first time, all-out nuclear war would inevitably entail extensive death and destruction within the United States. Since it was impossible to ensure that escalation could be avoided once nuclear weapons of any sort were used anywhere in the world, the threat to use them thereafter must be restricted to crises involving areas absolutely essential to the United States: noncommunist Europe and the Western Hemisphere.

Although the stage was thus set for a policy

of "flexible response" resting on conventional forces, Eisenhower's reluctance to spend large sums on defense prevented him from strengthening the army. For the same reasons of fiscal prudence he also steadfastly resisted public and congressional pressure to disperse SAC aircraft more widely, begin a crash program of ballistic missile development, and spend tens of billions on fallout shelters. In August 1958, when the Department of Defense and some scientists warned him that discontinuation of nuclear testing would endanger further evolution of American tactical nuclear weapons, Eisenhower overrode their objections and announced a moratorium on atmospheric testing.

American aviation technology made restraint possible. Beginning in August 1955, the United States regularly flew reconnaissance aircraft over the Soviet Union. Dubbed U-2's, these extremely high-altitude, gliderlike jets soared above the reach of Soviet air defenses. They returned with photographs proving that the Soviet Union had not built a massive offensive nuclear striking force, despite the technological capacity to do so. Thus Eisenhower could proceed at a measured pace with deployment of ICBM's and intermediate-range ballistic missiles (IRBM's), including the submarine-launched Polaris. He also could accurately describe Democratic presidential candidate John F. Kennedy's alleged "missile gap" as a "fiction." What Eisenhower could not do was win Soviet acquiescence to any form of inspections, and therefore negotiations in the United Nations for the limitation of nuclear armaments remained deadlocked throughout his presidency.

Kennedy may have been perpetrating what one observer has called a "pure election fraud," but it is more likely that he agreed with the militant congressmen and senators in his own party who disliked Eisenhower's restrained defense spending. In any event, upon becoming president in January 1961, Kennedy learned that a gap indeed existed—but that it was favorable to the United States. At that time America possessed at least 200 operational strategic missiles of varying range, while the Soviet Union probably had no more than sixteen. Despite this substantial nuclear advantage in missiles alone, in February 1961 Kennedy requested congressional permission to strengthen America's deterrent forces by accelerating the acquisition of second-generation, solid-propellant, land-based ICBM's and nuclear-powered Polaris submarines. In a clear reversal of Eisenhower's fiscal conservatism, Kennedy decided to "develop the force structure necessary to our military requirements without regard to arbitrary or predetermined budget ceilings."

The new president also reversed his predecessor by enlarging the nonnuclear, or conventional, forces of the United States. During the tense summer of 1961, Kennedy capitalized on the Berlin crisis resulting from sharply increased Soviet pressure to expel the Western powers from Berlin by persuading Congress to add a supplemental $3.2 billion to the defense budget. With these funds he increased the armed services by 300,000 men and sent 40,000 more troops to Europe. This deployment underscored Kennedy's commitment to "flexible response," a strategy resting largely on nonnuclear weaponry. From the outset he improved the electronic "fail safe" devices designed to prevent accidental firing of tactical nuclear weapons, discouraged planning involving use of such weapons, and retarded their technological evolution. These restrictions weakened NATO, which remained numerically inferior to the Red Army, by denying to the alliance the equalizing potential of clean and extremely low-yield tactical nuclear weapons. Thus massive retaliation remained the only real deterrent to a Russian military thrust into Western Europe; and as the Soviets enhanced their ability to devastate the United States in any strategic nuclear exchange, massive retaliation became increasingly less reassuring to the NATO countries—and presumably less credible to the Soviet Union.

One reason for the Soviet nuclear buildup of the 1960's was the ambiguity of American strategy. Secretary of Defense Robert S. McNamara, who served under both John F. Kennedy and Lyndon B. Johnson, increased the number of American ICBM's from about 200 to 1,000, completed the construction of forty-one submarines carrying 656 Polaris missile launchers, directed the development of the multiple independently targeted reentry vehicle (MIRV), and continuously kept a large portion of SAC B-52 bombers in a high state of alert. While some of these measures, notably

the conversion to MIRV's, came late in the decade, McNamara's determination to maintain great strategic nuclear superiority over the Soviet Union was apparent from the beginning of the Kennedy administration.

Equally obvious was the possibility that a huge increase in the American stockpile would create a "first strike" capability whereby the United States could preemptively attack and destroy the Russian nuclear striking force, thus making Soviet retaliation largely ineffective if not altogether impossible. The Soviets had lived with similar fears since 1945; but nuclear-tipped ballistic missiles are virtually impossible to stop, and thus Kennedy's increase of those weapons deepened old apprehensions.

As if to allay suspicion, on 26 March 1961 the president promised, "Our arms will never be used to strike the first blow in any attack." Secretary McNamara publicly described his strategy as one of "assured destruction," that is, guaranteeing that enough of the American nuclear arsenal survived any Russian first strike to permit a retaliatory blow that would destroy the Soviet war machine.

Despite these reassurances that the United States would not strike first, Soviet Premier Nikita Khrushchev announced in August 1961 that he was breaking the three-year-old moratorium on nuclear testing in the atmosphere. Worried by the dangers of radioactive fallout, Kennedy at first restricted his reaction to resumption of underground testing; but in April 1962 he resumed atmospheric testing to develop more sophisticated warheads and thereby prevent the Soviet Union from scoring a technological breakthrough that would eliminate American nuclear superiority.

Reinvigoration of the strategic arms race in 1961 constituted the background to the first major nuclear war scare. Kennedy's decision to resume atmospheric testing frustrated the Soviet grasp for nuclear equality with the United States, and Khrushchev soon sought a cheap and quick adjustment of the strategic imbalance by emplacing medium-range ballistic missiles (MRBM's) in Cuba. By doing so, he also hoped to enhance his fading image as a supporter of overseas communist regimes, thereby answering hard-liners in Moscow and Peking who deplored his efforts to ease tensions with the West.

NUCLEAR WEAPONS AND DIPLOMACY

On 14 October 1962, American U-2 reconnaissance aircraft photographed the Cuban missile sites while they were still under construction. For a week the Kennedy administration debated its response, finally settling upon a naval blockade of further shipments of offensive missiles. As he announced his decision to the world on 22 October, President Kennedy also warned that if ballistic missiles were launched from Cuba against any country in the Western Hemisphere, the United States would counter with a "full retaliatory response upon the Soviet Union." While massing troops in Florida for a possible invasion of Cuba, the president insisted that the Soviet Union remove the missiles already on the island.

The crisis lasted for another week and was highlighted by a last-minute Soviet attempt to extract a quid pro quo from the United States: removal of American IRBM's from Turkey. Kennedy formally refused the demand, but his brother, Attorney General Robert F. Kennedy, privately assured Soviet Ambassador Anatoly Dobrynin that once the Cuban crisis passed, the American missiles would be withdrawn. With that assurance Khrushchev capitulated and agreed to remove the Soviet missiles from Cuba. His attempt to rectify the unfavorable strategic imbalance had been thwarted by a president who interpreted the Russian MRBM's as a dangerous alteration in at least the appearance of American strategic superiority. Khrushchev accepted what in fact was a global humiliation because the overwhelming United States nuclear superiority left him no alternative but national suicide.

The reverberations following the Cuban missile crisis continued throughout the 1960's. The continental European members of NATO were shaken by the unilateral way in which America went to the brink of nuclear holocaust without consultation with its allies. French President Charles de Gaulle reaffirmed his determination to reduce European economic and military dependence upon the United States. In January 1963 he vetoed British membership in the Common Market on the grounds that British membership "would appear as a colossal Atlantic community under American domination and direction." Simultaneously, he denounced Kennedy's plan for a multilateral nuclear force as a device for perpetuating American control over the actual use of nuclear weapons by the West. To end his own subservience to the United States, de Gaulle pressed the development of a French atomic striking force, the *force de frappe;* gradually withdrew his military services from the NATO command; and ordered removal of NATO headquarters from French soil.

The impact of the missile crisis on Soviet-American relations was tragically paradoxical. On the one hand, the humiliating Soviet retreat strengthened the militants in the Kremlin who favored increased defense expenditures. They resolved that in future crises the Soviet Union would deal with the United States as a nuclear equal. On the other hand, leaders in both countries were chastened by having been faced with total nuclear destruction. On 29 October 1962, in the very act of capitulating, Khrushchev set the tone for further accommodation: "We should like to continue the exchange of views on the prohibition of atomic and thermonuclear weapons, general disarmament, and other problems relating to the relaxation of international tension."

For some months Kennedy hesitated. Then, on 10 June 1963, in a speech at American University, he made a passionate appeal for peace as "the necessary rational end of rational men." Coupled with various Anglo-American diplomatic initiatives, Kennedy's speech broke the impasse in superpower negotiations. Within weeks Britain, the Soviet Union, and the United States formally agreed to refrain from testing nuclear weapons in outer space, in the atmosphere, or under water. In September the Senate ratified the Test Ban Treaty by a vote of 80 to 19.

The discontinuation of atmospheric experiments within two years of resumption was a major diplomatic development, but there had been disconcerting technological advances during the tests. The Soviet Union detonated hydrogen weapons in the range of twenty-five megatons. By mounting these enormously destructive warheads on ICBM's, the Soviet Union could seriously threaten the entire American land-based strategic retaliatory system, however well the United States "hardened" its missile launching sites. Only the Polaris submarines remained relatively invulnerable. Rather than match the Soviet accomplishment in extremely high megatonnage, the United States developed MIRV's that could be aimed with great precision at multiple targets, an accomplishment beyond the grasp of Soviet technology. Thus, with smaller warheads American strategic missile forces could do as much damage to the Soviet Union as the Russians could do to the United States.

During the 1960's these new creations were integrated into the operational nuclear striking forces of the two countries, with the result that by the early 1970's nuclear parity at last existed between the two superpowers. This equality destroyed once and for all any probability of an American first strike, as well as the likelihood of an American strategic nuclear response to an attack on Western Europe by the Red Army.

Strategic nuclear equality was unacceptable to Republican presidential candidate Richard M. Nixon in 1968. In words reminiscent of Kennedy's eight years earlier, Nixon denounced the "security gap," deplored the concept of parity, and promised to restore clearcut American superiority. But the legacy Nixon inherited was far different from that which Kennedy had inherited. In 1968 the United States was mired down in the deeply dehumanizing, morally outrageous, and extremely costly war in Vietnam. That war had sapped the vitality from the administration of Nixon's predecessor, Lyndon B. Johnson. It would do the same to any presidential administration if continued, and thus Nixon entered office vaguely committed to terminating it. While he would take four years to do so, the fact that he was able to look beyond Vietnam from the outset gave him an advantage over Johnson, whose advisers repeatedly glimpsed the light of victory "at the end of the tunnel," only to find it had mysteriously receded when they reached the chronological point where it was thought to have been.

With campaign rhetoric behind him, Nixon was able to gauge the strategic reality more coolly, and under the influence of his senior foreign policy adviser, Henry Kissinger, he concluded that nuclear parity between the superpowers was unavoidable, given the technological evolution of the 1960's and the limitation imposed by the Vietnam War on spending for nuclear weapons. Early in 1969 the president dismissed superiority as unattainable and

announced for "sufficiency," a politically palatable euphemism for parity.

After some initial hesitation, Nixon also accepted a Soviet suggestion to begin bilateral talks aimed at limiting the strategic arms race, which was threatening to enter a new and even more costly phase with the Russian construction of an antiballistic missile (ABM) defense system around Moscow. With the usual inexorability of the arms race, the United States was on the verge of beginning its own ABM system, despite the staggering technological obstacles and the great financial cost. To appease militants in Congress and ensure that the Russians appreciated his hardheadedness and determination to match the Soviet Union, weapons system for weapons system, Nixon promised to continue development and deployment of an ABM system at the same time that he urged negotiations. He was successful, and in November 1969 the Strategic Arms Limitation Talks (SALT) began in Helsinki.

SALT proved to be the most meaningful Soviet-American negotiations since those culminating in the Test Ban Treaty of 1963. During the Johnson administration, the Soviet Union and the United States had negotiated a nuclear nonproliferation treaty that the General Assembly of the United Nations endorsed in June 1968, but it was a hollow document because several of the nonnuclear powers declined either to sign it or vote for it at the United Nations. SALT, by contrast, had meaning because bilateral discussions between nuclear equals were held.

In one crucial respect, technology facilitated negotiations. Since the beginning of the nuclear age, the United States had included a viable inspection system as part of any strategic arms limitations agreement, and the Soviet Union just as stubbornly refused to expose itself to foreign eyes. The U-2 spy planes permitted limited American aerial surveillance of the Soviet Union, but in 1960 when one was shot down their usefulness there was ended. However, a revolutionary age of aerial reconnaissance dawned in the 1960's with the advent of orbiting space satellites. Henceforth, it would be possible for the United States to maintain regular electronic, photographic, and infrared surveillance of the entire Soviet Union. Thus Soviet ballistic missile tests, nuclear explosions, and preparations for full-scale war could be detected from space. On-site inspections were no longer necessary to ensure compliance with any arms limitation agreement.

After protracted negotiations, the first phase of SALT reached fruition. On 26 May 1972 the Soviet Union and the United States agreed by treaty to limit deployment of ABM's. Delegates of the two superpowers also initialed a five-year interim agreement on offensive strategic nuclear weapons systems. In essence, the United States conceded to the Soviet Union an advantage in large missiles with enormously destructive warheads and the Soviet Union conceded to the United States the countervailing advantage of MIRV's, that is, smaller missiles armed with numerous and highly accurate warheads. By this agreement the Soviet Union and the United States formally recognized their nuclear parity.

Nixon's acceptance of atomic equality did not deter him from relying on nuclear weapons in his conduct of foreign and military policy. For example, during the 1973 Yom Kippur War in the Middle East, he authorized a full alert of American strategic forces to discourage intervention by Soviet airborne troops. Similarly, as he progressively reduced the size of the United States Army, he permitted his advisers to revive plans for using tactical nuclear weapons. In January 1971, when speaking about the American defense posture for 1972 through 1976, Secretary of Defense Melvin B. Laird said: "For those levels in the deterrent spectrum below general nuclear war, the forces to deter Soviet and Chinese adventures clearly must have an adequate war-fighting capability, both in limited nuclear and conventional options."

After Nixon's resignation, President Gerald R. Ford continued to seek the same ends in nuclear diplomacy. Together with Kissinger, who remained in the administration as secretary of state, Ford sought to extend the interim five-year limitation on the offensive strategic arms race, due to expire in October 1977. The negotiations to achieve this end were dubbed SALT II, but in the Senate and elsewhere, militants like Henry Jackson of Washington alleged Soviet violations of the 1972 arms limitation agreement and proclaimed the necessity of restoring nuclear superiority. Thus hobbled,

Ford and Kissinger passed the unresolved arms limitation problem to President James E. Carter in January 1977.

Complicating the issue for the new administration were two recent advances in nuclear weapons technology: the American cruise missile, a terrain-hugging weapons system of phenomenal precision, and the Soviet Backfire bomber. As each side attempted to exclude its new delivery vehicle from any strategic arms limitation, it encountered determined resistance to such exclusion from the other superpower. Some domestic critics interpreted Carter's effort to develop and deploy the cruise missile without negotiated restraint as a calculated ploy to retain the technological superiority characteristic of American nuclear policy since the dawn of the atomic age.

In 1946, in a book entitled *The Absolute Weapon,* Bernard Brodie and a small group of academic strategists had argued for nuclear equality between the United States and the Soviet Union. "Neither we nor the Russians," they wrote, "can expect to feel even reasonably safe unless an atomic attack by one were certain to unleash a devastating atomic counterattack by the other." For more than twenty years American presidents disregarded the admonition that, among nuclear nations, the greatest mutual security lies in individual insecurity. Then, when technology made the balance a reality, Richard M. Nixon, the first president unquestionably possessed of the statesmanlike vision and courage to accept parity, proved tragically flawed as an American politician and human being. Whether Nixon's successors can resist chauvinistic politicians who would renew the costly and chimerical search for clear-cut American nuclear superiority over the second-strongest nation on earth is the overriding foreign policy question of the last half of the 1970's.

BIBLIOGRAPHY

See Gar Alperovitz, *Atomic Diplomacy: Hiroshima and Potsdam* (New York, 1965), the first book to pose the revisionists' questions; Bernard Brodie, ed., *The Absolute Weapon: Atomic Power and World Order* (New York, 1946), the first scholarly argument for a balance of terror; Richard G. Hewlett and Oscar E. Anderson, Jr., *The New World, 1939–1946* (University Park, Pa., 1962), the first volume of the history of the United States Atomic Energy Commission (AEC); Richard G. Hewlett and Francis Duncan, *Atomic Shield, 1947–1952* (University Park, Pa., 1969), the second volume of the AEC's history, written with unflagging precision and based on the agency's documents, and *Nuclear Navy, 1946–1962* (Chicago–London, 1974), an extremely detailed study of Admiral Hyman Rickover's struggle for a nuclear-powered submarine, the first step toward the Polaris system; Samuel P. Huntington, *The Common Defense; Strategic Programs in National Politics* (New York–London, 1961), the best survey of 1945–1960, by a pioneer in the study of strategy; Morton A. Kaplan, *S.A.L.T.: Problems and Prospects* (Morristown, N.J., 1973), a glimpse of the intricacies of arms limitations by a distinguished observer; Edward A. Kolodziej, *The Uncommon Defense and Congress, 1945–1963* (Columbus, Ohio, 1966), a good summary of the military arguments presented to Congress each year, with ample attention to the case made for increasing the nuclear capacity of the air force and, to a lesser extent, the other services; Walter La Feber, *America, Russia, and the Cold War 1945–1973,* 3rd ed. (New York, 1976), a careful portrait of the diplomatic context shaping nuclear policies;

Alva Myrdal, *The Game of Disarmament; How the United States and Russia Run the Arms Race* (New York, 1976), a critical analysis of the arms race from the perspective of an advocate of disarmament; Harvey M. Sapolsky, *The Polaris System Development; Bureaucratic and Programmatic Success in Government* (Cambridge, Mass., 1972), a provocative explanation of why weapons systems are built; Martin J. Sherwin, *A World Destroyed: The Atomic Bomb and the Grand Alliance* (New York, 1975), a well-received argument that atomic diplomacy began long before Truman became president; and Herbert York, *Race to Oblivion: A Participant's View of the Arms Race* (New York, 1970), a disturbing criticism by a disillusioned nuclear scientist who was present at the creation.

[See also ALLIANCES, COALITIONS, AND ENTENTES; BLOCKADES AND QUARANTINES; THE COLD WAR; CONGRESS AND FOREIGN POLICY; CONTAINMENT; DÉTENTE; DISARMAMENT; IDEOLOGY AND FOREIGN POLICY; INTERNATIONAL ORGANIZATION; NATIONAL SECURITY; POLITICS AND FOREIGN POLICY; PROTECTORATES AND SPHERES OF INFLUENCE; PUBLIC OPINION; REALISM AND IDEALISM; REVISIONISM; TREATIES; THE TRUMAN DOCTRINE; UNCONDITIONAL SURRENDER.]

OPEN DOOR INTERPRETATION

William Appleman Williams

A SIGNIFICANT NUMBER of historians and other commentators have viewed the Open Door notes of 1899 and 1900 as the culmination of earlier attitudes, objectives, and policies, and as a coherent and decisive formulation of the major forces affecting American diplomacy during the century after 1865. But such people are too different (and too separated in time) to be jumbled together as a school. They are not, for example, defined by the ideological, institutional, personal, generational, and political affinities that characterized the Frankfurt School of Marxist sociologists that flourished from the 1930's through the 1960's, and that produced a clearly defined body of analysis and interpretation. Hence, it is more helpful to speak of an Open Door interpretation of American foreign relations that has been advanced, from the 1890's to the present, by a disparate group of policymakers and politicians, bureaucrats, nonacademic intellectuals, and university and college teachers.

That odd assortment of people has nevertheless shared, however obliquely, the conviction that the Open Door policy is the keystone of twentieth-century American diplomacy. Elected policymakers, for example, as well as the bureaucrats they ushered into positions of influence, have used it as the intellectual vantage point from which to view and deal with the world. Such people have defined the policy as the touchstone of their dialogues—and confrontation—with the American public and other countries. The Open Door policy has been their idiom of thought, discourse, and action: it defines American perceptions and objectives, and hence those who criticize or oppose the policy have been viewed as problems if not enemies. Germany was thus a troublemaker

long before Adolf Hitler, Japan long before Hideki Tojo, and Russia long before Josef Stalin.

Elihu Root and Henry L. Stimson operated within the framework of the Open Door policy when they served as secretaries of war, as well as during their tenures as secretaries of state. William Jennings Bryan thought within that framework prior to World War I just as surely as Charles Evans Hughes, Cordell Hull, and James S. Byrnes did in later years. And President Theodore Roosevelt and President Woodrow Wilson (and others) worked within the idiom that had been stated by President William McKinley even before Secretary of State John Hay announced it to the chancelleries and the publics of the world. Historian A. Whitney Griswold made the central point very neatly in his study *The Far Eastern Policy of the United States* (1938): "It is wrong, perhaps, to say that Hughes stole Wilson's thunder, for Wilson himself had stolen Hay's."

The contextual persuasiveness of the Open Door outlook among American bureaucrats becomes apparent during a routine survey of the volumes in the State Department's published record, as offered in its *Bulletin* and *Papers Relating to the Foreign Relations of the United States*. Indeed, the student grows weary of the references to the Open Door policy: he is inclined to consider it a meaningless ritual save for the seriousness with which it is repeatedly used to explain and justify American actions. Another kind of evidence is provided by the testimony (before congressional committees, as well as in memoirs) of such influential bureaucrats as William S. Culbertson, John Van Antwerp MacMurray, Joseph Clark Grew, and George F. Kennan.

Kennan, an influential foreign service officer and scholar, provides a particularly striking example of the power of the *Weltanschauung* of the Open Door. Writing as a historian in *American Diplomacy: 1900–1950* (1951), he damned the Open Door policy (and its underlying outlook) as idealistic, moralistic, legalistic, unrealistic, and ineffective. But his own zealous proposal to contain, and thereby drastically change, the Soviet Union through the global deployment of American moral, economic, political, and military power was designed to realize the objectives of Secretary Hay's original notes: a world open to American ideals and influence. Kennan was initially proposing—whatever his later denials, caveats, and remorse—an exponential escalation of President McKinley's deployment of American power against the Boxer Rebellion in China.

Because China was the initial subject of the Open Door notes, the early commentators focused their analyses of the policy upon its operation in Asia. While some observers (and participants) felt that the government ought to act more vigorously against what they considered to be the more restrictive policies of Japan, Russia, and Germany (and even China), they generally agreed that Secretary Hay's integration of moralism, ideology, political strategy, and economic expansion provided a definitive statement of the need and the wisdom of extending the area of Anglo-American freedom and enlarging the American marketplace without war. Even leading Populists, otherwise bitterly critical of the McKinley administration, admitted that the policy addressed the basic issues. The editors of the *Prairie Farmer,* for example, urged their readers in 1900 to elect expansionist politicians. And *Wallace's Farmer* was enthusiastic about the prospect of using "our moral advantage" to expand a "valuable" trade.

Three very different people—Brooks Adams, Theodore Roosevelt, and Woodrow Wilson—promptly placed the Open Door policy within a broader—and even more dynamic—intellectual context. Adams, the grandson of President John Quincy Adams (and the brother of Charles Francis and Henry Adams), was the most original—and eccentric—of that unusual group. He suffered from those differences in two ways: he never became famous,

and his major idea became associated with another person.

From the late 1880's to the publication of *The Law of Civilization and Decay* in 1894, Adams developed an explanation of world civilization that defined westward expansion as the key to progress, prosperity, and culture. The centers of civilization had moved ever westward until, in the 1890's, the scepter was passing from Paris and London to New York. That meant to Adams that the United States, if it was to seize its hour, had to move westward across the Pacific to dominate Asia. Otherwise Russia or another country would become the next center of world power and civilization. Adams then published a series of magazine articles on foreign policy, collected in 1900 as *America's Economic Supremacy,* in which he praised Hay's Open Door notes as a basic strategy for the United States and advocated a vigorous imperial policy—including the containment of Russia. In his view, Hay was "the only minister of foreign affairs in the whole world who grasped the situation."

Adams and his history-on-the-spot exerted a significant influence on Theodore Roosevelt (even though the latter did once remark that he thought Adams was "half-crazy"); but, in the larger arena, Adams lost out to the formulation of a similar idea offered by Frederick Jackson Turner. Adams was a disillusioned and acerbic Boston Brahmin writing history in the petulant frustration of having lost power, while Turner was an excited and romantic Midwestern poet-historian who stirred the mind of the public. In December 1893 Turner offered "The Significance of the Frontier in American History," a dramatic reinterpretation of American history that explained the nation's democracy and prosperity in terms of westward expansion from Virginia and Boston to Oregon, Alaska, and Hawaii.

Turner was not as overtly imperial as Adams. He even seemed sometimes to imply that a native form of socialism was as appropriate to the end of continental frontier expansionism as overseas expansion into Asia and other regions. But his stress on past expansion, and his interpretation of the outward push from 1897 to 1901 as a natural continuation of the earlier rush across the continent, left his readers with the idea that the Open Door policy was the new frontier. Certainly Theodore Roosevelt and Woodrow Wilson read that message in his essays, and took that idea from their correspondence and conversations with him.

Roosevelt was primed for Turner by Adams (and by his romantic cowboy interludes in the Dakota Territory), and his role in acquiring the Philippines and Cuba completed this transformation into what a psychologist might call a true believer. American expansion was a crusade for the Open Door virtues of peace, democracy, and prosperity. Roosevelt was sometimes discouraged by the difficulties of implementing the outlook in the face of opposition by other nations, or by the reluctance of the public to support the measures he considered desirable; but his commitment to the *Weltanschauung* remained firm: "We advocate the 'open door' with all that it implies."

Not only did Roosevelt view the Open Door policy as the extension of the Monroe Doctrine to Asia; he moved in 1905–1906 to extend the policy to Africa. His discussions with Secretary of State Elihu Root led to one of the clearest expressions of the way in which the open door interpretation guided such policymakers. Seeking to prevent either France or Germany from establishing exclusive control over Morocco, Root advised American negotiators that "here, again, the 'open door' seems to be the sound policy to advocate." He then emphasized that it was vital "that the door, being open, shall lead to something; that the outside world shall benefit by assured opportunities, and that the Moroccan people shall be made in a measure fit and able to profit by the advantages of the proposed reform."

A very similar view was held and acted upon by President Woodrow Wilson. During the late 1880's he had met and talked with Turner at Johns Hopkins University, and the results were impressive. As a historian and political scientist on his way to the White House, Wilson used Turner's frontier thesis to explain much of American history. "All I ever wrote on the subject," he once commented, "came from him." That remark qualifies as one of Wilson's unusual acts of intellectual generosity, and therefore mirrors his usual arrogance by giving Turner too much credit. Wilson was an idealis-

tic missionary crusader in behalf of American virtues and economic supremacy in his own right, and added his particular insights to the American political system.

Even so, Wilson-as-historian leaned very heavily on Turner. "The days of glad expansion are gone, our life grows tense and difficult," he wrote in 1896 in explaining the crisis of the 1890's. Five years later, after Hay's Open Door notes, he considered such expansion a "natural and wholesome impulse." "Who shall say," he added, "where it will end?" In 1902 he published the four-volume *History of the American People,* which made it clear that the historian-as-politician-as-would-be-world-leader viewed economic expansion as the frontier to replace the continent that had been occupied. A section in volume V (which reads like a close paraphrase of some essays written by Brooks Adams) recommended increased efficiency in government so that the United States "might command the economic fortunes of the world." He concluded his analysis by stressing the need for markets—markets "to which diplomacy, and if need be power, must make an open way."

Wilson classically revealed his involvement with the Open Door *Weltanschauung* during the 1915 confrontation with Japan over its Twenty-One Demands on China. He explained to Secretary of State William Jennings Bryan that the basic objective was "the maintenance of the policy of an open door to the world." Thereafter Bryan periodically reminded various individuals and groups that the president's policy was to "open the doors of all the weaker countries to an invasion of American capital and enterprise." The principal importance of these and earlier quotations in this historiographical context lies not in revealing the policy per se, but in suggesting how early policymakers were intellectuals developing and applying an Open Door interpretation of American foreign relations.

Moreover, even before Wilson was elected, a few historians and political scientists had recognized the importance of the policy in that sense. Archibald C. Coolidge, for example, in *The United States as a World Power* (1908), called the Open Door outlook "one of the cardinal principles of American policy." John A. Hob-

OPEN DOOR INTERPRETATION

son, the perceptive English liberal who initiated the critical Western study of imperialism (1902), was the first scholar to recognize the pervasive nature of the Open Door *Weltanschauung*. Viewing it as the key to American policy, and reacting with a favorable judgment, he argued in an essay contributed to *Towards a Lasting Peace* (1916) that the policy and its underlying outlook provided the basis for lasting peace and prosperity.

That statement was almost a prediction, for in January 1918 President Wilson presented in his Fourteen Points a program that was clearly a product of the Open Door *Weltanschauung*. He not only used (consciously or unconsciously) phrases from Hay's original notes, but the encompassing idiom of what he called "the only possible program" for peace was clearly an Open Door view of the world. The historian-become-policymaker and the historian as analyst-turned-public-commentator had reached an unplanned consensus.

The ensuing debates over Wilson's program, and the causes of the war and American intervention, buried Hobson's insight. His approach was ignored and unexplored for many years; and even when it was revived, it was done without any overt recognition of his pioneering effort. That did not mean, however, that the Open Door policy and its underlying outlook were wholly neglected. But that is the essence of the historiographical question: the issue involved whether or not historians (and other commentators) recognized that the Open Door policy was in truth the expression of a broad understanding of America and its relationship with the world.

Defined more formally in philosophical terms, the problem concerned a choice between a Cartesian world and a Spinozan world. Most American historians who came to maturity between 1895 and 1950 were Cartesians; they accepted a world composed of discrete atomistic units, some of which sometimes interacted with each other much as various billiard balls hit this time one ball and next time another ball. This led to what came to be known as the interest-group approach: individual A or P, or association D or S, exerted a determining influence upon decision F or Z.

Such an approach produced in history, as it did in science, some stimulating—if limited—

research and analysis. Thus in *Americans in Eastern Asia* (1922), Tyler Dennett could perceive "the Reassertion of the Open Door Policy" during the McKinley administration, but within a few pages assert that it was all "a purely temporary expedient." But Alfred L. P. Dennis' "The Open Door in China," in his *Adventures in American Diplomacy* (1928), used Dennett to suggest the long-term development of a guiding outlook. He cited Dennett's summary of the situation in 1858: the United States "desired for its citizens an open door to trade." Then he, too, retreated to call it all "an expedient." Revealing the ambivalence of early postwar scholarship, Dennis next quoted a comment that reminds one of Root and Wilson: "The policy of the Open Door . . . is the one and only policy. . . . Neither is it any use keeping the door open without insuring that the room on the other side of the door is in order."

Dennett was at his best on the broader nature of the Open Door policy a few years later when, in *John Hay: From Poetry to Politics* (1933), he was the first historian to sense the role of Brooks Adams in developing a world view that guided Hay and other policymakers. But the key figure of the interwar years was Charles Austin Beard. The magnificent study *The Rise of American Civilization* that he and Mary Ritter Beard first published in 1927 talked candidly about the turn-of-the-century expansion as "Imperial America," and they hinted at the development of an imperial *Weltanschauung* that was crystallized in the Open Door policy.

The Beards perceptively saw the origins of that outlook in Secretary of State William H. Seward's mid-nineteenth-century vision of a global American empire. Their description of the Open Door policy made the point that it integrated three elements—while "designed with realistic and practical ends in mind, the policy of the open door also had a lofty moral flavor"—but they did not develop it as a *Weltanschauung*. They said nothing of Theodore Roosevelt's extension of the policy to Africa, for example, and barely mentioned it in dealing with the later diplomacy of Secretary of State Charles Evans Hughes.

That curiously titillating performance can be explained by two considerations: the Beards were writing a sweeping essay rather than a

706

study of foreign policy per se, and Charles Beard was in the process of modifying his theory of knowledge and causation. His early work was grounded in an orthodox scientific-atomistic conception of reality that led him into a sophisticated interest-group analysis of history and politics (as in *The Economic Basis of Politics* [1916] and *An Economic Interpretation of the Constitution* [1913]). There is strong evidence, however, that even as those books were being published, Beard was turning away from his methodology. That became apparent between 1928 and 1937, when he wrote a great deal about the problem. Beard had referred to various German antipositivists as early as 1913, and their influence reappeared in *The American Party Battle* (1928), in which he discussed the weaknesses of his earlier theory. He then opened a direct confrontation with the issue in two books and an article in 1934: *The Idea of National Interest, The Open Door at Home,* and "Written History as an Act of Faith" (*American Historical Review* [January]).

Beard did not break completely free of the atomistic, interest-group theory of reality in *The Idea of National Interest,* but he did place the conflict between urban and agrarian interests in a much broader context. He spoke most directly about the question near the end of the book, remarking that the danger of the atomistic, Cartesian view of the world was in "limiting the understanding of the whole." That enriched the meaning of his earlier references to such intellectual heirs of Spinoza as Georg Wilhelm Hegel, Karl Marx, Max Weber, Frederich Meinecke, Karl Huessi, Karl Mannheim, Wilhelm Dilthey—and even Albert Schweitzer.

The issue was the ongoing dialogue between Descartes and Spinoza: the discrete, atomistic conception of reality versus the view that all things are related to each other. Given the American intellectual environment of those years, Beard was engaged in a lonely, courageous, and difficult task of reexamining his *Weltanschauung* in his middle years (see Lloyd Sorenson, "Charles Beard and German Historiographical Thought," in *Mississippi Valley Historical Review* [September 1955]). He did not, however, develop and use the new approach in a rigorous manner. The results can be seen in *The Discussion of Human Affairs* (1936), "Currents of Thought in His-

toriography" (*American Historical Review* [April 1937]), and *The American Spirit* (1942).

Instead, Beard veered off into a quasi-biographical approach, interpreting foreign policy after 1934 as largely the result of Franklin Delano Roosevelt's power drive and inability to deal with the domestic crisis. Those books, *American Foreign Policy in the Making, 1932–1940* (1946) and *President Roosevelt and the Coming of the War* (1948), raised troublesome questions; but Beard's personalizing of policy neglected broader issues. Hence his methodological explorations were ultimately developed by others who returned to Beard after they had come to the concept of an Open Door *Weltanschauung* along different lines.

In the meantime, however, the study of the Open Door policy was dominated by A. Whitney Griswold's *The Far Eastern Policy of the United States* (1938). Sensing that the Open Door was more than just a policy, he offered, for example, the suggestion that President Wilson and Secretary of State Charles Evans Hughes had transformed Hay's notes into a way of perceiving and thinking about foreign relations, and indicated that Cordell Hull's dedication to that outlook had more than a little to do with the subsequent confrontations with Germany and Japan. But all he said explicitly was that the Open Door was a "time honored American principle."

The concept of a principle emerging from the pragmatic needs and demands of various interest groups, and then becoming a *Weltanschauung,* was the analytical and interpretive tool that Beard had tried to forge between 1925 and 1935. Though they did not reveal his consciousness of purpose, three historians did advance that work during the decade after Griswold. Fred Harvey Harrington was the most intelligent and sophisticated interest-group historian of his generation; and, if he had remained a historian, he would probably have gone beyond Beard in the application of a more subtle methodology. Harrington, along with William Best Hesseltine, his friend and colleague at the University of Wisconsin, had a genius for integrating biography and policy in a way that implicitly transcended interest-group analysis.

Harrington's study of American policy in Korea, *God, Mammon, and the Japanese* (1944), culminated in a three-page passage that implicitly revealed the broad outlook of Theodore Roosevelt and other early architects of the Open Door *Weltanschauung*. Sylvester K. Stevens provided a related approach in *American Expansion in Hawaii, 1842–1898* (1945). A third book, Edward H. Zabriskie's *American-Russian Rivalry in the Far East . . . 1895–1914* (1946), displayed the post-Beardian ambivalence in American historiography. Zabriskie (like Harrington) placed the protagonists in a broad framework, and even suggested that they operated within an encompassing overview; but he never delineated that outlook.

At the end of the war, therefore, Beard's methodological explorations had neither been exploited directly nor reinforced by parallel investigations. The account of what happened next is complicated, as with all intellectual history, but the essentials are reasonably clear. To speak in the idiom of nuclear physics, a highly charged field was penetrated by highly charged particles. The environment was defined primarily by the history department of the University of Wisconsin: a great tradition was reinvigorated by the stimulating and contrasting minds of such scholars as Paul Knaplund, Paul Farmer, Robert Reynolds, and Gaines Post in European history, and Merrill Jensen, Hesseltine, and Harrington in American history. But other scholars in related fields, such as Hans Gerth in sociology and Frederick J. Hoffman in literature, were also a vital part of the ensuing nuclear reaction that was triggered by the arrival in 1946–1947 of hundreds of excited and hungry veterans who wanted to become excellent historians.

An unusually large number of them achieved that objective during the next four years, and went on to make important contributions in every field of American history. The major elements involved in the part of that process that produced what came to be known as the Open Door interpretation can be defined as follows: the ongoing intellectual interaction among the professors, among the students, and between those groups; the broad training in European as well as in American history, and in related disciplines; and the particular genius of Harrington. Thus, what emerged is best understood as the result of a true community that flowered for most of two decades.

The story can be told through focus on William Appleman Williams, though he explicitly insists that the result was a communal product and, furthermore, that it involved the work of scholars who are not usually identified as part of the "Wisconsin School" of diplomatic history. Given his exposure to the history faculty, the vital elements in Williams' development were his previous training in mathematics and science and his work with Gerth. Gerth gave Williams a broad knowledge of the methodology of *Weltanschauung* (including the serious study of Marx) and helped him to begin developing it as a tool for the study of foreign relations. Williams thus came to Beard twice: first as a beginning graduate student who read him as an interest-group historian and later, educated by Gerth, viewing him as a man struggling briefly with the concept of *Weltanschauung*.

Williams first experimented with that methodology in *American-Russian Relations, 1784–1947* (1952), as in his discussion of the influence of Brooks Adams; but he was not fully in command of the approach, and the effort to open the orthodox form of the monograph to include such analysis posed severe additional difficulties. The next phase of his work cannot be fully understood outside his friendship with Charles Vevier, a fellow student in Harrington's seminar, for they often did primary research together over the next three years and exchanged notes and ideas on a regular basis. Vevier's *The United States and China, 1906–1913* (1955) interpreted the specific events of those years within the broad framework of a knowing effort by decision makers to act upon the Open Door view of the world.

Also in 1955, Williams provided a clear example of how he was developing and using the concept of *Weltanschauung* in his study of the way that Frederick Jackson Turner's frontier thesis and John Hay's Open Door notes were related parts of the same overview ("The Frontier Thesis and American Foreign Policy," in *Pacific Historical Review* [November 1955]). He next used the methodology in dealing with contemporary foreign policy ("The American Century: 1941–1957," in *Nation* [November 1957]) and in offering a broad analysis of the revolutionary and early national period ("The Age of Mercantilism: An Interpretation of the American Political Economy," in *William and Mary Quarterly* [October 1958]).

Shortly after he had returned to Wisconsin as a member of the faculty, Williams published *The Tragedy of American Diplomacy* (1959), an interpretive essay on twentieth-century foreign policy. Although it came to be viewed rather narrowly as the basis for the "Open Door interpretation," and as a critique of policy after 1944, the book actually dealt with the development of a *Weltanschauung* through the interaction and integration of ideas, interest-group pressures, and the dynamic processes of marketplace capitalism. That more complicated nature of the approach was shortly underscored by Vevier, just before he left history to help build the University of Wisconsin at Milwaukee. His "American Continentalism: An Idea of Expansion, 1845–1910" (*American Historical Review* [January 1960]) was a subtle interpretation of the shift from continental conquest to overseas expansion.

As Williams has repeatedly pointed out, he and others working in the idiom of an Open Door *Weltanschauung* learned much from other scholars who favored a different approach. Charles C. Campbell's *Special Business Interests and the Open Door Policy* (1951), for example, made it clear that the Open Door policy was an idea—and an ideal—that embraced the practical demands of many different groups. And Paul Schroeder's early and perceptive *The Axis Alliance and Japanese-American Relations* (1958) remains a revealing analysis of the way that Secretary of State Cordell Hull's intense commitment to the Open Door outlook defined the ultimately violent confrontation with Japan.

Williams continued his own work in *The Contours of American History* (1961), a broad interpretation of American history based on the argument that the United States has developed under three major world views, and in *The Roots of the Modern American Empire* (1969), an effort to provide a quasi-monographic history of how one *Weltanschauung* matures and then infuses and influences its successor. But the methodology and the interpretation took on lives of their own as the people who participated in Williams' seminar at Wisconsin began to produce their own articles and books.

As a teacher, Williams was graced with an unusual number of exceptional students, the legacy of the department's preeminence during the late 1940's and early 1950's. Perhaps his most important contribution was to give them their heads, to encourage them to explore the great resources of the university faculty, and to push them to realize the very best that was within themselves. The way that some of them received and used his version of the methodological tool of *Weltanschauung* makes the point. Martin J. Sklar, for example, produced the striking essay "Woodrow Wilson and the Political Economy of Modern United States Liberalism" (*Studies on the Left* [1960]). And James Weinstein, one of Richard Hofstadter's most perceptive students, who entered and was influenced by the Wisconsin milieu, wrote the excellent *The Corporate Ideal in the Liberal State, 1900–1968* (1968).

If Williams had operated more traditionally, directing and controlling his seminar in a narrow and orthodox manner, then the subsequent professional discussion (and gossip) about a "Wisconsin School" would have more substance. As it happened, however, the students—and their students—went their own ways. One need only consider the impressive trio who worked with Harrington as well as Williams. Walter LaFeber's first book, *The New Empire: An Interpretation of American Expansion, 1860–1898* (1963), dealt with intellectuals (and other ideamongers) more as an interest group than as craftsmen of a *Weltanschauung*. In a later study, *America, Russia, and the Cold War, 1945–1960* (1967), he further refined that process. But one of his students, David Green (*The Containment of Latin America* [1971]), did more in the way of using a world view to explain a regional policy.

Thomas J. McCormick offered an imaginative marriage, so to speak, of Harrington and Williams in an exquisite study, *China Market: America's Quest for Informal Empire, 1893–1901* (1967). McCormick was deceptively empirical, for while his pages were filled with facts that no one else had uncovered, and his style was almost arid, he nevertheless constructed an account of how an expansionist *Weltanschauung* (in his own idiom, "informal empire") came into being at the turn of the century.

Lloyd C. Gardner's initial study, *Economic Aspects of New Deal Diplomacy* (1964), seemed more interest-group–oriented than it was: his climactic chapter, "Restoring an Open World," made the point about the power of Secretary of State Hull's world view with an almost fey sense of humor. He quoted Harry Hopkins telling President Roosevelt (p. 283) that Prime Minister Churchill ought to be "disabuse[d]" of the idea that Hull's persistence about the Open Door policy was only "a pet hobby." In a later and unusually sophisticated volume, *Architects of Illusion: Men and Ideas in American Foreign Policy, 1941–1949* (1970), Gardner transcended Beard by using the intellectual biography to explain the development of a world view shared by many top policymakers. Gardner's students used that approach with great effectiveness in dealing with the various aspects of the origins of the outlook and its later manifestations.

The ahistorical mistake involved in personalizing the Open Door interpretation—and the methodology of Spinoza, Marx, and Dilthey—around Williams is revealed in the work of many other historians. Robert Freeman Smith, for example, demonstrated in *What Happened in Cuba* (1963) that Harrington produced many students who moved beyond the interest-group methodology. And Stephen E. Ambrose made it clear, in *Rise to Globalism: American Foreign Policy, 1938–1970* (1971), that Hesseltine was a key figure in that milieu.

Finally, the approach also attracted younger European historians who knew independently, and perhaps better, the philosophical roots in Spinoza, Marx, Dilthey, George Lukacs, and the Frankfurt School. Perhaps the most stimulating work has been done by Hans-Ulrich Wehler, as in *Der Aufsteig des amerikanischen Imperialismus* (1974). With enviable finesse he treats the process through which interests, problems, and ideas produce a *Weltanschauung*.

Given their variations on a theme, and their energy, it is not surprising that the protagonists of the Open Door interpretation have provoked much comment. Many of those who have responded favorably, however, have been as inattentive to the essentials of the methodology as have the critics—who have also overemphasized the influence of Williams and who have not differentiated and discussed the primary issues. An excellent example of the latter failure is provided by Arthur S. Link's commentary (in *The Higher Realism of Woodrow Wilson and Other Essays* [1971]) on Carl P. Parrini's *Heir to Empire. United States Diplomacy, 1916–1923* (1969).

Link acknowledges that Parrini (a member of the Williams seminar) is correct in arguing that Wilson advocated Open Door expansionism, but then comments that Wilson's motives were the best—"the slow and steady improvement of mankind through the spread of a reformed and socially responsible democratic capitalism" (p. 79). Link not only misses the integration of economic and idealistic elements in Wilson's outlook that is stressed by Williams, Sklar, and Parrini, but further confuses their description and analysis of the consequences of that world view with the attribution of evil motives to Wilson. He also fails to credit Wilson, his own hero, with being a perceptive capitalist who understood the system's need for imperial expansion.

A few scholars have discussed the issues with greater insight and balance. Warren F. Kimball's "The Cold War Warmed Over" (*American Historical Review* [October 1974]) ranges far beyond his announced subject. And Joan Hoff Wilson's exploration of the subject in *Ideology and Economics: United States Relations with the Soviet Union, 1918–1933* (1974) is an example of her discerning insight into the primary problems of post-Beardian historiography. Such keen commentary underscores the judgment of Melvyn Leffler in "The Origins of Republican War Debt Policy, 1921–1923: A Case Study in the Applicability of the Open Door Interpretation" (*Journal of American History* [December 1972]). Williams and other advocates of his approach have "compelled all diplomatic historians to grapple with a complex set of criteria that heretofore had been frequently minimized" (p. 601).

THE OPEN DOOR POLICY

Richard W. Van Alstyne

THE OPEN DOOR is a political metaphor that has pertained to China since about 1898. Allegedly it is a policy unique to the United States. Secretary of State Dean Acheson so treated it in 1949 after the Chinese Communists had locked and barred the door. Admitting the communist victory, Acheson nevertheless remarked, "Meanwhile our policy will continue to be based upon . . . our friendship for China, and our traditional support for the Open Door and for China's independence and administrative and territorial integrity." Burdened with ambiguities, the phrase was seldom defined even during the years when it was common usage; and it accumulated a number of meanings so varied as to render it meaningless. "We stand for the Open Door," declared the editors of the *New Republic* magazine in 1921, thus rendering it a simple article of faith. Or it could be treated as a similitude of the Monroe Doctrine, as was done in the *New York Times* (16 January 1918): "The Open-Door in China, a Principle of Foreign Policy to be maintained like the Monroe Doctrine." One of that newspaper's prominent correspondents, Thomas F. Millard, an ardent advocate of a strong policy regarding China, wanted the Open Door given special mention in the Covenant of the League of Nations. It should "be included on the same basis as the Monroe Doctrine," urged Millard, "in any reservation the Senate might make to the Covenant." Millard felt that the Open Door should be known as the Hay Doctrine because, he asserted, John Hay had originated it in a series of diplomatic notes he had addressed to the principal treaty powers in 1899. "The Hay Doctrine," wrote Millard, "means that other nations shall not impose their institutions, or their Government, on the Chinese without their con-

sent, and that all foreign nations will have in China equal commercial, financial and industrial rights, privileges and opportunities . . ." (5 August 1919).

Actually, neither the phrase nor the policy originated with John Hay. The phrase was common usage in Britain in 1898, and the *New York Times* picked it up from there. "We believe," wrote the editor (24 November 1898), "that the *New York Times* was for some months alone among American journals in urging that we should join the demand of Great Britain for the open door in the Far East. . . ." As the British understood and practiced it, the Open Door meant free trade or equality of commercial opportunity, a much simpler version than Millard's. President William McKinley's definition resembled that of the British, though phrased in negative terms: "no advantages in the Orient which are not common to all."

Meanwhile, John Hay having been brought back from his ambassadorship in London in September 1898 to be made secretary of state, the *New York Times* led the way not merely in linking his name with the Open Door but also in enlarging upon the concept. "If Mr. Hay had been in the State Department a year ago," it lamented (17 March 1899), "the Far Eastern question would have worn a much more cheerful aspect for American manufacturers and merchants than it wears today." The Open Door now meant world peace and prosperity; hence "it is clearly our duty to maintain it with all the resources at our command. It is the true mission that we have to carry out as a 'world power.'"

By the middle of 1900, the Open Door, in the view of the *Times,* was primarily an American policy; Britain was merely cooperating. Ex-

THE OPEN DOOR POLICY

cerpts from two editorials (18 and 24 July 1900) illustrate this intellectual metamorphosis. Under the rubric "America directs world's policy," the *Times* affirmed:

> That is practically what the United States under Mr. Hay's lead has done. The nations of the world, all guided by famous statesmen with established reputations, were taken by surprise by the Chinese crisis and halted, irresolutely waiting for a leader. In that emergency the leader was found. He was the quiet gentleman in Washington. . . . He did not announce himself as the leader of the nations. . . . He simply stepped in . . . and the nations recognized instinctively that a man of power had come. They have followed him like lambs ever since. [As the Chinese crisis unfolds] the conviction is growing that the solution of the great problem now upon the world will in the end depend more upon John Hay than upon any other man in the world.

Returning to the theme six days later, the *Times* declared: "the moral leadership of the powers has been practically established at Washington." China, weakened and exposed to dangerous plots, will naturally "turn to us as a friend whose disinterestedness has been demonstrated. . . . We stand ready to do our duty to humanity and to ourselves in China without ulterior and selfish designs." And "of course" this problem "has from the first been wisely guided by the firm and sure hand of Secretary Hay."

Two years later (12 July 1902) another editorial enlarged upon "Our Triumph in China." The Chinese were grateful; the British and European press gave Hay the credit for

> . . . enabling Europe to extricate itself from a situation humiliating to China, injurious to the Powers concerned, and dangerous to the peace of the world. . . . We shall reap advantages from our good behavior. But it would be absurd to pretend that our treatment of China was motived by interest. It was evidently instigated by the same spirit of justice and kindness by which the work of the State Department under Mr. Hay has been animated, and that goes near to making good his own description of the Golden Rule as the basis of American diplomacy.

So in 1900 the millennium was at hand. America, leading the nations, stood before the Open Door, clad in all the virtues. Disinter-

estedness, unselfishness, friendship for China—these were the words of the American catechism. Dean Acheson a half-century later could do no more than recite the faith. This essay will probe more deeply into the mythology of the Open Door, but first it will have recourse to substantive history. The dates of the first *New York Times* editorials, published in 1898 and 1899, indicate that the process of idealizing the Open Door—of depicting it only in terms of abstractions—began at once, even before John Hay had put his name to the diplomatic notes (September 1899) that bear the label. In other words, the myth took hold before the policy itself was formulated. In realizing this we should reflect upon the power of myth in history.

The substance, though not the name, of the Open Door lay in the Chinese treaty system that dated from the Treaty of Nanking (1842), which ended the First Opium War between Great Britain and China. There were five original treaty ports—Canton, Amoy, Foochow, Ningpo, and Shanghai—but many others were added in the course of the century, particularly after the Second Opium War, waged by the British and French in 1856–1860. Historians have stigmatized the method as "gunboat diplomacy"; but other powers, first among them the United States, obtained the same concessions. Nationals of the various treaty powers were enabled to import their goods subject to a uniform tariff of 5 percent imposed under the treaties and collectible by the Chinese customs service. All of the treaties contained the most-favored-nation clause, which guaranteed that any new right or privilege obtained by any of the treaty powers automatically applied to them all.

However, because of Chinese resentment against the treaties foisted upon them and because of the ingrained corruption of the native customs service, three institutions separate from the treaties were developed to make the system work. All three were British in origin: the crown colony of Hong Kong, an open port from 1843, which demonstrated quick success as the entrepôt to the trade of south China; the International Settlement of Shanghai, an autonomous city where foreigners might reside and do business that developed as the gateway to the trade of the Yangtze Valley; and the

THE OPEN DOOR POLICY

Inspectorate of Maritime Customs, which started as a model customshouse at Shanghai and subsequently opened offices at all the other treaty ports. Under the direction of Sir Robert Hart, the inspectorate earned a reputation for honesty and efficiency in the collection of duties.

The Open Door label comes from the international rivalries and concession hunting that moved to the fore in China after the Sino-Japanese War (1894–1895). The British-controlled Shanghai Chamber of Commerce may have been the first to hit upon the phrase in its demand that the whole of China be opened to foreign trade. The German seizure of Kiaochow (November 1897), followed by the Russian sequestration of the Liaotung Peninsula in Manchuria, precipitated a sense of crisis in Britain, whose long dominance of the China trade appeared threatened. A lengthy debate on the situation took place in the House of Commons in January 1898, during the course of which two of the government speakers, Arthur Balfour and Michael Hicks Beach, invoked the Open Door by name in answer to the special rights in the leaseholds obtained by the other powers. J. W. Bengough, a popular Canadian cartoonist, poet, and lecturer, published a poem entitled "The Open Door," in the *New York Times* on 3 September 1898. The poem, in nine stanzas, amusingly but accurately describes how Britain appealed to America to support the Open Door.

> John Bull spake out in accents clear,
>   With something of the lion's roar,
> (His cousin Sam was standing near)—
>   "Hello! You there on China's shore,
>   There's got to be an Open Door!
> What say you, Sam?"
>   Cries Sam, "Encore!"
>
> "This wholesale changing of the map
>   By the great powers everywhere
> May be all right—and I'm the chap
>   Who takes the cake, they all declare,
>   But with the world my cake I share,
> What say you, Sam?"
>   Cries Sam, "Ah, there!"
>
> "The 'Open Door' for one and all,
>   Free trade in every blessed spot
> Where I am ruler—at the pole
>   Or in the tropics; cold or hot—

> Fair field for all the blooming lot—
> What say you, Sam?"
>   Cries Sam, "That's what!"
>
> "I've got some millions to be fed,
>   And markets I must somehow get;
> My life depends upon my trade:
>   All round the world I spread my net,
>   And for free commerce I am set,
> What say you, Sam?"
>   Cries Sam, "You bet!"
>
> "I've got no use for Chinese walls—
> We want no more, but rather fewer—
> And, by my ten-pound cannon balls,
>   And first-class battleships galore,
>   This sort of thing I won't endure—
> What say you, Sam?"
>   Cries Sam, "Why sure!"
>
> "My policy all around is Peace.
>   My mission is to spread the light,
> I rule the waves that war may cease,
>   But in my arm's resistless might,
>   And for free markets I will fight!
> What say you, Sam?"
>   Cries Sam, "That's right!"
>
> "Say 'sphere of influence' if the phrase
>   More diplomatically flows
> Than 'Open Door'—but don't you raise,
>   My friends, lest you become my foes,
>   Trade barriers: we may come to blows—
> What say you, Sam?"
>   Cries Sam, "That goes!"
>
> The Gang—ah, pardon me—the Powers
>   Retire to think a season, so
> John turns to Sam and says; "Tis ours,
>   Not mine alone, but ours, to show
>   The path on which world trade must go,
> Hey, Sam?"
>   Cries Sam, "It-is-you-know!"
>
> "In fack, I calkilate," says he,
>   " 'Twould be a ruther grand affair
> If out thar on the Yellow Sea,
>   With your old flag mine should appear;
>   My duty in this thing seems clear,
> What say you, John?"
>   Cried Bull, " 'Ear! 'Ear!"

Bengough may have been a bit early, but he was a keen observer nonetheless. Alarmed at the prospect that production would so outrun consumption that the domestic market would be glutted and prices collapse, American businesses had begun looking for markets in "undeveloped" portions of the world, notably in Latin America and the Orient. "Our manufacturers have outgrown or are outgrowing the home market," announced the National Association of Manufacturers (NAM) when it was organized in 1895, and the "expansion of our foreign trade is [the] only promise of relief." Other industrial nations shared this fear of a surplus, but ambition and belief that markets and avenues to greater wealth could be found tended to supersede fears. "A vast inert mass of humanity" (Secretary of State Walter Gresham's phrase), China was the great lure, as it had been for centuries.

A scramble by financiers in 1895 to lend money to China to pay off the war indemnity extorted by Japan was among the first moves; and extensive new treaty rights secured by the Japanese, and automatically made available to the other treaty powers, made Japan, in the eyes of the British and Americans, the natural champion of the Open Door. "We must make our plans," the NAM announced in 1897, "to secure our full share of the great trade which is coming out of the new industrial era in the Orient." By 1899 American confidence, fired by the acquisition of islands from Spain, was prepared to translate "full share" as "the lion's share." With peace and the Open Door secured, "the world is ours commercially." And with the Philippines as "pickets of the Pacific standing guard at the entrances to trade with the millions of China, . . . it would be possible for American energy to . . . ultimately convert the Pacific Ocean into an American Lake."

The quotations are from members of the American Asiatic Association, formed in 1898 from an earlier committee and composed of corporations, individual businessmen, public figures such as the mayor of New York, and former diplomats who had served in the Orient, notably Charles Denby, minister to China (1885–1898), and John Barrett of the legation in Bangkok, Siam (1894–1898). "For five years," wrote Barrett in the *North American Review,* "I have hammered away in reports to the Government, letters to Chambers of Commerce, and contributions to newspapers, magazines, and reviews . . . with the hope of thus awakening our Government . . . to an appreci-

ation of the splendid field [in the Orient] awaiting their best efforts." Studies of Barrett's activities and of the Asiatic Association show that they fulfilled their purpose in arousing public sentiment and in bringing influence to bear upon the government.

There was also the American China Development Company, which set out in 1896 to obtain a concession to build a railway from Peking to Hankow. Some of the outstanding business and professional men in America were shareholders in this concern, and it had the support of Grover Cleveland's administration. In China, Denby exulted that this would be the opening wedge for an "almost limitless field of financial and industrial operations [that] will be occupied, dominated and controlled by Americans." The contract fell through, but the company's project illustrates two important new developments that were taking place in China: an international race for railway concessions, the nature of which affected the whole concept of the Open Door as practiced under the treaty system, and government backing required by financiers as a prerequisite for speculative enterprises involving heavy capital investment.

Equality of capital investment is quite different from equality of commercial opportunity, and would seem impracticable without special concessions and government guarantees against ruinous competition. In the United States itself there had been overbuilding of railroads and construction of parallel lines, resulting in bankruptcies. Yet that was what was now proposed for China: to the concept of the Open Door in trade was to be added the concept of the "territorial integrity and administrative independence" of China so that the weak central government at Peking might be coerced by foreign governments into granting concessions to rival financiers and entrepreneurs. This was not a part of the original British Open Door policy, which was quite prepared to meet foreign competition in the trade of the Yangtze Valley, where it held a better than two-thirds control. But to welcome foreign rivals seeking special concessions in this vast area was not to be expected.

In sponsoring the promotional activities of Lord Charles Beresford, the American Asiatic Association achieved noticeable results in advancing its cause. Beresford, arriving in San

THE OPEN DOOR POLICY

Francisco from China in February 1899, represented the Associated Chambers of Commerce of Great Britain and had been working to popularize the Open Door in that country. John Hay knew him there, and personally entertained him when he came to Washington. But Beresford's success lay principally in the field of building opinion—in his after-dinner speeches and in his book *The Break-up of China,* published in England and widely read in America. An excerpt from one of his speeches in New York (March 1899) illustrates how the myth of helping China was beginning to take shape:

> We have a big, honest idea of what should be done with trade and commerce, and we have, even better than that, a grand, chivalrous, noble sentiment in regard to what should be done with weaker nations . . . I hope our friendliness will be cemented into an everlasting friendship, for I am absolutely certain that if that is so, not only will it push the interests of trade and commerce, but it will push the interests of humanity and of Christianity.

Apparently Beresford was making a bid to America to formulate its own policy independent of the British, for he declared: "The integrity of China should be assured, because without the integrity of China there is no use in talking about the open door." Advocates of a unilateral Open Door policy called attention to the analogy of the Monroe Doctrine; just as the United States "guaranteed" Latin America against Europe, so would it guarantee the "integrity" of China.

Beresford's speeches struck a sour note with William W. Rockhill, an American career diplomat and friend of Hay who had reason to feel himself better informed regarding China than the Englishman was. Collaborating with another friend, Alfred Hippisley, an Englishman who had had more than a quarter-century of experience with the Chinese Inspectorate of Maritime Customs, Rockhill was at this time preparing drafts of diplomatic notes that he hoped Hay would submit to the European powers as a formal statement of American policy. Beresford's assistance was "unnecessary . . . over here to carry out what must be recognized by all as *our* policy in China." Nevertheless, Rockhill inserted "integrity" into the draft of the note in-

tended for the British government, and the concept was subsequently formalized in a circular that Hay dispatched to the powers in July 1900.

In September 1899 Hay approved and sent Rockhill's notes to the powers—Britain, Germany, Russia, Japan, Italy, and France, in that order. The basic idea, which was originally Hippisley's, was to save the treaty system from eclipse by the leased ports. Each of the powers was asked to agree that it would not interfere with any treaty port situated inside any "so-called 'sphere of interest' or leased territory" it might have in China; that the existing treaty tariff would apply to any port that might be leased and that it would be administered by the Chinese inspectorate; and that in the matter of harbor dues and railroad charges over lines built, controlled, or operated within its sphere, it treat the merchandise belonging to the citizens of other nationalities on the same basis as the merchandise belonging to its own citizens or subjects. In other words, the notes assumed that the Open Door ("free enterprise system," in modern American parlance) would continue to function normally under the treaties.

Rockhill and Hay both recognized, however, that the spheres of interest—notably those of Germany, Russia, and France—were accomplished facts and that railways and other forms of capital investment would be exclusive to these powers in their respective spheres. This of course fell short of the original intent, which saw meaning in the Open Door only if it was equated with "integrity." But Hay and even Rockhill were too cautious to make this an issue, nor were they really initiating a policy for the United States: they were appealing for cooperation from the other powers—which they did not get, especially from Russia, which already had a large vested stake in Manchuria. At best theirs was a policy of "eat your cake and have it too." Ironically, not only was China not informed, much less consulted, but it was requested "that no arrangements . . . be entered into . . . which shall be to the disadvantage of American commerce."

So poorly informed were Hay and his advisers on real conditions in China that they took no note of the bitter xenophobia among the masses, which was manifested in riots and attacks on foreigners that increased in violence

715

and frequency in 1898. Phrases like "Open Door" and "integrity and independence" were mere abstractions in the face of these formidable forces of popular revolt. Rockhill and Hay prepared their notes in an intellectual vacuum, believing, like the missionaries, that China could be "saved" and its government stabilized by diplomacy and by advice that America stood ready to give. Hay himself remained undeceived by the idealistic legend already being shaped around his name. "Talk of the papers," he remarked to John Bassett Moore, the former assistant secretary of state, "about 'our pre-eminent moral position giving us the authority to dictate to the world' is mere flapdoodle." Hay made this remark just as his July 1900 circular was going out to the powers. To cope with the Boxer uprising (Peking was now under siege), the American Asiatic Association demanded "a strong policy . . . for the protection of life and property, and the safeguard of the large investments planned. . . ." To meet the emergency in Peking, the McKinley administration dispatched 5,000 troops from the Philippines; an international relief expedition was assembled at Tientsin, and it broke the siege in August.

Meanwhile, in his circular Hay informed the powers that "The policy of . . . the United States is to seek a solution which may bring about permanent safety and peace to China, preserve Chinese territorial and administrative entity, protect all rights . . . and safeguard for the world the principle of equal and impartial trade with all parts of the Chinese Empire." The circular contributed to this myth, but the practical settlement was arranged in conjunction with the other powers in September 1901. A fresh indemnity of $333 million, to be apportioned among the powers, was exacted from China (the financing to be accomplished through an international loan), and various servitudes imposed.

Rockhill was the American delegate to this conference and proved effective in scaling down the amount of the indemnity. But he continued to view China only from an American perspective. China must be reformed according to the American model, and the Chinese must be punished for acting so wickedly. They must adopt the concepts and institutions of the Western nation-states, but it would take

armed might to bring this about. The United States got the credit for being the friend of China against Europe, but the "friendship" rested on the tenuous basis of a smaller claim for indemnity. The differences were matters of degree and not of principle. In 1901 the Open Door and "integrity" were further from reality than ever, and the rivalry among the powers was so strong that those who knew the situation feared the outbreak of a general war. In his *Education,* Henry Adams "laughed at Hay for his helplessness" and saw the central issue as the "inevitable struggle for the control of China."

Meanwhile, in 1900 the United States Navy expressed itself in favor of a base on the China coast, singling out the Chusan Archipelago off the mouth of the Yangtze and Samsah Bay in Fukien province as desirable in relation to Manila; and the American consul at Amoy, thinking more in commercial terms, suggested a lease of that port. From Peking, E. H. Conger, the American minister, made an even more startling proposal: acquire a lease of the whole of Chihli Province, including apparently the Chinese capital itself. "We ought to be ready," he recommended, "either by negotiation or by actual possession, to own and control at least one good port from which we can potently assert our own rights and effectively wield our influence." Hay himself endorsed the navy's request, and President McKinley, according to Hay, was "inclined to favor the policy of seizing a port in China, and getting a foothold there, as other powers had done." Samsah Bay was the first choice and, imagining that Japan and Britain would collaborate with the United States, Hay sounded out the Japanese on the subject only to have the phrases of his July circular thrown back at him. So ended for the time being the covert American move to participate in the carving up of China. Ambitions were by no means satiated but, considering the rebuff received from Japan, it was deemed safer to fall back on the pretense of the Open Door.

Beginning in 1905, during the Russo-Japanese War, a determined attempt was made by the United States to open the door, but it was no longer the door of the treaty ports. These were now secondary in importance to the prospects for the sale of durable goods, products of the industrial revolution, and the placing of venture capital. The Open Door was, to quote Herbert Croly of the *New Republic* magazine, "a matter of building railroads, tapping natural resources, founding industries and of seeking those changes in Chinese political and social organization which would equip it to stand the strain of modern industrialism."

Russia's success with the Trans-Siberian Railroad turned attention toward Manchuria. A Russian concession obtained from China (1896) to build a direct line, the Chinese Eastern, that would shorten the distance to Vladivostok, and a branch line (the South Manchurian) to run south from Harbin to the newly leased port of Dalny (Talien), pointed to the opening of this new frontier. Conger wrote a report on this matter in September 1901, the month of the Boxer settlement. Dalny (subsequently renamed Dairen) soon superseded Vladivostok as the main outlet, and the railway ". . . open[ed] up to settlement and development the only great territory, still left on the globe, so favored with soil and climate as to promise great agricultural development and . . . trade progress."

Being "contiguous" to the United States, Manchuria was America's "new West"—the phrase of Willard Straight, the young and ambitious Cornell graduate whom Theodore Roosevelt appointed consul general at Mukden (1906). Straight's vivid expressions, found in his voluminous private papers, illustrate the direction American thinking was taking at this time but, as a recent historian, Michael H. Hunt, has shown, a group of young officials in the State Department were shaping policy while leaving it to Straight to play the role of front man. Among these were F. M. Huntington Wilson, the assistant secretary of state, William Phillips, Henry Fletcher, and others "schooled in the imperatives of economic expansion."

Hay's Open Door doctrine was good diplomatic leverage to use on Russia and Japan. (By its victory in war, Japan had forced Russia to give up all its rights in south Manchuria and had taken Russia's place as America's principal rival.) The American government would exert pressure on Tokyo and St. Petersburg to share ownership of the railways with American financiers; and once the latter obtained a foothold, they would eventually take monopoly control and convert Manchuria into an American sphere of influence. It was playing the "Great Game of Empire," as Straight candidly outlined the scheme.

Hay's "Open Door" was supposed to be a demonstration of friendship for China, but paradoxically the United States was enforcing its laws barring the "heathen Chinee" from entering the country. Legislation aimed at coolie labor originated with an act of Congress passed in 1882, but subsequent legislation put obstacles in the path of other Chinese seeking temporary sojourn in the country. Special certificates were required of even merchants and students before they were allowed to enter. An act passed in 1902 reached the ultimate in the exclusion policy by giving the commissioner-general of immigration a free hand to impose such regulations as he chose. How fanciful is the legend of the "traditional friendship" between America and China!

Repeated efforts to induce the Japanese and Russians to admit American capitalists having failed, the government of President William Howard Taft tried a new approach through Peking. Under the theory of "independence and integrity," China would charter a new north-south railway across Manchuria to compete with the Japanese line and, if necessary, force it into bankruptcy. Faced with this threat, Japan and Russia might agree to turn their railways over to China, which would purchase them with funds supplied mainly by American and British sources. The nominal control would be China's, but the real control would be vested in an international banking consortium. Through the New York banks, American heavy industry would at least get its share of the Chinese market. This scheme has gone down in history as the Knox neutralization plan, named for Philander C. Knox, Taft's secretary of state.

The Taft administration also pushed for an equal share in a railway promotion scheme for the Yangtze Valley (1909). Bankers who declined to act without government guarantees were told they had a "duty" to the United States to provide these opportunities; the Chinese were informed that it was all for their benefit. President Taft told them he had "an intense personal interest in making the use of American capital in the development of China an instrument for the promotion of China, and an increase of her national prosperity without entanglements or creating embarrassments affecting the growth of her independent political power and the preservation of her territorial integrity." But the terms written into the proposed loan were designed to carry China in exactly the opposite direction, and they stirred up bitter resentment. Neither Taft nor any of the numerous men in and out of government who were promoting these schemes were conscious of putting a match to a revolution almost ready to flare up.

The mythology of the Open Door, moreover, reaches beyond these outright schemes of empire and enters the realm of altruism. Taft's honeyed words, addressed to the prince regent in Peking, were not intentionally misleading. They echoed the convictions of the Protestant churches and their missionaries who had long labored to "bring Christ" to the heathen, and strongly believed in material and social reform. They also reflected the optimism of the Progressive movement that had captured the American imagination. Industrialist Charles R. Crane of Chicago, mining engineer Herbert Hoover, railroad organizer John Hays Hammond, Red Cross worker Mabel Boardman, and sociologist Edward A. Ross were typical of those Progressives with a special interest in China. They held that American skill and reforming capacity could remodel that "awakening" country in the image of the United States.

William Jennings Bryan conceived of "progressive civilization" being carried to China by Christianity and labor-saving machinery. Yale-in-China set its sights on the education and "uplifting of leading Chinese young men toward civilization." This group of idealists hoped to develop an institution modeled after their alma mater. "For God, for China and for Yale" was their motto. The YMCA established itself in Shanghai in 1899 with the multiple purpose of providing living quarters for visiting American businessmen, sponsoring lectures on industrial education, working to ameliorate slum conditions, and spreading the Christian gospel. "The door stands open before us by a miracle. . . . The world is ours," said a speaker at a convention of the NAM (1909); but missionaries and social reform groups were equally sure of themselves. With an eye on the mis-

sionaries in particular, Mark Twain poked fun at these people as "the blessings of civilization trust."

China, however, was "awakening," as the revolution in 1911 made clear. Here was the "new republic" ready to model itself after the United States. Woodrow Wilson voiced this widely held belief and accorded the regime of Yüan Shih-kai speedy diplomatic recognition. In his *History of the American People,* published in 1902, Wilson had sounded the note of realpolitik: China was "the market for which statesmen as well as merchants must plan and play their game of competition, the market to which diplomacy, and if need be, power, must make an open way." Wilson rebuffed the New York bankers—he campaigned against the "organized power of money"—but he assumed that, given "a fair field and no favor" (the original notion of the Open Door), the United States would emerge at the top of the heap. There should be no cooperation with the European powers. "We ought to help China in some better way"—which, put into practice through a new minister to Peking, meant advancing the interests of American business. War and revolution, however, were not good for business, especially with Japan pushing to the fore.

Like Bryan, Wilson clung to certain notions, one of which was that membership in an evangelical Christian church was a necessary prerequisite for the ambassadorship to China. Paul S. Reinsch, son of a Lutheran pastor and an active member of the Wisconsin group working to improve China, was their man. Reinsch's panacea for China was industrialization, and accordingly he sought opportunities for American corporations. Under his prompting, Wilson reversed himself in 1916 by reviving the banking consortium. The move was meant to prop up the crumbling regime of Yüan Shih-kai, whom Bryan in 1912 had hailed as leader of a "United States of China." Such scanty knowledge of China as Wilson possessed came from missionary friends and acquaintances, notably from Methodist Bishop J. W. Bashford, a prominent figure among the Americans in Peking whose opinions carried weight in his home country. Senator William E. Borah of Idaho, later the declared foe of Japan, spoke in similar language (1916): aversion to European influence in the Orient, a powerful navy in the Pacific to check Japan, faith in American "free enterprise" but fear that without foreign markets, economic stagnation would set in. There was no real distinction between Borah's ideas (and Wilson's) and those of such earlier imperialists as Senator Albert Beveridge of Indiana and Brooks Adams, who had argued for American world supremacy.

Civil war was now chronic in China—ten major outbreaks occurred between 1915 and 1922. The best-known was the May Fourth Movement of Peking students infuriated by Japanese aggressions and demanding reforms that would revolutionize China and abolish the treaty system. Chinese revolutionaries condemned the treaties as "unequal"—they were the instruments by which the Western powers had imposed their will on China. Out of this movement emerged the Kuomintang, a conglomerate of nationalists and communists centered in Canton. The American educator-philosopher John Dewey, who contributed numerous articles to the *New Republic,* was an onlooker during the disorders in 1919 and thought that the United States had an "unparalleled opportunity" in meeting these new forces that had come to the fore in China. Dewey had learned to appreciate the viewpoints of the Chinese students who came to him at Columbia University. Paradoxically, however, the "unequal treaties" constituted the Open Door; and when the *New Republic* affirmed its belief in the Open Door, it is not clear what it believed in. The phrase was an aritcle of faith, but in practice it could not be separated from the "unequal treaties."

At the Paris Peace Conference (1919) and again at the Washington Naval Conference (1921), the Chinese delegation demanded that the treaties be abolished. But none of the powers, the United States included, was prepared for this step. The Russian Bolsheviks, feared and outlawed by the Western powers and having nothing to lose in China, volunteered to relinquish Russian treaty rights and, by so doing, made friends with the Kuomintang. Under Sun Yat-sen the latter had aroused the masses in the "rights-recovery" movement. The treaty powers, however, recognized only the military regime at Peking that survived Yüan Shih-kai. This regime was still the symbol of China's "independence and integrity," but it was hemmed in by enemies and confined to the vicinity of Peking.

As Jerry Israel well put it, China itself was a myth, but the myth was too strong to be ignored. At the Washington Conference, Charles Evans Hughes stood in the shoes of John Hay, but the shoes were much larger than Hay's: the United States was now the leading power, and its secretary of state spoke with a stronger voice. As in 1899 there were advocates of a unilateral policy aimed at all-out support of the Peking government. Thus Herbert Hoover adivsed Hughes to negotiate a $250 million loan to China, "conditional upon the elimination of the Communists and the creation of a much stiffer internal administration." Such a program of course called for even stronger medicine than the nineteenth-century gunboat diplomacy responsible for the Open Door in the first instance. But the international scene confronting Hughes was too complex for him to heed such advice, and the secretary of state really had no choice but to fall back upon the myth. The other powers, including China, readily covenanted the following:

1. To respect the sovereignty, the independence, and the territorial and administrative integrity of China.

2. To provide China the fullest and most unembarrassed opportunity to develop and maintain for itself an effective and stable government.

3. To use their influence for the purpose of effectually establishing and maintaining the principle of equal opportunity for the commerce and industry of all nations throughout the territory of China.

4. To refrain from taking advantage of conditions in China in order to seek special rights or privileges that would abridge the rights of subjects or citizens of friendly states and from countenancing action inimical to the security of such states.

Thus John Hay's Open Door principles received international sanction in their widest possible context: they formed the text of the Nine-Power Treaty, one of the leading accords reached at the Washington Conference. Literally the treaty was an attempt to apply the

Golden Rule to international relations. In Christian mythology China was Paradise; on earth it had to be looked for in the lower regions.

The gap continued to widen. Still leading the treaty powers, the United States obtained tariff autonomy for China in 1925–1926—the first breach in the treaty system, but with an effect mainly, if not entirely, on paper. While the conference was sitting in Peking, the city was under siege and American minister John Van Antwerp MacMurray, witness to another civil war, characterized the regime as a mere pawn of military factions and advised Washington to cancel recognition. But Secretary of State Frank B. Kellogg felt it necessary to keep the myth alive. To act upon the factual situation as reported by the minister was to confess failure and bring disrepute to the government at home. Soon thereafter the Kuomintang fought its way through to the north, and in 1928 it took over the central government. Further tragedies awaited China, however: the Kuomintang found an avowed enemy in the Chinese Communists, and civil war began anew, to be terminated twenty years later with the complete victory of the communists.

Meanwhile, Japan won an easy victory in Manchuria and proceeded with its ambitions for a Japanese "New Order for Greater East Asia," in which China, subdued and stabilized under Japanese rule, would be central. The Kuomintang, the Chinese Communists, the Japanese—all three aimed to bring down the treaty system and reopen the door, if at all, on their respective terms. Paradoxically, the United States made this its object too, but put all of its eggs into the Kuomintang's basket, relying on friendship and common victory in war to transform the myth into a living reality. By a new set of treaties concluded with Nationalist China in 1943, it put its legal capstone in place: the Open Door was preserved, but all the special rights were abrogated. The basic premises behind these treaties being at fault, the myth of the Open Door in all its materialist and idealistic ramifications became a lost cause in 1948. One is left to conjecture why the secretary of state then took refuge in the tired phrases of 1900.

The paradox of the Open Door lies in the fact that it never was real. At the very time it was conceived and identified as a distinctive American policy, powerful forces were inexorably at work against it: the leaseholds and spheres of interest that failed in World War I, the short-lived Japanese claims to hegemony over East Asia, and—strongest and most enduring of all—the development of a resistance movement within China itself. American diplomacy in the half-century from Hay to Acheson was ineffective; it could not get past the stage of verbalizing its objectives. But on both sides of the Open Door an elaborate mystique was created; and so China, as the great market for American industry and as the great beneficiary of American charity and goodwill, penetrated the American mentality so deeply that nothing short of total disillusionment at the hands of the Chinese Communists could rouse it from its dream.

BIBLIOGRAPHY

Thomas H. Buckley, *The United States and the Washington Conference, 1921–22* (Knoxville, Tenn., 1970), examines this conference, ostensibly for naval arms limitation, with reference to international power relationships. Charles S. Campbell, *Special Business Interests and the Open Door Policy* (New Haven, Conn., 1951), is an important pioneer work in showing how the policy was intended to serve American business. Michael H. Hunt, *Frontier Defense and the Open Door: Manchuria in Chinese-American Relations, 1895–1911* (New Haven, Conn., 1973), is important for its revision of other works of comparatively recent authorship. Hunt establishes the identity of officials inside the State Department who were more influential than Willard Straight in playing "the great game of [an American] empire" in Manchuria. Akira Iriye, *Pacific Estrangement: Japanese and American Expansion, 1897–1911* (Cambridge, Mass., 1972), is particularly good in comparing Japanese and American ideas of world expansion. The author has the advantage of a command over Japanese sources, but is traditional in his treatment of "John Hay's Open Door Policy." Jerry Israel, *Progressivism and the Open Door: America and China, 1905–1921* (Pittsburgh, Pa., 1971), is a stimulating monograph of original scholarship that identifies the Open Door with the Progressive movement. Li Tien-yi, *Woodrow Wilson's China Policy, 1913–1917* (New York, 1952), is an authoritative analysis showing the influence of evangelical Christianity on Wilson's Far Eastern diplomacy. Robert McClellan, *The Heathen Chinee: A Study of American Attitudes Toward China, 1890–1905* (Columbus, Ohio, 1971), competently analyzes American exclusionism, and examines the dichotomy between this expression of xenophobia and the contemporaneous ambition to "civilize" China. Thomas J. McCormick, *China Market: America's Quest for Informal Empire, 1893–1901* (Chicago, 1967), is an incisive study written within the framework of realpolitik. Delber L. McKee, *Chinese Exclusion Versus the Open Door Policy, 1900–1906: Clashes Over China Policy in the Roosevelt Era* (Detroit, Mich., 1977), is rich in detail regarding American exclusionism, particularly the act of 1902 and the retaliatory Chinese boycott. McKee emphasizes the contradictions between exclusion on the one hand and the "open door" on the other, and concludes that of the two exclusion was the stronger. Ralph Eldin Minger, *William Howard Taft and United States Foreign Policy: The Apprenticeship Years 1900–1908* (Urbana, Ill., 1975), contains a chapter on Taft's visit to China in 1907 and his sympathetic reactions to the ideas of Thomas F. Millard and Willard Straight. Richard W. Van Alstyne, *The United States and East Asia* (London–New York, 1973), a synthesis of the changing pattern of relations between the United States and China and Japan from the eighteenth century to the present, capitalizes on the invaluable scholarly literature published since World War II. Paul A. Varg, *The Making of a Myth: The United States and China,* *1897–1912* (East Lansing, Mich., 1968), is a contribution to the mythology of American policy toward China. Charles Vevier, *The United States and China, 1906–1913: A Study of Finance and Diplomacy* (New Brunswick, N.J., 1955), is a closely documented study of the interaction of American government and finance in promoting the economic penetration of China. Marilyn B. Young, *The Rhetoric of Empire: American China Policy, 1895–1901* (Cambridge, Mass., 1968), is a fine monograph analyzing the interaction of American and Chinese nationalisms. Edward H. Zabriskie, *American-Russian Rivalry in the Far East: A Study in Diplomacy and Power Politics, 1895–1914* (Westport, Conn., 1973), is of prime importance in understanding Russian reactions to American policy.

[*See also* IDEOLOGY AND FOREIGN POLICY; IMPERIALISM; MISSIONARIES; THE MOST-FAVORED-NATION PRINCIPLE; NATIONALISM; OPEN DOOR INTERPRETATION; POWER POLITICS; PROTECTORATES AND SPHERES OF INFLUENCE; TREATIES.]

PACIFISM

Charles Chatfield

THE MEANING of "pacifism" altered in Anglo-American usage during World War I. Before 1914 the word had been associated with the general advocacy of peace. In wartime, "pacifism" was used to denote the refusal to sanction or participate in war on grounds of principle, an ancient doctrine associated with the nonresistance of the early Christian church or the traditional "peace" churches, such as the Mennonites, Quakers, and Brethren. This absolute opposition to war was joined with support for peace programs to produce modern, liberal pacifism. The broad usage is still current in Europe and, to some extent, in the United States; and so the significance of changes in the conception is somewhat lost.

The shift in conceptualization of pacifism is the key to its significance for American foreign policy, however. Once this is understood, it is possible to interpret pacifism as simultaneously the core of several modern peace movements and, ironically, a source of factionalism among peace workers; it is also possible to relate pacifism to the foreign-policymaking process.

Pacifism, although absolutely opposed to war, never has been confined to antiwar movements. It has been a way of life for individuals and religious sects, and it has characterized peace organizations founded after wars. Thus, pacifism contributed to the formation of the first peace groups after the Napoleonic Wars, notably the American Peace Society (1828). It was the basis of the Garrisonian New England Non-Resistance Society, founded in 1838 by abolitionists and others dissatisfied with the moderate position of the American Peace Society, and of the Universal Peace Union, founded in 1866 by Alfred A. Love in the wake of the collapse of peace societies during the Civil War.

The history of pacifism in the United States was treated by Merle Curti and Devere Allen in the 1930's in connection with their histories of peace movements, but little more was written for a generation. During the decade of controversy about the Indochina war the subject acquired new importance, and by then a substantial body of sources had become available, notably in the Swarthmore College Peace Collection. Recent historians have studied peace societies for their governing assumptions, social characteristics, and organizational dynamics, as well as for their importance to the formation of foreign policy; and Peter Brock has put American pacifists in the context of their European antecedents and contemporaries.

The modern conceptualization of pacifism draws upon the tradition of nonresistance in the Christian religion, strains of philosophical anarchism and socialism, nineteenth-century internationalism, and a religious conception of social responsibility. These four elements were brought together in the context of World War I.

The oldest element of modern pacifism is the tradition of religious nonresistance that was formed in the first three centuries of the Christian church, under Roman rule. Abandoned for the concept of just war, in fact by the time of Constantine I and in theory with Saint Augustine, nonresistant pacifism appeared again with Christian sects in the medieval era. It emerged in the Protestant Reformation, notably under Peter Chelčický and the Unity of the Brethren (Bohemian Brethren) in the fifteenth century and among the Anabaptists. From the sixteenth through the eighteenth centuries, it was institutionalized in the writings and practice of "peace" churches: the Men-

PACIFISM

nonites, the Quakers, and the Brethren. Non-resistance characterized the leaders of the first organized peace movements in the United States in the early nineteenth century, and it was officially recognized as ground for exemption under the conscription systems of the Civil War and World War I. Large numbers of Mennonites and Brethren immigrated to the United States late in the nineteenth century, often to escape conscription. Traditional nonresistance implied not only the repudiation of violence and warfare but, frequently, dissociation from government, based as it was on physical force.

In the second half of the nineteenth century, traditional nonresistance was supplemented by anarchism deriving from the religious inspiration of Leo Tolstoy and from the philosophical anarchists who repudiated violence. In addition, some leading European socialists took the position that national wars were instruments of class action and that they should be boycotted by workers. In the United States during World War I these elements of pacifism became important because American law provided for conscientious objection based only on religious opposition to fighting and not that derived from secular or political principles or directed against conscription. Furthermore, the majority position of the Socialist party then condemned American involvement, thus bringing socialists to the antiwar cause.

Also during the second half of the nineteenth century, nonresistance was supplemented by organized internationalism as a force motivating peace advocacy. In some measure this derived from the humanistic traditions of Hugo Grotius and Immanuel Kant; and it evolved into programs for international law, international arbitration, and even international organization. In some measure, too, internationalism derived from classical economists who, like Jeremy Bentham, repudiated mercantilism and advocated free trade. Internationalism was buttressed by Americans' tendency to assume that their institutions would produce harmonious progress if written on a world scale, and it garnered the enthusiastic support of men of means and prestige in the years before World War I. It is important in the development of modern pacifism because its institutional and world views, and even some

of its programs, were incorporated into the encompassing policy platforms of pacifists.

A fourth element of modern pacifism was the sense of social responsibility that derived from antebellum evangelical religion and from analyses of industrialism and urbanism about the turn of the century. The reform spirit, the transnational outlook, and the political philosophy of liberal pacifism were rooted in two decades of Social Gospel and Progressive activity that preceded World War I.

Upon the outbreak of that conflict, most traditional internationalists supported the Allied cause and, increasingly, became reconciled to American intervention. When the United States entered the war, they viewed the crusade as the vehicle of international organization and tried to write their views into the Allied war aims, notably in the case of the League of Nations.

Meanwhile, between 1914 and 1917 several organizations were formed in opposition to Woodrow Wilson's preparedness program, in opposition to intervention, and in support of absolute pacifists (nonresistant and liberal): the American Union Against Militarism (1915–1921), which was succeeded by the National Council for Prevention of War; the Women's Peace Party (1915), which was succeeded by the United States Section of the Women's International League for Peace and Freedom; the Fellowship of Reconciliation (1915), which was supplemented in 1923 by the War Resisters' League; and the American Friends Service Committee (1917). These groups became the institutional base of modern pacifism in the United States.

The leaders of these and other wartime pacifist organizations were predominantly Progressives and, with few exceptions, were religious. They included Jane Addams and Emily Balch, directors of Hull House and Denison House settlements; Crystal Eastman, an ardent suffragette and expert on the legal aspects of industrial accidents; her brother Max Eastman, who edited two radical literary journals, *Masses* and *Liberator;* Norman Thomas, later the leader of the Socialist party; Roger Baldwin, long-time director of the American Civil Liberties Union; Rufus Jones, a Quaker historian; Paul Jones, an Episcopal bishop; and John Haynes Holmes, a Unitarian pastor. They identified with transnational ideologies, whether religious, humanitarian, or socialist; but politically they were pragmatists in the Progressive tradition. They believed in the ultimate worth of the individual, but they appreciated the influence of social institutions upon personal development.

They associated with antiwar radicals, with whom they were persecuted. Indeed, the American Civil Liberties Bureau was formed by pacifists in 1917 for the defense of conscientious objectors and radicals during the war. Leading pacifists identified force as an instrument of social control and associated violence with authoritarianism. They therefore associated their own quest for peace with a commitment to social justice, so that they combined complete opposition to war with the spirit of reform and internationalism. Their organized expression of this belief during World War I marks the beginning of modern, liberal pacifism and the development of an activist core of the peace movements in recent American history.

Peace and antiwar movements can be viewed, institutionally, as a single element of the foreign-policymaking process. To draw a distinction between them is legitimate with regard to specific foreign policy issues—that is, specific wars—but not with regard to the process of policy formation. Taken together, peace and antiwar movements in all periods of United States history have been coalitions of separate groups aligned variously with regard to different policy issues. These constituencies have combined to influence public policy either directly through the professional expertise of peace advocates (as in the case of numerous projects of the Carnegie Endowment) or through political lobbying, or indirectly through public opinion. In any case, pacifists have been relevant to the policymaking process in terms of the broader peace movements, and they cannot be evaluated apart from them.

There is one possible exception to this observation: the contribution made by pacifist pressure groups to the administration of conscription and the treatment of conscientious objectors. In this case pacifist pressure groups acted directly upon government agencies and substantially affected policy formation.

Efforts on behalf of conscientious objectors

have taken essentially three forms. First, pacifists representing the peace churches, the ecumenical Fellowship of Reconciliation, and, just prior to World War II, the secular War Resisters' League lobbied to broaden the basis of exemption. At the outset of World War I objectors were exempted only if they belonged to churches with creedal positions against military service, and even then they were legally exempted only from fighting. Provisions were broadened administratively during the war to include all religious objectors. Since then exemption has been expanded by court decision to include philosophical authority embodying a universal principle, and recently leading churchmen and church bodies have endorsed the principle of selective objection to war on political grounds.

Second, pacifists have lobbied in support of administrative agencies that would remove objectors from military jurisdiction, in recognition of those who object to conscription per se. The Civilian Public Service of World War II was the result of such pressure, although it proved to be an unsatisfactory solution. Various forms of exemption for civilian jobs since that time represent attempts to accommodate pressure from pacifists, buttressed as it often is by church bodies and liberals who recognize conscientious objection as an authentic ethical choice even when they do not endorse it as a preferred one.

Third, pacifists have lobbied for amnesty for conscientious objectors following each war of this century. The basic rationale for amnesty is that objectors are really political prisoners, although the laws of the United States do not recognize political crimes and treat objectors as criminals. The Vietnam War was distinguished by the number of men who publicly deserted from the military and those who fled the country to escape the draft; this created a situation where pacifists found themselves joined in their demand for amnesty by nonpacifists interested in political and social reconciliation. Insofar as conscientious objection has become recognized as a legitimate ethical option and a form of protest, it has ceased to become the exclusive concern of pacifists.

Even with regard to conscientious objection, therefore, the influence of pacifists must now be evaluated in relation to that of the general peace movements. Consequently, the significance of pacifism cannot be measured with exactness, although its qualitative influence can be suggested.

Pacifists affected peace coalitions in which they participated by their cultivation of a political base in specific publics and, in the Cold War period, by their development of new techniques of nonviolent protest. They also gave distinctive emphases to movements in which they were associated: transnational orientation, moral thrust, and skepticism about the efficacy of force.

Pacifists were drawn together both by their opposition to World War I and by their isolation from the American public during the conflict. Increasingly, they became committed to a campaign against all future wars. They cooperated with peace advocates who had supported the war effort as a vehicle of internationalism and who, in the 1920's, maneuvered for the adoption of the League of Nations, the World Court, and treaties to outlaw war. But pacifists also systematically cultivated constituencies that had been largely neglected by other peace workers: religious bodies, college youth, Christian youth organizations, and labor. Although their primary appeal was to repudiate warfare altogether, pacifists also educated the public on international relations and recruited support for specific legislation, notably arms limitation.

By the mid-1930's, a core of pacifist leaders had developed a network of support groups, a political base from which they tried to build a public consensus for strict neutrality. They engineered the $500,000 Emergency Peace Campaign with this goal in mind. Occasionally they were able to translate public opinion into congressional positions, and they considerably reinforced popular resistance to overseas involvement. In the course of the neutrality controversy, however, internationalists affiliated with the League of Nations Association gradually broke from their coalition with pacifists and organized a popular campaign for collective security arrangements. In this respect, the activity of pacifists heightened the political organization of the interwar peace movement.

During World War II pacifists were largely isolated from political influence except insofar as they cooperated with prowar internationalists to popularize the proposed United Nations Organization. They remained isolated after the war, as the world seemed to polarize between the United States and the Soviet Union and collective security was reinterpreted in terms of Cold War containment, still ostensibly in the service of internationalism.

A concomitant of cultivating labor and reform constituencies for peace had been supporting domestic reform programs. Increasingly, pacifists developed techniques of nonviolent direct action (often modeled on the example of Mohandas Gandhi), which they employed on behalf of labor and especially in the civil rights struggle. By the time of the Reverend Martin Luther King's campaign to desegregate buses in Montgomery, Alabama (1955–1956), a few pacifists had considerable experience with these forms of protest. In 1957 a small band of them took advantage of the loosening of Cold War tensions and an accelerating concern over nuclear testing to form two new organizations: the National Committee for a Sane Nuclear Policy (SANE) and the Committee for Nonviolent Direct Action. The former was a coalition with liberals; the latter represented the activist pacifist core, and it employed the tactics of nonviolent direct action to dramatize the coalition campaign against nuclear arms, tactics that were also applied in the antiwar coalition after 1965. In this respect, pacifists contributed to the development of techniques with which a minority might challenge a majority consensus on foreign policy. Thus, their participation contributed to organizational changes in the peace movement after World War I.

Pacifists have not evolved a vision of foreign policy as coherent as collective security or its counterpart, containment. Nonetheless, they have shared distinctive qualities, including a transnational orientation, a moral thrust, and a skepticism about the efficacy of military force.

The transnational orientation of nineteenth-century pacifists was largely religious and resulted from the dualism of Christian perfectionism, which assigned different roles to religious bodies and secular societies. This element was supplemented by the antistate individualism of philosophical anarchists and the class analysis of socialists. But none of these elements yielded specific implications for foreign policy.

PACIFISM

In the twentieth century the transnational perspective of pacifists was secularized, but it remained essentially ethical and humanistic rather than political. It was oriented to the quality of life and the equitable distribution of power rather than to the political relations of states. In this sense, leading pacifists found World War I, for all its magnitude, irrelevant to the solution of fundamental world problems. They eventually supported the League of Nations, but they harbored the reservation that such international organizations were inadequate vehicles for change and human welfare.

They even formed their own international associations. The International Fellowship of Reconciliation (IFOR, 1919), the Women's International League for Peace and Freedom (WILPF, 1919), and the War Resisters' International (WRI, 1921) have had substantial leadership from Americans, such as John Nevin Sayre (IFOR) and Emily Balch (WILPF). The American Friends Service Committee has had a worldwide Quaker base. These organizations linked otherwise isolated pacifists in many lands and often provided support and succor for conscripted war resisters. They cooperated in relief and reconstruction projects, and they occasionally tried to influence foreign relations. They have complemented national groups seeking to modify foreign policy.

As early as 1915, American women participated in an international citizens' campaign for mediation that was the origin of the "peace expedition" to Europe financed by Henry Ford. Following the war, Quaker and IFOR teams visited the former belligerents to do relief and reconstruction work. In the 1920's pacifists propagated revisionist histories and moralizing tracts to stimulate disillusionment and reinforce their interpretation that warfare is an inevitable product of state rivalry. They attacked military preparedness, which, they averred, is the cause of war. Thus, WILPF and IFOR coordinated attempts in several nations to generate support for disarmament in connection with the Geneva conference of 1932–1934. The outstanding pacifist analyst of international affairs was Kirby Page, who argued in the 1930's that traditional European rivalries had vitiated the League of Nations and would lead to a second world war unless a new foundation could be built for international relations. Ironically,

although pacifists viewed historical revisionism as the basis for a realistic assessment of traditional diplomacy and a justification for radically internationalizing world power, many Americans used it as their justification for a new isolationism.

As the world crisis worsened, pacifists strengthened their international ties. The WILPF had Dorothy Detzer as its lobbyist in Washington, and Frederick Libby's National Council for the Prevention of War had an observer at Geneva to coordinate lobbying efforts in the United States with world events. English pacifists were brought to the United States to speak on behalf of neutrality. And an attempt at direct intervention was made in 1937 when IFOR sponsored coordinated visits by George Lansbury and other pacifists to European heads of state, including Adolf Hitler and Benito Mussolini, in a vain effort to discover some basis for averting war.

Following World War II some pacifists, notably Abraham J. Muste, sought to build a new basis for a transnational foreign policy. By the 1950's Muste had come to view the Third World as the fulcrum for a world policy beyond the bipolar terms of the Cold War. This hope was extended in the 1960's by non-pacifist radicals; but as a basis for foreign policy lobbying it was eclipsed by the campaign against nuclear arms that focused on the United States-Soviet Union détente and by the crusade against the war in Vietnam that built a large coalition by including protest groups with domestic rather than world concerns. Nonetheless, the American Fellowship of Reconciliation, together with other pacifist elements of the coalition and IFOR, mounted an ambitious attempt to coordinate Vietnamese Buddhist and American antiwar efforts, played a significant role in publicizing the existence and persecution of those opposed to war in South Vietnam, sent teams to North Vietnam, and tried to coordinate the development of public opinion in Europe and the United States.

Despite their considerable activity abroad, pacifist groups in the United States have placed their national constituencies first and have given decidedly fewer resources to the development of a world network. In this respect they have been subject to the very national priorities they have sometimes decried.

PACIFISM

The moral emphasis of nineteenth-century pacifism was individualistic. Pacifists tended to assume that good people would make a good world. Twentieth-century pacifists, however, reflected the Progressive emphasis on social environmentalism. They included war among the social institutions in which good men and women become enmeshed, with devastating consequences. Accordingly, leading pacifists made pacifism an expression of social ethics; and their journal, *The World Tomorrow* (published 1918–1934), became the most forthright exponent of the Social Gospel. "If war is sin," wrote Kirby Page, then it must be abjured and overcome by every available stratagem. Their essentially moral outlook enabled several pacifist leaders to transcend the narrow allegiances to specific programs that set so many internationalists at odds with one another.

In the 1920's, for example, Page and his colleagues made futile attempts to devise a plan of unity between the advocates of a World Court and of a general treaty to outlaw war. Similarly, in the 1930's pacifists were able to write an umbrella platform that attracted nonpacifist internationalists to their Emergency Peace Campaign, with its neutralist bias. In 1957 a pacifist nucleus stimulated the formation of both the National Committee for a Sane Nuclear Policy and the Committee on Nonviolent Action in order to enlist both liberal and pacifist constituencies in action against nuclear arms. And in the 1960's a generalized sense of moral outrage accounted for much of the cohesion of the organized antiwar movement. It was the basis on which pacifists could associate with groups having nonpacifist political biases.

The very sense of moral commitment that led to comprehensiveness in some circumstances engendered division in others. Ideologies often have served as standards of factional loyalty within out-of-power groups, and the principle of total repudiation of violence and warfare sometimes functioned in this way among pacifists or in coalitions they joined.

A few examples may illustrate this problem. The American Peace Society was impelled by a sense of moral obligation, but it was wracked by factional disputes related to the question of whether to prohibit all wars or only aggressive ones. Again, in World War I absolute pacifism was both the cohesive element of pacifist orga-

nization and the reason that prowar liberals refused to work with pacifists even for liberal goals. WILPF, formed just after the war, included pacifists Jane Addams and Emily Balch; but the coalition was too broad for Fanny Garrison Villard and other absolutists, who created the separate Women's Peace Society. Early in the 1930's both the Fellowship of Reconciliation and the Socialist party were sharply divided over how completely they should renounce violence in a potential class struggle. Socialists never recovered from the political effects of that controversy, and they also were faced with the theoretical issue of whether to support an antifascist war.

By 1938 pacifist groups were united against intervention, but they tended to withdraw from political action in order to prepare communities of believers for the coming crisis. During the war the pacifist community was divided over the implications of its moral commitment to conscientious objection, and its support groups disagreed about the limits of cooperation with Civilian Public Service, the administrative agency for objectors.

The antiwar movement of the 1960's was no more immune to factionalism than its predecessors, and the division was often over conflicting principles. Divisive issues included whether to exclude communists from coalitions, whether to criticize North Vietnamese and communist policy in the context of analyses of American involvement, tactics for demonstrations, and organizational principles within the movement. Protest during the Vietnam conflict was united under a generalized sense of moral outrage; but it also was divided by the question of allegiance to specific principles, of which the total repudiation of violence and authoritarianism was one.

In any case, pacifists have reinforced an essentially ethical interpretation of national interest: that world interest should be a criterion of national policy, and that the concomitants of peace are change as well as order, justice as well as stability. This moral thrust is not unique to pacifists, but it has been sharpened by their participation in American peace movements.

Skepticism, no less than belief, has characterized pacifist propaganda and attitudes. Indeed, modern pacifism was formed in opposition to a popular war and to the power assumed by government in it. That skepticism became a valuable credential when disillusionment followed the war. Pacifists themselves have assiduously propagated skepticism about the justness of specific wars, the credibility of war aims, and the constructive potential of victory. For more than half a century they have challenged the general claim that preparedness deters warfare and the specific claims of military security needs. From Woodrow Wilson's preparedness campaign of 1916 through legislative battles over arms spending in the 1920's to the question of nuclear arms in the 1950's, from the inauguration of conscription in 1917 through its reinstatement in 1940 to the introduction of a peacetime draft in 1948, pacifists constituted a core of political opposition. They challenged not only programs but also the rationale for them. Some pacifists also marshaled economic and anti-imperialist interpretations of war to expose the economic linkages of warfare and to challenge official explanations of foreign policy. And they propagated skepticism about the efficacy of American intervention abroad, whether public or covert, whether in World War I or in Latin America, in Cold War containment or in Southeast Asia.

Skepticism about the use of military power and the rationale for violence has been extended to systematic inquiries about the nature of power by pacifists and nonpacifists, who built first on the experience of Mohandas Gandhi and then on American reform experience. Recent scholarship has tried to put nonviolent application of social force on a systematic and empirical basis and has begun to explore its implications for national security. In this sense the study of nonviolence is no longer confined to ethical pacifism.

Skepticism about foreign policy and governmental accountability is endemic to pacifism. It is the inheritance of the nonresistants and the experience of the peace sects. It was reinforced when pacifists were persecuted or were isolated from serious consideration. It is the concomitant of the values of the faith—individual worth, harmony, brotherhood—contrasted as they are with articles of foreign policy such as national interest, conflict, and sovereignty. It follows from the pacifist emphasis on a transnational orientation and moral commitment, as against foreign policy based on national inter-

est and pragmatic choices. It is at the heart of the demand that foreign policy be tested publicly by the very values it purports to secure. Skepticism is not unique to pacifism, but it has been significantly sharpened in the American peace movement as a result of pacifist activity.

Foreign policymaking can be interpreted as the process of relating national interest to international situations. A crucial stage of the process is the definition of national interest, and it is at this point that ideals are related to concrete self-interests. A given principle of American institutions is that policy choices should be subject to public scrutiny and popular pressure. Accordingly, coalitions of peace advocates are essential in a democratic republic . because they serve the twin functions of providing independent education about international affairs and of organizing public opinion and translating it into political pressure.

Pacifism, as a motivating concept, has had significance for foreign policymaking in terms of the influence of its exponents upon peace coalitions. They have broadened the popular base of pressure, stimulated political organization, and developed techniques with which minorities may challenge majority consensus. They also have imbued the peace movements with the distinctive qualities of their transnational orientation, moral thrust, and skepticism about the efficacy of military force to bring about orderly change or an equitable distribution of world power. Furthermore, organized pacifists have occasionally played independent roles in consensus formation, notably in the resistance to preparedness and intervention in World War I, in the neutrality controversy of 1935–1937, and in the protest against the Indochina conflict. They also have attempted to abolish conscription and to liberalize the treatment of conscientious objectors.

Most people who repudiate violence and war on the basis of pacifist beliefs have not been politically active. But even their faith is significant for American foreign policy in two respects. First, in its conduct of foreign relations, including warfare, the nation has been obligated to protect principled dissent from persecution or repression. The fact that this rule has been abrogated does not minimize its constraint on the foreign policy process. Second, the definition of national interest and power is subject to openly advocated alternative conceptions. Whatever the merits of pacifist judgments on specific policies, the free existence of pacifism and its political expression constitute a significant index of the consistency of foreign policy-making with democratic institutions.

BIBLIOGRAPHY

Devere Allen, *The Fight for Peace* (New York, 1930), written by a journalist and editor who advocated war resistance and political activism, this substantial volume remains an important source of pacifist thought and history. Peter Brock, *Pacifism in the United States From the Colonial Era to the First World War* (Princeton, 1968), is the best history of the subject, thorough in its coverage of pacifism in sects, peace churches, and antebellum reform, but less adequate on the twentieth century; it is based on primary research, is carefully documented, and includes a valuable bibliography. Peter Brock, *Twentieth-Century Pacifism* (New York, 1970), is a brief and balanced text that is the only available treatment of pacifism from an international viewpoint. Peter Brock, *Pacifism in Europe to 1914* (Princeton, 1972), is a necessary, comprehensive, and thoughtful background for an understanding of the religious and philosophical origins of pacifism. Charles Chatfield, *For Peace and Justice: Pacifism in America, 1914–1941* (Knoxville, Tenn., 1971; rev. ed., New York, 1973), traces the development of modern, liberal pacifism through the interwar period in relation to peace coalitions and foreign policy issues, and also in relation to reform movements, emphasizing the relationship between thought and political history; the book includes an extensive bibliographical essay. Merle Curti, *Peace or War: The American Struggle, 1636–1936* (New York, 1936), is a balanced, chronological narrative that has not been surpassed for its treatment of the period; pacifism is treated in relation to the broad peace coalition. Sondra Herman, *Eleven Against War: Studies in American Internationalist Thought, 1898–1921* (Stanford, Calif., 1969), although not a history of pacifism per se, develops important paradigms of thought through which liberal pacifists such as Jane Addams are related to other internationalists. C. Roland Marchand, *The American Peace Movement and Social Reform, 1896–1918* (Princeton, 1972), analyzes the peace movement comprehensively and relates it to pacifism in terms of important sociological paradigms; the work includes a comprehensive bibliography. David Patterson, *Toward a Warless World; The Travail of the American Peace Movement, 1887–1914* (Bloomington, Ind., 1976), is a narrative account of the rise of the modern peace and internationalist movement with particular attention to organizational roles, social origins, and attitudes; the book reflects careful, comprehensive scholarship. Gene Sharp, *The Politics of Nonviolent Action* (Boston, 1973), is a massive treatise that combines extended documentation of nonviolent political campaigns with a typological organization to yield a conceptual framework for his interpretation of power; the work illustrates the secularization of pacifism in contemporary political thought. Lawrence Wittner, *Rebels Against War: The American Peace Movement, 1941–1960* (New York, 1969), is a work in which pacifists provide, to a large extent, the thread of continuity, although Wittner describes shifting and contending patterns within the coalition; the book includes an extensive bibliography.

[*See also* COLLECTIVE SECURITY; CONSCRIPTION; DISARMAMENT; DISSENT IN WARS; IDEOLOGY AND FOREIGN POLICY; INTERNATIONALISM; INTERVENTION AND NONINTERVENTION; ISOLATIONISM; PEACE MOVEMENTS; PUBLIC OPINION.]

PAN-AMERICANISM

Thomas L. Karnes

ACCORDING TO Joseph B. Lockey, the closest student of Pan-Americanism's early days, the adjective "Pan-American" was first employed by the *New York Evening Post* in 1882, and the substantive "Pan-Americanism" was coined by that same journal in 1888. The convening of the first inter-American conference in Washington the next year led to wider usage of the first term about 1890 and popularization of Pan-Americanism in the early years of the twentieth century. While the terms have since become familiar expressions to most of the reading public in the Western Hemisphere, their connotation remains vague. Broadly defined, Pan-Americanism is cooperation between the Western Hemisphere nations in a variety of activities including economic, social and cultural programs, declarations, alliances, and treaties—though some authorities narrow the definition to include political action only. Yet, the specific definition must always be partly in error; the broad one borders on the meaningless.

Pan-Americanism is more easily traced than defined. In the middle of the nineteenth century, various "Pan" movements achieved popularity as adjuncts or exaggerations of the powerful nationalism of the times, throwbacks to ancient Pan-Hellenism. Pan-Slavism was perhaps the first to acquire some measure of fame; Pan-Hellenism revived about 1860, and was followed by Pan-Germanism, Pan-Islamism, Pan-Celtism, Pan-Hispanism, and others. Probably all these "Pan" movements share certain predicates: their believers feel some unity, some uniqueness—perhaps superiority—and they share mutual interests, fears, history, and culture. In short their similarities make them different from the rest of the world, and they combine for strength. Pan-Americanism, however, fails to meet most of those criteria and must fall back upon the weaker elements of a common geographical separation from the rest of the world and something of a common history.

From early colonial times, Western Hemisphere peoples believed that they were unique. Statesmen of the Americas, both North and South, were united in affirmation that some force—nature, or perhaps God—had separated the Old World and the New World for a purpose; and this isolation in an unknown land had brought a common colonial experience that deserved the name of "system." Among leaders who saw and described this division was Thomas Jefferson; Henry Clay often argued before Congress for its preservation; Simón Bolívar acted upon it; and President James Monroe's doctrine most fundamentally assumes it.

What were the elements of this American system? First was independence, defined by Clay as freedom from despotism, either domestic or European. Americans believed in a common destiny, a body of political ideals, the rule of law, and cooperation among themselves (at least when threatened from the outside). In later years Secretary of State James G. Blaine saw these factors strengthened by commerce; the Brazilian statesmen Joaquim Nabuco and José Maria da Silva Paranhos, baron Rio Branco, talked of a common past; Woodrow Wilson thought he saw a unique American spirit of justice.

No American could ignore his geography. He had moved to, or been born in, an underpopulated continent, where the strife of Europe was put aside, and mobility, vertical or horizontal, was easily achieved. Nature isolated the American, and that isolation would produce a different man.

But the most apparent difference between the American and his European cousin was in the form of government. The vastness of America enhanced the individual's worth, and the right of each person to have a share in his government found fertile soil in America. Thus, when the colonies struggled to their freedom in the half century after 1789, most deliberately chose the unfamiliar republican form of government that would safeguard the rights of citizens to choose those who would govern them. Inevitably some constitutions were copied, but that was the plagiarizing of words; the ideas were pandemic. (That a few nonrepublican administrations arose was a matter singularly ignored and always easily explained away to anyone who pursued the puzzle.) From Philadelphia to Tucumán in the Argentine, new constitutions proclaimed that the Americans had a new way of life and a new form of government to insure its continuance.

Nowhere were these American ideas better expressed than in paragraphs of the presidential address that became known as the Monroe Doctrine. Monroe asserted a belief in the existence of two worlds, one monarchical and one republican; the new was closed to further colonization by the old, and neither should interfere with the other. Third parties were not to tamper even with regions in America that were still colonies. Whether America's will to protect this separation was based upon geography or, ironically, the British fleet, the doctine expressed what Americans believed and would fight to preserve.

At times Americans have been carried away with the enthusiasm of their rhetoric and have found unifying interests where they did not exist. Proponents have often spoken of the existence of a common heritage, a statement with limited application, for in the hemisphere there is no common language, culture, or religion. Contrary to most "Pan" movements, Pan-Americanism has little basis in race or ethnicity; and it seems scarcely necessary to belabor the cultural diversity of the persons who bear the name American. If heritage were the chief basis of community, Spanish-Americans would have their strongest ties with Spain, Brazilians

with Portugal, the Anglo-Americans with Great Britain, and so on. Nor can Pan-Americanism ignore those millions of African heritage or those who are indigenous to America. Language and religion are even more varied than race in America, and can offer no more means of unification.

Finally, consideration must be given to the geographical basis for Pan-Americanism. It is a fact that the Americans occupy their own hemisphere and that they are comfortably separated from the disturbances of Europe by great seas. Clearly this isolation leads to some community of interest. The danger lies in exaggeration, for the modern traveler soon learns that in terms of dollars, hours, or miles, much of the United States is far closer to Europe than it is to most of Latin America; and Buenos Aires is far closer to Africa than it is to New York or Washington. In short, it is a fallacy to contend that the Americas are united by their proximity to one another. The Americans, North and South, occupy the same hemisphere, and that does present an important mythology and symbolism to the world. More than that cannot be demonstrated.

Who are the Pan-Americans? No one has ever established requirements for membership nor set forth the procedures by which a people can become part of the elect. Form of government played a more or less clear part; the American nations all seemed to understand that colonies could not participate in Pan-American movements, but that local empires (the only one bearing that title for any duration was Brazil) were welcome. Nations sent delegates to the various conferences called during the nineteenth century primarily because they were invited by the host, not because of any established rules. Thus some meetings that are classified as Pan-American might have had delegates from only four or five states. After 1889 nearly all of the republics of the hemisphere took part.

The proliferation of new states in the years following World War II is reflected in Pan-Americanism; and former British colonies, no matter how small (and perhaps unviable), seem to be welcomed into the American family. Canada must be considered as special; it has frequently been offered formal membership, and there would appear little logic in its absten-

PAN-AMERICANISM

tion from American affairs, but generally the Canadians have preferred their own route.

A nation can also be excommunicated. Cuba, even though it continued to have diplomatic relations with some American states, was drummed out of the family and had commercial sanctions imposed upon it for its behavior toward other members.

What, then, is Pan-Americanism? What is its purpose? How does it go about its work? What has it achieved? Given its shifting focus, its frequently amorphous structure, and its imprecise definition, has it been, and will it likely prove to be, a significant force in world affairs?

Pan-Americanism most often expresses itself through international conferences, very loosely joined in the early years, highly structured in more recent decades. In the nineteenth century, conferences were often called to seek combined action against some specific problem. In the twentieth century, sessions have been scheduled long in advance and have had wide-ranging agendas. Attendance at the latter meetings has neared unanimity; in the early days it was irregular, made the worse by slow communications. The record is filled with accounts of delegations not formed in time or sent too late to take part in the proceedings. A final distinction is clear: while in recent times the impetus usually has come from the United States, during the nineteenth century almost all of the leadership came from Spanish America, often to the exclusion of the Anglo-Americans and Portuguese-Americans. Some writers, in fact, seeking to divide Pan-Americanism chronologically, have classified the years 1826–1889 as the "old," or Spanish-American, period of the movement.

The first, and most ambitious, of the Spanish-dominated meetings was the responsibility of one man, Simón Bolívar, hero of Latin American independence. Long before any other leader, Bolívar dreamed of a strong league of American states leading to permanent military and political cooperation. Initially, at least, Bolívar thought of a confederation of only the Spanish-American states, if for no other reason than their common struggle for freedom from Spain. Although not a visionary, Bolívar in 1815 predicted the creation of some fifteen Latin American states after the defeat of Spain. Nevertheless, he struggled

against this kind of atomization. In defeat and in victory his plan never disappeared, and by 1818 he (somewhat inaccurately) wrote to an Argentine friend, "We Americans should have but a single country since in every other way we are perfectly united."

By the 1820's the freedom of most of the Latin American colonies seemed assured, and the United States and other neutrals began extending diplomatic recognition to the new governments. The time was ripe for Bolívar to renew his plan, and in 1822 he persuaded the government of Gran Colombia to send emissaries to the other South American nations, delivering preliminary bases for a confederation as well as invitations to a conference to discuss the plan. The visits resulted in several treaties, but Bolívar sought much more.

In December 1824 he renewed his call for an "amphictyonic body or assembly of plenipotentiaries," confident that the military struggle was at an end and that the new states could plan for "a hundred centuries." Bolívar's notice was addressed to "the American republics, formerly Spanish colonies," and therefore omitted several American states. He sought the presence of Great Britain, however, because he felt that without British support the Americans would be lost; he also permitted the Netherlands to send an observer, apparently without an invitation. Bolívar had ignored both the United States and Brazil, which, of course, were not "formerly Spanish colonies"; but when their attendance was sought by other Latin Americans, he interposed no objection.

Bolívar's classical training caused him to see Panama as the modern counterpart of the Isthmus of Corinth, to which he frequently referred, and he selected Panama as the site of the conference. That unsavory little town had many defects as a center for an international conference, and every delegate seems to have taken ill during the sessions; but it did have the advantage of a central location. In June 1826 the representatives of Peru, Gran Colombia, Mexico, and the Central American Federation met and planned the first steps toward Pan-Americanism.

Technically speaking, attendance was much greater, for in time Gran Colombia was to be divested of Venezuela, Ecuador, and Panama; and in 1838 the Central American Federation was split into its original five parts, which became the republics of Guatemala, El Salvador, Honduras, Nicaragua, and Costa Rica. In that sense the four nations accounted for eleven future Latin American republics. But what of the others? The United Provinces of La Plata already evidenced the isolationism and antipathy to alliances that were to mark the policy of its successor state, Argentina. Even more self-contained was Paraguay, which simply declined to be represented. Brazil, Chile, and Bolivia exhibited some interest, but for various reasons failed to get their delegates to Panama.

The United States, as a neutral in the Spanish colonies' rebellions against Spain, could quite properly have declined the invitation; but some members of President John Quincy Adams' administration, led by Secretary of State Henry Clay, were eager to join in any movement toward inter-American cooperation. In the United States Congress strong opposition arose. This sentiment had little to do with Latin America, but was based on the purely partisan goals of harassing the administration. The debate, a major one, lasted so long that final approval came too late. One delegate died en route to Panama; the other made no effort to travel to that town but journeyed instead to Mexico, where the Spanish-American statesmen planned further meetings.

Rivalries, both petty and large, soon appeared at Panama. Some states professed to fear Bolívar's ambitions; others wanted only a temporary league to complete the independence of America from Europe. Even the role of the British at the sessions was debated. Probably on account of the climate and unsanitary conditions, the Panama Congress lasted less than one month; nevertheless, it concluded a treaty of perpetual union, league, and confederation (a strange combination of clashing terminology) that contained thirty-one articles for a permanent confederation of the signatories and the means to promote this formal cooperation of the states. In addition, the delegates agreed to a convention describing the rules for future meetings and two conventions providing for combined military forces, their support, and their operation.

Each representative signed all of the agreements, then left—some for home, some for the village of Tacubaya near Mexico City, where they planned to reconvene if their governments deemed the effort worthwhile. Some informal talks were held at Tacubaya, but no formal sessions ever took place and the Panama Congress had to stand upon its completed work. With one exception the various national legislatures failed to ratify any of the agreements; Gran Colombia, despite the surprising opposition of Bolívar, ratified them all.

In only one regard can the Panama Congress be looked upon as a success: the fact of its existence perhaps made the holding of future such conferences a bit easier. Little else was accomplished. Why did it fail so badly? The end of the threat from Spain and the beginnings of civil strife all over Latin America had coincided to make the congress a forum for expressing the new republics' distrust of one another. Furthermore, most conferences do not achieve world-shaking consequences, and Panama was a noble experiment. Obviously far ahead of its time, its aims were appropriate to any time.

The failure of the Panama Congress also demonstrated that its prime mover, Bolívar, had changed his mind about the vast confederation of states and would concentrate instead upon establishing a tight federation of the Andes with himself as permanent dictator. This change left a leadership vacuum in Pan-Americanism that was briefly filled by Mexico. Despite rapid shifts from conservative to liberal administrations, the Mexican government for a decade followed a policy of urging the South American states to consummate some of the plans drafted at Panama and help protect the region against the possibility of European intervention. Armed with a proposal for a treaty of union, and calling for renewal of the Panama discussions, Mexican ministers were dispatched to several capitals. Mexico was willing that the meetings be convened in almost any convenient spot, but the suggestion received little support. This first bid of 1832 was repeated in 1838, 1839, and 1840, by which time Mexico was becoming increasingly frightened by the American presence in Texas. However, the other nations lacked Mexico's concern, and the proposals did not result in even one conference. Only when the South Americans feared for their own security did they decide to band together again.

733

The immediate threat came from General Juan José Flores, a Venezuelan-born conservative, who had been Ecuador's first president. During his third term he had been exiled by a people tired of his rotating with the liberals in the presidency. A vain and dictatorial man, Flores went to Europe for help and appeared to be successful in raising private troops and a fleet to restore him to the presidency. Anticipating an invasion by Spain or Great Britain, the government of Peru invited the American republics to meetings at Lima in December 1847. The sessions lasted until March 1848, even though it was known by that time that the British government would prohibit the sailing of the fleet.

The Lima Conference was thus the second of the "old" or Spanish-dominated conferences. In attendance were ministers from Colombia, Chile, Bolivia, Ecuador, and Peru. The United States was invited and sent J. Randolph Clay as a nonparticipating observer. Four treaties were concluded, most of them concerning mutual assistance. Once again, only Colombia ratified even one.

The city of Santiago, Chile, was the site of the third Pan-American conference under Spanish-American auspices. By the middle of the nineteenth century the United States was replacing Spain, France, and other European states as the chief threat to Latin America's territorial integrity. It had just acquired through warfare more than one-third of Mexico, and Yankee filibusters seemed to be threatening the security of several Caribbean territories. The conference was called because Ecuador proposed granting the United States the right to mine guano on the Galápagos Islands. Ecuador's neighbors on the Pacific Coast were disturbed by this invitation, and Chile even broke diplomatic relations for a time. Lumping objectives together, the republics of Peru, Ecuador, and Chile sent delegations to Santiago in 1856 to draft plans for another confederation and to agree upon joint measures for handling filibustering and other "piratical" expeditions. The result was the Continental Treaty, dealing with many aspects of international law, filibustering, and acts of exiles, as well as the usual nod in the direction of a confederation. Significantly, while all of the nations of Latin America were urged to join, even Portuguese-speaking Brazil,

the United States was not invited to attend the conference or to join the confederation. But once more failure ensued. The Continental Treaty was not ratified.

The fourth and last of the old Spanish-American conferences, which took place at Lima, Peru, in 1864, was the consequence of the weakness of so many of the Latin American states. United States preoccupation with its Civil War allowed a series of dangerous European flirtations in the American hemisphere. Spain claimed the reannexation of the Dominican Republic in 1861; Spain, Great Britain, and especially France threatened, and then invaded, Mexico; and Spain occupied Peru's Chincha Islands to collect debts under the pretext that Peru was still Spain's colony. At Colombia's suggestion, the Peruvian foreign office in 1864 invited all of the former Spanish colonies to a conference at Lima to take up the matter of intervention by foreign powers in the affairs of the hemisphere. The United States and Brazil were ignored; states attending included Chile, Argentina, Venezuela, Colombia, Guatemala, and El Salvador, in addition to Peru. The Lima Congress failed to negotiate with Spain for the withdrawal of its troops from the Chincha Islands; and when the delegates turned their full attention to the usual grand treaty of confederation, the failure was just as complete. Once again no nation ratified any of the agreements. The end of the American Civil War and the renewed preoccupation of Spain and France with domestic and foreign problems account for the departure of those two nations from their Latin American adventures.

The War of the Triple Alliance (1865–1870), which pitted Paraguay against a loose league of Uruguay, Brazil, and Argentina, and the War of the Pacific (1879–1884), in which Chile easily mastered Bolivia and Peru, left bitter residues that in the short run meant the end of any program of Pan-Americanism led by Spanish-American republics. Although a few technical and nonpolitical conferences were held in the next few years, Pan-Americanism was discarded until the United States assumed the responsibility.

United States leadership marks the beginning of the "new" Pan-Americanism, dating from the 1880's and differing significantly from the "old." The four early conferences had been dominated by Spanish-American states concerned with problems that, while not exclusively Spanish-American, seemed to threaten those states particularly. The meetings were usually provoked by the threat of outside aggression, and the solutions sought were political and military in nature. While the delegates undoubtedly left some heritage for subsequent hemispheric programs, they revealed a near-tragic ability to draft agreements that were perfect in purpose and in language but acceptable to none of the ratifying bodies of the individual states. The "new" Pan-Americanism, less racial in structure and less ambitious in scope, sought, and could obtain, agreement on low-profile issues, thus giving at least an impression of solid growth and occasional unanimity. These factors, spurred by the pressure of United States size and prestige, meant far greater participation in the conferences and the building of Pan-Americanism into an institution of imposing size and machinery.

Credit for inaugurating the new series of Pan-American conferences rests with James G. Blaine, who, passed over for the presidential nomination in 1880, had been selected by James A. Garfield as secretary of state. Blaine had a genuine interest in Latin America, at least in part because of his admiration for Henry Clay. He saw two problems in hemispheric relations for which he diagnosed the single common solution of Pan-Americanism. The first was an unfavorable trade balance caused by the North Americans' large purchases of Latin America's raw materials and the small sales of manufactured goods to the same area in return.

Equally distressing to Blaine were several ongoing disputes. The worst of these was the War of the Pacific, in which Bolivia had already been decisively defeated by Chile, whose troops were occupying Lima, Peru, and giving every indication of doing permanent damage to that republic by vast territorial acquisitions. In addition, several boundary disputes threatened the stability of Latin America and provoked Blaine into assuming the unpopular role of peacemaker. Blaine's intentions were better than either his methods or his agents, and he incurred significant displeasure from Latin Americans during his brief term in office. When President Garfield was assassinated, Blaine decided that he could not work with the new president, Chester A. Arthur. Before leaving the State Department, however, Blaine was able to promote a call for the first International Conference of American States in Washington, D.C.

Blaine's immediate successor had no interest in the conference, and withdrew the invitation. The movement was renewed a few years later by Congress, and the First International Conference convened in 1889, when, by coincidence, the secretary of state was again James G. Blaine. All of the American states except the Dominican Republic (the absence was due to United States failure to ratify a trade treaty with its tiny neighbor) sent delegations of high caliber. With some opposition Blaine was chosen chairman of the sessions, a post in which he demonstrated considerable tact and skill. The delegates were entertained lavishly and given an impressive and fatiguing 6,000-mile railroad tour through the industrial heart of the nation as far as Chicago. Back at work, the delegates could not agree upon Blaine's customs union, opposition coming as much from some United States congressmen as from Argentina, chief spokesman for the producers of raw materials who wanted open markets. In its stead a program of separate reciprocal trade treaties was recommended; a few were instituted, decades ahead of the subsequent and popular Good Neighbor program of the 1930's. An ambitious arbitration treaty was watered down in conference, nullified by a minority of delegations, and ratified by no one.

The solid results of this conference were few. The nations represented at Washington established the International Union of American Republics for the collection and distribution of commercial information; the agency to execute this command was created in Washington as the Commercial Bureau of the American Republics, supervised by the United States secretary of state. This bureau met regularly, expanding in both size and functions and becoming a useful agency to the American states, though a far cry from the Pan-Americanism of Bolívar's day.

The delegates to the First International Conference had not scheduled any future meetings; but about 1899, since the International Union had been established for ten years, many statesmen concluded that another conference should be held. The Commercial Bureau, which provided the only continuity for the International Union, selected Mexico City as the site for the second conference and handled the drafting of agenda and invitations.

In this fashion the institutionalization of the International Conferences of American States developed. To reduce the appearance of United States domination, the conferences were held in the various Latin American capital cities, presumably in time meeting in all of them had the series continued that long. The record of attendance was very high, frequently unanimous; only once were as many as three states absent (from Santiago, Chile, 1923). The frequency of the sessions varied, but four- or five-year intervals were the norm.

INTERNATIONAL CONFERENCES OF AMERICAN STATES*

First	Washington, D.C.	1889–1890
Second	Mexico City	1901–1902
Third	Rio de Janeiro, Brazil	1906
Fourth	Buenos Aires, Argentina	1910
Fifth	Santiago, Chile	1923
Sixth	Havana, Cuba	1928
Seventh	Montevideo, Uruguay	1933
Eighth	Lima, Peru	1938
Ninth	Bogotá, Colombia	1948
Tenth	Caracas, Venezuela	1954
Eleventh†		

*World wars account for the occasional irregularities in scheduling.
†Scheduled at various times for Quito, Ecuador, but indefinitely postponed.

The issues recurring most prominently at these meetings were arbitration, hemispheric peace, trade, the forcible collection of debts, United States dominance of the organization, and intervention by one state in the affairs of another. A number of problems arose about 1938, closely related to World War II and its possible spread to America. Structural changes were numerous. The major alterations included the substitution in 1910 of the name Pan-American Union for the Commercial Bureau, and in popular usage Pan-American Conference replaced the name International Conference of American States. At Bogotá in 1948

the Organization of American States (OAS) became the parent organ, and a new Pan-American Union was made the permanent secretariat of the organization.

Specific accomplishments of these many conferences were more modest. Resolutions, conventions, and treaties were often debated, but compromise was endless and major solutions rarely reached or ratified. One exception was the Gondra Treaty of 1923, designed to create machinery for the peaceful settlement of American disputes. This treaty was the basis for similar machinery in the later OAS.

From time to time some delegates expressed their dismay that Pan-Americanism was taking no steps toward the confederacy so often praised, but the majority clearly preferred the use of the Pan-American Union as a sounding board for international public opinion and an agency that moved slowly in the settlement of specific problems.

A change was apparent in the 1920's, once the glow of World War I selflessness disappeared. That war had removed the last European threat to the security of Latin America; it had thrust the United States for the first time into a position of economic dominance in Latin America; and it had brought no modification in the United States claim to the right to intervene in another state's affairs when the former's security was threatened. As of 1924, United States forces occupied Nicaragua, Haiti, the Dominican Republic, and Honduras; had the legal right to intervene in Cuba and Panama; and had badly strained relations with Mexico. Irrespective of fault, strong pressures were growing inside the United States, as well as outside, to bring some alteration in this picture.

Festering and covered over at Santiago in 1923, the issue popped into the open five years later at Havana. Latin Americans now publicly expressed their disappointment at the United States return to its prewar isolationism and increasingly protested that nation's use of intervention in the Caribbean area. Never before had a conference debated the right of one state to interfere in the affairs of another; at Havana speaker after speaker rose to condemn the United States practice, often in their utterances claiming the incompatibility of intervention and Pan-Americanism. The presence of President Calvin Coolidge and the defense of former Secretary of State Charles Evans Hughes made little difference in Latin American attitudes. The United States could prevent the passage of condemnatory decrees, but the attack upon intervention was merely delayed while Pan-Americanism hung in the balance.

The "new" or second stage of Pan-Americanism drew to a close around 1930. Contrasted with the "old," this period was marked by more concern for nonpolitical objectives, technical and social. The "old" had been geographically more restrictive and often purely Spanish; the "new" was deliberately hemispheric in scope, and the leadership clearly rested with the United States. But by the 1920's the other nations were growing restive under United States dominance, just as they were becoming increasingly outspoken about United States intervention in Latin American affairs.

Change came gradually at first, then more dramatically in the 1930's. Many United States citizens found themselves questioning the value of interventions that were so often accompanied by bloodshed and so rarely brought about change for the better; the State Department became increasingly sensitive to charges that it sought only to defend giant business abroad; and the military responsible for carrying out the interventions found little glory and less appreciation from the citizenry. President-elect Herbert Hoover made a goodwill trip to Central and South America to demonstrate his methods of improving relations, and while in office he ended the occupation of Nicaragua and commenced measures to terminate the Haitian intervention.

Much of Hoover's work, however, was nullified by his high tariff policy; his government never received the acclaim popularly accorded within Latin America to his successor, Franklin D. Roosevelt. The Good Neighbor program, at first intended for global application, soon narrowed itself to a skillful wooing of Latin America. Pan-Americanism never sustained such prodding from Washington or such acceptance in Latin America. Of course, this was Pan-Americanism as seen by the United States, and it did not always achieve universal acceptance. Sometimes too glossy, and frequently expensive, it was reasonably sincere even when some cultural programs insulted the in-

telligence of the Latin Americans. But under the veneer was a solid construction of goodwill, and the makers—Sumner Welles, Cordell Hull, and Roosevelt—understood the Latin American need for equality and dignity. Perhaps these three policymakers were led farther down the road than they had planned. In the Montevideo Conference of December 1933, Secretary Hull's vote made unanimous the Convention on the Rights and Duties of States, the major article of which declared, "No state has the right to intervene in the internal or external affairs of another."

In the same month President Roosevelt made a formal address, in which he affirmed that the nation would no longer engage in armed intervention. Action followed. American troops were withdrawn from Haiti, and new treaties ended the right of the United States to interfere in the affairs of Cuba and Panama. A potentially explosive question raised by Mexico's expropriation of vast foreign oil holdings was accepted by the administration as a matter of concern only to Mexico and the oil companies. In questions of diplomatic recognition, the Roosevelt government ended the morality test of the Woodrow Wilson days and generally (but not always) recognized as legitimate even revolutionary governments not very popular in Washington. The Hull reciprocal trade program, which resembled the goals of Secretary Blaine four decades before, did not revive world trade; but it did yield dividends in friendship and set a precedent for major postwar agreements. And for the first time Pan-Americanism had a financial basis, found in the Export-Import Bank and later in Lend-Lease and various United States agencies. Another precedent—granting and lending large sums—drew criticism from many corners of the hemisphere; but some of the accomplishments, especially in sanitation, transportation, and health, were as astonishing as they were overdue. Finally, through its Office of Inter-American Affairs, the United States boldly entered the field of cultural affairs, seeking to tell the nation's story to its neighbors for the first time.

Meanwhile, by 1938, Pan-Americanism faced its greatest trial—the threat of another war, a war whose weapons could span the protective Atlantic. The American states had previously declared their solidarity against outside aggression; but by the time of the Lima conference, aggression seemed much more of a possibility. The result was a nonbinding, but effective, resolution to consult among themselves when the peace of any American republic was threatened. The new machinery built for such consultation was the organization of the several foreign ministers, who could be called together at the initiative of any one of them.

The Lima conference was the last regular meeting of the American states until after the war; but on three occasions the foreign ministers were asked to consult in the fashion prescribed at Lima, and their work proved essential to the continuity of Pan-Americanism when world-scale military agreements were taking precedence.

The first meeting of the foreign ministers took place in Panama City after the German invasion of Poland in September 1939. To protect their neutrality, the ministers agreed upon a safety zone south of Canada, and extending an average of 300 miles out to sea around the remainder of the hemisphere. Belligerent nations were warned to commit no hostile act within this zone. Within a matter of weeks the zone was violated by both the British and the Germans, and frequent ship scuttlings in American waters in 1940 made the zone something of a nullity. More important, however, was the unanimity of the Americans in their resolve to keep the war away.

The second meeting of the Consultation of the Ministers of Foreign Affairs (the full title of these sessions) followed the fall of France to the Germans in June 1940. Again at the urging of the United States, the ministers met at Havana, Cuba, in July to discuss the question of European colonies in the Western Hemisphere and the danger of their falling into German hands. They agreed upon the Act of Havana, which provided that if a non-American state (Germany) should attempt to obtain from another non-American state (France, for example) any islands or other regions in the Americas, one or more American states would step in to administer such territory until it was able to govern itself freely or it had been restored to its previous status. Fear that the Axis powers might attempt to occupy some of the many possessions in America was real enough; however, no such attempt was made.

The ministers also affirmed the Declaration of Reciprocal Assistance and Cooperation for the Defense of the Nations of the Americas, the gist of which was that an attack upon the sovereignty of any American state was to be treated as an attack upon them all, a further broadening or multilateralizing of the Monroe Doctrine in process since 1933.

The third and last wartime meeting of the foreign ministers convened at the request of Chile and the United States as a consequence of the Japanese attack upon Pearl Harbor. The statesmen met at Rio de Janeiro in January 1942, by which time ten American nations, including the United States, had declared war upon the Axis powers. The United States military services were not anxious for the participation of underequipped Latin American forces in a global struggle. They agreed with many of the ministers that the proper gesture would be to sever diplomatic relations, eliminating the Axis ministries in America and thus helping to reduce the flow of classified information to those governments. However, a strong declaration requiring the American states to break relations (favored by Secretary Hull) was so rigidly opposed by Argentina and Chile that the United States delegation, led by Sumner Welles, settled for a milder version that merely recommended such an action. The issue was deeper than one of semantics, for the Argentines were doing more than expressing their usual reluctance to appear to be following United States policy; the Argentine military was actually pro-German and gave considerable help to the Axis in the war years. The ministers at Havana also drafted a number of resolutions on subversives, war production, and trade.

Toward the close of the war the American states met in the Inter-American Conference on the Problems of War and Peace at Mexico City in February. 1945. Uninvited Argentina was conspicuously absent. Much concerned with the place of Pan-American regionalism in the plans for the proposed United Nations, the Americans insisted upon their right to protect themselves without having to seek the approval of the Security Council. Ultimately this demand was approved in the United Nations Charter. The conference also recommended that Argentina, after declaring war on the Axis, be permitted to participate in the San Francisco sessions that formalized the United Nations. The delegates drafted the Act of Chapultepec, which required the states to conclude a treaty of reciprocal assistance, a treaty on the settlement of disputes, and a new regional arrangement that would substitute a permanent treaty for the various informal agreements underlying the inter-American association in the past.

The first of these, an elaborate set of methods for keeping the peace, was concluded in 1947 at a special conference in Rio de Janeiro. The remaining two matters were taken up at Bogotá, Colombia, the following year, when the next regular International Conference of American States (the ninth) convened. This conference was nearly destroyed when the assassination of a popular Liberal party leader was followed by citywide rioting, a reflection, perhaps, of Latin disillusionment over the absence of some sort of Marshall Plan for that region. Nevertheless, the sessions were completed. The treaty for the pacific settlement of disputes was signed, but with so many additions and amendments that several states failed to ratify it.

The major achievement was the reorganization of the entire inter-American system by the Charter of the Organization of American States (OAS), the first permanent treaty basis for the old structure. The charter declares the principles upon which the organization is based and the necessity for such machinery welded into the United Nations framework. Briefly, the OAS accomplishes its purposes by means of the following:

1. The Inter-American Conference, the supreme organ of the OAS, meeting every five years to decide general policy and action.

2. The Meeting of Consultation of Ministers of Foreign Affairs, called to discuss urgent matters and to serve as the organ of consultation.

3. The Council of the Organization of American States, meeting in permanent session and composed of one delegate from each member state. The council takes cognizance of matters referred to it by the agencies listed above, and supervises the Pan-American Union.

4. The Pan-American Union is the general secretariat of the OAS, with a wide variety of functions. In addition there are several organs of the council, specialized organizations, and special agencies and commissions.

In the 1960's several amendments were made to the OAS charter, the most fundamental being the replacement of the Inter-American Conference with an annual General Assembly. (The last Inter-American Conference was held at Caracas, Venezuela, in 1954, when the OAS was badly torn by the issue of communism in the hemisphere.)

The rise of communism as a threat in Latin America unquestionably provoked the feeling among many Americans that the Pan-American movement needed a long-range program to improve the economy there, or many of the treaties and agreements would become hollow. The first organized economic assistance to Latin America had been a part of the Good Neighbor program of the 1930's. Another precedent had been set in the Point Four Program of the Truman administration, and in 1958 the president of Brazil, Juscelino Kubitschek, had suggested some kind of "Economic Pan America." Both the OAS and the United Nations considered recommendations for financial help to the underdeveloped nations of the hemisphere.

Little was accomplished, however, until the revolution in Cuba, led by Fidel Castro, convinced the administration of President John F. Kennedy in 1961 that a giant program of economic aid was essential to prevent a number of other American states from following the path to Castroism. Kennedy pledged $1 billion per year over a ten-year period as the United States contribution to what became known as the Alliance for Progress, an admission that his nation had departed from its traditional premise that private investment and technical assistance programs were sufficient for the steady development of the region. The Latin Americans were to raise a total of $80 billion in investment capital over that ten-year period. Machinery for the Alliance was built in 1961 at Punta del Este, Uruguay; the aim was to increase the per capita wealth of participating Latin American states by 2.5 percent each year for ten years. The revolutionary elements of the Alliance, the vast amount of cooperative spending, and the strict requirements (such as reforming tax laws) to be met before a grant could be approved raised high hopes in the minds of many Americans.

Most of these hopes were to be dashed. While gross national product rose substantially, the net gains were meager when adjusted for the increase in population. Many of the most significant projects were postponed or destroyed because pressure groups in Latin America would not tolerate the reforms that were prerequisite to the grants of money. Expectations were probably too high, the inertia too vast; not even the United States government had experience in administering programs on such scale. Red tape, small graft, confused aims—all played their roles. Latin Americans wanted a larger share in the decision making; the United States government wanted to give them less. From all over the hemisphere came cries of failure as loud and as dramatic as the first pronouncements of unlimited success. The completion date was moved from 1970 to 1979. The aid continued in reduced form, but an ominous shadow could be seen in the increasing number of questions raised in Congress about the validity of any foreign aid program.

Pan-Americanism has taken yet one other shape in recent years. Ironically it is a form of Blainism-without-Blaine. Beginning about 1960, regional groups of Latin America have slowly, often timidly, worked toward some form of customs union. Generally they have been able to agree upon a common tariff against goods entering their region as well as a reduction or even abolition of tariffs against one another. Most successful in this program has been the Central American Common Market, made up of the five states of Central America, whose ultimate aim was to accomplish the complete integration of their economic systems, including manufacturing, currency, banking, as well as tariffs. The Central American Common Market was badly jolted by the 1969 "Soccer War" between Honduras and El Salvador, but it has shown signs of recovery. A similar agency is the Latin American Free Trade Association of Argentina, Bolivia, Brazil, Chile, Colombia, Ecuador, Mexico, Paraguay, Peru, Uruguay, and Venezuela, whose steps toward economic union have been shorter along a more difficult road. There is probably no room for the United States in these leagues; escape from the economic power of that nation is, in fact, one of the purposes of these common markets. Since their aims are not political, but economic, few persons find fault. Their sights are set a little lower than the grand Bolivarian dream, and therefore they may hit the target.

Among its many publications the Organization of American States distributes a small pamphlet entitled "A Dream That Became a Reality," a brief sketch of the present inter-American system. The conclusion implicit in that name is probably a fair assessment; the Pan-American system is a reality. It is a force, a qualified success. More than that the careful chronicler should not declare. The OAS has few wildly enthusiastic supporters; its achievements are too few, its activities too mundane. (Probably its nearest approach to a dramatic accomplishment was helping to settle the Honduras-El Salvador "Soccer War.") Neither has the OAS many enemies—there are no movements accompanied by cries of "Get the U.S. out of the OAS." To which one must add, regrettably, that probably most Americans, North and South, have very little idea of what OAS stands for, literally or figuratively.

Once Pan-Americanism was dominated by a theme, Pan-Hispanic Americanism, which is no longer evident. At times it has suffered from pure negativism–a Yankeephobia, always capable of eruption. Historian Arthur P. Whitaker has suggested that the idea of a hemisphere community has just about disappeared as the United States turns its attention not to Latin America but to Cold War and a far greater concern with Europe and Southeast Asia. Pan-Americanism without the United States is a cultural exercise. Pan-Americanism with the United States has great potential; but until Latin America is important enough in Washington to command greater attention than the other seasonal "crises" that the world faces, the neighbors to the south will probably continue to complain of neglect.

BIBLIOGRAPHY

R. N. Burr and R. D. Hussey, eds., *Documents on Inter-American Cooperation*, 2 vols. (Philadelphia, 1955), includes well-selected and well-edited documents from 1810 to 1948. Alexander DeConde, *Herbert Hoover's Latin American Policy* (Stanford, Calif., 1951), pushes the origins of the Good Neighbor policy back at least to the Hoover administration. Federico G. Gil, *Latin America–United States Relations* (New York, 1971), is a popular survey of the subject, providing broad, not intensive, coverage. Samuel Guy Inman, *Inter-American Conferences, 1826–1954* (Washington, D.C., 1965), gives accounts, both personal and official, by perhaps the most zealous of the specialists on Latin America and includes intimate information available from no other source. Thomas L. Karnes, *The Latin American Policy of the United States* (Tucson, Ariz., 1972), contains documents with narrative bridges to show Latin America as an issue in United States policy. James B. Lockey, *Pan-Americanism; Its Beginnings* (New York, 1920), is a detailed, sympathetic study of the movement from independence through the end of the Panama congress of 1826. J. Lloyd Mecham, *The United States and Inter-American Security, 1889–1960* (Austin, Tex., 1961), is one of the foremost studies of Pan-Americanism, a detailed, chronological approach to all the major conferences. Graham H. Stuart and James L. Tigner, *Latin America and the United States,* 6th ed., rev. (En-glewood Cliffs, N.J., 1975), is a new comprehensive text. Arthur P. Whitaker, *The Western Hemisphere Idea: Its Rise and Decline* (Ithaca, N.Y., 1954), is a stimulating study of Pan-Americanism as an idea and how time has destroyed much of the buttressing of hemispheric relations. Bryce Wood, *The Making of the Good Neighbor Policy* (New York, 1961), is an examination of the Good Neighbor policy that emphasizes its origin in the failure of earlier interventions. [*See also* DOLLAR DIPLOMACY; FOREIGN AID; IMPERIALISM; INTERVENTION AND NONINTERVENTION; ISOLATIONISM; MANIFEST DESTINY; THE MONROE DOCTRINE; PEACEMAK-ING.]

PEACEMAKING

Berenice A. Carroll

"PEACEMAKING" appears to be a commonplace term, easily understood. On closer examination, it is much more elusive. Dictionaries define it tautologically as "the making of peace"; standard encyclopedias do not recognize it as a topic for separate entry; and, surprisingly, it seldom appears in scholarly works in the fields of international relations and peace research, though somewhat more often in the literature of the peace movement.

Where it does appear, the term "peacemaking" is used in four senses:

1. Settlement or termination of a war or dispute by explicit agreement among the belligerent parties or others ("peace settlements");

2. The process of transition from hostility to amity, or from war to peace ("ending hostilities and preferably also resolving the active issues of war"—R. F. Randle), with or without explicit agreement;

3. The development of procedures and institutions to facilitate conflict resolution, or termination or prevention of wars or conflicts ("pacific settlement of disputes");

4. Efforts to create the foundations or conditions for lasting peace ("The conscientious objector is a conscientious peacemaker"—*The Pacifist Handbook,* 1940).

THE STUDY OF PEACEMAKING

The number of scholarly works explicitly devoted to "peacemaking" is small, and almost all limit their concern to peace settlements, particularly peace settlements by explicit agreement. Thus Richard B. Morris' *The Peacemakers* deals with the negotiation of the settlement of the American Revolution, and Harold Nicolson's *Peacemaking 1919,* as well as Arno J. Mayer's *Politics and Diplomacy of Peacemaking, 1918–1919,* with the settlement reached at the end of World War I. Robert Randle, in *The Origins of Peace: A Study of Peacemaking and the Structure of Peace Settlements,* makes clear in the preface: "Although I have dealt with a number of aspects of peacemaking, I have concentrated mainly upon the structure and content of *peace settlements.*" In a later work, while recognizing that peacemaking studies embrace "all matters relating to the transition from a state of war to a state of peace," including "an analysis of the conditions prompting the parties to move toward peace," Randle still places central emphasis upon settlements by explicit agreement. Thus in Randle's summation, peacemaking studies include first, study of the peace negotiations; second, "an analysis of the form, content and meaning of the peace settlement"; and finally, "a study of the impact of the war and its settlement, including consideration of any postwar negotiations aimed at completing, amending or improving the settlement, a history of the implementation of its terms, and its value as precedent for the management or resolution of future disputes."

This focus on agreed peace settlements is consistent with the position, generally accepted in the field of international law, that "The most frequent mode of terminating a war . . . is a treaty of peace, negotiated either while operations continue or after the conclusion of a general armistice." This was generally true of wars between recognized members of the international system in the period prior to World War II; but since 1945 fewer peace treaties have been concluded, and truce or armistice agreements have "tended in some respects to move forward to the place of the old treaty of peace."

For a general understanding of peacemaking, however, it must be recognized that a great many wars, or large-scale hostilities, end without any agreed settlement—for example, by outright conquest, annexation, or military rule of foreign territory; by suppression of insurrectionary forces; or by overthrow of an existing regime and its replacement by a new government. In such cases, the study of peacemaking must be oriented mainly to "an analysis of the conditions prompting the parties to move toward peace."

This analysis of "the causes of peace" presents difficulties as great as analysis of the causes of war. While the latter has received much more attention, there is no consensus among scholars on the solution of either problem. With respect to the causes of peacemaking, debate has centered upon the relative importance of selected events, conditions, or policies in inducing a belligerent to make peace: battle victories, war costs, "unconditional surrender" policies, misperception, coalition diplomacy, secrecy, the role of mediators, and domestic politics are among the factors most often treated as relevant to the process of ending or prolonging hostilities.

In reality, all these and other factors enter into the calculations of belligerents weighing the prospects for peace; and it is unlikely that any simple formula could lead us to predict which would be "decisive" in any given case. The problem, while still neglected, has received closer attention in recent years. Special issues of the *Journal of Peace Research* (December 1969) and of *Annals of the American Academy of Political and Social Science* (November 1970) were devoted to the topic "How Wars End." Robert F. Randle's *The Origins of Peace* (1973) was followed by David Smith's *From War to Peace: Essays in Peacemaking and War Termination* (1974). Nevertheless, the study of peacemaking is still a new and undeveloped field, and no systematic analytical overview of the subject has yet appeared.

ATTITUDES TOWARD PEACEMAKING

Throughout its history the United States has sought to project an image of dedication to peace and to peacemaking. George Washington, in his Farewell Address, exhorted Ameri-

cans to avoid "overgrown military establishments which, under any form of government, are inauspicious to liberty," and urged: "Observe good faith and justice toward all nations. Cultivate peace and harmony with all." Nearly two centuries later, President John F. Kennedy was obliged to acknowledge that, far from "cultivating peace and harmony," the United States found itself "caught up in a vicious and dangerous cycle in which suspicion on one side breeds suspicion on the other and new weapons beget counterweapons"; nevertheless, he too exhorted Americans to turn their attention to "the most important topic on earth, world peace":

> What kind of peace do I mean? What kind of peace do we seek? Not a *Pax Americana* enforced on the world by American weapons of war. Not the peace of the grave or the security of the slave. I am talking about genuine peace . . .—not merely peace for Americans but peace for all men and women, not merely peace in our time but peace for all time.

But the record of the behavior of the United States in regard to both "peace in our time" and "peace for all time" has been ambiguous at best.

Certainly there have been strong traditions of antimilitarism, internationalism, and pacifism in American society. The history of peace movements in the United States, reaching back at least to the formation of the New York, Massachusetts, and Ohio Peace Societies in 1815, is long and rich, and can lay claim to having influenced the peace settlements in a number of wars or other conflicts, most prominently in World War I. On the level of governmental action, the long-term peacemaking efforts of the United States have focused on the development of international legal and institutional instruments for pacific settlement of disputes and peacekeeping by international organizations. The Rush-Bagot Convention (1817) established a lasting basis for disarmament on the long border between the United States and Canada, and the Treaty of Washington (1871) provided for the resolution of other outstanding issues (boundary and fisheries questions, and the *Alabama* claims) by a court of arbitration.

The United States has also given strong support to the formulation of treaties of arbitration, both voluntary and compulsory, though the Senate has as strongly resisted acceptance of compulsory arbitration without significant reservations. The United States has also shown itself willing and even eager to extend its services as mediator, and has had some success in this role—for example, in mediating the Russo-Japanese peace settlement of 1905. Finally, the United States has sometimes adopted the role of peacemaker on a global scale, taking the initiative in the establishment of the Permanent Court of International Justice and the League of Nations. Though the United States never joined the League and even declined to become a party to the Statute of the Permanent Court, it later played a major role in the establishment and development of the United Nations, and has accepted (though with major reservations) the jurisdiction of the new International Court of Justice as reconstituted under the United Nations Charter.

There has also been strong interest in the United States in the development of techniques of peacekeeping and other approaches to conflict resolution. On the governmental level, United States involvement in "peacekeeping" operations has unfortunately been associated with the large-scale use of military force, especially in Korea. Nevertheless, on the level of independent citizen action and professional research, there has been widespread interest in peacekeeping without the use of military force and in nonviolent modes of conflict resolution at international as well as domestic and interpersonal levels.

FORMAL PEACE AGREEMENTS

In the period between 1775 and 1945, the United States entered into a great many treaties or other formal peace agreements, of which the overwhelming majority were treaties with the Indian nations or tribes.

Five major wars between the United States and recognized foreign states were concluded by peace treaties: the American Revolution (Treaty of Paris, 3 September 1783); the War of 1812 (Treaty of Ghent, 24 December 1814); the Mexican War (Treaty of Guadalupe Hidalgo, 2 February 1848); the Spanish-American War (Treaty of Paris, 10 December 1898); and World War I. The United States Senate de-

clined to ratify the Treaty of Versailles and associated treaties negotiated by President Woodrow Wilson at the conclusion of World War I, but the United States subsequently signed separate treaties of peace with Germany (Berlin, 25 August 1921), Austria (Vienna, 24 August 1921), and Hungary (Budapest, 29 August 1921). No treaties were signed and ratified by the United States with Bulgaria and Turkey, and the Soviet Union was absent from the entire peace settlement.

A number of lesser foreign wars or partial engagements of the United States were also concluded by treaties of peace: the Moroccan War (treaty of 28 June 1786), the Tripolitan War (Treaty of Tripoli, 3 June 1805), two Algerian wars (treaties of 1795 and 1815), the second Opium War (Treaty of Tientsin, 18 June 1858), and the Boxer Rebellion (Treaty of Peking, 7 September 1901). The United States–French undeclared naval war (Quasi-War) of 1798–1800 was also settled by a formal convention of 30 September 1800.

WAR ENDINGS WITHOUT FORMAL SETTLEMENTS

The United States has been involved in a considerable number of undeclared foreign wars or "interventions," particularly in the twentieth century. Such wars typically were not concluded by formal agreement but were ended rather by United States suppression of opposition, military rule, unilateral imposition of terms, or, in some cases, unilateral withdrawal of United States forces. These undeclared wars include the suppression of the Philippine independence movement in 1899–1902; the Siberian interventions of 1918–1921; numerous interventions in Cuba, Haiti, Mexico, Nicaragua, Panama, and the Dominican Republic; and military interventions in civil wars in Greece, China, Korea, Lebanon, Indochina, and others since World War II.

A study of American peacemaking must give some attention to the way the United States has handled the conclusion of civil wars and insurrections. The distinction between these and "foreign wars" becomes somewhat doubtful when we recall that the United States itself originated in an insurrectionary war. When an

PEACEMAKING

incumbent government is obliged to concede statehood and separate territorial sovereignty to rebel belligerents, the ending of the conflict takes on the character of a settlement between sovereign states. On the other hand, the treatment accorded to defeated belligerents in civil wars and insurrections often is not significantly different from the treatment accorded to defeated foreign nations in colonial wars of conquest or interventions.

The United States has experienced a substantial number of insurrections or rebellions, including at least thirty-five slave uprisings, at least five significant domestic insurrections or civil conflicts, the great Civil War of 1861–1865, and other types of conflicts such as large-scale riots, vigilante expeditions, and violent labor disputes. The United States government has consistently refused to give the rebels or rioters any recognized status as belligerents, and these conflicts have all been terminated by piecemeal suppression of the disturbances.

This was true even for the Civil War, in which the refusal of the United States government to negotiate with the rebel forces affected both the duration of hostilities and the character of the outcome. Efforts of the Confederate generals Robert E. Lee and Joseph E. Johnston to negotiate terms of general surrender with Union generals Ulysses S. Grant and William T. Sherman were expressly rejected by both President Abraham Lincoln and President Andrew Johnson. Far from welcoming the opportunity to put a rapid end to the fighting, on 3 March 1865 Lincoln instructed Grant "to have no conference with General Lee, unless it be for the capitulation of General Lee's army, or on some minor or purely military matter." Furthermore, Grant was "not to decide, discuss, or confer upon any political questions. Such questions the President holds in his own hands, and will submit them to no military conferences or conventions. Meantime you are to press to the utmost your military advantages."

Similarly, when Sherman, unaware of this directive to Grant, later met with Johnston and drafted terms for a general surrender of the Confederate forces remaining after Lee's surrender at Appomattox, the draft agreement was sharply rejected by President Johnson and his cabinet. Sherman was authorized to accept only the surrender of the army commanded by

Johnston, and to engage in no negotiations. As Sherman observed, this policy meant that the war might continue indefinitely in sporadic engagements with dispersed "guerrilla bands." Indeed, while the Civil War formally terminated one year later with a proclamation by President Johnson (2 April 1866), some hostilities continued even after that date and a separate proclamation was required to end the fighting in Texas (20 August 1866).

While the position taken by Lincoln and Johnson appears at first sight to be based primarily on the principle of civilian control over vital political and civil questions, it must be observed that it was not particular political terms drafted by the generals that were rejected, but any conference or negotiation between the military leaders for terms of general surrender. Nor was the United States government itself willing to negotiate with the Confederate government or its generals. In contrast, in both World War I and World War II, general surrender or armistice agreements were received and signed by military leaders of the Allied armies: Marshal Ferdinand Foch, general-in-chief of the Allied armies in France, signed the armistice agreement for the Allies in World War I. In 1945 Lieutenant General Walter Bedell Smith, chief of staff to General Dwight D. Eisenhower, signed the German instrument of surrender, while General Douglas MacArthur signed the Japanese surrender agreement for the Allied powers in World War II. Though the terms of these documents were determined ultimately by the civilian authorities, the Allied governments did not hesitate to have the military leaders receive the surrenders and, indeed, accorded them considerable influence on the formulation of surrender terms and occupation policies.

It seems probable that the refusal of the presidents during the Civil War to approve the receipt by either Grant or Sherman of general surrender by Lee or Johnston was less a question of military versus civilian control of policy than it was a question of refusing to treat with any party claiming to represent or exercise general authority in or over the Confederate states or forces. Such a position is characteristic of incumbent governments faced with insurrectionary forces, not only at the cost of prolonging armed hostilities but even at the cost of making impossible a settlement based on mutual accord and amity.

PEACEMAKING WITHOUT PEACE: THE INDIAN WARS

In *Custer Died for Your Sins* (1969), Vine Deloria wrote that "Indian people laugh themselves sick" when they hear American whites charge Soviet Russia with breaking treaty agreements: "It would take Russia another century to make and break as many treaties as the United States has already violated" in its dealings with American Indians. In the century between 1778 and 1871, the United States government made some 370 treaties with Indian tribes and nations. About one-third of these were peace treaties, but it is open to question what relationship should be understood between these treaties and "peacemaking" as construed above.

Since 1871 the United States has declined to sign treaties with Indian tribes, though it has continued to sign "agreements" understood to have the same binding force as treaties. The difference lies in rejection of the notion that the Indian tribes should be recognized as independent nations. Prior to 1871 this had been a matter of dispute, subject to varying interpretation and practice. In 1828 President John Quincy Adams declared that at the establishment of the United States, "the principle was adopted of considering them as foreign and independent powers. . . ." But in 1831, in the case of *Cherokee Nation* v. *Georgia,* Chief Justice John Marshall gave the majority judgment of the Supreme Court that the Indians were "domestic dependent nations," not to be considered "a foreign state in the sense of the Constitution. . . ." However, the Supreme Court was closely divided on the issue. In their dissent Justice Smith Thompson and Justice Joseph Story argued that the history of past treatment of the Indians led irresistibly to the conclusion that "they have been regarded, by the executive and legislative branches of the government, not only as sovereign and independent, but as foreign nations or tribes, not within the jurisdiction nor under the government of the states within which they were located."

Moreover, while Chief Justice Marshall maintained that the Indians were not "foreign states in the sense of the Constitution" with respect to the jurisdiction of the Supreme Court, he acknowledged that for other purposes the Cherokee nation clearly did have the character of "a state, as a distinct political society, separated from others, capable of managing its own affairs and governing itself. . . . The numerous treaties made with them by the United States recognize them as a people capable of maintaining the relations of peace and war, of being responsible in their political character for any violation of their engagements, or for any aggression committed on the citizens of the United States by any individual of their community." The following year, in the related case of *Worcester* v. *Georgia,* Marshall reaffirmed as the judgment of the Court that treaties with the Indians had the same standing as treaties with other nations:

> The constitution, by declaring treaties already made, as well as those to be made, to be the supreme law of the land, has adopted and sanctioned the previous treaties with the Indian nations, and consequently admits their rank among those powers who are capable of making treaties. The words "treaty" and "nation" are words of our own language, selected in our diplomatic and legislative proceedings, by ourselves, having each a definite and well understood meaning. We have applied them to Indians as we have applied them to the other nations of the earth. They are applied to all in the same sense.

The first treaty of peace made by the United States government was with the Delaware Indians in 1778, at Fort Pitt (Pittsburgh). This was in fact a treaty of alliance between the United States and some of the Delaware tribes, at a time when most of the Indians of Ohio and New York, including the Delawares, were fighting on the side of the British in the Revolutionary War. The treaty repudiates the allegations of "enemies of the United States" who have "endeavoured by every artifice to possess the Indians with an opinion that it is our design to extirpate them, and take possession of their country; to obviate such false suggestions, the United States guarantee to said nation of Delawares, and their heirs, all their territorial rights in the fullest and most ample manner as bounded by former treaties." Similar guarantees were reiterated numerous times in succeeding years—for example, in 1790, when President George Washington assured the Iroquois Nations that the United States government would "protect you in all your just rights. . . . You possess the right to sell, and the right of refusing to sell your lands. . . . The United States will be true and faithful to their engagements."

In reality, the United States repeatedly violated these engagements, systematically dispossessing the Indian tribes of their lands and depriving them of their traditional means of subsistence, utilizing every means to hand including force and fraud, trickery and bribery, and finally murder, arson, and massacre. Though no war was ever declared by Congress against an Indian nation, one may well name the entire period of white colonization of the territory now comprising the United States the "Four Hundred Years' War." By 1872, this protracted war had reduced the Indian population from an estimated one million before the arrival of the colonists to some 300,000. By that time the Delawares, who had been assured in 1778 that it was only the "false suggestions" of "enemies of the United States" that it was "our design to extirpate them, and take possession of their country," had been driven from their native territory and so reduced and dispersed that the report of the commissioner of Indian affairs for 1872 mentioned only eighty-one Delawares, living with the Wichitas in Indian Territory.

In the present context, three main points are salient about the relations between the United States and the Indian nations: first, the consistent failure of the United States government to adhere to commitments made in numerous treaties of peace and amity; second, the outright resistance of many officers of the United States Army, and many state and federal government officials, to making peace with Indians on any terms other than unconditional surrender, removal to reservations, or, if necessary, extermination; and third, the use of peace treaties as weapons of war.

Although the full history of "broken peace pipes" has yet to be written, one may read parts of it in such works as Helen Hunt Jackson's *A Century of Dishonor* (1881), Dee Brown's *Bury My Heart at Wounded Knee* (1971), and Vine De-loria's *Of Utmost Good Faith* (1971). With respect to peacemaking, the effect of the most glaring atrocities, such as the Sand Creek massacre, was to shut all doors to peace. On 29 November 1864, Colonel John M. Chivington and Major Scott Anthony led 700 men to slaughter and mutilate some 200 Indians, encamped at Sand Creek under assurances from Anthony himself that they would be under the protection of Fort Lyon. As Dee Brown concluded: "In a few hours of madness at Sand Creek, Chivington and his soldiers destroyed the lives or the power of every Cheyenne and Arapaho chief who had held out for peace with the white men. After the flight of the survivors, the Indians rejected Black Kettle and Left Hand, and turned to their war leaders to save them from extermination."

Despite the hideousness of this and other massacres, far more Indians were killed and driven off their lands by the devices of dishonest, dictated, and disregarded peace treaties. Among the clearest examples of this was the case of the Cherokees. First persuaded by treaty commitments in 1785–1791 that the United States "solemnly guarantee to the Cherokee nation all their lands" not expressly ceded in the treaties, the Cherokees refrained from making war despite many hostile encounters with whites and the illegal entry onto their lands of numerous white settlers. Pressured into ceding more territory by treaty in 1817, some of the Cherokees began to move west of the Mississippi; but many refused to sign the treaty and most of the Cherokees clung stubbornly to their traditional lands. In 1829, however, the state of Georgia adopted an act that annexed their whole territory to the state and deprived them of all legal and political rights, annulling "all laws made by the Cherokee nation, . . . either in council or in any other way," and providing that "no Indian . . . shall be deemed a competent witness in any Court of this State to which a white man may be a party." The Cherokees sought to challenge this in the Supreme Court, but were discouraged by the Indian Removal Act of 1830, the refusal of the Supreme Court to hear their case in 1831, and the refusal of President Andrew Jackson to implement the more favorable decision of the court in *Worcester* v. *Georgia* (1832).

Under these circumstances, some of the

Cherokees were induced to sign the Treaty of New Echota (1835), relinquishing all the Cherokee lands east of the Mississippi (encompassing territory in four southern states exceeding in size the states of Massachusetts, Rhode Island, and Connecticut) in return for $5 million and seven million acres west of the Mississippi. The treaty again assured the Cherokees that the new lands ceded to them "shall in no future time, without their consent, be included within the territorial limits or jurisdiction of any State or Territory." Whether they recognized that these assurances would be as worthless as earlier ones, or simply preferred their ancestral lands, most of the Cherokees refused to sign the Treaty of New Echota; in 1837 General John Ellis Wool reported that the Cherokee people "uniformly declare that they never made the treaty in question." Nevertheless, at the expiration of the stipulated time the United States Army appeared to carry out the removal, "in obedience to the treaty of 1835." Fifteen thousand Cherokees were forcibly evicted under conditions of such inadequate food, shelter, and sanitation that 4,000 died on the long trek west. Thus in retrospect, treaty-making takes on the appearance of the most deadly weapon employed by the whites in their war to wrest the continent from the Indians; to persuade, trick, or coerce them into giving up their lands; and to reduce them to a remnant of their former numbers.

TREATY-MAKING VERSUS PEACEMAKING

The experience of the American Indians is the most glaring example, but by no means unique, illustrating the limitations of treaty-making as a model for peacemaking. It is widely recognized that so-called "peace settlements," explicit agreements for the termination of a particular war or dispute, may fail to resolve key issues in dispute, and may even plant the seeds for new hostilities.

In the case of World War I, for example, President Woodrow Wilson resisted strong pressures from political opponents at home to demand "unconditional surrender" as the only basis for a settlement of the war with Germany, but he was later obliged to make many concessions weakening or contradicting the principles of his Fourteen Points, and forcing Germany to accept dictated terms of peace. When the Senate declined to ratify the resulting Treaty of Versailles, it was in the setting of a national campaign portraying the treaty terms and even the Covenant of the League of Nations as a betrayal of hopes for a lasting peace. Senator Henry Cabot Lodge argued before the Senate on 12 August 1919:

> Whatever may be said, it [League of Nations] is not a league of peace; it is an alliance, dominated at the present moment by five great powers, really by three, and it has all the marks of an alliance. The development of international law is neglected. The court which is to decide disputes brought before it fills but a small place . . . it exhibits that most marked characteristic of an alliance—that its decisions are to be carried out by force. Those articles on which the whole structure rests are articles which provide for the use of force; that is, for war.

Nor did the opposition to the treaty as a provocation of future wars come only from the right. Indeed, the first organized group to condemn the Treaty of Versailles was the Women's International League for Peace and Freedom, whose international congress at Zurich, meeting 12–17 May 1919, declared:

> This International Congress of Women expresses its deep regret that the terms of peace proposed at Versailles should so seriously violate the principles upon which alone a just and lasting peace can be secured, and which the democracies of the world had come to accept.
> By guaranteeing the fruits of the secret treaties to conquerors, the terms of peace tacitly sanction secret diplomacy, deny the principles of self-determination, recognize the right of the victors to the spoils of war, and create all over Europe discords and animosities, which can only lead to future wars.
> By the demand for the disarmament of one set of belligerents only, the principle of justice is violated and the rule of force continued [Jane Addams, *Peace and Bread in Time of War*].

One may argue that the Treaty of Versailles was not so bad as its opponents portrayed it, that its terms were less harsh than they might have been, that the disarmament of Germany was a first step toward the general disarmament that the treaty envisaged for the future, and that the League of Nations, imperfect as it was, offered a framework for international cooperation and peace that would have been effective had it been given responsible support and leadership by the United States and other great powers. One may argue that the failure of the peace settlement of 1919 was less a consequence of its internal flaws than of its abandonment in the subsequent years, first by the withdrawal of the United States and then by successive retreats by other major signatories (especially Great Britain and France), particularly from the treaty's provisions for general disarmament and for collective action against breaches of the peace. These questions are still debated; nevertheless, it is probable that disillusionment with the settlement of 1919 contributed to the failure to arrive at any general peace settlement in World War II, and perhaps to the near abandonment of treaties of peace as a mode of terminating hostilities in the period since 1945.

Doubts concerning the necessity and advisability of concluding a treaty of peace at the end of World War II were expressed in the work on planning for peace during the last years of the war. In the report "Procedures of Peacemaking: With Special Reference to the Present War," the Legislative Reference Service of the Library of Congress pointed out in August 1943 that the Declaration of the United Nations bound the signatories not to conclude a separate peace. Nevertheless, the report noted:

> The world-wide scope of the present war and the multitude of problems which its settlement entails constitute a strong temptation for the solution of certain questions independently of the over-all settlement. . . . Even the major problems of boundaries, of federations, and of economic and political alliances among foreign States, insofar as the United States is not directly committed, might be thus decided without these decisions ever appearing in the text of a treaty which the United States would be called upon to ratify. . . . The cessation of hostilities in different parts of the world may be far from simultaneous. . . . And should a prolonged interval intervene between the end of the fighting in the main theatres of war and the definitive peace, the situation

might become so deeply influenced by decisions made and regimes established in the meantime, that the peace conference might find its freedom of action considerably prejudiced. As a result of this development, the peace treaty or treaties may lose a great deal of their importance.

This analysis proved remarkably close to the actual course of events at the end of World War II. As one text summed it up: ". . . peacemaking was a long-drawn-out process which never quite ended but turned into the cold war between the Soviet Union and its wartime allies." The wartime conferences at Casablanca, Teheran, Yalta, and Potsdam laid down some of the principles and specific terms of the postwar arrangements, including the demand for "unconditional surrender" of the Axis powers; the policy of "complete disarmament, demilitarization and dismemberment of Germany"; the establishment of the United Nations; and various specific provisions relating to the Far East and Eastern Europe, particularly Poland. Nevertheless, many key issues were left imprecise or totally unresolved, and all the agreements were understood to be provisional pending a final peace treaty. By the time the peace conference convened in Paris, however, the situation had indeed become "so deeply influenced by decisions made and regimes established in the meantime" that the formulation of a general peace settlement acceptable to all the major participants had become impossible.

Thus no general treaty settlement of World War II in Europe was concluded; the peace treaty with Japan was delayed until 1951, and was not signed by the Soviet Union. Nor have peace treaties been concluded in other wars fought by the United States in recent decades. No peace treaty followed the armistice in the Korean War, concluded at Panmunjom in July 1953. The withdrawal of United States forces from Vietnam was arranged by a cease-fire agreement of 28 January 1973. Although this was called "An Agreement Ending the War and Restoring Peace in Vietnam," it was actually, as Randle has noted, "a military settlement without the concomitant political settlement that completes the peacemaking process." Moreover, the withdrawal of United States uniformed forces did not end the war or restore

PEACEMAKING

the peace; fighting continued among the Vietnamese and other Indochinese belligerents for more than two years.

On the whole, the United States has held an image of peacemaking as "sitting down around the table to negotiate." But with the exception of the early period of its history in relations with European powers, especially Great Britain, the United States has not had a strong record of making peace on negotiated terms, such as to establish a lasting basis of concord. The terms of the treaties with Mexico in 1848, Spain in 1898, and Germany in 1919 were essentially dictated, as were the terms of surrender of the Axis countries in World War II. In the latter cases, the United States was obliged to negotiate at least with its own allies. In World War I, negotiation with allies may have cost the United States the freedom to negotiate with the opposing belligerents; but in World War II, it was the declared policy of the United States to achieve "unconditional surrender." This was also the policy most often adopted by the United States in dealing with insurgents, both domestic, as in the Civil War, and foreign, as in the Philippines. Moreover, in dealing with the American Indians, the United States has shown that negotiating treaties may be a device not to establish peace but to disarm, defeat, and gradually drive an opponent into a dependent condition.

The United States has sometimes sought to ameliorate the harshness of terms imposed on defeated enemies by financial awards (payments and annuities to Indians, $15 million to Mexico for 40 percent of its territory from Texas to California) or postwar programs of aid and rehabilitation (loans to Germany after World War I, the Marshall Plan after World War II). Even in this respect, however, the provision of aid has been more generous and given on less humiliating terms to powerful opponents, especially those of the Caucasian race, than to those peoples of different race and culture who have found themselves in the path of "manifest destiny" and United States global expansion, whether American Indians, Filipinos, or Vietnamese.

It may be that there is no better symbol of the paradoxes in the history of United States peacemaking than dubbing the Colt .45 "The Peacemaker." Yet it may be hoped that the voices will be heard of those other peacemakers who hold with Jane Addams that peace cannot be secured merely by the temporary conclusion of fighting, but "only as men abstained from the gains of oppression and responded to the cause of the poor; that swords would finally be beaten into plowshares and pruning hooks, not because men resolved to be peaceful, but because the metal of the earth would be turned to its proper use when the poor and their children should be abundantly fed," and when peace came to be conceived "no longer as an absence of war, but the unfolding of worldwide processes making for the nurture of human life."

BIBLIOGRAPHY

The classic study of war termination and peace treaties from the standpoint of international law is Coleman Phillipson, *Termination of War and Treaties of Peace* (London, 1916). A more recent treatment of legal aspects of abatement and termination of war may be found in Julius Stone, *Legal Controls of International Conflict* (New York, 1959), bk. III, ch. 23.

A number of articles that survey relevant literature and suggest general perspectives on peacemaking and war termination are Berenice A. Carroll, "How Wars End: An Analysis of Some Current Hypotheses," in *Journal of Peace Research* (December 1969); and "War Termination and Conflict Theory," in *Annals of the American Academy of Political and Social Science*, 392 (1970); Janice Gross Stein, "War Termination and Conflict Reduction, or, How Wars Should End," in *Jerusalem Journal of International Relations*, 1 (1975); and Wallace J. Thies, "Searching for Peace: Vietnam and the Question of How Wars End," in *Polity*, 7 (1975).

Robert F. Randle, *The Origins of Peace: A Study of Peacemaking and the Structure of Peace Settlements* (New York, 1973), offers a broad-ranging analysis of peace settlements based on a systematic study of numerous wars of selected types. Fred C. Iklé, *Every War Must End* (New York, 1971), provides a briefer, more impressionistic treatment of problems in trying to bring wars to conclusion.

Collections of articles on war termination from varied perspectives may be found in *Journal of Peace Research* (December 1969), guest ed., Berenice A. Carroll; *Annals of the American Academy of Political and Social Science*, 392 (1970), guest ed., William T. R. Fox; and David S. Smith, ed., *From War to Peace: Essays in Peacemaking and War Termination* (New York, 1974).

Pertinent works on negotiation and pacific settlement of disputes include Fred C. Iklé, *How Nations Negotiate* (New York, 1964); Arthur Lall, *Modern International Negotiation: Principles and Practice* (New York, 1966); and United Nations Secretariat, *Systematic Survey of Treaties for the Pacific Settlement of International Disputes, 1928–1948* (Lake Success, N.Y., 1949), which updates a similar survey by the League of Nations (*Arbitration and Security: Systematic Survey of Arbitration Conventions and Treaties of Mutual Security Deposited With the League of Nations* [1927]). David Wainhouse et al., *International Peace Observation* (Baltimore, 1966), provides a valuable survey of seventy cases of peace observation by the League of Nations, the United Nations, and the Organization of American States, and offers recommendations for strengthening the peacemaking role of the United Nations.

Among other works relevant to particular aspects of peacemaking are: Devere Allen, *The Fight for Peace* (New York, 1930), a history of the American peace movement and American internationalism; Joan Bondurant, *Conquest of Violence* (Princeton, 1958), an important analysis of Gandhian philosophy and techniques of nonviolent action and nonviolent peacemaking; and Elise Boulding, "The Technology of Peacemaking," Report for the Center for Research on Conflict Resolution (Ann Arbor, Mich., 1962), a brief survey of social science research in the United States, relevant to peacemaking in the general sense, in the period 1932–1962; Paul Kecskemeti, *Strategic Surrender: The Politics of Victory and Defeat* (Stanford, Calif., 1958), which analyzes surrender as a strategic and political concept, and unconditional surrender as a policy, with reference to the French, Italian, German, and Japanese surrenders in World War II; Barbara Stanford, *Peacemaking: A Guide to Conflict Resolution of Individuals, Groups and Nations* (New York, 1976), which attempts to apply the insights of contemporary peace and conflict studies to peacemaking at different levels, from individual to international; Wilcomb E. Washburn, *The American Indian and the United States: A Documentary History,* IV (New York, 1973), which contains pertinent peace treaties and legal decisions, with interpretive introductions.

[*See also* ALLIANCES, COALITIONS, AND ENTENTES; ARBITRATION, MEDIATION, AND CONCILIATION; COLLECTIVE SECURITY; DISARMAMENT; THE FOURTEEN POINTS; INTERNATIONALISM; INTERNATIONAL LAW; INTERNATIONAL ORGANIZATION; INTERVENTION AND NONINTERVENTION; PACIFISM; PEACE MOVEMENTS; REPARATIONS; TREATIES; UNCONDITIONAL SURRENDER.]